A COMPANION TO GREEKS ACROSS THE ANCIENT WORLD

BLACKWELL COMPANIONS TO THE ANCIENT WORLD

This series provides sophisticated and authoritative overviews of periods of ancient history, genres of classical literature, and the most important themes in ancient culture. Each volume comprises approximately twenty-five to forty concise essays written by individual scholars within their area of specialization. The essays are written in a clear, provocative, and lively manner, designed for an international audience of scholars, students, and general readers.

ANCIENT HISTORY
Published
A Companion to the Roman Army
Edited by Paul Erdkamp
A Companion to the Roman Republic
Edited by Nathan Rosenstein and Robert Morstein-Marx
A Companion to the Roman Empire
Edited by David S. Potter
A Companion to the Classical Greek World
Edited by Konrad H. Kinzl
A Companion to the Ancient Near East
Edited by Daniel C. Snell
A Companion to the Hellenistic World
Edited by Andrew Erskine
A Companion to Late Antiquity
Edited by Philip Rousseau
A Companion to Ancient History
Edited by Andrew Erskine
A Companion to Archaic Greece
Edited by Kurt A. Raaflaub and Hans van Wees
A Companion to Julius Caesar
Edited by Miriam Griffin
A Companion to Byzantium
Edited by Liz James
A Companion to Ancient Egypt
Edited by Alan B. Lloyd
A Companion to Ancient Macedonia
Edited by Joseph Roisman and Ian Worthington
A Companion to the Punic Wars
Edited by Dexter Hoyos
A Companion to Augustine
Edited by Mark Vessey
A Companion to Marcus Aurelius
Edited by Marcel van Ackeren
A Companion to Ancient Greek Government
Edited by Hans Beck
A Companion to the Neronian Age
Edited by Emma Buckley and Martin T. Dinter
A Companion to Greek Democracy and the Roman Republic
Edited by Dean Hammer
A Companion to Livy
Edited by Bernard Mineo
A Companion to Ancient Thrace
Edited by Julia Valeva, Emil Nankov, and Denver Graninger
A Companion to Roman Italy
Edited by Alison E. Cooley
A Companion to the Etruscans
Edited by Sinclair Bell and Alexandra A. Carpino
A Companion to the Flavian Age of Imperial Rome
Edited by Andrew Zissos
A Companion to Science, Technology, and Medicine in Ancient Greece and Rome
Edited by Georgia L. Irby
A Companion to Greeks Across the Ancient World
Edited by Franco De Angelis
A Companion to Sparta
Edited by Anton Powell

A Companion to Classical Athens
Edited by Sara Forsdyke
A Companion to Ancient Agriculture
Edited by David Hollander and Timothy Howe
A Companion to Ancient Phoenicia
Edited by Mark Woolmer
A Companion to Roman Politics
Edited by Valentina Arena and Jonathan R. W. Prag
A Companion to the Archaeology of the Roman Empire
Edited by Barbara Burrell
A Companion to the City of Rome
Edited by Amanda Claridge and Claire Holleran
A Companion to Rome and Persia, 96 BCE–651 CE
Edited by Peter Edwell
A Companion to Assyria
Edited by Eckart Frahm
A Companion to North Africa in Antiquity
Edited by Bruce Hitchner
A Companion to the Achaemenid Persian Empire
Edited by Bruno Jacobs and Robert Rollinger
A Companion to the Hellenistic and Roman Near East
Edited by Ted Kaizer
A Companion to the Archaeology of Early Greece and the Mediterranean
Edited by Irene S. Lemos and Antonios Kotsonas
A Companion to Euripides
Edited by Robin Mitchell-Boyask
A Companion to Greco-Roman and Late Antique Egypt
Edited by Katelijn Vandorpe
A Companion to the Archaeology of Ancient Egypt
Edited by Josef W. Wegner

LITERATURE AND CULTURE
Published
A Companion to Classical Receptions
Edited by Lorna Hardwick and Christopher Stray
A Companion to Greek and Roman Historiography
Edited by John Marincola
A Companion to Catullus
Edited by Marilyn B. Skinner
A Companion to Roman Religion
Edited by Jörg Rüpke
A Companion to Greek Religion
Edited by Daniel Ogden
A Companion to the Classical Tradition
Edited by Craig W. Kallendorf
A Companion to Roman Rhetoric
Edited by William Dominik and Jon Hall
A Companion to Greek Rhetoric
Edited by Ian Worthington
A Companion to Ancient Epic
Edited by John Miles Foley
A Companion to Greek Tragedy
Edited by Justina Gregory
A Companion to Latin Literature
Edited by Stephen Harrison

A Companion to Greek and Roman Political Thought
Edited by Ryan K. Balot
A Companion to Ovid
Edited by Peter E. Knox
A Companion to the Ancient Greek Language
Edited by Egbert Bakker
A Companion to Hellenistic Literature
Edited by Martine Cuypers and James J. Clauss
A Companion to Vergil's Aeneid and its Tradition
Edited by Joseph Farrell and Michael C.J. Putnam
A Companion to Horace
Edited by Gregson Davis
A Companion to Families in the Greek and Roman Worlds
Edited by Beryl Rawson
A Companion to Greek Mythology
Edited by Ken Dowden and Niall Livingstone
A Companion to the Latin Language
Edited by James Clackson
A Companion to Tacitus
Edited by Victoria Emma Pagán
A Companion to Women in the Ancient World
Edited by Sharon L. James and Sheila Dillon
A Companion to Sophocles
Edited by Kirk Ormand
A Companion to the Archaeology of the Ancient Near East
Edited by Daniel Potts
A Companion to Roman Love Elegy
Edited by Barbara K. Gold
A Companion to Greek Art
Edited by Tyler Jo Smith and Dimitris Plantzos
A Companion to Persius and Juvenal
Edited by Susanna Braund and Josiah Osgood
A Companion to the Archaeology of the Roman Republic
Edited by Jane DeRose Evans
A Companion to Terence
Edited by Antony Augoustakis and Ariana Traill
A Companion to Roman Architecture
Edited by Roger B. Ulrich and Caroline K. Quenemoen
A Companion to Sport and Spectacle in Greek and Roman Antiquity
Edited by Paul Christesen and Donald G. Kyle
A Companion to Plutarch
Edited by Mark Beck
A Companion to Greek and Roman Sexualities
Edited by Thomas K. Hubbard
A Companion to the Ancient Novel
Edited by Edmund P. Cueva and Shannon N. Byrne

A Companion to Ethnicity in the Ancient Mediterranean
Edited by Jeremy McInerney
A Companion to Ancient Egyptian Art
Edited by Melinda Hartwig
A Companion to the Archaeology of Religion in the Ancient World
Edited by Rubina Raja and Jörg Rüpke
A Companion to Food in the Ancient World
Edited by John Wilkins and Robin Nadeau
A Companion to Ancient Education
Edited by W. Martin Bloomer
A Companion to Ancient Aesthetics
Edited by Pierre Destrée & Penelope Murray
A Companion to Roman Art
Edited by Barbara Borg
A Companion to Greek Literature
Edited by Martin Hose and David Schenker
A Companion to Josephus in his World
Edited by Honora Howell Chapman and Zuleika Rodgers
A Companion to Greek Architecture
Edited by Margaret M. Miles
A Companion to Aeschylus
Edited by Peter Burian
A Companion to Plautus
Edited by Dorota Dutsch and George Fredric Franko
A Companion to Ancient Epigram
Edited by Christer Henriksén
A Companion to Religion in Late Antiquity
Edited by Josef Lössl and Nicholas Baker-Brian
A Companion to Ancient Greece and Rome on Screen
Edited by Arthur J. Pomeroy
A Companion to Late Antique Literature
Edited by Scott McGill and Edward Watts
A Companion to Ancient Egyptian Religion
Edited by Martin Bommas
A Companion to Classical Studies
Edited by Kai Broderson
A Companion to Latin Epic, ca. 14–96 CE
Edited by Lee Fratantuono and Caroline Stark
A Companion to Ancient Near Eastern Art
Edited by Ann C. Gunter
A Companion to Aegean Art and Architecture
Edited by Louise A. Hitchcock
A Companion to Ancient History in Popular Culture
Edited by Llyod Llewellyn-Jones

A COMPANION TO GREEKS ACROSS THE ANCIENT WORLD

Edited by

Franco De Angelis

WILEY Blackwell

This edition first published 2020
© 2020 John Wiley & Sons, Inc.

All rights reserved. No part of this publication may be reproduced, stored in a retrieval system, or transmitted, in any form or by any means, electronic, mechanical, photocopying, recording or otherwise, except as permitted by law. Advice on how to obtain permission to reuse material from this title is available at http://www.wiley.com/go/permissions.

The right of Franco De Angelis to be identified as the author of the editorial material in this work has been asserted in accordance with law.

Registered Office
John Wiley & Sons, Inc., 111 River Street, Hoboken, NJ 07030, USA

Editorial Office
111 River Street, Hoboken, NJ 07030, USA

For details of our global editorial offices, customer services, and more information about Wiley products visit us at www.wiley.com.

Wiley also publishes its books in a variety of electronic formats and by print-on-demand. Some content that appears in standard print versions of this book may not be available in other formats.

Limit of Liability/Disclaimer of Warranty
While the publisher and authors have used their best efforts in preparing this work, they make no representations or warranties with respect to the accuracy or completeness of the contents of this work and specifically disclaim all warranties, including without limitation any implied warranties of merchantability or fitness for a particular purpose. No warranty may be created or extended by sales representatives, written sales materials or promotional statements for this work. The fact that an organization, website, or product is referred to in this work as a citation and/or potential source of further information does not mean that the publisher and authors endorse the information or services the organization, website, or product may provide or recommendations it may make. This work is sold with the understanding that the publisher is not engaged in rendering professional services. The advice and strategies contained herein may not be suitable for your situation. You should consult with a specialist where appropriate. Further, readers should be aware that websites listed in this work may have changed or disappeared between when this work was written and when it is read. Neither the publisher nor authors shall be liable for any loss of profit or any other commercial damages, including but not limited to special, incidental, consequential, or other damages.

Library of Congress Cataloging-in-Publication Data
Name: De Angelis, Franco, editor.
Title: A companion to Greeks across the ancient world / edited by Franco De Angelis.
Description: Hoboken : Wiley, 2020. | Series: Blackwell companions to the ancient world | Includes bibliographical references and index.
Identifiers: LCCN 2019053490 (print) | LCCN 2019053491 (ebook) | ISBN 9781118271568 (hardback) | ISBN 9781118341360 (adobe pdf) | ISBN 9781118341377 (epub) | ISBN 9781119675228 (paperback)
Subjects: LCSH: Hellenism. | Greeks–Foreign countries–History. | History, Ancient.
Classification: LCC DF77 .C6958 2020 (print) | LCC DF77 (ebook) | DDC 938–dc23
LC record available at https://lccn.loc.gov/2019053490
LC ebook record available at https://lccn.loc.gov/2019053491

Cover Design: Wiley
Cover Image: ©Nikolayenko Yekaterina/Shutterstock

Set in 10/12.5pt Galliard by SPi Global, Pondicherry, India

Printed in the United States of America

SKY10122829_072425

Contents

Maps   xi
Illustrations and Tables   xiii
Abbreviations   xv
Notes on Contributors   xvii
Acknowledgments   xxiii

Introduction: Greeks across the Ancient World   1
Franco De Angelis

PART I   Approaches, Ancient and Modern   11

1. Mobility in the Ancient Greek World: Diversity of Causes, Variety of Vocabularies   13
   Michela Costanzi

2. English-Speaking Traditions and the Study of the Ancient Greeks outside their Homelands   37
   Lela M. Urquhart

3. French-Speaking Traditions and the Study of Ancient Greeks outside their Homelands   53
   Michel Gras

4. German-speaking Traditions (including the Habsburg Empire) and the Study of the Ancient Greeks outside their Homelands   69
   Martin Mauersberg

5. Italian-Speaking Traditions and the Study of the Ancient Greeks outside their Homelands   85
   Franco De Angelis

6. Tsarist Russian, Soviet, and Post-Soviet Traditions and the Study of Ancient Greeks outside their Homelands   101
   Sergey Saprykin

7	Models of Culture Contact and Cultural Change: Moving Beyond National and Linguistic Traditions *Christoph Ulf*	119

PART II Regional Case Studies 137

8	Phoenicians and Greeks as Comparable Contemporary Migrant Groups *Brien K. Garnand*	139
9	Neo-Assyrian through Persian Empires *Robert Rollinger*	173
10	Greeks in Iron Age Central Europe: Patterns of Interaction and Change *Peter S. Wells*	199
11	Anatolia *Andrew Brown*	221
12	Greeks on the Island of Cyprus: "At home" on the Frontiers *Maria Iacovou*	247
13	Southern Italy *Gianfranco Adornato*	273
14	Sicily *Justin St. P. Walsh*	295
15	The Adriatic Sea and Region *Maria Cecilia D'Ercole*	317
16	Cyrenaica *Gerald P. Schaus*	339
17	Egypt *Joseph G. Manning*	363
18	The Phocaeans in the Far Western Mediterranean *Joan Sanmartí*	385
19	The Northern Aegean *Despoina Tsiafaki*	409
20	The Black Sea *Pia Guldager Bilde†, Søren Handberg, and Jane Hjarl Petersen*	431
21	The Greeks in the East in the Hellenistic Period *Gerassimos G. Aperghis*	459

PART III	Themes	**481**
22	Greeks and Cultural Development in the Pre-Roman Mediterranean *Tamar Hodos*	483
23	Relations with Homelands: *Apoikia* and *Metropol(e)is* *Frank Bernstein*	499
24	The Making of Greece: Contributions from the Edges *Raimund J. Schulz*	513
Index		529

Maps

The first three maps in this list illustrate several different chapters. They are grouped separately as part of the front matter of this volume, and reference is made to them in the relevant chapters. The remaining maps are embedded in individual chapters.

Map 1	Map of Greece and Asia Minor.	xxiv
Map 2	The western Mediterranean.	xxv
Map 3	Map of the Hellenistic world.	xxvi
8.1	The Near East.	145
8.2	Mediterranean resources.	152
8.3	Island sites with their *peraea*: Aradus (ʿRWD); Gades (ʾGDR); Motya (MṬW); Pithecussae.	154
8.4	Island sites with their *peraea*: Tyre (ṢR); Sulcis (SLKY) and Enosis (ʾY NSM); Syracuse; Emporiae and Neapolis-Indica.	155
8.5	Plateau sites: Sidon (ṢDN); Panormus (ṢYṢ); Selinus.	157
8.6	Peninsula sites: Carthage (QRTḤDŠT) and Utica (ʿTQ); Tharrus and Othoca (ʿTQ); Corcyra and Buthrotum.	158
10.1	Greek-Iron Age central Europe.	200
11.1	Anatolia.	222
12.1	Cyprus with main sites relevant to the discussion; areas in dark grey around the Troodos mark the location of the pillow lavas, which contain rich copper deposits.	249
18.1	The far western Mediterranean within the pre-Roman Mediterranean.	386
19.1	The northern Aegean.	410
20.1	Map of the Black Sea area with major Greek settlements indicated.	432

Maps

Illustrations and Tables

Figures

7.1	Four possible interdependent parameters and their influences on cultural actors.	129
9.1	"Greek" gift-bearers (Delegation XII) on the eastern Apadāna staircase in Persepolis carrying balls of wool and folded lengths of cloth.	178
9.2	"Greek" gift-bearers (Delegation XII) on the northern Apadāna staircase in Persepolis carrying balls of wool and folded lengths of cloth.	179
11.1	The city wall at Phocaea preserved in the Maltepe tumulus.	229
11.2	Reconstruction of the east façade of the Temple of Athena at Assos.	234
11.3	The Taş Kule tomb with false door.	235
11.4	Wild Goat ware oenochoe, Ionian, ca. seventh century BC.	236
12.1	Salamis. Silver siglos (10.59 g), Evelthon (ca. 530/520 BC). Obverse with reclining Ram; syllabic inscription with the king's name.	255
12.2	Idalion. 1/3 of silver siglos (3.51 g), Stasikypros (ca. 460–450 BC). Obverse with Sphinx seated to left; syllabic inscription with the king's name in shorthand.	255
12.3	Paphos. Cypro-syllabic inscription of the royal family of Onasicharis, king of Paphos, son of King Stasis of Paphos (late sixth century BC). 98 cm.	256
12.4	Kition. Silver siglos (10.70 g), Baalmilk I (ca. 479–449 BC). (a) Obverse with Herakles striding and Phoenician inscription right; (b) reverse with seated lion and Phoenician inscription.	256
12.5	Salamis. Silver-plated siglos (8.28 g.), Evagoras I (ca. 411–374 BC). (a) Obverse with bearded Herakles and syllabic inscription with king's name; (b) reverse with he-goat, syllabic inscription with royal title [pa] and alphabetic E, the initial of Evagoras.	261
12.6	Paphos. Cypro-syllabic inscription of Nikokles, king of Paphos and priest of *wanassa*, and son of Timarchos, king of Paphos (last quarter of fourth century BC). 113 cm high × 37 cm wide.	262

16.1	View from Cyrene's theater down across the middle plateau to the sea.	340
16.2	Apollo sanctuary with the acropolis (left), and Fountain of Apollo (in cliff face).	345
16.3	Sphinx from a votive deposit found outside the city walls, mid-sixth century BC.	356
16.4	Temple of Zeus.	356
16.5	North necropolis, Archaic portico tombs.	357
18.1	Plan of main topographic and archaeological features of Massalia.	390
20.1	Classical lekythos in the shape of Aphrodite appearing from a seashell. From Phanagoria. Height 17 cm.	436
20.2	Gilded *gorytos* (bow case) of the early Hellenistic period with depictions of episodes in the life of Achileus. From the Chertomlyk Barrow in the Dnieper area. 46.8 by 27.3 cm.	438
20.3	Honorary decree depicting the three Bosporan rulers, Spartokos II, Pairisades I, and Apollonios.	441
20.4	Alabaster pyxis from Archaic grave in Olbia. Naukratis. Second half of the sixth century BC. 11.7 cm. Alabaster. Olbia necropolis, 1912. Burial no. 64.	442
20.5	Grave stele from Chersonesos. Anthropomorphic representation in *Naiskos*. Local limestone. Height 26 cm; width 20.5 cm; thickness 14.5 cm.	444
20.6	One-handled cup by the Eretria Painter from Apollonia showing Thracian warriors. Preserved height ca. 14 cm.	446
20.7	Eminakos coin from Olbia with a depiction of Herakles stringing a bow.	448
20.8	Fragment of a wall from the Aphrodite shrine in Nymphaion covered with a multi-colored painting of the Ptolemaic warship "Isis." Plaster and painting with encaustic coating. 160 by 60 cm. First half of the third century BC.	450

Tables

7.1	A summary of the motivations of migrants according to their social status.	122
7.2	A Summary of the different perceptions of migrants and their transferred items.	125
7.3	A Summary of the different types of contact zones and their power features.	126

Abbreviations

The abbreviations used in citing journal titles, epigraphic corpora, standard works of reference, and ancient authors and their works follow those in the fourth edition of *The Oxford Classical Dictionary* (Oxford: Oxford University Press, 2012), edited by Simon Hornblower and Anthony Spawforth, pp. xxix–liii. Any other abbreviations can be found in their respective chapters.

Notes on Contributors

Gianfranco Adornato is Professor of Greek and Roman Art and Archaeology at the Scuola Normale Superiore, Pisa. He was Visiting Scholar at the Getty Research Institute, Los Angeles (2012), member of the scientific committee of the Royal Museums in Turin (2015), and Visiting Palevsky Professor at the University of California, Los Angeles (2018). His main fields of interest are: Archaic, Classical, and Hellenistic Art (he edited *Scolpire il marmo. Importazioni, artisti itineranti, scuole artistiche nel Mediterraneo antico*, Milan 2010); Archaic Rome, architecture, and cults; the Western Greek world and its colonization (he is author of *Akragas arcaica. Modelli culturali e linguaggi artistici di una città greca d'Occidente*, Milan 2011, and scientific director of the *Locri Survey*); artistic practice and drawings in the ancient world; the reception of Greek art in Roman contexts (he co-edited *Restaging Greek Artworks in Roman Times*, Milan 2018); aesthetics and technical terminology in literary sources; and Winckelmann and ancient literary sources.

Gerassimos G. Aperghis obtained degrees in Engineering from Cambridge and Caltech. After a career in computers, he received a Doctorate in Ancient History from University College London in 2000. His dissertation, *The Seleukid Royal Economy*, was published in 2004. Since 2005 he has been an Honorary Research Fellow at University College.

Frank Bernstein studied in Düsseldorf and Oxford. Following positions at the universities of Duisburg, Mainz, and Bielefeld, he now holds a Chair for Ancient History at the Johann Wolfgang Goethe-Universität Frankfurt am Main. His teaching seeks to pay tribute to a political reading of the legacy of the classical world in line with the Nietzschean approach. His research covers both Greek and Roman history. Bernstein is particularly interested in the political history of religions (see his work on the *Ludi publici*, Stuttgart: Franz Steiner Verlag, 1998) and the complex phenomenon of "Archaic Greek Colonization" (such as his study *Konflikt und Migration*, St. Katharinen: Scripta Mercaturae Verlag, 2004). Recent projects include an analytical study of the pragmatics and semantics of collective oblivion, as a prelude to preparing a monograph which will seek to offer contrasting considerations on the irritating particularity of pacification among the Greeks and the Romans.

Pia Guldager Bilde† was, before her untimely death on January 10, 2013, Associate Professor at Aarhus University. From 1993 to 2002, she was Director of the Museum of Antiquity at that same university. She took part in the Nordic excavations of the Castor and Pollux temple on the Forum Romanum in Rome (1983–1985), and led the excavations of an imperial villa at Lake Nemi south of Rome in 1998–2002. Between 2002 and 2010, she was Director of the Danish National Research Foundation's Centre for Black Sea Studies.

Andrew Brown is Assistant National Finds Advisor for Iron Age and Roman Coinage at the British Museum. He holds a PhD in Archaeology from the University of Bristol focused on the Iron Age Troad and is Iron Age lead for the Çaltılar Archaeological project.

Michela Costanzi is Associate Professor of Greek History and Archaeology UPJV-Université d'Amiens, E.A. 4284 TrAme. She is Director of the French archaeological mission at Halaesa, Sicily. Her publications deal with the foundation of Greek cities in the Mediterranean, especially Sicily, southern Italy, and Libya, with a particular interest in secondary foundations (cities established by Greeks who did not come from the Greek homeland, but from already founded cities). She is also interested in other types of non-Greek foundations in Sicily in the Classical, Hellenistic, and Roman periods.

Franco De Angelis is Professor and Distinguished University Scholar at the University of British Columbia. He specializes in the development of ancient Greek culture outside Greece, in terms of both similarities to and differences with its place of origin. His most recently published work on the subject is *Archaic and Classical Greek Sicily: A Social and Economic History* (New York: Oxford University Press, 2016). He is co-editor of *The Archaeology of Greek Colonisation: Essays Dedicated to Sir John Boardman* (revised paperback edition Oxford: Oxford University School of Archaeology, 2004) and editor of *Regionalism and Globalism in Antiquity: Exploring their Limits* (Leuven: Peeters, 2013).

Maria Cecilia D'Ercole is a Professor (Directrice d'Études) at the École des Hautes Études en Sciences Sociales, in Paris. She specializes in cultural and economic contacts in the ancient Mediterranean, in Greek and Roman colonization, in ancient Adriatic trade and landscape, and in ancient carved ambers. She is the author of several articles and volumes; her most recent books are *Histoires Méditerranéennes. Aspects de la colonisation grecque de l'Occident à la mer Noire (VIIIe–IVe siècles av. J.-C.)* (Arles: Éditions Errance, 2012) and *Ambres gravés. La collection du département des Antiquités grecques, étrusques et romaines du Musée du Louvre* (Paris: Éditions du Louvre-Somogy, 2013).

Brien K. Garnand is an Assistant Professor in the Classics Department at Howard University. His interdisciplinary research interests straddle the Greco-Roman and Near Eastern Mediterranean, its languages and literatures, its archaeology and history. In particular, he focuses on interactions of Greeks and Phoenicians in the central Mediterranean and North Africa. He has undertaken extensive archaeological fieldwork and archival research, including excavations at Mt. Polizzo in Sicily and field survey on Meninx, and is currently preparing archaeological reports for the *tophet* at Carthage.

Michel Gras is a historian and archaeologist. He was Director of Research at the CNRS (1985–2011) and Director of l'École française de Rome (2003–2011). He was in charge of the French research at Megara Hyblaea, Sicily, between 1994 and 2003. Since 2012, he has been a foreign member of the Accademia dei Lincei, Italy.

Søren Handberg is Associate Professor at the Department of Archaeology, Conservation and History at Oslo University. In 2012–2015 he was Assistant Director of the Danish Institute at Athens. His research has focused mostly on the Greek settlements in Magna Graecia and the Black Sea region. Since 2013 he has conducted excavations in the ancient Greek city of Kalydon in Aetolia in Greece.

Tamar Hodos is Reader in Mediterranean Archaeology at the University of Bristol. A world-leading expert on the Mediterranean's Iron Age archaeology, she has written *Local Responses to Colonisation in the Iron Age Mediterranean* (London: Routledge, 2006) and most recently edited *The Routledge Handbook of Archaeology and Globalization* (London: Routledge, 2017).

Maria Iacovou is Professor of Prehistoric and Protohistoric Archaeology in the Department of History and Archaeology of the University of Cyprus. Her work focuses on political economies in relation to the island landscape of Cyprus from a long-term, diachronic perspective. Since 2006, she has been directing the Palaepaphos Urban landscape Project (https://ucy.ac.cy/pulp/).

Joseph G. Manning is the William K. and Marilyn Milton Simpson Professor of History and of Classics at Yale University. He specializes in Hellenistic history with particular focus on the legal and economic history of Ptolemaic Egypt. His interests lie in governance, reforms of the state, legal institutions, formation of markets, and the impact of new economic institutions (coinage, banking) on traditional socioeconomic patterns in the ancient world. Much of his previous work has been devoted to the understanding of the interactions between Greek and Egyptian institutions in the Ptolemaic period and the new state formation of the Ptolemies that was driven by these interactions as well as longer term historical forces. His approach, thus, has been to examine Ptolemaic Egyptian society as a whole, striking a balance between state aims and local responses to these aims, and deploying both the Egyptian and the Greek material to fuller effect. Manning is the author of several books, including *Land and Power in Ptolemaic Egypt. The Structure of Land Tenure* (Cambridge: Cambridge University Press, 2003), and *The Last Pharaohs. Egypt under the Ptolemies, 305–30 BC* (Princeton: Princeton University Press, 2010). His current research involves examining climate change and dynamic modeling of Hellenistic societies.

Martin Mauersberg is Lecturer in Ancient History at the Leopold-Franzens Universität Innsbruck. His research interests include the perceptions of the past in Antiquity and Reception Studies. He recently published a monograph on ancient and modern perceptions of "Greek colonization": *Die "griechische Kolonisation." Ihr Bild in der Antike und der modernen altertumswissenschaftlichen Forschung* (Bielefeld: transcript, 2019).

Jane Hjarl Petersen is Associate Professor at the Department of Classical Studies at the University of Southern Denmark. Her research has focused on burial customs in the Black Sea colonies in a comparative perspective with colonies in Magna Grecia. She has conducted fieldwork in the Black Sea region as well as Southern Italy.

Robert Rollinger holds a PhD (1993) and Habilitation (1999) in Ancient History from Leopold-Franzens Universität Innsbruck, where since 2005 he has been full Professor in the department of Ancient History and Ancient Near Eastern Studies. Between 2011 and 2015 he was Finland Distinguished Professor at the Department of World Cultures, University of Helsinki, and Research Director of the project "Intellectual Heritage of the Ancient Near East." His main research interests are Greek historiography, intercultural contacts between East and West, and ancient Near Eastern history of the first millennium BCE.

Joan Sanmartí is Professor at the University of Barcelona. He has also been Visiting Professor at the University of Chicago (2009) and the University Paul Valéry Montpellier III (2013). He has been a member of the Institute of Catalan Studies (International Academic Union) since 2007. He has also been a member of the Committee of Archaeology of the Autonomous Government of Catalonia since 1997. His research has mainly focused on the rise and development of complex societies in pre-Roman Iberia and the northeastern Maghreb, as well as the evaluation of the respective roles in those processes of endogenous evolution and the relationships with the Greek and Phoenician societies. This activity has involved important fieldwork in central and southern coastal Catalonia, in the Balearic Islands, and since 2006 in Tunisia (Althiburos project).

Sergey Saprykin is Professor and Head of the Department of Ancient History of the Moscow State University. He is also leading fellow-researcher in the Institute of World History of the Academy of Sciences of Russia.

Gerald P. Schaus is Emeritus Professor of Archaeology and Classical Studies, Wilfrid Laurier University. He has excavated and published material from the Demeter Sanctuary, Cyrene. He is currently publishing the Canadian excavation results from the acropolis sanctuary at Stymphalos, Greece. He co-edited *Onward to the Olympics: Historical Perspective on the Olympic Games* (Waterloo, ON: Wilfrid Laurier University Press and The Canadian Institute in Greece, 2007).

Raimund J. Schulz is Professor of History with particular reference to Ancient History at the University of Bielefeld. His interests cover the history of the sea in antiquity, war, and the emergence of ancient empires. His publications include *Die Antike und das Meer* (Darmstadt: Primus, 2005), *Athen und Sparta*, 5th ed. (Darmstadt: WBG, 2015), *Kleine Geschichte des antiken Griechenland*, 2nd ed. (Stuttgart: Reclam, 2011), and *Feldherrn, Krieger und Strategen. Krieg in der Antike von Achill bis Attila* (Stuttgart: Klett-Cotta, 2012).

Despoina Tsiafaki holds a doctorate in Classical Archaeology and is Director of Research at the "Athena" Research Center, Xanthi Department, Greece. Her research focuses on the archaeology of the northern Aegean, ancient ceramics, and Digital Humanities. She has published extensively on the archaeology of the region, and on the relations between Greeks and Thracians. She is the author of a monograph on Thracian myths in Attic art and co-editor of a volume on the archaeology of Macedonia and Thrace.

Christoph Ulf is Professor Emeritus of Ancient History at the University of Innsbruck. His main research interests focus on the history of Archaic Greece, the development of sociopolitical identities, cultural interactions, sport and competition in ancient societies, and the impact of political beliefs on ancient and modern historiography.

Lela M. Urquhart is the Senior Communications and Development Specialist for the Getty Research Institute in Los Angeles, California. Her research focuses on the archaeology of the ancient western Mediterranean, and specifically on the connections between colonization, religious change, and state formation in Sicily and Sardinia.

Justin St. P. Walsh is Associate Professor of Art History and Archaeology at Chapman University. He has published on Greek pottery and relations between ancient European cultures. Walsh's primary archaeological expertise is in Sicily. He currently directs an excavation at Cástulo, Spain, and is co-Principal Investigator of the International Space Station Archaeological Project. He is the author of *Consumerism in the Ancient World: Imports and Identity Construction* (London: Routledge, 2014).

Peter S. Wells is Professor of Anthropology at the University of Minnesota. His research focus is later European prehistory. Publications include *The Barbarians Speak: How the Conquered Peoples Shaped Roman Europe* (Princeton: Princeton University Press, 1999) and *How Ancient Europeans Saw the World: Vision, Patterns, and the Shaping of the Mind in Prehistoric Times* (Princeton: Princeton University Press, 2012).

Acknowledgments

I most grateful to Haze Humbert, my original commissioning editor, who, many years ago, approached me with the idea of this volume. She saw the project develop from idea, through book proposal, to contract, and continued to serve as its commissioning editor as contributors were invited to participate in the volume and contracts issued to them. She and her staff provided advice and support of all kinds, without which this project would not have gotten off the ground. Her successor, Jennifer Manias, has continued to show this project the same commitment and support, and has taken this project now through to publication. I am very grateful to her. I am also very grateful to Ajith Kumar, my project editor, Sakthivel Kandaswamy, my production editor, and their respective teams, who have been responsible for the editing and production side of the publication process. I thank all the contributors for their hard work and patience, and for believing in the project from start to finish. I must also thank my former graduate student Andrei Mihailiuk, who translated Chapters 1 and 3 into English from their French originals. The final word of thanks, though not the least in any sense, is due to Tara Connolly, who not only lived with the entire project, but who also acted as my editorial assistant in the final phase of work needed to put the volume into press.

Bloomsbury, London
August 2019

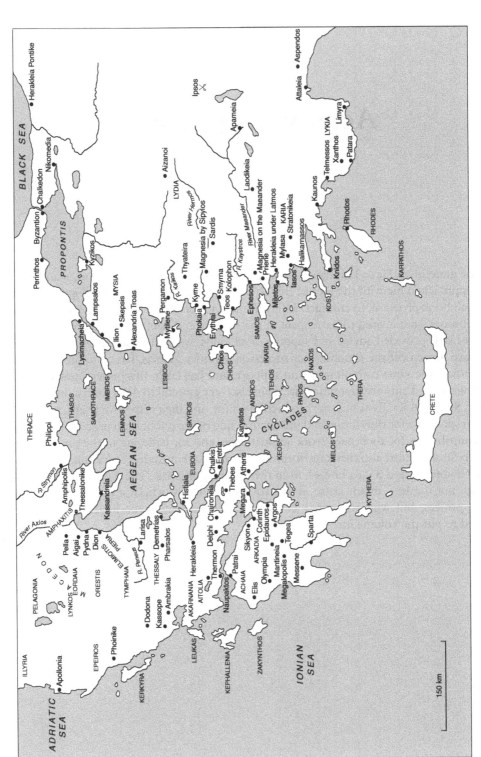

Map 1   Map of Greece and Asia Minor.

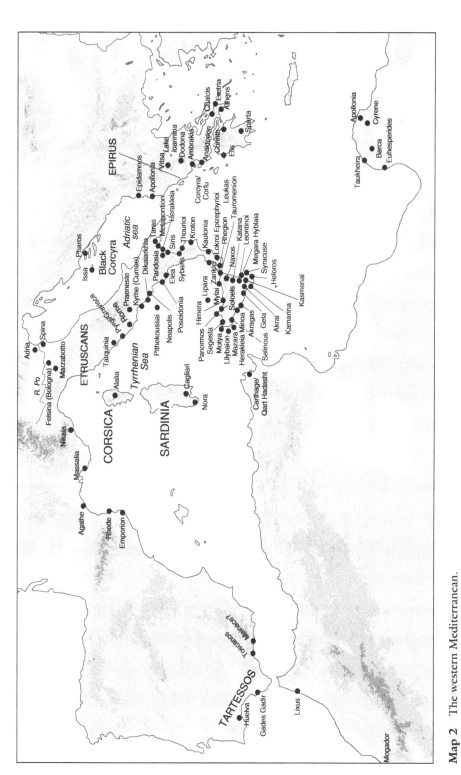

Map 2 The western Mediterranean.

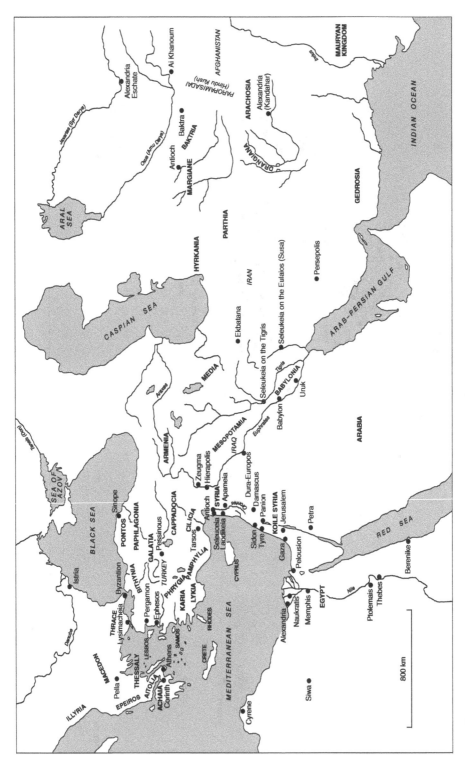

Map 3 Map of the Hellenistic world.

Introduction: Greeks across the Ancient World

Franco De Angelis

"*Tutta la storia greca era considerata dagli antichi, in buona parte, storia di apoikiai*"

(Mazzarino 1966, 1:111).[1]

The Greeks across the ancient world discussed in this *Companion* migrated, either permanently or temporarily, between the Early Iron Age and Hellenistic period (traditionally dated to ca. 1000–30 BC) (see Maps 1–3). This volume focuses on the regions where the migrants went, the new lives that they created there, and the connections that they maintained with home and with other Greeks and non-Greeks. Our approaches to and knowledge of this subject have grown and developed in unprecedented ways since the late 1980s, and it is the purpose of this *Companion* to bring together leading specialists to take stock of these scholarly advances. In this Introduction, I discuss the growth and development of the subject over the past generation, and how the present volume positions itself with regard to these. Let us start by outlining four crucial developments leading up to this *Companion*.

The collapse of the Soviet Union and Communist East Bloc in Central and Eastern Europe represents the first development. These regions were once home to ancient Greek settlements on their coasts (including Albania, Bulgaria, Croatia, Georgia, Rumania, Russia, and Ukraine) and played host to a variety of interactions with the hinterlands beyond. National and regional scholarly research traditions emerged there in modern times to study these ancient Greeks, just as they did elsewhere in western European countries and their colonies overseas. Communism and the Cold War kept these two scholarly worlds largely apart, but the disappearance of these barriers has opened up opportunities. Scholars today have easier access to this Bloc and its past and present research and vice versa, thanks also in part to the development of the internet during this same time, exposing these two worlds to each other.

A Companion to Greeks Across the Ancient World, First Edition. Edited by Franco De Angelis.
© 2020 John Wiley & Sons, Inc. Published 2020 by John Wiley & Sons, Inc.

At the same time as world politics were shifting, the practices of ancient historians were also changing, to such a degree that they comprise the second scholarly development of note (Davies 2002). Ancient history's traditional foci on written sources as evidence and on avoiding comparative approaches began to diminish (Ampolo 1997, 79–82). By focusing on surviving written evidence, a powerful canon restricted to a handful of questions and states (especially Athens) had been created. To counterbalance this, scholars had to face three important methodological challenges. The first is the ancient Greeks' penchant for local and regional traditions of historiography, which often survived in fragmentary form or not at all (Momigliano 1979, 169; cf. Vlassopoulos 2007, 15–17). This meant coming to terms with the silences of the written record and with the careful handling of the external perspectives of any surviving written sources (such as the accounts by Athenians regarding the Spartans or Sicilians). Second, it also entailed a search for alternative forms of evidence. Archaeology became important for the writing of Greek history, with the understanding that it is the only form of evidence that could bring together all the different regions and communities of the ancient Greek world (Roberts 2000, 99–100, 113, 131; Gosden 2004; Vlassopoulos 2007, 222–223). Lastly, Greek history's traditional canon began to broaden even further as the plea to study "Third Greece" (a term originally coined for overlooked states in Greece beyond Athens and Sparta: Gehrke 1986) came to be heeded. These three methodological challenges combined to loosen the straitjacket around the discipline.

Soon the concept of "Third Greece" and the crucial role of archaeological evidence came to be applied to ancient Greeks outside Greece (De Angelis 2003; Tsetskhladze and De Angelis 2004). This application set a third scholarly development into motion and raised a whole new series of questions. The primacy of particular parts of the ancient Greek world was also heavily molded by the incorrect modern practice of labeling all ancient Greek city-states outside Greece proper as "colonies." This practice can be traced back to the early Renaissance, with a mistranslation of the ancient Greek word *apoikiai* ("homes away from home") into "colonies," and gained considerable momentum with modern Greek state formation and European colonial expansion in the nineteenth and twentieth centuries (McNeal 1991; Morris 1994; Shanks 1996; De Angelis 1998; Osborne 1998; Haagsma, den Boer, and Moormann 2003; Moore, Macgregor Morris, and Bayliss 2008). Such a misleading label and connection extended the model of modern nationalist history writing to ancient Greece and encouraged a number of modern beliefs and practices with which we still grapple today. In general, nationalist histories showed no interest in migrants: once they left, they left the nation's historical imagination (Harzig, Hoerder, and Gabaccia 2009, 1; Constantinides 2015, 16). Not surprisingly, a similar lack of interest extended to the ancient Greek migrants who left Greece. When they received any attention, it only emphasized their inferiority, with Greece proper representing the "center" of an imperial-like system that treated regions outside it as an underdeveloped or undeveloped "periphery" (see most recently De Angelis 2019, and Chapters 22–24 in this volume). As a result, it was usually assumed, though without much supporting evidence, that fully formed ancient Greek civilization in Greece was exported to the "colonies," and that Greek culture overseas completely depended on it. No cultural developments worth reporting sprang from the edges of the Greek world (as noted by Frisone and Lombardo 2007, 183). In addition, there was the widespread assumption that the ancient Greek settlers encountered "native" populations who were inferior and easily overrun. The "natives" contributed little or nothing to shaping the development of ancient Greek culture overseas, let alone at home (for some challenges to these views, see Snodgrass 1986, 9; Malkin 1994, 2001, 2011; De Polignac 1995; Lomas 2000; Hall 2002). In any case, the fusion of Greeks and natives and their cultures was regarded as something baneful, causing the Greeks to become debased in a way that further justified ignoring them and focusing on the "purer" Greeks of Greece. Racism and other contemporary issues and anxieties raised by nationalism, colonialism, and imperialism of the nineteenth and twentieth centuries reverberated through the minds of contemporary scholarship on ancient Greece (see Chapters 2, 4–5 in this volume).

In the 1980s the subject was ripe for postcolonial scrutiny. The unsuitable ways in which modern imperialism and colonialism negatively affected the study of ancient Greece began to be put under the microscope. Part of this included the first attempts to calculate the size and number of all ancient Greek states (Ruschenbusch 1985). Since then, it has come to be appreciated that Greeks may have founded over 500 "colonies" (or about one-third to one-half of the total number of Greek city-states in the Archaic and Classical periods), which may have been home to more than 40% of the total ancient Greek population (see Hansen and Nielsen 2004; Hansen 2006). This realization coincided with another new perspective on how the Mediterranean's ecology was essentially microregional. Generally, no one region possessed all the resources it needed, and this imposed mobility on its inhabitants who were thus more interconnected and interdependent than scholars had earlier imagined (Horden and Purcell 2000; for a pioneering attempt to apply these ideas to Greek history, see Schulz 2008, as well as his chapter in this volume, see Chapter 24). In other words, the Greeks and their "colonies" could not be separated from one another. This threw into stark relief the need to integrate the ancient Greeks outside Greece into accounts of ancient Greek history in a much more systematic and comprehensive way than ever before (De Angelis 2009, 48–49; 2019; Gras 2016, 243). Decolonization of the modern world had finally caught up with the study of the ancient Greeks, opening a door onto a largely unexplored world as far as the overall narrative of Greek civilization goes, which still tends to be dominated by a well-established grand narrative of great battles, famous individuals and monuments, and big developments, like democracy, centered on the ancient Greeks of the Aegean basin area (for recent examples, see Pomeroy et al. 2008; Sansone 2009).

The fields of mobility, migration, and diaspora studies followed logically upon the foregoing development and represent the fourth and final development to impact the study of ancient Greeks outside Greece. The combination of mobility, migration, and diaspora studies acknowledged, once and for all, the ongoing maintenance of meaningful contacts between migrants and their place of origin and that these relationships needed to be viewed as a two-way dialogue. This was part of a trend discernible in nationalist history, where mobility, migration, and diaspora, along with everything that they entailed, gained in respectability as subjects of inquiry (Manning 2005; Sheller and Urry 2006; Koser 2007; Cohen 2008; Harzig, Hoerder, and Gabaccia 2009; Livi-Bacci 2012; Kenny 2013; Cohen and Sheringham 2016; Isabella and Zanou 2016). The most conscious and comprehensive application of these ideas to antiquity has been in a series of recent French books prepared in connection with the *agrégation* (the examination required to gain access to teaching posts at the secondary level in France: Avram 2012; Boillet, Barat, and Costanzi 2012; Bouffier 2012; Capdetrey and Zurbach 2012; D'Ercole 2012; Martinez-Sève 2012; Schwentzel et al. 2013). The intersection with mobility, migration, and diaspora studies provides a larger comparative intellectual framework that can help invigorate the study of the ancient Greeks. It supplies us, for instance, with the valuable reminder that "colonization" illustrates but one part of a wider range of possible ways to discuss mobility, migration, and diaspora, which are also about forced and voluntary migrations to procure slave labor or mercenaries. It is also about where the Greeks did not succeed or where others subordinated the ancient Greeks.

These four developments collectively represent a major turning point over the past generation. Here lies the opportunity. Most work on Greek migrations and diasporas continues to focus on the first generation or two of the foundation period (Boardman 1999; Tsetskhladze 2006–2008), and makes little attempt to integrate this roughly other half of the ancient Greek world into a new, more up-to-date historical account (points I argue for in De Angelis 2009). From a suppressed and peripheral role in the study of the ancient Greeks, the subject matter of this *Companion* has emerged as a needed component in understanding better the growth and development of Greece and the Mediterranean. The writing of new, more comprehensive histories of the ancient Greeks fills a niche, and this *Companion* seeks to contribute to that. The *Companion* will do much, we hope, to mute recent opinions that the study of Greek history and Greek "colonization" sit parked in a state of crisis because they have reached a crossroads, if not an impasse (see, respectively, Roberts 2000, 99–100; Purcell 2005, 115). An opportunity exists, therefore, to seize upon Santo Mazzarino's declaration quoted at the outset. It remains now to turn to outlining the overall approach and contents of this volume.

There are 24 chapters divided into three parts. Part I contains seven chapters that deal with ancient and modern approaches to discussing ancient Greeks outside their homelands. What have ancient and modern people thought about this phenomenon for better or for worse, and what do we make of these inherited ideas today? What sorts of models exist to frame culture contact and culture change? Chapter 1, by Michela Costanzi, provides a thorough overview of ancient terminology and concepts, and how they have been understood and translated in modern times. Chapters 2–6 build on this and focus on the intellectual traditions that used one of the five main scholarly languages to write about ancient Greek migrations and diasporas – English (Lela Urquhart), French (Michel Gras), German (Martin Mauersberg), Italian (Franco De Angelis), and Russian (Sergey Saprykin). The purpose of these chapters is to expand our horizons beyond previous scholarly treatments (for which need I have argued elsewhere: De Angelis 2009, 52–53).[2] Our five chapters throw much new light on the subject and help fill a gap in the existing scholarly literature on the classical tradition (De Polignac and Levin 2006; Kallendorf 2007; Moore, Macgregor Morris, and Bayliss 2008; Tsingarida and Verbanck-Piérard 2008; Bradley 2010; Stephens and Vasunia 2010), including in that series of recent French books just mentioned. We should not regard our chapters solely as "national versions of an international phenomenon" (to quote the great Arnaldo Momigliano: 1977, 1). They also reveal the preceding attitudes and views that national traditions had to deal with, as well as the transnational nature of all this scholarship. Our chapters help fill a gap, but they do not exhaust the possibilities, for other case studies remain to be written on, for example, the

Greek, Turkish, Dutch, Swedish, and Spanish scholarly traditions (for the latter, see already Sanmartí, Chapter 18, below). The seventh and final chapter in Part I, by Christoph Ulf, seeks to cut across these various national and linguistic traditions by considering the full range of theoretical models and frameworks (for example, the middle ground, network theory, and code-switching) recently used to understand and contextualize ancient Greek migrations and cultural interactions. According to the late Jerry Bentley (2011, 344), a pioneer in the development of world history:

> There is no major paradigm for the analysis of cultural developments that flow from cross-cultural interactions and exchanges – no coherent body of theory or analysis, for example, analogous to the modernization or world-system school of thought on modern political economy. World historians have worked out no common approach to the study of cultural developments, nor have they even adopted any settled vocabulary or analytical convention for the investigation of cultural developments.

A similar goal seems worthwhile pursuing for the study of ancient Greek mobilities, migrations, and diasporas. Ulf's chapter represents an important foray in this regard. The first and seventh chapters by Costanzi and Ulf which begin and conclude Part I frame the subject in broad terms and show the great variety of words and ways to approach it. The five chapters sandwiched in between their chapters demonstrate the rather limited modern interpretations of this breadth of approaches and remind us of the subject's other dimensions.

Part II concentrates on regional case studies and contains 14 chapters, which form the volume's core. It begins with three chapters (8–10) on regions and peoples with whom Greeks primarily exchanged in some form or another. The chapters cover Phoenicians, the other contemporary migrant group across the Mediterranean (Brien Garnard), Greeks living as subjects in the Neo-Assyrian, Neo-Babylonian, and Persian Empires (Robert Rollinger), and Greek–Celtic interactions in central Europe (Peter S. Wells). The remaining chapters deal with regions, from Central Asia to the western Mediterranean, in which Greeks established states, sometimes in synergy with other local pre-existing cultures. Two of these chapters (17 and 21), by Joseph G. Manning and Gerassimos George Aperghis, pick up where Robert Rollinger's left off by focusing on the Ptolemaic and Seleucid Empires forged out of Alexander the Great's conquest of the Persian Empire. The other chapters discuss regions to which Greeks had migrated in the Early Iron Age and Archaic period. They include chapters (13–16 and 19–20) on the most commonly discussed regions of Greek "colonization," such as southern Italy (Gianfranco Adornato), Sicily (Justin St. P. Walsh), the Adriatic (Cecilia D'Ercole), Cyrenaica (Gerald P. Schaus), the northern Aegean (Despoina Tsiafaki), and the Black Sea (the late Pia Guldager Bilde, Søren Handberg, and Jane Hjarl Petersen). There are also three chapters (11–12 and 18) on Anatolia, Cyprus, and France and the Iberian Peninsula by, respectively, Andrew Brown, Maria Iacovou, and Joan Sanmartí, all regions acknowledged as omissions in a recent major work (Vlassopoulos 2013, xvi).

United by their basic structure, Part II's 14 chapters consist of a sketch of the geography and people(s) resident in these regions at the time of contact and how they related to the Greek states established there. A long-duration perspective has been taken, so that these regional histories can be fully viewed and put into context (just as those scholars who study modern Hellenism have long been doing: Bruneau 1992; Prévélakis 1995). All the authors received the tall order of writing ambitious chapters to synthesize a great deal of material. By looking carefully at individual regions of the ancient Greek world outside Greece, this regional approach leads to a different picture of the whole (Burke 2004, 43–46; cf. also Vlassopoulos 2007, 228–235). Taking a microhistory approach based on individual case studies reveals why ancient Greek culture at the edges was often diverse and regional in character in ways different from that of Greece proper, itself culturally unharmonized to begin with (Dougherty and Kurke 2003). Nicholas Purcell (2003, 21) has argued that Mediterranean history should be approached in this way, on the basis of frontier studies that pay special attention to the fluctuating character of its borders (cf. also Frisone and Lombardo 2007, 181–182). The Mediterranean differs, says Purcell, because of its edges. These chapters provide grist to his mill.

Three chapters meant to bring together wider themes emerging from the volume's first two parts embody Part III. In Chapter 22, Tamar Hodos considers the role played by Greeks in cultural development in the pre-Roman Mediterranean and steers a balanced course between Hellenocentrism and outright dismissal (so too recently Vlassopoulos 2013, 322). Instead of swinging the pendulum from one extreme to the other, she summarizes superbly the evidence for the impact of Greeks on the lives of others. In Chapter 23, Frank Bernstein looks back to Greece and reexamines relations with these homelands. He shows that such relations, normally described as between "colony and mother city," were actually quite limited and usually overemphasized in earlier scholarship working in a colonialist mindset. He provides a fresh perspective and review of the evidence, supplying much food for thought on this important matter. In Chapter 24, the volume's final, Raimund J. Schulz discusses very impressively the contributions made by the edges of the Greek and non-Greek worlds to the making of Greece itself. He reveals the interconnected and integrated nature of the different regions of the Greek and non-Greek worlds in a manner that serves as a fitting close to the volume and brings us full circle to Chapter 1 by Costanzi on the varieties of mobility and their outcomes.

This *Companion* has by no means exhausted all the possible avenues in the study of the Greeks across the ancient world. But it is hoped that it will act as a positive and helpful stride in the development of scholarship and teaching. With this intention in mind, every attempt has been made to make the contents of this volume accessible to as wide an audience as possible: to upper level undergraduate students, graduate students, specialists, and other teachers/researchers of Classical antiquity, as well as to non-specialist teachers and researchers who want to access the latest research and thinking on ancient Greek mobilities, migrations, and diasporas.

NOTES

1 "All of Greek history was considered by the ancients, in large part, the history of *apoikiai*."
2 Two examples can be used to illustrate the need for this part of the *Companion*. First, in Albania, the ancient Greeks have never formed a distinct field of study and instead

are always discussed in terms of being Illyrianized and not any more advanced than the native cultures with whom they came into contact (Mano 1998; cf. also Bejko and Hodges 2006). Second, Carla Antonaccio (2007, 214) has stated that there was much more native-Greek integration in the Black Sea than elsewhere settled by the ancient Greeks. Was this really so? Before such a conclusion can be drawn, one needs to wonder whether this evidence for integration has been especially crafted by Soviet archaeology and history due to their focus, for obvious reasons given the Soviet Union's ideological agenda (Trigger 2006, 334–341), on investigating how ordinary people lived and on delineating ethnic diversity. Cf. Petersen 2010, 301: "Understanding the research history of both Russian/Soviet and Western scholarship was a central issue in my initial approach to this 'new' study area, and many correlations and interpretations which I have met along the way have become much clearer to me in the light of the social and political contexts in which they were created."

REFERENCES

Ampolo, Carmine. 1997. *Storie greche. La formazione della moderna storiografia sugli antichi Greci*. Turin: Einaudi.

Antonaccio, Carla. 2007. "Colonization: Greece on the Move, 900–480." In *The Cambridge Companion to the Archaic Greek World*, edited by H. Alan Shapiro, 201–224. Cambridge: Cambridge University Press.

Avram, Alexandru. 2012. *Les diasporas grecques du VIIIe siècle à la fin du IIIe siècle av. J.-C. (Bassin méditerranéen, Proche-Orient)*. Paris: Bréal.

Bejko, Lorenc, and Richard Hodges, eds. 2006. *New Directions in Albanian Archaeology: Studies presented to Muzafer Korkuti*. Oxford: Oxbow.

Bentley, Jerry. 2011. "Cultural Exchanges in World History." In *The Oxford Handbook of World History*, edited by Jerry H. Bentley, 344–360. Oxford: Oxford University Press.

Boardman, John. 1999. *The Greeks Overseas: Their Early Colonies and Trade*, 4th ed. London: Thames & Hudson.

Boillet, Pierre-Yves, Claire Barat, and Michela Costanzi. 2012. *Les diasporas grecques du VIIIe s. au IIIe s. avant J.-C.* Paris: Dunod.

Bouffier, Sophie, ed. 2012. *Les diasporas grecques du détroit de Gibraltar à l'Indus (VIIIe siècle av. J.-C.-fin du IIIe siècle av. J.-C.)*. Paris: Sedes.

Bradley, Mark, ed. 2010. *Classics and Imperialism in the British Empire*. Oxford: University Press.

Bruneau, Michel. 1992. "L'Hellénisme. Un paradoxe ethno-géographique de la longue durée." *Géographie et cultures*, 2: 45–74.

Burke, Peter. 2004. *What is Cultural History?* Cambridge: Polity.

Capdetrey, Laurent, and Julien Zurbach, eds. 2012. *Mobilités grecques. Mouvements, réseaux, contacts en Méditerranée, de l'époque archaïque à l'époque hellénistique*. Bordeaux: Ausonius.

Cohen, Robin. 2008. *Global Diasporas: An Introduction*, 2nd ed. London: Routledge.

Cohen, Robin, and Olivia Sheringham. 2016. *Encountering Difference: Diasporic Traces, Creolizing Spaces*. Cambridge: Polity.

Constantinides, Stephanos. 2015. "The Greek Diaspora." *Études helléniques/Hellenic Studies*, 23(2): 14–21.

Davies, John K. 2002. "Greek History: A Discipline in Transformation." In *Classics in Progress: Essays on Ancient Greece and Rome*, edited by T. Peter Wiseman, 225–246. Oxford: University Press.

De Angelis, Franco. 1998. "Ancient Past, Imperial Present: The British Empire in T.J. Dunbabin's *The Western Greeks*." *Antiquity*, 72: 539–549.

De Angelis, Franco. 2003. *Megara Hyblaia and Selinous: The Development of Two Greek City-States in Archaic Sicily*. Oxford: Oxbow.

De Angelis, Franco. 2009. "Colonies and Colonization." In *The Oxford Handbook of Hellenic Studies*, edited by Georges Boys-Stones, Barbara Graziosi, and Phiroze Vasunia, 48–64. Oxford: Oxford University Press.

De Angelis, Franco. 2019. "Conclusions." In *Une autre façon d'être Grec: interactions et productions des Grecs en milieu colonial. Actes du colloque international organisé à Amiens (Université Jules Verne Picardie) et Paris (ANHIMA), 18–19 novembre 2016*, edited by Michela Costanzi and Madalina Dana, 435–447. Leuven: Peeters.

De Polignac, François. 1995. *Cults, Territory, and the Origins of the Greek City-State*. Trans. Janet Lloyd. Chicago: Chicago University Press.

De Polignac, François, and Sonia Levin, eds. 2006. "Histoires helléniques. De quelques enjeux culturels, idéologiques et politiques de l'archéologie de la Grèce ancienne." *European Review of History*, 13(4): 509–676.

D'Ercole, Maria Cecilia. 2012. *Histoires méditerranéennes. Aspects de la colonisation grecque de l'Occident à la mer Noire (VIIIe-IVe siècles av. J.-C.)*. Arles: Errance.

Dougherty, Carol, and Leslie Kurke, eds. 2003. *The Cultures within Ancient Greek Culture: Contact, Conflict, Collaboration*. Cambridge: Cambridge University Press.

Frisone, Flavia, and Mario Lombardo 2007. "Periferie? Sicilia, Magna Grecia, Asia Minore." In *Storia d'Europa e del Mediterraneo, vol. 3: Grecia e Mediterraneo dall'VIII sec. a.C. all'Età delle guerre persiane*, edited by Maurizio Giangiulio, 177–225. Rome: Salerno.

Gehrke, Hans-Joachim. 1986. *Jenseits von Athen und Sparta. Das Dritte Griechenland und seine Staatenwelt*. Munich: Beck.

Gosden, Chris. 2004. *Archaeology and Colonialism: Culture Contact from 5000 BC to the Present*. Cambridge: Cambridge University Press.

Gras, Michel. 2016. "Observations finales." In *Conceptualising Early Colonisation*, edited by Lieve Donnellan, Valentino Nizzo, and Gert-Jan Burgers, 243–246. Turnhout: Brepols.

Haagsma, Margriet, Pim Den Boer, and Eric M. Moormann, eds. 2003. *The Impact of Classical Greece on European and National Identities: Proceedings of an International Colloquium, held at the Netherlands Institute at Athens, 2–4 October 2000*. Amsterdam: Gieben.

Hall, Jonathan M. 2002. *Hellenicity: Between Ethnicity and Culture*. Chicago: Chicago University Press.

Hansen, Mogens Herman, and Thomas Heine Nielsen, eds. 2004. *An Inventory of Archaic and Classical Poleis: An Investigation conducted by the Copenhagen Polis Centre for the Danish National Research Foundation*. Oxford: Oxford University Press.

Hansen, Mogens Herman 2006. *Polis: An Introduction to the Ancient Greek City-State.* Oxford: University Press.

Harzig, Christiane, Dirk Hoerder, and Donna Gabaccia. 2009. *What is Migration History?* Cambridge: Polity.

Horden, Peregine, and Nicholas Purcell 2000. *The Corrupting Sea: A Study of Mediterranean History.* Oxford: Blackwell.

Isabella, Maurizio, and Konstantina Zanou, eds. 2016. *Mediterranean Diaspora: Politics and Ideas in the Long 19th Century.* London: Bloomsbury.

Kallendorf, Craig W. 2007. *A Companion to the Classical Tradition.* Oxford: Blackwell.

Kenny, Kevin. 2013. *Diaspora: A Very Short Introduction.* Oxford: Oxford University Press.

Koser, Khalid. 2007. *International Migration: A Very Short Introduction.* Oxford: Oxford University Press.

Livi-Bacci, Massimo. 2012. *A Short History of Migration.* Trans. Carl Ipsen. Cambridge: Polity.

Lomas, Kathryn. 2000. "The Polis in Italy: Ethnicity, Colonization, and Citizenship in the Western Mediterranean." In *Alternatives to Athens: Varieties of Political Organization and Community in Ancient Greece*, edited by Roger Brock and Stephen Hodkinson, 167–185. Oxford: Oxford University Press.

Malkin, Irad. 1994. "Inside and Outside: Colonisation and the Formation of the Mother City." In *ΑΠΟΙΚΙΑ*, edited by Bruno D'Agostino and David Ridgway, 1–9. Naples: Istituto Universitario Orientale.

Malkin, Irad, ed. 2001. *Ancient Perceptions of Greek Ethnicity.* Cambridge, MA: Harvard University Press.

Malkin, Irad. 2011. *A Small Greek World: Networks in the Ancient Mediterranean.* Oxford: Oxford University Press.

Manning, Patrick. 2005. *Migration in World History.* New York: Routledge.

Mano, Aleksandra. 1998. "The Evolution of the Albanian Archaeological Thinking about the Hellenic Colonization of Southern Illyria." *Illyria*, 23(1–2): 135–137.

Martinez-Sève, Laurianne, ed. 2012. *Les diasporas grecques du VIIIe à la fin du IIIe siècle av. J.-C.* Pallas vol. 89. Toulouse: Presses universitaires du Midi.

Mazzarino, Santo. 1966. *Il pensiero storico classico.* 2 vols. in 3 pts. Bari: Laterza.

McNeal, Richard A. 1991. "Archaeology and the Destruction of the later Athenian Acropolis." *Antiquity*, 65: 49–63.

Momigliano, Arnaldo. 1977. *Essays in Ancient and Modern Historiography.* Oxford: Blackwell.

Momigliano, Arnaldo. 1979. "The Rediscovery of Greek History in the Eighteenth Century: The Case of Sicily." *Studies in Eighteenth-Century Culture*, 9: 167–187.

Moore, James, Ian Macgregor Morris, and Andrew J. Bayliss, eds. 2008. *Reinventing History: The Enlightenment Origins of Ancient History.* London: Institute of Historical Research.

Morris, Ian. 1994. "Archaeologies of Greece." In *Classical Greece: Ancient Histories and Modern Archaeologies*, edited by Ian Morris, 8–47. Cambridge: Cambridge University Press.

Osborne, Robin. 1998. "Early Greek Colonization? The Nature of Greek Settlement in the West." In *Archaic Greece: Problems and Evidence*, edited by Nick Fisher and Hans van Wees, 251–269. London: Duckworth.

Petersen, Jane H. 2010. *Cultural Interactions and Social Strategies on the Pontic Shores: Burial Customs in the Northern Black Sea Area c. 550–270 BC*. Aarhus: Aarhus University Press.

Pomeroy, Sarah B., Stanley M. Burstein, Walter Donlan, and Jennifer T. Roberts. 2008. *Ancient Greece: A Political, Social, and Cultural History*, 2nd ed. New York: New York University Press.

Prévélakis, Georges. 1995. "Les espaces de la diaspora hellénique et le territoire de l'État grec." In *Diasporas*, edited by Michel Bruneau, 99–112. Montpellier: GIP Reclus.

Purcell, Nicholas. 2003. "The Boundless Sea of Unlikeness? On Defining the Mediterranean." *Mediterranean Historical Review*, 18(2): 9–29 (reprinted with same pagination in Irad Malkin, ed., *Mediterranean Paradigms and Classical Antiquity*. London: Routledge, 2005).

Purcell, Nicholas. 2005. "Colonization and Mediterranean History." In *Ancient Colonizations: Analogy, Similarity and Difference*, edited by Henry Hurst and Sara Owen, 115–139. London: Duckworth.

Roberts, Jennifer. 2000. "Sociology and the Classical World." *Arion*, 8(2): 99–133.

Ruschenbusch, Eberhard. 1985. "Die Zahl der griechischen Staaten und Arealgrösse und Bürgerzahl der 'Normalpolis'." *Zeitschrift für Papyrologie und Epigraphik*, 59: 253–263.

Sansone, David. 2009. *Ancient Greek Civilization*, 2nd ed. Oxford: Oxford University Press.

Schulz, Raimund J. 2008. *Kleine Geschichte des antiken Griechenland*. Stuttgart: Reclam.

Schwentzel, Christian-Georges, Madalina Dana, Stéphane Lebreton, and Franck Prêteux. 2013. *Les diasporas grecques VIIIe–IIIe s.*, 2nd ed. Neuilly: Atlande.

Shanks, Michael. 1996. *Classical Archaeology of Greece: Experiences of the Discipline*. London: Routledge.

Sheller, Mimi, and John Urry. 2006. "The New Mobilities Paradigm." *Environment and Planning A*, 38: 207–226.

Snodgrass, Anthony M. 1986. "La formazione dello stato greco." *Opus*, 5: 7–21.

Stephens, Susan A., and Phiroze Vasunia, eds. 2010. *Classics and National Cultures*. Oxford: Oxford University Press.

Trigger, Bruce G. 2006. *A History of Archaeological Thought*, 2nd ed. Cambridge: Cambridge University Press.

Tsetskhladze, Gocha R., ed. 2006–2008. *Greek Colonisation: An Account of Greek Colonies and Other Settlements Overseas*. 3 vols. Leiden: Brill.

Tsetskhladze, Gocha R., and Franco De Angelis, eds. 2004. *The Archaeology of Greek Colonisation. Essays dedicated to Sir John Boardman*, revised paperback edition of 1994 original. Oxford: Oxbow.

Tsingarida, Athéna, and Annie Verbanck-Piérard, eds. 2008. *L'Antiquité au service de la Modernité? La reception de l'antiquité classique en Belgique au XIXe siècle*. Brussels: Timperman.

Vlassopoulos, Kostas. 2007. *Unthinking the Greek Polis: Ancient Greek History beyond Eurocentrism*. Cambridge: Cambridge University Press.

Vlassopoulos, Kostas. 2013. *Greeks and Barbarians*. Cambridge: Cambridge University Press.

PART I

APPROACHES, ANCIENT AND MODERN

CHAPTER ONE

Mobility in the Ancient Greek World: Diversity of Causes, Variety of Vocabularies[1]

Michela Costanzi

Since the beginning of the 1990s, the question of mobility has been at the center of a renewed reflection in historical studies, especially within the ancient period. The past two decades saw a transition from a very marginal vision of this phenomenon[2] to a new approach which, first off, frames the Mediterranean as the site, since the Archaic period, of all kinds of migration, individual and collective (Gras 1995; Stazio 2000; cf. Moatti 2012, 40), and then imposes a vision of this fluid space as the scene for traffic, exchange, and diverse and complex movements.[3]

The work of Claudia Moatti has only confirmed the importance of mobility which, beyond just pushing people to move with objects in tow, also takes on precise forms, and has political, social, economic, and cultural consequences (Moatti 2004, 2007; Moatti and Kaiser 2007, 2009; Moatti, Kaiser, and Pébarthe 2009). Tracing the historiography of the concept of mobility, she remarks that since we cannot doubt that mobility lies at the heart of ancient as well as modern and contemporary societies, then this concept alone encompasses a large variety of movements and displacements. It also underlines how "behind a unifying [modern] vocabulary lies a great diversity of realities," which range from mass movements (for which we most often use the term *migration*, referring interchangeably to colonization, exodus, or flight, etc.) to individual mobility (called generally or imprecisely *foreigner*, who could just as easily be an alien, nomad, or guest, etc.). Moatti denounces the uniformity of this modern lexicon, which reduces the complexity of these experiences and relations, and argues for "the necessity to start from the ancient vocabulary."[4] But were the ancient Greeks really aware of different types of movement, conveyed in a specific and precise vocabulary? Or is their vocabulary reductive and unvarying from the start?

This study presents a few examples to identify different forms of mobility and their causes, and to analyze the terms used in ancient sources. One should not expect an exhaustive

---

A Companion to Greeks Across the Ancient World, First Edition. Edited by Franco De Angelis.
© 2020 John Wiley & Sons, Inc. Published 2020 by John Wiley & Sons, Inc.

glossary here. The examples, which come from literary and epigraphic sources of the Archaic to Hellenistic periods, illustrate a sampling of the terms used by ancient authors.[5] Among the many categories of mobility, I will endeavor to go deeper into some of the most significant ones, so as to identify a specific lexicon. I will at times study certain problems raised by the vocabulary of modern authors on this subject.

Categories of Mobility

From the Archaic to the Hellenistic periods, the sources clearly show that the Greeks were in constant movement for numerous reasons. Modern thinkers interpret this with great variety: for some, mobility is a condition of everyday life, just as much in times of peace as war;[6] for others, the practice of traveling, though not foreign to the ancients, was nevertheless not as common as now, for political and social reasons (hostility, wars) and practical reasons (distance, the precariousness of routes, and modes of transport), implying a different concept and command of space (Marasco 1978, 15–29). The reality is that, despite difficulties, the majority of ancient Greeks traveled incessantly, pushed by all sorts of motives and without the aid of our modern modes of transport.

As Thucydides (1.2.1–2) relates, "in ancient times" the Greeks were already emigrating and leaving their homes with ease:

> It appears, for example, that the country now called Hellas had no settled population in ancient times; instead there was a series of migrations (μεταναστάσεις), as the various tribes, being under the constant pressure of invaders who were stronger than they were, were always prepared to abandon (ἀπολείποντες) their own territory. There was no commerce.... the use they made of their land was limited to the production of necessities; they had no surplus left over for capital, and no regular system of agriculture.... they showed no reluctance in moving from their homes (οὐ χαλεπῶς ἀπανίσταντο), and therefore built no cities of any size or strength... (trans. Warner 1954).

The primary agent of mobility during the Archaic period is certainly colonization, which is to say the foundation of cities outside of Greek territory, more or less autonomous and independent of the metropolis. In the Classical period, colonies were founded as part of the constitution of the Athenian Empire, different from the cleruchies established during that same time. In the Hellenistic period, Alexander founded colonies throughout his eastern expedition, all bearing his name, as well as some other less important establishments. Thereafter, Hellenistic kings often resorted to the metonymy of ancient cities as they transformed and adapted to the new Greek presence.

Moreover, commerce drove Greeks to the extreme borders of the Mediterranean, touching the coastlines to the east and west, from which they moved inland. The more they traveled, the greater their reputation, and the further they went. Sanctuaries generated remarkable mobility as well. Private visits included Greek individuals consulting oracles at sanctuaries for personal or healing reasons. Public visits involved the political life of the city and the flow of its official representatives, *oikistai*, *theoroi*, ambassadors, and emissaries. Sanctuaries were equally a meeting place for athletes and artists. For education, Greek students and teachers were drawn to and from the great centers of Hellenic culture, like Athens or Alexandria in Egypt.

While the above forms of mobility are done freely, others by contrast involve constraint and violence: ostracisms, exiles, migrations of populations, and marriages across borders and cultures. Hence all Greeks moved about, and not just those among the elite. This list of the categories of mobility is incomplete, and in turn these categories can only be unevenly developed. By organizing them into two groups – mass mobility and personal mobility – I am forced to choose certain categories which seem particularly significant to highlight their causes and reasons for their associated vocabulary. I will leave aside mobility linked to colonization, which has already received ample commentary.[7] Nevertheless, concerning Archaic colonization I cannot avoid the debate sparked by modern language.

Mass Mobility

Greeks left home (in general, the colonial expedition and the settlement itself were indifferently called *apoikia*, "away from home") for many reasons,[8] and settled themselves all along the perimeter of the Mediterranean and the Black Sea. These newly founded cities multiplied, reproducing cities of their own (the colonies of colonies were also called *apoikiai*).

The related lexicon has already been analyzed many times before (Casevitz 1985; Costanzi 2010; De Wever and Van Compernolle 1967; Virgilio 1971–1972). The current trend, among specialists and non-specialists alike, is to use a new term to identify this phenomenon: diaspora has been appearing increasingly in works concerning Greek history to designate mobility in general (Garland 2014 uses it to indicate Greeks who are forced to leave and settle elsewhere, especially political exiles), but more precisely colonization (Martinez-Sève 2012). According to some, this word purports to replace the term colonization, which has been almost universally contested since it relates to modern and contemporary events. So the word diaspora, some claim, "decolonizes" the current vocabulary and avoids confusion between ancient and modern historical realities (Osborne 1998; Étienne 2010). Since, however, it seems to me to introduce other precise connotations, making it neither more neutral nor more appropriate than colonization, I will stop for a moment on this question.

The noun διασπορά, it is true, comes from ancient Greek. It is constructed from the verb διασπείρειν (to distribute, disperse, disseminate), which itself comes from the verb σπείρειν (to sow, seed, or scatter like grain). Though the verb is already attested by the fifth to fourth centuries BC in Isocrates (*Philippus* 104; *Letter to Dionysius* 6) to refer to spreading the word and fame, Xenophon (*An.* 1.8.25; *Hell.* 5.1.25) to refer to scattering troops and spreading noise, and Aristotle (*Meteorology* 369a) to refer to releasing heat, the substantive does not appear before the third century BC. It was a neologism invented by Greek-speaking Jewish scribes working on a translation of the first five books (*Torah*) of the Hebrew Bible (*Tanakh*). One should clarify that the word diaspora never translates those terms issuing from the Semitic root *glh* (the verb *galah*, "to exile," or the substantives *golah/galouth*, "exile"), though we may claim that as a general rule. In the Septuagint, the Greek terms *apoikia*, *paroikia*, and *meitoikesia* translate the words related to colonization, whereas *diaspora* seems to have always been associated with the idea of "dispersion," and to notions of dishonor, divine retribution, or banishment. In most cases, this dispersion did not take place, but was only potential (Casevitz 2002; Dufoix 2012a, 2012b). The substantive noun reappeared in Plutarch (*Sol.* 32.4) to describe the "scattering" of Solon's ashes after his death. Yet other authors use it to describe the "dispersal of the soul" in the body or the "discord of parts" (Philo, *De praemiis et poenis* 115; Clem. Alex., *Protrepticus* 88). Certain Greek Christian authors of the Low Empire used the word to signify "dispersion" or "dissemination," applying it to ethnic groups, such as the Jews after the annexation of Judaea and the destruction of Jerusalem's temple by Titus (70 AD), as well as after the destruction of Jerusalem by Nebuchadnezzar (587 BC). Thereafter, one encounters the word *diaspora* in one of the first Modern Greek (Vaclos 1659) dictionaries from the seventeenth century to express the dispersal of Greeks in the modern period. After the appearance of the concept of nation-state, the word would come to designate, in many modern languages, all dispersed ethnic and/or religious groups. The diaspora includes all those living outside of national borders, scattered across the world, who share a common feeling of alienation from their homeland, to which they feel close and hope to return (Bruneau 1995, 2005, 2007). In France, the word appears in 1929's Larousse dictionary, relating once again to Jewish realities. Up until the end of the 1960s, it did not designate those ethnic communities forced into migration by economic or political factors. It was not until the 1970s that it gained this distinct and in many cases unwarranted use, evoking all sorts of migrants, deported groups, and refugees (for an overview, see Avram 2012, 10–12).

Claudia Moatti writes that the notion of diaspora, no matter the word's historical origins, is today emancipated from that origin (Moatti 2012, 45–46). For her, it is characterized by an initial dispersal, forced or voluntary, from the host community, as well as a persistent social and spiritual link with origins. Since it can be applied to different forms of mobility, it can be applied equally to ancient colonization. Michel Casevitz (2012, 87) remarks that the word diaspora can identify things other than the Jewish diaspora.

The lack of correspondence between the idea of Greek colonization and the term diaspora, already evident in the Septuagint, but even more its association with certain communities (particularly the Jewish community), does not permit us to use this word without causing grave confusion. To me, the wish to "decolonize" Archaic colonization (Osborne 1998) to then "diasporize" it (Étienne 2010), replacing one controversial word with another that raises just as many difficulties, does not seem methodologically correct.

Franco De Angelis (2009, 52; 2010, 252) has proposed using the word *apoikia* to identify the colony and *apoikiazation* for the process of its creation. This way of proceeding, to me more logical, permits us to avoid designating ancient phenomena with words that have taken on precise meanings. One difficulty arises, however; though English permits the creation of neologisms (*apoikiazation*), for other languages (French or Italian) this possibility is hardly conceivable. According to Andreas Morakis (2011, 460 n. 1), it would be better to use *apoikia* for the colony and *apoikismos* for colonization. In his opinion, taking this term from Modern Greek is justifiable since it preserves the use of *apoikiai* for colonies. In fact, this word is already present in Aristotle and Diogenes Laertius to signify the foundation of a colony (Arist., *Pol.* 5.5.3; Diog. Laert, 9.20). Even the word *apoikisis* is attested in Dionysius of Halicarnassus (3.31). Nevertheless, Morakis continues to use the words *colony* and *colonization*, proving just how difficult it is to adopt a new vocabulary.

With this all considered, it would perhaps be good to put the terms of the question back in order. After all, in the modern era we took up words that the Latins had already used to define cities founded by the Greeks.[9] At the same time, the Greeks who spoke of the Roman Empire and its colonies used the words *apoikia, apoikoi,* and *apoikizein* (e.g., Dion. Hal. 3.31 on the first cities founded by Rome). These terms already seem to be more or less synonymous, capable of adapting to situations that do not correspond perfectly. The Humanists revived this tradition, and in the modern period we simply reused these same root words and adapted them to yet different realities. I believe, therefore, that once the problem of the lexicon's flexibility is explained to students so that they avoid confusion, for specialists the inevitable parallels between ancient and modern colonization seem in the end more appropriate than those brought to mind by the word diaspora. While this term may permit us to imagine certain elements linked to departure in particular (its violence, its sometimes obligatory character and ensuing heartbreak), it is far less relevant with regard to the causes and specifics of this phenomenon (reasons for departing, the organizing of the expedition with its necessary rituals, the types of establishments across which this phenomenon expresses itself and the different sorts of relations it permits in new territories; the hope of returning one day, if it exists, is less present than the will to go and found other, yet more distant colonies).

The founded settlements have a dominant agricultural character. Far away from the *oikos*, another is recreated where the base element is the *kleros*, for trade and exchange with Greeks and the local population alike. One should certainly not speak of a "colonial empire" in antiquity, even if a certain will to dominate was not totally absent. One should equally not imagine a dependent link between the colony and its metropolis, though connections with the homeland remained privileged and strong (or at least they could strengthen at a given moment, on the basis of temporary necessity rather than sentimental attachment). Moreover, the word *metropolis* first appears in Pindar (*Pyth.* 4.20; *Nem.* 5.8) and Thucydides (1.34; 3.92), underlining that there was already a relation between daughter city and its motherland. Those settlements founded by the Greeks, therefore, are justifiably colonies, so I will use this word regularly and without quotation marks.

Forced Migrations of Populations

Populations are forced to relocate for many different reasons, war being the principal cause.[10] Tyrants are another common motive. According to Thucydides (6.9–23), when evaluating the Sicilian cities before his expedition, Alcibiades remarked that they were not a great power since, populated by a large number of people of different origins, they change and acquire citizens easily (καὶ ῥᾳδίας ἔχουσι τῶν πολιτῶν τὰς μεταβολὰς καὶ ἐπιδοχάς). For Thucydides, mobility is a typical element of colonial cities and constitutes weakness. The exchange (*métabolai*) and admission (*épidochai*) of new citizens often take place under the constraint of tyrants.

In Sicily, between the fifth and fourth centuries, forced migrations are linked to the policies of the Deinomenids (Maddoli 1980, 67–102; Asheri 1980, 145–158; Vattuone

1994). Herodotus (7.154–156) recounts that Gelon, a brilliant general under Hippocrates's tyranny, took hold of Gela after the tyrant's death. He accomplished this with the help of the *Gamoroi*, who had been formerly driven out (ἐκπίπτειν) by the people and the *Killyroi*, their slaves. In the process of bringing them back (κατάγειν) from Casmenai to Syracuse he managed to take possession of the former as well. From then on, he became tyrant of Syracuse, leaving Gela to his brother Hieron. He fortified the city and brought in (ἄγειν) all the Camarinians after completely leveling theirs, and did much the same for more than half of Gela's citizens. Besieging Megara Hyblaea and forcing its citizens to yield, he brought in (ἄγειν) the *Pacheis* ("fat ones"), to make them citizens, and he sold and expelled the rest from Sicily (ἀπέδοτο ἐπ'ἐξαγωγῇ ἐκ Σικελίης). Diodorus relates that Hieron, after expelling (ἀνιστάναι more precisely means "to make stand up") the inhabitants of Naxos and Catania from their cities, sent over (ἀποστέλλειν, "to snatch in order to send off") new inhabitants of his choice, among them five thousand Peloponnesians, and just as many Syracusans.[11] He changed Catania's name (μετονομάζειν) to Aetna, and portioned out (κατακληρουχεῖν) his and his neighbor's territories. The Naxians and Catanians, expelled (ἀνιστάναι) from their homelands, were forced to live in Leontini with its original inhabitants (μετοικίζειν). In 461 BC, the Syracusans, allied with Douketios, attacked Catania and chased off (ἐκπίπτειν) those who were settled (κατοικίζειν) under Hieron. So they recovered their homeland, while other Catanians took possession of Inessa, renaming it Aetna.[12] According to Diodorus (12.54.7; 12.83.1), in 424 BC all of Leontini's inhabitants set off to live with (μετοικίζειν) the citizens of Syracuse (on which, see Vanotti 1995). Thucydides (5.4.2–6) writes that the *dynatoi* of the city demanded Syracuse's help in expelling the *demos*, who as a consequence scattered themselves abroad (πλανεῖν, in the passive). A large number of *dynatoi* left Leontini and settled in Syracuse (ἐκπλεῖν, meaning they set out by sea, and then settled in, οἰκεῖν), but they soon decided to go back (according to Thucydides, they left Syracuse and took hold of (καταλαμβάνειν) a part of Leontini's territory).

Other examples of forced migrations exist, such as in Athens, where between 411 and 307 BC several non-democratic regimes succeeded one another, leading to deaths, exiles, transfers, and actual deportations. Thus, during the tyranny of Phocion (322–318 BC) (Bearzot 1985, 1994), after Antipater successfully imposed himself on Athens, many citizens were for reasons of the census excluded from citizenship and forced to leave en masse (μετιστάναι) for Thrace, where Antipater offered them a territory to colonize (Diod. 18.18.4–5). This migration was a true deportation, stimulated by Antipater's political motivations and by his wish for permanent exile. In fact, by the time of the collapse of Phocion's government in 318 the exiles had resettled (Diod. 18.66.5; Plut., *Phocion* 32–34; cf. Bearzot 1994, 155–163). The word that Diodorus uses here, κάθοδος, generally indicates a "return," very often for exiles.[13]

The events that displace or transfer populations are therefore expressed with verbs linked to the actions of these tyrants, who chase (ἐκπίπτειν), expel (ἀνιστάναι), send off (ἀποστέλλειν), lead (ἄγειν), bring back (κατάγειν), banish (μετιστάναι), lead settlers en masse (μετοικίζειν), and settle them (κατοικίζειν). The prefixes of these verbs seem to have a certain value which does not always carry into modern translations; they indicate a coercion. Among these verbs, ἀνιστάναι does not simply mean "to expel" but "to make stand up, so as to make leave." The word ἀποστέλλειν does not signify "to send off" but "to be snatched up and sent away." In addition, the verbs μετιστάναι and μετοικίζειν carry the idea of mass action. More than simple movement, these verbs express the result of involuntary action imposed by some authority. The nouns for "exodus" or "mass departure" under force of circumstances or of tyrants, ἀνάστασις (Thuc. 2.14.2) and ἐξαγωγή (Hdt. 7.156), are rare. Once again, authors mostly employ verbs, and the prefixes serve to express the violent obligation of leaving, while nominal second elements do not necessarily carry the idea of movement. Those who are forced to leave in exile are normally defined by active or passive participles of the verbs ἐκβάλλειν and ἐκπίπτειν, respectively "those who were expelled" and "those who were driven out," or by other verbal forms that indicate the action by which tyrants drove out and alienated them (Forsdyke 2005; Montiglio 2005, 30–37; Garland 2014). Often authors use the verb φεύγειν/φυγεῖν as well as the word φυγάδες. This last term appears in Diodorus to indicate all of the "fugitives" of the different Sicilian cities (11.76.2; 12.83.1), but is used by other authors to designate "people in flight" and the "banished" (Hdt. 1.150; 3.138; Xen. Hell. 5.2.10). Sometimes these people return, and Diodorus again uses the word φυγάδες to indicate all of the Greek exiles that Alexander the Great called back in 324 BC.[14]

Personal Mobility

Greeks also had an appetite for travel for pleasure. By Herodotus's (1.29–30) account, after a sea voyage (the verb ἐκπλεῖν indicating the action of setting sail, leaving by boat) Solon arrived (ἀφίκνεσθαι) at the palace of Croesus, at the time when his reign was at its height and Sardis, flourishing and rich, saw visits from all the sages of Greece. The pretext (πρόφασις) for this voyage was a simple curiosity for knowledge, but more specifically to see the world (θεωρίη).[15] However, as is soon explained, this trip is the means for Solon to avoid revoking one of the laws he instituted in Athens. With Solon's arrival, Croesus emphasizes his wanderlust (πλάνη) that pushes him to visit new countries.[16] This word expresses travel undertaken for the pleasure of wandering and travel itself. In a chapter of the *Politics* dedicated to natural resemblances, Aristotle speaks of those who tour the world (… τινὲς τῶν τὰς τῆς γῆς περιόδους πραγματευομένων) without going into any more detail (Arist., *Pol.* 2.3.9). During the Hellenistic era, "travel amateurs" existed and are spoken of as such by their contemporaries. The term φιλαπόδημος seems to have been invented by Xenophon (*Hell.* 4.3.2) to describe a Spartan, Dercylidas, sent out all across Greece to announce the victories of his king, Agesilaus. Dercylidas is described as pleased because he is so fond of travel. Thereafter, we encounter this word in Dicaearchus of Messina, who calls the Chalcidians and those living on the island of Euboea, among other things, "travel amateurs," φιλαπόδημοι (59.30, 261). Pollux mentions this term in his *Onomasticon* (6.168). We find it as well in Artemidorus (*Onirocriticon* 1.80), among a list of professional travelers (navy commanders, pilots, merchants) and vagabonds. Another family of terms, ἄλητης/ἀλάεσθαι, identify the condition of being a vagabond, whether by choice or by necessity.[17]

At the end of the Bronze Age, pushed by commercial interests, the Greeks traced Phoenician routes, moving east and west across the Mediterranean (Giangiulio 1996, 497–502; Domínguez 2007, 132–155). Beginning in the Archaic period, by then a world of cities generated by their own colonization, they traded with other Greeks and locals from the most distant cities. The terms normally used to identify commerce and merchants are ἐμπορία, ἐμπόριον, and ἔμπορος.[18] Ἐμπορία as meaning "commerce by sea" is present in Hesiod (*Op.* 646) as well as Herodotus (3.139), though we find it used in Thucydides (1.2.2) to signify commerce in general.[19] The ἐμπόριον is the "place of commerce," a site not far from the port or the coast, or on an island, arrived at by ship (Thuc. 1.100.2; Hdt. 1.165). It can also designate a place of commerce farther inland (Dion. Hal. 7.20). An ἔμπορος is "one who travels for commercial activities" (Hdt. 2.39; Thuc. 6.31) but can also signify a "wholesale merchant," (Pl., *Prt.* 313d) as opposed to a κάπηλος or "retail merchant" (Hdt. 2.41). *Emporoi* get around by boats they do not own and often share with other *emporoi*. The ship's owner is called a *naukleros* (Vélissaropoulos 1980). The verb ἐμπορεύεσθαι evidently expresses the action of "traveling for business" (*Syll.*³ 1166). All of these words derive from πόρος/πείρειν, which indicates the action of "traveling," whether it is down a river or across a sound, and not from πορεία/πορεύειν. This word derives from the former, and designates the "path" and thus the voyage, especially by land, but also by sea, and not necessarily for commercial reasons. Thucydides recounts that Athens, short of money and cutting costs, immediately sent back the Thracians who arrived after Demosthenes's departure. Since they were crossing the Euripus Strait (πορεύεσθαι δι'Εὐρίπου), their commander received the order to use the Thracians during their passage to harm Athens' enemies as much as possible (Thuc. 7.29).

Regarding modes of transport for traders, travelers on land and sea, Herodotus's (2.178) text on the Greeks in Egypt contains, besides the verb that expresses their arrival in Egypt (ἀφίκνεσθαι), the verb ναυτίλλεσθαι ("to navigate by sea"), which describes those merchants who are only passing through.[20] Based on Herodotus's text, one understands that Greeks in transit gained certain advantages by merit of their trade, such as the ability to honor their gods at sanctuaries predicated on their mobility, but without any particular term to state so.

The orators inform us on the activities of Greek merchants (Pébarthe 2007, 162–166). Their speeches use terms for commercial travel that are taken from the common lexicon for navigation. Demosthenes, in his *Against Lacritus* (3, 20, 25, 28), reports an action mounted by Androcles against Lacritus over a borrowed ship, whose recovery the orator defends. The loan was granted by an Athenian, Androcles, and a Euboean, Nicostratos, to two merchants from Phaselis, Artemo and Apollodorus. The proceedings, however, only concern Androcles against Artemo's brother, who was probably deceased. Three thousand drachmas were borrowed to mortgage a boat for a voyage from Athens to Pontus and then back again. The term employed only once to indicate this "roundtrip voyage" is ἀμφοτερόπλους; the term ἑτερόπλους designates a "one-way trip," either going away or returning. In general, however, the author prefers resorting to periphrases, such as εἰς τὸν Πόντον καὶ πάλιν Ἀθήναζε to say a "voyage to Pontus with a return trip to Athens," or expressions such as ἀφίκνεσθαι δεῦρο for a "return trip."

The vocabulary for merchant travel is thus mainly connected to sea journeys. The verbs ἀποπλεῖν, ἐκπλεῖν, καταπλεῖν, and συμπλεῖν suggest the idea of making a trip away or back by sea, and their prefixes impart a more specific character: ἀποπλεῖν and ἐκπλεῖν emphasize the moment of departure, while καταπλεῖν indicates the action of arriving by sea, of approaching and making land.[21]

Mercenaries traveled for work (Tagliamonte 1994; Bettalli 1995, 2013; Baker 1999; Trundle 2004). In Sicily, for example, tyrants called on the services of both foreign and Greek soldiers. Foreign sovereigns hired Greek mercenaries in turn, as was the case with the pharaohs Psammetichus I and Psammetichus II in Egypt, and Cyrus the Younger in Asia Minor. The word *epikouros* is used often in Herodotus and Thucydides, and up to the end of the fifth century to indicate a mercenary.[22] Its origin is uncertain, but it is likely that we would find it in a lost verb whose root generated the Latin *currere* ("to run"). The word identifying mercenaries would thus carry the idea of movement within itself. Generally, the sources go about describing mercenaries as soldiers who receive a *misthos* ("a payment") (*misthophoroi*), or they specify their origin. These include the Ionians in Egypt[23] (such as Pedon of Priene, mercenary under Psammetichus I,[24] and the mercenaries of Teos, Colophon, and Ialysos under Psammetichus II[25]), or the Greeks of Asia Minor in Croesus's army.[26] We also find Arcadians among the mercenaries under Gelon and Hieron of Syracuse (Paus. 5.27.1–7). By the end of the fifth century BC the word *xenos* begins to appear in the literary sources to define mercenaries, even if they were Greek soldiers (Diod. 11.48.3; 11.72.3; cf. Gauthier 1971, 57).

In general, the kings who employed mercenaries compelled them to move about with them (ἀνιστάναι specifically means "to make rise," to draw them from one place to another: Hdt. 2.154; Diod. 1.66). In his *Anabasis*, Xenophon left us the most important account of the activities of Greek mercenaries, specifically those in the service of Cyrus the Younger against his brother Artaxerxes, successor of Darius, the Great King, to overthrow him and assume power. Cyrus calls on the mercenaries of Asia Minor and reunites them in Sardis:

> he also sent word to Clearchus to come (ἥκειν) to him with the entire army which he had, and to Aristippus to effect a reconciliation with his adversaries at home and send (ἀποπέμπειν) him the army which he had; and he sent word to Xenias the Arcadian, who commanded for him the mercenary force in the cities, to come (ἥκειν) with his troops ... (Xen., *An.* 1.2.1–2; trans. Brownson 1922).

As the levying of mercenary troops is described in these terms, their different movements are retraced in stages, which are measured in parasangs (Hdt. 2.6; 5.53; 6.42).

In Clearchus's first speech to his soldiers, who, suspecting that they were being led against the Great King, did not wish to continue the expedition, the general says:

> Then when Cyrus' summons came, I took you with me and set out, in order that, if he had need of me, I might give him aid in return for the benefits I had received from him. But you now do not wish to continue the march with me; so it seems that I must either desert you and continue to enjoy Cyrus' friendship, or prove false to him and remain with you (Xen., *An.* 1.3.4–5; trans. Brownson 1922).

The verb πορεύεσθαι expresses the act of Clearchus setting out with the mercenaries, which generally means "traveling on foot," and making a journey by land, as was already observed. Clearchus's continuation of the trip with the mercenaries is described with the verb συμπορεύεσθαι, whose prefix underlines the troops' movement as a group.

The word which serves as the title of Xenophon's (*An.*, 1.4.9; 3.1.1) work merits a few observations; ἀνάβασις indicates the rising expedition from the coast of Asia Minor to the inland. Thus the term only properly suits the first part of the account. Thereafter, the Greeks descend to central Asia toward the Euxine Sea, which they reach at Trapezus (κατάβασις), and walk the length of the sea as far as Pergamon (παράβασις). Xenophon was not the first to use the term ἀνάβασις, but he was the first to lend it this technical sense of a "march toward the interior."[27] Xenophon and other authors use it to designate the "act of mounting a horse" (Xen., *Eq. mag* 3.11), the "summit of a mountain" (Hdt. 7.223; Thuc. 7.42; Xen., *An.* 4.1.10), the "ascent of a ramp in a tower" (Hdt. 1.181), or the "waters of a river" (Diod. 1.36.7 referring to the Nile). The term κατάβασις is used by Xenophon (*An.* 5.2.26; 5.2.28; 5.5.4) to describe the mercenary troops' march from central Asia to the coast of the Euxine Sea. Other authors generally use it to indicate a "descent," a "downward path,"[28] but also, for example, the "descent to hell" (Hdt. 7.223). The word παράβασις normally defines the act of "marching" and "crossing" (Plut. *Phil.* 60); it can signify "to make a digression" (Strab. 1.2.2) or "a deviation" (Arist., *Pol.* 1307b33); in comedy, it designates the "act of advancing," in particular the staging of the chorus who advance toward the public. In Xenophon the word designates the mercenaries' journey, as they skirt the southern coast of the Euxine Sea all the way to Pergamon (Xen., *An.* 7.8.26).

In describing the movement of those soldiers called on by pharaoh or foreign king, Herodotus and Xenophon borrow verbs that express displacement from one place to another in a common and standard manner, even in different contexts. No particular term, however, is used to describe this type of movement, except perhaps the word *epikouros*, which originally could define someone who marches against an enemy. On the other hand, it is interesting to note how mercenaries become *xenoi*; even Greeks are foreigners, probably in relation to the person who hires them. Certain terms can take on a more technical definition: the words ἀνάβασις, κατάβασις, and παράβασις are used in Xenophon to indicate the direction of his soldiers' march. However, these words, which are not used in this sense by other authors (save Diodorus and Arrian), would never attain the status of terms linked specifically to mercenaries' movements.

Professionals who possess a *techne* and practice their rare and specialized skills everywhere in the Greek world, pass from place to place. Among them are the λιθουργοί ("stonemasons"),[29] sculptors and construction workers. The mobility of these craftspeople depends on their reputation, which grows with their travels. Their mobility is propelled by the artisans' own self-promotion and city patronage (Jockey 2009, 139). Can we isolate a specific vocabulary for their movements? We find an interesting reference in Pausanias to the wanderings of the mythical artisan, and stoneworker *par excellence*, the famous Daedalus: because of his art, his taste for travel (ὁμοῦ τῇ τέχνῃ τῆς πλάνης τε εἵνεκα), and his misfortunes, he won fame the world over.[30] His voyages, undertaken for the simple pleasure of wandering (πλάνη), figure among the causes of his celebrity.

Nevertheless, the mobility of stonemasons is attested mainly in inscriptions, particularly the texts that record building expenses for the great Greek sanctuaries. Attic records very often reveal the geographic origins of workforces, by way of two clues: the demotic that qualifies the artisan-citizens, and the formula οἰκῶν ἐν for artisan-metics (Feyel 2006, 341–168). In this way we discover that most of the artisans who worked on sanctuaries in

Eleusis and Athens (the Erechtheion) came from Megara, Corinth, and Boeotia, even if there were some exceptions (from Samos or Chios). By contrast, the building records for the sanctuaries at Delphi and Delos mention artisans coming from the most distant regions of the Greek world: a Crotoniate at Delphi (*CID* II, 51, ll. 6–10), and at Delos there was one artisan each from Byzantium (*Délos* 116), Sinope (*Délos* 629), and Mytilene (*Délos* 63). The texts thus inform us that both locals and foreigners worked at these construction sites (Feyel 2007, 90–91, figures 1–2). Despite being named at multiple sites, these artisans are often unknown. However, some very well-known elite artists were also itinerants. Scopas of Paros (fourth century BC) was the traveling sculptor *par excellence* (Palagia 2000, 209–225), as attested in literary sources which permit us to imagine his travels. Ethnic signatures on works found in sanctuaries illustrate the wide demand for these masters, who roam to different building sites (Marcadé 1953–1957), without any specific vocabulary to qualify their movement.

Physicians, another category of Greeks possessing a *techne*, were in demand all across the Greek world (Phillips 1981; Jouanna 1995, 1997; van der Eijk 1999; Samama 2003; Massar 2005). They traveled extensively, pausing for one or several years, before setting off again. In his treatise *The Best Physician is also a Philosopher* (3), Galen of Pergamon teaches us that Hippocrates traveled a lot, saying that all good physicians must travel and visit all of Greece. Travel is thus part of the life and career of a good physician who wants to increase their knowledge and salary (Jouanna 1997, 813). Among the literary sources, Herodotus (3.129–132), writing about an accident suffered by Darius I, recounts how Democedes of Croton became court physician to the Great King in the sixth century BC. He was Aegina's public physician and, because of his renown, he was hired with a much higher salary as Athens' public physician. The next year he was hired by Polycrates of Samos, for a yet higher salary, just before becoming court physician for Darius and Atossa.

Epigraphic texts, however, are our primary source of information on these professional travelers. The Athenian decree for the physician Phidias of Rhodes, dating to 304–303 BC, tells us that this doctor left Rhodes for Athens, where his devotion won him public praise (Samama 2003, n. 7). An honorific decree teaches us that Apollonius of Miletus, at the end of the second century BC, was present as a physician in Tinos (Samama 2003, n. 165), though he had traveled previously and worked as a public physician on other islands (l.7 : ἀποδημῶ[ν τε] καὶ δημοσι ἐ[ν ἄλλαις νήσοις…]) (Samama 2003, n. 166). The honorific decree in Gortyn for Hermias of Kos informs us that he, after working as Gortyn's public physician, having been elected and sent out by the city of Kos (l. 2–4: χε[ιρο]|τονηθένς ὑφ'ὑμίων καὶ ἀποστευνθεὶς παρ'ἀμὲ ἰα|τρός), requested permission to return home (l. 17–18: ἐπεὶ δὲ ἐπευθὼν ἐπὶ τὰν ἐσκλησίαν | ἀξίωσε ἀμὲ ἀφέμεν αὐτὸν ἐς τὰν ἰδίαν…) (Samama 2003, n. 126). Just as Herodotus does not use any specific word in reference to Democedes, and describes his movements by listing which cities called for him at different times, in the same manner we find in inscriptions the verb ἀποδημεῖν, which normally indicates the act of "moving away," or "being away from home" – in other words, traveling (as seen in Apollonius's inscription). We also find the verbs ἀποστέλλειν, "to send off" (there is always the strong idea of separation with the prefix ἀπο-), and ἀφιέναι, "to let go," to express the act of returning home (such as in Hermias's inscription). Physicians are thus generally called on by somebody, be it a city or a king, and the employer releases them to set out for another destination or return home. The term περιοδευτής, used by such later authors as Galen and Athanasius, signals the rounds a physician would make from patient to patient.[31]

Athletic contests, especially the Panhellenic games, involved great travel. Athletes, who mostly came from aristocratic families, found their names inscribed on lists of winners or on monuments commemorating their victories in all of the sanctuaries of the *periodos*: Olympia, Delphi, Nemea, and the Isthmus of Corinth. *Periodos* to begin with names a "way around" something.[32] In Aristotle, the word signifies a "trip around a country" or "world tour."[33] He also uses it more specifically to name the "tour of sanctuaries" made in Attica by the Athenian *ephebes* and their keepers (Arist., *Ath. Pol.* 42.3) to understand the outline and extent of the territory they will have to defend. So when did the term *periodos* gain the sense of a "complete tour of the four great Panhellenic sanctuaries," on the occasion of these international gatherings that cycled every four years? It seems to have first appeared in later literary sources, probably first in Arrian (end of the first/beginning of second century AD). In the *Manual of Epictetus* (3.25.5), on the subject of happiness, the author says that the struggle for happiness is not like that of an athletic contest; if you give up, you can begin the fight again as soon as you find your bearings and regain your strength, rather than have to wait four years for the "return of new Olympic contests." In his *Deipnosophistae*, Athenaeus of Naucratis (10.415a) speaks about Herodorus of Megara, who, during the siege of Argos by Antigone's son Demetrios, succeeded in exciting the soldiers' zeal by playing his two trumpets; he had apparently been "ten times the victor in the circuit of sacred games" (ἐνίκησε δὲ τὴν περίοδον δεκάσις).

The word *periodos* also appears in inscriptions. In an Amphictyonic law from 380 BC it refers to the inspection of sacred land and does not yet relate to the tour of Panhellenic sanctuaries (*CID* IV.1). We encounter the latter sense in inscriptions from the Imperial era: one inscription in Athens mentions a sprinter who won at the Panhellenic and Panathenaic games, accomplishing a "complete period" (*periodos teleios/a*) (*BÉ* 1987, 572). The word *periodonikes*, which designates an "athlete who won at all four Panhellenic contests," is used by Philo of Alexandria (*Virt.* 193). He observes that having noble parents means nothing for whomever is not noble in spirit, as one who suffers a long bout of consumption cannot find any solace in the family reputation for athletic prowess among the victors at Olympia and all the contests of the *periodos* (ἐν Ὀλυμπιονίκαις ἢ περιοδονίκαις). One funerary inscription from the Imperial period honors a Seleucid citizen, whose victories yielded him multiple citizenships and who is the first to accomplish a "complete period" (here the phrase probably refers to the games at Olympus, Rome, Delphi, Nemea, Athens, the Isthmus, etc.) (*BÉ* 1993, 602).

Other forms of movement tied to sanctuaries, such as oracle consultation, did not produce any particular vocabularies. The tablets at Dodona (Lhôte 2006) or the references to Delphi's oracles in literary sources (Parke and Wormell 1956) simply show that these sanctuaries provoked mobility for many centuries. One significant example from Delphi is the many consultations made with the Pythian oracle preceding the foundation of Cyrene in Libya, as recounted by Herodotus (4.150–156). In the Theraean version of the story, Grinnus, the king of Thera, travels to Delphi twice. On the first occasion, he must provide a hecatomb, as was normal practice when consulting this oracle. Though he probably came to interrogate the oracle on questions concerning Thera, in an unexpected response, the Pythia ordered him to found a colony. The verb indicating his first trip to Delphi is ἀφικνέσθαι, and his return ἀπέρχεσθαι. For the second visit, Herodotus does not even use a verb for movement and instead, in paraphrasis, he relates how the Pythia responded to the Theraeans by insisting that they found Cyrene. The same words appear in the Cyrenean version, in which Battus leaves three times to consult the oracle.

On the occasion of Panhellenic contests, artists also traveled to sanctuaries. Certain ones are cited as members of associations, and as such traveled all over the Greek world (Hunter and Rutherford 2009). A certain Pythocles, known from an epigram carved into a statue base in the Peloponnese that his brother had erected for Hermione (*IG* IV.682), was a musician who held the position of choral leader for the association of Dionysiac *technitai*[34] in several *Soteriae* at Delphi. He also won a combined 12 prizes at the Pythian, Isthmian, and Nemean games, though he achieved victories in musical contests in Boeotia and outside of Greece as well. The inscriptions of the artists' victories permit us to follow their movements from one sacred place to another across the Greek world.

There were also the *theoroi*, traveling sanctuary representatives who were received by the *theorodokoi* of different cities (Perlman 1995, 2000). No specific vocabulary exists for their movements: it is the mechanisms and circuits of their travel that are clues, through a linguistic formula, which puts the name of the city in the dative, preceded by ἐν, and the name and patronym of the *theoredokos* in the nominative. Among the epigraphic documents that constitute the bulk of evidence on this subject, the Hellenistic "Great List,"[35] which lists the names of the cities and *theorodokoi* that received Delphi's *theoroi*, is a particularly reliable tool for retracing these officials' itineraries.[36] As for ambassadors (Habicht 2001), a third-century BC inscription, which stresses the dangers and difficulties of the voyages these people faced, even during trips of tens of kilometers, such as the route from Istros during the rule of the Getic king Zalmodegikos (*IGLSkythia* I.8), demonstrates how no specific lexicon existed to describe these movements.

The same goes for cultural mobility, the last category of personal mobility. Starting especially in the Hellenistic period, a large number of youths, wishing to broaden their knowledge, made way to the cultural centers of the Greek world (Natali 1996). Teachers, who conducted their lessons in gymnasiums and schools both public and private, traveled as well from all over (*Insc. Perg.*, 12, ll. 7–9, 34–36; *IG* XII.9.235, ll. 9–13; cf. Massar 2007). Athens was renowned for its philosophical schools (Habicht 2000, 123–129). Isocrates (*Antid.* 224, 226) speaks of his pupils who crossed the sea (πλεῖν) to see him, and remarks on how disposed they are to spend money and take risks, coming all the way from Sicily or Pontus for instruction. The Athenian ephebic lists, citing foreigners with their ethnicities after the Athenians, meaning that they did not (or at least did not always) have citizenship (Perrin-Saminadayar 2005, 2007, 470–475), show the importance of this cultural mobility for young people. Among the foreigners cited on the Athenian ephebic lists, between 123–122 and the end of the first century BC, seven Heracleots are recorded, probably from Pontus (Perrin-Saminadayar 2007, 476, table 22). One Heracleot is also found on the list of ephebes for the years 119–118 at Delos, as well as one Sinopean in 123–122, and yet other young people from around the Euxine Sea in the same years (Dana 2011, 51–53). These documents are very important for revealing the cultural rapport between Athens and the Euxine Sea (*IG* II².1008–1009, 1011; *IDélos*, 2593, 2598). It is possible that these youths arrived in Athens from their Pontic cities following a veritable network. Or, for example, we could imagine that they got around because their families traveled for work (Dana 2011, 51–53). In all cases, the vocabulary used in these texts, which are nothing more than long lists of names with ethnicities, shows that no precise term was prescribed for the movement of these ephebes. The mention of ethnicity permits specialists interested in cultural relations between Greek cities to infer that travel of this category was frequent.

Conclusion

> Behind a unifying [modern] vocabulary lies a great diversity of realities ... the multi-dimensionality of travel, and the multiplicity of foreign regimes all implicate the concepts we use to identify these phenomena. Hence the necessity of starting from the ancient vocabulary (Moatti 2012, 42).

The present contribution, born out of a necessity to study the causes of ancient Greek mobility and to understand how conscious these people were of the importance and scope of this phenomenon, is an attempt to learn if the ancient vocabulary on this subject is richer, more varied, and more precise than the modern one.

Through the course of this brief review, the principal elements of the question that have emerged are as follows: the Greeks described in literary and epigraphic sources are in incessant motion and the forms their travel take are as varied as their causes. What is evident right away is that there are two large families of mobility: mass migration and individual travel.

Individuals sometimes moved because of a simple desire for travel, a pure curiosity. Travelers also included sanctuary visitors, Greeks who went, for example, to the sanctuaries at Dodona or Delphi seeking answers from oracles to specific questions. Sanctuaries regularly sent out *theoroi* as well to meet people in different Greek cities and announce the sacred festivals, which attracted athletes and artists. Study trips commonly occurred; however, individual mobility was generally related to specific professions such as merchants, as well as mercenaries, stonemasons, physicians, teachers, and any specialists with a *techne* that gave them renown. With a few exceptions, the lexicon generally consists of banal terms for movement and some formulaic phrases about the individual's relocations. The texts do not normally offer any specific terms to distinguish the movements of categories of people, nor the circumstances and status of these foreign traveling specialists (Lonis 1992; Moatti 2004, 2007, 2012) who submitted to identity checks, a practice which is not well described in the sources but has been lucidly studied (Lefèvre 2004). Descriptions show how citizenship was conferred to them in many cities, that their mobility and skills were regularly controlled (Lefèvre 2010), and that the benefits they procured offered stability.

Mass migrations are ordinarily related to situations of necessity or constraint in the frame of political life in a city, of a community. From the Archaic to Hellenistic periods, colonization is the most significant agent of mass movement. The modern vocabulary on this point has proven to be the most problematic, due to the necessity to find a word that generally describes this phenomenon (diaspora, apoikiazation, apoikismos). But one must concede that the Greeks themselves never felt the need to define a normal part of their everyday life with one generic noun. The word colony, used since the Romans, as well as the word colonization have the double advantage of raising fewer problems, and are in the end more appropriate than the word diaspora.

Forced migration, exile, and the transfer of populations are linked to a variety of situations generating vocabulary which, unspecifically, shows constraint and necessity. While there is an abundant use of verbs expressing the act of making to leave, chasing out, expelling, and forcing to live with a new city's inhabitants (with a particular importance given to prefixes), corresponding nouns are relatively rare. Exiles and the banished are identified by the same words. It is possible to conclude, therefore, that ancient Greeks did not create a specific vocabulary for each form of displacement. Even substantive nouns for indicating general movement are rare: μεταβολαὶ (the act of tossing/being tossed in the middle), μετοικέσεις (the act of living together), and μεταναστάσεις (the act of making to leave together) are all used in different contexts.

The social and sometimes political consequences of such movements help us better understand this phenomenon. The Greeks did not clarify mobility with words for its different forms and conditions. Today scholars face so many difficulties when endeavoring to find precise definitions that describe the movements and status of migrating people. Yet again, we attempt to pass an ancient phenomenon through today's prism, as the following chapters will reveal. Inevitably, the end result is that the words seem deficient or inappropriate.

NOTES

1 Translated from the French by Andrei Mihailiuk.
2 Finley 1973, 1975, 1976, 1984: by the end of the 1980s, the model proposed by Moses Finley of ancient societies as "face-to-face societies" considered mobility as quantitatively marginal; we knew that there were population movements, colonization in particular, but we did not yet grasp the scope of the phenomenon, not just historically, but politically, socially, technologically, and culturally as well. Cf. Moatti 2012, 39–40.
3 The vision of Braudel 1949 was called into question by that of Horden and Purcell 2000. See also Naso 2006.
4 Moatti 2012, 42. Malkin (2012, 224–225) underlines the wide application of the word *mobility*, which covers the phenomenon of colonization, but which is applied equally to the displacement of mercenaries, traders, and even seers and wandering poets.
5 I use mostly historical sources, and in some rare instances poetry. I am particularly interested in historical actors, without considering the movements of gods, heroes, and other dramatic characters. My analysis of substantives and verbs is mainly based on Chantraine 1999, *ad vv.*, and Liddell and Scott 1996, *ad vv.*, as well as the volumes of the *Thesaurus Linguae Graecae*, *ad vy*, adding my own personal observations on prefixes.
6 André and Baslez 1993, 11. I cannot share the authors' opinion that the Greeks naturally had a "calling for travel, linked indissolubly to adventure" (8), since the Greeks traveled mainly for very practical reasons; but I share their idea that travel is a condition that characterizes their everyday life.

7 I refer to just a few essential works. For colonization in the Classical period: Gauthier 1973; Bearzot 1995; Brun 2005; Pébarthe 2009. For the Hellenistic period: Cohen 1978, 1995, 2006; Briant 1998; Capdetrey 2007.
8 Here are just a handful of titles from a vast bibliography on Archaic colonization. For different aspects of the phenomenon: Osborne 1998; Boardman 1999; Tsetskhladze 2006–2008; De Angelis 2009; 2010; Malkin 2009, 2011. For different regions: Asheri 1979; Bats 1992; Pugliese Carratelli 1996; Grammenos and Petropoulos 2003–2007; van Dommelen 2005.
9 For example: Cic., *Cat.* 1.8 (on the Greek colonies founded by consent of the oracle in Asia, Sicily, and South Italy); Liv. 8.24 (Heraclea, *colonia* of Tarentum, and so a colony of a colony); Sall., *Iug.* 19.9 (Cyrene, *colonia Theraeon*).
10 Garland 2014, 88–94, with a final lexicon of the words used. Thuc. 2.14.2: the Peloponnesians were about to arrive at Athens, and so the Athenians withdrew the women and children from the countryside. He relates, however, that since the masses were habituated to living in the countryside, the *anastasis* (exodus) was especially difficult.
11 Diod. 11.49.1–3. Haillet 2001 prefers not to insist on the value of prefixes (ἀνιστάναι is "to chase," ἀποστέλλειν "to send"; I choose to translate μετοικίζειν with "to make live with" rather than his "to reinstall").
12 Diod. 11.76.3. Haillet 2001 translates the text's ἐκτήσαντο as "to found," a translation which corresponds better with ἐκτίσαντο, the word given in the footnotes. I prefer to translate it as "to take possession."
13 See also Hdt. 1.60–61, to indicate the return of Peisistratus, taken from power for the first time, and Thuc. 8.81.1 for the return of Alcibiades after he leaves Tissaphernes.
14 Diod. 18.8.4. For an example in inscriptions, see the *Diagramma* of Ptolemy of Cyrene (Bencivenni 2003, 105–108).
15 Legrand 1970 translates πρόφασις as "admitted reason" and θεωρίης as "curiosity." I prefer "pretext" and "observation."
16 Legrand translates πλάνη as "curiosity," but I think that, respecting its etymology, one can translate it as "wanderlust."
17 Hdt. 3.52: Periander addresses his son, who prefers the life of a vagabond (βίος ἀλήτης) over staying with his father; Hdt. 4.97: during Darius's expedition against the Scythians, Cöes advises the king not to destroy a floating bridge on the Istros in case they're defeated and need to retreat, and to avoid being forced to wander astray (ἀλάεσθαι).
18 On commerce, just a few references in a very rich bibliography: Bresson and Rouillard 1993; Gras 1995; Reed 2003; on movement related to commerce: Giangiulio 1996; Domínguez 2007.
19 The word πρᾶξις/πρῆξις (Hom., *Od.* 3.72; *Hymn to Apollo* 397) also indicates commerce (Mele 1979) but does not include the idea of movement.
20 On the distinction between resident Greeks and Greek merchants in transit, see Bresson 2000, 13–26.
21 On the institutional significance of terms such as ἔισπλους, ἔκπλους, etc., see Bresson 2007.

22 For example, Arch. fr. 15 and 216; Hdt. 2.163 for 30000 *epikouroi* under Apries, on the march against Amasis; Hdt. 3.120, for the mercenaries of Polycrates of Samos; Thuc. 6.55.3 for the mercenaries of the tyrant Hippias; maybe Hdt. 6.39 for the mercenaries enrolled by Miltiades; Xenophon, however, only uses the word twice, *An.* (4.5.1; 5.8.21).
23 Greek mercenaries were in the service of the Saites up until Egypt's conquest by the Persians in 525, see Laronde 1995; Agut-Labordère 2012.
24 *SEG* XXXVII.994; Masson and Yoyotte 1988.
25 Bernand and Masson 1957; Braun 1982, 50 (with a dating error: when Braun says that Psammetichus II ruled from 595 to 589 and dates his expedition, during which he employed these mercenaries, to the third year of his reign, he says 591 and not 593).
26 Xen. *Cyr.* 6.2.9–11: there were also Thracian, Phoenician, and Assyrian mercenaries, etc.; Xenophon writes that the Ionians, Aeolians, and just about all of the Greeks settled in Asia Minor were forced to march with Croesus (σύν Κροίσῳ ἠναγκάσθαι ἕπεσθαι).
27 Arrian uses this word as the title to his *History of Alexander*, probably in reference to the ascent of Alexander's army toward the innermost regions, and certainly influenced by Xenophon, whom he admired and was inspired by; cf. Brunt 1976, xiii–xiv.
28 Polyb. 3.54.5 (the route descending the Alps) and 11.15.7 (the slope of a ditch); Diod. 14.25.7 (the path heading toward the sea) and 14.28.5 (the access corridors in villages for beasts of burden), in reference to the same expedition by Cyrus the Younger against the Great King.
29 Hellmann 2000; Jockey 2009. The word is found, for example, in Thuc. 4.69.2; 5.82.6.
30 Paus. 7.4.5. In Casevitz and Lafond (2000) πλάνη is curiosity for travel; I prefer translating it as "wandering" or "a taste for, pleasure in wandering." See n. 16 above.
31 It is in this sense, rather, that one probably ought to interpret this word, behind which Jouanna (1997) sees traveling physicians with their transfers from city to city.
32 Hdt. 1.163: Arganthonius gives money to the Phocaeans so they can surround their city with a wall, the perimeter (περίοδος) of which measures a good number of stades; Hdt. 5.49: "Aristagoras, according to the report of the Lacedaemonians, produced a bronze tablet, whereupon the whole circuit (περίοδος) of the earth was engraved."
33 Arist., *Pol.* 2.3.9 on natural resemblances: "This indeed is said by some of those who write of travels round the world."
34 On these artistic associations (choral leaders, musicians, actors, poets, etc.) that formed after the death of Alexander the Great, see Le Guen 2001; Aneziri 2003. See also *IG* V.2.118.
35 Karila-Cohen 2005. Three lists of *theorodokoi* exist in Delphi: the first, fragmentary, is from the fifth century (Daux 1949, 12); the other two are from Hellenistic times, among them the "Great List" of 650 lines, which indexes 300 cities (Plassart 1921).
36 See Dana 2011, 91–95, for a very interesting discussion of the route along the coast of the Euxine Sea.

REFERENCES

Agut-Labordère, Damien. 2012. "Plus que des mercenaires! L'intégration des hommes de guerre grecs au service de la monarchie saïte." *Pallas*, 89: 293–306.

André, Jean-Marie, and Marie-Françoise Baslez. 1993. *Voyager dans l'Antiquité*. Paris: Fayard.

Aneziri, Sophia. 2003. *Die Vereine der dionysischen Techniten in Context der hellenistischen zur Geschichte, Organisation und Wirkung der hellenistischen Technitenvereine. Historia Einzelscriften*, 163. Wiesbaden: F. Steiner.

Asheri, David. 1979. "La colonizzazione greca." In *La Sicilia antica*, vol. 1 edited by Emilio Gabba and Georges Vallet, 89–142. Naples: Storia di Napoli e della Sicilia.

Asheri, David. 1980. "Rimpatrio di esuli e ridistribuzione di terre nelle città siceliote, ca 466–461." In Φιλίας Χάριν. *Miscellanea di studi classici in onore di Eugenio Manni*, vol. 1, 145–158. Rome: G. Bretschneider.

Avram, Alexandru. 2012. *Les diasporas grecques du VIIIe siècle à la fin du IIIe siècle av. J.-C.* Paris: Breal.

Baker, Patrick. 1999. "Les mercenaires." In *Armées et sociétés de la Grèce classique. Aspects sociaux et politiques de la guerre aux Ve et IVe s. av. J.-C.*, edited by Francis Prost, 240–255. Paris: Errance.

Bats, Michel, Armelle Guilcher, Mireille Pagni, et al., eds. 1992. *Marseille grecque et la Gaule. Actes du colloque international d'histoire et d'archéologie et du Ve congrès archéologique de Gaule méridionale, Marseille, 18–23 novembre 1990*. Lattes: Association pour la diffusion de l'archéologie méridionale and Aix-en-Provence: Université de Provence.

Bearzot, Cinzia. 1985. *Focione tra storia e trasfigurazione ideale*. Milan: Vita e Pensiero.

Bearzot, Cinzia. 1994. "Esili, deportazioni, emigrazioni forzate in Atene sotto regimi non democratici." In *Emigrazione e immigrazione nel mondo antico*, edited by Marta Sordi, 141–167. Milan: Vita e Pensiero.

Bearzot, Cinzia. 1995. "Motivi socio-demografici nella colonizzazione ateniese del V secolo: promozione o relegazione?" In *Coercizione e mobilità umana nel mondo antico*, edited by Marta Sordi, 61–88. Milan: Vita e Pensiero.

Bencivenni, Alice. 2003. *Progetti di riforme costituzionali nelle epigrafi dei secoli IV–II a.C.* Bologna: Lo Scarabeo.

Bernand, André, and Olivier Masson. 1957. "Les inscriptions grecques d'Abou-Simbel." *Revue des Études Anciennes*, 70: 3–10.

Bettalli, Marco. 1995. *I mercenari nel mondo greco. I. Dalle origini alla fine del V sec. a.C.* Pisa: ETS.

Bettalli, Marco. 2013. *Mercenari: il mestiere delle armi nel mondo greco antico. Età arcaica e classica*. Rome: Carocci.

Boardman, John. 1999. *The Greeks Overseas: Their Early Colonies and Trade*. 4th ed. London: Thames & Hudson.

Braudel, Fernand. 1949. *La Méditerranée et le monde méditerranéen à l'époque de Philippe II*. Paris: A. Colin.

Braun, Thomas F.R.G. 1982. "The Greeks in Egypt." In *The Cambridge Ancient History*, vol. 3.3, 2nd ed., edited by John Boardman and Nicholas G. L. Hammond, 32–56. Cambridge: Cambridge University Press.

Bresson, Alain. 2000. *La cité marchande*. Bordeaux: Ausonius.
Bresson, Alain. 2007. "L'entrée dans les ports en Grèce ancienne: le cadre juridique." In *Gens de passage dans les villes méditerranéennes, de l'Antiquité à l'époque moderne. Procédures de contrôle et de identification*, edited by Claudia Moatti and Wolfgang Kaiser, 37–78. Paris: Maisonneuve & Larose and Aix-en-Provence: Maison méditerranéenne des sciences de l'homme.
Bresson, Alain, and Pierre Rouillard, eds. 1993. *L'Emporion*. Talence: Université Bordeaux III and Paris: Centre Pierre.
Briant, Pierre. 1998. "Colonizzazione ellenistica e popolazioni del Vicino Oriente: dinamiche sociali e politiche di acculturazione." In *I Greci. Storia cultura arte società*, vol. 2:3, edited by Salvatore Settis, 309–333. Turin: G. Einaudi.
Brun, Patrice. 2005. *Impérialisme et démocratie à Athènes. Inscriptions de l'époque Classique*. Paris: A. Colin.
Bruneau, Michel. 1995. "Espaces et territoires de diasporas." In *Diasporas*, edited by Michel Bruneau, 5–23. Montpellier: Reclus.
Bruneau, Michel. 2005. "Les mots de la diaspora grecque: société, état et diaspora." In Les Diasporas, *2000 ans d'histoire*, edited by Lisa Anteby-Yemini, William Berthomière, and Gabriel Sheffer, 79–89. Rennes: Rennes University Press.
Bruneau, Michel. 2007. "Comment définir la diaspora grecque?" In *Arméniens et Grecs en diaspora: approches comparatives. Actes du colloque européen et international organisé à l'École française d'Athènes (4–7 octobre 2001)*, edited by Michel Bruneau et al., 19–28. Athens: École française d'Athènes.
Brunt, Peter A. 1976. *Arrian. Anabasis I. Books 1–4*. London: Heinemann.
Capdetrey, Laurent. 2007. *Le pouvoir séleucide. Territoire, administration, finances d'un royaume hellénistique (312–129 avant J.-C.)*. Rennes: Rennes University Press.
Casevitz, Michel. 1985. *Le vocabulaire de la colonisation en grec ancien. Etude lexicologique: les familles de ktizo et de oikeo-oikizo*. Paris: Klincksieck.
Casevitz, Michel. 2002. "D'Homère aux historiens romains: le grec du Pentateuque alexandrine." In *Le Pentateuque. La Bible d'Alexandrie*, edited by Cécile Dogniez and Marguerite Harl, 636–649. Paris: du Cerf.
Casevitz, Michel. 2012. "A propos de l'expression 'les diasporas grecques'." In *Mobilités grecques. Mouvements, réseaux, contacts en Méditerranée, de l'époque archaïque à l'époque hellénistique*, edited by Laurent Capdetrey and Julien Zurbach, 87. Bordeaux: Ausonius.
Casevitz, Michel and Yves Lafond. 2000. *Pausanias. Description de la Grèce. Tome VII (livre VII: l'Achaïe*. Paris: Les Belles Lettres.
Chantraine, Pierre. 1999. *Dictionnaire étymologique de la langue grecque. Histoire des mots. Avec Supplément*. 2nd ed. Paris: Klincksieck.
Cohen, Getzel. 1978. *The Seleucid Colonies: Studies in Founding, Administration and Organisation*. Wiesbaden: F. Steiner.
Cohen, Getzel. 1995. *The Hellenistic Settlements in Europe, the Islands and Asia Minor*, vol. 1. Berkeley: University of California Press.
Cohen, Getzel. 2006. *The Hellenistic Settlements in Syria, the Red Sea Basin and North Africa*, vol. 2. Berkeley: University of California Press.
Costanzi, Michela. 2010. "Les colonies de deuxième degré de l'Italie du Sud et de Sicile: une analyse lexicologique." *Ancient West & East*, 9: 87–107.

Dana, Madalina. 2011. *Culture et mobilité dans le Pont-Euxin. Approche régionale de la vie culturelle des cités grecques.* Bordeaux: Ausonius.

Daux, Georges. 1949. "Liste delphique de théarodoques." *Revue des Études Grecques*, 62: 1–30.

De Angelis, Franco. 2009. "Colonies and Colonization." In *The Oxford Handbook of Hellenic Studies*, edited by Georges Boys-Stones, Barbara Graziosi, and Phiroze Vasunia, 48–64. Oxford: Oxford University Press.

De Angelis, Franco. 2010. "Colonies and Colonization, Greek." In *The Oxford Encyclopedia of Ancient Greece and Rome*, vol. 2, edited by Michael Gagarin, 251–256. Oxford: Oxford University Press.

De Wever, Josette, and René Van Compernolle. 1967. "La valeur des termes de colonisation chez Thucydide." *Antiquité Classique*, 36: 461–523.

Domínguez, Adolfo. 2007. "Mobilità umana, circolazione di risorse e contatti di culture nel Mediterraneo arcaico." In *Storia d'Europa e del Mediterraneo. I. Il mondo antico. Sezione II. La Grecia. Vol. III: Grecia e Mediterraneo dall'VIII sec. a.C. all'Età delle guerre persiane*, edited by Maurizio Giangiulio, 131–175. Rome: Salerno.

Dufoix, Stéphane. 2012a. *La Dispersion. Une histoire des usages du mot diaspora.* Paris: Amsterdam.

Dufoix, Stéphane. 2012b. "Des usages antiques de *diaspora* aux enjeux conceptuels contemporains." *Pallas*, 89: 117–133.

Étienne, Roland. 2010. "Historiographie, théories et concepts." In *La Méditerranée au VIIe siècle av. J.-C. (essai d'analyses archéologiques)*, edited by Roland Étienne, 2–26. Paris: de Boccard.

Feyel, Christophe. 2006. *Les artisans dans les sanctuaires grecs aux époques classique et hellénistique à travers la documentation financière en Grèce.* Athens: École française d'Athènes.

Feyel, Christophe. 2007. "Le monde du travail à travers les comptes de construction des grands sanctuaires grecs." *Pallas*, 74: 77–92.

Finley, Moses, ed. 1973. *Problèmes de la terre en Grèce ancienne.* Paris: Mouton.

Finley, Moses. 1975. *L'Économie antique.* Trans. Max P. Higgs. Paris: de Minuit.

Finley, Moses. 1976. "Colonies: An Attempt at a Typology." *Transactions of the Royal Historical Society*, 26: 166–188.

Finley, Moses. 1984. *Economie et société en Grèce ancienne.* Trans. Jeannie Carlier. Paris: La Découverte.

Forsdyke, Sara. 2005. *Exile, Ostarcism, and Democracy. The Politics of Expulsion in Ancient Greece.* Princeton: Princeton University Press.

Garland, Robert. 2014. *Wandering Greeks: The Ancient Greek Diaspora from the Age of Homer to the Death of Alexander the Great.* Princeton: Princeton University Press.

Gauthier, Philippe. 1971. "Les *xenoi* dans les textes athéniens de la seconde moitié du Ve siècle av. J.-C." *Revue des Études Grecques*, 84: 44–79.

Gauthier, Philippe. 1973. "A propos des clérouquies athéniennes du Ve siècle." In *Problèmes de la terre en Grèce ancienne*, edited by Moses Finley, 163–178. Paris: Mouton.

Giangiulio, Maurizio. 1996. "Avventurieri, mercanti, coloni, mercenari. Mobilità umana e circolazione di risorse nel Mediterraneo arcaico." In *I Greci. Storia cultura arte società*, vol. 2:1, edited by Salvatore Settis, 497–525. Turin: G. Einaudi.

Grammenos, Dēmētrios, and Elias Petropoulos, eds. 2003–2007. *Ancient Greek Colonies in the Black Sea*. 2 vols. Thessaloniki: Archaeological Institute of Northern Greece and Oxford: Archaeopress.

Gras, Michel. 1995. *La Méditerranée archaïque*. Paris: A. Colin.

Habicht, Christian. 2000. *Athènes hellénistique. Histoire de la cité d'Alexandre le Grand à Marc Antoine*. Trans. Martine and Denis Knoepfler. Paris: Les Belles Lettres.

Habicht, Christian. 2001. "Tod auf der Gesandtschaftsreise." In *Studi Ellenistici XIII*, edited by Biagio Virgilio, 9–17. Pisa: Istituti editoriali e poligrafici internazionali.

Haillet, Jean. 2001. *Diodore de Sicile. Bibliothèque Historique. Livre XI*. Paris: Les Belles Lettres.

Hellmann, Marie-Christine. 2000. "Les déplacements des artisans de la construction en Grèce d'après les *testimonia* épigraphiques." In *L'artisanat en Grèce ancienne: les productions, les diffusions. Actes du colloque de Lyon, 10–11 décembre 1998. Travaux et recherches*, edited by Francine Blondé and Arthur Muller, 265–280. Villeneuve-d'Ascq: Université Charles-de-Gaulle-Lille 3.

Horden, Peregrine, and Nicholas Purcell. 2000. *The Corrupting Sea: A Study of Mediterranean History*. Oxford: Blackwell.

Hunter, Richard, and Ian Rutherford, eds. 2009. *Wandering Poets in Ancient Greek Culture. Travel, Locality and Pan-Hellenism*. Cambridge: Cambridge University Press.

Jockey, Philippe. 2009. "D'une cité à l'autre. Brèves réflexions sur la mobilité des artisans de la pierre dans l'Antiquité Classique." In *Le monde de l'itinérance en Méditerranée, de l'Antiquité à l'époque moderne. Procédures de contrôle et d'identification*, edited by Claudia Moatti, Wolfgang Kaiser, and Christophe Pébarthe, 139–159. Bordeaux: Ausonius.

Jouanna, Jacques. 1995. *Hippocrate*. Paris: Fayard.

Jouanna, Jacques. 1997. "Il medico tra tempio, città e scuola." In *I Greci. Storia cultura arte società*, vol. 2:2, edited by Salvatore Settis, 795–815. Turin: G. Einaudi.

Karila-Cohen, Karine. 2005. "Les Pythaïstes athéniens et leurs familles: l'apport de la prosopographie à la connaissance de la religion à Athènes au IIe siècle avant notre ère." In *Prosopographie et histoire religieuse. Actes du colloque tenu à l'Université Paris XII-Val de Marne les 27 et 28 octobre 2000*, edited by Marie-Françoise Baslez and François Prévot, 70–83. Paris: de Boccard.

Laronde, André. 1995. "Mercenaires grecs en Egypte." In *Entre Egypte et Grèce*, 29–36. Paris: Académie des Inscription et des Belles Lettres.

Lefèvre, François. 2004. "Contrôle d'identité aux frontière dans les cités grecques. Les cas des entrepreneurs étrangers et assimilés." In *La mobilité des personnes en Méditerranée, de l'Antiquité à l'époque moderne. Procédures de contrôle et documents d'identification*, edited by Claudia Moatti, 99–125. Rome: École française de Rome.

Lefèvre, François. 2010. "Le contrôle des compétences dans les cités grecques." *Journal des Savants*, 1: 3–10.

Legrand, Philippe-Ernest. 1970. *Hérodote. Histoires. Livre I Clio*. Paris: Les Belles Lettres.

Le Guen, Brigitte. 2001. *Les associations de technites dionysiaques à l'époque hellénistique*. Nancy: Association pour la diffusion de la recherche sur l'Antiquité.

Liddell, Henry George, and Robert Scott. 1996. *A Greek-English Lexicon. With a Revised Supplement*, 9th ed. Oxford: Clarendon Press.

Lhôte, Eric. 2006. *Les lamelles oraculaires de Dodone*. Geneva: Droz.
Lonis, Raoul, ed. 1992. *L'étranger dans le monde grec. Actes du colloque organisé par l'Institut d'Etudes Anciennes, Nancy, mai 1987*. Nancy: Nancy University Press.
Maddoli, Gianfranco. 1980. "Il VI e V secolo." In *La Sicilia antica*, vol. 2:1, edited by Emilio Gabba and Georges Vallet, 1–102. Naples: Società editrice storia di Napoli e della Sicilia.
Malkin, Irad. 2009. "Foundations." In *A Companion to Archaic Greece*, edited by Kurt A. Raaflaub and Hans van Wees, 373–394. Chichester: Wiley Blackwell.
Malkin, Irad. 2011. *A Small Greek World*. Oxford: Oxford University Press.
Malkin, Irad. 2012. "Diaspora, réseau: le poids des mots, le choix des images. Entretien." *Tracés. Revue des Sciences Humaines*, 23: 221–235.
Marasco, Gabriele. 1978. *I viaggi nella Grecia antica*. Rome: Edizioni dell'Ateneo.
Marcadé, Jean. 1953–1957. *Recueil de signatures de sculpteurs grecs*. 2 vols. Paris: de Boccard.
Martinez-Sève, Laurianne, ed. 2012. *Les diasporas grecques du VIIIe à la fin du IIIe siècle av. J.-C*. Pallas vol. 89. Toulouse: Presses universitaires du Midi.
Massar, Natasha. 2005. *Soigner et servir: histoire sociale et culturelle de la médicine grecque à l'époque hellénistique*. Paris: de Boccard.
Massar, Natasha. 2007. "Les maîtres itinérants en Grèce : techniciens, sophistes, philosophes." In *Lieux de savoir. Espaces et communautés*, vol. 1, edited by Christian Jacob, 786–804. Paris: Albin Michel.
Masson, Olivier, and Jean Yoyotte. 1988. "Une inscription ionienne mentionnant Psammétique Ier." *Epigraphica Anatolica*, 11: 171–179.
Mele, Alfonso, ed. 1979. *Il commercio greco arcaico. Prexis ed emporia*. Naples: Centre Jean Bérard.
Moatti, Claudia, ed. 2004. *La mobilité des personnes en Méditerranée, de l'Antiquité à l'époque moderne. Procédures de contrôle et documents d'identification*. Rome: École française de Rome.
Moatti, Claudia. 2007. "De la *peregrinatio* comme stratégie intellectuelle dans l'Empire romain au IIe siècle de notre ère." *Mélanges de l'École française de Rome. Italie et Méditerranée modernes et contemporaine*, 119: 129–136.
Moatti, Claudia. 2012. "Mobilités et circulations: approches historiographiques et conceptuelles." In *Mobilités grecques. Mouvements, réseaux, contacts en Méditerranée, de l'époque archaïque à l'époque hellénistique*, edited by Laurent Capdetrey and Julien Zurbach, 39–52. Bordeaux: Ausonius.
Moatti, Claudia, and Wolfgang Kaiser, eds. 2007. *Gens de passage dans les villes méditerranéennes, de l'Antiquité à l'époque moderne. Procédures de contrôle et de identification*. Paris: Maisonneuve & Larose.
Moatti, Claudia, and Wolfgang Kaiser. 2009. "Mobilità umana e circolazione culturale nel Mediterranneo dall'età classica all'età moderna." In *Migrazioni, Storia d'Italia, Annali 24*, edited by Paola Corti and Matteo Sanfilippo, 5–20. Turin: Einaudi.
Moatti, Claudia, Wolfgang Kaiser, and Christophe Pébarthe, eds. 2009. *Le monde de l'itinérance en Méditerranée, de l'Antiquité à l'époque moderne. Procédures de contrôle et d'identification*. Bordeaux: Ausonius.
Montiglio, Silvia. 2005. *Wandering in Ancient Greek Culture*. Chicago: Chicago University Press

Morakis, Andreas. 2011. "Thucydides and the Character of Greek Colonisation in Sicily." *Classical Quaterly*, 61: 460–492.

Naso, Alessandro, ed. 2006. *Stranieri e non cittadini nei santuari greci*. Grassina: Le Monnier Università.

Natali, Carlo. 1996. "Lieux et écoles de savoir." In *Le savoir grec*, edited by Jacques Brunschwig and Geoffrey Lloyd, 229–249. Paris: Flammarion.

Osborne, Robin. 1998. "Early Greek Colonization? The Nature of Greek Settlement in the West." In *Archaic Greece: New Approaches and New Evidence*, edited by Nick Fisher and Hans van Wees, 251–269. London: Duckworth for Classical Press of Wales.

Palagia, Olga. 2000. "Skopas of Paros and the 'Pothos'." In *Paria Lithos: Parian Quarries, Marble and Workshops of Sculpture. Proceedings of the First International Conference on the Archeology of Paros and the Cyclades, Paros 2–5 October 1997*, edited by Demetrio Schilardi and Dora Katsonopoulou, 209–225. Athens: Edkóseis Díktynna.

Parke, Herbert W., and Donald E.W. Wormell. 1956. *The Delphic Oracle*. 2 vols. Oxford: Blackwell.

Pébarthe, Christophe. 2007. "Commerce et commerçants à Athènes à l'époque de Démosthène." *Pallas*, 74: 161–178.

Pébarthe, Christophe. 2009. "Emigrer d'Athènes. Clérouques et colons aux temps de la domination athénienne sur l'Egée au Ve siècle a.C." In *Le monde de l'itinérance en Méditerranée, de l'Antiquité à l'époque moderne. Procédures de contrôle et d'identification*, edited by Claudia Moatti, Wolfgang Kaiser, and Christophe Pébarthe, 367–390. Bordeaux: Ausonius.

Perlman, Paula. 1995. "ΘΕΩΡΟΔΟΚΟΥΝΤΕΣ ΕΝ ΤΑΙΣ ΠΟΛΕΣΙΝ. Panhellenic *Epangelia* and Political Status." In *Sources for the Ancient Greek City-State. Symposium August, 24–27 1994*, edited by Mogens Herman Hansen, 113–164. Copenhagen: The Royal Danish Academy of Sciences and Letters.

Perlman, Paula. 2000. *City and Sanctuary in Ancient Greece: The Theorodokia in the Peloponnese*. Göttingen: Vandenhoeck & Ruprecht.

Perrin-Saminadayar, Éric. 2005. "Images, statues et accueil des étrangers à Athènes à l'époque hellénistique." In *Le barbare, l'étranger: images de l'autre. Actes du colloque organisé par le CERHI, Saint-Etienne, 14 et 15 mai 2004*, edited by Didier Nourrisson and Yves Perrin, 67–91. Saint-Etienne: Saint-Etienne University Press.

Perrin-Saminadayar, Éric. 2007. *Education, culture et société à Athènes. Les acteurs de la vie culturelle athénienne (229–88): un tout petit monde*. Paris: de Boccard.

Phillips, Eustace D. 1981. *Aspects of Greek Medicine*. London: Thames & Hudson.

Plassart, André. 1921. "La liste des théodoroques." *BCH*, 45: 1–85.

Pugliese Carratelli, Giovanni, ed. 1996. *I Greci in Occidente*. Milan: Bompiani.

Reed, Charles. 2003. *Maritime Traders in the Ancient Greek World*. Cambridge: Cambridge University Press.

Samama, Evelyne. 2003. *Les médecins dans le monde grec. Sources épigraphiques sur la naissance d'un corps medical*. Geneva: Droz.

Stazio, Attilio, ed. 2000. *Magna Grecia e Oriente mediterraneo prima dell'età ellenistica. Atti del XXXIX Convegno di Studi sulla Magna Grecia, Taranto 1–5 ottobre 1999*. Taranto: Istituto per la storia e l'archeologia della Magna Grecia.

Tagliamonte, Gianluca. 1994. *I figli di Marte: mobilità, mercenari e mercenariato italici in Magna Grecia e Sicilia*. Rome: G. Bretschneider.

Tsetskhladze, Gocha, ed. 2006–2008. *Greek Colonisation: An Account of Greek Colonies and Other Settlements Overseas.* 3 vols. Leiden: Brill.

Trundle, Matthew. 2004. *Greek Mercenaries from the Late Archaic Period to Alexander.* London: Routledge.

Vaclos, G. 1659. *Thisavros tetraglossos.* Venice.

van der Eijk, Philip. 1999. *Ancient Histories of Medicine.* Leiden: Brill.

van Dommelen, Peter. 2005. "Urban Foundations? Colonial Settlement and Urbanization in the Western Mediterranean." In *Mediterranean Urbanization, 800–600 BC*, edited by Robin Osborne and Barry Cunliffe, 143–167. Oxford: Oxford University Press.

Vanotti, Gabriela. 1995. "Leontini nel V secolo, città di profughi." In *Coercizione e mobilità umana nel mondo antico*, edited by Marta Sordi, 89–106. Milan: Vita e Pensiero.

Vattuone, Riccardo. 1994. "'Metoikesis.' Trapianti di popolazioni nella Sicilia greca fra VI e IV sec. a.C." In *Emigrazione e immigrazione nel mondo antico*, edited by Marta Sordi, 81–113. Milan: Vita e Pensiero.

Vélissaropoulos, Julie. 1980. *Les nauclères grecs. Recherches sur les institutions maritimes en Grèce et dans l'Orient hellénisé.* Geneva: Droz.

Virgilio, Biagio. 1971–1972. "I termini della colonizzazione in Erodoto e nella tradizione preerodotea." *Atti della Accademia delle Scienze di Torino*, 106: 345–406.

FURTHER READING

The literary and epigraphic sources that form the basis of the reconstruction put forth in this chapter always repay further reading for the rich insights they offer on individual and mass mobility in the ancient Greek world. Several of the items cited in the References above provide ideal secondary reading on various aspects of the subject. The starting point, as emphasized in this chapter, is all the sole-authored and edited works of Claudia Moatti. Reliable general accounts in English approach the question of wandering among the ancient Greeks in various ways: see in particular Garland 2014; Hunter and Rutherford 2009; Montiglio 2005. On the foundation of cities, see Malkin 2009.

CHAPTER TWO

English-Speaking Traditions and the Study of the Ancient Greeks outside their Homelands

Lela M. Urquhart

In the foreword to T.J. Dunbabin's *The Greeks and their Eastern Neighbours*, Sir John Beazley outlined the roles held by the Greeks and the people with whom they interacted in their overseas activities. "In the West," Beazley claimed, "the peoples with whom the Greeks came into contact were at a more primitive stage of development …; in the East … the position was the reverse" (1957, ix). This comment, made in the waning years of the British Empire, speaks to several currents within Anglophone studies of Greek history outside of the Aegean during the 1950s: the categorization of Greek and non-Greek populations in dichotomous terms, the concept of a single process of cultural diffusion that originated in the East and culminated in the West, and the idea of "contact" itself. Each is discernible in Beazley's declaration. Also apparent, however, is the outline of a more deeply seated historiographic paradigm, one that used the example of ancient Greek colonization as a point of reference for thinking through contemporary colonialism. As British classicist and then-President of Corpus Christi College at Oxford University Richard Livingstone pronounced, "These ages, with which we have spiritual affinities and which have anticipated our problems, have a special interest and instructiveness for us. They are our Doppelgänger" (1935, 117–118).

This chapter outlines the emergence of this and other historiographic traditions that have marked Anglophone scholarship on the Greeks outside their homelands. In 1984, Jean-Paul Morel noted that a number of thematic waves related to the continuity of colonization from the Bronze to the Iron Age, the motives of Greek colonization, and the political history of the colonies had risen and fallen in scholarly interest. The aim of this chapter is not to apply Morel forensics to the state of scholarship three decades later, but rather to analyze the long-term development of certain traditions in the historiography of English-speaking scholars. Three themes stand out: the marginalization of the overseas Greeks in narratives of Greek history; the definition of Greek settlements abroad as *apoikiai, poleis*,

---

A Companion to Greeks Across the Ancient World, First Edition. Edited by Franco De Angelis.
© 2020 John Wiley & Sons, Inc. Published 2020 by John Wiley & Sons, Inc.

or *emporia*; and the relationship between Greeks and non-Greek populations. Such slants on the scholarship have developed in tandem with broader trends in ancient Greek history and archaeology, and with the changing sociopolitical, cultural, and intellectual climates of predominantly English-speaking parts of the world.

Motherlands, Colonies, and the Marginalization of Greeks on the Margins

Studies of the ancient Greeks outside the Aegean first appeared in the eighteenth century, but relatively infrequently and cursorily. Political shifts toward looser federations in Europe and a growing enthusiasm for narrative history made the Greek past more scholastically appealing during the 1700s (Pagden 1995), but the lack of fit between Greece's fragmented *poleis* and participatory citizen institutions and the still-dominant historiographical model of successive empires and cultures made the writing of Greek narrative history challenging (Akça Ataç 2006; Jenkyns 1980; Momigliano 1984). Greek history, moreover, primarily consisted of Aegean political events, with historical episodes outside mainland Greece being minimized, as seen in the work of John Potter (*Archaeologia Graeca*, 1697–1706) and Temple Stanyan (*Grecian History*, 1756). The position Stanyan took toward colonial history, for instance, was that it was inconsequential. Greece was, he wrote,

> ... so well peopled that it was common upon any little Pique, or ill Success in a Battle, to throw themselves out in Colonies; which by this means were planted not only in Sicily and Italy, but several other Parts of Europe and Asia. But to avoid Tediousness and Repetition, we shall mention the chief of 'em in their proper places, and return to the Messenians ... (1756, 110).

This abbreviated discussion of Greek colonies contrasts with later works. As Momigliano (1984) and others (e.g., Ceserani 2012, 103; Vlassopoulos 2010, 32) have shown, the use of antiquity as a filter for modern political debates went hand in hand with the elevated relevance of colonization to British political culture in the mid-eighteenth century. By the 1760s and 1770s, issues surrounding the American colonies made the comparability of ancient and modern colonization (and particularly the legal/juridical relationships between homelands and colonies) especially pertinent. In debates over the 1765 Stamp Act, those endorsing the Government position perceived colonies as expressions of imperial power and grandeur but also as submissive to metropolitan Britain (Greene 2013, 91–93). The Opposition, by contrast, stressed the commercial returns of empire over state power and colonial affection over obedience. According to one author in the pamphlet *State of the British and French colonies in North America, with Respect to the Number of People, Forces, Forts, Indians, Trade and Other Advantages* (1755, 63–64), the colonists thought of themselves as "branches of the same *British* tree, tho' transplanted in a different soil," and did not believe that they had "forfeited their *British* rights by that removal."

The underlying contention of the Opposition was that governmental supporters had failed to recognize the uniqueness of Britain's success and the absence of historical parallels for early modern European empires (Greene 2013, 98–99). Modern colonies were characterized by an entirely "new species of colonization," the London agent for Barbados, Samuel Estwick, explained. Unlike Greek colonies, which were the products of "excursions of people to ease a country surcharged with inhabitants," or Roman colonies, which had "been planted among various nations to over-awe, and hold them in subjection," modern colonies were "colonies of *commerce*," a feature that differentiated them essentially "from every other species of colonization that is known" (Estwick 1776, 93–94). In making this claim, Estwick and other Opposition proponents directly responded to the Government definition of "colonising" as "the act of a powerful and parental people," being "to a state what propagating is to a family" (*Colonising, or a Plain Investigation of that Subject; with the Legislative, Political and Commercial View of the Colonies,* 1774). Colonies, such logic suggested, were "merely offshoots of their sponsoring state and as such had no 'other political ground or national object, than the good of the *common weal*,' … defined narrowly as the 'advantage of that government, to which all their enterprises should point'" (quoted in Greene 2013, 92). Colonies thus grew like the branches of a tree, bearing the fruit of the state, but always dependent on the parent-state's healthy roots.

Such debates infiltrated the first in-depth looks at Greeks outside their homelands, some of which were explicitly conducted to contribute to ongoing discussions over the Americas. William Barron, for example, used the ancient "free states" and their colonies to argue in favor of American taxation (Barron 1777, 3). But Barron was only able to make the example of Greek colonialism work by conflating colonies, subjects, and allies. Prior to the Persian wars, "the mother-country was glad to exonerate herself, for her own peace and safety; and she expected no benefit from her colonists, because she possessed no resources to protect them, or to secure any advantages to be derived from them. The only principle … of connection which did exist … was that of affection" (Barron 1777, 74). To Barron, this situation changed with the growth of Sparta and Athens; their respective alliance-based "empires" demanded protection via large fleets and armies, both of which required a treasury, one that could only be supplied by taxes. According to Barron, such circumstances raised the Athenians to their "most favorable juncture … and they succeeded to their utmost with it" (Barron 1777, 74.). For Barron, the analogy worked, but only by synonymizing "allies" and "colonies."

The first full English-language studies of ancient Greece were published by John Gillies (1786) and William Mitford (1784–1818), by which time an awareness of non-Aegean Greek history was more widespread. The side effects of the recent American experience linger in both Gillies and Mitford: anti-republican sentiments are apparent and a premium was put on Greek "unity" (cf. Gillies 1786, 1:35), perhaps faint forms of self-appeasement by some British scholars who continued to consider the Americans rebels and the Revolution a subversive act (Ceserani 2012, 111). Gillies emphasized that Greek history formed an "unbroken narrative" (1786, 1:vi), in which "the establishment of new colonies in many distant parts of Europe as well as of Asia and Africa" and other events worked alongside the "improvement of those singular institutions which tended to unite, to polish, and to adorn the scattered and still spreading branches of the Grecian race through every part of the world" (Gillies 1786, 1:93). The primacy of the motherland over the colonies is also explicit. Mitford situated the colonies of southern Italy and Sicily in a position of dependency, characterizing them as in "constant intercourse with the country of their forefathers" (1784–1818, 2:254). The achievements of the colonial Greeks and the significance of episodes of colonial history also were closely evaluated based on the impact they had on Aegean Greece; according to Gillies, for example, the Greek war against the Persians overshadowed campaigns against the Carthaginians because it was "not confined to the extremities"; it "reached and shook the centre of Greece," and it "embraced all the great nations of antiquity, together with the scattered communities of Grecian extraction in every part of the world" (1786, 1:377–378).

British scholars salvaged more from the British-ancient Greek colonial analogy by spinning colonization as a civilizing process. If defined as a stretching of geographical boundaries and culture, British colonization was a success, despite past military losses. Starting in the nineteenth century, treatments of Greek history increasingly cast overseas colonists as civilization-bearers departing the Aegean for resettlement among distant barbarian populations. "Hellenization" – a model of cultural change stipulating the transfer of Greek culture to non-Greek populations – made its first concrete appearance among those nineteenth-century works. George Grote, the banker-historian whose more liberal-oriented *History of Greece* (1846–1856) responded to the earlier work of Gillies and Mitford, defined Hellenization as

> the ascendency of a higher over a lower civilization ... the working of concentrated townsmen ... upon dispersed, unprotected, artless villages, who could not be insensible to the charm of that superior intellect, imagination, and organization. (1846–1856, 3:495–497).

He argued further that the Hellenization of "native" populations had transformed backwater lands (inhabited by people "of rude pastoral habits, dispersed either among petty hill-villages, or in caverns hewn out of the rock," (Grote 1846–1856, 3:494) as the ancient Italians were described) into a land of towns, wealth, and sophistication that rivaled the mainland *poleis*. Embedded in this image of ancient "native" populations were, of course, a number of assumptions about European superiority that had formed in response to British overseas expansion. These assumptions, moreover, framed colonization as a process primarily affecting "barbarian" areas, an interpretation that in turn worked to conceptually and narratologically marginalize Greeks living beyond the Aegean.

A closer look at Grote's model reveals this process more clearly. His formulation of Hellenization was not one of simple displacement – that of native by Greek culture. It was one, rather, of fusion. Based on various measures of colonial culture, he made the case for a "fusion of the two races in the same community, though doubtless in the relation of superior and subject, and not in that of equals" (1846–1856, 3:494–495). Fusion colors Grote's notion of cultural and political change throughout the sections on colonization, but its consistent semantic underpinning is ethnic: to Grote, the colonists had received a "considerable infusion of blood, of habits, and of manners, from the native Sikels" (1846–1856, 3:498–499). As such, they were not to be considered "pure" Greeks. While this reckoning shows that neither Grote nor Victorian historiography more generally were exempt from broader biases regarding concepts of race and nation (Turner 1981, 213–233; Challis 2010), it also reveals the logic behind the qualification of Greek colonists as "important but outlying" to Grote's overarching narrative of Greek history (Ceserani

2012, 219). The mixture with "the native element" had predisposed Italiot and Siceliot Greeks toward "unrestrained voluptuous license" and prevented them "from partaking in that improved organisation" that characterized Athens and other Aegean city-states (Grote 1846–1856, 1:ix; 183–184).

Much of the privilege attached to the Aegean homeland in nineteenth-century Greek histories can naturally be ascribed to factors of evidence. Though antiquarian studies of sites outside of mainland Greece had been in circulation since the eighteenth century and Hellenic antiquities held mass appeal, historical accounts of the Greeks outside of the Aegean drew dominantly on literary sources until the mid twentieth century. The literary tradition plays up foundational moments over other aspects of colonization, generally framing colonies as the propagations of individual Aegean cities. Given the vagueness of the tradition, the task that befell historians was "to fill the gaps as best they could" (Cook 1946, 70), but within the parameters of what the texts spoke. Such inductive methods combined with the narrative bent toward foundation stories meant that, from the outset, the metropolis-to-colony relationship was basic to scholarly interpretations.

The literary tradition took on new dimensions, however, as it responded to the crescendo of classical archaeological activity conducted in Europe, northern Africa, and Asia Minor from the late 1800s on. Material evidence produced during these years made the ancient non-Greek populations among whom Greek colonists had settled more tangible, the effects of which can be seen in T.J. Dunbabin's work, *The Western Greeks* (1948), which combined written and archaeological evidence to yield a complex social and economic history of western Greek settlement, and included "native" populations (De Angelis 1998). Excavations also shed light onto the post-foundation lives of the colonies, lengthening the temporal framework within which most studies of colonization had been performed. For all these advances, however, the authority of the literary record remained solid, enduring long enough into the 1970s for the claim to be made that,

> The literary sources on Greek colonisation may be small in bulk, but they will always remain the most important. Archaeology cannot provide us with the precise and detailed knowledge we often obtain from a literary account. Cyrene will, I imagine, always be the best known of early Greek colonial enterprises – because of Herodotus, not the spade (Graham 1971, 36).

Moreover, despite the widening berth of topics related to the study of ancient colonization, the metropolis-to-colony relationship and questions of how to characterize it would continue to feature strongly in Anglophone studies. Echoing the arguments of Revolution-era Opposition pamphlets, Connop Thirlwall in 1860 argued that motherlands and colonies shared "filial affection" rather than feelings of "dependence on the one side or a claim of authority on the other" (1860, 110). Nearly a century later, Dunbabin devised a colonial formula defined by relations of dependency between mother-country and colony (cf. 1948, vii), an approach heavily influenced by his own status as a "colonial," as Franco De Angelis (1998, 545–546) has shown. The rationale supporting the perception of this relationship had changed, but its remarkable endurance neatly attests to the strength of its grip on Anglophone historiography.

Apoikiai, *Emporia*, and the *Polis*

Though the motherland-to-colony relationship was not absent from later studies (cf. Graham 1964; Hansen and Nielsen 2004, 63–87), the characterization of Greek settlements outside the Aegean did change significantly in the late 1960s and 1970s. This transformation was at least partly due to the partition of "British" scholarship into independent "American," "Canadian," and "Australian" disciplinary traditions, wherein colonies were construed as places of autonomous innovation, tension, and experimentation. This was portrayed, for example, in the mid-century work of New Zealander A.D. Trendall, who argued for the influence of southern Italy and Sicily in Classical Greek vase painting and production.

By 1976, the American-born scholar Moses Finley had dismissed the utility of the term "colony" on the basis of the anachronistic parallels it encouraged. His snub marked a departure from earlier rhetorics of dependency, but more important was Finley's suggestion that the essential quality of the Archaic overseas Greek and Phoenician settlements was that "they were all, from the start, independent *city-states*, not colonies" (Finley 1976, 173–174, italics added). Finley's critique heralded the beginning of a long process of reflexive, lexical dissection among Anglophone scholars in which the (mis)translation of *apoikiai*, the word used by Classical writers to describe ancient settlements made outside the Aegean, and the misappropriation of modern imperial language were of central concern (e.g., Osborne 1998, 252; Owen 2005; Tsetskhladze 2005, xxxviii–xli; Van Dommelen 2002, 121). His critique also registered the new attention in the 1970s to the ancient Greek *polis*. Where earlier studies had presumed that *apoikiai* were only made by pre-established *poleis* (thereby equating "metropolis" and the state form of the *polis*), the newer studies suggested that *apoikiai* were where *polis* ideology and implementation had first been both necessitated and incubated; from *apoikiai*, the idea of the *polis* moved back to Hellas.

Other chapters in this volume discuss more concretely the ways in which *apoikiai* have been examined as city-states. It is more to the purpose here to understand how this reconceptualization of early Greek overseas settlements as (the) early *poleis* created a somewhat new line of thinking within the historiography. The substitution in mentality that occurred by looking at Greek overseas settlements less as colonies – sites dependent on a motherland for their political and cultural identity – and more as *poleis* – independent city-states – allowed for Aegean and non-Aegean Greek settlements to be brought into a less imbalanced comparative framework: *all* of the settlements made during the late Iron Age and early Archaic periods could now be seen as developmental *poleis*. And because overseas settlements were established on a blank slate, they theoretically operated as petri dishes for investigating the significant features of the early Greek city-state and the Archaic period in a more distilled way.

The impact of this shift has been manifested widely across the scholarship of the past 40 years. Among Anglophone scholars, the influential work of Anthony Snodgrass, Irad Malkin, Robin Osborne, David Ridgway, Carol Dougherty, Ian Morris, Jonathan Hall, and Carla Antonaccio (among many others) can all be said to reflect this tendency toward a more inclusive view of Greek history as it occurred outside of mainland Greece. Snodgrass has certainly been one of the pioneers: having coined the Archaic period as "the age of experiment," his work has also implied that, in many ways, the colony operated as an archetypical experiment in the formation of a community, both conceptually and physically (1980, 40–42; 119–121). Irad Malkin has pursued these implications further:

> The need implied in colonization to create a society *ex novo* required conceptualizing what the social unit was and what the ideal type should be. Colonization, while creating new *poleis*, provided also the opportunity for refining and defining the *polis* both in practice and in theory … In short, it is our opinion that colonization contributed just as much to the rise of the *polis* as it was dependent on this "rise" for its own existence (1987, 263).

The colony as polis *par excellence* has also been a major theme of French historiography, as Michel Gras (Chapter 3, this volume) discusses. With the translation of François De Polignac's *La Naissance de la cité grecque* into English, the French tradition of scholarship that combined structuralist-oriented theory with archaeological data (often derived from sites led by French archaeologists) converged with the work of Anglophone scholars. De Polignac traced the formation of *polis* societies via the emergence of sanctuaries, particularly sanctuaries in "ex-centric" locations that worked to take possession of territory and consolidate social integration through religious participation (1995, 33–36, 74, 98–106).[1] As John Pedley (2005, 55) has recognized, De Polignac's model is best tested by non-mainland Greek sites, given that in the "new worlds" created by Greek overseas migrations, "poleis and their sanctuaries were created at one fell swoop on what to the Greeks was virgin territory." Interestingly, recent explorations of colonies as political communities and the tentative suggestions that the hallmarks of Greek *polis* ideology (such as egalitarianism, restrictions on displays of wealth, and collective decision-making) are first found overseas have a historiographical precedent. Thirlwall (1860), for instance, suggested that Greek colonies and the idea of democracy were fundamentally linked:

> The maritime position and pursuits of the colonies, and the very spirit in which they were founded was highly unfavourable to the permanence of an aristocratical ascendancy. A powerful and enterprising commonalty soon sprang up, and the natural tendency of the state toward a complete democracy could seldom be restrained, except by the adoption of a liberal standard of property (Thirlwall 1860, 112).

Democracies resulted from "the absence of all restraint" and "the abolition of the monarchical form of government, which probably took place everywhere within a few generations after the first settlement, though the good was balanced by great evils" (Thirlwall 1860, 116). To Thirlwall, then, the political experiment conducted in the colonies was a detriment.

Finley's claim that *apoikiai* were *poleis* engaged another aspect of the *apoikia* debate, which was the distinction between *apoikiai* and *emporia*. Translated as "trading stations" or "ports-of-trade," *emporia* were often represented opposite *apoikiai* on the scale of Greek overseas settlements. Elsewhere they were interpreted as the embryonic phases of later bona fide colonies, a model especially implemented in Soviet scholarship for the Black Sea region (cf. Noonan 1973; see also Saprykin, Chapter 6, this volume). Regardless of the model, *apoikiai* and *emporia* were, for a very long time, represented in the scholarship in binary terms: *apoikiai* were *poleis* containing urban centers and agricultural territory, while *emporia* were ephemeral coastal way stations without political identities (e.g. Morel 1975). The motivations for their settlement were also explained reductively: expansion was either commercially driven, resulting in *emporia*, or agrarian-motivated, resulting in *apoikiai*.

Though not formally apparent in the scholarship until the 1960s, the roots of the *apoikia* and *emporion* dichotomy can perhaps be traced back to the 1920s and early 1930s when trade gained prominence in studies of Greek history. As noted earlier, studies of Greek colonization had sometimes used the role of commerce to contrast ancient and modern colonization. By the 1920s, though, modern British colonialism was itself oriented increasingly around the creation of an imperial economy fed by the discoveries and exploitation of resources found outside the British motherland, new definitions of luxury, and the creation of British cultural oases in the "native" deserts of the colonial possessions (Darwin 1980, 664–665). In the context of ancient scholarship, the famous "trade before the flag" argument laid out by Alan Blakeway (1932–1933, 1935) summoned this aspect of the British Empire. Blakeway used samples of early pottery found across the western Mediterranean to argue against the customary explanation that colonies "were planted solely as a means of solving the problem of over-population in old Greece in areas suitable for the production of corn, and without commercial intent" (1932–1933, 170–171). The stimulus for Greek population movements out of the Aegean, he contested, was driven more by commercial opportunity than demographic necessity, a situation that closely reflected contemporary British colonial policy in Africa, Asia, and the West Indies.

Considerable problems with Blakeway's chronology opened his argument to critique (e.g., Beazley 1944; Dohan 1942). But his insistence on the involvement of Greeks in precolonial trade activities nevertheless changed the tone of the discussion in that it offered a different explanation for an early Greek diaspora out of the Aegean and, more significantly, privileged social and economic factors over the political narrative embedded in the literary tradition. The work additionally augmented an already idealized view of the Greeks through both the typological classification of pottery into categories of Greek originals versus native imitations and the dismissal of the idea that non-Greeks like the Phoenicians were involved in early trading ventures (Blakeway 1932–1933, 170).

Blakeway's latter suggestions resonated with other research happening at the time. Excavations in the East, particularly those led by Leonard Woolley in the late 1930s at Al Mina, had revealed connections between Greek and Levantine groups, but were interpreted to entitle the Greeks. Al Mina was presented as a Euboean-founded port that became the node connecting "East" and "West," an interpretation based in part on Eurocentric, Orientalizing views of trade in the eastern Mediterranean (Gill 1994, 105–106). Woolley's comment that in modern Alexandretta in the 1930s, "heads of business firms are seldom Syrians, and it is likely to have been so in the past" (1938, 16) insinuates such views, while his assertion that the merchants at Al Mina "must have been Greeks" makes the position explicit (Woolley 1938, 15). In combination with Blakeway's argument that trading movements in the West began with the Greeks, the scholarship on Al Mina, and more generally on the connection between Greece and the East, painted a picture of the Greeks as the principal movers and shakers in a process of Mediterranean-wide cultural transformation, achieved via the mechanism of commercial initiative and exchange: as stated by Giorgio Buchner, the Greeks [Euboeans], "having possession of Al Mina in the East and Pithekoussai in the West .... were from about 775–700 BC, the masters of trade between the Eastern

Mediterranean and Central Italy" (1966, 12; see also Ridgway 1973). Within this paradigm, the Phoenicians and other Eastern groups were reduced to the roles of producers of "minor oriental trinkets" (Boardman 1964, 215), who were not spurred to establish "regular trading posts or colonies until Greek example and competition led them to similar undertakings" (Boardman 1964, 60), images that drew heavily on contemporary ethnic and cultural stereotypes (Mackenzie 2005; Said 1978). This downplaying of the importance of the Phoenicians has, in turn, impacted models of Phoenician colonization appreciably: most Phoenician overseas settlements have long been thought of as *emporia*, contrary to Greek "colonies" or *apoikiai* (Aubet 2001). The *apoikia* versus *emporion* schema thus has also implicated the cultural or ethnic opposition of Greeks and Phoenicians and recursively engaged the modern construct of Occident and Orient (Said 1978, 39–60).

Greeks and Non-Greeks

Historiographically, non-Greek populations have held an important, though variable, role in English-language narratives of Greek overseas expansion. To characterize the issue of Greek and non-Greek or native interaction as a "tradition" within Anglophone scholarship is to flatten somewhat the vertiginous distance separating studies produced prior and successive to the emergence of postcolonialism in scholarly discourse. Studies of non-Greek populations from the past 40 years clearly approach the question of Greek–native interaction from a very different place than scholarship of the eighteenth through mid-twentieth centuries, which generally embraced the concept of Hellenization and accepted it "axiomatically as an inevitable outcome of mere contact between 'barbarians' and 'civilized' Greeks" (Dietler 2005, 56). Despite the chasm separating the approaches of recent from earlier studies, visualizing them as a single tradition of interest in Greek and non-Greek interaction has its advantages.

Eighteenth-century Hellenism transformed the interpretive framework in which antiquity was perceived as the inverse of modernity into one that was internally comparative. Under this ideological mantle, the Greeks became the standard-bearers of civilization to whom all other ancient societies aspired. As colonial encounters between Greeks and non-Greek groups were increasingly incorporated into narrative histories, this ranked way of looking at past societies was molded to reflect a modern Western consciousness, itself replete with notions of the synonymity of colonization and civilization and inherent Western superiority (Dietler 2005, 56). A hermeneutical feedback loop was thereby created: in the past, native non-Greek populations were not only culturally disadvantaged, they were barbarians, devoid of civilization. In the present, modern colonialism continued the civilizing mission originally carried out by Greeks (Van Dommelen 1997, 19–23; Dietler 2010).

This inverse relationship between Greeks and natives is perceptible in Anglophone scholarship of the late 1700s and 1800s. Gillies, for example, wrote that,

> Wherever the spirit of enterprise diffused their settlements, [the Greeks] perceived ... the superiority of their own religion, language, institutions, and manners; and the dignity of their character and sentiments eminently distinguished them from the general mass of nations whose territories they invaded, and whom they justly denominated Barbarians (Gillies 1786, 1:289–290).

Mitford likewise labeled Italy and Sicily as regions "scarcely known but by name," full of "imaginary monsters and real savages," and "barbarian inhabitants" (Mitford 1784–1818, 2:345). Barbarism also entailed passivity and acquiescence to the cultural offerings of the Greeks. To Thirlwall, the Greeks of Liguria gained and requited the "good-will" of Celtic tribes "by diffusing among them the arts of civilised life, and Grecian usages and letters" (1860, 2:122), while to Grote, Hellenization was meted out by Greek colonists to inferior and desperate natives (1846–1856, 3:496).

Such one-way cultural assimilation by native populations was an assumption that nicely paired with another unfounded postulate: their political submission. The historian and politician Edward Freeman, for example, equated any political independence of the indigenous population with their continued barbarism, and stipulated further that the Sikels saw the Greeks as their conquerors and masters (1891–1894, 1:133; 155). This dualism is, of course, a well-known pattern within Anglophone historiography. However, the discrepant ways in which earlier studies conceptualized interaction between Greeks and non-Greeks have been less recognized.

Three models of engagement seem to have been articulated in studies prior to the mid-twentieth century. The first was shaped around the idea that Greeks and non-Greeks were fixed, homogeneous, and distinct entities that, despite coming into "contact" with one another, did not engage beyond the dynamic of active colonizer to passive native. Thirlwall, for instance, wrote that ancient local Africans were "even said to have served as guides to the [Greeks], whom they found useful neighbors, as a European colony would be to the Bedouins who now range over the same tracts. But their habits must have kept the two races completely apart from each other" (1860, 2:108–109). Nearly a century later, this model endured: Dunbabin represented Italic groups as racially inferior and drew a line between Greek and native populations (De Angelis 1998, 542–544), saying that he was inclined "to stress the purity of Greek culture in the colonial cities" and found "little to suggest that the Greeks mixed much with Sikel or Italian peoples, or learnt much from them" (Dunbabin 1948, vi).

A second model, expressed via the idea of fusion, advanced deeper levels of interaction between Greeks and non-Greeks. Grote represented relations between Greeks and local populations intimately, seeing them driven by needs for intermarriage and "breeding" (e.g., 1846–1856, 3:176, 530). He applied the idea of mixing to nearly all cases of Greek settlement overseas, musing that colonies were composed of different sections of people, both Greek and non-Greek. "Such was usually the case," he stated, "in respect to all emigrations, and hence the establishments thus planted contracted at once, generally speaking, both more activity and more instability than was seen among those Greeks who remained at home." Superficially, Grote made space for bilateral cultural exchange, acknowledging indigenous influence on Greek settlers in the areas of language, coinage, weights and measures, "taste, habits, and ideas," and religion (1846–1856, 3:496). Below the surface, however, presumptions of native racial inferiority clearly prevailed; indeed, as seen earlier, it was, at least in part, the mingling of Greek settlers and Italic peoples that led to his subordination of colonies within Greek history overall.

Edward Freeman's (1891–1894) articulation of colonial interaction constitutes a third, if somewhat singular, historiographical model. For Freeman, Greek colonization, as pitted against Phoenician expansion, functioned as the embarking point of a continuous "rivalry" between the Aryan West and Semitic East, a narrative likely informed by Freeman's personal involvement in the Balkan uprising against the Ottomans. Within this framework, indigenous populations were presented demeaningly, even by the standards of late nineteenth-century imperial Britain (Shepherd 2005, 29); as non-"colonizing powers" (i.e., the Greeks and Phoenicians), indigenous groups were basically historically irrelevant. Freeman did admit a degree of indigenous influence on the Greeks, however; Sicily was "a land of Greek settlers among earlier inhabitants who were not driven out, but with whom the colonists had large dealings, teaching them many things and learning some things from them" (1891–1894, 1:103–104). This position makes sense when seen in conjunction with his overarching theory of western European ascendancy: by submitting to the Greeks, the natives – whom Freeman labeled "Aryans," "Europeans," and "from the same stock" that would produce Rome, the successor to Greece in his narrative of West–East "strife" – would be allied to them politically, thus forming a cohesive unit against the "Semitic" threat posed by the Phoenicians-Carthaginians. In this scheme, Freeman produced an alternative model of colonial interaction that did not abandon the idea of native inferiority, but saw indigenous groups as the lesser of two evils when compared to the Phoenicians.

These examples show that ancient native populations could have agency in scholarship prior to the mid- to late twentieth century, though nearly always in a way that reinforced Hellenocentrism. Any sense of agency in the earlier scholarship also pales in comparison to recent postcolonialism-influenced studies. Modern scholars have critiqued earlier interpretations and representations of ancient colonization heavily, framing their own work as a reaction against the hegemonic discourse of imperialism. Not coincidentally, the strongest criticism has come from scholars based in former British imperial territories (cf. De Angelis 2003; Dietler 2005, 2010; Fossey 1991; Hodos 2006; Shepherd 2005), all of whom have used temporal and regional contextualization to shift away from the reification of colonialism, as well as "colonial" and "indigenous" categories. North American scholars especially adapted the work of anthropologists working on "New World" culture contact and acculturation (cf. Cusick 1998) to the ancient Mediterranean. Although "acculturation" is now recognized as overly simplistic (e.g., Whitehouse and Wilkins 1989), current studies build on ideas first posed in earlier acculturation studies, but reframe the interaction of Greeks and non-Greeks in terms of reciprocity, hybridization and hybridity, Middle Grounds, and identity (cf. Antonaccio 2003; Gosden 2004; Malkin 2004). Collectively, the contributions of these and other scholars turn a reflective eye upon earlier historiography, while also demonstrating the wider accommodation being made for non-Greeks in studies of the Greeks outside their homelands.

Conclusion

Frank Turner (1981, 8–9) once noted that interpretations of Greek history have, since the eighteenth century, been closely associated with national intellectual contexts, all of whose studies reflect particular "preoccupations of the national culture." This argument finds particularly fertile applicability in the specific case of studies of the Greeks outside their homelands by Anglophone scholars. It has been the intent of this chapter to identify some of the significant traditions related to this field of scholarship, and to describe the ways in which such traditions have been articulated through the sociopolitical contexts of the eighteenth, nineteenth, and early to mid-twentieth centuries. It has shown how the experiences of modern colonialism and imperialism have shaped and been shaped by the ancient Greek example, while also revealing how certain ideas, though recurrent, can be differently motivated and intended. In exploring the historiographical development of the Greeks overseas, it is hoped that contemporary scholars are reminded of the continued significance of studying ancient "colonization" while also being vigilant to the meaning and effects of our own involvement in an intellectual landscape defined by the experiences of former colonial regimes and contemporary global systems.

NOTE

1 Articulated in 1984 in French in *La naissance de la cité grecque: cultes, espace et société, VIII–VII siècles avant J.-C.*

REFERENCES

Akça Ataç, Cemile. 2006. "Imperial Lessons from Athens and Sparta: Eighteenth-Century British Histories of Ancient Greece." *History of Political Thought*, 27: 642–660.

Antonaccio, Carla. 2003. "Hybridity and the Cultures within Greek Culture." In *The Cultures within Ancient Greek Culture: Contact, Conflict, Collaboration*, edited by Carol Dougherty and Leslie Kurke, 57–74. Cambridge: Cambridge University Press.

Aubet, Maria Eugenia. 2001. *The Phoenicians and the West: Politics, Colonies and Trade*, 2nd ed. Cambridge: Cambridge University Press.

Barron, William. 1777. *History of the Colonization of the Free States of Antiquity Applied to the Present Contest Between Great Britain and her American Colonies*. London: T. Cadell.

Beazley, John. 1944. "Review of Dohan, *Italic Tomb Groups*." *Classical Review*, 58: 30–31.

Beazley, John. 1957. *Foreword to T.J. Dunbabin, The Greeks and their Eastern Neighbours*. London: Society for the Promotion of Hellenic Studies.

Blakeway, Alan. 1932–1933. "Prolegomena to the Study of Greek Commerce with Italy, Sicily and France in the Eighth and Seventh Centuries B.C." *The Annual of the British School at Athens*, 33: 170–208.

Blakeway, Alan. 1935. "'Demaratus': A Study of Some Aspects of the Earliest Hellenisation of Latium and Etruria." *The Journal of Roman Studies*, 25: 129–149.

Boardman, John. 1964. *The Greeks Overseas*. Baltimore: Penguin.

Bradley, Mark, ed. 2010. *Classics and Imperialism in the British Empire*. Oxford: Oxford University Press.

Buchner, Giorgio. 1966. "Pithekoussai, Oldest Greek Colony in the West." *Expedition*, 8: 4–12.

Ceserani, Giovanna. 2012. *Italy's Lost Greece: Magna Graecia and the Making of Modern Archaeology*. Oxford: Oxford University Press.

Challis, Debbie. 2010. "'The Ablest Race': The Ancient Greeks in Victorian Racial Theory." In Bradley 2010: 94–120.

Colonising, or a Plain Investigation of that Subject; with the Legislative, Political and Commercial View of the Colonies. 1774. London: printed for J. Brotherton and others.

Cook, Robert Manuel. 1946. "Ionia and Greece in the Eighth and Seventh Centuries B.C." *JHS*, 66: 67–98.
Cusick, James. 1998. *Studies in Culture Contact: Interaction, Culture Change, and Archaeology*. Carbondale: Southern Illinois University.
Darwin, John. 1980. "Imperialism in Decline? Tendencies in British Imperial Policy between the Wars." *The Historical Journal*, 23(3): 657–679.
De Angelis, Franco. 1998. "Ancient Past, Imperial Present: The British Empire in T.J. Dunbabin's *The Western Greeks*." *Antiquity*, 7: 539–549.
De Angelis, Franco. 2003. *Megara Hyblaea and Selinous*. Oxford: Oxford Monographs in Archaeology.
De Polignac, François. 1995. *Cults, Territory, and the Origins of the Greek City-State*. Trans. Janet Lloyd. Chicago: Chicago University Press.
Dietler, Michael. 2005. "The Archaeology of Colonization and the Colonization of Archaeology: Theoretical Challenges from an Ancient Mediterranean Colonial Encounter." In *The Archaeology of Colonial Encounters: Comparative Perspectives*, edited by Gil Stein, 33–68. Santa Fe: School of American Research Press.
Dietler, Michael. 2010. *Archaeologies of Colonialism: Consumption, Entanglement, and Violence in Ancient Mediterranean France*. Berkeley: University of California Press.
Dohan, Edith Hall. 1942. *Italic Tomb Groups in the University Museum*. Philadelphia: University of Pennsylvania Press.
Dunbabin, Thomas J. 1948. *The Western Greeks: The History of Sicily and South Italy from the Foundation of the Greek Colonies to 480 BC*. Oxford: Clarendon Press.
Estwick, Samuel. 1776. *A Letter to the Reverend Josiah Tucker*. London: J. Almon.
Finley, Moses. 1976. "Colonies: An Attempt at a Typology." *Transactions of the Royal Historical Society*, 26: 167–188.
Fossey, John. 1991. *Proceedings of the First International Congress on the Hellenic Diaspora from Antiquity to Modern Times*. Amsterdam: Gieben.
Freeman, Edward. 1891–1894. *A History of Sicily from the Earliest Times*. 4 vols. Oxford: Clarendon Press.
Gill, David. 1994. "Positivism, Pots and Long-distance Trade." In *Classical Greece. Ancient Histories and Modern Archaeologies*, edited by Ian Morris, 99–107. Cambridge: Cambridge University Press.
Gillies, John. 1786. *The History of Ancient Greece: Its Colonies and Conquests from the Earliest Accounts till the Division of the Macedonian Empire in the East*. 2 vols. Philadelphia: John Marot.
Gosden, Chris. 2004. *Archaeology and Colonialism: Cultural Contact from 5000 BC to the Present*. Cambridge: Cambridge University Press.
Graham, A. John. 1964. *Colony and Mother City in Ancient Greece*. Manchester: Manchester University Press.
Graham, A. John. 1971. "Patterns in Early Greek Colonisation." *JHS*, 91: 35–47.
Greene, Jack. 2013. *Evaluating Empire and Confronting Colonialism in Eighteenth-Century Britain*. Cambridge: Cambridge University Press.
Grote, George. 1846–1856. *A History of Greece*. 12 vols. London: John Murray.
Hansen, Mogens Herman, and Thomas Nielsen, eds. 2004. *An Inventory of Archaic and Classical Poleis*. Oxford: Oxford University Press.

Hodos, Tamar. 2006. *Local Responses to Colonization in the Iron Age Mediterranean*. London: Routledge.

Hurst, Henry, and Sara Owen, eds. 2005. *Ancient Colonizations: Analogy, Similarity and Difference*. London: Duckworth.

Jenkyns, Richard. 1980. *The Victorians and Ancient Greece*. Cambridge, MA: Harvard University Press.

Livingstone, Richard. 1935. *Greek Ideals and Modern Life*. Cambridge, MA: Harvard University Press.

Mackenzie, John. 2005. "Empires of Travel: British Guide Books and Cultural Imperialism in the 19th and 20th centuries." In *Histories of Tourism: Representation, Identity and Conflict*, edited by John Walton, 19–38. Clevedon: Channel View Publications.

Malkin, Irad. 1987. *Religion and Colonization in Ancient Greece*. Leiden: Brill.

Malkin, Irad. 2004. "Postcolonial Concepts and Ancient Greek Colonization." *Modern Language Quarterly*, 65: 341–364.

Mitford, William. 1784–1818. *The History of Greece*. 5 vols. London: T. Cadell and W. Davies.

Momigliano, Arnaldo. 1984. "The Rediscovery of Greek History in the Eighteenth Century: The Case of Sicily." In *Studies in Eighteenth-Century Culture 9*, edited by Roseann Runte, 167–187. Madison: University of Wisconsin Press.

Morel, Jean-Paul. 1975. "L'expansion Phocéenne en Occident: dix années de recerches (1966–75)." *Bulletin de correspondance hellénique*, 99: 853–896.

Morel, Jean-Paul. 1984. "Greek Colonization in Italy and in the West: Problems of Evidence and Interpretation." In *Crossroads of the Mediterranean*, edited by Tony Hackens, Nancy Holloway, and R. Ross Holloway, 123–161. Providence: Center for Old World Archaeology and Art, Brown University.

Noonan, Thomas. 1973. "The Origins of the Greek Colony at Panticapaeum." *American Journal of Archaeology*, 77: 77–81.

Osborne, Robin. 1998. "Early Greek Colonization? The Nature of Greek Settlement in the West?" In *Archaic Greece: New Methods and New Evidence*, edited by Nick Fischer and Hans van Wees, 251–269. London: Duckworth.

Owen, Sara. 2005. "Analogy, Archaeology and Archaic Greek Colonization." In Hurst and Owen 2005: 5–22.

Pagden, Anthony. 1995. *Lords of All the World: Ideologies of Empire in Spain, Britain, and France, c. 1500–1800*. New Haven: Yale University Press.

Pedley, John. 2005. *Sanctuaries and the Sacred in the Ancient Greek World*. Cambridge: Cambridge University Press.

Potter, John. 1697–1706. *Archaeologia Graeca; or, The Antiquities of Greece*. London: printed for J. Knapton and others.

Ridgway, David. 1973. "The First Western Greeks: Campanian Coasts and Southern Etruria." In *Greeks, Celts and Romans*, edited by Christopher and Sonia Hawkes, 5–38. Totowa, NJ: Rowman & Littlefield.

Said, Edward. 1978. *Orientalism*. New York: Vintage Books.

Shepherd, Gillian. 2005. "The Advance of the Greek: Greece, Great Britain and Archaeological Empires." In Hurst and Owen 2005: 23–44.

Snodgrass, Anthony. 1980. *Archaic Greece: The Age of Experiment*. London: J.M. Dent.

Stanyan, Temple. 1756. *Grecian History*. London: Jacob Tonson and S. Draper.

State of the British and French colonies in North America, with Respect to the Number of People, Forces, Forts, Indians, Trade and Other Advantages. 1775. 63–64. London: printed for A. Millar.

Thirlwall, Connop. 1860. *History of Greece.* London: printed for Longman, Rees, Orme, Brown, Green & Longman and John Taylor.

Tsetskhladze, Gocha. 2005. "Revisiting Ancient Greek Colonisation." In *Greek Colonisation: An Account of Greek Colonies and Other Settlements Overseas*, vol. 1, edited by Gocha Tsetskhladze, xxiii–lxxxiii. Leiden: Brill.

Turner, Frank. 1981. *The Greek Heritage in Victorian Britain.* New Haven: Yale University Press.

Van Dommelen, Peter. 1997. *On Colonial Grounds: A Comparative Study of Colonialism and Rural Settlement in First Millennium BC West Central Sardinia.* Leiden: Faculty of Archaeology.

Van Dommelen, Peter. 2002. "Ambiguous Matters: Colonialism and Local Identities in Punic Sardinia." In *The Archaeology of Colonialism*, edited by Claire Lyons and John Papadopoulous, 121–147. Los Angeles: Getty Research Institute.

Vlassopoulos, Kostas. 2010. "Imperial Encounters: Discourses on Empire and the Uses of Ancient History during the Eighteenth Century." In Bradley 2010, 29–53.

Whitehouse, Ruth, and John Wilkins. 1989. "Greeks and Natives in South-east Italy: Approaches to the Archaeological Evidence." *In Centre and Periphery: Comparative Studies in Archaeology*, edited by Tim Champion, 156–162. London: University of London, Institute of Classical Studies.

Woolley, Charles Leonard. 1938. "Excavations at Al Mina, Suedia I: The Archaeological Report." *JHS*, 58: 1–30.

FURTHER READING

Isaac, Benjamin. 2004. *The Invention of Racism in Classical Antiquity.* Princeton: Princeton University Press.

Lambroupoulos, Vassilis. 1993. *The Rise of Eurocentrism.* Princeton: Princeton University Press.

Lianeri, Alexandra, ed. 2011. *The Western Time of Ancient History: Historiographical Encounters with the Greek and Roman Pasts.* Cambridge: Cambridge University Press.

Lombardo, Mario, et al., eds. 2012. *Alle origini della Magna Grecia: mobilità, migrazioni, fondazioni. Atti del cinquantesimo Convegno di Studi sulla Magna Grecia, Taranto 1–4 ottobre 2010.* 3 vols. Taranto: Istituto per la Storia e l'Archeologia della Magna Grecia. Especially the chapters by Carmine Ampolo and Emmanuele Greco and Mario Lombardo on 1:11–34 and 35–60.

Lyons, Claire, and John Papadopoulos, eds. 2002. *The Archaeology of Colonialism: Issues and Debates.* Los Angeles: Getty Research Institute.

Stein, Gil, ed. 2005. *The Archaeology of Colonial Encounters: Comparative Perspectives.* Santa Fe: School of American Research Press.

Trigger, Bruce. 2006. *A History of Archaeological Thought.* 2nd ed. Cambridge: Cambridge University Press.

CHAPTER THREE

French-Speaking Traditions and the Study of Ancient Greeks outside their Homelands[1]

Michel Gras

The Century When it all Began

The year was 1705. Did the French consul at Tripoli, Claude Lemaire, know that in visiting Cyrene – a city founded in the seventh century by Greeks from Thera, which itself came from Sparta – he would in his own manner inaugurate a long tradition of scholarship?

The year was 1745. A young scholar, 23-year-old Jean-Pierre de Bougainville, decided to respond to a challenge posed by the Académie Royale des Inscriptions et Belles-Lettres: *What were the rights of the Greek home cities over their colonies? The colonies' obligations toward their home cities? The mutual commitments between one and the other?* These questions would guide him through an accelerated career: becoming permanent secretary of this academy in 1754, when he was only 32 years old, he died prematurely in 1763 at age of 41. A tragic fortune shattered before its time. Bougainville had a brother, seven years his junior. Louis-Antoine was one of the great French explorers of the eighteenth century, a companion of Montcalm in the defense of Québec, embedded in history for circumnavigating the globe (1767–1769), for his active participation in the American War of Independence in 1779, and for having given his name to an exotic flower brought back from Brazil: *la bougainvillée* or *le bougainvillier*, a colonial flower.

Who were the promoters of this contest? Besides Nicolas Fréret, permanent secretary of the Académie Royale since 1742, one might think rather of the count of Caylus, who became a member at this time, and who had already journeyed to South Italy and Sicily between April and June of 1715. However, a jurist must have also participated in the project's definition (Malesherbes?). They probably drew their line of questioning from one of Fontenelle's dialogues, a fictional meeting between the great Spanish explorer Fernando Cortés and the Aztec prince Montezuma II. Bougainville, who cites Fontenelle, defends

---

A Companion to Greeks Across the Ancient World, First Edition. Edited by Franco De Angelis.
© 2020 John Wiley & Sons, Inc. Published 2020 by John Wiley & Sons, Inc.

Cortés's point of view. Thus, Greek "colonization" emerges under the patronage of the Spanish conqueror, or at least the image that eighteenth-century men had of him.

Bougainville knew his Classical sources, in particular those commented on by Henri Valois in 1634. He identified the concept of the *apoikia*, distinguishing it from contemporary "colonies," evoking instead "migrations" and "transmigrations." He also recognized the *kleros*, and this over 200 years before Ettore Lepore and Moses Finley.

The year is now 1772. The Académie renewed its challenge with a theme from current affairs: *On the State and Types of Colonies of Ancient Peoples*. Guillaume de Sainte-Croix came out victorious in 1779, at the height of the War of Independence. Like Fontenelle and Bougainville, Sainte-Croix was raised a Jesuit, but wished to make a career as a mariner. Renouncing his faith, he directed his passion toward his studies. He took the opposite view of Bougainville and defended the colonies from their home cities: "all history is contemporary." In the background, it was the English colonial model that was really being attacked.

Again in 1784, Emmanuel de Pastoret won a competition on *The influence of Rhodian Maritime Laws on the Greek and Roman Navies*. Feeling let down on this point, in 1788 Abbé Barthélémy, a great friend of Caylus and Sainte-Croix, took revenge in his *Voyage du jeune Anacharsis*, depicting the relations between colonies and founding cities in a positive light.

Thus, Désiré Raoul-Rochette, who came out the victor in 1813 with his *Histoire critique de l'établissement des colonies grecques*, was not the first to write on this subject, as is often said in the official historiography advanced by Jean Bérard in his 1941 book, and by Finley in a 1976 conference. He was following his predecessors, like Wladimir Brunest de Presle, the winner in 1842 for his *Recherches sur l'établissement des Grecs en Sicile*.

Through its innovative policy, there is no doubt that the Académie played a decisive role in the emergence of a modern historical view of Greek emigration. But in framing it in a historical context where colonialism dictated international politics, it cast the Greek "removal" (*apoikia*) as a first phase in the colonial phenomenon. We are all tied to this story.

This dynamic place between scholarship, the sea, and exploration is the catalyst that explains the birth of this thinking and the weight that it acquired in historiography. Greek "colonization" is a child of eighteenth-century France. Anglo-Saxon historiography followed suit with Barron in 1777 and Gillies in 1786. Later (1948), Thomas Dunbabin took British colonization as his referent.

Greek "colonization," therefore, was first of all a scholarly discourse, legitimated by contemporary colonial experiences. It would take the "Grand Tour," the publication of the Tables of Heraclea in 1754, the first reliefs from Paestum, and Sir William Hamilton's collection fever in Naples from 1764 to actually spark an interest in the *realia*, the sites, and the works. French scholars and practical men were thus working on two parallel tracks, even if they progressively came into contact.

Fieldwork began with Honoré de Luynes at Metapontum in 1833 after an interval at Velia starting in 1828. This was the big moment for the Instituto di Corrispondenza Archeologica, founded in 1829. De Luynes was accompanied by his architect, Jean-Louis Debacq. He dug around a pile of columns and capitals which distinguish Temple A – a temple to Hera and not Apollo – in the heart of the Greek city. But these early attempts in the field would not resume for a long time. The French did not really return to the Greek city sites until 1911 with the École française d'Athènes' (EFA) work in Thasos. Returning to Italy would take even longer. Jean Hulot had made a preliminary report on Selinous in 1906 (before his 1910 publication with Fougères), and Jean Bérard started a memoire on Metapontum (below) in 1934, a century after Caylus. But one must wait until 1949 for new fieldwork, with the École française de Rome (EFR) at Megara Hyblaea, and then in 1951 with the arrival of Madeleine Cavalier at Lipari.

At Metapontum and in South Italy, François Lenormant continued Caylus's work in 1879 and 1881. The son of Charles Lenormant was in good hands with a Hellenophile father, who had even published a review of Duke of Luynes's *Metapontum* (Lenormant 1833), regretting that it was not a full-fledged monograph (*Annales de l'Institut de correspondance archéologique*, 1833, 292–299). This southern exploration appears to have launched a long season of study for Lenormant. He was accompanied by Felice Barnabei, right-hand man of Giuseppe Fiorelli, the director general then at the height of his glory. He evoked the opening of a dig at Velia for the young EFR, based at the Farnese Palace since 1875. Velia, for him, would become a revelation, more so than Paestum where the tourists annoyed him. He interceded at Taranto and amassed a collection of terracottas – there was still some of the antiquarian in him, this man of transition and contradictions, before 1887 and the opening of Taranto's museum. His two great works of 1881 (*La Grande Grèce. Paysages et histoire*) and 1883 (*A travers l'Apulie et la Lucanie*) ring like manifestos; indeed, these were his legacy after the death of their author in 1883. In a preliminary report to Fiorelli about his achievements, he concluded: "The history of the Greek colonies of southern Italy ... is an essential chapter in the general history of Hellenism." Charles Picard used these same terms to recognize the tragic loss of Jean Bérard in 1957. Today, these words are no longer vainly rhetorical but a matter of fact. The academic world only admitted after much reluctance that Greek history is not just the history of Athens and Sparta.

Victor and Jean Bérard, from the Sea to the Earth

A second great moment is that of the Bérard family, both father and son. Victor Bérard (1864–1931) and Jean Bérard (1908–1957), with their coherent and complementary outlooks, put the Greek Mediterranean back into the center of French historiography – like a boomerang too, after the passing of the Lenormants, another father-son duo (Brun and Gras 2010). And the two French schools, first in Athens, and then in Rome, can boast of acting as launching pads for these two scholars.

It all began in 1887 with the arrival of Victor Bérard at the EFA. He was already showing his wanderlust: from Greece to Albania, Macedonia, and then Anatolia. He kept in his mind the lessons of Paul Vidal de la Blache, who taught him geography at the École Normale Supérieure. Bérard was an inheritor of the French school of geography and would all his life be a devourer of spaces, especially maritime spaces. Indeed, the Bérards would always be more comfortable with space than with time and chronological debates. From 1896, Victor Bérard taught ancient geography at the École des Hautes Études but also at the École Supérieure de Marine. He did not focus anymore on specific regions – the experience of his thesis on Arcadian cults was quite enough. He instead treated Greek mobility across the Mediterranean as his frame, both geographical and cultural, using nothing other than the Homeric text as his instrument (Bérard 1929a, 1929b). Thus was born the *Phéniciens et l'Odyssée* and then the *Navigations d'Ulysse*. It was effusive and evocative work, certainly eclipsed by the evolution of the historical method, even if it remains terribly captivating and suggestive. Victor Bérard knew how to grab the reader and embellish his research. Admittedly, it had the tendency of replacing the Phoenicians with the Euboeans, but this does not really matter in the end. The work is what it is, take it or leave it. With its innumerable topographical references, Bérard succeeded in making the Mediterranean known, an achievement that would later belong to Braudel and then Horden and Purcell, who gave him the cold shoulder somewhat. However, Bérard had a model in mind as well, even if he did not use that vocabulary.

It is the *Odyssey* that would serve as witness to the changing of the guards between father and son. By the time his father passed in 1931, Jean Bérard had not yet shown his determination to work on the Greek Mediterranean (Brun and Gras 2010). His Master's thesis was on the voyages of Saint Paul in Asia Minor and the region's economic conditions – a question of itineraries, certainly, but most of all a subject worth studying. Now it was up to him to fulfill what his father did not have time to do, notably the *Album odysséen* which he held so dear. Charles Picard advised the young EFR member to write his dissertation on Metapontum. This was the turning point. Jean Bérard took up where de Luynes and Lenormant left off by writing a definitive work for posterity. From 1935 to 1940, at Paris, and then again at Rome, he built a base for future studies.

La colonisation grecque de l'Italie méridionale et de la Sicile dans l'Antiquité: L'histoire et la légende is like a medallion in which the two sides complete each other. Today, the historical component outweighs the mythological component. Legend was a link to his father and to Homeric *nostoi*. The genius of Jean Bérard was to comprehend that we cannot leave ourselves tossed round by the sea's waves, but that we need to anchor ourselves to something other than Odyssean locales, dear to his father, but so uncertain. One must attach Greek history of the Mediterranean to its *poleis*, as well as the cities of southern Italy and Sicily, well-situated since the sixteenth century (Fazello for Sicily). One must take stock of the literary data site by site.

Jean Bérard's antiquarian colleagues at the EFR traditionally followed the model of a monograph on a single ancient city, a model which launched the careers of their predecessors such as Fernique on Praenesta (1880), Audollent on Roman Carthage (1901), and Dubois on Pozzuoli (1908). Michel Clerc, at the end of his career in 1929, published *Massalia*, a superb monograph on the only Greek city in French territory. Wuilleumier chose Tarentum, on which he wrote his thesis, published in 1939. Heurgon attached himself to pre-Roman Capua – admittedly not Greek, but central in Greek Campania – which was published from 1937. All of them were Latinists, like Perret who, in Paris, wrote an additional dissertation on Siris. After the war, the Athenians continued the tradition with monographs by Chamoux on Cyrene (1953) and Pouilloux on Thasos (1954). Recently, the publication of a first volume on Illyrian Apollonia continues this tradition but in the context of collaborative work (Dimo 2007; see also Bresson, Ivanchik, and Ferrary 2007).

Jean Bérard inherited his father's love for the outdoors. Because of his career, Jean was unable to fulfill Charles Lenormant's dream of writing a monograph on Metapontum. He broadcast a message to the future in his 1941 preface:

> The present work was not conceived as a self-contained piece. Rather it should be seen as a primer for future research, which can be undertaken by people other than myself, who only wishes to mark its direction and define its method.

To mark his desire to build for the future, he drafted as a supplementary work his *Bibliographie topographique des principales cités grecques de l'Italie méridionale et de la Sicile dans l'Antiquité*, which became the basis for a recently completed project by Giuseppe Nenci and Georges Vallet (*Bibliografia topografica della colonizzazione greca in Italia e nelle isole tirreniche*). One may take note of the slip from "Greek cities" to "Greek colonization".... In its second edition, published in 1957 shortly before his death, Jean Bérard showed his interest in archaeology, absent in the first edition. The excavations of Luigi Bernabò Brea and Madeleine Cavalier at Lipari, and those of Georges Vallet and François Villard at Megara Hyblaea, seem to address the very questions that he was asking. The transition had taken place and was carrying itself out despite Bérard's death.

Vallet and Villard both chose research subjects that were in line with their elders, at least superficially. It was not necessary to write simple monographs, neither on Marseille (already studied by Clerc) nor on Rhegion (Reggio) and Zancle (Messina). One must credit Bérard for opening the window and considering the Western Greek "colonial" world as an ensemble (Lévêque 1964; Clavel-Lévêque 1977; Casevitz 1985; Gras 1985; Rouillard 1991; Lamboley 1996; Colonisation 1999), a vision which Anne Jacquemin (EFA 1977) would later complete with Delphic vision (Jacquemin 1999).

Ceramics and Commerce

Vallet and Villard were not obligated to follow in Jean Bérard's footsteps. For them, there was no question of showing filial piety. Vallet's rude words of introduction in his dissertation, published in 1958, would have seemed particularly hurtful to Bérard, who was part of his jury in 1956:

> It is hardly acceptable to base conclusions on hypotheses, no matter how seductive and brilliant they might be. The date of the *Odyssey* or the accounts from which it is composed are so uncertain, the locales it suggests so arbitrary, and the whole enterprise so questionable that it is vain to pretend drawing even useless facts for our subject. It would therefore be better to pass these problems in silence.

It was an indictment against Victor Bérard and an invitation to turn the page. It was chosen to lean on the work of the son while absolving it from that of the father. The novelty of his approach came from a criticism by François Villard, an expert in Greek ceramics. To revive the study of Greek cities, Villard convinced Vallet of the necessity to direct attention not to the archaeology in a global context (as Dunbabin had done), but to the ceramology. It was a matter of going beyond Paolo Orsi's findings from his many and productive explorations in east Sicily and Calabria, and using ceramics as a chronological and economic marker.

Chronology was the weak point of Bérard's model. Villard had the ambition of constructing a reliable and tightened chronology of the different pottery styles from Corinthian Geometric and Protocorinthian up to Attic, for which he could lean on Sir John Beazley's work. He understood that the grave furnishings published by Orsi did not provide any solutions and that the stratigraphy of the residences could allow for more precision. Like Vallet, he closely emulated Courbin's work at Argos in 1952 to arrive at thorough stratigraphic readings. In 1948, he proposed a project to EFR's director Grenier and Syracuse's superintendent Bernabò Brea to excavate Megara Hyblaea's Archaic residential layers, refining its dates from stratified ceramics.

On the cultural plane he used ceramics, once they were firmly dated, to reconstruct commercial rhythms through the import of vases. In two articles, published in 1961 and 1963 (reprinted in Vallet 1996), Vallet and Villard laid out the principals that would guide them to Marseille as if on the Strait of Messina. When he gave his thesis the provocative but legitimate subtitle "essai d'histoire économique," Villard wished to demonstrate the new direction he was taking with ceramics – a direction indebted to the innovative observations of Alan Blakeway from the 1930s, but that went even further. This method proved fruitful. It was extended and expanded upon in the 1970s and beyond Italy, the south of France, and Spain (Gras, Morel, and Rouillard).

Nevertheless, ceramics began to show their limits when applied to chronology. Despite Vallet and Villard's efforts, they did not yield a decisive relative chronology of the Greek cities' foundations in Sicily, producing gaps that were too small (as between Syracuse and Megara Hyblaea). The scraps of Megarian stratigraphy were nothing compared to the impressive layers at Argos, and Hellenistic disruptions further complicated the picture. However, from this point forward, it was possible to identify multiple and countless junctions between different sites, further refining this essential tool that could not remain exclusive.

As a counterpoint one must read Edouard Will's major work, based on a monograph of Corinth (yet another one at that!) published in 1955. The work styled itself as a political history of the great Greek metropolis, careful not to fall into the trap of historical modernism, which flourished at the end of the last century. Indirectly, Will's efforts became very important for avoiding some of the downward spirals that archaeology can lead to. This line of study, however, could not have any great future if it ignored archaeology's input; Will himself gladly acknowledged this in his lucidity.

Southern France: The Birth of a Field Laboratory

During the 1960s and 1970s, the study of the Western Greek world saw a sudden growth as much in Languedoc as in Provence. In Provence, Clerc's (above) large summary monograph did not produce an immediate effect, and Vasseur's pioneering, though little-known work at the beginning of the twentieth century, did not save Marseille from remaining "an antique city without antiquities," to use one local scholar's expression. One has to wait until after the war before the research truly takes off. Henri Rolland, Director of Antiquities at Provence-North, focused on Provence's interior and knowledge of its essential sites to grasp the impact of Phocaean Hellenism on its territories. His action at Saint-Blaise should be underlined, as well as at Glanum, for a long time an important training ground. At Marseille, Fernand Benoit's intervention was key. This old member of the EFR (1922–1924) was an archivist, but his arrival at Marseille's Borély Museum in 1942, and his directorship of Provence's historical antiquities, created the necessary dynamic. In 1965, his *Recherches sur l'hellénisation du Midi de la Gaule*, a dense but very rich work, was read by all of the young archaeologists training in southern France. His efforts were further developed by Villard's work (above).

The postwar climate was marked by a reunion of French, Italian, and Catalan archaeologists. One should mention Nino Lamboglia's efforts in training French archaeologists in Liguria (Bordighera) at the Institute of Ligurian Studies, which published a journal, the *Revue d'études ligures* (or *Rivista di studi liguri*). In this way a common thread was woven between Liguria and Catalonia by way of southern France. Etruscan studies, closely related to questions in Greek scholarship, also developed after Massimo Pallottino's voyage through these regions in 1949.

Another process was taking place in Languedoc. Jean Jannoray, an old member of the EFA (1934) who was nominated for Montpellier's Faculty of Letters and the directorship of historical antiquities at Languedoc-Roussillon, wrote a regional archaeological thesis in the form, once again, of a site monograph (an *oppidum* at Languedoc, near Béziers). *Ensérune: Contribution à l'étude des civilisations préromaines de la Gaule méridionale* (1955) had an enormous regional impact, building on the pioneering work of Odette and Jean Taffanel at Mailhac, a large Iron Age site near Narbonne. Jannoray's premature death did not slow things down. His successor at both posts, Hubert Gallet de Santerre (1915–1991), another "Athenian" (and General Secretary of the EFA from 1949 to 1953), took the reins. His efforts toward the development of regional archaeology were crucial. Through a weekly seminar, he trained generations that would remain active over the following decades. All the while they fostered the birth of a veritable center for archaeology in Languedoc, which expressed itself to its full extent from the Rhône to the Pyrenees. This explains, among other factors, the success of the large archaeological operation undertaken at Lattes (Michel Py, Dominique Garcia, and many others with the aid of Guy Barruol), which will for a long time remain the key to analyzing Hellenization in the south. André Nickels's endeavors as director of antiquities – sadly too brief because of his premature death – also had great influence, in particular his work at the site of Agde (Nickels, Marchand, and Schwaller 1989).

In Provence, Benoit's work was extended by the implantation in Aix-en-Provence of research teams returning to France after the decolonization of North Africa. It was then possible to establish an important urban archaeological project in Marseille (at the site of the Bourse), which played a large role in the transformation of French urban archaeology and in the development of rescue archaeology. It also had an impact on the training of its students around Maurice Euzennat and François Salviat, two academics from Aix schooled in Athens and Rome, who also became directors of antiquities after Rolland and Benoit. The heritage of this site – which provided important documentation – would be revived and managed under the executive operation of the Centre National de la Recherché Scientifique (CNRS), and the coordination of Henri Tréziny (EFR 1977) would prove crucial in creating a record of excavations (1989). Numerous recent publications, as well as one volume of an archaeological map of Gaul, demonstrate that Marseille is no longer an antique city without antiquities but a field laboratory in which all members of today's French archaeological community actively work (Bats and Tréziny 1986; Hermary, Hesnard, and Tréziny 1999; Hermary and Tréziny 2000; Rothé and Tréziny 2005).

The dynamism of southern France has increasingly been influencing Spanish (especially Catalan) and Italian centers, also active in their own right. From this point forward, Marseille is a scientific base (even if the local authorities are not always conscious of this), but unfortunately this dynamism has not touched Corsica. Despite the uncovering of a large Etruscan necropolis of the fifth to second centuries in Aléria, the Phocaean Greek presence, alluded to by Herodotus in the case of Alalia, remains almost unknown today. This region, which has everything to make it central from our point of view, including its geographical position, has remained on the fringes, far more so than Sardinia, which has more successfully inserted itself into Mediterranean debates.

Roland Martin and Urban Spaces

The endearing career of Roland Martin can serve as introduction to such an analysis. Educated at the EFA (1938), and the author of an important thesis on the Greek agora (1951), Martin held an original and cross-disciplinary place with his approach to Greek urbanism (Martin 1974). From Thasos to Selinous, he had a strong influence on the French and Italian archaeologists working at Megara Hyblaea as well as at Paestum, Velia, Naxos, Syracuse, and Kamarina, not forgetting Marseille or the Greek East (by way of Paul Bernard). Through his guidance and, by 1965, his Parisian seminar at the École Pratique des Hautes Études, he contributed in placing architecture and urbanism at the heart of archaeological and even historical thought surrounding Greek *poleis*. In founding the CNRS's *Service* of ancient architecture in 1958 (which later became the Institut de recherche sur l'architecture antique), Martin had, in accord with Pouilloux and Vallet, created a common workspace for architects and archaeologists. His principal collaborators, starting with the Romanian architect Dinu Theodorescu in 1969, were major players on a number of Greek sites.

Thasos is an important case. Martin made first contact with this EFA site in May of 1939. The agora of Thasos had been located in 1921–1923. At this time, no other agora for a Greek *apoikia* had been identified insofar as Paolo Orsi, in the West, had not studied them as such. This was, therefore, an important step toward a global scientific view of a city founded *ex nihilo* (in this case by the Parians in the seventh century). The subject of Martin's thesis on the Greek agora was first suggested by Charles Picard (who had also guided Bérard toward Metapontum some years before; see above). But even if he did make an important contribution to this subject in 1959, Martin did not concentrate on the agora alone. He contended with issues of urban organization all across the globe, and many of his later studies draw from these observations, including those which deal with fortifications. It is no accident that many of Roland Martin's students have worked on fortifications (from Garlan to Leriche and Tréziny). Greek fortifications are not a peripheral element but a key factor in understanding urbanism, and their study really only makes sense within that context. It was with Martin at Thasos that this approach was born.

We will not be surprised then to see Martin's influence on Vallet and the Swiss architect Paul Auberson when they, in the 1970s, confronted the question of urban space at Megara Hyblaea, and especially the surroundings of the agora (identified in 1957), which led to their 1976 publication (Vallet, Villard, and Auberson 1976). In an indirect way, Thasian research had a strong influence. And Martin's impact would even spread to Selinous when, in 1973, he was invited by the superintendent, Tusa, which permitted Juliette de La Genière to locate the agora (1985), thanks to the work of Theodorescu.

A sectorial approach based in national research traditions must, nevertheless, acknowledge the strong affinity between Italian and French research during the 1970s and 1980s. The roles of Dinu Adamesteanu, Antonino Di Vita, Emanuele Greco, Giorgio Gullini, Ettore Lepore, Roland Martin, Giuseppe Nenci, Paola Pelagatti, Georges Vallet, and Giuseppe Voza must be underlined. Data taken from such sites as Naxos, Karamina, Himera, Lipari, Megara Hyblaea, Poseidonia, Selinous, Syracuse, and Velia were combined to create a global research dynamic. The *Centre Jean Bérard* in Naples, founded by Vallet in 1966, not to mention the Scuola Normale Superiore in Pisa and the Congress of Tarentum, make up the privileged centers of this dialogue.

On sites where modern constraints are less of a concern, one must ask, on a case by case basis, if the urban space was defined from the start or if it came out of gradual development. The debate raged on and persists today at Thasos, as the two arguments divide specialists. At Megara Hyblaea, by contrast, the data permit the view of an early definition of this space and of stability over two centuries (Gras, Tréziny, and Broise 2004). The results of German research at Selinous (Mertens) paint a similar picture.

The case of Megara Hyblaea, as important as it is, should not for all that become a model. It is only one scenario among so many others that are still poorly understood. Were there coherent systems for the cultural identity of the Greeks (Achaean, Corinthian, Euboean, Laconian, Megarian, Parian) or are these just variations on a common base (which would then justify the idea of a global Greek identity)? These complex questions are made even more so if we envisage treating cities of the first phase (end of the eighth century and beginning of the seventh century) alongside those from the sixth century. As much as it is reasonable to think (though one must first prove it) that Kamarina in the sixth century took on an urban form that had strong links with Syracusan tradition, it is just as unreasonable to apply Megara Hyblaea in understanding Phocaean urbanism in Greek Marseille. A century is a world away in this western milieu, which learned much between 700 and 600. And we should not forget the question of the *emporion* (Bresson and Rouillard 1993).

Between *Apoikiai* and *Emporia*

In this subject as well, French research owes a lot to Italian studies and the teachings of Lepore and Alfonso Mele. Through his regular chronicles and assessments of the Phocaean world starting in 1966, Jean-Paul Morel (EFR 1960) gave unity to a subject that would have otherwise been divided.

The question of *emporia* is not, strictly speaking, part of the record of the first phase of emigrations, although we sometimes ask if Pithecusae might not follow this model. It is better to discard this approach if we want the concept of *emporion* (and the *emporia* with which it is bound) to retain the rigor that Mele demanded of it (the *emporia* commerce that succeeds *prexis* commerce). It is not until the end of the seventh century and certainly the sixth century that we must envisage this question without falling into the opposite excess which, surprisingly, holds to exclude Mediterranean emporic commerce from the sixth century since the word does not first appear until Herodotus around 450 (Bresson and Rouillard 1993). This strange argument by Hansen has been recently revived without the necessary verification. It is indefensible if one only remembers that *emporia* are presented by Herodotus as the basis of Phocaean commerce before the destruction of Phocaea, and therefore before 545. And this is without mentioning Naucratis, an *emporion* founded near an Egyptian city, as proven by Jean Yoyotte, nor the Heraion at the mouth of the Sele near Poseidonia, whose calling is yet bigger (Juliette de La Genière).

Effectively, in the sixth century, the record cannot be avoided. Is Massalia an *apoikia* in the sense of cities from the end of the eighth century? The answer is no, as is shown by the relation between Massalia and Ampurias. In effect, Ampurias was born as an *emporion*, which is self-evident (Ampurias = Emporion) and matches with the data of our Catalan colleagues on the *Palaiopolis* of Ampurias. Then, near the middle of the sixth century, Massalia seizes upon this site which in fact becomes a direct dependency of the Phocaean city. We see that we can no longer call Massalia a simple *emporion* and a non-*polis*. Would not an *emporion* be incapable of politically dominating another? This argument seems better to me in any case than that which advances the regularity of Marseille's development in the sixth century to the extent that the little *emporia* of the Etruscan coast (Regisvilla, Fonteblanda) show a regularity of plan without in any way affirming the status of the *polis*.

The record is even more jumbled as Alalia is undocumented for the 20-year phase preceding the Battle of Alalia (565–545 BCE), and it is not a given that these potential remains will one day be identified. In the absence of precise data on Phocaea (the pioneering research of Félix Sartiaux in 1913, 1914, and 1920) and Lampsacus, there remains Velia, which is not an *emporion* but more like a little Massalia which also has a limited first establishment (the "polygonal village"). We must therefore understand what Massalia is, which is less simple than it sounds. Indeed, the sources complicate matters by preserving the memory of a possible second foundation in 540.

This double tradition, however, could lead us on the right track. Massalia's urban space is limited at 20 ha. Compare this figure to the 60 ha of Syracuse and Megara, which are among the smallest *apoikiai* of the eighth and seventh centuries. One should not forget Metapontum's 150 ha nor Poseidonia's 120 ha, this latter city contemporary with Massalia. It is not even in the same league. This urban space, however, evolved rapidly, and progressively swelled. At first there was only the Saint-Laurent and probably the Moulins hills acting as an acropolis; the Carmes hill was not occupied until about 500. This pattern is the opposite of what we see at Megara Hyblaea, with a static urban space over two centuries. Expansion with each generation or thereabouts, like at Marseille, assumes a particular model of stable occupation of an urban space. The Phocaean model appears original. Appraisal of the research on Marseille's urban space is therefore important.

Territories

Vallet's report at the 1967 Congress of Tarentum helped introduce this issue to French historiography. The innovative contribution of Agnès Rouveret and Serge Gruzinski (1976), which cross-referenced data from Magna Graecia with colonial Mexico, gave a new and more anthropological dimension to this vision. Fieldwork developed in varied directions: southern Gaul, Metapontum, Calabria (Mercuri 2004), the Black Sea (since the French work of Aleksandra Wasowicz and up until Christelle Müller 2010), and finally, post 1993, around the Adriatic with research in Salento and then Apollonia in Albania (Cabanes, Lamboley, and Quantin). A collected volume gives the measure of this activity as part of international research (Tréziny 2010). The classic concepts of Hellenization or Greek diffusion, as well as the center and the periphery, give way to more complex models founded on increasingly rich and multiform documentation that demands fine periodization.

A History of Style

This is another line which emerged out of French scholarship. It takes its inspiration from the work of Pierre de La Coste Messelière (EFA 1921) and Ernst Langlotz. It was Francis Croissant (EFA 1964) who traced out contours with rigor and method based on his analysis of Archaic protomes from Asia Minor, as well as his attention to all plastic forms, beyond material and dimensions. Claude Rolley (EFA 1961) applied his know-how to sculpture and Greek bronzes by redeeming those long-forgotten from the western domain. Croissant's (1983) approach underlined the pertinence of stylistic analysis for understanding cultural identities, taking into global consideration the archaeological object, whose dimensions – functional and formal – must not be separated. The analysis of sculpture from Greek cities in the Achaean domain of southern Italy is essential here. It is about understanding how a community (*polis*), through its artists and artisans (two categories that were less remote then than in contemporary society), succeeds in creating a "local style" both in its uniqueness and in its occult links, on display with other styles. In short, it is style as the identity of the *polis*. This approach is a far cry from vague notions of influence or *koine*, crude concepts which often serve to mask ignorance or the inability to analyze complex mental and artistic developments in the transmission and diffusion of models. It is style as a cultural signature.

This global approach, which gathers the alleged specialists of archaeology (ceramic, bronze, terracotta, painting) around a coherent vision, implementing all of the necessary knowledge toward an understanding of the Greek city, is essential in the study of a "Greek adventure" (Pierre Lévêque 1964) at the scale of the entire Archaic Mediterranean. Such an approach does not content itself with being seen as an accumulation of bilateral relations between "metropolis" and "colony."

Conclusion

This archaeology of a "colonial" knowledge and know-how shows at what point archaeology, in reviving it, subscribed to a traditional history of Greek colonization which, since the war, has been hard put in renewing problems of research stemming from tired readings of the literary sources. The rare attempts at tackling something beyond the writing of student textbooks include those by François de Polignac (EFR 1981), nourished by the teachings of Jean-Pierre Vernant, Pierre Vidal-Naquet, and Marcel Detienne, whose work raises a Greek consciousness and an ensemble of rituals, as well as a global reading of the *polis*. More recently, Maria Cecilia D'Ercole traced her path with her *Histoires méditerranéennes* (2012), at the intersection of several historiographies (see also Rouillard 2009; Avram 2012).

Finally, there is the work done on the writing of colonial societies. Michel Lejeune, with his linguistic knowledge, gave this subject a decisive forward thrust. Catherine Dobias-Lalou (2000, on Cyrene) and Laurent Dubois (1989–2008) fall in this vein, not forgetting the onomastic studies of Olivier Masson. Epigraphic sources are here called upon, notably sacred laws, curse tablets (Selinous), or contracts (Pech-Maho in Languedoc or Elephantine in Egypt). It remains to be hoped that discoveries, such as the 150 inscribed lead tablets from Kamarina (1987) recording the registration of citizens into a phratry, multiply. This would open up another big opportunity for analyzing the interior function of societies in Greek *poleis*. It is one great hope for historians who are a little deprived of documentation.

Today, new issues have been delineated. A "new frontier" has been opened since 1989 in Eastern Europe and, in turn, the east bank of the Adriatic and the Black Sea coast (Bresson, Ivanchik, and Ferrary 2007). Here, French scholarship could lean on a tradition marked earlier by Marcelle Lambrino's pioneering 1938 book on the Archaic ceramics of Histria. The work made its mark on the excavators at Megara Hyblaea (in *Megara II*, 1964), but most of all, it opened the way for a rich collaboration between French and Romanian researchers through the appointment of ceramologist Pierre Dupont. In a grander scheme, those working in these regions (no less peripheral than those in the western Mediterranean), including Pierre Cabanes in Albania, Pierre Lévêque in Georgia, and Véronique Schiltz and Jean-Paul Morel in the Black Sea, will be crucial in forging new paths.

NOTE

1 Translated from the French by Andrei Mihailiuk.

REFERENCES

Avram, Alexandru. 2012. *Les diasporas grecques du VIIIe siècle à la fin du IIIe siècle av. J.-C.* Paris: Bréal.

Bats, Michel, and Henri Tréziny, eds. 1986. *Le territoire de Marseille grecque*. Aix-en-Provence: Edisud.

Benoit, Fernand. 1965. *Recherches sur l'hellénisation du Midi de la Gaule*. Aix-en-Provence: Ophrys.

Bérard, Jean. 1941. *La colonisation grecque de l'Italie méridionale de la Sicile dans l'Antiquité*. Paris: BEFAR, de Boccard.

Bérard, Victor. 1929a. *Les Phéniciens et l'Odyssée*. Paris: A. Colin.

Bérard, Victor. 1929b. *Les navigations d'Ulysse*. Paris: A. Colin.
Bresson, Alain, and Pierre Rouillard, eds. 1993. *L'emporion*. Paris: de Boccard.
Bresson, Alain, Askold Ivanchik, and Jean-Louis Ferrary, eds. 2007. *Une koinè pontique. Cités grecques, sociétés indigènes et empires mondiaux sur le littoral nord de la Mer noire*. Bordeaux: Ausonius.
Brun, Jean-Pierre, and Michel Gras, eds. 2010. *Avec Jean Bérard 1908–1957. La colonisation grecque. L'Italie sous le fascisme*. Rome: EFR.
Casevitz, Michel. 1985. *Le vocabulaire de la colonisation en grec ancien*. Paris: Klincksieck.
Chamoux, François. 1953. *Cyrène et la monarchie des Battiades*. Paris: de Boccard.
Clavel-Lévêque, Monique. 1977. *Marseille grecque. La dynamique d'un empire marchand*. Marseille: Laffitte.
Clerc, Michel. 1929. *Massalia. Histoire de Marseille dans l'Antiquité*. Marseille: Laffitte.
Colonisation. 1999. *La colonisation grecque en Méditerranée occidentale. Actes de la rencontre scientifique en l'honneur de Georges Vallet* (1995). Rome: EFR.
Croissant, Francis. 1983. *Les protomés féminines archaïques. Recherches sur les représentations du visage dans la plastique grecque de 550 à 480 av. J.-C*. Paris: BEFAR, de Boccard.
D'Ercole, Maria Cecilia. 2012. *Histoires méditerranéennes*. Paris: Errance.
Etienne, Roland, ed. 2010. *La Méditerranée au VIIe siècle av. J.-C. (essais d'analyses archéologiques)*. Paris: de Boccard.
Dimo, Vangjel, Philippe Lenhardt, and François Quantin, eds. 2007. *Apollonia d'Illyrie, 1. Atlas archéologique et historique*. Rome: EFR.
Dobias-Lalou, Catherine. 2000. *Le dialecte des inscriptions grecques de Cyrène*. Karthago, XXV. Paris: Peeters.
Dubois, Laurent. 1989–2008. *Inscriptions dialectales de Sicile*. Rome: EFR, 1. Paris: EPHE, 2.
Gras, Michel. 1985. *Trafics tyrrhéniens archaïques*. Rome: BEFAR, EFR.
Gras, Michel. 1995. *La Méditerranée archaïque*. Paris: A. Colin.
Gras, Michel, Henri Tréziny, and Henri Broise. 2004. *Mégara Hyblaea 5. L'espace urbain d'une cité grecque de Sicile orientale*. Rome: EFR.
Hermary, Antoine, Antoinette Hesnard, and Henri Tréziny. 1999. *Marseille grecque. 600–49 av. J.-C. La cité phocéenne*. Aix-en-Provence: Edisud.
Hermary, Antoine, and Henri Tréziny, eds. 2000. *Les cultes des cités phocéennes*. Aix-en-Provence: Edisud.
Jacquemin, Anne. 1999. *Offrandes monumentales à Delphes*. Paris: BEFAR, de Boccard.
Jannoray, Jean. 1955. *Ensérune. Contribution à l'étude des civilisations préromaines de la Gaule méridionale*. Paris: BEFAR, de Boccard.
Lamboley, Jean-Luc. 1996. *Les Grecs d'Occident. La période archaïque*. Paris: SEDES.
Lenormant, Charles. 1833. "Compte rendu de l'ouvrage de MM. le duc de Luynes et Debacq *Métaponte*." *Annales de l'Institut de correspondance archéologique*, 5: 292–299.
Lenormant, François. 1881. *La Grande Grèce. Paysages et histoire*. Paris: A. Lévy.
Lenormant, François. 1883. *A travers l'Apulie et la Lucanie*. Paris: A. Lévy.
Lévêque, Pierre. 1964. *L'aventure grecque*. Paris: A. Colin.
Martin, Roland. 1951. *Recherches sur l'agora grecque*. Paris: BEFAR, de Boccard.
Martin, Roland. 1974. *L'urbanisme dans la Grèce antique*. 2nd ed. Paris: Picard.

Mercuri, Laurence. 2004. *Eubéens en Calabre à l'époque archaïque. Formes de contact et d'implantations*. Rome: BEFAR, EFR.

Müller, Christel. 2010. *D'Olbia à Tanais. Territoires et réseaux d'échanges dans la mer Noire septentrionale aux époques classique et hellénistique*. Bordeaux: Ausonius.

Nickels, André, Georges Marchand, and Martine Schwaller. 1989. *Agde. La nécropole du premier âge du fer*. Paris: CNRS.

Polignac, François de. 1995. *Naissance de la cité grecque*. Paris: La Découverte.

Pouilloux, Jean. 1954. *Recherches sur l'histoire et les cultes de Thasos*. Paris: BEFAR, de Boccard.

Rothé, Marie-Pierre, and Henri Tréziny. 2005. *Marseille et ses alentours (Carte archéologique de la Gaule 13/3)*. Paris: CID.

Rouillard, Pierre. 1991. *Les Grecs et la péninsule ibérique du VIIIe au IVe siècle avant J.-C*. Paris: de Boccard.

Rouillard, Pierre, ed. 2009. *Portraits de migrants, portraits de colons*. Paris: de Boccard.

Rouveret, Agnès, and Serge Gruzinski. 1976. "'Ellos son come niños.' Histoire et acculturation dans le Mexique colonial et l'Italie méridionale avant la romanisation." *MEFRA*, 88(1): 159–219.

Tréziny, Henri, ed. 2010. *Grecs et indigènes de la Catalogne à la mer Noire*. Paris: Errance.

Vallet, Georges. 1958. *Rhégion et Zancle. Histoire, commerce et civilisation des cités chalcidiennes du détroit de Messine*. Paris: BEFAR, de Boccard.

Vallet, Georges. 1996. *Le monde colonial grec d'Italie du Sud et de Sicile*. Rome: EFR.

Vallet, Georges, François Villard, and Paul Auberson. 1976. *Mégara Hyblaea 1. Le quartier de l'agora archaïque*. Rome: EFR.

Vernant, Jean-Pierre. 1962. *Les origines de la pensée grecque*. Paris: Maspero.

Villard, François. 1960. *La céramique grecque de Marseille (VIe –IVe siècles). Essai d'histoire économique*. Paris: BEFAR, de Boccard.

Will, Edouard. 1955. *Korinthiaka. Recherches sur l'histoire et la civilisation de Corinthe des origines aux guerres médiques*. Paris: de Boccard.

Wuilleumier, Pierre. 1939. *Tarente: des origines à la conquête romaine*. Paris: BEFAR, de Boccard.

FURTHER READING

Bérard, Jean. 1941. A synthesis of the literary sources with analysis by city.

D'Ercole, Maria Cecilia. 2012. A recent work with historiographical approaches and in-depth analyses on particular themes (land, institutions, the Euboeans, Corinth, the Black Sea, Marseilles, etc.).

Etienne, Roland, ed. 2010. A volume of essays with lateral analyses of chronology, writing, distributions, sanctuaries, and styles.

Gras, Michel. 1995. A synthesis of the Archaic Mediterranean's landscapes, routes, territories, memory, values, and distributions.

Gras, Michel, Henri Tréziny, and Henri Broise. 2004. An analytical archaeological overview, quarter by quarter, of an *apoikia*, as well as an analysis of the layout of the urban land plots.

Polignac, François de. 1995. A brilliant book on the emergence of the world of cities.

Tréziny, Henri, ed. 2010. A broad panorama of archaeological results for the Greek world in contact with local populations.

Vallet, Georges. 1996. A collection of the main articles of Vallet (sometimes in partnership with Villard) on Greek colonization.

Vernant, Jean-Pierre. 1962. A major book on Greek rationality.

Villard, François. 1960. A pioneering and classic work on the relationship between pottery and economic history.

CHAPTER FOUR

German-Speaking Traditions (including the Habsburg Empire) and the Study of the Ancient Greeks outside their Homelands

Martin Mauersberg

The following pages will provide a panoramic view of the evolution of knowledge of the phenomenon conventionally called "Greek colonization" in German-speaking scholarship.[1] This geographical restriction requires a caveat: Due to the transnational connectedness of classical scholarship, it is not self-evident to distinguish national "schools." This is of course also true for research concerning the Greeks outside of Greece. Adolf Holm (1830–1900), for instance, dedicated his three-volume *Geschichte Siciliens im Alterthum* (1869–1897) not only to the eminent German scholar Ernst Curtius but also to George Grote. The Sicilian scholar Michele Amari (1806–1889) initiated Adolf Holm's move to the University of Palermo in 1876, and between 1884 and 1897 he held a post at the University at Naples. Or, Désiré Raoul-Rochette's (1789–1854) four-volume *Histoire critique de l'établissement des colonies grecques* from 1815 was considered as the standard work on "Greek colonization" in Germany throughout the nineteenth century. Thus, it should not cause surprise to learn that there are more similarities than differences in the national scholarly traditions.

It is even more difficult to subdivide German-speaking scholarship into its constituent parts: Germany and the German-speaking regions of Switzerland and the Habsburg Empire. German-speaking *Altertumswissenschaften* were closely interconnected as scholars and their works moved easily: the Swiss, Jacob Burckhardt (1818–1897), whose famous *Griechische Kulturgeschichte* will be discussed below, spent a part of his studies in Berlin, one of the gravitational centers for classical scholarship. Johann Oehler (1857–1921), who taught at the *Gymnasium* in the Austrian town Linz, wrote the lemma *"apoikia"* in the *Realencyclopädie der classischen Altertumswissenschaften* (hereafter abbreviated to *RE*). The general political circumstances furthered this connectedness, as the rising nationalism created a cross-border feeling of belonging to the German "Volk." It has to be underlined that the German Empire was

---

A Companion to Greeks Across the Ancient World, First Edition. Edited by Franco De Angelis.
© 2020 John Wiley & Sons, Inc. Published 2020 by John Wiley & Sons, Inc.

founded only in 1871, uniting different kingdoms, states, and princedoms under the Prussian crown, while in the "Vielvölkerreich" Austria the "Deutsche Frage"[2] remained unresolved.

In summary, when writing about German-speaking traditions, one has to observe that there are no inherent "national" ways of writing history. The starting point should be the practice of the scholarly production of knowledge understood as the result of individual scholarly exploits of the leeway in concrete spatiotemporal circumstances – and the (changing) perceptions of the concept "nation" is one of them! Only in this sense can differences between an English-speaking and a German-speaking tradition be approached.

Changing Perspectives on "Colonization"

Knowledge of "Greek colonization" is a cluster consisting of different paradigms, axiomatic assumptions, and structural circumstances plus the corresponding interpretation of ancient written sources and, progressively, archaeological data. These elements are affected by fluctuations and mutations in the course of time. Nevertheless, knowledge of "Greek colonization" is less characterized by rapid changes, remaining quite stable due to a *colonial paradigm* that proved highly influential until recently: colonization was seen as a universal, yet foremost European phenomenon. This allowed comparative analyses of different eras and provided classicists with material to fill the gaps that their material left. This approach was bolstered in the second half of the nineteenth century by a strong scientific sentiment that advocated the possibility of deducing natural laws from human or societal behavior: colonization was a "Naturprozeß" (Burckhardt 1982, 4:67), a natural process, following its "allgemeinen Entwicklungsgesetzen, welche das koloniale Leben beherrschen"[3] (Pöhlmann 1889, 378). A foundational work for this approach was the historian and economist Wilhelm Roscher's (1817–1894) highly influential *Kolonien, Kolonialpolitik und Auswanderung* (first ed. 1848), who intended to write the "Grundzüge einer Naturlehre der Kolonien."[4]

Modifications to the knowledge of "Greek colonization" primarily occurred because of changes in the perception of colonization itself in the course of the nineteenth century. Dietrich Hermann Hegewisch (1740–1812), who wrote the first monograph in German on "Greek colonization" (Hegewisch 1808), advocated a cultural definition of colonization: An emigration in which cultural and linguistic bonds between emigrants and the "Vaterland" persisted (1808, 149). Political relations were not a necessary part of this definition. This broad definition was consistent with the perception of "Greek colonization," as there was a unanimous agreement on its most defining character: the independence of Greek "colonies." The recurrent term to characterize this link was "Pietätsverhältnis," relation of piety, often illustrated with the metaphor of an emancipated child's reverence to its home, which was borrowed from ancient sources (e.g., Plato *Leg.* 754b–d).

This cultural definition moved into the background, when the factor of political domination became more important in the wake of European imperialism. Thus, "Greek colonization" increasingly became an exceptional case of colonization.

Specific national perspectives become obvious, when illustrative comparisons with a more recent past are introduced: According to his understanding of "colonization," Hegewisch was able to list German emigrants in New England as examples of "German" "colonies" (Hegewisch 1808, 149).

Later in the century, Ernst Curtius (1814–1896) presented "Greek colonization" as "diaspora" in his programmatic speech *Die Griechen als Meister der Colonisation* (held to honor the birthday of Kaiser Wilhelm I at the Friedrich-Wilhelms-Universität Berlin, today's Humboldt Universität, in 1883). This underlined the aspect of cultural bonds between independent *apoikiai* and their *metropoleis* and opened the possibility to compare "Greek colonization" with the situation of contemporary Germany, where a political debate raged whether to obtain colonies or not:

> Nächst den Griechen hat kein Volk der Erde das, was es an Kraft besitzt, so zu einem Gemeingute der Menschheit gemacht, wie die Deutschen. Nach allen Richtungen haben sie den Ocean, der unser Mittelmeer ist, überschritten; in allen überseeischen Continenten haben sie die Wälder gelichtet, den Boden urbar gemacht, den Samen ausgestreut.[5] (1892, 107)

Greeks did not create a colonial empire in the Archaic period, yet they disseminated civilization in the Mediterranean basin. This was their "große weltgeschichtliche That,"[6] as Robert Pöhlmann (1889, 373) put it in his *Grundzüge der politischen Geschichte Griechenlands*, part of the multivolume standard work *Handbuch der klassischen Altertumswissenschaft*. "Greeks," as the forefathers of modern European civilization, possessed the most advanced culture of the first millennium BC in the eyes of the nineteenth century. Thus, their presence in non-Greek regions must have had *a priori* most beneficial effects on local populations. Adolf Holm described the difference between the "Phoenician" and the "Greek" impact in Sicily as follows:

> Die Völkerschaften, welche wir bis jetzt als Bewohner Siciliens kennen gelernt haben, waren ihrer ganzen geistigen Begabung nach nicht im Stande, der Insel eine hohe geschichtliche Stellung zu verleihen. Die Sikaner und Sikeler scheinen nicht einmal die so höchst nothwendige und weniger gebildeten Stämmen sonst meistens innewohnende Eigenschaft eines hervorragenden kriegerischen Sinnes besessen zu haben, und das Hinzukommen der Phönicier, die in ihren Kolonien auf der Insel vorzugsweise als Kaufleute und Fabrikanten auftraten, konnte der Urbevölkerung zwar gewisse Fertigkeiten des praktischen Lebens bringen, war aber zur Beförderung einer innerlichen Entwicklung derselben zu höherer Bildung nur wenig geeignet. Alles ward anders, als Griechen sich auf Sicilien niederliessen.[7] (1870, 108)

If the lack of a hierarchical relation between *apoikia* and *metropolis* was seen as typical for "Greek colonization" (and atypical for colonization), the views of the relation between "colonizer" and "colonized" matched the general ideas of European colonization. "Greeks" were not necessarily conquerors, although if necessary one assumed that they had no problem in taking possession of a strip of land, proof of which could be shown, for instance, in the correspondent statements in Thucydides's description of the "Greek" settlement of Sicily (Book VI).

An important factor for the description of "colonial" contacts was the determination of the causes for "Greeks" to "colonize." The colonial paradigm proved highly influential here. Overpopulation was seen as the main push factor, but also the establishing of trading posts, "Handelsfaktoreien," was thought to have been a potent motive for emigration.

Yet, in contradistinction to "Phoenicians," "Greeks" were not seen as traders *per se*. Jacob Burckhardt expressed this juxtaposition as follows:

> Allein der wesentliche Grund ihres [the "Greek" colonies'] Daseins ist [...] nicht der Handel, derselbe dient den Auswanderern vielmehr nur als Mittel, um als freie Bürgerschaften zu leben und ihre Kräfte zu erproben.[8] (1982, 4:68–69)

Trade was on the one hand the most important channel for the diffusion of "Greek" culture, and on the other hand an explanation for the more peaceful character of "Greek colonization." Ernst Curtius wrote:

> Im Allgemeinen aber kann Handelsvölkern nur mit friedlichen Verhältnissen gedient sein, und darum suchten sich die ionischen Griechen auch mit den Barbaren baldmöglichst auf Friedensfuß zu stellen. Sie kamen nicht als Eroberer; sie wollten die Eingeborenen nicht austreiben, sie traten überall mit geringer Mannschaft großen Massen gegenüber. Darum mussten sie dieselben zu gewinnen, sich ihnen dienstfertig und nützlich zu erweisen suchen;[9] (1874, 1:450)

The idea of the distribution of civilization to less developed "people" was increasingly used to legitimatize the colonial system in the nineteenth century, and the perception of "Greek" colonizers adapted itself to those visions. They were the first to fulfill the European civilizing mission and served to illustrate the bright side of colonization: Like their successors centuries later, the "Greeks" brought with them the blessings of culture that almost automatically transformed the colonized.

What made the phenomenon in the eyes of the nineteenth century also "colonial" was the "fact" that *apoikiai* were the product of state-planned emigrations. Whereas in the eighteenth century "colony" had been more or less equated with "emigration," the factor of organization now became – in accord with modern colonial experience – increasingly important. As already pointed out, Hegewisch defined "colony" as "jede große Anzahl Menschen, die aus einem Lande, wo sie lange wohnten, weggeht und sich in einem andern Lande niederläßt"[10] (1808, 149). He defended adamantly, true to his definition, the inclusion of the emigrations to Asia Minor in the "Greek colonization" against attempts to exclude them as "Völkerwanderungen." Scholars, however, became increasingly restrictive because of a more narrow vision of colonization, as an *a priori* organized endeavor. The emigrations to Asia Minor were seen as part of the formative phase of the political landscape of Greece. Only when this was accomplished, Greek *poleis* were able to send away "colonies" – in accordance with Thucydides's outline of Greek history (Thucydides 1.12). They were "colonies," as they conformed at least in some aspects to the contemporary understanding of colonization: be it only because of the initial organization of the *apoikia* and the subsequent "Pietätsverhältnis" in the case of the "Greek colonization."

Those features were its defining elements, and their abolition signaled the transition to subsequent phases of "Greek colonization." Starting with the fifth century BC, *metropoleis* sought to control their "colonies" more directly, defying the "Pietätsverhältnis," whereas the *poleis* lost their independence under Macedonian rule and thus the possibility to play an active role in the "Pietätsverhältnis" between an initially organizing *metropolis* and its *apoikia*.

From a German perspective, the Greek example could provide some lessons. To Curtius the "Greeks" were "masters of colonization," and their example served to reflect on the importance of national unification: it would give the Germans overseas, at least symbolically, a homeland. For this he praised the Prussian king, Wilhelm, now the first Kaiser of the German Empire, in his speech and pitied the "Greeks", who were not able to create a unified homeland. Yet, their example taught that there was hope for a "people" that was late in the "colonial" struggle:

> Sie haben saure Lehrjahre durchgemacht und die Meeresnähe lange Zeit wie einen Fluch empfunden. Das mußte sie ihnen sein, so lange fremde Völker das Meer beherrschten, phönikische Kaperschiffe urplötzlich im Morgennebel auftauchten, die Eingeborenen mit buntem Tand an den Strand lockten, die Söhne und Töchter des Landes in unerreichbare Ferne fortschleppten. Auch in größerer Zahl wurden sie fortgeführt, um fremder Colonialpolitik als Material zu dienen, bis sie allmählich ihren Feinden das Handwerk ablernten, eigene Schiffe zimmerten und sich schaarenweise zusammenthaten, um in steten Beutezügen die erlittene Unbill an den älteren Seevölkern zu rächen.[11] (1892, 97)

The "Greek" People/Race/State(s)/Nation(s)

"Peoples" were perceived as entities with essentialized inherent properties. For historiography this was an important tool, as it allowed generalizations on the basis of statements in written sources referring to isolated cases: what was true for them must be true for the whole "people" concerned. This was especially valuable for Classics, given the scarcity of information preserved in ancient sources, not least for the time of "Greek colonization." Thus, scholars were able to assemble a catalog of "Gründungsgebräuche," customary acts when founding an *apoikia*, by compiling various isolated statements.

In the nineteenth century this paradigm witnessed a significant shift from the view of culturally defined "peoples" inhabiting a certain region and being shaped by its environmental factors to genetically determined "races." Concerning "Greek colonization," this manifested itself notably in the descriptions of contacts, which gained space next to the permanent main point of interest, the political relations between *apoikiai* and *metropoleis*, not least due to the increased awareness of the "Greeks" as civilizers. The gap between "Greeks" and "barbarians" broadened, as not only cultural but also racial factors divided them. Jacob Burckhardt was quite clear in this respect:

> Trotz Vermählung mit den Frauen des Landes getrauten sich die Griechen, ihr Blut griechisch zu halten, und da sie den Willen dazu hatten, was ihnen bei ihrer Furcht vor dem barbarisch werden sehr nahe gelegen haben muß, setzten sie es auch durch.[12] (1982, 4:74)

In the "Age of Empire" it became unimaginable that a colonizing people might lose its racial pureness, even if intermarriage was admitted. The recurrent use of labels like

"Mischlinge" (Curtius 1874, 1:443) or "Mischrasse" (Burckhardt 1982, 4:67) for populations living on the fringes of *apoikiai* were the logical consequence of this dichotomization in opposing racial blocs.

Next to their superior culture, another inherent quality of the "Greeks" was identified in their constant striving for independent polities. Robert Pöhlmann put it in the following way:

> In dieser unendlichen Zerstreuung der Griechen fast über den ganzen Länderkreis der Mittelmeerwelt fand der tief im Nationalcharakter wurzelnde Trieb nach individueller Gestaltung ihres Gemeinwesens reichste Befriedigung. Nirgends hat die Kolonisation zu umfassenden Staatenbildungen geführt; und wo der Versuch zur Gründung einer wirklichen Kolonialherrschaft gemacht ward, wie z.B. von Korinth im ionischen Meere und an der Adria, da kam es zu Kolonialkriegen [...], welche die Tendenz zu partikularer Absonderung nur verschärfen konnten.[13] (1889, 376)

From the perspective of a nineteenth century obsessed by the question of national unification, this was at the same time the "Greeks'" Achilles's heel.

One of the landmarks in the development of German *Altertumswissenschaften* was the self-definition as science that produces methodologically and autonomously historical knowledge in a deliberate contrast to a "before," when there was only the compiling of ancient statements. A central pillar was the reconstruction of the "Wesen," the essential nature of states, that is, the reconstruction of their constitutions, laws, and policies to enable a better understanding of the past. Paradigmatic for this development were works like Wilhelm Wachsmuth's *Hellenische Alterthumskunde aus dem Gesichtspunkte des Staates* or Karl Friedrich Hermann's *Lehrbuch der griechischen Staatsalterthümer*. For "Greek" history this meant writing the history of their (city-)states, seen as necessarily isolated political entities given the assumed basic property of the "Greek" people. This struck a chord in the German-speaking world in the early nineteenth century when the *Altertumswissenschaften* began, as the German "people" were equally divided in various political units. Another important factor of this focus on political entities, one could call it a *polit-ontological paradigm*, was that people, states, and nations became historical actors. This had its effects on the reconstruction of "Greek colonization:" The *polis* was seen as its main force, corresponding perfectly with the notion of colonization as the result of state action and the reconstructions of "Gründungsgebräuche" as its manifestations.

Yet, despite the diagnosed "Greek" political fragmentation, it seemed logical that people possessed superordinate "national" institutions that served as uniting elements. Scholars found institutions with cultic qualities in the "Greeks'" case, indicating a high, even primordial age (cf. Pöhlmann 1889, 377). One was the Delphic oracle. Its importance for "Greek colonization" and the apparent success of its prophecies were rationalized by the accumulation of knowledge brought to Delphi by visitors from all over the Mediterranean (e.g., Curtius 1874, 1:467–468; Burckhardt 1982, 4:69). Thus, not only written sources confirmed this perception, but also the axiomatic assumptions concerning the inherent properties of people's respective nations.

Overpopulation versus Trade

Knowledge of "Greek colonization" sat at the intersection of the colonial and the polit-ontological paradigm. This presents itself also when looking at the reconstructions of its causalities. "Colonization" was perceived in the eighteenth century as a subtype of migration. Especially early "colonies," like those of the "Greeks," were seen more as the result of necessity than of utility (e.g., Heyne 1785, 296–297), which found its confirmation in the *loci classici* of Plato (*Leg.* 798b–c) and Seneca (*Helv.* 7). It was Arnold Herrmann Ludwig Heeren (1760–1842), Professor of History in Göttingen, who furthered an economic approach toward the history of colonization, as his works circled around the triad "Politik," "Verkehr" (transportation), and "Handel" (trade). According to him, a new era started with the dissemination of the "Greeks": that of the "colonization" of European peoples (Heeren 1826, 9). Trade especially was seen as a major force in history; it was modern European colonization that resulted in an unprecedented connectedness of modern nations based on commerce, while the fusion of economics and politics was not yet that profound in antiquity. Still, progressively there were "states" with a high degree of symbioses between trade and politics, not least in a "colonial" context:

> Auch die Griechischen Colonieen wurden theils aus politischen Gründen, theils des Handels wegen gestiftet. Das Erste gilt fast ohne Ausnahme von allen Pflanzstädten, welche das Mutterland selber anlegte; das Andere von denen die wiederum Töchter von Pflanzstädten waren, welche durch ihren Handel sich schon aufgeschwungen hatten; - und fast alle Griechischen Colonieen sind mehr oder weniger Handelsstädte geworden, wenn sie auch bey ihrer Anlage nicht dazu bestimmt waren.[14] (Heeren 1810, 196–197)

Greek "colonies" were envisioned as examples for the beneficial effect that political freedom could have on the progress of polities:

> Allein eben durch diese Unabhängigkeit so vieler Pflanzstädte, die fast ohne Ausnahme in den glücklichsten Gegenden der Erde, unter dem schönsten Himmel angelegt, und durch ihre Lage selbst zur Schiffahrt und zum Handel aufgefordert waren, mußte die Cultur der Hellenischen Nation überhaupt nicht nur die größten Fortschritte machen, sondern auch eine Vielseitigkeit erhalten, wie sie die Cultur keiner anderen Nation der damaligen Welt erhalten konnte.[15] (Heeren 1810, 197–198)

Progress was the necessary result of (economic) freedom. In this regard, Heeren openly followed Adam Smith. Even if ancient sources hardly refer to trade as a cause for the foundation of an *apoikia*, the colonial logic, enriched with this economic facet, provided a rationale: the main factors for "Greek colonization" were overpopulation *and* trade. This proved enduring, even when the enlightened emphasis on the factor of freedom was dropped in the era of imperialism.

There was a certain leeway for scholars with regard to which of these two causes they deemed more important. Curtius or Burckhardt for instance followed a more universalizing approach, focusing on the role of sociocultural structures. Therefore, trade and the colonial paradigm played an important role in their description of Greek history. In alignment with this perspective, the Croatian scholar Josef Brunšmid (1858–1929) could deduce the following causes of the Greek settlements in an essay dedicated to inscriptions and coins of the Greek cities on the Dalmatian coast (then part of the Habsburg Empire) – the contribution of archaeological research at that time:

> Für ihre Begründung konnte, da bei den bedürfnislosen Barbaren ein rentables Absatzgebiet für Producte des hellenischen Kunst- und Gewerbefleisses nicht vorausgesetzt werden darf, neben strategischen Gründen nur die Rücksicht auf den Bernsteinhandel maßgebend sein.[16] (Brunšmid 1898, i)

Other scholars, like Pöhlmann, put more weight on the polit-ontological paradigm: "Colonization" was principally a state-run endeavor *ergo* following a state's interests or reacting to circumstances that menaced its stability – such as overpopulation. In this perspective trade was an important and beneficial side effect.

This fusion of political and economic properties of "Greek colonization" was generally shared by European scholarship. However, a peculiarity of German-speaking scholarship was a partition of those two causes according to ethnic subdivisions – witnessing the unbroken importance of ethnic categories. Oehler wrote in the *RE*:

> Im Westen finden wir Korinthos und Chalkis auf Euboia mit zahlreichen Colonien, die wie die milesischen den Handelsinteressen dienten, während die Achaier mehr Ackerbaucolonien am tarantischen Golfe anlegten.[17] (1894, 2824)

The different Greek *ethnē* were associated with distinctive, inherent properties. This allowed the attribution of certain causes to their "colonization": Achaeans and Dorians were farmers, Ionians (but also the Corinthians – a flaw in the rationale) traders.

The 1920s witnessed an attack on this coexistence of causalities. Johannes Hasebroek (1893–1957) denied in his book *Staat und Handel im alten Griechenland* (1966; 1st ed. 1928) one of the central implications of the colonial paradigm: the importance of trade. He pointed out that "Greek" states functioned differently from modern European ones, a perspective that owed much to the influence of Max Weber (see Näf 1995, 281, 295–297 for Hasebroek's role in Classics, not least for Moses I. Finley):

> Die griechische Kolonisationstätigkeit der vorhellenistischen Zeit steht fast ausschließlich entweder im Dienste eines rein politischen Imperialismus oder im Dienste der Nahrung, d. h. die griechische Kolonie ist fast immer: keine Handelskolonie, sondern Militär- (Eroberungs-) Kolonie oder Ackerbaukolonie.[18] (Hasebroek 1966, 111)

Like Heeren, Hasebroek points to differences between the premodern and the modern world. However, whereas Heeren used his comparative approach to introduce an economic perspective on antiquity, Hasebroek denounced its anachronistic excesses (1966, 114), as exemplified by Ulrich Wilcken (1862–1944), who wrote in his *Griechische Geschichte*:

> Hatte nach der Mitte des 2. Jahrtausends die politische Machtentfaltung den Anstoß zur Expansion gegeben, so war jetzt der wirtschaftliche Aufschwung der Hauptgrund für die Kolonisation. Es galt, Rohstoffe für das heimische Gewerbe und neue Absatzgebiete für Handel mit dessen Produkten zu gewinnen.[19] (1926, 64)

For Haasebroek, ancient states did not follow a "Handelspolitik" to comply with their trade interests and their industry. The premodern state aimed primarily at the subsistence of its citizens; thus overpopulation was the only logical explanation for "Greek colonization" (1966, 110–116).

Although Hasebroek's role in German-speaking *Altertumswissenschafen* declined during the Nazi regime (he chose to retire following a denunciation in 1937, at the age of 44), his antimodernist attack proved to be enduring. Helmut Berve (1896–1979), whose career on the contrary advanced with the new regime (see Rebenich 2001), saw in his influential *Griechische Geschichte* (1931) "Greek" "colonies" primarily as "Ackerbaukolonien," agricultural colonies:

> Erst später, infolge der großen sozialen und wirtschaftlichen Bewegung des 7. Jahrhunderts treten Gründungen andern Zwecks auf, die man jedoch nur mit starkem Vorbehalt als Handelskolonien bezeichnen darf.[20] (1931, 112)

One has to point out that the idea of a "Volk's" "natural" need of expansion, even more if it is restricted in its "Lebensraum" – a key term in Nazi ideology (cf. Chapoutot 2012, 407–414) – acquired immediate relevance in the first half of the twentieth century and especially following the territorial losses after World War I. Berve's introductory remarks to his chapter "Die Kolonisation" are exemplary in this regard (as they are tragically prophetic!):

> So karg bemessen ist der anbaufähige Boden auf der hellenischen Halbinsel, daß jede dem Landbau ergebene Bevölkerung nach wenigen Generationen ihn als zu eng empfinden, das dringende Verlangen nach seiner Erweiterung verspüren muß. Die Erfüllung dieses Wunsches kann auf zweierlei Art gefunden werden: entweder man versucht mit Gewalt das Land des Nachbarn und dadurch den notwendigen Lebensraum zu gewinnen – so taten es die Spartaner gegenüber Messenien – oder ein Teil der Bevölkerung entlastet durch Auswanderung die Heimat und sucht sich in der Ferne ein neues, weiteres Land.[21] (1931, 110)

"Colonization" was now the taking of the possession of land, wrestled from inferior local populations (see for instance Berve 1931, 115 and 117; for a description of the colonial aspects of the German occupation of Eastern Europe see Furber and Lower 2008, and for the role of ancient models see Chapoutot 2012, 414–422). Additionally, the perception of the "Greeks" as farmers strengthened the dichotomy to a more economically oriented "Semitic" "colonization."

This shift in the evaluation of the causes of "Greek colonization" was accordingly not due to a better understanding of the past. One anachronistic perception of "colonization" was exchanged for another that was more consistent with contemporary axioms. "Greeks" persisted as prototypes for "Indo-Germanic" colonizations because of the farmer-warrior cliché, even if the Roman Empire served as primary source of inspiration for Nazi ideology (cf. Chapoutot 2012, 339–424).

Texts and Pots

German-speaking *Altertumswissenschaften* was characterized by continuity in the first decades after World War II: Many scholars kept their positions, others, after a short phase of unemployment due to denazification, were reintegrated relatively quickly into the university system. Helmut Berve, for instance, took up university posts again, starting in 1949, and his *Griechische Geschichte* saw two more editions (see Bichler 1989 and Rebenich 2005). Therefore, it is no surprise that knowledge of "Greek colonization" saw in its basic outline hardly any modification.

Nevertheless, there were some shifts, the most important one due to an increasing use of a so far marginal variable in scholarly reconstructions: archaeology. In particular, the question of causality was affected, as the presence of "Greek" remains on the shores of the Mediterranean had to be accounted for. Hermann Bengtson (1909–1989) wrote in his repeatedly edited *Griechische Geschichte* (which originated in the time of his exclusion from the university system from 1945 to 1949 because of his involvement in the Nazi era – see Rebenich 2009):

> Mit dem Streben nach neuem Ackerland verbinden sich, und zwar von allem Anfang an, handelspolitische Gesichtspunkte. Für die bedeutende Ausweitung der griechischen Schiffahrt und des griechischen Handels in jener Periode, die der Kolonisation unmittelbar vorausgeht, liegen zuverlässige Angaben bisher nur für den Westen vor. An nicht weniger als 30 Stellen im Raum von Apulien bis Marseille ist griechischer Import, vor allem von Vasen, im 8. und 7. Jahrhundert durch Bodenfunde nachgewiesen; die Vasen stammen aus dem Bereich nahezu der gesamten griechischen Welt, aus Kreta, von den Kykladen, aus Böotien und Korinth. Es sprechen sogar Anzeichen dafür, daß man schon in der ersten Hälfte des 9. Jahrhunderts v. Chr. mit griechischen Künstlern in Etrurien, in Falerii und Tarquinii, ja sogar mit einer spürbaren ersten Hellenisierung des etruskischen Kunsthandwerks rechnen darf.[22] (1960, 89–90)

Trade made a huge comeback (cf. also the "Einleitung" in Langlotz 1963), even if Hasebroek's *Staat und Handel im alten Griechenland* was reissued in 1966.

Ultimately, the question whether overpopulation or trade was the main factor for "Greek colonization" had to be left open. Anneliese Mannzmann displayed a pragmatic approach in her lemma "Ἀποικία" in *Der kleine Pauly*, an abbreviated version of the monumental *Real Encyclopädie* that was edited between 1964 and 1975, and turned to more important matters:

> Sich darüber zu streiten, ob Überbevölkerung und Landnot oder Handelsinteressen die Koloniegründungen veranlaßt haben, ist unergiebig, da vielleicht, trotz vorliegender materieller Voraussetzungen, die von Fall zu Fall zu prüfen sind, die Zugkraft der Polisidee so groß war, daß diese Staatsform sich weltweit verwirklichen mußte. Man kann hier von staatlichem τόκος sprechen, einer Vermehrung aus sich selbst, die wiederum die Tendenz zur Weitererzeugung in sich trägt.[23] (1964, 435)

A noticeable element in postwar *Altertumswissenschaften* was a growing austereness concerning holistic, and in the Nazi era, openly ideologically based, generalizations about essentialized qualities of "Greeks" and "Romans." The focus shifted to a more factual, descriptive approach, not least toward the analysis of political systems (cf. Bichler 1989, 81), thus in a way a return to the German-speaking *Altertumswissenschaft*'s foundations: the polit-ontological paradigm.

Research on "Greek colonization" turned toward the "Greeks'" (the prototypical *zoa politika*) basic political manifestation: the *polis* and the issue of the relations between *apoikiai* and *metropoleis*. The diagnosed austereness affected in the case of "Greek colonization" more the colonial than the polit-ontological paradigm, which proved more enduring: the basic feature of *apoikiai*, their independence, was due to the "ausgeprägte politische Individualismus der Griechen, der im allgemeinen eine Beherrschung der Kolonie durch die Mutterstadt verhindert hat,"[24] as Bengtson (1960, 89) put it. Yet, scholars became more cautious concerning generalizing views of the *polis*, too. As one conceded that the development of the Greek *polis* and "Greek colonization" proceeded simultaneously, there was room for different forms (see for instance Seibert 1963).

Alternatively, scholars focused on the *longue durée*; the role of the Mediterranean landscape and the question of the occupation of land were taken into the equation (see Kirsten 1958 and Blumenthal 1963). Not only was the view of the "Greeks'" political progressiveness enduring, but also that of their cultural progressiveness – the image of the foundational role of "Greek" culture for the European self-consciousness remains unbroken as "Greek colonization" was "unter welthistorischen Gesichtspunkten hochbedeutende Kulturmission"[25] (Bengtson 1960, 21). Accordingly, the epithet "great" could be attributed to the Archaic "Greek colonization" to distinguish it from older (i.e., the Mycenaeans) or later forms (e.g., Bengtson 1960, 66). Even if an openly racial/racist terminology more or less vanished, some underlying – and older! – patterns of thought were prevailing (cf. Bichler 1989, 79f.). The archaeologist Ernst Langlotz's (1895–1978) portrayal of *Die Kunst der Westgriechen* was no exception:

> Naturgemäß konnten die meisten Griechenstädte im fernen Osten und Westen nicht dicht bevölkert werden. Die ersten Siedler waren reine Griechen. Durch die manchen Städten unvermeidliche Blutmischung in den folgenden Generationen entstand allmählich jenes Bevölkerungssubstrat, das Politik, Kunst und Kultur einer Kolonie entscheidend bestimmt hat.
>
> Durch diese Tatsache hat sich der griechische Geist und seine Gestaltwerdung in der bildenden Kunst in Kolonien oft nicht so rein erhalten, um dem Einfluß prähistorisch gebliebener vor den Städten wohnender Barbaren sich immer ganz verschließen zu können, menschlich, religiös und auch künstlerisch. Aber gerade durch diese Verschmelzung und geistige Assimilierung der Urbevölkerung ist der geistige Samen der Griechen im Umkreis ihrer Städte besonders fruchtbar geworden und hat neue Kulturen entstehen lassen.[26] (1963, 9)

A Postcolonial Epilogue

In the wake of the various turns and -isms in the second half of the twentieth century, fundamental pillars of knowledge in Classics underwent reevaluation. There was an opening for approaches borrowed from other disciplines like sociology, ethnology, or anthropology, and accordingly new ways of interpreting ancient societies that affected knowledge of "Greek colonization." Additionally, the intensification of archaeological research made available new information concerning the settlements overseas as well as cultural contacts. Archaeology lost its status as proverbial "handmaiden to history" and became an equal partner, thus contributing new perspectives. Nevertheless, this development had more impact on Classics than in the rigid disciplinary system of German *Altertumswissenschaften*. This was one reason why the initiative in research on "Greek colonization" went to other countries. Another cause was a decline in interest in this thematic field. This finds its expression in the fact that the current important question of intercultural contacts was not dealt with either by Anneliese Mannzmann in her lemma in *Der kleine Pauly*, nor by Walter Eder (1941–2009) in his entry on the "'Grosse' griechische Kolonisation" in *Der neue Pauly* (1999), the complete revision of the *RE* (though see recently Ulf 2009). The focus rests on the description of (multiple) causes, the foundation and the relations of *apoikiai* to their *metropoleis*, that is, the political aspects of the phenomenon.

Equally important was the crumbling of the colonial paradigm after the end of European colonization and the impact of postcolonial studies. Universalized ideas, not least concerning the relationship of "colonizers" versus "colonized," came under scrutiny, even more so as the awareness of the anachronism of applying the colonial model to Greek antiquity grew (Eder 1999, 646; Bernstein 2004, 28). "Greek colonization" is understood (again) more as a migratory phenomenon than a colonization. With the replacement of the homogenizing concept of "Volk" with the more open category "Kultur" and the problematization of the perception of antiquity as direct precursor of modern Europe, scholarship tends to highlight the complexity of the phenomenon instead of looking for overall answers on how "Greeks" "colonized" (cf. Bernstein 2004, 22–23; Ulf 2009, 92). The perception that the Archaic period was a time of significant change in Greece itself became generally accepted; therefore, the idea of an *a priori* fixed overall "Greek" colonizing procedure has declined and the heterogeneity of the phenomenon has been highlighted.

NOTES

1 For a more comprehensive discussion of the modern perception of "Greek colonization," including in German-, French-, and English-speaking scholarship, see Mauersberg 2019. All the German quoted in this chapter has been translated in the notes below.

2 The so-called German Question alludes to the political discourse concerning the role of "Germans" in the Austrian "multiethnic empire". That is, the question whether the German-speaking parts should be integrated in to an overall "German" political entity or not.

3 "[…] general laws of development, ruling colonial life."

4 "Outline of a natural model of colonies."

5 "Besides the Greeks, no people on earth made what it possessed of strength into a common property of humanity like the Germans. They have crossed the ocean, our Mediterranean, in all directions; they have cleared forests in all overseas continents, have made the soil arable and sowed the seeds."

6 "great deed in world history."

7 "The people whom we have gotten to know so far as inhabitants of Sicily were not capable of giving the island an advanced historical status because of their overall intellectual capability. Sicani and Sicels seem to have not even possessed, like other less educated people, a highly necessary bellicose sense. The arrival of the Phoenicians, acting in their colonies on the island particularly as merchants and manufacturers, could teach the native population some skills of practical life but did not further their inner development toward higher education. Everything changed once the Greeks settled in Sicily."

8 "Solely the essential reason of their [the "Greek" colonies'] being is […] not trade. It served the emigrants rather as a means to live as free citizenries and to test their strength."

9 "But in principal only peaceful relations suit the purpose of trading people; that is why Ionian Greeks sought to find peace with the Barbarians as soon as possible. They did not come as conquerors; they did not want to expel the natives, everywhere they faced in small numbers great masses. Thus they had to win them over, to be of service and of use to them."

10 "[…] each larger quantity of persons that leaves the country where they lived for a longer time and settles in another country."

11 "They have endured bitter years of apprenticeship and felt the vicinity of the sea as a curse for a long time. It had to be like that as long as foreign people ruled the sea: Phoenician privateers suddenly appeared in the morning mist, lured the natives with gay bric-a-brac to the shores, and dragged the sons and daughters of the country in inaccessible distance. They were carried away even in larger numbers to serve as material for a foreign colonial policy until they learned from their enemies the craft, built their own ships, and gathered together in order to take revenge for the injustice suffered by the older seafaring people in constant raids."

12 "Despite marriage with the women of the country, the Greeks aspired to keep their blood Greek; and because they had the will to do what must have been very close to their fear of becoming barbarian, they succeeded."

13 "In this infinite dissemination of the Greeks almost over the whole Mediterranean world, the instinct, deeply rooted in the national character, to drive toward an individual organization of their communities found its fullest satisfaction. Nowhere did the colonization lead to the erection of an encompassing state; and where there were attempts to obtain actual colonial rule, as for instance by Corinth in the Ionian and Adriatic Seas, colonial wars resulted […], that only could aggravate the tendency toward isolation."

14 "Greek colonies were founded partly because of political reasons and partly because of trade. The first was true almost without exception for all plantations installed by the mother-country itself; the latter for those being daughters of plantations, already boomed by means of trade; – and almost all Greek colonies became more or less trading-cities, even if they were not founded as such."

15 "Exactly because of the independence of so many plantations, installed almost without exception in the luckiest regions of the earth, under the most beautiful sky, and because of their location prompted to navigation and trade, the culture of the Hellenic nation made not only greatest progress, but also developed a versatility like no other nation of that era."

16 "Responsible for their foundation, next to strategic reasons, could only have been the consideration of the trade in amber, as the wantless Barbarians provided no lucrative market area for the products of Hellenic art and industry."

17 "In the west there are Corinth and Euboean Chalcis with numerous colonies that served, like those of Miletus, trade interest, while the Achaeans installed rather farming colonies in the Tarentine Gulf."

18 "The Greek colonial endeavor of pre-Hellenistic times served almost exclusively either a mere political imperialism or reasons of subsistence; this means a Greek colony is almost always: no trade colony, but a military colony (a colony of conquest) or a farming colony."

19 "If the pursuit of political power was the impetus to expansion after the middle of the second millennium, now economic growth was the main reason for colonization.

It was necessary to acquire raw materials for the domestic industry as well as new markets for its products."

20 "Only later, due to the great social and economic upheavals of the seventh century, do foundations for other reasons occur, which one can call trade colonies only with strongest reservation."

21 "Arable land on the Hellenic peninsula is so scarce, that every population bound to agriculture must perceive it as too narrow after a few generations and feel the urge to enlarge it. There are two ways to fulfill this wish: either one tries to win by force the land of the neighbor and thus the necessary living space – as the Spartans did with Messenia – or a part of the population relieves the homeland by emigration and seeks a new, wider land in the distance."

22 "The pursuit of arable land was, since the beginning, connected with trade politics. For the immense increase of Greek navigation and trade in the period immediately before the colonization movement reliable information is only available for the west. At no fewer than 30 places between Apulia and Marseilles, Greek imports, mostly vases, are attested through finds; theses vases came from almost everywhere in the Greek world, from Crete, from the Cyclades, from Boeotia and Corinth. There are even indications of Greek artists in Etruria, in Falerii and Tarquinii, in the first half of the ninth century and for a noticeable first Hellenization of Etruscan arts and craft."

23 "To quarrel whether overpopulation and scarcity of land or trade interests caused the founding of colonies is unproductive, as perhaps, despite concrete material predispositions, which have to be evaluated from case to case, the attraction of the *polis*-idea was so important that this form of state had to fulfill itself worldwide. One can speak of a stately *tokos*, a reproduction from itself that comprised the tendency to propagate itself."

24 "[…] the Greek's distinct political individualism, that prevented the control of a colony by its mother-city."

25 "[…] in the perspective of world history a highly relevant cultural mission."

26 "Naturally, most of the Greek towns in the far east and west were not densely populated. The first settlers were pure Greeks. In some towns, unavoidable mixing of blood in subsequent generations gradually developed a subordinate population that decisively shaped a colony's politics, art, and culture. Because of this fact, the Greek spirit and its incorporation in visual arts in colonies was often not preserved in such a way as to be able always to be completely closed to the influence of Barbarians in their prehistoric stage, living outside the towns, humanely, religiously, and also artistically. But it is precisely due to this amalgamation and mental assimilation of the natives that the intellectual seed of the Greeks became especially fertile and produced new cultures."

REFERENCES

Bernstein, Frank. 2004. *Konflikt und Migration: Studien zu griechischen Fluchtbewegungen im Zeitalter der sogenannten Großen Kolonisation*. St. Katharinen: Scripta Mercaturae.

Bengtson, Hermann. 1960. *Griechische Geschichte: Von den Anfängen bis in die Römische Kaiserzeit*, 2nd ed. Munich: Beck.

Berve, Helmut. 1931. *Griechische Geschichte: Erste Hälfte: Von den Anfängen bis Perikles*. Freiburg: Herder and Co.

Bichler, Reinhold. 1989. "Neuorientierung in der Alten Geschichte?" In *Deutsche Geschichtswissenschaft nach dem Zweiten Weltkrieg (1945–1965)*, edited by Ernst Schulin, 63–85. Munich: Oldenbourg.

Blumenthal, Ekkehard. 1963. *Die altgriechische Siedlungskolonisation im Mittelmeerraum unter besonderer Berücksichtigung der Südküste Kleinasiens (Tübinger geographische Studien, Heft 10)*. Dissertation, Tübingen.

Brunšmid, Josef. 1898. *Die Inschriften und Münzen der griechischen Städte Dalmatiens*. Vienna: A. Hölder.

Burckhardt, Jacob. 1982. *Griechische Kulturgeschichte*, 2nd ed. 4 vols. Munich: Deutscher Taschenbuch.

Chapoutot, Johann. 2012. *Le nazisme et l'Antiquité*. Paris: Presses universitaires de France.

Christ, Karl. 2006. *Klios Wandlungen. Die deutsche Althistorie vom Neuhumanismus bis zur Gegenwart*. Munich: Beck.

Curtius, Ernst. 1874. *Griechische Geschichte*, 4th ed. 3 vols. Berlin: Weidmannsche Buchhandlung.

Curtius, Ernst. 1892. "Die Griechen als Meister der Colonisation." In *Alterthum und Gegenwart: Gesammelte Reden und Vorträge. Bd. 3. Unter drei Kaisern*, edited by Ernst Curtius, 96–109. Berlin: Wilhelm Hertz.

Eder, Walter. 1999. "Kolonisation. I. Allgemein. IV. 'Grosse' griechische Kolonisation. VI. Alexander der Grosse und Hellenismus." In *Der Neue Pauly: Enzyklopädie der Antike*, vol. 6, edited by Hubert Cancik and Helmuth Schneider, 646–647, 653–664, 665–666. Stuttgart: J.B. Metzler.

Furber, David, and Wendy Lower. 2008. "Colonialism and Genocide in Nazi-occupied Poland and Ukraine." In *Empire, Colony, Genocide: Conquest, Occupation, and Subaltern Resistance in World History*, edited by Dirk A. Moses, 372–400. New York: Berghahn Books.

Hasebroek, Johannes. 1966. *Staat und Handel im alten Griechenland: Untersuchungen zur antiken Wirtschaftsgeschichte*. Hildesheim: Georg Olms. Originally published in 1928.

Heeren, Arnold Herrmann Ludwig. 1810. *Handbuch der Geschichte und Staaten des Alterthums, mit besonderer Rücksicht auf ihre Verfassungen, ihren Handel und ihre Colonien*, 2nd ed. Göttingen: Johann Friedrich Röwer.

Heeren, Arnold Herrmann Ludwig. 1826. *Ideen über die Politik, den Verkehr und den Handel der vornehmsten Völker der alten Welt, Band 3: Europäische Völker, Erste Abtheilung: Griechen*, 4th ed. Göttingen: Vandenhoek & Ruprecht.

Hegewisch, Dietrich Hermann. 1808. *Geographische und historische Nachrichten, die Kolonien der Griechen betreffend*. Altona: Johann Friedrich Hammerich.

Heyne, Christian Gottlob. 1785. "De veterum coloniarum iure eiusque caussis." In *Opuscula Academica*, vol. 1, edited by Christian Gottlob Heyne, 290–309. Göttingen: Johann Christian Dieterich.

Holm, Adolf. 1870–1897. *Geschichte Siciliens im Alterthum*. 3 vols. Leipzig: Wilhelm Engelmann.

Hurst, Henry, and Sara Owen, eds. 2005. *Ancient Colonizations. Analogy, Similarity and Difference*. London: Duckworth.

Kirsten, Ernst. 1958. "Raumordnung und Kolonisation in der griechischen Geschichte." In *Historische Raumforschung II. Zur Raumordnung in den alten Hochkulturen (Forschungs- und Sitzungsberichte der Akademie für Raumforschung und Landesplanung, Band 10)*, edited by Kurt Brüning, 19–24. Bremen: Walter Dorn Verlag.

Langlotz, Ernst. 1963. *Die Kunst der Westgriechen*. Munich: Hirmer.
Mannzmann, Anneliese. 1964. "Ἀποικία." In *Der kleine Pauly: Lexikon der Antike*, vol. 1, edited by Konrat Ziegler and Walther Sontheimer, 434–435. Stuttgart: Alfred Druckenmüller.
Mauersberg, Martin. 2019. *Die "griechische Kolonisation." Ihr Bild in der Antike und der modernen altertumswissenschaftlichen Forschung*. Bielefeld: transcript.
Näf, Beat. 1995. "Deutungen und Interpretationen der griechischen Geschichte in den Zwanziger Jahren." In *Altertumswissenschaft in den 20er Jahren: Neue Fragen und Impulse*, edited by Hellmut Flashar, 275–302. Stuttgart: Franz Steiner.
Nippel, Wilfried. 2013. *Klio dichtet nicht. Studien zur Wissenschaftsgeschichte der Althistorie*. Frankfurt: Campus.
Oehler, Johann. 1894. "Ἀποικία." In *Paulys Realencyclopädie der classischen Altertumswissenschaften*, 1:2, edited by Georg Wissowa, 2823–2836. Munich: Alfred Druckenmüller.
Pöhlmann, Robert. 1889. "Grundzüge der politischen Geschichte Griechenlands." In *Handbuch der klassischen Altertumswissenschaft in systematischer Darstellung. Dritter Band: Geographie und politische Geschichte des klassischen Altertums*, edited by Iwan Müller, 355–464. Nördlingen: Beck.
Rebenich, Stefan. 2001. "Alte Geschichte in Demokratie und Diktatur: Der Fall Helmut Berve." *Chiron*, 31: 457–496.
Rebenich, Stefan. 2005. "Nationalsozialismus und Alte Geschichte: Kontinuität und Diskontinuität in Forschung und Lehre." In *Elisabeth Charlotte Welskopf und die Alte Geschichte in der DDR*, edited by Isolde Stark, 42–64. Stuttgart: Franz Steiner.
Rebenich, Stefan. 2009. "Hermann Bengtson und Alfred Heuß: Zur Entwicklung der Alten Geschichte in der Zwischen- und Nachkriegszeit." In *Alte Geschichte zwischen Wissenschaft und Politik. Gedenkschrift Karl Christ*, edited by Volker Losemann, 181–208. Wiesbaden: Harrassowitz.
Seibert, Jakob. 1963. *Metropolis und Apoikie: Historische Beiträge zur Geschichte ihrer gegenseitigen Beziehungen*. Dissertation, Würzburg.
Ulf, Christoph. 2009. "Rethinking Cultural Contacts." *Ancient West & East*, 8: 81–132.
Wilcken, Ulrich. 1926. *Griechische Geschichte im Rahmen der Altertumsgeschichte*. Munich: Oldenbourg.

FURTHER READING

For a more comprehensive survey of the modern perception of "Greek colonization" as well as the ancient discourse on the phenomenon, see Mauersberg (2019). On the dialectics between modern perceptions and "Greek colonization" (although without a specific discussion of German-speaking *Altertumswissenschaften*) see, for instance, Hurst and Owen (2005). Or see the contributions to the Discussion section in *Ancient West & East* 10 (2011). On the history of *Altertumswissenschaften* in general, see Christ (2006) and Nippel (2013).

CHAPTER FIVE

Italian-Speaking Traditions and the Study of the Ancient Greeks outside their Homelands

Franco De Angelis

Even before creating their nation-state in 1861, Italian-speaking scholars incorporated ancient Greeks into their historical accounts. These uses responded to contemporary Italian concerns, particularly the political control by outsiders in pre-unification Italy, the North–South divide that emerged shortly after unification, and the rise and fall of ancient Rome as a model in concert with nationalism, fascism, imperialism, and colonialism. While some of these issues are not unique to the Italian tradition, what makes it stand out from others is that ancient Greeks actually once lived in Italy and its former colonies (Momigliano 1968, 48; Corcella 1999, 53–54). English- and German-speaking scholars strongly self-identified with the ancient Greeks and took the lead in producing narratives about them, often in an idealized manner, thanks to a Romanticism that was lacking in Italian scholarship (Momigliano 1987, 59–89, 161–178; Ampolo 1997, 70; Zecchini 2013). By contrast, Italian scholarship on the ancient Greeks outside their homelands was on the front lines of this historical phenomenon and had other competing historical concerns, most notably ancient Rome. In these ways, scholarship developed differently and merits its own chapter.

The discussion will be divided into three major periods: (i) pre-unification Italy until 1861 characterized by outside rule; (ii) the Italian nation-state from 1861 to the close of World War II in 1945 characterized by hyper-nationalism; and (iii) the period thereafter to the present characterized by internationalism. Important developments first emerged in all these three periods, although some continued to resonate and recur in later periods, which only emphasizes their overlapping nature.

A Companion to Greeks Across the Ancient World, First Edition. Edited by Franco De Angelis.
© 2020 John Wiley & Sons, Inc. Published 2020 by John Wiley & Sons, Inc.

Pre-unification Italy: Monarchies and Invasions

The centuries before Italian unification in 1861 were characterized by two main historical phenomena: the Kingdoms of Sicily and Naples, and the conquest of Italy and its incorporation into the French Empire by Napoleon Bonaparte. Both had effects on the study of the ancient Greeks in Magna Graecia (southern Italy) and Sicily.

The Kingdoms of Sicily and Naples were the dominant political entities in the southern half of Italy from the thirteenth century until Italian unification. The Kingdom of Sicily controlled most of the southern Italian mainland, until it separated in 1282. Although the mainland kingdom continued to be known as the Kingdom of Sicily, it is most commonly referred to as the Kingdom of Naples to avoid confusion. The two kingdoms remained separate until 1816, when the Kingdom of Naples reasserted control over the other, to create the multiethnic Kingdom of Two Sicilies. A constant feature of both kingdoms was their rule by absolute monarchies of local and foreign origins. Their exercise of political and legal authority brought to mind ancient Rome, which acted as an obvious source of inspiration for these monarchies (Salmeri 1993, 273; Ceserani 2012, 20), as was the case generally around the world where monarchs ruled kingdoms and/or empires (Pagden 1995). From ancient Rome historical models were sought, by both rulers and ruled, to help understand their present political circumstances. The conquerors wanted to know how to treat their subjects and provinces in terms of taxation and other obligations, as well as what to offer in return. The same held for their subjects, who also sought faults with this form of governance.

The ancient Greeks had to compete for a place in the historical mindset of these centuries. Marginality ensued, but not complete disregard. The antiquarian tradition of scholarship that emerged in the sixteenth century and involved its customary "tell-all" regional investigations naturally had to include some mention of the ancient Greeks who had once occupied the lands of the Kingdoms of Sicily and Naples (Salmeri 1991, 1992, 61–96; 1993). For Magna Graecia, the Dominican friar Leandro Alberti (1479–1552) traveled from Bologna to southern Italy to undertake research. He included in his *Descrittione di tutta Italia* ("Description of all of Italy"), published in 1550, the first known collection of ancient evidence to appear in print (Ceserani 2012, 32). His account foreshadowed the trouble of comfortably finding a place for Magna Graecia's cultural diversity in Italy's history. He also recognized the greater antiquity of Magna Graecia vis-à-vis Rome and concluded that the former had happened earlier, which, given the absence of an obvious parallel with ancient Rome in a world ruled by monarchies, helped to put more distance between the ancient Greeks and the present. For Sicily, it was Tommaso Fazello, another Dominican friar, who, born there at Sciacca, inaugurated the inclusion of the ancient Greeks in published antiquarian accounts, with the appearance in 1558 of his *De Rebus Siculis Decades Duae* ("On Sicilian Things in Two Volumes"). Fazello's lasting legacy is that he defined what constituted Sicilianness: locals maintained their core identity by subsuming the impact of successive invaders into the island's rich cultural fabric (Momigliano 1979, 178–179; Ceserani 2000, 175–177; 2012, 20). What Alberti, Fazello, and still other antiquarians also exposed was that reliance on ancient Rome was inherently flawed. This ultimately established the door through which later scholarship on earlier antiquity could proceed.

These orientations continued into the seventeenth century, taking their place alongside new scholarly developments. Here one notes in particular Alessio Simmaco Mazzocchi (1684–1771), the Italian priest, who, thoroughly trained in several ancient languages and archaeology, specialized in the Bible (Ceserani 2012, 40–68). Mazzocchi, educated in and around Naples during the time of the great Neapolitan philosopher/jurist/historian Giambattista Vico, similarly continued probing into the pre-Roman past of Italy and likewise had little sympathy for the ancient Greeks. Mazzocchi postulated that ancient Greek settlers, such as Pythagoras, learned much from ancient Italians and owed their survival, as at Cumae, to them. The ancient Italians were themselves migrants connected with the Bible. The ancient Greek cities of Italy were "fictive and legendary" (Ceserani 2012, 58–59): Paestum's temples, for example, were believed to be Phoenician. In the late seventeenth and early eighteenth centuries, Italian scholarship distanced itself even further from the ancient Greeks, playing down their contributions in favor of Italic and other peoples.

In the late eighteenth century, two interrelated developments originating outside Italy impacted scholarship in other important ways. The crucial spark was the French Revolution and the emergence of the French Empire ruled by Napoleon Bonaparte (1804–1814), which had major reverberations all across Europe. It led to a second, spin-off development: the will for self-determination and political independence, which coincided with the transition from Enlightenment to Romanticism. The winds of change blew in both Europe and their New World colonies, where it began with the American Revolution. Ancient Rome started generally to fall out of favor as the dominant role model. European powers reassessed their settlement and colonization policies and came to favor mercantile endeavors and federalist associations. Ancient Greece thus served as the better model (Pagden 1995, 126–155). Ancient Greece, and the Romantic Movement more generally that accompanied it, also affected those kingdoms and empires challenged by independence movements, as with the transformation of Bonaparte himself in official portraiture away from bulky Enlightenment ideology toward that of a more dashing and dynamic Romantic figure. Hellenism, therefore, took on a new and important role in shaping identity and actions over the next two centuries. As part of this, many learned travelers set out from their home countries to acquire firsthand experience of ancient Greece, wherever possible (Momigliano 1979, 1980; Ceserani 2000, 2012, 77–133). At first, this meant southern Italy and Sicily controlled by the Kingdoms of Sicily and Naples, as Greece was still under Ottoman Turk rule, which made travel trickier. That drastically changed after the Greek War of Independence (1821–1832), which led to the creation of the modern nation-state of Greece (for the ramifications, see next section).

How did these two developments play out in Italy's case? It was business as usual with a new twist. The distance between local and foreign scholars widened even further in the early nineteenth century (Ceserani 2012, 77–133). Foreign scholars, despite their new-found interest in ancient Greece, encountered Italian scholars who remained steadfast, pretty much continuing to espouse the same kinds of views as their predecessors had. To take one example, Francescantonio Grimaldi, in his three-volume work *Riflessioni sopra l'ineguaglianza tra glia uomini* ("Reflection on the Inequality between Men"), considered the ancient Greek settlers in Italy barbarians who migrated when Greece was still in its early uncivilized period (Ceserani 2012, 121–122). He argued that Greeks were attracted to lands of abundant produce, fighting against the natives in settling them, like Europeans in the Indies and Americas, and helping to accelerate "our" cultural development. Nevertheless, Grimaldi had no time for partisans of the ancient Greeks who saw in them only their virtues and not their vices.

Concurrently, Bonaparte's conquests generally shook up Italian historical consciousness. Antiquity came to have greater importance (De Francesco 2013, 17–18). The Kingdom of Italy, a client state of the French Empire, was created on March 17, 1805, and signaled the new political reality. Italians sought to carve out and protect their regional identities through recourse to historical writing. Vincenzo Cuoco, the Naples-based polymath (1770–1823), published in 1806 a novel called *Platone in Italia*, whose fictional setting involved an editor presenting the transcription of an ancient Greek manuscript, found in Heraclea in southern Italy, where in reality amazing bronze inscriptions were discovered in 1732 (Ceserani 2012, 122–128; De Francesco 2013, 29–50). Here ancient Italians were yet again presented as teachers of the ancient Greeks, perhaps a message to Naples' elite who were too involved in foreign culture to appreciate the history of ancient Italy beneath their very noses. Unsurprisingly, Cuoco gave Italian origins to key ancient Greek figures such as Homer and Pythagoras, and in general Italic civilization was regarded as superior to the Greek. The Etruscans led this Italic civilization because of their internationalism. They were Pelasgians who had colonized Greece and other regions and acted as cultural intermediaries between these colonies and Italy (De Francesco 2013, 38–41). Laudably, Cuoco tried to redress the growing imbalances in the emerging historiography of ancient Greece, and, despite the obvious problems with his work, his ideas have had a lasting influence on the Italian conception of Greek southern Italy.

Giuseppe Micali's (1768–1844) work written in this period has also had a long-lasting impact on the scholarship of ancient Italy (Pallottino 1991, 6–10, 18–21). Micali, born in Livorno (Leghorn) in northern Italy, came from a family involved in the antiquities trade, often visited by Grand Tour travelers, and so took naturally to becoming a historian/archaeologist (De Francesco 2013, 51–83). Antonino De Francesco has summed up well the main tenets of Micali's work published in 1810:

> In his *Italia avanti il dominio dei romani* ('Italy before Roman Rule') Micali focused on the antiquity of the Italic peoples to demonstrate how a high degree of civilization had already been achieved before the Romans, which would then to a large extent be sacrificed by the latter's work of assimilation. In this reconstruction of a pre-Roman past, Micali, despite insisting on an element of autochthony for the country's peoples, was careful to keep them all distinct from one another and took care not to speak of their substantial uniformity. In his opinion, not only were the Italic peoples different from one another, they were also far from similar to the Greeks, who in fact brought great changes to the anthropological profile of the southern regions of Italy. From a different point of view, he also underlined how another people, the Gauls, overthrew the Etruscans in the northern regions and drove them away, thus distancing the Italic peoples from a common cultural process.

Micali elaborated on and revised this thesis in another work, *Storia degli antichi popoli italiani* ("A History of the Ancient Peoples of Italy"), published in two volumes in 1832. The anti-Romanism of his first work is played down here, probably because of the collapse of the French Empire in Italy and elsewhere in the meanwhile (De Francesco 2013, 60).

In both works, Micali criticizes the ancient Greeks, whose settlement in Italy involved violent aggression and thus was not beneficial overall (De Francesco 2013, 54–66).

Micali's work, perhaps more than Cuoco's contemporary work, resonated with and contributed to the future Italian nationalist project (De Francesco 2013, 19–20). While Cuoco argued that ancient Italy was under Etruscan leadership and ethnicity, Micali saw ancient Italy as made up of a plurality of cultures. Micali's totalizing approach, unlike Cuoco's, appealed to later Italian nationalists, who soon after launched their project. This nationalism ushers in a second important period in scholarship.

Nationalism 1861–1945: The Rise and Fall of Ancient Rome

Unification of an independent Italian nation-state, ruled at first by a constitutional monarchy, made Rome the capital because of its ancient glories. Nationalism took this association to extreme heights that had other ramifications for the study of the ancient Greeks. This applied both to the ancient Greeks who once lived on Italian soil and to those ancient Greeks elsewhere brought into Italy's fold via its imperialism and colonialism.

Revealing the glories of ancient Rome through the spade was modern Italy's way of nation building and gaining glory against rivals. This also entailed prohibiting archaeological excavations in Italy and its future colonies by other nations (Dyson 2006, 98–99; Barbanera 2015, 52–96). These colonies began to be acquired from the 1880s onward. Imperial expansion occurred in two ways, in the crevices between other larger and better established imperial powers, like England and France, and in the vulnerable ruins being left behind by a declining Ottoman Empire. This meant attention was directed primarily to Libya, the Horn of Africa, and the Dodecanese Islands in the Aegean Sea. Such expansion was naturally couched, where possible, in terms of reclaiming lands that once belonged to Italy via the Roman Empire (Altekamp 2000, 2004; La Rosa 1986; Munzi 2001, 2004a, 2004b; Petricioli 1990; Troilo 2012; D'Ercole 2013). Inspiration from ancient Rome increased substantially with Fascist dictator Benito Mussolini's seizure of power (1922–1943), which saw the emergence of an ultra-nationalist cult of *Romanitas* (Canfora 1976; Cagnetta 1979; Salmeri 2004; Arthurs 2013).

Italian imperialism and colonialism were not restricted to its colonial possessions. At the time of Italian unification, the peninsula's northern and southern halves were divided into two polarized blocks encompassing the Piedmontese north and the Bourbon south (Verdicchio 1997; Moe 2002; De Francesco 2013). The Piedmontese half, which drove state formation, envisioned itself as the true and primary Italy and looked down on the Bourbon half as uncivilized barbarism. This polarization became accentuated within two decades of Italian unification, especially after some southern regions turned to armed resistance to challenge the north's imposition of power. The national government could not comprehend why the benefits of the liberal state were being rejected by these southerners (De Francesco 2013, 134). Explanations and guidance were needed, and one of the prime solutions for our purposes was the development of a school of criminal anthropology founded by Cesare Lombroso, which argued that southern Italian culture as a whole must be classified as racially inferior. This made Italy's use of racism unique, creating a peculiar national configuration (D'Agostino 2002, 320), the so-called Southern Question discourse, in which Italy's southern regions were viewed in contemporary Orientalist and neo-colonialist terms (Schneider 1998). This occurred intentionally, at the same time as Italy began its imperial expansion in Africa (Verdicchio 1997, 27). This discourse was also extended to earlier periods of history, including the ancient Greek period, but again that was something that non-Italian traditions of scholarship had already been doing. One thinks particularly of the Englishman George Grote, the father of modern narrative history on ancient Greece, who regarded the fusion of Greeks and natives in ancient Italy as resulting in the racial debasement of the ancient Greeks, and thus their inferiority vis-à-vis the untainted homeland Greeks (see Urquhart, Chapter 2 this volume).

The Southern Question discourse continues to be felt still today, despite attempts by Mussolini to neutralize it to promote national unity (D'Agostino 2002, 338). It and Italy's close association with ancient Rome do much to help us understand why between 1861 and 1945 most Italian scholarship was devoted to ancient Rome (Treves 1962; Momigliano 1966; Ampolo 1997; Ceserani 2012, 17–267). Of those scholars who published on ancient Greece, their views were often colored by foreign scholarship which dominated this field (Manni 1977; Ampolo 1997). That is because, as we have already seen, ancient Greece had generally been the role model for other western European nations and their colonies, former and current, since the later eighteenth century. Another reason why scholars also looked to Greece for their ancient Greek history has to do with a problem that became clear to Italian and foreign scholars during their Grand Tour visits to Italy. The paucity of ancient writings to study Greek Italy and the regional nature of ancient Greek culture presented unique challenges to all scholars, given that archaeology was practically non-existent and historiographical models were generally structured around empires, kingdoms, and, increasingly, nation-states (Ceserani 2012, 80, 100–101, 112, 128). This helps to explain why foreign and sometimes Italian scholars resorted to making comparisons between ancient Greek and modern colonies (Gabba 1991; Ampolo 2012; Ceserani 2012). Both historical phenomena involved migration from a homeland, but comparison reinforced a questionable practice from which we are still trying to disentangle ourselves. The creation of the Greek nation-state, following liberation from the Ottoman Turks, only exacerbated the practice. Ancient Greek history was inserted into a nationalistic historical framework that imagined Athens, selected as the capital of this new nation-state in 1834, as the metropolis and the Greeks beyond Greece as its colonists (Vlassopoulos 2007). In this regard, the long shadow of marginalization inevitably began to be cast on regions "colonized" by the ancient Greeks, such as southern Italy and Sicily. The ancient Greeks were made to be colonizers very much in the mold of modern empires, dominating their neighbors with their superior culture and colonies, while being lesser and secondary to Athens and the homeland.

While some Italian scholars, like Paolo Orsi (an Austrian by birth who later took up Italian citizenship), followed this line of thinking (Leighton 1986; La Rosa 1987; Orsi 1991), most Italian scholars continued to follow the older line, reinvigorating and amplifying it in light of current circumstances. We can illustrate the development of scholarship in this period via the long careers of three notable scholars, Ettore Pais (1856–1939), Emanuele Ciaceri (1869–1944), and Biagio Pace (1889–1955).

Pais, born to a Piedmontese mother and Sardinian father of noble stock, moved from Turin to Sardinia at age seven. He later met Giuseppe Garibaldi, the builder of the Italian nation, although this had little impact on Pais's earliest work, which contained negative attitudes to ancient Rome in Sardinia and a focus on its pre-Roman history and monuments (Ridley 1975–1976, 520–522; Salmeri 1992, 1993, 265–298; Ampolo 1997, 98–99; Polverini 2002). Pais continued with this approach in Sicily, when he became chair of ancient history in Palermo. Pais and other scholars from Sicily and Sardinia were accustomed to being treated in a secondary and peripheral manner by the newly created Italian state based in Rome and concluded that these regions must have been in this same position in antiquity.

Italy's political fortunes in the late nineteenth and early twentieth centuries impacted Pais's approach, for we witness a softening of attitudes to ancient Rome and its modern counterpart (Cagnetta 1994). Pais argued that Italy's history should begin not, as usual, with the barbarian invasions of Late Antiquity, but with ancient Rome. He frequently mentioned Italy's politics in these years, such as her defeat at Adowa (Adua), the annexation of Tripolitania, and the rise of Mussolini (Ridley 1975–1976, 515–516; Cagnetta 1994, 212–221). Toward the end of his life, Pais (1934) published an article comparing the merits of ancient Greek and Roman civilization, in which he maintained that ancient Rome's detractors had gone too far in upholding Hellenism. Ancient Rome kept Greek civilization alive and made big contributions to politics and society in ways that ancient Greeks did not. Rome also inherited from Greek Syracuse its traditional enmity with Carthage in getting involved in Sicily. For this reason Pais (1894) included the ancient Greeks in his historical accounts, but really only as a prelude to the proper understanding of ancient Rome.

Ciaceri was born in Sicily and spent most of his life studying and teaching in other parts of Italy, from Padua, through Pisa, to Naples (Ciaceri 1994; Ampolo 2012; Ceserani 2012, 255–260). Although a student of Pais, Ciaceri chose, for reasons unknown, not to include Sicily, despite being a Sicilian, in his great three-volume work, *Storia della Magna Grecia* ("History of Great Greece"), published between 1924 and 1932. More distance was put between Magna Graecia and Sicily, which later scholars increased only further. While Fascist rhetoric sought to deny the Southern Question, and Orsi and others (like Umberto Zanotti Bianco, a vocal opponent of Fascism) undertook archaeological excavations in many ancient Greek cities, including searching for mythically wealthy Sybaris, to understand the region's ancient agricultural success and so to help curb its modern poverty and emigration (Esposito and Leo 2006; Ceserani 2012, 244, 263–266), Ciaceri continued to highlight the contributions of ancient Italians to Greek civilization. For herein, he argued, lay the remarkable development of the ancient Greeks in Italy, and therefore more work on the Italic character of Greek civilization was required. His reconstructions included a theory about overlapping native Italic and Greek religious spaces, the former establishing the basis of the latter. Some of the other elements Ciaceri emphasized go back ultimately to the sixteenth century, but with a new twist. Pythagoras was now transformed into a proto-Duce, who brought order and spiritual leadership to Magna Graecia, uttering, like Mussolini, words that became doctrine. However, unlike earlier scholarship, Ciaceri avoided comparing ancient native Italians to American "redskins" (to use his word, which was the parlance of the time), as that only raised the question of their respective racial inferiority. However, he did like the favorable comparison of the mixture of ancient Greeks and Italics in the way that was happening to modern Italian immigrants around the world.

Pace was another Sicilian whose work also well reflects these years (Ampolo 2012; Giammellaro 2012a; De Angelis 2016, 15–16). His prime achievement was a four-volume history of ancient Sicily published between 1935 and 1949 (volume one appeared posthumously in a second edition), a synthesis of archaeological and historical data available up to the outbreak of World War II. Pace wanted to put the study of ancient Sicily on a completely new footing by avoiding the positivist historical approach characteristic of the time and by introducing a unified interpretive vision that it lacked before and even afterwards (Pace 1958, vii–viii; cf. Bonacasa 1977, 680–681). Pace studied all peoples and materials, practicing a kind of total history in the way advocated by his teacher Antonino Salinas (Salmeri 1993, 296–297). In Pace's vision, the ancient Greeks were just another player in the island's ancient history (Caputo 1955, 104–107; Momigliano 1979, 185–186; Salmeri 1993, 297–298). This was in keeping with wider Sicilian attitudes, in which other periods of history (Muslim, Norman, and Angevin) were of greater interest and often served as models (Momigliano 1979, 1987, 121–134). Because of the diverse peoples and cultures involved in Italian history, national scholarship appreciated the world history and comparative perspectives of Italian and foreign scholars alike (Manni 1977, 22–26; Mazzarino 1977, 8–9).

Pace's nationalism grew through Italian archaeological work in the Levant before and after World War I and through his involvement in the upper echelons of Fascist politics (Caputo 1955, 83–85, 92–95; Rizza 1971, 347–348). Pace gradually softened his anti-ancient Rome attitudes, as his own place in Italy changed, and concluded that the Roman period in Sicily did not represent one of decline and decadence (Pace 1958, 393–397). Italian national unity under the Fascists allowed and encouraged regionalism, which Pace pursued in his life and work. Thus, in his history of ancient Sicily, he returned to Fazello's line from the sixteenth century, in which the impact of ancient Greek and other cultures coming to Sicily from outside was subsumed under a strictly Sicilian lens. Pace maintained that there was a Sicilian genius at work. He was ready to accept native influences on Greek culture and to see the island as a place of cultural innovation and dynamism, including in the sphere of Greek art (Arias 1976, 41–42, 101; Mazzarino 1977, 14–15; Salmeri 1991, 295). Here too Pace belonged to the anti-classicism trend in Italy of discussing the autonomy and value of Italic art vis-à-vis its Greek counterpart (Barbanera 2015, 122–128).

Pace's scholarship should not be dismissed out of hand because of his Fascist commitments. His scholarship has in some regards stood the test of time (Arias 1976, 36–40; La Rosa 1987, 722, 726–727). The same holds for Pais and Ciaceri. Like Pace, both essentially maintained that the ancient Greeks in Italy were enriched by the local cultures they encountered. All three were literally "native interlocutors" (Corcella 1999, 55; cf. Giammellaro 2013). One does not have to agree with all the details of this line of argument, revised, now and then, thanks to newer evidence (Ceserani 2012, 264). It is, rather, the underlying premise – essentially, postcolonialism and middle ground theory *avant la lettre* – that remains valid (for the subsequent appreciation of Ciaceri, see Ceserani 2012, 270).

Other scholars applied this tradition in two possible ways. One way was to undertake regional studies of various kinds (Mazzarino 1939; Pareti 1959, a synthesis based on earlier work: cf. Giammellaro 2012b). The second way sought, more courageously, to venture into the larger debate regarding center and periphery in the ancient Greek world. The presence of ancient Greek "colonies" in southern Italy, Sicily, and Libya (controlled by Italy between 1912 and 1943) provided Italian scholars with different perspectives. The dominant line of thinking, established by non-Italian scholarship, was that Greece was the model by which these "colonies" had to be judged in all respects. The debate was especially intense in the field of art, then generally viewed as the highest form of cultural expression, though not so much among Italian scholars, like Pace, who tried to break the usual link that archaeology was art history (Bonacasa 1977, 681). Nevertheless, a rigid canon for Greek art was already in place, in which "colonial Greek" products, if their existence was not denied outright (since colonies were supposed to dutifully import the manufactures of their homelands), were treated as derivative, provincial, and never quite measuring up to Greece's artistic excellence (Settis 1994; Siracusano 2009, 76–78; Ceserani 2012, 3; Marconi 2012; De Angelis 2016, 14–19, 248–249, who all note the ongoing nature of this debate). The Italian reaction was the development of the anti-classicism trend mentioned earlier. Fodder for the Italian argument also came from Libya. Even though Italian colonial archaeology focused on the Roman period, many important discoveries relating to the Greek period were also made, especially at Cyrene. The early discoveries there of various forms of sculpture permitted Silvio Ferri (1931) to advance the idea of "autoevolution" for Cyrene's artistic development and more generally as a theory (cf. Settis 1994, 880). Instead of viewing the matter in terms of degradation, and of a pre-established hierarchical order between "colony and metropolis" (that other contemporary Italian scholars were also skeptical about: Ciccotti 1931, 132), Ferri argued for internal dynamics involving the independent picking and choosing of artistic elements and their incorporation into something new without any value judgments (Bonacasa 1977, 682). Ferri (1923) also used the newly excavated evidence from Cyrene to contribute to bigger discussions of ancient Greek religion. In sum, his work and that of other Italian scholars operating in this mold can today be considered as ahead of its time and still valid, as most scholars working in zones of cultural contact would agree with empowering local actors with agency and with allowing without value judgment for similarities *and* differences in the development of ancient Greek culture.

The Postwar Internationalism: Greeks as Olive Branch?

The end of World War II around the world ushered in a new era of international cooperation and collaboration. In Italy, the supranationalism that identified with ancient Rome abated substantially, and other approaches, questions, and traditions emerged in line with the times that represent a new phase in scholarly developments.

Although Italy surrendered to the Allies in 1943, almost two years before the official end of World War II in Europe, it was nevertheless considered part of the losing side. In 1947, the Italian Empire was formally abolished, resulting in the loss of its colonies and a return to its original national base. Italian archaeologists and historians continued to be involved in the projects launched under imperial administration, but that willingness on the part of the international community not to exclude Italians required a major adjustment on the Italian home front. Part of the olive branch that Italy extended to the world was the opening of its doors to foreign-led archaeological excavations that were previously banned. This had immediate, positive effects. New questions and methodologies were introduced, the latter being particularly welcome after the "big pick and dig around" grand monuments mentality that characterized many Italian archaeological projects under Fascism (Barbanera 2015, 132–148, 161–167). Foreign archaeologists could now excavate, at long last, the rich ancient Greek cities that existed on Italian soil. In Sicily, for example, this got under way in 1948 with the French work at Megara Hyblaia, and the American work at Morgantina in 1955. Systematic surface surveys of archaeological landscapes started to follow within a generation. Italian scholars immediately recognized the value of these projects for the proper understanding of ancient Sicily and its Hellenism, since it also suited their longstanding temperament of using archaeology to write history (Manni 1990–1991, 26–27, 49). In general, Italian scholarship, at the urging of the great Arnaldo Momigliano (1968), consciously turned to ancient Greece in the postwar period, but in a way that learned from the excesses of Nazism and the idealized Romanticism that ultimately gave rise to it, and that brought to the table the best of what Italian scholarship had to offer. Italian scholarship decolonized itself and that of others, and took its place on the world stage of ancient Greek scholarship as a whole that marks a complete break with the past.

The new spirit of international collaborative scholarship was also manifested via the creation of conferences spearheaded in the early 1960s by Ettore Lepore in Naples for Magna Graecia and by Eugenio Manni in Palermo for Sicily (Barbanera 2015, 187–188; De Angelis 2016, 19). Methodology was extremely important in these and other Italian initiatives. Besides the need to combine archaeology and history, as already mentioned, it also entailed drawing on comparative inspiration from other historical periods. The ancient Greeks in Italy were thus conceived of as examples of frontier history (Corcella 1999, 60–68), so that the give and take between Greeks and Italics could be embedded in the less emotionally charged supranationalistic scholarly environments of previous decades. In interpreting the past, the main vehicle was Marxism, as Italian politics and society moved decidedly to the left after World War II (D'Agostino 1991, 57–59; Dyson 2006, 217–218; Barbanera 2015, 168–176). Marxism's ground-up approach to history provided a methodological and theoretical framework championed by Antonio Gramsci, and quashed by the Fascists, that embraced big and small players, oppressors and oppressed, and ideologies, to write more social and economic histories (Lepore 2000). Consequently, the full range of people to be found on these ancient Italian frontiers were part of the story. As in previous decades, non-Greek populations continued to be important (Romanelli 1962, 1972). While the impact of ancient Greeks was not diminished, the uncritical "Hellenization" of those who came into contact with them was reevaluated (Gallini 1973; Canfora 1987), most dramatically by Momigliano (1975) in a study entitled *Alien Wisdom: The Limits of Hellenization* (see recently Zecchini 2013). These reevaluations were all well ahead of their time, their significance increased by a related phenomenon: the messages of Italian scholarship have also been transmitted around the world via its diaspora (Verdicchio 1997, 90–135, 153–154; D'Agostino 2002).

This started before World War II with the Sicilian-born and Harvard-trained historian Vincent Scramuzza, who spent most of his career teaching at Smith College. Scramuzza's approach was hybrid, straddling the mindsets of both sides of the Atlantic. He arrived in New Orleans as a young man and, like so many immigrants, immediately felt the strong forces of assimilation. As was customary in English-speaking scholarship, Scramuzza (1939) drew parallels between ancient Greek and English colonization, even claiming that the decline of the ancient native Sicilians was owed to the devastating effects of alcohol, much in the same way as had happened in the New World. While no ancient evidence to substantiate this comparison exists, it is a product of that period before World War II in which anthropology sought to explain the destruction of native cultures in North America. Scramuzza (1938) was often called upon to review Italian works, such as those of Biagio Pace, for English-language journals, and rightly predicted that one day, when the obvious scholarly excesses brought on by the charged political climate of the world had passed, much would be found true in them. Contemporary to Scramuzza is Momigliano. Being Jewish, he was forced to leave Italy because of Fascism's adoption of anti-Semitic racial laws in 1938. He spent the rest of his life teaching in England, the United States, and, well after the war, in his native Italy (Polverini 2006). Momigliano represents the towering example of what Scramuzza and still other scholars, whether born in Italy and now residing abroad (e.g., Ceserani 2012; Marconi 2012) or born abroad to Italian parents (e.g., Antonaccio 2001; De Angelis 2016), understand instinctively and gravitate toward – the complexities of cultural encounters. All these scholars act as natural vectors between different traditions and are helping to shape an ongoing scholarly dialogue (see now Donnellan, Nizzo, and Burgers 2016).

Conclusions

Italian-speaking traditions and the study of the ancient Greeks outside their homelands represent a unique chapter in the history of this field of scholarship. Right from the sixteenth century, the presence of ancient Greeks in Italy presented two challenges to historical writing. The availability of written sources and how to fit these Greeks into the history of Greece and Italy was one. The other revolved around gauging the Greek impact on ancient Italy, made all the more relevant owing to the fact that control of Italy from the Middle Ages on similarly involved struggles between internal and external powers. A unique set of dynamics emerged, and polarized positions often resulted and continued until well after World War II. Italian scholarship tended to view ancient Greeks as just another people who both taught and learned from others, especially, of course, ancient "Italians," whereas foreign scholarship tended to exalt ancient Greeks in often idealized accounts. It was only after World War II that the ancient Greeks became a subject in their own right in Italy. Since then, scholarship has reached out internationally, slowly maturing to become the scholarly force that it is today.

REFERENCES

Altekamp, Stefan. 2000. *Rückkehr nach Afrika: italienische Kolonialarchäologie in Libyen, 1911–1943*. Cologne: Böhlau.
Altekamp, Stefan. 2004. "Italian Colonial Archaeology in Libya 1912–1942." In *Archaeology under Dictatorship*, edited by Michael Galaty and Charles Watkinson, 55–71. New York: Kluwer.

Ampolo, Carmine. 1997. *Storie greche. La formazione della moderna storiografia sugli antichi Greci*. Turin: Einaudi.

Ampolo, Carmine. 2012. "Gli storici del XIX e XX secolo di fronte alla colonizzazione greca in Occidente." In *Alle origini della Magna Grecia: mobilità, migrazioni, fondazioni. Atti del cinquantesimo Convegno di Studi sulla Magna Grecia, Taranto 1–4 ottobre 2010*, 3 vols., vol. 1, edited by Mario Lombardo, 11–34. Taranto: Istituto per la Storia e l'Archeologia della Magna Grecia.

Antonaccio, Carla Maria. 2001. "Ethnicity and Colonization." In *Ancient Perceptions of Greek Ethnicity*, edited by Irad Malkin, 113–157. Cambridge, MA: Harvard University Press.

Arias, Paolo Enrico. 1976. *Quattro archeologi del nostro secolo. Paolo Orsi, Biagio Pace, Alessandro Della Seta, Ranuccio Bianchi-Bandinelli*. Pisa: Giardini.

Arthurs, Joshua. 2013. *Excavating Modernity: The Roman Past in Fascist Italy*. Ithaca, NY: Cornell University Press.

Barbanera, Marcello. 2015. *Storia dell'archeologia classica in Italia. Dal 1764 ai giorni nostri*. Rome: Laterza.

Bonacasa, Nicola. 1977. "Orientamenti della cultura archeologica in Sicilia." In *La presenza della Sicilia nella cultura degli ultimi cento anni*, 2 vols., no stated editor(s), 2: 676–684. Palermo: Palumbo.

Cagnetta, Mariella. 1979. *Antichisti e impero fascista*. Bari: Dedalo.

Cagnetta, Mariella. 1994. "Pais e il nazionalismo." *Quaderni di Storia*, 39: 209–225.

Canfora, Luciano. 1976. "Classicismo e fascismo." *Quaderni di Storia*, 3: 15–48.

Canfora, Luciano. 1987. *Ellenismo*. Rome: Laterza.

Caputo, Giacomo. 1955. "Il pensiero di Biagio Pace e l'archeologia italiana." *Dioniso*, 18: 83–121.

Ceserani, Giovanna. 2000. "The Charm of the Siren: The Place of Classical Sicily in Historiography." In *Sicily from Aeneas to Augustus: New Approaches in Archaeology and History*, edited by Christopher Smith and John Serrati, 174–193. Edinburgh: Edinburgh University Press.

Ceserani, Giovanna. 2012. *Italy's Lost Greece: Magna Graecia and the Making of Modern Archaeology*. New York: Oxford University Press.

Ciaceri, Emanuele. 1994. "Scritti in memoria di Emanuele Ciaceri." *Sileno*, 20: 8–116.

Ciccotti, Ettore. 1931. "Il problema demografico nel mondo antico." *Metron*, 9(2): 111–165.

Corcella, Aldo. 1999. "La frontiera nella storiografia sul mondo antico." In *Confini e frontiera nella grecità d'Occidente. Atti del trentasettesimo convegno di studi sulla Magna Grecia, Taranto, 3–6 ottobre 1997*, edited by Attilio Stazio and Stefania Ceccoli, 43–82. Taranto: Istituto per la storia e l'archeologia della Magna Grecia.

D'Agostino, Bruno. 1991. "The Italian Perspective on Theoretical Archaeology." In *Archaeological Theory in Europe: The Last Three Decades*, edited by Ian Hodder, 52–64. London: Routledge.

D'Agostino, Peter. 2002. "Craniums, Criminals, and the 'Cursed Race': Italian Anthropology in American Racial Thought, 1861–1924." *Comparative Studies in Society and History*, 44: 319–343.

De Angelis, Franco. 2016. *Archaic and Classical Greek Sicily: A Social and Economic History*. New York: Oxford University Press.

De Francesco, Antonino. 2013. *The Antiquity of the Italian Nation: The Cultural Origins of a Political Myth in Modern Italy, 1796–1943*. Oxford: Oxford University Press.

de Haan, Nathalie, Martijn Eickhoff, and Marjan Schwegman, eds. 2008. *Archaeology and National Identity in Italy and Europe 1800–1950*. Fragmenta no. 2. Turnhout: Brepols.

D'Ercole, Maria Cecilia. 2013. "Archeologia e politica fascista in Adriatico." *Annali della Scuola Normale Superiore di Pisa Classe di Lettere e Filosofia*, 5: 359–401.

Diaz-Andreu, Margarita. 2007. *A World History of Nineteenth-Century Archaeology: Nationalism, Colonialism, and the Past*. Oxford: Oxford University Press.

Donnellan, Lieve, Valentino Nizzo, and Gert-Jan Burgers, eds. 2016. *Conextualizing Early Colonization. Archaeology, Sources, Chronology and Interpretative Models between Italy and the Mediterranean*. 2 vols. Rome: Palombi Editori for the Royal Netherlands Institute in Rome and Brussels: Belgian Historical Institute in Rome.

Dyson, Stephen L. 2006. *In Pursuit of Ancient Pasts: A History of Classical Archaeology in the Nineteenth and Twentieth Centuries*. New Haven: Yale University Press.

Esposito, Arianna, and Giovanna Leo. 2006. "Archéologie, histoire et politique nationale (1860–1970): l'Italie méridionale et Sybaris." *European Review of History/Revue Européene d'Histoire*, 13: 621–642.

Ferri, Silvio. 1923. *Contributi di Cirene alla storia della religione greca*. Ricerche e testi di storia e letteratura religiose, no. 2. Rome: Libreria di Cultura.

Ferri, Silvio. 1931. "Sul concetto d'arte ed archeologia 'coloniali'." *La Nuova Italia*, 2(8): 295–299. Reprinted in *Opuscula* (Florence: Felice Le Monnier, 1962), 79–86.

Gabba, Emilio. 1991. "Colonie antiche e moderne." *Scienze dell'Antichità*, 5: 601–614.

Gallini, Clara. 1973. "Che cosa intendere per ellenizzazione. Problemi di metodo." *Dialoghi di Archeologia*, 7: 175–191.

Giammellaro, Pietro. 2012a. "Biagio Pace e la Sicilia antica." *Studi Storici*, 53: 391–420.

Giammellaro, Pietro. 2012b. "Indigeni, Greci e Fenici negli studi siciliani di Luigi Pareti." In *EPI OINOPA PONTON. Studi sul Mediterraneo antico in ricordo di Giovanni Tore*, edited by Carla Del Vais, 353–361. Oristano: S'Alvure.

Giammellaro, Pietro. 2013. "Il problema della presenza fenicia in Sicilia nella storiografia italiana nazionalista e fascista: Ettore Pais, Emanuele Ciaceri, Biagio Pace." In *Fenícios e Púnicos por terra e mar. Actas do 6° Congresso Internacional de Estudos Fenícios e Púnicos*, edited by Ana Margarida Arruda, 159–165. Lisbon: Centro de Arqueologia da Universidade de Lisboa.

Guidi, Alessandro. 1996. "Nationalism without a Nation: The Italian Case." In *Nationalism and Archaeology in Europe*, edited by Margarita Diaz-Andreu and Timothy C. Champion, 108–118. London: University College London Press.

La Rosa, Vincenzo, ed. 1986. *L'archeologia Italiana nel Mediterraneo fino alla seconda Guerra mondiale*. Catania: Centro di Studi per l'archeologia greca.

La Rosa, Vincenzo. 1987. "'Archaiologhia' e storiografia: quale Sicilia?" In *Storia d'Italia Regioni dall'unità a oggi: la Sicilia*, edited by Maurice Aymard and Giuseppe Giarrizzo, 701–731. Turin: Einaudi.

Leighton, Robert. 1986. "Paolo Orsi (1859–1935) and the Prehistory of Sicily." *Antiquity*, 60: 15–20.

Lepore, Ettore. 2000. *La Grande Grèce: aspects et problèmes d'une "colonisation" ancienne. Quatre conférences au Collège de France (1982)*. Naples: Centre Jean Bérard.
Manni, Eugenio. 1977. "La Sicilia antica nella storiografia straniera degli ultimi cento anni." In *La presenza della Sicilia nella cultura degli ultimi cento anni*, 2 vols., no stated editor(s), vol. 1, 19–31. Palermo: Palumbo.
Manni, Eugenio. 1990–1991. "Processo storico e metodologia nel pensiero di Eugenio Manni." *Kokalos*, 36–37: 3–50.
Marconi, Clemente. 2012. "Sicily and South Italy." In *A Companion to Greek Art*, vol. 1, edited by Tyler Jo Smith and Dimitris Plantzos, 369–396. Oxford: Wiley Blackwell.
Mazzarino, Santo. 1939. "Kottabos siculo e siceliota." *Atti dell'Accademia nazionale dei Lincei: Rendiconti*, 15: 357–378.
Mazzarino, Santo. 1977. "La presenza della Sicilia nel pensiero storico dopo l'Unità: premesse originarie e problemi generali." In *La presenza della Sicilia nella cultura degli ultimi cento anni*, 2 vols., no stated editor(s), 1: 3–18. Palermo: Palumbo.
Moe, Nelson. 2002. *The View from Vesuvius: Italian Culture and the Southern Question*. Berkeley: University of California Press.
Momigliano, Arnaldo. 1966. "Gli studi italiani di storia greca e romana dal 1895 al 1939. In *Cinquant'anni di vita intellettuale Italiana 1896–1946*, 2nd ed., edited by Carlo Antoni and Raffaele Mattioli, 93–121. Naples: Edizione Scientifiche Italiane.
Momigliano, Arnaldo. 1968. "Prospettiva 1967 della storia greca." *Rivista Storica Italiana*, 80: 5–19. Reprinted in *Quarto contributo alla storia degli studi classici* (Rome: Edizioni di Storia e Letteratura, 1969), 43–58.
Momigliano, Arnaldo. 1975. *Alien Wisdom: The Limits of Hellenization*. Cambridge: Cambridge University Press.
Momigliano, Arnaldo. 1979. "The Rediscovery of Greek History in the Eighteenth Century: The Case of Sicily." In *Studies in Eighteenth Century Culture*, vol. 9, edited by Roseann Runte, 167–187. Madison: University of Wisconsin Press.
Momigliano, Arnaldo. 1980. "La riscoperta della Sicilia da T. Fazello a P. Orsi." In *La Sicilia antica*, edited by Emilio Gabba and Georges Vallet, vol. 1.3, 767–780. Naples: Società editrice storia di Napoli e della Sicilia.
Momigliano, Arnaldo. 1987. *Ottavo contributo alla storia degli studi classici e del mondo antico*. Rome: Edizioni di Storia e Letteratura.
Munzi, Massiliano. 2001. *L'epica del ritorno. Archeologia e politica nella Tripolitania italiana*. Rome: L'Erma di Bretschneider.
Munzi, Massiliano. 2004a. *La decolonizzazione del passato. Archeologia e politica in Libia dall'amministrazione alleata al regno di Idris*. Rome: L'Erma di Bretschneider.
Munzi, Massiliano. 2004b. "Italian Archaeology in Libya: From Colonial Romanità to Decolonization of the Past." In *Archaeology under Dictatorship*, edited by Michael Galaty and Charles Watkinson, 73–107. New York: Kluwer.
Orsi, Paolo. 1991. *Atti del convegno Paolo Orsi e l'archeologia del '900, Rovereto 12–13 maggio 1990*. Rovereto: Musei Civici di Roverto.
Pace, Biagio. 1935–1958. *Arte e civiltà nella Sicilia antica*. 4 vols. Milan: Dante Alighieri.
Pagden, A. 1995. *Lords of All the World: Ideologies of Empire in Spain, Britain and France c. 1500–c. 1800*. New Haven: Yale University Press.
Pais, Ettore. 1894. *Storia della Sicilia e della Magna Grecia*. Turin: Carlo Clausen.

Pais, Ettore. 1934. "Romanità e ellenismo." *Historia*, 8: 3–16.
Pallottino, Massimo. 1991. *A History of Earliest Italy*. Trans. Martin Ryle and Kate Soper. London: Routledge.
Pareti, Luigi. 1959. *La Sicilia antica*. Palermo: Palumbo.
Petricioli, Marta. 1990. *Archeologia e Mare Nostrum. Le missioni archeologiche nella politica mediterranean dell'Italia 1898/1943*. Rome: Valerio Levi.
Polverini, Leandro, ed. 2002. *Aspetti della storiografia di Ettore Pais*. Naples: Edizioni Scientifiche Italiane.
Polverini, Leandro, ed. 2006. *Arnaldo Momigliano nella storiografia del Novecento*. Naples: Edizioni Scientifiche Italiane.
Ridley, Ronald T. 1975–1976. "Ettore Pais." *Helikon*, 15–16: 500–533.
Rizza, Giovanni. 1971. "Ricordo di Biagio Pace." *Archivio Storico per la Sicilia Orientale*, 67: 345–355.
Romanelli, Pietro, ed. 1962. *Greci e Italici in Magna Grecia. Atti del primo Congresso di Studi sulla Magna Grecia, Taranto, 4–8 novembre 1961*. Naples: L'Arte Tipografica.
Romanelli, Pietro, ed. 1972. *Le genti non greche della Magna Grecia. Atti dell'undicesimo Convegno di studi sulla Magna Grecia, Taranto, 10–15 ottobre 1971*. Naples: L'Arte Tipografica.
Salmeri, Giovanni. 1991. "Grecia vs Roma nella cultura siciliana dal XVII al XX secolo." In *Römische Geschichte und Zeitgeschichte in der deutschen und italienischen Altertumswissenschaft während des 19. und 20. Jahrhunderts*, edited Karl Christ and Emilio Gabba, 275–297. Como: Edizioni New Press.
Salmeri, Giovanni. 1992. *Sicilia romana: storia e storigrafia*. Catania: Giuseppe Maimone.
Salmeri, Giovanni. 1993. "L'antiquaria italiana dell'ottocento." In *Lo studio storico del mondo antico nella cultura italiana dell'Ottocento*, edited by Leandro Polverini, 265–298. Naples: Edizioni Scientifiche Italiane.
Salmeri, Giovanni, ed. 2004. *Fascismo e antichità. Tra retorica e pratica*. Pisa: PLUS.
Schnapp, Alain. 1996. *The Discovery of the Past: The Origins of Archaeology*. Trans. Ian Kinnes and Gillian Varndell. London: British Museum Press.
Schneider, Jane, ed. 1998. *Italy's "Southern Question": Orientalism in One Country*. Oxford: Berg.
Scramuzza, Vincent M. 1938. "Review of Pace 1935." *Classical Philology*, 33: 335–338.
Scramuzza, Vincent M. 1939. "Greek and English Colonization." *American Historical Review*, 44: 303–315.
Settis, Salvatore. 1994. "Idea dell'arte greca d'Occidente fra Otto e Novecento: Germania e Italia." In *Storia della Calabria. Età antica e romana*, edited by Salvatore Settis, 855–902. Rome: Gangemi.
Siracusano, Anna. 2009. *Arte greca: un'interpretazione*. Messina: Di.Sc.A.M.
Treves, Piero. 1962. *Lo studio dell'antichità classica nell'Ottocento*. Milan: Riccardo Ricciardi.
Trigger, Bruce G. 2006. *A History of Archaeological Thought*. 2nd ed. Cambridge: Cambridge University Press.
Troilo, Simona. 2012. "'A Gust of Cleansing Wind': Italian Archaeology on Rhodes and in Libya in the Early Years of Occupation (1911–1914)." *Journal of Modern Italian Studies*, 17: 45–69.

Verdicchio, Pasquale. 1997. *Bound by Distance: Rethinking Nationalism through the Italian Diaspora*. Madison, NJ: Fairleigh Dickinson University Press.

Vlassopoulos, Kostas. 2007. *Unthinking the Greek Polis: Ancient Greek History beyond Eurocentrism*. Cambridge: Cambridge University Press.

Zecchini, Giuseppe, ed. 2013. *L'ellenismo come categoria storica e come categoria ideale*. Milan: Vita e Pensiero.

FURTHER READING

The most important sources on this topic are naturally written in Italian. For readers wishing to pursue further with little or no Italian, the growing trend to discuss Italian developments in wider comparative perspective is leading to more and more of the relevant scholarship being written in English (e.g., Schnapp 1996; Trigger 2006; Diaz-Andreu 2007). While helpful to a degree, such accounts are often limited in length and scope depending on their narrative needs. Another growing trend which provides a solution to this, because of its ability to access thoroughly original sources, is to consult scholarship written in English by Italians or individuals of that and other origins using original sources. In this connection, highly recommended are the following works which supply considerably more details on the topics raised in this chapter: D'Agostino 1991; Guidi 1996; Moe 2002; Altekamp 2004; Munzi 2004b; Dyson 2006; de Haan, Eickhoff, and Schwegman 2008; Ceserani 2012; Troilo 2012; De Francesco 2013; De Angelis 2016, 4–27.

CHAPTER SIX

Tsarist Russian, Soviet, and Post-Soviet Traditions and the Study of Ancient Greeks outside their Homelands

Sergey Saprykin

Russian classical scholarship has strong traditions in studying ancient Greek culture in the Black Sea and Central Asia. The achievements of this scholarship have been discussed in various ways over the years. Our main task here is to highlight some of its results relating to Hellenic civilization in these regions during Tsarist, Soviet, and post-Soviet times.

Greeks in the Black Sea

The Black Sea witnessed active cultural interaction between Greek, Roman, and barbarian cultures. Hellenic traditions there stood in close relation with barbarian ones. The study of the northern coast of the Black Sea began at the end of the eighteenth/early in the nineteenth century (Zastrozhnova 2013). The first field trips to record the Greek monuments were undertaken by Peter S. Pallas, Heinrich K. E. Kehler, Peter Köppen, Frederic Dubous de Montpéreux, and Pavel Sumarokoff. They raised interest and stimulated archaeological excavations. Paul Dubrux worked at Panticapaeum on the Mithridates Hill, and in the 1830s–1840s investigations were conducted on the banks of Lake Akhtanizovskaya and on the barrows Kul-Oba, Zolotoy, and Tsarskij. Archaeological travel focused on locating sites mentioned in Greek sources. Ivan A. Stempkovskij initiated work in this field mostly in the regions of Cimmerian Bosporus, southwestern Taurica, Lower Bug, Lower Dniester, and the Lower Dnieper (Zhebelev 1923, 103–105; 1953, 13–15; Tunkina 2002, 25–190). The foundation of museums in Theodosia (1811), Odessa (1825), and Kerč (1826) intensified classical archaeology in eastern Crimea and Taman peninsula. Anton B. Ashik (1848–1849) first summarized the results relating to

---

A Companion to Greeks Across the Ancient World, First Edition. Edited by Franco De Angelis.
© 2020 John Wiley & Sons, Inc. Published 2020 by John Wiley & Sons, Inc.

the Bosporan Kingdom. In 1854, the excellent edition *The Antiquities of Cimmerian Bosporus, kept in the Emperor's Museum of Hermitage* started. It included a publication of monuments of ancient art along with some archaeological reports on the excavations in Kerč and environs.

In the 1860s–1870s, large-scale excavations in eastern Crimea, Kuban, and the steppe areas of the Dnieper region occurred. In the 1880s, research in Panticapaeum produced many important materials – grave-chambers with excellent paintings and decoration, Ionian and Attic pottery, sepulchral reliefs, Greek inscriptions, which enlarged the understanding of religion, ideology, and burial customs. Russian archaeologists excavated the barrows at Bolschaya Bliznitza, Vasjurina Gora, Artjukhov, Semibratnie on the Taman peninsula, Aleksandropolskij, Tchertomlyk, and Solokha in the Dnieper steppes. Ludolf E. Stephani, a head keeper of the Hermitage Museum, was responsible for publishing the most impressive finds.

Regular archaeological research in the Tauric Chersonesus in southwestern Crimea began in 1888. It uncovered new information concerning topography, chronology, and organization of the city and its *chora* (Sorochan, Zubar, and Marchenko 2000, 26–42; Zubar 2009, 5–10). The most systematic excavations in Olbia, a Milesian colony on the Lower Bug, started in 1900 by Boris V. Pharmakovskij, helped to reveal the cultural and urban face of the Hellenic *poleis* on the northern Black Sea coast (Pharmakovskij 1902, 1–20; 1903, 1–113; 1906, 1–32; Karasev 1976, 13–21). Ernst R. von Stern (1909, 139–152) was the first to attribute the site on the Berezan Island to the earliest Greek *apoikia*.

The intensification of archaeological investigations produced large-scale publications of narrative sources. Vasiliy V. Latyschev (1896–1906), in collaboration with other scholars, translated numerous Greek, Roman, and Byzantine sources. Greek and Latin inscriptions from the Caucasus were published by Ivan Pomialowskij (1881) and Latyschev (1900–1901; 1916). Latyschev (1887, 1909), through his epigraphic studies, discussed the state institutions of Olbia and Bosporus. Pavel O. Burachkoff (1884) published a catalog of ancient coins from the northern Black Sea coast; Alexander L. Bertie-Delagard (1907) classified them in accordance with their exact weights and attribution. They all remain the most complete collections of sources on history, religion, culture, and military affairs of the Greeks and the Romans on the Black Sea coast. Narrative sources and epigraphy helped in the locating of ancient sites, in perceiving their political and administrative character, system of magistracies and power, demography, and onomastics. They stimulated the study of trade, economy, political history, state institutions, and relations with the natives. Henceforth, Russian classical scholarship worked out two main approaches of how to study ancient history.

The first one ("pan-Hellenic") envisaged that the Greek institutions and traditions were taken as decisive factors in *polis* development and as the main force in creating power and state institutions, social and political relations, ideology and culture (Latyschev 1887; Pharmakovskij 1915; Tolstoy 1918). From this viewpoint, von Stern (1909, 139–152) studied Greek colonization, along with the political and social structures of the Hellenic *poleis*. All these works relied mostly on the material from Olbia. The second approach was linked to Michail I. Rostovtzeff, who investigated the historical development of ancient states on the northern coast of the Black Sea and their cultural interactions with Scythians, Sarmatians, Sindians, and Maeotians. He initiated excavations of barrows, carefully studying the material and different traces of the sepulchral cult of the barbarians and the Greeks, as well as the decorative painting of grave-chambers at Bosporus. Summarizing the results of archaeological research of the northern Black Sea states and outlining its main task in future, Rostovtzeff wrote that Russian classical archaeology needed systematic and regular excavations of Greek centers with the goal of finding proto-Hellenic settlements, and careful excavation and research on barrows and barbarian graves in the non-Greek sites in Dnieper, Bug, Kuban, and Lower Volga regions (Rostovtzeff 1912, 1914, 1922, 1931).

So by 1917, Russian classical scholarship posed a number of important questions about Greek colonization, Hellenization, and barbarization of local populations (later dubbed "the process of Sarmatization"), some features of *polis* development and its crisis, and the problem of Hellenism. One should also point to the forms of urban and state organization, power, and the relations between Greeks and natives. A very important question was the arrangement of the *chora* and land possessions. All these problems, present from 1917 to 1991, remain the same today.

Tsarist Russian and eastern European classical scholarship before World War II uncovered few archaeological materials, hindering progress in solving the problem of Greek colonization. Only in the second half of the twentieth century could such questions as precolonial contacts, dates of founding colonies, and their character in the first years of existence, become clear. The earliest contacts Greeks had with the Black Sea were shown to belong to the second millennium BC (Lordkipanidze 1996, 21–46). The Phoenicians and Carians were previously thought to antedate the Greeks there (Rostovtzeff 1922, 65; Zhebelev 1953, 51, 196), but modern archaeology does not find any traces of them there (Iessen 1947, 51; Shelov 1970, 45; Brashinkij 1981, 84; Kacharava and Kvirkvelia 1991, 123). In any case, this old supposition inspired Soviet scholars to investigate the Greeks' "precolonial contacts," a theory which was rather popular in the second half of the twentieth century (Gajdukevič 1971; cf. Blawatskij 1954, 8).

The main task of researchers from the former USSR (including the East Bloc countries Ukraine and Georgia) was to establish foundation dates for the Greek colonies. After extensive archaeological excavations, scholars confirmed that Ionians from Miletus widely settled the region (Kuznetsov 1991, 31–37). The first Milesian settlements appeared in the first half of the seventh century BC in Istria (Blawatskaya 1952, 23; Alexandrescu 1962, 49–69; Alexandrescu and Schuller 1990, 9–102) and Sinope (Maximova 1956; Ivantchik 1998, 297–330). The next stage of penetration goes back to the late seventh century BC (Apollonia Pontica: Panayotova 1998, 97; Lazarov 1998, 86–89; Berezan [ancient Borysthenis]: Solovyov 1999). The recent discovery of Archaic Greek pottery in Olbia (Buiskikh 2013) and Panticapaeum, along with some building remains in the latter (Kuznetsov and Tolstikov 2017, 137), allows their foundation dates to be moved to the late seventh century BC. But most colonies were dated to the turn of the seventh/sixth centuries BC and to the early sixth century BC (Odessos: Toncheva 1967; Tomi: Stoian 1961, 245; 1962; as well as Amisos, Nikonion, Nymphaeum, Myrmekion, and Hermonassa). Scholars from the former USSR and modern Georgia revealed that the oldest Greek pottery in coastal Colchis belongs to the second quarter of the sixth century BC, which is why the Hellenic cities of Ionic origin – Dioskurias, Phasis, Hyenos – appeared closer to the second half of the century (G. Lordkipanidze 1978; O. Lordkipanidze 1979;

Tsetskhladze 1992). It is now clear that Mesembria was founded at the end of the sixth century BC by Megara, Byzantium, and Chalcedon (Velkov 1969, 15; Lazarov 1998, 90), and that Callatis, the colony of Heraclea Pontica (another Megarian foundation on the southern Black Sea coast, founded in 554 BC), was first colonized in the late sixth century BC. The main *apoikiai*, however, appeared only at the beginning of the fourth century BC (Avram 1999, 9–22; Saprykin 2011, 146–149). Debates long raged over the foundation of Chersonesus Taurica, another Heraclean colony (Tymenev 1938, 251; Belov 1948, 34; Chtcheglov 1992; Saprykin 1997, 69–72 arguing for a date of 422 versus the late sixth-century date proposed by Zolotarev 1993; Vinogradov 1997, 397–419). Recent analysis of all the relevant material and historical context has provided formidable arguments for a later date in the middle or even last third/quarter of the fifth century BC (Stoyanov 2007, 125; Tokhtasyev 2007, 110; Buiskikh 2008; Saprykin 2011, 151–154).

Soviet scholars proposed that Greeks first founded *emporia* (trading stations) where local tribes could trade with them (Iessen 1947, 76; Belov 1948, 32; Blawatskij 1954, 16; 1959, 11). Some Bulgarian scholars supported this view, arguing that a highly developed Thracian economy attracted Greeks to trade. As a result, Greek colonies were founded at local settlements (Velkov 1988, 269–271; cf. Fol and Dimitrov 1984, 97–99). Georgian scholars thought that Greek colonies in Colchis were initially *emporia* (Boltunova 1963, 155), as economy and statehood in Colchis were highly sophisticated and hindered the formation of *poleis* (Lordkipanidze 1977, 1979a, 193). The "emporium theory" and another closely related one – "the theory of bilateral colonization" – were long popular in Soviet scholarship. With a certain amount of ideology behind them, they helped to prove that local populations allowed Greeks to hold firm on the coasts of the Black Sea, and that the Greeks greatly impacted the indigenous population in their attempts to create tribal states (Sokolskij and Shelov 1959, 48–54).

These ideas go back to theories dominant in Russian classical scholarship before 1917 and between the 1920s and 1950s. They were based on the discovery of Archaic Greek pottery taken as evidence for commercial relations between Greeks and Cimmerians, Sindians, Maeotians, and Scythians. This trade was controlled by tribal elites (Knipovič 1935, 106), who were encouraged to take up residence in Greek *apoikiai* (Gajdukevič and Kaposhina 1951, 162–187; Iwanova 1951, 188–203; Knipovič 1955, 178). The main arguments centered on the early settlers' dugouts and semi-dugouts, which were considered to be barbarian dwellings (Solovyov 1999, 121–132), the flexed position of bodies in burials (Kaposhina 1956), barbarian weaponry (arrowheads, spearheads, and swords), and handmade pottery in the Greek cities and their cemeteries (Marchenko 1988).

Today these ideas have been seriously revised. Dugouts and semi-dugouts are considered to be early Greek dwellings (Kryzhitskij 1993, 41), and the Archaic burials with weapons are completely Hellenic (Lapin 1966, 206; Zubar and Son 2007, 19). When Greeks settled the northern Black Sea coast, practically no indigenous population lived there, except probably at Sindica. This could have hardly stimulated any precolonial commercial contacts between Greeks and barbarians, and by no means corresponds to the scenario of "bilateral colonization" between barbarians and Greeks. It also contradicts the supposition that barbarian elites and Greeks were interested in settling in common. On the eastern Black Sea coast, Greeks did not face a strong Colchian Kingdom, as some Georgian scholars seem to think, but a weak and crumbling political union of several tribal entities transitioning to early statehood (Voronov 1979, 274). The excavations in the Greek cemetery at Pichvnari (western Colchis) convincingly proved that early Hellenic colonists preferred to settle and live apart from the local population (Kakhidze 1975, 92). This became a key argument against the idea of communal life between Greeks and barbarians in the early *apoikiai*. But some Bulgarian and Romanian researchers still insist on the active participation of Thracians in the lives of the early Greek settlers in Thrace and Dobrudja (Toncheva 1956, 51; Danov 1960, 73; Pippidi 1984, 108).

The main approach to Greek colonization in the Black Sea, now supported by many Russian scholars, contains four dimensions: (i) the process was caused by economic and political conditions of *polis* development in the Aegean; (ii) there were no *emporia*; rather Greek *apoikiai* started as organized communities, and not as a result of commerce with locals; (iii) on arrival the settlers cultivated the territory, having provided themselves and their reinforcements with plots of land, an indispensable condition for arranging any colony (Košelenko and Kuznetzov 1992, 6–28); (iv) trade was a secondary task and became important after living conditions had stabilized.

Another important problem for eastern European classical scholars is connected with turning the Greek colonies into *polis* centers and the creation of *polis* territory. Russian, Bulgarian, and Romanian researchers (and less so Czech and Polish scholars) brought to light two main aspects: (i) the political, social, and state structures of the Hellenic cities along with their cultural and religious traditions taken from their mother-cities; (ii) the impact of indigenous societies on Greeks, and vice versa. The latter were actively studied by Tsarist Russian scholars. Later Soviet scholars analyzed new material from Scythia, Maeotika, and Sindica (Kallistov 1952, 5–10; Blawatskij 1964a; 1964b), and Bulgarian and Romanian scholars from the Getae and Thracians. In the nineteenth and early twentieth centuries, scholars mostly studied the internal political situation, foreign policy, culture of the Greek *poleis*, and their position vis-à-vis their barbarian neighbors. For Thrace and the Getae, they chiefly paid attention to the great impact of local culture, which was sometimes exaggerated (Pârvan 1928). They actively promoted the idea of how their economic interests prevailed over those of Greeks (Danov 1947, 1982). The same approach was typical for some Soviet scholars, who advanced the idea of barbarians having a greater interest in the development of *polis* economy (Sokolskij 1961, 123–136). But new material proved direct Greek impact on the development of local societies.

The earliest Ionian settlers initially lived in small rural communities, not in centralized *apoikiai*, and in some places cultivated vast agricultural territories in the Lower Dniester, Lower Bug, and Lower Dnieper (Kryzhitskij et al. 1999). In other parts of the Black Sea, Greeks obtained land by treaty with local kings and dynasts, and they had to live close to or in indigenous rural communities (Blawatskaya 1952 20–25; Kacharava and Kvirkvelia 1991, 29, 156; Vinogradov 2005, 221–225). Greeks sometimes subjugated local populations by force, having displaced them from fertile land or even enslaved them and other Greeks who had arrived earlier, particularly in areas of Doric settlement (Heraclea Pontica, Byzantium, Callatis, Tauric Chesonesus). In the 1930s–1950s, Soviet scholars proposed that local populations played a great role in turning the *apoikiai* into *poleis*, as their representatives were included into civic structures (Kaposhina 1956; Murzin 1984, 45; Marchenko 2005, 63). This problem still remains under-studied; local populations made up only a small part of the *polis*'s citizens (Vinogradov 1981, 131–148).

This conclusion corresponds to what some Russian Tsarist scholars had said, but with a new twist added by Soviet and post-Soviet scholarship: namely, the "secondary colonization process." This held that the later arrivals of settlers (*epoikoi*) could not meet the property qualification for citizenship because they were unable to acquire plots of land. It was a condition for political and social struggle, and many Greeks had to leave their colonies to move to other places. As a result, the Black Sea coast was settled by numerous Hellenic settlements, and Greek civilization spread to the hinterland.

Regular excavations in the rural territory of the Greek cities began in the second half of the twentieth century and continue today. In Olbia, Chersonesus, and Bosporus, the results convincingly showed that the foundation of small coastal towns happened in converting *apoikiai* into *poleis*, for the purpose of providing land for their citizens and arranging contacts with indigenous populations. The secondary colonization process enlarged the agrarian hinterland with country estates, farmhouses, and trading stations, allowing Greeks to spread their power over locals, gradually turning them into dependents and semi-dependents (Maslennikov 1998, 77–95). At the same time, barbarian elites moved to Greek cities, in accord with a longstanding view, already from Tsarist times, that indigenous elites sought to profit from the Greek city-states' economies and agriculture with their surplus grain. But the supposition that Greek *poleis* were exclusively commercial seems incorrect, as they had their own agrarian territory. Friendly local dynasts and chiefs sometimes allowed Greeks to obtain land in order to get mutual benefits from its exploitation, which helped to generate local commerce.

According to Rostovtzeff (1922, 61), the Greeks had to arrange close relations with the Scythians. The creation of Thracian and Scythian states in the late sixth to fifth centuries BC coincided with the organization of *polis* territory. The Scythian elite became familiar with the Hellenic mode of life and even lived in Greek cities and helped Greek craftsmen sell their products. But from the third century BC, Scythian power weakened with the arrival of Sarmatian tribes. Soviet scholars, on the other hand, were convinced that the barbarian kingdoms sought to subjugate the Greeks and establish a protectorate over them. They also thought that from 480 BC the Bosporus was a mixed Greek-barbarian kingdom, created under direct threat of the Scythians (Vinogradov 1997, 100–132; 2012). Some scholars also asserted that Olbia, Chersonesus, Istria, Callatis, and Bosporus, in the fifth to fourth centuries BC, having expanded into barbarian regions, functioned very much like typical Hellenistic kingdoms (Zhebelev 1953), in which land was royally owned (Krouglikova 1975; Maslennikov 1998). The general idea of proto-Hellenism was also promoted for the Black Sea, formulated first here before the Macedonian conquest of the Persian Empire (Blawatskij 1985, 95–132; Sokolskij and Shelov 1959, 61; cf. Sokolskij 1955, 199–204; 1961, 123–136; Frolov 1996, 56–58).

These ideas have now been shown to be incorrect (Shelov-Kovediaev 1985, 182–186). There was no Scythian protectorate, and Greek states developed into typical *poleis*. The Bosporan state as an alliance (*symmachia*) of Greek cities was formed not earlier than the first half of the fourth century BC, but not in 480 BC, as earlier scholars believed. The creation of the Bosporan state was due to internal *polis* development, which remained in place until the late second century BC. So we can hardly claim that Bosporus's land was "royal" property (Saprykin 2003, 11–35; 2006, 273–288; Zavoikin 2013).

All Black Sea Hellenic states at that time were typically *polis* by character. From the early fifth century BC, and mostly in the fourth century BC, we find barbarian elite mounds near the most important Greek cities, as well as the coin mints of some Scythian kings. This was not linked with the "Scythian protectorate," but obviously appeared as barbarian elites were keen to interact with Greeks, as Russian scholars before 1917 had correctly noted. Native cultivators who worked on Greek lands afforded barbarian elites the possibility of profiting from selling a part of their production. This testifies not to the vassalage of barbarians, but to the desire to use the *polis* economies to acquire personal wealth. That was the real basis of Hellenization and the syncretism of Hellenic and barbarian culture.

Another important scholarly problem concerns the crisis of Greek states. Russian scholars before 1917 and after admitted that the economic situation worsened in the early third century BC because of the migrations of Sarmatians and Celts. The pressure put on the Greek *poleis* led to agricultural decline, especially in regard to the exportation of grain, and to other economic and social problems. Some scholars insisted on complete crisis; others confined the decline to the recalibration of relations caused by the new ethnopolitical situation, perhaps in turn accentuated by the establishment of Mithridates Eupator's rule in the northern Black Sea region. Barbarization (i.e., Sarmatization) throughout practically the whole Black Sea region was another cause of lasting crisis (Zhebelev 1953, 52, 149–152; Blawatskij 1959, 22–30; Gajdukevič 1955, 1971, 303–332; Kastanayan 1959, 208–214). Closer study reveals that the Greek states were in a comparative crisis: after stagnating in the first three-quarters of the third century BC, craft production, trade, and other parts of their economies continued to function, albeit at a reduced scale. Any deep crisis took place not earlier than the mid- to late second century BC and coincided with the Sarmatian migrations (Shelov 1984, 16–18; Vinogradov, Marchenko, and Rogov 1997, 93–103), as well as the actions of the Getae, Thracians, and Scythians in Dobrudja. The latter established early states that expanded at the expense of the Greek cities, leading to a serious contraction. The Bosporan Kingdom also was not spared, forced to pay tribute to the Sarmatians, but it withstood better thanks to its agricultural hinterland, which allowed Greeks to survive longer.

This relates to the question of Hellenism. In the Hellenistic period, one has traditionally spoken of the "process of Hellenization" spread by Greek *poleis*. The Romans supported Hellenistic traditions either by including the Greek states into the Empire or simply by maintaining allies. But Greeks still kept their *polis* traditions. The Bosporan dynasty of Tiberii Julii actively involved local barbarians, chiefly Sarmatians and Maeotians, into its agrarian economy, which they developed on royal lands. This stimulated settlement of the royal *chora* and entangled the barbarians in Hellenic traditions, all of which laid the groundwork for quickly overcoming the economic and political crisis. The Romans simply continued this (Saprykin 2003, 11–35; 2018). The problem of barbarization (i.e., "Iranianism") put forward by Russian scholars before the October Revolution was also actively studied by Soviet scholars. Barbarization was believed to have begun in early times. Recent studies, however, show active barbarization not earlier than the mid-third century AD, while earlier it was simple Hellenization of the barbarians. That is why Sarmatization can hardly indicate any crisis in the Black Sea region. What has only been accepted since the Tsarist scholarship is the crisis of the Greek *poleis* from the first half of the third century BC.

Greeks in Central Asia[1]

Theophilus Bayer (1738) represents the first Russian attempt to study Hellenic culture in Central Asia (Bactria, Sogdiana, Margiana, Parthiena). In the nineteenth century, scholars began to study the campaigns of Alexander of Macedon in western Turkestan, the history of the Greco-Bactrian Kingdom, historical geography, and narrative sources (Grigoriev 1867, 1881). In 1913, Rostovtzeff discussed the historical development of Hellenistic Central Asia and was the first to point out elements of Greek cultural heritage. But scholars were still mostly interested in historical geography, the spread of Hellenistic influence in Bactria, and the political and military history of Alexander (Bartold 1916).

Regular excavations in the 1920s changed that and brought to light rich archaeological complexes linked with Greek and local post-Hellenistic traditions. In-depth study of all the evidence revealed considerable Greek impact on history and traditions in Central Asia (Masson 1933). In the 1930s, The State Hermitage Museum began to publish pieces of Greek and Bactrian art which documented syncretism of Greek and local cultural traditions, correctly identified as the result of Greco-Macedonian presence in Central Asia (Trever 1940, 1947). But Soviet ideology obliged scholars to study such problems from the viewpoint of class struggle and the national liberation movement. Some scholars asserted the popular idea that Central Asians were constantly fighting for independence from their Greco-Macedonians conquerors (Tolstov 1940).

After World War II, archaeological research took place on the monuments of Parthiena and Margiana, the Parthian rural sites near the foothills of Kopet-Dag, ancient Nysa, monuments in the northern part of Merv Oasis, and ancient Sogdiana in Bactria (Uzbekistan and Tadjikistan). This revealed new material to study Hellenization, previously discussed only on the basis of literary sources and coins. Many monuments, for example the site Mansur-depe (second to first centuries BC), were influenced by Hellenistic cultural traditions. The Greek sculpture from ancient Nysa testifies to the syncretism of art and ideology in Parthia, based on Hellenistic artistic principals and closely linked with ancient Greeks (Masson and Pugachenkova 1954; Košelenko 1977). Parthian kings used Greek and Iranian traditions, having taken their prototypes from them for different goods (Pugachenkova 1969; Pilipko 2001).

Margiana (Merv Oasis), a part of the Achaemenid Empire and later those of Alexander and Seleucus, became part of the Greco-Bactrian Kingdom (Smirnova 1999). The city and countryside were planned according to Greek principles (Košelenko 1977; Zavyalov 2007). The development of archaeology and historical geography encouraged the mapping of different regions, particularly the monuments of ancient Margiana, which was one of the main tasks of Soviet scholarship in the 1970s to 1990s (Staviskij 1977b).

Greek colonists also invaded Sogdiana, as shown by Hellenistic pottery found in Aphrosiab (Shishkina 1975). The excavations in southern Tadjikistan at Takhti-Sangin and in northern Afghanistan in the cemetery of Tilla-tepe revealed the clearest Greek influence in Bactria. Takhti-Sangin is famous for a temple of Oxus (modern Amoudarja), dated to the time of the Seleucids and the Greco-Bactrian rulers (Pichikian 1991; Litvinskij and Pichikian 2000; Litvinskij 2001, 2010). The many finds included Greek sculpture from the Asia Minor school (Pichikian 1991; cf. Litvinskij 2004), a Greek dedicatory inscription of the first half of the second century BC (Litvinskij, Vinogradov, and

Pichikian 1985), and molds for casting bronze cauldrons with Greek inscriptions dedicated to Oxus (Ivantchik 2011). The Tilla-tepe finds included many pieces of Hellenistic toreutics, jewelry made by Greek and Bactrian craftsmen, which bear Chinese and Scytho-Sarmatian traditions with many Greek features (Sarianidi 1989). A sepulchral Greek inscription, found by Soviet archaeologists on the site of Zhiga-tepe in northern Afghanistan (Krouglikova 1979), as well as Greco-Bactrian and other Hellenistic coins, allowed scholars to begin to study the economic and political networks (Rtveladze and Pidaev 1981; Rtveladze 1987; Zeimal 1983). These finds helped to establish the view that Bactria, as a part of the Seleucid Empire and then as an independent Hellenistic state, had intensive contacts with the eastern Mediterranean, thanks to the presence of Greek and Macedonian soldiers, colonization, and the Seleucids' direct involvement. Until the last third of the twentieth century, Soviet historians studied the syncretism of Greco-Macedonian and local cultures in a general historical context without analyzing local cultural phenomena, whereas scholars from local republics preferred to exaggerate indigenous traditions.

Some Soviet scholars postulated that the creation of new cities and military settlements of Greeks and Macedonians helped to surmount the inner contradictions of Alexander's empire. The use of former cities and sites became the main argument in discussing whether only Greek and Macedonian colonization promoted urban development (Masson and Romodin 1964). This theory was based on the fact that Central Asia, like the ancient Near East, was one of the cradles of the most ancient agrarian civilizations, with urban and settlement structures appearing long before Greeks arrived. That is why the impact of Hellenic colonization and culture in Central Asia was minimal (Litvinskij and Ranov 1998), the quantity of Greek and Macedonian cities was not so great, and the political goal was to strengthen the military and administrative presence of the Greco-Macedonians (Shofman 1975). Another line of thinking disparaged Greco-Macedonian influence: the Greek cities could hardly spread Hellenic traditions among the economically and socially dissociated local population (Bokschanin 1960–1966). Others admitted that Greco-Macedonian colonization was rather strong. The uprising of the Greeks in Bactria and Sogdiana in 323 BC showed that the policy of colonizing the East, without taking into account the interests of Hellenic settlers, was doomed to fail. That is why a new Greek social organization appeared – the eastern Hellenistic *polis* – an ideal form of coexistence between the interests of the syncretic eastern Greek monarchy and a large number of Greek subjects. It became the background for developing socioeconomic and administrative relations in the Seleucid Empire. Scholars also confirmed the significant impact of Greek cultural traditions in different regions of Parthia and Margiana (Košelenko 1966, 1977, 1979; Staviskij 1977a).

Post-Soviet Russian scholars have argued for a significant role for Greek and Macedonian colonists in state formation in Hellenistic Central Asia. The decline and fall of the Greeks' power in late second century BC coincided with their activity in northwestern India, which coincided with the emergence of a new Greco-Indian Kingdom. It was convincingly proven that the conquerors who settled in Central Asia with Alexander carried out a well-formulated policy of erecting cities to secure their hegemony over local inhabitants. At the same time, the "minor cities" (which served as regional agricultural centers) had a limited part to play in Hellenization because of their smaller populations. These "minor cities" did not become *poleis* and played the specific role of mediating between the regional administration and agrarian periphery (Golubtzova 1990; Gaibov, Košelenko, and Serditykh 1992).

LIST OF ABBREVIATIONS

IAK	*Izvestiya Imperatorskoj arkheologicheskoj Komissii*
IAN	*Izvestiya Akademii Nauk*
IBAI	*Известия на Българския археологически инсТиТуТ*
IGAIMK	*Izvestiya Gosudarstvennoj Akademii istorii materialnoj kultury*
IVAD	*Известия на ВарненскоТо археологическо дружесТво*
KSIA	*Kratkie soobschenija Instituta arkheologii*, Academy of Sciences (USSR, Russia)
PIFK	*Problemy istorii, filolgii, kultury*
VDI	*Vestnik drewnej istorii*
ŹMNP	*Zhurnal Ministerstva narodnogo prosveschenija*

NOTE

1 I am very grateful to Sergey V. Novikov, assistant professor of the Moscow State University, for references on Central Asia.

REFERENCES

Alexandrescu, Peter. 1962. "Autour de la date de foundation d'Histria." *Studii classice*, 4: 49–69.
Alexandrescu, Peter, and Wolfgang Schuller, eds. 1990. *Histria*. Konstanz: Konstanz University Press.
Ashik, Anton. 1848–1849. *The Bosporan Kingdom*, vols. 1–3. Odessa: Tipografia. Naiman (in Russian).
Avram, Alexandru. 1999. "Histoire de Callatis." In *Inscriptions grecques et latines de Scythie Mineure. Vol. III: Callatis et son territoire*, edited by Alexandru Avram, 3–84. Bucharest: Editura Enciclopedică.
Bartold, Vasiliy. 1916. "The Greco-Bactrian State and Its Spread to the North-East." *IAN*, VI.10, 823–828 (in Russian).
Bayer, Teophilus. 1738. *Historia regni Grecorum Bactriani*. Saint Petersburg: Tipografia Academiae Scientiarum.
Belov, Grigory. 1948. *Chersonesus Taurica*. Leningrad: State Hermitage (in Russian).
Bertie-Delagard, Alexander L. 1907. *Corrections to Burachkoff's Common Catalog of Coins*. Moscow: Tipografia Gerbek (in Russian).
Blawatskaya, Tatiana. 1952. *The West Pontic Cities in VII–I Centuries B.C.* Moscow: Academy of Sciences of the USSR (in Russian).

Blawatskij, Vladimir. 1954. "Archaic Bosporus." In *Materials and Studies on Archaeology of the North Black Sea Littoral*, edited by Maria Kobylina, 7–44. Moscow: Academy of Sciences of the USSR (in Russian).

Blawatskij, Vladimir. 1959. "Process of Historical Development of Ancient States in the North Black Sea Littoral." In *Problems of History of the North Black Sea Coast in Antiquity*, edited by Alexey Smirnov, 7–39. Moscow: Academy of Sciences of the USSR (in Russian).

Blawatskij, Vladimir. 1964. "The Impact of Ancient Culture on the Countries of the North Black Sea Coast (VII–IV c. BC)." *Soviet Archaeology*, 2: 13–26 (in Russian).

Blawatskij, Vladimir. 1964b. "The Impact of Ancient Culture on the Countries of the North Black Sea Coast (IV c. BC–III c. AD)." *Soviet Archaeology*, 4: 25–35 (in Russian).

Blawatskij, Vladimir. 1985. *Ancient Archaeology and History*. Moscow: Nauka (in Russian).

Bokschanin, Anatoliy. 1960–1966. *Parthia and Rome. The Appearance of a System of Political Dualism in the Near East, I–II*. Moscow: MSU (in Russian).

Boltunova, Anna. 1963. "Ancient Cities of Georgia and Armenia." In *Ancient City*, edited by Anna Boltunova, 153–169. Moscow: Academy of Sciences of the USSR (in Russian).

Brashinkij, Iosif. 1981. "The Greeks and Barbarians on the Lower Don and in the North-Eastern Littoral of the Sea of Azov in the VI–IV c. BC." In *The Demographic Situation in the Black Sea Littoral in the Period of the Great Greek Colonization*, edited by Otar Lordkipanidze, 84–92. Tbilisi: Mezniereba (in Russian).

Buiskikh, Alla. 2008. *Spatial Planning Development of Chersonesos of Taurica in Antiquity*. Simferopol: National Academy of Sciences Ukraine and Demetra (in Russian).

Buiskikh, Alla. 2013: *Archaic Painted Pottery from Olbia*. Kiev: Starodavnij Svit (in Russian).

Burachkoff, Pavel. 1884: *A Common Catalogue of Coins which Belonged to the Hellenic Colonies on the Northern Coast of the Black Sea in Antiquity*. Odessa: Tipografia Schultze (in Russian).

Chtcheglov, Alexandre. 1992. *Polis et chora. Cité et territoire dans le Pont-Euxin*. Paris: Les Belles Lettres.

Danov, Christo. 1947. *The West Pontic Coast of the Black Sea in Antiquity*. Sofia: Bulgarian Academy of Sciences (in Bulgarian).

Danov, Christo 1960. "Thracian Penetration into the Greek Cities on the West Coast of the Black Sea." *Klio*, 37: 73–80.

Danov, Christo 1982. *The Thracians*. Sofia: Narodna Prosveta (in Bulgarian).

Fol, Alexander, and Straschimir Dimitrov, eds. 1984. *History of Dobrudja*, vol. 1. Sofia: Bulgarian Academy of Sciences (in Bulgarian).

Frolov, Eduard. "Pre-Hellenism in the Greek West (To the Problem of Relations 'Polis-Monarchy' and 'Hellenes-Barbarian' Relations)." *PIFK*, 1: 53–60 (in Russian).

Gaibov, Vasif, Gennadiy Košelenko, and Zoia Serditykh. 1992. "Hellenistic East." In *Hellenism: East and West*, edited by Elena Golubtzova, 10–58. Moscow: Nauka (in Russian).

Gajdukevič, Viktor. 1955. "History of Ancient Cities of the Northern Black Sea Coast." In *Ancient Cities of the North Black Sea Littoral*, edited by Viktor Gajdukevič and Maria Maximova, 164–187. Moscow and Leningrad: Academy of Sciences of the USSR (in Russian).

Gajdukevič, Viktor. 1971. *Das Bosporanische Reich.* Berlin: Akademie-Verlag.
Gajdukevič, Viktor, and Svetlana Kaposhina. 1951. "To the Question on Local Elements in Culture of Ancient Cities of the North Black Sea Coast." *Soviet Archaeology*, 15, 162–187 (in Russian).
Golubtzova, Elena, ed. 1990. *Hellenism: Economy, Policy, Culture.* Moscow: Nauka (in Russian).
Grigoriev, Vasiliy. 1867. "The Greco-Bactrian Kingdom." *ŽMNP*, 136: 321–359 (in Russian).
Grigoriev, Vasiliy. 1881. "Alexander of Macedon's Campaign in Western Turkestan." *ŽMNP*, 217: 24–67 (in Russian).
Iessen, Alexander. 1947. *Greek Colonization of the North Black Sea Littoral.* Moscow: State Hermitage (in Russian).
Ivantchik, Askold. 1998. "Die Gründung von Sinope und die Probleme der Anfangsphase der Griechischen Kolonisation des Schwarzmeergebietes." In *The Greek Colonisation of the Black Sea Area. Historical Interpretation of Archaeology*, edited by Gocha Tsetskhladze, 297–330. Stuttgart: Franz Steiner.
Ivantchik, Askold. 2005. *Am Vorabend der Kolonisation. Das nördliche Schwarzmeergebiet und Steppennomaden des 8.–7. Jhs. V. Chr. in der klassischen Literaturtradition: Mündliche Überliferung, Literatur und Geschichte.* Moscow: Paleograph (in Russian).
Ivantchik, Askold. 2011. "New Greek Inscriptions from Takhti Sangin and the Problem of the Origin of Bactrian Art." *VDI*, 4: 110–132 (in Russian).
Iwanova, Anna. 1951. "Local Motifs in the Decorative Sculpture of Bosporus." *Soviet Archaeology*, 15: 188–203 (in Russian).
Kacharava, Daredjan, and Guram Kvirkvelia. 1991. *Cities and Sites of the Black Sea Coast in Antiquity.* Tbilisi: Mezniereba (in Russian).
Kakhidze, Amiran. 1975. *Ancient Monuments of the East Black Sea Coast (Greek Necropolis at Pichvnari).* Batumi: Sabchota Adjara (in Georgian).
Kallistov, Dmitriy. 1952. *The North Black Sea Coast in Antiquity.* Moscow: Uchpedgiz (in Russian).
Kaposhina, Svetlana. 1956. "On Scythian Elements in the Culture of Olbia." In *Olbia and the Lower Bug in Antiquity*, edited by Viktor Gajdukevič, 154–189. Moscow: Academy of Sciences of the USSR (in Russian).
Karasev Alexey. 1976. "B.V. Pharmakovskij and Olbia." In *Artistic Culture and Archaeology of the Ancient World*, edited by Nikolay Sokolskij, Iosif Braschinskij, Ksenija Gorbunova, et al., 13–22. Moscow: Nauka (in Russian).
Kastanayan, Elena. 1959. "The Period of Late Hellenism in the History of Bosporan Cities." In *Problems of History of the North Black Sea Coast in Antiquity*, edited by Alexey Smirnov, 205–219. Moscow: Academy of Sciences of the USSR (in Russian).
Knipovič, Tatiana. 1935. "To the Question of Trading Relations of Greeks with the Region of Tanais River in VII–V Centuries BC." *IGAIMK*, 104: 90–110 (in Russian).
Knipovič, Tatiana. 1955. "Main Lines of Artistic Development in the Cities of the North Black Sea Coast in Ancient Epoch." In *Ancient Cities of the North Black Sea Littoral*, edited by Viktor Gajdukevič and Maria Maximova, 164–187. Moscow: Academy of Sciences of the USSR (in Russian).

Košelenko, Gennady. 1966. *The Culture of Parthia*. Moscow: Nauka (in Russian).
Košelenko, Gennady. 1977. *Motherland of the Parthians*. Moscow: Sovetskiy khudozhnik (in Russian).
Košelenko, Gennady. 1979. *Greek Polis in the Hellenistic Orient*. Moscow: Nauka (in Russian).
Košelenko, Gennady, and Vladimir Kuznetzov. 1992. "Greek Colonization of Bosporus (in Connection with Some Common Problems of Colonization)." In *Essays of Archaeology and History of Bosporus*, edited by Gennady Košelenko, 6–28. Moscow: Nauka (in Russian).
Krouglikova, Irina. 1975. *Agriculture of Bosporus*. Moscow: Nauka (in Russian).
Krouglikova, Irina, ed. 1979. *Ancient Bactria. Materials of the Soviet-Afghan Archaeological Expedition*, vol. 2. Moscow: Nauka (in Russian).
Kryzhitskij, Sergey. 1993. *Architecture of Ancient States of the North Black Sea Coast*. Kiev: Naukova dumka (in Russian).
Kryzhitskij, Sergey, Anna Rusiaeva, Valentina Krapivina, et al. 1999. *Olbia. The Antique State in the Northern Black Sea Area*. Kiev: National Academy of Sciences Ukraine and Demetra (in Russian).
Kuznetzov, Vladimir. 1991. "Early *Apoikiai* of the North Black Sea Coast." *KSIA*, 204: 31–37 (in Russian).
Kuznetzov, Vladimir, and Vladimir Tolstikov, eds. 2017. *Panticapaeum and Phanagoria: Two Capitals of the Bosporan Kingdom*. Moscow: GMII im. Puschkina (in Russian).
Lapin, Vladimir. 1966. *Greek Colonization of the Black Sea Coast*. Kiev: Naukova dumka (in Russian).
Latyschev, Vasiliy. 1887. *Studies in the History and State System of the City of Olbia*. Saint Petersburg: Tipografia Balashova (in Russian).
Latyschev, Vasiliy. 1896–1906. *Scythica et Caucasica e veteribus scriptoribus graecis et latinis*. Saint Petersburg: Imperatorskaia Akademiia Nauk.
Latycshev, Vasiliy. 1900–1901, 1916. *Inscripitiones antiquae orae septentrionalis Ponti Euxini graeca et latinae*, vol. 1–2, 4. Saint Petersburg: Imperatorskaia Akademiia Nauk.
Latycshev, Vasiliy. 1909. *ΠΟΝΤΙΚΑ*. Saint Petersburg: Imperatorskaia Akademiia Nauk (in Russian).
Lazarov, Michail. 1998. "Notizen zur Griechischen Kolonisation am westliche Schwarzen Meer: Schriftquellen und archäologische Denkmäler." In *The Greek Colonisation of the Black Sea Area. Historical Interpretation of Archaeology*, edited by Gocha Tsetskhladze, 85–95. Stuttgart: Franz Steiner.
Litvinskij, Boris. 2001. *The Temple of Oxus in Bactria (South Tadjikistan), vol. 2: The Bactrian Armament in Ancient East and Greek Context*. Moscow: Vostochnaia literatura (in Russian).
Litvinskij, Boris. 2004. "Hellenistic Sculptures from the Temple of Oxus." *VDI*, 1: 202–223 (in Russian).
Litvinskij, Boris. 2010. *The Temple of Oxus in Bactria (South Tadjikistan), vol. 3. Art, Artistic Craft, Musical Instruments*. Moscow: Vostochnaia literatura (in Russian).
Litvinskij, Boris, and Igor Pichikian. 2000. *The Hellenistic Temple of Oxus in Bactria (South Tadjikistan)*, vol. 1. Moscow: Vostochnaia literatura (in Russian).
Litvinskij, Boris, and Vadim Ranov. 1998. *History of the Tadjik People*, vol. 1. Duschanbe: Academy of Sciences of the Republic of Tajikistan (in Russian).

Litvinskij, Boris, Juri G. Vinogradov, and Igor Pichikian. 1985. "The Votive Offering of Atrosokes from the Temple of Oxus in Northern Bactria." *VDI*, 4: 84–110 (in Russian).
Lordkipanidze, Guram. 1978. *Colchis in the VI–II centuries BC*. Tbilisi: Mezniereba (in Russian).
Lordkipanidze, Otar. 1977. *To the Problem of Greek Colonization of the East Black Sea Coast (Colchis)*. Tbilisi: Mezniereba (in Russian).
Lordkipanidze, Otar. 1979a. "To the Problem of Greek Colonization of the East Black Sea Coast (Colchis)." In *Problems of Greek Colonization of the Northern and Eastern Black Sea Littoral*, edited by Otar Lordkipanidze, 187–256. Tbilisi: Mezniereba (in Russian).
Lordkipanidze, Otar. 1979. *Ancient Colchis*. Tbilisi: Sabchota Sakartvelo (in Russian).
Lordkipanidze, Otar. 1996. "La geste des Argonautes dans les premières épopées grecques sous l'angle des premiers contacts du monde grec avec le littoral pontique." In *Sur les traces des Argonautes*, edited by Otar Lordkipanidzé and Pierre Lévêque, 21–46. Paris: Les Belles Lettres.
Marchenko, Konstantin. 1988. *Barbarians as a Part of Population of Berezan and Olbia*. Leningrad: Nauka (in Russian).
Marchenko, Konstantin. 2005: "The Greeks and the Barbarians of the Northwestern Black Sea Coast." In *Greeks and Barbarians of the Northern Black Sea Coast in the Scythian Period*, edited by Konstantin Marchenko, 42–136. Saint Petersburg: Aleteia (in Russian).
Maslennikov, Alexander. 1998. *Hellenic Chora on the Edge of Oikumene. Rural Territory of the European Bosporus in Antiquity*. Moscow: Indrik (in Russian).
Masson, Michail. 1933. Coin Finds, Registered in Central Asia in 1930–1931. Materialy Uzkomstarisa 5. Tashkent (in Russian).
Masson, Michail, and Galina Pugachenkova. 1954. "Parthian *Rhytons* of Nysa." *Proceedings of the South Turkmenistan Archaeological Complex Expedition 4*. Ashkhabad: Academy of Sciences of Turkmenistan (in Russian).
Masson, Vadim, and Vadim Romodin. 1964. *History of Afghanistan*, vol. 1. Moscow: Nauka (in Russian).
Maximova, Maria. 1956. *Ancient Cities of the South-East Black Sea Coast*. Moscow: Academy of Sciences of the USSR (in Russian).
Murzin, Vjacheslav. 1984. *The Scythian Archaics of the Northern Black Sea Coast*. Kiev: Naukova Dumka (in Russian).
Panayotova, Kristina. 1998. "Apollonia Pontica: Recent Discoveries in the Necropolis." In *The Greek Colonisation of the Black Sea Area. Historical Interpretation of Archaeology*, edited by Gocha Tsetskhladze, 97–113. Stuttgart: Franz Steiner.
Pârvan, Vasil. 1928. *Dacia*. Cambridge: Cambridge University Press.
Pharmakovskij, Boris. 1902. "The Grave-Chamber of Eurisibius and Arete." *IAK*, 3: 1–20 (in Russian).
Pharmakovskij, Boris. 1903. "The Excavations of the Ancient Olbia Necropolis in 1901." *IAK*, 8: 1–113 (in Russian).
Pharmakovskij, Boris. 1906. "The Excavations in Olbia in 1902 and 1903." *IAK*, 13: 1–306 (in Russian).
Pharmakovskij, Boris. 1915. *Olbia*. Petrograd: Levenson (in Russian).

Pichikian, Igor. 1991. *Culture of Bactria. Achaemenid and Hellenistic Periods.* Moscow: Nauka (in Russian).
Pilipko, Viktor. 2001. *Ancient Nysa. Main Results of Archaeological Study in the Soviet Period.* Moscow: Nauka (in Russian).
Pippidi, Dionys. 1984. *Parerga.* Bucureşt: Editura Academiei Republicii Populare Romîne.
Pomialowskij, Ivan. 1881: *Greek and Latin Inscriptions of the Caucasus.* Saint Petersburg: Imperatorskaia Akademiia Nauk (in Russian).
Pugachenkova, Galina. 1969. "The Throne of Mithridates I from Parthian Nysa." *VDI*, 1: 161–171 (in Russian).
Rostovtzeff, Michail. 1912. *The Kingdom of Bosporus and the South Russian Barrows.* Saint-Petersburg: Tipografia Smirnova (in Russian).
Rostovtzeff, Michail. 1913. "Hellenistic Asia in the Seleucid Period." *Scientific Historical Journal*, 1: 54–63 (in Russian).
Rostovtzeff, Michail. 1914. *Ancient Decorative Painting in South Russia.* Saint Petersburg: Iz-vo IAK (in Russian).
Rostovtzeff, Michail. 1922. *Iranians and Greeks in South Russia.* Oxford: Clarendon.
Rostovtzeff, Michail. 1931. *Scythien und der Bosporus.* Berlin: H. Schoetz & Co.
Rtveladze, Edvard. 1987. *Ancient Coins of Central Asia.* Tashkent: Iz-vo literatury i iskusstva im. G. Guliama (in Russian).
Rtveladze, Edvard, and Shakirdzhan Pidaev. 1981. *Catalogue of Ancient Coins of South Uzbekistan.* Tashkent: Fan (in Russian).
Saprykin, Sergey. 1997. *Heracleia Pontica and Tauric Chersonesus before Roman Domination.* Amsterdam: A.M. Hakkert.
Saprykin, Sergey. 2003. "The Kingdom of Bosporus: From Tyranny to the Hellenistic Monarchy." *VDI*, 1: 11–35 (in Russian).
Saprykin, Sergey. 2006. "The *Chora* in the Bosporan Kingdom." In *Surveying the Greek Chora: Black Sea Region in a Comparative Perspective*, edited by Pia Guldager Bilde and Vladimir Stolba, 273–288. Aarhus: Aarhus University Press.
Saprykin, Sergey. 2011. "The Doric Colonization of the Black Sea." In *In Klios Reich*, vol. 1, edited by Iia Majak, 128–162. Moscow: Akademie-Leibnitz, MSU (in Russian).
Saprykin, Sergey. 2018. *Ancient Black Sea Littoral.* Moscow: Christian Humanities Academy Russia (in Russian).
Sarianidi, Viktor. 1989. *Temple and Necropolis at Tilla-tepe.* Moscow: Nauka (in Russian).
Shelov, Dmitriy. 1970. *Tanais and the Lower Don in the III–I Centuries BC.* Moscow: Nauka (in Russian).
Shelov, Dmitriy. 1984. "History of the Northern Black Sea Ancient States." In *Ancient States of the Northern Black Sea: Archaeology of the USSR*, edited by Gennadiy Košelenko, Irina Krouglikova, and Vjacheslav Dolgorukov, 8–25. Moscow: Nauka (in Russian).
Shelov-Kovediaev, Fedor. 1985. "History of Bosporus in the VI–IV Centuries BC." In *The Ancient States on the Territory of the USSR 1984*, edited by Anatoly Novoseltsev, 5–187. Moscow: Nauka (in Russian).
Shishkina, Galina. 1975. "Hellenistic Pottery of Afrosiab." *Soviet Archaeology*, 2: 60–78 (in Russian).
Shofman, Arkadiy. 1975. "Urban Activity of Alexander of Macedon." *Klio*, 57: 123–145 (in Russian).

Smirnova, Nataliya. 1999. "Finds of Seleucid and Greco-Bactrian Coins at the City-Site Giaour-kala (Turkmenistan)." *Numismatics and Epigraphy*, 16: 242–265 (in Russian with English summary).

Sokolskij, Nikolay. 1955. "On the Period of Hellenism in the Northern Black Sea Coast." *VDI*, 4: 199–204 (in Russian).

Sokolskij, Nikolay. 1961. "Mutual Relations of Ancient States and Tribes of the North Black Sea Coast." In *Griechische Städte und einheimische Völker des Schwarzmeergebietes*, edited by Johannes Irmscher and Dmitrii Schelow, 123–136. Berlin: Akademie-Verlag (in Russian).

Sokolskij, Nikolay, and Dmitriy Shelov 1959. "Historical Role of Ancient States of the North Black Sea Coast." In *Problems of History of the North Black Sea Coast in Antiquity*, edited by Alexei Smirnov, 40–62. Moscow: Academy of Sciences of the USSR (in Russian).

Solovyov, Sergey. 1999. *Ancient Berezan. The Architecture, History and Culture of the First Greek Colony in the Northern Black Sea*. Leiden: Brill.

Sorochan, Sergey, Vitaly Zubar, and Leonid Marchenko. 2000: *The Life and Death of Chersonesus*. Charkov: Majdan (in Russian).

Staviskij, Boris. 1977a. *To the South of the Iron Gates*. Moscow: Sovetskiy khudozhnik (in Russian).

Staviskij, Boris 1977b. *Kushanian Bactria: Problems of History and Culture*. Moscow: Nauka (in Russian).

Stoian, Iorgu 1961. "La città pontica di Tomis." *Dacia*, 5: 245–273.

Stoian, Iorgu. 1962. *Tomitana. Contribuţii epigrafice la istoria cetaţii Tomis*. Bucureşt: Editura Academiei Republicii Populare Romîne.

Stoyanov, Roman. 2007. "Some Notes on the Time and Causes for the Foundation of Chersonesus Taurica." *VDI*, 2: 125–144 (in Russian with English summary).

Tolstoy, Ivan. 1918: *The White Island and Taurica on Pontus Euxeinus*. Saint Petersburg: 2 State Tipografia (in Russian).

Toncheva, Goranka. 1956. "Thracian Influence in Odessus." *IVAD*, 10: 51–60 (in Bulgarian).

Toncheva, Goranka. 1967. "Archaic Materials from Odessus." *IBAI*, 30: 157–180 (in Bulgarian).

Tokhtasyev, Sergey. 2007. "Towards the Onomasticon and Dating of Chersonesian Ostraka." *VDI*, 2: 110–125 (in Russian with English summary).

Tolstov, Sergey. 1940. "Rise and Fall of the Empire of the Hellenistic 'Extreme Orient'." *VDI*, 3–4: 194–209 (in Russian).

Trever, Kamilla. 1940. *Monuments of Greco-Bactrian Art*. Moscow: Academy of Sciences of the USSR (in Russian).

Trever, Kamilla. 1947. "Alexander of Macedon in Sogd." *Voprosy istorii*, 5: 112–122 (in Russian).

Tsetskhladze, Gocha R. 1992. "Greek Colonization of the Eastern Black Sea Littoral (Colchis)." *Dialogues d'Histoire Ancienne*, 18: 213–258.

Tunkina, Irina. 2002: *Russian Scholarship on Classical Antiquities of the South of Russia (18th–Middle of 19th Century)*. Saint Petersburg: Nauka (in Russian).

Tymenev, Alexander. 1938. "Chersonesian Etudes." *VDI*, 2: 245–275 (in Russian).

Velkov, Velizar. 1969. "Mesambria-Mesembria-Nessebre: situation, recherches, notes historiques." In *Nessebre I*, edited by Teofil Ivanov, 9–28. Sofia: Académie bulgare des sciences.

Velkov, Velizar. 1988. "Pontic Thrace and Its Interrelations with the Greek World in the 12th–4th Centuries." In Local Ethno-Political *Entities of the Black Sea Area in the 7th–4th Centuries BC*, edited by Otar Lordkipanidze, 264–280. Tbilisi: Mezniereba.

Vinogradov, Juri A. 2005. "The Cimmerian Bosporus." In *Greeks and Barbarians of the Northern Black Sea Coast in the Scythian Period*, edited by Konstantin Marchenko, 211–296. Saint Petersburg: Aleteya (in Russian).

Vinogradov Juri A. 2012. "The Pages of History of Bosporan Archaeology: The Period of the Imperial Archaeological Commission (1859–1917)." *Bosporos Studies*, 27: 3–364 (in Russian).

Vinogradov Juri A., Konstantin Marchenko, and Eugeny Rogov. 1997. "The Sarmatians and the Perishing of 'The Great Scythia'." *VDI*, 3: 93–103 (in Russian with English summary).

Vinogradov, Juri G. 1981. "The Barbarians in the Prosopography of Olbia in the 6th to 5th Centuries BC." In *The Demographic Situation of the Black Sea Littoral in the Period of Great Greek Colonization*, edited by Otar Lordkipanidze, 131–148. Tbilisi: Mezniereba (in Russian).

Vinogradov, Juri G. 1997. *Pontische Studien*. Mainz: Philip von Zabern.

von Stern, Ernst R. 1909. "Die griechische Kolonisation am Nordgestade des Schwarzen Meeres im Licht archäologischer Forschung." *Klio*, 9: 139–152.

Voronov, Juri. 1979. "Some Problems of the Social History of Northern Colchis in the Epoch of Greek Colonization." In *Problems of Greek Colonization of the Northern and Eastern Black Sea Littoral*, edited by Otar Lordkipanidze, 274–279. Tbilisi: Mezniereba (in Russian).

Zastrozhnova Evgenija. 2013. *The History of Archaeological Research of Phanagoreia (late 18th Century to 1940)*. Unpublished PhD dissertation, Institute of History of Material Culture, Saint Petersburg (in Russian).

Zavoikin, Alexey 2013. *The Creation of the Bosporan State: Archaeology and Chronology of the Territorial State's Formation*. Simferopol: National Academy of Sciences Ukraine and Demetra (in Russian).

Zavyalov, Viktor. 2007. "The Fortifications of the City Gyaur kala, Merv." *Proceedings of the British Academy*, 133: 313–329.

Zeimal, Eugeny. 1983. *Ancient Coins of Tadjikistan*. Duschanbe: Donisch (in Russian).

Zhebelev, Sergey A. 1923. *Introduction to Archaeology*. Petrograd: Nauka i schkola (in Russian).

Zhebelev, Sergey. 1953. *The North Black Sea Littoral*. Moscow: Academy of Sciences of the USSR (in Russian).

Zolotarev, Michail. 1993. *Chersonesian Archaics*. Sevastopol: M.I. Zolotarev (in Russian).

Zubar, Vitaly. 2009. *A Chronicle of Archaeological Research at Chersonesus-Cherson and Its Environs (1914–2005)*. Simferopol: National Academy of Sciences Ukraine and Demetra (in Russian with English summary).

Zubar Vitaly, and Natalia Son. 2007. *The Northwestern Black Sea Coast in Antiquity*. Simferopol: National Academy of Sciences Ukraine and Demetra (in Russian with English summary).

FURTHER READING

Ivantchik (2005) is a detailed study of Greek colonization of the northern Black Sea, particularly in regard to myths, foundations, and relations with indigenous populations. Blawatskij (1985) is a collection of articles also devoted to the archaeology, history, and culture of the Greek states on the northern coast of the Black Sea. For the west coast of the Black Sea, Danov (1947) is still the basic account for anyone wishing to learn more about the Greeks and their neighbors. This very distinguished author has also written many articles on this question in various other European languages.

From these general overviews, we move to works on specific themes. Kryzhitskij (1993) delves deeply into the architecture of the Greek cities and their territories on the northern Black Sea coast. Buiskikh (2008) complements this with a complete study of the ancient urban planning of Tauric Chersonesus and demonstrates the close links between city planning and the creation of *chora*, including the land division system. Chtcheglov (1992) uses mostly archaeological material in its discussion and complements the previous work with its focus on the *chora* of Tauric Chersonesus. His work contains detailed descriptions of country estates and farms as well as discussing the relations between Chersonesus and the Crimean Scythians. Saprykin (1997) provides a detailed account written in English of the Tauric Chersonesus and its mother city Heraclea Pontica. Topics include its foundation and the impact of the Heraclean state system on the Tauric Chersonesus's institutions, foreign policy, and relations with its neighboring peoples. Gajdukevič (1971) is a full study of the Bosporan Kingdom from the time of Greek colonization to Late Antiquity. It is based on complex analysis of literary, epigraphic, numismatic, and especially archaeological sources. Rostovtzeff (1931) has stood the test of time with its excellent account of all source types for the Bosporan Kingdom and its relations with Scythia and Sarmatia.

On Bactria, the following works are essential for anyone seeking further reading: Litvinskij and Pichikian 2000; Litvinskij 2001; Litvinskij 2010. These works provide a full and detailed publication of the archaeological material from the temple of Oxus set in the context of the region's Hellenization and the impact of local traditions on the Greeks.

CHAPTER SEVEN

Models of Culture Contact and Cultural Change: Moving Beyond National and Linguistic Traditions

Christoph Ulf

Cultural contact and cultural change are not possible without the movement of people and objects. For this reason, it makes good sense to look at the corresponding models that help explain both phenomena also from the perspective of migration (cf. Haug 2000; Massey and Taylor 2004). This has the added advantage that the explanations and rationales for migration explicitly operate with such models. If these models are systematically placed in relation to one another, a background emerges which highlights that the various rationales and explanations for cultural contacts in the ancient world are based on similar, if not the same, models.

Migration Theories

In the oldest serious attempt to arrive at a theory-based understanding of migration, Ernest George Ravenstein (1889) founded his thinking on the very general hypothesis that people wish to improve their material wellbeing. He claimed that this explained why excess populations migrate from underdeveloped to better developed regions. This fundamental assumption was complemented by the idea, among others, that the number of migrants decreased proportionately to the growing geographical distance, therefore making "short journey migration" the most attractive form of migration. Ravenstein also assumed that migration increased as transportation routes and industry became better developed. On the whole, he thought that migration was positive because he equated a lack of migration with stagnation.

A Companion to Greeks Across the Ancient World, First Edition. Edited by Franco De Angelis.
© 2020 John Wiley & Sons, Inc. Published 2020 by John Wiley & Sons, Inc.

Macro Theories

This attempt at explaining migration by the means of population geography contains important concepts that have multifariously shaped the debate right up to the present day. It can barely be separated from the macro-economic approaches, which not only assume the existence of different labor markets, but also assert that economic activity tends to lead to a state of global economic equilibrium. In this model, migration is determined by push and pull factors, which are pivotal in deciding whether or not migration is an option. It is assumed, among other things, that the potential places of destination display different opportunities, which determine how attractive they are to the migrant. These only vaguely definable factors are presumed to have an effective power with reference to the basic classical economic principle of supply and demand and the postulated rational choice actor (cf. Pribram 1986).

Another frequently advocated macro approach is to analyze the interplay between population, organizational structure, technology, environment, and migration. Where the ecological perspective is accentuated, the idea is to establish an equilibrium between the population size and its sustenance organization. In the theory of a world system, the migration of people follows the transfer of goods and capital between capitalistic industrial states and less industrialized countries (Sassen 1991). This assertion is based on the assumption that there is an expanding global market, which breaks down into centers and peripheries. Whereas this theory affirms that pull factors are at work, a different macro model places the emphasis on push factors. According to this model, the motivation for individuals to migrate is triggered by structural and anomic tensions to which social positions are exposed in a social fabric. Migration is seen as a way of relieving such tensions, for example, as a response to an imbalance of power and status.

A recent approach, preferably used in so-called prehistory, refers to new bioarchaeological and biogeoarchaeological methods (stable isotope, DNA, biodistance analyses) to demonstrate that people migrated in the past. There is a tendency to assume that migration was a common fact of life in the past (van Dommelen 2014). From the angle of globalization theories, similar conclusions are drawn (Hodos 2017).

Micro Theories

Whereas the macro concepts attempt to identify laws which apply irrespective of time and space, and to which the actors are subject, micro explanations for migration are based on the decisions of individuals. In micro-economic, neo-classical theory, the individual with his income and his human capital resources is seen as the unit of analysis; migration is seen as investment in human capital. In this calculation, the decision to migrate arises when migration leads to a net gain for the rational actor. Under these conditions, it is reasonable to assert that individuals with different skills and abilities, or even entire households, can also expect different yields in human capital as a consequence of migration and that the psychological and material cost of migration differs for each individual (Boyd 1989). In these cases, migration flows are a consequence of the sum of cost–benefit calculations. Micro-economic approaches of this kind presuppose macro-economic approaches in many respects.

Decision theory models place the individual at the center of analysis much more consistently than the above. Push and pull factors are not considered here as "objective" factors but are subject to the individual ways in which they are perceived by potential migrants (Haug 2008). The resulting evaluations are included in the personal cost–benefit calculation, which can be carried out in accordance with three different modes: purposive-rational mode, traditional mode, short-run hedonistic mode. An important factor in arriving at a decision is how the "utility" of the place of residence as well as the place of destination is assessed. As a consequence, it is assumed that these individual expectations are formed in line with social and cultural norms as well as by individual characteristics such as the willingness to take risks and the ability to adapt, and that they have a serious influence on deciding in favor of or against migration.

The Social and Cultural Context of Migration

This lays bare an obvious shortcoming of the macro models, whose very broadly defined general assumptions are not suited to explaining trends or the dimensions of migration with any degree of accuracy (Radu 2008). The resulting necessity to substantiate these assumptions by including social contexts also means having to forego their claim for universal validity. They must, therefore, be replaced with more nuanced methods of analyzing migrant judgments and expectations that must not be tainted with the postulate of the rational actor from classical economic theory. On the other hand, the explanatory power of such methods of analysis is greatly reduced where the migrants are not embedded in structured contexts.

Offering a path out of this dilemma, a migration system has been developed that regards the migrant's place of origin and place of destination as a social space representing a reality independent of geographical and political frontiers (Faist 1997). The migrating individuals are connected to one another in this space by dynamic and flexible social networks as emigration and immigration networks. The strong or weak personal relationships within these networks consequentially lead to phenomena such as chain migration or circular migration (Boyd 1989).

Recently, a tendency can be observed to replace migration by mobility including any form of human movement or travel. Therefore, the stress is on connectivity and the ensuing various kinds of (cultural, social, political, etc.) interactions (van Dommelen and Knapp 2010; Gill, Caletrio, and Mason 2011; Mac Sweeney 2016).

Migrants and their Motivations

Since cultural contacts in the ancient world are mostly considered from the point of view of migration, it is no coincidence that the explanations for migration swing back and forth between macro and micro approaches. The models used here fail to systematically assess the migrants' social and cultural context. Accordingly, the following will place the population groups side by side that have been distinguished as groups of migrants in the past. They are characterized by social status, their motivations, and their mobility behavior (Table 7.1).

Table 7.1 A summary of the motivations of migrants according to their social status.

Social status	Motivations	Movers
Elite(s)	Satisfying interests in the sociopolitical network	Intermittently mobile people moving to a limited extent
Outsiders, exiles/refugees, mercenaries	Search for physical, social, or economic security	People forced into mobility
Captives, slaves	Coercion	People forced to stay in one place
Itinerant diviners, wandering poets	Search for non-material benefit	People whose mobility is intrinsically motivated
Craftsmen, merchants	Search for benefits in the economic network	People whose mobility is motivated by economic factors
Itinerant craftsmen	Search for economic benefits	People motivated into intermittent mobility
Settlers	Search for economic and social benefits	People determined to change location

The motives of these groups of people not only differ for individual reasons but clearly also because of their different social, political, and economic contexts. The anthropological typing of societies (egalitarian societies, big-man societies, chiefdoms, city-states, monarchies) certainly delivers more strongly differentiated results in terms of characterization than is expressed by the frequently and solely used simple distinction between *polis* and *ethnos*. It has a direct or indirect bearing on the following brief descriptions of the different migrant groups.

Elite(s)

The anthropological theory that preindustrial societies were largely governed by the principles of a gift-giving economy is decisive for the idea that elites in the Mediterranean exchanged with one an other within the framework of a "peer polity" (Renfrew and Cherry 1987). The motives for people and objects to move are not (primarily) driven by an interest in trade, but by the necessity to preserve their social status by displaying prestige goods. It is important, however, to ensure that this principle is not simply generalized. The existence of different – and from a diachronic point of view – unstable exchange systems can be assumed. The networks often cited as being the basis for the exchange of goods (and people), therefore, need to be characterized more closely in each individual case; they should not under any circumstances be equated with mere trade networks (Malkin 2011).

Outsiders, Exiles/Refugees, and Mercenaries

Those people often cited in the sources who have no alternative than to leave their own sociopolitical community have a completely different social status. As far as the information available suggests, they are generally members of the elite who have to leave their place of origin for various reasons. The reasons for migrating may include forced flight, bowing together with a group of supporters to social pressure triggered by internal strife, or the (strategically) planned dismissal of a section of the developing state community. The motives of mercenaries differ from those of outsiders and refugees in that the former can determine the location and the duration of their stay at the place of destination (Haider 1996). Potential mercenaries are not, however, simply drawn to foreign climes by the potential financial gain but feel forced for different reasons to leave their place of residence.

A conflict theory which takes into account the different societies and their specific internal conflict zones would be helpful in analyzing and explaining the correlations in both cases (e.g., Coser 1965).

Captives and Slaves

Captives fall into their own separate group of migrants and differ from other forms of migration in that they have been denied the freedom to choose whether they wish to migrate; they are forced to live in a foreign place of residence. There is considerable evidence of captives in the monarchies bordering on the eastern and southeastern Mediterranean (e.g., Rollinger 2011). In terms of freedom of choice, slaves are assessed in a similar way to captives and were in evidence in large numbers in the space occupied by the Greeks. Both groups of people lose their former social status through war.

Itinerant Diviners and Wandering Poets

Walter Burkert (1983) identified the special kind of migrant who wanders from place to place as a diviner or magician, with the intention of spreading the religious ideas developed in the cultural contexts on the edge of the eastern Mediterranean (Rollinger 1996, 202–210). This group of people can be compared to wandering poets, who migrate in a limited "internal" wandering and stay in their places of destination, for example, at musical contests in funeral games, for a limited amount of time (Hunter and Rutherford 2009).

It can be assumed that pull factors are in evidence in that, equipped with their spectrum of ideas constituting an order, they react to a (religious) need that must have been in existence in the various societies in the (eastern part of the) Mediterranean.

Craftsmen and Merchants

The motives for engaging in trade are generally explained by the human need to improve one's economic situation. In terms of the motives for engaging in long-distance trade, this general assumption only gains significance if the economies characterizing each society are taken into consideration. In this context, it is necessary to determine the relationship between trade and the crafts, as well as the social status held by traders (Raaflaub 2004). It can generally be assumed that, in their role as producers, craftsmen were bound to a single location. The amount of time traders would stay in one place of residence varied but did not necessarily mean that they were integrated within the local population.

They alternate in relatively short intervals between cultural spaces and are thus predestined to develop their own behavioral patterns, including double and multiple identities.

Assuming they existed (Morgan 2009, 50), the itinerant craftsmen also form their own group of migrants. They decide to migrate of their own free will, based on the information available to them. Much the same applies to the choice and duration of residence. Their situation possibly corresponds most closely to a diaspora (Cohen 2004).

Settlers

The search for an – economically – improved lifestyle in a "new world" is a fundamental motivation for traders and settlers alike to migrate. The extent to which the migration of settlers can be regarded as a planned action is debatable. In order to find a solution to the undeniable logistical problems, the idea has frequently been raised that Delphi functioned as a kind of migration agency or "the headquarters of a colonial network" (Descoeudres 2008, 293–294). Since it is not possible to prove that there was an excess population as a trigger for migration (Scheidel 2013), a planning set-up of this kind is equally controversial. The main reason for this lies in the evidence that the concept of Greek "colonies" was greatly colored by the (alleged) analogy of colonialism in the era of European imperialism (De Angelis 1998; Dietler 2010; Mauersberg 2019).

This brief outline of the types of migrants in evidence in the ancient Mediterranean world shows that all rationales explaining why individuals migrate require – either implicitly or explicitly – models or exemplary assumptions. It is asserted that the principles of a gift-giving economy should be applied on the one hand, with the axiom of classical economic theory based on supply and demand appearing on the other. In addition, social, political, religious, and ideational motives are, likewise, listed as triggers for migration (Tsetskhladze 2006). The parallelism of these models gives rise to contradictions, which can partially be resolved when the migrants' sociopolitical context is considered. It cannot, however, be ignored that the models are based on the migrants and that the place of destination only comes into view rudimentarily from the angle of place utility. Moreover, it is not until the local population is included in the rationale that convincing models can be created to describe cultural contact.

The Relationship between Migrants and Local Populations

For a long time, the belief in a kind of automatic cultural diffusionism and associated cultural drift blocked from view the need to analyze the relationship between "colonialists" and "indigenous" populations (De Angelis 2013). This clearly simplifying macro concept was justified by the fact that the few Greek terms for the settlements created by migrants likewise reflect merely the migrant perspective. To show a pathway out of the ensuing debate over the definition of colony and colonialism (Lyons and Papadopoulos 2002), Franco De Angelis (2009) proposed choosing "*apoikia*" from the available ancient terms, whilst suggesting "apoikiazation" to describe the process of migration. This term can be easily linked to the concept of decision theory, according to which place utility fundamentally influences the decision to migrate. It does, however, once again place the migrant perspective at the center of attention as does the model of center and periphery.

This is not the case with the Mediterranean concept. Here, the assumption is that the Mediterranean forms a unit (the Black Sea is largely ignored). Accordingly, it forms a (natural) framework within which processes of exchange almost automatically arise from geographical realities. This model not only fails to define the edges or borders of the Mediterranean region and their connection to the "outside" world, but it represents yet another macro model that does not take into account the nuanced views of the actors in the Mediterranean region (Harris 2005). By contrast, attempts at isolating regional and local conditions in their relation to specifically definable "global" fields (Hales and Hodos 2010) come considerably closer to achieving this goal. This is because the attempt is also made to take into account the recipients of foreign people, objects, and ideas at the place of destination. The evidence of mixed settlements and so-called *enoikismoi* (single persons or small groups of foreigners living within a settlement) provides the context for an explanation of how migrants and local population first came in contact with one another.

Again, it is striking that these attempts do not turn explicitly to the tools of social psychology to make substantiated assumptions about the completely non-uniform expectations of migrants and their recipients (Brewer 2003). This is why this chapter proposes to take into account the psychologically often difficult situation that arises from contact between migrants and local populations when describing the relationship between both groups (Table 7.2).

Due to the "Greek" perspective, which dominated research for a long time, the actors were presumed to be mostly autonomous (Greek) individuals who judged foreignness and foreigners through the lens of their own interests and needs. The repercussions of encountering "otherness" on one's self-image subsequently came into view (Cartledge 1993).

Table 7.2 A summary of the different perceptions of migrants and their transferred items.

Migrants	*Perception of the migrants*	*Perception of the transferred items*
Members of the elite(s) and/or followers	Respected persons; short-term stay	Foreign prestige goods
Outsiders, exiles/refugees, Mercenaries	Accepted, but dependent persons; medium-term or long-term stay	Accepted, but dependent persons
Captives, slaves	Dependent persons; short-term to life-long stay	Persons/"commodities"
Itinerant diviners, wandering poets	Accepted outsiders; short-term stay	Tolerated/accepted foreign ideas
Craftsmen, merchants	Accepted foreigners; short-term to medium-term stay	Foreign purchased commodities
Itinerant craftsmen	Accepted foreigners; medium-term stay	Locally produced commodities
Settlers	Foreigners/enemies; life-long stay	Locally produced and transferred goods and commodities

It was the analysis of the effects of the real-life experience of foreignness before and after the Persian wars, however – characterized by a blend of rejection, admiration, and various forms of creative adoption – that finally kindled an appreciation of the complexity of the relationships between migrants and recipients, albeit still from the Greek perspective (Miller 1997).

In the context of these processes of perceiving foreignness, the "traveling concepts" have not yet been considered (Neumann and Nünning 2012). In this model, it is assumed that cultural thought patterns in the broadest sense, serving to provide orientation in one's own environment, constitute objects that are taken on by other persons or groups and can wander on their own. Even though these objects are admittedly exposed to changes on their wanderings, there is an insistence that they have to a certain extent an independent existence (Appadurai 1988).

In its tendency to emphasize the meaning of the object, the actor–network theory is not too far removed from the model of traveling concepts (Latour 2005). In this theory the objects tend to become actors themselves. If this attempt seems over the top, it should be remembered that in many cases actors do not make rational decisions but only react to influences that can also emanate from (new) objects. By the term and concept of agency, it is considered how big the leeway for actors in a certain historical situation can be.

Both concepts emanate from the idea that the meaning of objects and ideas changes as they are transferred from one cultural space to another. The moment one disposes of an object, the producer/owner loses the interpretative sovereignty over it (Crielaard, Stissi, and van Wijngaarden 1999). By considering the thus visible, unintended, und uncontrollable processes involved in the perception of objects, ideas, and people, it becomes apparent that the perception of migrants by the recipient, but also the perception of the recipients by the migrants, (can) continually change in these processes through mutual contact (Yntema 2000).

However, because of its micro approach, this method fails to identify whether the cited changes in meaning are also subject to certain conditions. This is where the model of contact zones comes in (Pratt 2008). It is assumed that besides the sociopolitical and cultural situation of the migrants and the local population, the relationship between the two must also be borne in mind. With the help of the criterion of power, this approach leads to a distinction between different zones of contact, not as physical but as sociopolitical spaces (Table 7.3; cf. Ulf 2009; Rollinger and Schnegg 2013).

Table 7.3 A summary of the different types of contact zones and their power features.

Types of contact zones	
Open Contact Zones: Distant relationship	**Contact Zones of Intense Contact**: Close relationship Contact zones with little use of power Middle Ground with latent asymmetrical power relations Contact zones with open use of power

The Open Contact Zone differs from the Zones of Intense Contact in the geographical distance between the contact partners. They are so far apart that they do not have to come into direct contact with one another. The connection between them is usually created by transmitters (merchants, itinerant craftsmen, gateway communities), but can also arise through short-term contact between members of the elite within the framework of a gift-giving economy. An important factor here is that it is impossible to usurp any form of power over the partner. Similarly, the transmitters can only be exposed to a limited amount of pressure, if the relationship between the partners is not to be jeopardized. The transregional festive locations (interregional sanctuaries) can be regarded as a special kind of open contact zone (Freitag and Haake 2019), where people of different origins can meet. These zones of time-limited encounters and cultural exchange are not burdened by power or any form of dependence. The transferred objects are completely adapted to the functional context of their new cultural space (Morgan 2009, 57–59).

In Zones of Intense Contact, the partners are in direct and personal contact with one other. The encounters in these contact zones are never completely free from attempts at exerting power over the respective partner.

In contact zones with little use of power, economic, ideological, and social dependence is defined by the specific interests of the partners. It generally involves obtaining coveted goods and products or metals that are in short supply in one's own region (critical of the demand for metals: Descoeudres 2008, 304–308). In terms of migration, one should think here of the situation of resident craftsmen or mercenaries, but also traders who engage in exchanges with the local population in the *emporia*. Their situation, their behavior, and the way in which they are judged by the local population is comparable to the situation faced by a diaspora community.

In the Middle Ground, which was identified by Richard White (1991) using the relationship between the Algonquin and the French in the late seventeenth century around the Great Lakes in Canada, the French were clearly the superior military force. Even so, using force toward the Algonquin would have damaged their common interests, which consisted in resisting the Hurons and engaging in the fur trade. To use the terminology from decision theory, it could be said that the relationship between both contact partners was defined by a cost–benefit calculation in the purposive rational mode. This explains why the relationship between the parties was frequently characterized by a targeted "mutual misunderstanding" that served their own interests.

In zones with open use of power, the exercising of coercive power in conjunction with the open use of violence is a normal tool for securing the dependence of "partners." How much and the kind of violence used is solely determined by the resulting cost. The relationship between the Greeks and local populations is likely to have frequently displayed such characteristics or at least assumed them in the course of time (Dougherty 2003). All forms of a port of trade likewise lead into relationships of this kind. The extent of violence used certainly appears to have a direct influence on the way in which foreign goods and ideas are received (Ulf 2009, 105–122).

The contact zone model foregoes macro models that, like classical economic theory, lay claim to general validity. It does, however, bring less prevalent macro models together with micro approaches. By applying power theory and social psychology, it is possible to set apart from one another social spaces of different sizes which can exist independently of and in parallel with one another within geographical spaces. This allows a nuanced and accurate description of local circumstances, in which contact partners appear as actors who act within the framework of prevailing power-political and cultural rules.

Culture, Cultural Contact, and Cultural Change

The path from the macro and micro models of migration research to the diverse factors that shape people's decisions to migrate and the complex relationship between migrants and local populations must also lead to the question of how migration and reception influence the cultural self-image of these two groups of people (Hall 2004; Kistler and Ulf 2012).

In this context, culture is not considered an area of values that can be separated from the everyday world; it is more a question of whether or to what extent culture represents a unit in its own right. An achievement of postcolonial studies was to point out that cultures are in a constant state of flux, and to give evidence of how open and permeable their boundaries are. This hardly disputable finding is the result of an analysis that approaches the object from the "outside."

Irrespective of this move to qualify culture as a distinct entity, which from an "etic" perspective is certainly justified and understandable, the fact remains that individuals, that is, taking an "emic" view, generally feel that they belong to a specific "culture" which they see as being clearly definable. The need to have a sense of belonging to such distinct units can be explained from a social psychological point of view by the individual need for security.

Figuration

What at first glance appears to be a contradiction can be clearly explained with the aid of the figuration concept, as this creates the necessary link between the micro and the macro perspective. Norbert Elias (2012) defined figuration as the interdependencies of the actions carried out between individuals, which develop into a pattern through repetition. This is easier to comprehend if the possible interdependencies are ordered with the help of four parameters (Figure 7.1; cf. Kistler and Ulf 2012, 34–55).

The model clearly shows that every change to any of the parameters has a direct influence on the actor. The question is how the changes in the parameters come about. From the individual point of view, such change arises from two factors in particular: changes in time and changes in space. In the course of a lifetime, every individual changes and also leaves his social space. The latter also occurs even if the location does not change because spaces are likewise exposed to change. Major changes naturally occur as a result of movement through space in the form of migration. Conversely, the introduction of new elements from the outside triggers changes to the parameters. For this reason, the reception of foreign goods and ideas causes the figuration to regroup.

Consumption

Dealing with the "new" need not explicitly find expression in the emic definition of what is considered one's own culture; individuals do not necessarily estimate the "new" to cause change in their own culture. In comparison, such changes are clearly discernible

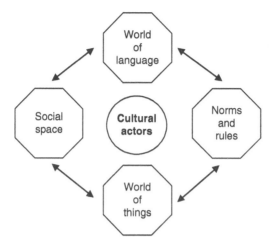

Figure 7.1 Four possible interdependent parameters and their influences on cultural actors.

from the etic perspective because influences of this kind entail changes to lifestyle. An important way of analyzing such changes is offered by the concept of consumption (Featherstone 2004).

This concept once again links up macro and micro perspectives. The fundamental theory states that consumption consists not only in the use and consumption of material goods but also in the reception, processing, and utilization of cultural information (Gabriel and Lang 2010). Consumption is thus directly linked to the parameters that define a figuration, and therefore also to lifestyle. It is fair to assume that ancient societies, like modern ones, accommodated a certain spectrum of individual types of consumption (Ulf 2014; Kistler et al. 2015). Under this premise, the consumption model gives the possibility of choice (agency) back to the consumer, which from the point of view of macro-economics is generally denied.

By passing through cultural spaces, as occurs in migration, the consumers become cultural actors who make selections from the consumption opportunities open to them based on their own perspectives (Wiskermann and Nieberding 2004, 26).

This mechanism still applies when a counter-position to the dominating norms and expectations is assumed by consciously deviating from "normal" consumer behavior (Heimerdinger, Kistler, and Hochhauser 2013). How much room for deviation there is depends on the prevailing social conditions. The network model, which is being used with greater frequency, represents a viable means of demarcating the boundaries of this leeway.

Network

In the social network model individual actors form the nodes in the network; they are connected to the other actors by edges or ties (Wassermann and Faust 1999; Scott 2011). The ties between the actors do not form coincidentally, but are established selectively and in accordance with principles that steer the network. The actors are not distributed homogeneously either, but often form clusters. The contacts between the actors do not generally display the same intensity and frequency either. Frequently used contacts can also be shortcuts which, in the scheme of the network, means that individual nodes are skipped so that direct contact can be made with the desired partner, called the "small world effect" (Malkin 2011).

In the case of this model, a network is endowed with a decentralized structure. The shortcuts subvert the equality of the actors and can create a more or less well defined hierarchy. After all, the actors connected by shortcuts have better access to the material and immaterial resources due to the higher efficiency of their connections in the network. Thus they achieve a higher status, and this can break down a network if the inequality of the actors brings about its centralization.

Since the information about the past is always fragmentary, it seems more expedient to categorize historical networks with the help of a handful of main features. This notion is supported by the distinction made by Granovetter (1973, 1983) between different kinds of ties. He distinguishes between strong ties and weak ties. Strong ties, frequently used, close ties between actors and reinforce their common identity while, however, reducing the willingness to enter into new connections. The actors connected through weak ties display less social commitment to one another but are open to new ties and thus also interested in receiving new information. These nodes are the "bridges" and/or "structural holes" that connect a network to the outside world (Burt 1992). Actors in such positions in the network have to be flexible, adapt cognitively to new conditions on an ongoing basis, and be willing and able to cope in different contexts.

Cultural Change

Analyzing the motives that prompt people to migrate has shown that economic networks do not have their own inner life, but form part of sociopolitical and cultural networks. The appearance of the networks depends on the kind of societies involved and the social status of the migrants. Significant factors for characterizing the relationship between the migrants and the local population include the migrants' duration of residence, the possible ways in which foreignness can be perceived, and the different types of contact zones. All these factors influence the appearance of a figuration in which every individual is embedded.

If cultural contacts are considered as movements within different migration systems, in which people have different motives (social, economic, political) for migrating and which are defined by various conditions (sociopolitical contexts, social status, figuration, network), then the distinction needed to characterize networks of strong and weak ties can also be applied when describing the process of cultural change. It can, therefore, be purported that cultural change is triggered either by the changes within "a culture" itself or by external influences.

Assuming that societies are made up of different networks (Ulf 2009, 101–103), the weak ties function as bridges between these networks. The existence of counter-cultures is a clear indication of this. After all, counter-cultures seldom aim to destroy the existing social system, but exist in different forms of subcultures, as well as in concepts and discourses, that aim to relativize and thus also change the dominant norms in their historical confinement (Heimerdinger et al. 2013). Societies that attempt to suppress the various discourses as far as possible close down the flow of new information, much in the same way as networks with strong ties. Conversely, similar to the network with weak ties, societies that permit contradicting discourses and counter-cultural behavior display the necessary flexibility to actively handle and cope with unavoidable changes. In this case, the counter-culture is not deemed to interfere with the balance of a society, but is seen as an opportunity to use the new information to release the creativity needed to overcome unprecedented difficulties. The consequences are a change in the perception and reception of what was previously rejected, a new dominant form of consumption, and the acceptance of a new (hybrid) lifestyle.

The same can be observed in the behavior of societies. This is made quite clear by the easily recognizable relationship between network theory and the contact zone model (Ulf 2009, 102–122). It is easy to see that networks with weak ties and an intensive reception of information conflict with the rejection of foreignness that exists in intense contact zones which, in turn, correlates with a strong self-identity, that is, with networks with strong ties. Cultural change is fundamentally rejected here; however, this does not mean that it does not occur, even subtly. Conversely, networks with weak ties in intense contact zones with little use of power or in the middle ground also have their place. Here, the actors have the opportunity to add new information to their own knowledge but also to use this knowledge. This situation has an undeniable influence on the consumption behavior of the actors in these social spaces, or in other words: it not only allows but even accelerates cultural change (cf. Archibald 2013).

Societies that are flexible in this way and are open to cultural change are, like flexible networks, well equipped to deal with the appearance of new conditions, because they are endowed with a particularly high creative potential (Mathis-Moser and Mertz-Baumgartner 2012). To exaggerate somewhat, it could be said that the readiness to accept cultural changes represents a survival principle. The necessity of cultural change is only ignored where an exclusive identity is to be maintained for ideological and power-political reasons. The justification for this is derived from the claim that there are essential cultural units which, in reality, largely are reifications.

REFERENCES

Appadurai, Arjun, ed. 1988. *The Social Life of Things: Commodities in Cultural Perspective.* Cambridge: Cambridge University Press.

Archibald, Zofia H. 2013. "Innovation and the Transmission of Knowledge in Antiquity: A Look at Current Network Models." In *Regionalism and Globalism in Antiquity: Exploring Their Limits*, edited by Franco De Angelis, 23–39. Leuven: Peeters.

Boyd, Monica. 1989. "Family and Personal Networks in International Migration: Recent Developments and New Agendas." *International Migration Review*, 23(3): 638–670.

Brewer, Marilynn B. 2003. *Intergroup Relations*, 2nd ed. Buckingham: Open University Press.

Burkert, Walter. 1983. "Itinerant Diviners and Magicians: A Neglected Element in Cultural Contacts." In *The Greek Renaissance of the Eighth Century B.C. Tradition and Innovation*, edited by Thomas Hägg, 115–119. Stockholm: Swedish Institute in Athens.

Burt, Ronald S. 1992. *Structural Holes: The Social Structure of Competition*. Cambridge, MA: Harvard University Press.

Cartledge, Paul A. 1993. *The Greek: A Portrait of Self and the Others*. Oxford: University Press.

Cohen, Robin. 2004. *Global Diasporas: An Introduction*. Abingdon: Routledge.

Coser, Lewis. 1965. *The Functions of Social Conflict*. London: Routledge.

Crielaard, Jan Paul, Vladimir Stissi, and Gert Jan van Wijngaarden, eds. 1999. *The Complex Past of Pottery: Production, Circulation and Consumption of Mycenaean and Greek Pottery. Sixteenth to Early Fifth Centuries BC*. Amsterdam: Gieben.

De Angelis, Franco. 1998. "Ancient Past, Imperial Present: The British Empire in T.J. Dunbabin's *The Western Greeks*." *Antiquity*, 72: 539–549.

De Angelis, Franco. 2009. "Colonies and Colonization." In *The Oxford Handbook of Hellenic Studies*, edited by George Boys-Stone, Barbara Graziosi, and Phiroze Vasunia, 48–64. Oxford: Oxford University Press.

De Angelis, Franco. 2013. "Introduction: Approaches to the Movement of Ancient Phenomena Through Time and Space." In *Regionalism and Globalism in Antiquity: Exploring Their Limits*, edited by Franco De Angelis, 1–12. Leuven: Peeters.

Descoeudres, Jean-Paul. 2008. "Central Greece on the Eve of the Colonisation Movement." In *Greek Colonisation: An Account of Greek Colonies and Other Settlements Overseas*, vol. 2, edited by Gocha R. Tsetskhladze, 289–382. Leiden: Brill.

Dietler, Michael. 2010. *Archaeologies of Colonialism: Consumption, Entanglement, and Violence in Ancient Mediterranean France*. Berkeley: University of California Press.

Dougherty, Carol. 2003. "The Aristonothos Krater: Competing Stories of Conflict and Collaboration." In *The Cultures within Ancient Greek Culture: Contact, Conflict, Collaboration*, edited by Carol Dougherty and Leslie Kurke, 35–56. Cambridge: Cambridge University Press.

Elias, Norbert. 2012. *What is Sociology?* Dublin: University College Dublin Press.

Faist, Thomas. 1997. "From Common Questions to Common Concepts." In *International Migration, Immobility and Development*, edited by Tomas Hammar, Grete Brochmann, Kristof Tamas, and Thomas Faist, 247–276. Oxford: Berg.

Featherstone, Mike. 2004. *Consumer Culture and Postmodernism*. London: SAGE.

Freitag, Klaus, and Matthias Haake, eds. 2019. *Griechische Heiligtümer als Handlungsorte. Zur Multifunktionalität supralokaler Heiligtümer von der frühen Archaik bis in die römische Kaiserzeit*. Stuttgart: Steiner.

Gabriel, Yiannis, and Tim Lang. 2010. *The Unmangeable Consumer*, 2nd ed. Thousand Oaks: SAGE.

Gill, Nick, Javier Caletrio, and Victoria Mason. 2011. "Introduction: Mobilities and Forced Migration." *Mobilities*, 6: 301–316.

Granovetter, Mark. 1973. "The Strength of Weak Ties." *American Journal of Sociology*, 78(6): 1360–1380.

Granovetter, Mark. 1983. "The Strength of Weak Ties: A Network Theory Revisited." *Sociological Theory*, 1: 201–233.

Haider, Peter W. 1996. "Griechen im Vorderen Orient und in Ägypten bis ca. 590 v. Chr." In *Wege zur Genese griechischer Identität. Die Bedeutung der frühcharchaischen Zeit*, edited by Christoph Ulf, 59–115. Berlin: Akademie Verlag.

Hales, Shelley, and Tamar Hodos, eds. 2010. *Material Culture and Social Identities in the Ancient World*. Cambridge: Cambridge University Press.

Hall, Jonathan. 2004. "Culture, Cultures and Acculturation." In *Griechische Archaik. Interne Entwicklungen – Externe Impulse*, edited by Robert Rollinger and Christoph Ulf, 35–50. Berlin: Akademie Verlag.

Harris, William V., ed. 2005. *Rethinking the Mediterranean*. Oxford: Oxford University Press.

Haug, Sonja. 2000. Klassische und neuere Theorien der Migration. Arbeitspapiere/Working Papers: Mannheimer Zentrum für Europäische Sozialforschung, 30. Mannheim: MZES.

Haug, Sonja. 2008. "Migration, Networks and Migration Decision-making." *Journal of Ethnic and Migration Studies*, 34(4): 585–605.

Heimerdinger, Timo, Erich Kistler, and Eva-Maria Hochhauser, eds. 2013. *Gegenkultur. Cultural Encounters and Transfers*, vol. 2. Würzburg: Königshausen & Neumann.

Hodos, Tamar, ed. 2017. *The Routledge Handbook of Archaeology and Globalization*. London: Routledge.

Hunter, Richard, and Ian Rutherford, eds. 2009. *Wandering Poets in Ancient Greek Culture: Travel, Locality and Pan-Hellenism*. Cambridge: Cambridge University Press.

Kistler, Erich, and Christoph Ulf. 2012. "Kulturelle Akteurinnen und Akteure – Die emische Konstruktion von Kultur und ihre Folgen." In *Kulturelle Akteure. Cultural Encounters and Transfers*, vol. 1, edited by Christoph Ulf and Eva-Maria Hochhauser, 21–69. Würzburg: Königshausen & Neumann.

Kistler, Erich, Birgit Öhlinger, Martin Mohr, and Matthias Hoernes, eds. 2015. *Sanctuaries and the Power of Consumption. Networking and the Formation of Elites in the Archaic Western Mediterranean World*. Wiesbaden: Harrassowitz.

Latour, Bruno. 2005. *Reassembling the Social: An Introduction to Actor-Network-Theory*. Oxford: Oxford University Press.

Lyons, Claire L., and John K. Papadopoulos, eds. 2002. *The Archaeology of Colonialism*. Los Angeles: Getty Publications.

Mac Sweeney, Naoíse. 2016. "Anatolian–Aegean Interactions in the Early Iron Age: Migration, Mobility, and the Movement of People." In *Of Odysseys and Oddities. Scales and Modes of Interaction between Prehistoric Aegean Societies and their Neighbours*, edited by Barry C. Molloy: 411–433. Oxford: Oxbow.

Malkin, Irad. 2011. *A Small Greek World: Networks in the Ancient Mediterranean*. Oxford: Oxford University Press.

Massey, Douglas S., and Edward J. Taylor. 2004. *International Migration: Prospects and Politics in a Global Market*. Oxford: Oxford University Press.

Mathis-Moser, Ursula, and Birgit Mertz-Baumgartner, eds. 2012. *Passages et ancrages en France. Dictionnaire des écrivains migrants de langue française (1981–2011)*. Paris: Honoré Champion.

Mauersberg, Martin. 2019. *Die "griechische" Kolonisation. Ihr Bild in der Antike und der modernen altertumswissenschaftlichen Forschung*. Frankfurt: Campus Verlag.

Miller, Margaret C. 1997. *Athens and Persia in the Fifth Century BC: A Study in Cultural Receptivity*. Cambridge: Cambridge University Press.

Morgan, Catherine. 2009. "The Early Iron Age." In *A Companion to Archaic Greece*, edited by Kurt A. Raaflaub and Hans van Wees, 43–63. Chichester: Wiley Blackwell.

Neumann Birgit, and Ansgar Nünning, eds. 2012. *Travelling Concepts for the Study of Culture*. Berlin: de Gruyter.

Pratt, Mary Louise. 2008. *Imperial Eyes: Travel Writing and Transculturation*, 2nd ed. Abingdon: Routledge.

Pribram, Karl. 1986. *A History of Economic Reasoning*. Baltimore: Johns Hopkins University Press.

Radu, Dragos. 2008. "Social Interactions in Economic Models of Migration: A Review and Appraisal." *Journal of Ethnic and Migration Studies*, 34(4): 531–548.

Raaflaub, Kurt A. 2004. "Archaic Greek Aristocrats as Carriers of Cultural Interaction." In *Commerce and Monetary Systems in the Ancient World: Means of Transmission and Cultural Interaction*, edited by Robert Rollinger and Christoph Ulf, 197–217. Stuttgart: Steiner.

Ravenstein, Ernest G. 1889. "The Laws of Migration: Second Paper." *Journal of the Royal Statistical Society*, 52: 241–301.

Renfrew, Colin, and John F. Cherry, eds. 1987. *Peer Polity Interaction and Socio-Political Change*. Cambridge: Cambridge University Press.

Rollinger, Robert. 1996. "Altorientalische Motivik in der frühgriechischen Literatur am Beispiel der homerischen Epen." In *Wege zur Genese griechischer Identität. Die Bedeutung der früharchaischen Zeit*, edited by Christoph Ulf, 156–210. Berlin: Akademie Verlag.

Rollinger, Robert. 2011. "Der Blick aus dem Osten: 'Griechen' in vorderasiatischen Quellen des 8. und 7. Jahrhunderts v. Chr. – eine Zusammenschau." In *Der Orient und die Anfänge Europas*, edited by Hartmut Matthäus, Norbert Oettinger, and Stephan Schröder, 265–281. Wiesbaden: Harrassowitz.

Rollinger, Robert, and Kordula Schnegg, eds. 2013. *Kulturkontakte in alten Welten: Vom Denkmodell zum Fallbeispiel*. Colloquia Antiqua 10. Leuven: Peeters.

Sassen, Saskia. 1991. *The Global City: New York, London, Tokyo*. Princeton: Princeton University Press.

Scheidel, Walter. 2013. "Demography." In *The Cambridge Economic History of the Greco-Roman World*, edited by Walter Scheidel, Ian Morris, and Richard P. Saller, 38–86. Cambridge: Cambridge University Press.

Scott, John. 2011. *Social Network Analysis: A Handbook*, 2nd ed. London: SAGE.

Tsetskhladze, Gocha R. 2006. "Revisiting Ancient Greek Colonization." In *Greek Colonisation: An Account of Greek Colonies and Other Settlements Overseas*, vol. 1, edited by Gocha R. Tsetskhladze: xxiii–lxxxiii. Leiden: Brill.

Ulf, Christoph. 2009. "Rethinking Cultural Contacts." *Ancient West & East*, 8: 81–132.

Ulf, Christoph. 2014. "Formen von Konsumption, Lebensstilen und Öffentlichkeiten von Homer bis Theognis." *Klio*, 96: 416–436.

van Dommelen, Peter. 2014. "Moving On: Archaeological Perspectives on Mobility and Migration." *World Archaeology*, 46: 477–483.

van Dommelen, Peter, and A. Bernard Knapp, eds. 2010. *Material Connections in the Ancient Mediterranean: Mobility, Materiality and Mediterranean Identities*. Abingdon: Routledge.

Wassermann, Stanley, and Katherine Faust. 1999. *Social Network Analysis: Methods and Applications*. Cambridge: Cambridge University Press.

White, Richard. 1991. *The Middle Ground. Indians, Empires, and Republics in the Great Lake Region, 1650–1815*. Cambridge: Cambridge University Press.

Wiskermann, Clemens, and Anne Nieberding, eds. 2004. *Die institutionelle Revolution. Eine Einführung in die deutsche Wirtschaftsgeschichte des 19. und frühen 20. Jahrhunderts*. Stuttgart: Steiner.

Yntema, Douwe. 2000. "Mental Landscapes of Colonization: The Ancient Written Sources and the Archaeology of Early Colonial-Greek Southeastern Italy." *BABesch. Annual Papers in Mediterranean Archaeology*, 75: 1–49.

FURTHER READING

De Angelis, Franco, ed. 2013. *Regionalism and Globalism in Antiquity: Exploring their Limits*. Colloquia Antiqua 7. Leuven: Peeters.

Dietler, Michael, and Carolina López-Ruiz, eds. 2009. *Colonial Encounters in Ancient Iberia: Phoenician, Greek and Indigenous Relations*. Chicago: Chicago University Press.

Malkin, Irad. 2011. *A Small Greek World: Networks in the Ancient Mediterranean*. Oxford: Oxford University Press.

Malkin, Irad, Christy Constantakopoulou, and Katerina Panagopoulou, eds. 2009. *Greek and Roman Networks in the Mediterranean*. Abingdon: Routledge.

Raaflaub, Kurt A., and Hans van Wees, eds. 2009. *A Companion to Archaic Greece*. Chichester: Wiley Blackwell.

Ulf, Christoph. 2009. "Rethinking Cultural Contacts." *Ancient West & East*, 8: 81–132.

Ulf, Christoph. 2020. "What Motivated People to Leave their Community According to the Texts of Archaic Greece." In *Connecting the Ancient World West and East*, edited by John Boardman, James Hargrave, Alexandru Avram, and Alexander Podossinov. Leuven: Peeters (forthcoming).

PART II
REGIONAL CASE STUDIES

CHAPTER EIGHT

Phoenicians and Greeks as Comparable Contemporary Migrant Groups

Brien K. Garnand

Few sources survive regarding Greek overseas ventures during the Archaic age, set down centuries after the events they describe. Regarding Phoenician expansion, our evidence is even more tenuous – we lack any mention of their own settlement history written in their own language, so we must rely on the fleeting attention of outsiders writing in Greek, Latin, Hebrew, and so on. We also lack archaeological evidence, since key cities have been poorly excavated or now lay concealed under later ancient occupation levels and modern buildings. We lack satisfactory answers about how Phoenicians conceived of their common identity, who initiated their colonial expansion and when, how they conceived of their cities, how they interacted with indigenes, and so on. This lack of evidence has been used to demonstrate how Phoenician settlements themselves somehow lacked rational urbanism. Thus our interpretation of Phoenician overseas expansion rests as much upon the methods used to extrapolate from limited evidence as it does upon the evidence itself. Instead of setting better-known Greek examples against the lesser-known Phoenician ones and emphasizing their dissimilarities, here our extrapolation depends upon analogy and comparison of settlement types and expansion patterns.

Classical scholars rarely take the entirety of the Mediterranean as their unit of analysis, with the era of colonial expansion a clear exception. From the eighth through the fifth centuries BCE, metropolitan Greeks sent out settlers from the Aegean and established independent settlements on land that they had seized; these sites became points of diffusion for Greek goods, alphabetic literacy, and urbanism (see Hodos, Chapter 22, this volume). They conceived of their habitable world as lying between the Pillars of Heracles and the River Phasis, and they settled along the sea like ants or frogs about a pond, along with "many other groups in many other such regions" (Plat. *Phaed.* 109B, cf. Cic. *Rep.* 2.9; Malkin 2011, 15). Classical scholars have focused primarily on the Greeks to the exclusion of other groups settled along the narrow coastal plain, leading them to ignore, downplay, or even erase the cultural contributions of the Phoenicians, although their alphabetic script, trade networks, and urban expansion (even beyond the Pillars) held precedence. When standard textbooks contrast these achievements with those of the Greeks, they reduce the Phoenician alphabet to non-vocalic signs, their trade to the exchange of baubles that seldom penetrated beyond the coastline, and their settlements to trading posts lacking territorial ambition. In this zero-sum equation, they use presumed deficiencies of the Phoenicians to explain Greek superiority.

While ancient authors consistently categorized Phoenician settlements as city-states, modern scholars have maintained a dichotomy that sets Greek agricultural settlements in opposition to Phoenician trading posts, a dichotomy that effectively denies the Phoenicians any prominence in the spread of urbanism. Instead of assuming that the unknown and the foreign provide points of contrast, we assume their diverse but synchronous and contiguous modes of expansion can provide points of comparison. While their expansion contributed to Mediterranean civilization, Greeks held no monopoly. Instead they, the Phoenicians, the Etruscans, and others created settlement networks through roughly similar, contemporary, and competitive processes.

Defining "Phoenician"

Ethnic distinctions between Greeks and Phoenicians have tended toward an essentialist notion of identity, a sort of unchanging national character, which fails to accommodate either the great variety of cultural attributes within these broader groups or the similarities between them. Their eastern homeland and their western settlements are "Phoenician" in the same imprecise way that metropolitan Aegean cities and their settlements are "Greek." Normally, neither group would have used such terms to describe themselves – in most situations they self-identified by their city of origin rather than by a broader ethnic marker. Modern standard periodization subdivides "Greeks" into Bronze Age Mycenaeans, then Iron Age Greeks, later Hellenistic kingdoms, but they could call themselves "Hellenes" throughout.[2] Likewise, modern scholars subdivide "Phoenicians" into Bronze Age Canaanites, Iron Age Phoenicians, and Punic Carthaginians, but they may well have called themselves "Canaanite" throughout, as they almost certainly did during the Iron Age, when their geographic neighbors and linguistic kin used this collective term to identify them.[3]

Metropolitan Greeks and those who settled abroad shared a sense of Hellenic kinship, language, religion, and culture (Hdt. 8.144), even though settlements established by ethnic subgroups within this broader identity (e.g., Dorians, Ionians) and their sub-subgroups, those sent by individual city-states (e.g., Corinth, Megara, Phocaea), employed diverse strategies regarding site selection and urban development. Although we might demonstrate how "Phoenicians" throughout the Mediterranean similarly shared a common language, religion, and culture, we can only surmise how they conceived of their common kinship or of their further divisions into ethnic subgroups. We have outsider (*etic*) conceptions of their collective identity, how they are depicted by foreign observers, but we lack Phoenician insider (*emic*) conceptions, how they perceived of their own identity (Sommer 2010, 134; cf. Hall 1997, 18–19). Inscriptions throughout the coastal cities of the eastern Mediterranean at the minimum provide a patrilineal self-ascription (e.g., son of PN), next they privilege self-ascription as member of a city-state (e.g., son of Tyre; Kaufman 2009), but we lack literary sources that might clarify how Phoenicians viewed their broader interconnections (Quinn 2018).

One might expect that the closely related, mutually intelligible Canaanite dialects of Hebrew and Phoenician would have fostered a sense of kinship and that these linguistic groups might have thought that they shared a common ancestor (e.g., Shem in the Table of Nations, Gen. 10–11); instead the Tanakh artificially designates the Canaanites as unrelated and accursed, marking them for enslavement and their territory for conquest (Gen. 9:20–27, 10:15–19).[4] Nevertheless, here we assume a broad Canaanite/Phoenician affiliation shared from one side of the Mediterranean to the other – speaking related dialects, using similar artifacts, worshiping the same gods – comparable to a shared Hellenic/Greek affiliation. Within this affiliation, again like the Greeks, there would have been varied orders of ethnic subdivision, with identity by city-state commonly holding the most salience.

Settlement Types

Modern scholars have tended to categorize Phoenician settlements with Greek terms, such as *apoikia*, *emporion*, or *enoikismos*. Before the sixth century BCE, they designate only Carthage as *apoikia* ("home away," i.e., *polis*, "city-state"), something of an agricultural exception to the presumed commercial enclave rule, with other settlements classified as *emporia* ("port of trade," e.g., Niemeyer 2000, 2006; Sommer 2009; Aubet 2013; cf. Demetriou 2013). This modern division rests upon an assumed Semitic proclivity for commerce to the exclusion of agriculture, upon an arbitrary assessment of the size and the utilization of a city's hinterland (*chora*), upon an assumption that our absence of evidence provides evidence of absence (e.g., lacking clear proof of territorial ambition, Phoenicians had none), and upon a preference for using rational Hellenic precedents to explain urbanism (e.g., Phoenician cities could develop only by borrowing Greek models). The *emporia* might also be dismissed as non-urban, or extra-urban, if considered temporary encampments of men (thus not self-reproducing communities), or simply enclaves of resident aliens without citizen rights. In any case, the Greek *apoikia*/Phoenician *emporion* dichotomy presupposes that the Greeks spread urbanism, legitimized by a sort of civilizing mission, and that they produced logical, well-ordered city plans, while Phoenicians offered nothing at best, irregular chaos at worst (Fumadó Ortega 2013). Certain modern ideological assumptions lie behind this dichotomy, assumptions that have led to a perceived moral disparity wherein noble Greek farmers could meet the property requirements necessary for their own service in the military, while base Phoenician merchants, subject to autocrats, paid mercenaries to do their fighting. In contrast, ancient authors gave credit to the Phoenicians for honoring their warriors (Arist. *Pol.* 1324B). At the same time, ancient sources considered moral inferiority not as something derived from their ethnic proclivities but from their geographic position, since Greek coastal commerce could corrupt just as easily as Phoenician (Cic. *Rep.* 2.7–9, cf. Plat. *Leg.* 704A–705A, Arist. *Pol.* 1327A).

Ancient authors admired Phoenician urbanism – Sidon was great, Tyre beautiful (e.g., Jos. 19:28–29; Ez. 27–28; cf. Strab. 16.12–27 [753–758]). Thus the clear delineation of urban categories and the depiction of *emporia* as trading posts seem modern preoccupations (following Graham 1964). Analysis of the semantic range of *emporion* undertaken by the Copenhagen Polis Centre has demonstrated, on the one hand, that the Greeks themselves used the term most often to describe the external port of trade of a *polis*, like Piraeus, rather than to designate a separate settlement category (Hansen 1997; 2006; cf. Bresson and Rouillard 1993; Bresson 2003; Demetriou 2013). On the other hand, ancient authors did not use *apoikia/polis* and *emporion* with any consistency, nor with mutual exclusivity – for example, Herodotus might categorize Olbia/Borysthenes as an *emporion* (Hdt. 4.17, 24), inhabited by citizens of a *polis* ("Olbiopolitae" 4.18; cf. Naucratis 2.178–179).

The third category of *enoikismos* ("in-dwelling") applied neither to Greek nor to Phoenician settlements in antiquity, but has been coined by modern scholars in order to explain Greek presence along the Levantine coast, describing clusters of workshops or storage magazines maintained by resident aliens (Riis 1970, 129, 158; Descoeudres 2002). Eventually the term transferred to the Phoenician presence in the Aegean and along the southern coast of Spain, namely to Maenace (mod. Toscanos) and to the Gephyraeans of Eretria (descendants of Phoenicians who had settled Thebes with Cadmus and had given Greeks their alphabet – Hdt. 5.57–58, Niemeyer in Tsetskhladze 2006, 149; 1993, 339; cf. Gras 2002, 194). Instead of using these outside categories, we might first understand Phoenician settlements in their own terms.

For "wall" or "citadel," Phoenician used QRT, a term that, through synecdoche, came to describe the walled city.[5] The toponym for Carthage (QRTḤDŠT, "new city") employs the term in direct correspondence with Greek *neapolis*. Besides the North African city, Phoenicians established a "Carthage" in Cyprus (likely Citium)[6] and in Spain (Carthago Nova), while certain other Phoenician settlements had their toponym translated into Greek as *neapolis*, for example, on Sardinia (mod. Santa Maria di Nabui),[7] in Byzacena (mod. Nābul), and in Tripolitania (Leptis Magna).[8]

This analogous, interchangeable nomenclature demonstrates that both the Greeks and the Phoenicians conceived of citizens creating new urban centers (QRT/*polis*) in the course of their overseas expansion. As for the urban features reproduced, one could expect to find a stronghold (fortified hilltop, peninsula, or islet); at the urban core an internal market (like the Greek *agora*) for local produce from the hinterland; and at the city's margin an external market (like the *emporion*) for secure and fair foreign exchange. Besides open-air markets, additional nodes of exchange included installations at city gates (*šaʿar*: cf. II Kg 7:1, 7:18; Niemeyer 2000, 107) and along thoroughfares (*ḥuṣôt*: I Kg 20:34).

Although we have no specific Phoenician/Punic parallel for the term *emporion*, bilingual inscriptions do translate the term MḤZ into Latin as either as "forum" (*KAI* no. 124) or as "administrator of a forum" (i.e., *aedile*, no. 130),[9] without designating whether the market was internal (like the Forum Romanum) or external (like the Forum Boarium). Similarly, the Akkadian term *kārum* applied equally to market officials and to their "river ports," as well as to inland markets not necessarily located along riverbanks.[10] The concept of the Phoenician merchant outpost derives in large part from the Middle Bronze Age Assyrian *kārum* at Kanesh (mod. Kültepe), well known due to its cache of administrative correspondence (Niemeyer 1990, 488; Aubet 2001, 108–109). Both the *kārum* and Phoenician settlements have been compared, again anachronistically, to the much later institutions of the "factory" (Portuguese *feitoria*), the *comptoir* (Hanseatic *Kontor*), and the *fondaco* (Arabic *funduq*).[11] In these contexts, resident aliens would manage warehouses or workshops in a city's "port of trade."[12] Such institutions secured the safety of merchants and their transactions, although resident alien rights would vary, as would their charter and their autonomy – for example, long-term private partnerships involving independent, hereditary firms managed by specific families; extraterritorial legal rights established and maintained by treaty agreements with their territory of origin; access to their own judicial mechanisms within the enclave. Excluding the *Report of Wenamun*, which may record the name of a trading house ("Werekter," Lichtheim 1976, 226), hypotheses concerning Phoenician trade institutions are founded not on any contemporary parallels but largely by analogy to examples either much earlier (e.g., Kanesh) or much later (e.g., Medieval enclaves).

Similar to *emporion* in Greek, the *kārum* in Akkadian could designate not just the external market but also the city-state as a whole (e.g., Emporiae), as when the Assyrians resettled Til-Barsip on the Euphrates as KAR-Shalmaneser and later Phoenician Sidon as KAR-Esarhaddon, both long-established cities that then served as Assyrian urban administrative centers. Or else the Assyrian *kārum* could designate a semi-dependent center of trade administered by resident aliens from a distant state (as at Kanesh). Otherwise, the *kārum* might well compare to the hypothetical *enoikismos* model, an enclave where foreign merchants used local wares and dwellings. In place of *kārum*, in Phoenician we find the term MḤZ, but used rarely and in late contexts. If it did have a semantic range similar to the Akkadian term, it might theoretically describe a city ("Portland"), a market ("port"), or a family firm ("importers"). In addition, during the reigns of Tiglath-pileser III and Esarhaddon, Assyrians used the term to label Levantine urban ports (*karāni*) and port-houses (*bīt-karāni*, Kuhrt 2002, 22–23; Kestemont 1983, 74–76; Parpola and Watanabe 1988, no. 5) to describe Phoenician trade institutions within their metropolitan cities.

Historical Context

In establishing the history of Greek expansion, much has been made of the Sicilian foundation dates in Thucydides. His meager list of founders and their cities of origin has allowed historians to establish causal relationships based upon the chronological order of the various waves of overseas settlement, and has allowed archaeologists to create ceramic typologies (assuming that excavated ceramics come from the earliest strata, cf. Morris 1996). Unfortunately, we lack a similar consistent list of Phoenician foundation dates, founders, and motherlands for ready comparison. We have various texts that report initial settlements either before the Trojan War, or somewhere between the mid-tenth to the mid- or late ninth century BCE.[13] Certain scholars have even suggested that the foundation dates of North African Phoenician colonies should be pushed even a century or more later, to the late eighth century BCE.

In the Late Bronze Age, Egyptian and Hittite Empires dominated the entire eastern Mediterranean littoral, with Canaanite/Phoenician cities from Byblus southward falling under the sway of Egypt. A cache of diplomatic correspondence deposited at Akhetaten (mod. Tell el-ʿAmarna) records how these small principalities shared in the cosmopolitan cuneiform culture of the region.[14] Migrations of so-called Sea Peoples contributed to the collapse of the large Near Eastern kingdoms and to the decline of Canaanite coastal principalities, roughly contemporary with the collapse of the Mycenaean kingdoms in the Aegean.[15] According to Philistus of Syracuse, during this era of migrations Carthage was founded by Zorus and Charchedon (eponyms for Tyre and Carthage, *BNJ* 556 F47; App. *Lib.* 1.1). Even given this account, and stray archaeological finds (Chiappisi 1961), we have insufficient material evidence to support a thirteenth- or twelfth-century Phoenician expansion.

This period of decline and collapse led to a significant change in political-administrative scale, shifting from large territorial kingdoms ("macro-states") to small autonomous cities ("micro-states," Hansen 2000, 16–17). Contemporaneous sources provide evidence for the relatively rapid recovery of Levantine coastal cities within a century of the collapse (ca. 1075 BCE: Lichtheim 1976, 226–227; Grayson 1991, A.O.87.3). We hear of Hiram of Tyre (ʾḤRM/Aḥīram, ca. 950 BCE) cooperating with Solomon in expeditions both to the east and to the west,[16] and of his campaign against an insubordinate tributary city ("Utica" or "Citium").[17] In the following dynasty, Ithobaʿal (ʾTBʿL, ca. 850 BCE) was said to have founded two cities: Botrus near Byblus and a certain Auza in North Africa.[18] Nevertheless, for these passing references we lack archaeological confirmation.

A complex system of highly developed autonomous city-states emerged in the Levant precisely at a time of "comparative backwardness and poverty" in Greece (Kuhrt 2002, 17). An inscription by Yariris of Carchemish (ca. 790 BCE) captures the multilingual, cosmopolitan context:

> … in our city's script [Luwian hieroglyphic], in the Tyrian script,[19] in the Assyrian script [Akkadian cuneiform] and in the Taimani script [Aramaic?], and I knew twelve languages. My lord gathered every country's son to me by (means of) travel for (the sake of) language, and he caused me to know every skill. (Hawkins 2000, 130–133, no. II.24 KARKAMIŠ A15*b*)

Like Carchemish, other residual Hittite states endured (e.g., Halpa) alongside Aramaean states (e.g., Damascus), but many cities in the region evade simplistic mono-cultural classification due to their linguistic diversity (e.g., Unqi, Yadiya). Phoenician cites occupied the coast (e.g., Aradus, Byblus, Sidon, Tyre), to their south were small principalities (e.g., Samaria/Israel, Jerusalem/Judah) and other coastal city-states (Philistia), while in Egypt rival cities sought dominance.

Significant Phoenician cultural presence in the merchant quarters of these small states might be considered a mode of expansion abroad. Starting in the ninth century BCE, in an arc stretching from Cyprus and Cilicia toward the Euphrates, city-state rulers or their officials set up inscriptions, commonly bilingual, for their Phoenician-speaking residents.[20] While these inscriptions may address resident aliens, they give no indication of foreign origin or subordinate status. In any case, Greeks considered Cilicia (Que) Phoenician territory,[21] with the northernmost limit of Phoenicia proper marked by the settlement of Myriandus in Alexandretta (Hdt. 4.38; *polis-emporion*: Xen. *An.* 1.4.6). Due to their proximity to the Phoenician *metropoleis*, enclaves in Cilicia and settlements on Cyprus

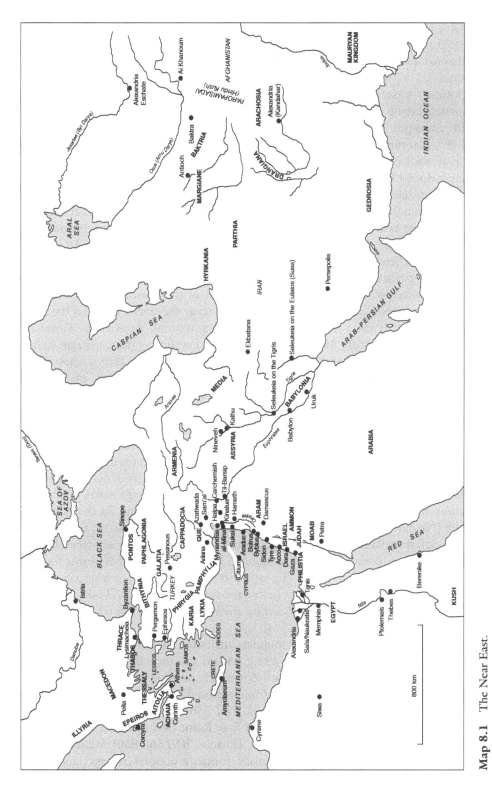

Map 8.1 The Near East.

presumably predated westward expansion. In the absence of evidence to the contrary, we assume that small ports and enclaves were dependent on nearby urban centers rather than being themselves independent, and assume that all participated in this regional system of small states.

In response to Assyrian expansion in the Levant and to the later Kushite expansion into Egypt, independent cities and principalities formed defensive alliances. Assyrian armies renewed campaigns into the Levant when Shalmaneser III subdued the upper Euphrates (856 BCE). Just three years later, Aramaean rulers of Damascus and Hamath led a broad coalition of small states against Shalmaneser at the Battle of Qarqar (853 BCE),[22] a coalition that included key northern Phoenician cities (Aradus, Byblus, Arqa, Ushnatu, and Sianu).[23] Meanwhile, southern Phoenician cities did not join the coalition but paid tribute[24] – bronze gates from the palace at Imgur-Enlil (mod. Balāwāt) depict an island ruler overseeing "tribute from the boats of the people of Tyre and Sidon: silver, gold, tin, bronze, wool, *lapis lazuli* and carnelian" (Grayson 1996, A.0.102.84, 102.66; Walters Art Museum 54.2335).[25] Southern Phoenician states bought a degree of autonomy through such tribute, a strategy that they maintained during the following centuries.

Our final literary context concerns the expansion of these southern cities to North Africa in the decades following the Battle of Qarqar, as the micro-states of the Levant replicated themselves even as they began losing autonomy to Assyria. Timaeus of Tauromenium (third century BCE) supplied the earliest version of the Carthaginian foundation saga, and he was followed by Pompeius Trogus (first century BCE), whose version is more complete.[26] The saga begins after the foundation of Utica (Just. 18.4) and the death of Mattan of Tyre (MTN), when a succession crisis set the faction of Pumayyaton (PMYTN, his son) against the faction of Zakarbaʿal (ZKRBʿL, his brother/son-in-law), a wealthy priest of Melqart. Aside from this romance, we find Pumayyaton on Menander's Tyrian king list (as Pygmaliōn) and perhaps on a ninth-century inscription from Sardinia (as PMY, *KAI* no. 46). After Pumayyaton murdered his uncle and seized the throne (ca. 820 BCE), his widowed sister, Elissa/Dido, fled with the remnants of her husband's faction and resources, first to Cyprus and then to Carthage. This saga offers etymological explanations for the name of Dido ("wanderer" due to her exile) and for the name of the Byrsa Hill ("oxhide" due to a ruse she used in order to claim the citadel, Gras 2002); it offers etiological explanations for cult practice (memorializing the self-immolation of Dido); and it offers romantic tales of unrequited love (Libyan Hiarbas yearns for Dido; Dido or her sister Anna for Aeneas). The saga also provided Carthage a suspicious parity and synchronicity with Rome, 38 years before the first Olympiad (*BNJ* 566 F60; Feeney 2007, 68–107), albeit with a founder befitting effeminate Phoenicians (cf. Aeneas's emasculation, Verg. *Aen.* 4.259-267).

Among the few cases where we have founders attributed to Phoenician settlements, the very existence of certain sites is uncertain (e.g., Auza) and the names of certain founders are contradictory and contrived (e.g., both Zorus/Charchedon and Elissa/Dido). In the case of Carthage, we have a wide variety of foundation dates – 50 years (App. *Lib*.1.1–2) or 30 years before the Trojan War (Philistus, *BNJ* 556 F47); after the fall of Troy but either 93 years (Liv. *Epit.* 51) or 56 years older than Rome (Vell. Pat. 1.6.4, cf. 1.2.3); or, finally, synchronous with Rome (814/3 BCE, Timaeus, *BNJ* 566 F60). We have only this one Phoenician foundation saga, a Hellenistic romance about Carthage, and we lack similar accounts for their other settlements. Such feeble and contradictory evidence makes the limited sources concerning Greek expansion seem robust.[27]

While the literary sources grant Phoenicians precedence, their deficiencies have led scholars to rely heavily upon archaeological data. By estimating foundation dates based solely upon the earliest finds of Greek finewares, certain modern scholars have offered dates in the late eighth century for Carthage, which would make the Phoenician expansion correspond closely with the Greek (Carpenter 1958), or even seem like a response to Greek expansion (e.g., Niemeyer 1990, 1993, 2000). Modern scholars also presume that the Phoenicians expanded in the eighth century in order to secure sources of raw materials, in particular metals that were needed to meet increasing Assyrian demands, providing further contrast to supposed Greek agricultural incentives (Frankenstein 1979; Sherratt and Sherratt 1993).[28]

Recent radiocarbon dates have undermined if not overturned the lower dates based upon Greek fineware typologies. Samples taken from Phoenician settlements, in both North Africa and Spain, fall within the last half of the ninth century BCE (i.e., 2800 to 2600/2500 BP).[29] The Carthaginian samples derive from a clay extraction pit that had collapsed upon itself (trench BM04, Docter et al. 2008), buried under later rubbish that sealed its early stratigraphic context. Samples from Onuba (mod. Huelva) and Gadir (mod. Cádiz) also derive from an early context (González de Canales, Serrano, and Llompart 2006; Gener et al. 2015). Besides these results, similar early radiocarbon dates from the east at Dora have led to a broad reassessment of early Iron Age Phoenician ceramic typologies and chronologies (Gilboa and Sharon 2003, Gilboa, Sharon, and Boaretto 2008), a reassessment that continues unabated.[30]

In addition, epigraphers have dated inscriptions from Nora and Bosa in Sardinia, and from Onuba in Spain, to the late ninth century BCE.[31] These paleographic dates, alongside the radiocarbon samples, would confirm that Phoenician expansion began before the Assyrians had asserted more direct control over the Levantine coast (eighth century BCE). As a result, we should revise the most common explanation for Phoenician expansion, namely that they sought raw materials in order to meet tribute demands, since westward settlement predates steep Assyrian levies. Although early artifacts may still indicate precolonial commercial exchange before settlement ("trade before the flag"), it remains difficult to differentiate between an ephemeral trading presence and an attempt at permanent settlement.

Comparative Urban Organization

Scholars within Classical and Ancient Near Eastern Studies have staked competitive claims to priority concerning the development of authentic city-states (Hodos 2009). The micro-states of the Levant that emerged following the Bronze Age collapse established themselves well before the village clusters in Greece coalesced into city-states, but their precedence does not necessarily demonstrate any particular influence. Nevertheless, the fact that the Phoenicians organized themselves at the scale of autonomous cities before the Greeks has led some to argue that Levantine micro-states served as models for the development of the Greek *polis* (e.g., Snodgrass 1980, 32–34; Drews 1979; Gschnitzer 1988; de Geus 2001).

In the course of Mediterranean-wide urban expansion, a "new city" (Neapolis/ QRTḤDŠT) could adopt formal metropolitan characteristics, a defining moment in the development of the city-state through institutional replication. Here again, the Phoenicians well preceded the Greeks (according to radiocarbon dating) or were at the very least their near contemporaries (according to fineware typologies). As claims to Greek priority have fallen, the disciplinary competition has shifted to the originality and quality of their respective civic institutions (e.g., Raaflaub 2004a, 2004b).[32] The tendency to promote the contributions and institutions of one ethnic group and to demote the other presumes essential, distinct ethnic characteristics, ignoring the fact that ancient authors recognized both institutional parity and Phoenician priority, and ignoring the fact that Greeks, Phoenicians, and indigenes intermingled.

The *poleis* of Greece developed along divergent trajectories – settlements of different sizes grew at different rates in varied locations. No common Greek state ever coalesced from these myriad cities – each had its own calendar, cult, coinage, manufacturing specialties, artistic styles, local script, and so on. Some controlled extensive territory with large populations (e.g., Athens), others remained relatively insignificant (e.g., the four *poleis* of tiny Ceos); some pursued the noble arts of war (e.g., Sparta), others the vulgar commercial arts (e.g., Corinth, Hdt. 2.165–167; Cic. *Rep.* 2.7–9; cf. Plat. *Resp.* 590C). Although, on the one hand, we have evidence demonstrating how Greek *poleis* differed, they and their overseas settlements are treated as a coherent whole. On the other hand, Greeks and Phoenicians organized their settlements similarly, yet we emphasize their presumed differences. In some cases, Greeks and Phoenicians even settled side by side. The traditional binary contrast between Greek agricultural and Phoenician commercial settlements may have little more than a grain of truth (Whittaker 1974, 59).

From the eleventh to eighth centuries BCE, Phoenician metropolitan cities enjoyed relative autonomy, monopolizing legitimate violence both externally (waging war, upholding treaties) and internally (maintaining order). Although the Copenhagen Polis Centre specifically excluded non-Greek city-states from their analyses (e.g., Hansen 1997b, 10), Levantine Phoenician states and their overseas settlements would meet their criteria for designation as *poleis* (e.g., autonomy, perimeter walls, local mint, etc.),[33] just as they had met the criteria of ancient authors. When such criteria are applied consistently, Greek and Phoenician settlements have similarities as significant as their differences.

Besides the formal characteristics of city-states, political institutions were replicated overseas. The mixed constitution of Carthage – combining administration by one, by few, and by many – attracted the admiration of both Greeks and Romans.[34] As was the case in metropolitan Greek cities during the ninth to eighth century BCE, in Phoenicia the hereditary monarch (MLK, "king") normally held executive power, except for a brief period during the sixth century when magistrates ruled Tyre (ŠPṬ/*sufes*, "judge").[35] Instead of the former, the latter institution of *sufes* migrated westward with overseas settlement.[36] Aside from Cypriote Carthage, which may have been administered by a Tyrian viceroy (SKN "steward," *KAI* no. 31), we have no indication that overseas settlements were under the direct political control of the *metropolis*, other than a tithe that some cities paid to the Tyrian temple of Melqart (Polyb. 31.12; Diod. Sic. 20.14; Arr. *Anab.* 2.24).

These magistrates presumably monopolized command over the military and key priesthoods, with such power checked by an advisory council of elders (RB/*rab* or 'DR/*'adîr*, "chief").[37] Council members may have been drawn specifically from ex-magistrates or more generally from an aristocracy that held significant economic power.[38] Finally, adult male citizens made up the assembly (ᶜM/ ᶜ*am*, "common people," Sznycer 1975), a body summoned by the Carthaginian magistrates where citizens confirmed legislation, elected military commanders, and spoke before their fellow citizens.[39] These political institutions advanced westward, perhaps at the very start of overseas settlement, although we have only late evidence.[40]

We would expect Phoenicians, like the Greeks, to have transferred political and cultural institutions abroad, as well as formal urban characteristics. They would establish a stronghold (islet, peninsula, plateau), a central place for exchange among citizens and a marginal place for foreign trade, places for worship and places for burial, a source of freshwater and a secure food supply, and so on. Before the sixth century, Greek settlements consisted of clustered houses, spread over a wide area and linked both to common sanctuaries and to a citadel, with an agglomerative urban plan rather than an angular grid. For the most part, Greek orthogonal urban plans developed later, after the initial foundation, with some possible exceptions (e.g., Megara Hyblaea, Metapontum). Similarly, we lack evidence for orthogonal plans in the initial phases of Phoenician settlement.

Private initiative did play some role in Greek expansion, as when enterprising merchants sought resources in the West (e.g., Colaeus of Samos and Sostratus of Aegina, Hdt. 4.152, cf. 1.163), or when disaffected nobles were pushed westward for reasons either personal (murder: Archias of Corinth, Plut. *Mor.* 772E–773B) or political (succession crisis: Dorieus of Sparta, Hdt. 5.41–48). But civic initiative also drove Greek overseas settlement, particularly in response to Persian expansion, as when Pentathlus led refugees away from Cnidus, or when Phocaeans abandoned their city in order to settle "Cyrnus" (Diod. Sic. 5.9; Hdt. 1.163–167). Aside from Hiram's reported cooperation with Solomon (suggesting direct royal/state support of commercial enterprise), and the romance of Dido/Elissa (suggesting that Tyrian political unrest led to the settlement of Carthage), we have little to indicate Phoenician motivations. For the sake of comparison, we presume that the same conditions, which led to population increase and food crises in Greeks cities, might likewise have led to crises in contemporary Phoenician cities, and that they, too, would have turned to overseas settlement for relief – pulled westward by the allure of resources and land, pushed westward by political or environmental pressures (Sall. *Iug.* 19.1–2, cf. Culican in *CAH* 1992, 485–486).

Finally, Phoenician overseas settlements did maintain the cultural practices of their metropolitan founders, according to the epigraphic evidence, which demonstrates the transfer of literacy (alphabetic scripts), as well as religious devotion (divinities in cult and theophoric elements of personal names) and ritual (formulaic votive dedications). Classical sources suggest that Levantine Phoenicians and those overseas respected their common kinship – not harming each other, as when the metropolitan cities refused to join Cambyses's campaign against Carthage (Hdt. 3.19); assisting each other, as when Carthage was expected to aid Tyre during the siege by Alexander (Diod. Sic. 17.40.3, cf. Just. *Epit.* 11.10.12, Curt. 4.3.19).

Impermanent or Dependent Non-Citizen Settlements

We find Greeks and Phoenicians together as resident alien merchants inhabiting the commercial quarters of cities throughout the Mediterranean, with these overseas venturers perhaps visiting seasonally while remaining citizens of their native city (cf. *Od.* 15.455–456). Like the independent settlements conforming to the *apoikia/polis* model, these enclaves might also import institutions from the mother city, but the material record left by resident aliens might not distinguish them from their host community. Again, we assume a common Mediterranean urban syntax for resident alien enclaves, mercenary encampments, and dependent commercial settlements.

In the Aegean, Phoenician residents set up inscriptions on Rhodes, Cos, and Delos, with enclaves and sanctuaries attested on Crete (Amyclaeum), Cythera (Punicus), and Thasus.[41] In Athens, particularly at the *emporion* of Piraeus, Phoenician residents set up inscriptions, often bilingual;[42] in the same way, Greek speakers set up votive dedications in North African Cirta (KRT).[43] At Syracuse in eastern Sicily, Phoenician resident aliens held property (which Dionysius seized along with their merchant ships, Diod. Sic. 14.46); at the very same time, Greeks were residents in the Phoenician west of the island (14.41, 53). In Italy, Greeks maintained cult to Hera (Uni) and Aphrodite (Turan) at Graviscae, the port and dependency of Tarquinia; meanwhile the Phoenicians maintained cult to ꜥAštart (Uni) at Pyrgi, a port and dependency of Caere.[44] In Egypt, the Greeks held a trading concession in Naucratis, granted by the ruler of Saïs; the Tyrians had a similar "encampment" at Memphis.[45] In the western part of the Nile Delta, Greek mercenaries were garrisoned at Pelusium, Phoenicians at Heroönpolis.[46] In the Northern Levant, Phoenicians settled Myriandus, north of the Orontes River; to the south of the river, Greeks inhabited modern al-Mīnāꜥ (although we can assume that both settlements were ethnically mixed).[47] Within this diverse range of settlements, from semi-dependent trading centers to mercenary encampments and resident aliens in merchant quarters, Phoenician and Greek settlement types corresponded and their settlers intermixed.

Quantifying independent presence in overseas settlements has proven difficult, as the case of al-Mīnāꜥ demonstrates (Waldbaum 1997; Lehmann 2005). At least three scenarios have been proposed for the site – first, an essentially Greek settlement (Boardman 1999, 38–54), or *polis-emporion*; second, a Phoenician or Aramaean city with a significant Greek enclave (*enoikismos*, Riis 1970); third, an entirely Levantine city (Descoeudres 2002). The poor documentation of undecorated ceramics has contributed to the site's contested categorization. The presence of foreign merchants at coastal sites may also predate the earliest attested fineware imports, since whenever these venturers used local wares they would have become less archaeologically visible. Instead of sharp ethnic divisions or open enmity, the varied groups inhabiting the cities of the eastern Mediterranean exhibited a "considerable degree of peaceful co-existence, mutual cultural exchange and even intermarriage" (Maier 1985, 38).

This multiethnic accommodation within settlements along the eastern Mediterranean littoral replicated itself in Phoenician expansion abroad, and their adaptation of indigenous and Greek material culture hampers the clear demarcation of their presence in overseas settlements. Sites such as Pithecussae and Maenace replicate a cosmopolitan mode of urbanism rather than an essentially Greek, Phoenician, or indigenous mode.[48]

Permanent Independent Citizen Settlements

The metropolitan cities of the Phoenicians/Canaanites occupied not only the coastline itself, but also key points along routes from the coast to the interior; not only islands and peninsulas, but plateaus between ravines. The island of Aradus (ʿRWD, mod. al-Arwād) dominated in Northern Phoenicia, controlling the coastal plain below the Bargylus Range, from the Orontes to the Eleutherus River, while Sidon (ṢDN, mod. Ṣaydā) and the island of Tyre (ṢR, mod. Ṣūr) dominated Southern Phoenicia, controlling the coastal plain below the Libanus Range, from the Eleutherus to the Acco Plain, at times extending their control even to the border of Egypt (Map 8.1). In the north, Phoenicians settled not only the coast but also along roads linking the coast to inland cities and river valleys – routes from Cilicia to the upper Euphrates, routes from the coast up the Orontes River to Unqi, and up the Eleutherus River to Emesa and Hamath and beyond. In the south, Tyre controlled routes up the Leontes River, and along the base of the Carmelus Range connecting to the sizeable inland Phoenician cities of Megiddo in the Esdraela and to Hazor in the upper Jordan Valley.[49] While the Tanakh designates large inland cities as Canaanite (i.e., Phoenician), Strabo distinguishes between Syrians farming inland and Phoenicians trading on the coast, and some modern scholars have emphasized the commercial rather than agrarian character of these metropolitan centers.[50] In any case, we might assume that the large settlements throughout the region were consumer cities that relied upon imports to support specialized labor.

Phoenician cities controlled these key nodes along routes of communication, extracting produce not only from the sea but also from the land. Mago of Carthage (ca. 200 BCE) wrote a 28-volume treatise recording traditional Phoenician practices in agriculture, horticulture, viticulture, and animal husbandry (even apiculture), which was translated both into Greek and into Latin at the request of the Roman Senate (Plin. *HN* 18.5 [22–23]), and he was often cited by Roman agricultural writers (e.g., Varro *Rust.* 1.1.8, 10; Colum. 1.1.10, 13). Metropolitan Phoenicians occupied well-watered sites with soils productive enough to support some of the more populous cities of the Levant. As they duplicated their urban centers across the Mediterranean, their site selection strategically targeted resources from both coastal plain and hinterland. The Phoenicians gained renown for their metalwork, and their early expansion targeted regions rich in copper, iron, lead, silver, and gold ores.

Assyria and Egypt sought beams to span their monumental structures, namely cedars from the Lebanon, and Phoenician shipbuilding required a variety of woods (and their metallurgy required fuel), so they harvested forests (Dietler and López-Ruiz 2009, 169–192). When Eratosthenes described Cyprus, the object of early Phoenician settlement, he first noted an abundance of olive, vine, and grain, next an abundance of copper and timber. Extraction of these resources formed an interrelated system – due to mining they cleared forests for charcoal, excess timber aided shipbuilding, and this clear-cutting opened land for agriculture (Strab. 14.6.5 [C684]).

Out of the sea they harvested mollusks of the genus *Murex*, from which they extracted their distinctive purple dye (Aristot. *Hist. an.* 5.15 [546B–547B], Plin. *HN* 9.124–138 [60]). Since each mollusk produced only a droplet, the volume required for this extraction left shell middens as evidence of their industry. They also pursued shoals of tuna across the Mediterranean to the Pillars of Heracles and beyond ([Aristot.] *Mir. ausc.* 844A

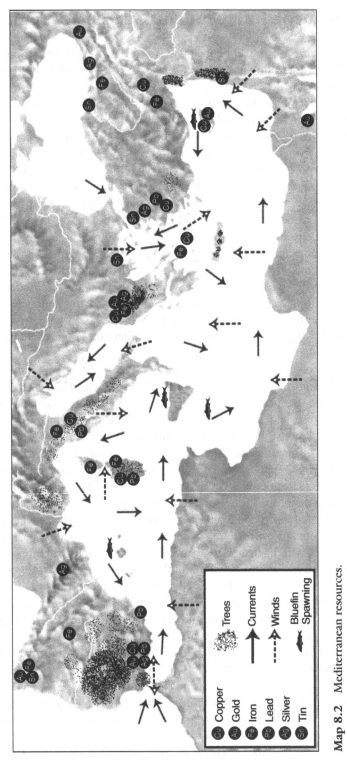

Map 8.2 Mediterranean resources.

[135–136]). They controlled not only the straits, where they could cull from the migrating shoals, but also spawning areas, and they used evaporation ponds in order to extract salt to cure their catch (Map 8.2). When they first sent settlers abroad, they sought not only fertile coastal plains suitable for a variety of crops, but interior mountains for ores and timber; not only ports for trade, but commercial fisheries and salt pans. Besides patterns of resource extraction, the Phoenicians also employed regular patterns of site selection, preferring locations easily defendable by sea, ideally with natural freshwater from springs or rivers, supplemented by artificial cisterns.

Whether Aradus in Northern Phoenicia joined in overseas expansion or not, the city fits this model of urban replication – a small but densely populated island, with multistoried structures, in control of the adjacent mainland *peraea* at Marathus (mod. ʿAmrīt) and Antaradus (mod. Ṭarṭūs). Strabo describes how, when besieged, the Aradians could ingeniously extract freshwater from a spring amidst the sea channel (16.2.13 [C753–754]), although they normally relied on cisterns and mainland springs, such as at the water-temple complex at Marathus (mod. *maʿabed*, Oggiano 2012).

Two stereotypical western settlements follow this settlement model, Gades (ʾGDR) and Motya (MṬW) (Map 8.3). Both densely inhabited, both exploited their adjacent coast – the former at Castillo Doña Blanca, at the mouth of the River Gaudalete;[51] the latter at Birgi with communication via a submerged causeway. In addition, both had monumental water-temples – on Gades at the Heracleium (i.e. Temple of Melqart, Strab. 3.5.7 [C172–173], Plácido 1993) and on Motya at the so-called Kothon (Spagnoli 2013). The modern overburden of Cadiz limits our knowledge of ancient Gades, but the foundations of house and perimeter walls on Motya reveal a dense urban fabric of multistoried buildings (Famà 2002, cf. Diod. Sic. 14.52).

Gades drew resources from the catchment of the River Baetis, positioned as it was near the mouth of that fertile and mineral-rich basin, and a series of early settlements along the southern Iberian coast also exploited the inland resources of the Baetica. From the Straits to Carthago Nova, settlers occupied stream mouths and estuaries, which provided freshwater as well as access to the interior.[52] Phoenicians made use of crops from the plain, timber and ores from the hills, and tuna from the sea. The region later became famous for its salted-fermented fish paste (*garum*, Lowe 2000). Motya, at the far western corner of Sicily, sat alongside the migratory path of tuna shoals (today culled during the *matanza*), as well as the salt flats used for preservation.

Tyre as *metropolis* provides the most relevant model for urban replication overseas, a densely populated island that controlled its adjacent mainland at Palaetyrus, where springs provided freshwater as supplement to their own offshore springs and cisterns (Map 8.4).[53] Strabo admired its multistoried structures, taller than those in Rome, if not its odiferous dye industry (Strab. 16.2.23 [C757]). Phoenician site selection sometimes focused on the exploitation of *Murex* – e.g., their most distant Atlantic settlement on the Insulae Purpurariae (MGDL, mod. Mogador, Plin. *HN* 6.201–203 [61]), and on Meninx in the Gulf of Syrte (mod. al-Qantara),[54] where middens provide evidence of local dye works (Plin. *HN* 9.127). However, we should assume that in every case they exploited as many resources as possible. Both Sulcis (SLKY) and Enosis (ʾY NSM), islands off of Sardinia, harvested not only the tuna shoals, which they cured by means of the latter's salt pans, but also timber and minerals from the interior, as well as crops from the coastal plain.[55]

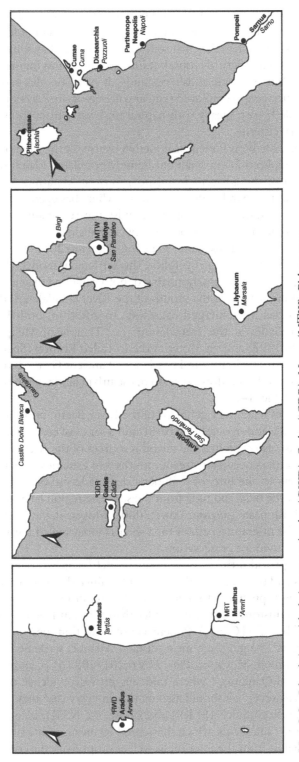

Map 8.3 Island sites with their *peraea*: Aradus (ᶜRWD); Gades (ᵓGDR); Motya (MṬW); Pithecussae.

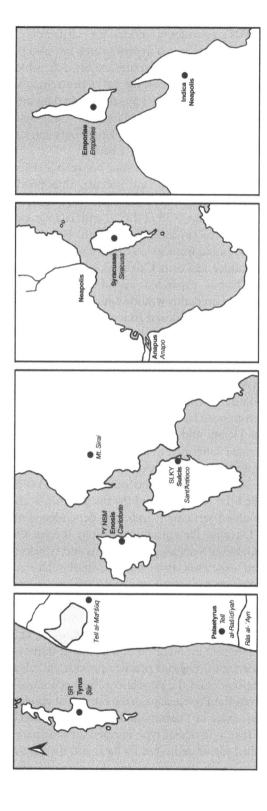

Map 8.4 Island sites with their *peraea*: Tyre (ṢR); Sulcis (SLKY) and Enosis (ʾY NSM); Syracuse; Emporiae and Neapolis-Indica.

Metropolitan Sidon (ṢDN) provides a model for settlements occupying plateaus between streams, which would offer not only freshwater but also places to beach ships; their escarpments, topped by walls, made such sites readily defensible; and alongside their banks were liminal sanctuaries (as at Sidon on the River Bostrenus, Map 8.5). This settlement type matches Panormus (ṢYṢ), bounded by streams feeding into its harbor. The city did not turn its back on the interior but exploited its fertile catchment basin (mod. Conca d'Oro). Greek Selinus fits this same pattern, on a plateau between streambeds, harbors in its estuaries, with extra-urban sanctuaries along its banks.

Phoenicians selected not only islands and plateaus, but readily defensible peninsulas and promontories, extending into estuaries or into the sea, thus providing paired harbors (Map 8.6). Early settlements at Lixus (LKŠ) and Utica (ʿTQ) occupied peninsulas extending into estuaries,[56] those at Carthage (QRTḤDŠT) and Tharros extending into the sea. In each of these cases, the Phoenician settlements controlled a fertile hinterland – e.g., Lixus practiced viticulture to judge from its coinage (Coll. Cores 712; cf. Strab. 17.3.4; Plin. *HN* 14.81, 120); produce came to Carthage from the surrounding countryside (Diod. Sic. 20.8); and Tharros expanded inland to Othoca (ʿTQ) and Neapolis (QRTḤDŠT). Ignoring their hinterlands would suggest that Phoenicians failed to recognize some of the most productive agricultural zones in the Mediterranean, since territories once controlled by Phoenicians – Africa, Sicily, and Sardinia – had become, by Cicero's time, Rome's three most reliable granaries (Cic. *Leg.Man.* 12 [34], cf. Joseph. *BJ* 2.383). The Corinthian colony at Corcyra, one of the wealthiest of Greek cities (Thuc. 1.25.4), occupied a peninsula with dual harbors, while on the adjacent mainland Buthrotum occupied a promontory extending into the bay of Pelodes. These Greek states also maximized local resource extraction from both land and sea – the Corcyraeans made two noteworthy statue dedications, one at Delphi and one at Olympia, each commemorating the same sensitive bull that had directed fishermen to a prodigious haul of tuna (Paus. 10.9.3–4).

Certain overseas island settlements may have been dependent rather than independent, at least initially, like the North African island of Acra (RʾŠ ŠYGʿN, mod. Rachgoun). Although it likely controlled the *peraea* around Portus Sigensis, at the mouth of the estuary, the name of the mainland settlement indicates dependence on Libyan/Numidian Siga, situated upstream. Likewise Phoenicians inhabited Iberian Onuba, dependent on Tartessus. At the time of Gelon of Syracuse, Phoenicians and Greeks competed for control over ports of trade that had some association with the Spartan Dorieus (Hdt. 7.158), who had failed to settle both Western Sicily (at Eryx) and Tripolitania (at the Kinyps River). If the former, these ports perhaps correspond to the settlements on islets and peninsulas mentioned by Thucydides (6.2); if the latter, perhaps those *emporia* in the Syrtis that Polybius described as having excellent hinterlands (*chora*, 3.23; cf. Malkin 1994, 201), although for both regions we find no mention of dependent status or precise locations.

The archaeological evidence of religious practice provides no clear formula for distinguishing between the temporary and the permanent, between initial dependence and full autonomy, particularly given the Phoenicians extensive use of ephemeral building materials (e.g., sun-dried brick), even in monumental religious architecture. One ingenious hypothesis has suggested that a particular type of open-air sanctuary found in the central Mediterranean, the so-called *tophet* dedicated to Baʿal and his consort Tinnit,[57] may preserve an expression of autonomous community and thus mark a useful distinction between

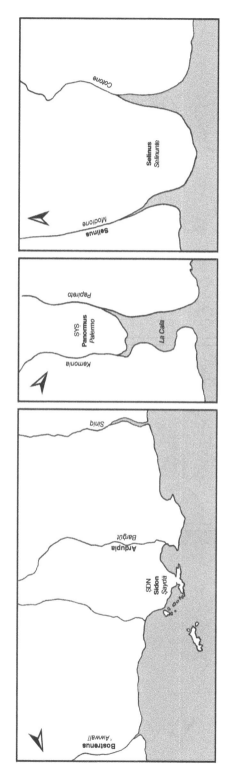

Map 8.5 Plateau sites: Sidon (ṢDN); Panormus (ṢYṢ); Selinus.

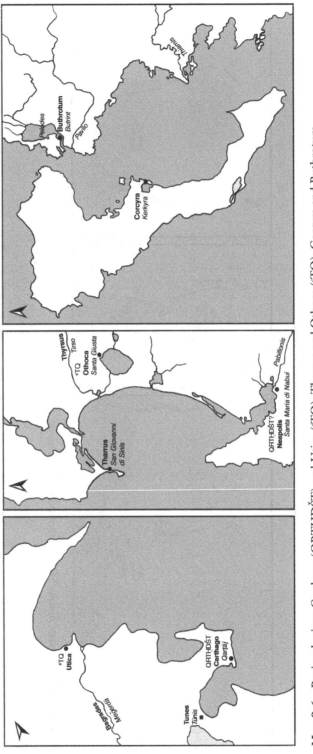

Map 8.6 Peninsula sites: Carthage (QRTḤDŠT) and Utica (ʿTQ); Tharrus and Othoca (ʿTQ); Corcyra and Buthrotum.

independent settlements and dependent trading centers, or between the diverse settlement zones (Aubet 2001, 215–217; D'Andrea and Giardino 2011). Nevertheless, literary texts offer few details as to how rites practiced there defined communities, and material remains from those cities where such sanctuaries have been found (e.g., Carthage, Hadrumetum, Motya, and Sulcis) differ little from those where they have yet to be discovered (e.g., Utica, Meninx, Gades, and Lixus).

Relations with local populations demonstrate independent foreign policy. Phoenicians may have relied in no small part on indigenes for food staples, or they may have dwelt among them, shared customs, and even intermarried (e.g., Libyphoenicians, Diod. Sic. 20.55.4).[58] Autonomous cities formed alliances with indigenes, for example, with the Libyans in North Africa and Elymians in Sicily, as Dorieus of Sparta discovered to his disadvantage (ca. 510 BCE, Hdt. 5.42, 46; cf. Thuc. 6.2; Diod. Sic. 4.23.3; Paus. 3.16.5), and with the Etruscans, as the Phocaeans discovered (ca. 535 BCE, Hdt. 1.163–167). In the latter case, Carthaginians maintained such a close commercial and defensive alliance with the Etruscans that, according to Aristotle, they seemed like citizens of the same state (*Pol.* 3.5.10–11 [1280A]); they later maintained similar close relations with the Romans (Polyb. 3.22–27). As in the eastern Mediterranean, economic and cultural intermingling marked Phoenician expansion westward. Greeks likewise cooperated with indigenes, dwelt among them, shared customs (e.g., Hdt. 4.170), and intermarried (e.g., 4.161).

At the start of Greek expansion, which Euboeans initiated to the west (e.g., Pithecussae and Zancle) and possibly to the east as well (e.g., al-Mīnāʿ), their trade routes and settlements overlapped with those of the Phoenicians. The rich tombs and *heroön* found between Chalcis and Eretria (mod. Lefkandi) demonstrate that the region also recovered comparatively quickly after the Late Bronze Age collapse, and Levantine imports demonstrate their connection to eastern markets. The island "famed for ships" not only appeared in Homeric verse (*Il.* 2.536–545, 4.464; *H. Hom.* 3.4, 219; cf. *Od.* 15.415), but hosted epic performances.[59] In these epics, elite warriors exchanged gifts in order to gain prestige (e.g., *Il.* 6.289, *Od.* 4.614–618; 15.115–119), but they left the exchange of trinkets for profit to the Phoenicians (*Od.* 8.159–164, cf. 15.415–484). Nevertheless, the Euboeans took an interest in the same resources in the same places as the Phoenicians (Rendeli 2005). Their earliest western settlement at Pithecussae resembled Gades – an island strategically located near a metal-bearing region soon exploiting its *peraea* at Cumae – and hosted a mixed population that included Aramaeans and Phoenicians (Ridgway 1992, 1999; Docter and Niemeyer 1994). At the same time, a number of Euboean toponyms appear in North Africa, suggesting that Greeks intermingled there as well (Gras 2002, 189–190, Lipiński 2004, 307–308).

Further Greek settlements followed soon after those of the Euboeans. Merchants from Corinth controlled only a narrow coastal plain and focused on banausic pursuits (Hdt. 2.167), yet they founded overseas settlements not just as commercial way-stations on the western coasting voyage but as productive agricultural centers, for example, Corcyra and Syracuse. Across Corinth's isthmus, land-poor and commercially minded Megara sent settlers west to Megara Hyblaea and then Selinus (De Angelis 2002), where they and the native Elymians shared citizen rights through intermarriage (Thuc. 6.6). Phocaean expansion in the western Mediterranean closely matched the Phoenician in terms of selecting settlement sites, trading in the far west with Tartessus (Hdt. 1.163), and competing for access to the Sardinian Sea. They founded Massalia, with satellite settlements extending from Nicaea to Emporiae across the Gallic Gulf, and later Velia in Italy (Hdt. 1.165–167; Thuc. 1.13). Some scholars assume that agricultural imperatives drove the Phocaeans, alongside their commercial interests, granting to them the honor of introducing olive and vine across the region (e.g., Cook in *CAH* 1982, 214), an honor that the Phoenicians might equally claim (Just. *Epit.* 43.4). Agricultural motives even adhere to the island of Emporiae, despite the settlement bearing a commercial name, having a limited territory, and acquiring a *peraea* joined in symbiosis with indigenes at the twin settlement of Neapolis-Indica (Strab. 3.4.8 [C160]; Liv. 34.9). In each case, scholars assume that Greek colonies settled by commercially minded Greek states hold the status of agricultural colony rather than trading post, while they assume the inverse for the Phoenicians.

While Greeks and Phoenicians both settled around the Sardinian Sea, classical scholars give the former precedence. Sometime between their foundation of Massalia (ca. 600) and Alalia on Corsica (ca. 565 BCE), they also expanded ephemerally into Spain at Hemeroscopium (mod. Dénia) and Maenace (mod. Toscanos), but these they soon abandoned, along with Alalia, after their defeat by a combined force of Phoenicians and Etruscans (ca. 540 BCE). In Sicily, the Phoenicians drove Greeks from the area west of the Halycus River (mod. Platani) and Himera Rivers (mod. Salso and Grande, 409–406 BCE), but Greek presence in Western Sicily maintains a privileged status. In contrast, the Carthaginian role in the resettlement of Hipponium receives comparatively little scholarly attention (e.g., Diod. Sic. 15.24, 379 BCE). Despite brief occupation or abandonment, Greek site names are remembered and mapped, the Phoenician forgotten; Greek periods of hegemony and processes of Hellenization are awarded greater import than eras of Orientalization and Phoenician hegemony.

The Corinthian island settlement at Syracuse matched the paradigm of Phoenician site selection, on the model of Aradus and Tyre – with protected harbors, with two freshwater springs (Arethusa on the island, Alpheus offshore), and with a fertile *peraea* that accommodated expansion (at Neapolis). Scholars imagine that Phoenician commercial enclaves found cooperation with indigenes expedient, requiring fewer resources than would subjugation. In contrast, Corinthian settlers of Syracuse and Corcyra employed a more coercive strategy of enslaving indigenes (Hdt. 7.155; Thuc. 1.55, 3.73; Phrynichus *Satyrs* F47), as did the Megarians at Heraclea Pontica (*BNJ* 348 F4; Strab. 12.3.4 [542]), although those same Megarians cooperated with the Sicels under Hyblon (Thuc. 6.4). We should assume again that both groups employed a range of strategies when interacting with local populations, given that perimeter fortifications belie benign and harmonious Phoenician occupation (Wagner 2007).

Whenever modern scholars demote Phoenician settlements to less-than-urban trading posts, their contributions to Mediterranean civilization decrease; whenever they promote Greek commercial quarters in foreign ports of trade to urban settlements, their contributions increase. Whenever scholars privilege Greek periods of hegemony and cultural influence, subsequent and sometimes even longer periods of Phoenician hegemony and cultural influence suffer. We should expect variation across the vast Mediterranean Sea as well as variation over time, and we can even make contrasting qualitative assessments of surviving material culture, yet the geographic, temporal, and qualitative variation within Greek states and within Phoenician states is as great as any differences between these broad groups. When the commercial centers of Corinth and Tyre are compared, their expansion produced a certain proportion of raw materials (including grain) for local consumption within settlements and a certain proportion for export, but any presumed differences in resource extraction for trade as opposed to agriculture have been determined by assumed inherent ethnic proclivities. Greeks participated fully in trade networks, Phoenicians farmed. The absolute ethnic dichotomy between agricultural settlements and trading posts has a foundation established on scholarly tradition more than on the evidence itself. Instead, Phoenicians and Greeks took part in the same Mediterranean-wide system, joined in competition and collaboration, seeking similar resources, taking advantage of similar opportunities, and employing similar strategies.

LIST OF ABBREVIATIONS

BNJ = Worthington, Ian, ed. 2013. *Brill's New Jacoby*. Leiden: Brill Online.
CAH = Boardman, John, Iorwerth E. S. Edwards, Nicholas G. L. Hammond, and Edmond Solleberger, eds. 1982–1992. *The Cambridge Ancient History*, vol. 3.1–3. Cambridge: Cambridge University Press.
KAI = Donner, Herbert, and Wolfgang Röllig. 1973–2002. *Kanaanäische und aramäische Inschriften, I–III*. Wiesbaden: Harrassowitz.

NOTES

1 This chapter benefited from the feedback of audiences at the University of Chicago (2003, cf. Dietler and López-Ruiz 2009), the University of Montreal (2006), the University of Toronto (2008), and the Washington Ancient Mediterranean Seminar at Catholic University (2018), as well as from the research assistance of Margaux Faris-Merkert.
2 On Greek ethnic identity, see Hall 1997; Demetriou 2013. On Phoenician identity, see van Dongen 2010; Quinn and Vella 2014; Bonnet 2014; Quinn; 2018.
3 One Hellenistic era inscription has been read with KNᶜN as an ethnic marker (e.g., Berthier and Charlier 1955, no. 102), and Augustine of Hippo (ca. 400 BCE) said that peasants of North Africa self-ascribed as "Chanani/Chananaei" (*Rom. inch. exp.* 13), although both of these may be "phantom" misreadings (Quinn 2018, 30–35). In any case, the modern subdivisions of Canaanite-Phoenician-Punic, however misleading as distinct ethnic markers, have proven expedient for historical and linguistic periodization.
4 In the Tanakh, Canaan sired Sidon, Aradus, and others, with his territory extending south to Gaza and east to the Jordan valley (Gen. 10:15–20). In Greek sources, Canaan and Phoenix served as alternate putative ancestors (Philo, *BNJ* 790 F2; Hecataeus, *BNJ* 1 F21, F272).
5 Hoftijzer and Jongeling 1995, s.v. *qrt*, Karatepe (*KAI* no. 26A II.9, 17; III.5, 7, 15; no. 26C IV.6, 17), with a semantic range similar to *polis* – "stronghold" (*acropolis*), "town" (*asty*, urban center), "country" (*chora*, center and its hinterland), or "state" (*koinonia*, cf. Hansen 1997a).

6 Citium likely served as residence for a viceroy (*KAI* no. 31.1–2, cf. *KAI* no. 37B), but Amathus and Limassol are also candidates (Lipiński 2004, 48–50).
7 *KAI* no. 68 (from Olbia), Amadasi Guzzo 1968.
8 See Scyl. 109–110, Str. 17, 3, 18; Plin. *HN* 5.27; possibly from MQMḤDŠ ("new site"), e.g., Macomades Maiores (mod. Sirte) and Macomades Minores (mod. Younga).
9 Ps 107:30 and restored at Is 23:10; originally designated a temple market (*Chicago Assyrian Dictionary* s.v. *māḫāzu*, "sacred water source," "town," or "harbor").
10 The term could signify (i) canal/river "embankment," or "quay wall," (ii) "quarter designated for traders," (iii) "community of merchants," or a position within such a community, and (iv) the "price of merchandise" (*Chicago Assyrian Dictionary* s.v. *kāru*).
11 Larsen 1976, 2000; Whittaker 1974, 58; Sommer 2009, 2010, 127 n. 61.
12 Polanyi distinguishes between competitive, modern free-market exchanges and regulated port-of-trade exchanges in antiquity (Polanyi 1963, 38; cf. Figueira 1984; Aubet 2013).
13 For a summary of the chronological issues, see Aubet in Sagona 2008.
14 Among others, Canaanite Byblus, Berytus, Sidon, Tyre, Acco, Hazor, and Megiddo corresponded with Egypt, with Byblus the most prolific (Moran 1992).
15 For example, Ugarit never recovered. On the one hand, the traditional refoundation of Tyre by Sidon (Joseph. *AJ* 8.3.1 [62]; Just. *Epit.* 18.3.5) and Tyre's absence from certain texts suggest decline (Grayson 1991, A.O.87.3), on the other, the city is mentioned in the *Report of Wenamun* (Lichtheim 1976, 226–227).
16 Expeditions to '*ōphīr* on the Red Sea (Kg 9:26–28, 10:11, 22:48–49) and Taršīš/Tartessus, either in Spain (I Kg 10:11, 22:48–49; Ez. 27:12; cf. Hdt.1.163; *De Phoenicia*, *BNJ* 794 F1; cf. Dietler and López-Ruiz 2009) or else on Sardinia or in Cilician Tarsus (Cross 1972; Lemaire 2000; Thompson and Skaggs 2013).
17 The manuscript variants in Greek (*Tituois, Iukeois, Hukaiois*) and Latin (*Titiceos*) have been restored as Uticaeans or Citians (*Itukaioi* or *Kitieusi*, Menander, *BNJ* 783 F4; Bunnens 1979, 140). Most scholars interpret this ethno-toponym as Cypriote Citium, although Lipiński proposes Acco (Lipiński 2004, 42 n. 23).
18 Botrus appears in the Amarna correspondence, so this would be its re-foundation (Moran 1992, no. 79); the location of Auza remains unknown (Menander, *BNJ* 783 F3).
19 Following Lanfranchi (2009, 130); cf. Hawkins, who relates "Suraean" to Urartian (2000, 130–133).
20 *KAI* nos. 23–28 and 214–215, 287; Hawkins 2000, 526 no. X46 İVRİZ 2; Tekoğlu and Lemaire 2000; Kaufman 2007; Lehmann 2008.
21 The eponymous ancestor Cilix was son of Phoenician Agenor, and brother of Cadmus, Phoenix, and Thasus (Apollod. 3.1; Schol. Eur. *Phoen.* 6; cf. Hdt. 7.91; Paus. 5.25.12), see n. 41.
22 Fantalkin (2006) suggests Aramaean expansion as the impetus for Phoenician overseas settlement.
23 The coalition continually met Shalmaneser in battle over the next decades, as recorded on the Kurkh Monolith (853 BCE), the Balawat Gates (850 BCE), the Calah Bulls (841 BCE), the marble tablet *Annals* (839 BCE), the Kurbaʻil Statue (839 BCE), and the Black Obelisk (827 BCE).
24 They had paid tribute to his father, Ashurnasirpal II (A.0.101.1–2); Tyre and Sidon were the only Phoenician cities represented at the inauguration of the Kalhu palace (mod. Nimrud, A.0.101.30 145).

25 Events on the Balawat Gates predate 844 BCE and depict tribute offered either by Ithoba‛al (887–856) or by Ba‛alazor (B‛L‛ZR, Badezōrus 856–830).
26 Timaeus (*BNJ* 566 F82), Trogus (Just. 18.4–6); see Scheid and Svenbro 1985.
27 We have no other founders mentioned outside of those listed here, and we rarely know the metropolis with any certainty. Although Tyre is often presumed the founder, Sidon competed for priority (cf. Strab. 1.2.33 [40]). For example, in the case of Leptis (mod. al-Khums), some considered Sidon *metropolis* (Sall. *Iug.* 78), others Tyre (Plin. *HN* 5.76). We have some secondary foundations recorded – e.g., Acholla from Melita (Steph. Byz. *s.v.* Ἄχολλα), Ebysus from Carthage (Diod. Sic. 5.16).
28 By 729 BCE the Tyrians paid 150 gold talents – if one *mina* weighed ca. 500 g, and one talent 60 *mina*, then this payment equaled ca. 4500 kg in gold.
29 See Nijboer and van der Plicht, in Docter et al. 2008; for Carthage (Docter et al. 2004; Nijboer 2004); Onuba (Nijboer and van der Plicht 2006); also Maenace (Pingel 2002; Brandherm 2006) and other adjacent sites, e.g., mod. Morro de Mezquitilla (Pingel 2006).
30 See Balmuth and Tykot 1998; Bartoloni and Delpino 2004; Sagona 2008; Brandherm and Trachsel 2008; Pappa 2012; cf. Tsetskhladze 2006, xxxviii–xxxix.
31 Nora: *KAI* no. 46; Bosa: *CIS* I.162; Onuba: González de Canales et al. 2000 (Huelva no. 4); Schmitz 2012.
32 For example, when Thucydides gives Phoenicians priority in Sicily (Thuc. 6.2), one can simply assert that he erred (Boardman 1999, 210).
33 Hansen and Nielsen 2004, 3–156; Weber established the criteria of (i) topographical and administrative self-containedness; (ii) sufficient population for (iii) division of labor and social differentiation; (iv) variety of building types; (v) urban lifestyle; (vi) functioning as a central place for a hinterland (as summarized by Davies 1997, 15).
34 Greeks: Arist. *Pol.* 1272b–1273b; Eratosthenes, *BNJ* 744 F8; Isoc. *Or.* 3.24; Polyb. 6.47–52; Romans: *De Carthagine*, *BNJ* 744 F9; Cato *Orig.* F80; Cic. *Rep.* 1 F3, in Non. 526M.
35 After the Babylonian siege (564–556 BCE), Tyre was ruled by "judges" (*dicastēs*: Menander, *BNJ* 783 F7, Joseph. *Ap.* 1.154–160; cf. Berossus, *BNJ* 680 F9a). The institution of *sufes* likely preceded or existed alongside the Tyrian monarchy, just as Israel was ruled by a *šōpēṭ* before the Davidic monarchy (e.g., Ju. 2:17–18; 1 Sam. 8).
36 For example, to Carthage (*KAI* no. 80), to Sardinia (*KAI* no. 66), to Sicily (Amadasi Guzzo 1967, Sic. 1), and to Spain (Liv. 28.37).
37 RB: Jb 32:9; Teixidor 1979; ʾDR: *KAI* nos. 119, 126, Sznycer 1975; Huss 1994, 333–334; Sommer 2010.
38 *De Cartagine*, *BNJ* 744 F4; these council members likely derived some portion of their wealth from trade (Is. 23:8; Ez. 26:16).
39 cf. ʿM ʾRṢ "people of the territory," *KAI* no. 10; ʿM ṢR "people of Tyre," no. 18; ʿM ṢDN "people of Sidon," no. 60.
40 Gschnitzer (1988) uses the later and better-known institutions to reconstruct the earlier and unknown; Raaflaub (2004a) repudiates this methodology.
41 Rhodes (Ialysus or Camirus, *KAI* no. 44); Cos and Delos (Briquel Chatonnet 2012); Amyclaeum, (mod. Kommos); purple dye-works at Punicus/Porphyrusa (mod. Avlemonas, Xen. Hell. 4.8.7, cf. Hdt. 1.105; Paus. 1.14.7; 3.23.1; Steph. Byz. s.v. Κύθηρα); Thasus (Hdt. 6.47; cf. also Hdt. 2.44; Paus. 5.25.12).

42 *KAI* nos. 53–60: four were set up by Phoenicians from Sidon (*KAI* nos. 53, 59, 60), one from Sidon via Ascalon (*KAI* no. 54, Stager 2005); two from Citium (*KAI* nos. 55, 57); one by a Phoenician speaker from Byzantium (*KAI* no. 56).
43 *KAI* nos. 175–177; Phoenician/Punic is almost entirely consonantal (save *matres lectionis*), but Cirta provides one inscription vocalized with Greek characters (*KAI* no. 175).
44 Caere also had a port at Punicum (mod. Santa Marinella), the name alone suggesting a Phoenician enclave.
45 The camp (*stratopedon*) seems a permanent concession with a temple to ʿAštart (Aphrodite), corresponding to the Hellenium and other Greek temples at Naucratis (Hdt. 2.112, 178–179; cf. Fantalkin 2006).
46 Pelusium (Hdt. 2.154); Heroönpolis (Lutz 2001). Egyptians and later Persians employed Greek, Carian, Phoenician, and Hebrew speaking mercenaries (Kaplan 2003).
47 Or Myriand(r)us (settlement of "10 000 men," Strab. 14.5; *Anab.* 1.4.6; Kestemont 1983, 1985; mod. Adatepe). While the port at al-Mīnāʿ could have served an adjacent settlement (mod. Hisallıtepe, Pamir in Tsetskhladze 2006), both were more likely dependencies of Pattina/Unqi (mod. Tell Tayinat – Lehmann 2005; Kestemont 1983, 66; 1985, 135), resembling nearby settlements at Poseidium (Diod. Sic. 19.79, Hdt. 3.91, mod. Raʿs al-Basīṭ), Betyllium (mod. Raʿs Ibn Hāniʾ), and Shuksi (Šuksu, mod. Tall al-Sūkās).
48 Scholars popularly use "network" theory, "middle ground," and "hybridity" when assessing these zones of interaction – van Dommelen 2005, 2006; Vives-Ferrándiz, 2008; Hodos 2010; Malkin 2011; on the problematic essentialist notion of "pure" necessary to posit the "hybrid," see Stockhammer 2013.
49 Megiddo (Jdg. 1:27, Joseph. 12.21) and Hazor (Joseph. 11, Jdg. 4) both corresponded with Egypt in the Amarna era (Moran 1992).
50 For example, *Brills New Pauly* describes Tyre as a "suitable trading post" and Aradus as a "commercial town" (*ss.vv.* "Aradus" and "Tyrus").
51 Although Strabo claimed that Phoenicians hardly exploited the coastal plain (Strab. 3.5.3 [C168–169]), the mainland settlement was once thought to predate that on the island itself (Ruiz Mata 1999), but older remains have now been found at the Teatro Comico of Gadir (Gener et al. 2015).
52 Cartia, adjacent to Calpe (mod. Gibraltar) on the estuary of the río Guadarranque; Malaca on the Guadalmedina; Maenace on the Vélez; Sexi (mod. Almuñécar) on the Secco and Verde; Abdera on the río Grande de Adra; Baria (mod. Vera) on the Almanzora; and finally Carthago Nova on its estuary (*testero*).
53 Palaetyrus lay adjacent to the spring at mod. Raʾs al-ʿAyn (cf. Menander, *BNJ* 783 F4).
54 In addition, the island had a saw settlement inland at mod. Būrgū, (Fentress 2009), near the mainland sites of Gigthis and Gergis.
55 Sulcis expanded inland as far as modern Monte Sirai and Pani Loriga.
56 Lixus on its estuary (mod. Wādī Lūkūs); Utica on the Bagradas (mod. Wādī Maǧarda).
57 For these distinctive sanctuaries, see Xella 2013, with full bibliography.
58 The term may simply designate location rather than ethnicity (Steph. Byz. s.v. Ἀβρότονον; Polyb. 3.33.15; Diod. Sic.17.113.2).
59 Chalcis traditionally hosted the contest (*certamen*) between Homer and Hesiod, cf. Hes. *Op.* 650–659.

REFERENCES

Amadasi Guzzo, Maria Giulia. 1967. *Le iscrizioni fenicie e puniche delle coloni in Occidente.* Rome: Istituto di studi.

Amadasi Guzzo, Maria Giulia. 1968. "Neapolis = Qrthdst in Sardegna." *Rivista degli studi orientali*, 43: 19–21.

Aubet, Maria Eugenia. 2001. *The Phoenicians and the West*, 2nd ed. Cambridge: Cambridge University Press.

Aubet, Maria Eugenia. 2013. *Commerce and Colonization in the Ancient Near East.* Cambridge: Cambridge University Press.

Balmuth, Miriam S., and Robert H. Tykot, eds. 1998. *Sardinian and Aegean Chronology.* Oxford: Oxbow.

Bartoloni, Gilda, and Filippo Delpino, eds. 2004. *Oriente e Occidente.* Rome: Istituti Editoriali Poligrafici Internazionali.

Berthier, André, and René Charlier. 1952–1955. *Le sanctuaire punique d'El-Hofra à Constantine, I–II.* Paris: Arts et métiers graphiques.

Boardman, John. 1999. *The Greeks Overseas*, 4th ed. New York: Thames & Hudson.

Bonnet, Corinne. 2014. "Greeks and Phoenicians in the Western Mediterranean." In *Companion to Ethnicity in the Ancient Mediterranean*, edited by Jeremy McInerney, 327–340. Chichester: Wiley Blackwell.

Brandherm, Dirk. 2006. "Zur Datierung der ältesten griechischen und phönizischen Importkeramik auf der Iberischen Halbinsel." *Madrider Mitteilungen*, 47: 1–23.

Brandherm, Dirk, and Martin Trachsel, eds. 2008. *A New Dawn for the Dark Age? Shifting Paradigms in Mediterranean Iron Age Chronology.* Oxford: Archaeopress.

Bresson, Alain. 2003. "Merchants and Politics in Ancient Greece: Social and Economic Aspects." In *Mercanti e politica nel mondo antico*, edited by Carlo Zaccagnini, 139–163. Rome: Bretschneider.

Bresson, Alain, and Pierre Rouillard, eds. 1993. *L'Emporion.* Paris: de Boccard.

Briquel Chatonnet, Françoise. 2012. "Communication: Les inscriptions phénico-grecques et le bilinguisme des Phéniciens." *CRAIBL*, 156.1: 619–638.

Bunnens, Guy. 1979. *L'expansion phénicienne en Méditerranée.* Rome: Institut historique belge de Rome.

Carpenter, Rhys. 1958. "Phoenicians in the West." *American Journal of Archaeology*, 62: 35–53.

Celestino, Sebastián and Carolina López-Ruiz. 2016. *Tartessos and the Phoenicians in Iberia.* Oxford: Oxford University Press.

Chiappisi, Stefano. 1961. *Il Melqart di Sciacca e la questione fenicia in Sicilia.* Rome: Bardi.

Cross, Frank M. 1972. "An Interpretation of the Nora Stone." *BASOR*, 208: 13–19.

D'Andrea, Bruno, and Sara Giardino. 2011. "Il tofet dove e perché." *Vicino e Medio Oriente*, 15: 133–157.

Davies, John K. "The 'Origins of the Greek *polis*'." In *The Development of the Polis in Archaic Greece*, edited by Lynette Mitchell and Peter J. Rhodes, 13–20. London: Routledge.

De Angelis, Franco. 2002. "Trade and Agriculture at Megara Hyblaia." *Oxford Journal of Archaeology*, 21(3): 299–310.

Demetriou, Denise. 2013. *Negotiating Identity in the Ancient Mediterranean*. Cambridge: Cambridge University Press.

Descoeudres, Jean-Paul. 2002. "Al Mina across the Great Divide." *Mediterranean Archaeology*, 15: 49–72.

Dietler, Michael, and Carolina López-Ruiz, eds. 2009. *Colonial Encounters in Ancient Iberia*. Chicago: University of Chicago Press.

Docter, Roald F., Fethi Chelbi, Boutheina Maraoui Telmini, et al. 2008. "New Radiocarbon Dates from Carthage." In *Beyond the Homeland*, edited by Claudia Sagona, 179–191. Leuven: Peeters.

Docter, Roald F., and Hans Georg Niemeyer. 1994. "Pithekoussai." *Annali di archeologia e storia antica*, 1: 101–115.

Docter, Roald F., Hans Georg Niemeyer, Albert J. Nijboer, and Johannes van der Plicht. 2004. "Radiocarbon Dates of Animal Bones in the Earliest Levels of Carthage." In *Oriente e Occidente*, edited by Gilda Bartoloni and Filippo Delpino, 557–577. Rome: Istituti Editoriali Poligrafici Internazionali.

van Dommelen, Peter. 2005. "Colonial Interactions and Hybrid Practices." In *The Archaeology of Colonial Encounters*, edited by Gil Stein, 109–142. Santa Fe: School for Advanced Research.

van Dommelen, Peter. 2006. "The Orientalizing Phenomenon: Hybridity and Material Culture in the Western Mediterranean." In *Debating Orientalization*, edited by Corinna Riva and Nicholas Vella, 135–152. London: Equinox.

van Dommelen, Peter, and Carlos Gómez Bellard, eds. 2008. *Rural Landscapes of the Punic World*. Oakville: Equinox.

van Dongen, Erik. 2010. "'Phoenicia': Naming and Defining a Region in Syria-Palestine." In *Interkulturalität in der Alten Welt*, edited by Robert Rollinger, Birgit Gufler, Martin Lang, and Irene Madreiter, 471–488. Wiesbaden: Harrassowitz.

Drews, Robert. 1979. "Phoenicians, Carthage and the Spartan *Eunomia*." *AJPh*, 100: 45–58.

Famà, Maria Luisa, ed. 2002. *Mozia. Gli scavi nella "Zona A" dell'abitato*. Bari: Edipuglia.

Fantalkin, Alexander. 2006. "Identity in the Making." In *Naukratis*, edited by Alexandra Villing and Udo Schlotzhauer, 199–208. London: British Museum.

Feeney, Denis. 2007. *Caesar's Calendar*. Berkeley: University of California Press.

Fentress, Elizabeth. 2009. "The Punic and Libyan Towns of Jerba." In *Phönizisches und punisches Städtewesen*, edited by Sophie Helas and Dirce Marzoli, 203–216. Mainz: von Zabern.

Figueira, Thomas J. 1984. "Karl Polanyi and Ancient Greek Trade." *Ancient World*, 10: 15–30.

Frankenstein, Susan. 1979. "The Phoenicians in the Far West." In *Power and Propaganda*, edited by Mogens T. Larsen, 263–294. Copenhagen: Akademisk Forlag.

Fumadó Ortega, Ivan. 2013. "Colonial Representations and Carthaginian Archaeology." *Oxford Journal of Archaeology*, 32(1): 53–72.

Gener, José Maria, Rafael Maya, Gemma Jurado et al. 2015. "Nuevos datos sobre el Kronion de Gadir: resultados de la intervención arqueológica en el Castillo de San Sebastián (Cádiz)." In *VII Encuentro de Arqueología del Suroeste Peninsular, Aroche-Serpa*, edited by Nieves Medina Rosales, 429–451. Huelva: Ayuntamiento de Aroche.

de Geus, Cornelius H.J. 2001. "Oriental Origins of the Greek City." In *The Greek City from Antiquity to Present*, edited by Kristoffel Demoen, 41–48. Leuven: Peeters.

Gilboa, Ayelet, and Ilan Sharon. 2003. *"An Archaeological Contribution to the Early Iron Age Chronological Debate."* BASOR, 332: 7–80.

Gilboa, Ayelet, Ilan Sharon, and Elisabetta Boaretto. 2008. "Tel Dor and the Chronology of Phoenician 'Pre-Colonisation Stages.'" In *Beyond the Homeland*, edited by Claudia Sagona, 179–191. Leuven: Peeters.

González de Canales, Fernando, Leonardo Serrano, and Juan P. Garrido. 2000. "Nuevas inscripciones fenicias en Tarteso." In *Actas del IV Congreso Internacional de Estudios Fenicios y Púnicos*, edited by Maria E. Aubet and Manuela Barthélemy, 227–238. Cadiz: Universidad de Cádiz.

González de Canales, Fernando, Leonardo Serrano, and Jorge Llompart. 2006. "The Pre-Colonial Phoenician Emporium of Huelva ca. 900–770 BC." *BABesch*, 81: 13–29.

Graham, Alexander J. 1964. *Colony and Mother City in Ancient Greece*. Manchester: Manchester University Press.

Grayson, A. Kirk. 1991–*1996. Assyrian Rulers of the First Millennium BC, I–II*. Toronto: Toronto University Press.

Gras, Michel. 2002. "Périples culturels entre Carthage, la Grèce et la Sicile au VIIIe siècle av. J.-C." In *Identités et cultures dans le monde méditerranéen antique*, edited by Cristel Müller and Francis Prost, 183–198. Paris: Publications de la Sorbonne.

Gschnitzer, Fritz. 1988. "Die Stellung der Polis in der politischen Entwicklung des Altertums." *Oriens antiquus*, 27: 287–302.

Hall, Jonathan. M. 1997. *Ethnic Identity in Greek Antiquity*. Cambridge: Cambridge University Press.

Hansen, Mogens H. 1997a. "*Emporion*: A Study of the Use and Meaning of the Term in the Archaic and Classical Periods." In *Yet More Studies in the Ancient Greek Polis*, edited by Thomas H. Nielsen, 83–105. Stuttgart: Franz Steiner.

Hansen, Mogens H. 1997b. "The Copenhagen Inventory of *Poleis* and *the Lex Hafniensis de Civitate*." In *The Development of the Polis in Archaic Greece*, edited by Lynette Mitchell and Peter J. Rhodes, 5–12. London: Routledge.

Hansen, Mogens H., ed. 2000. *A Comparative Study of Thirty City-State Cultures*. Copenhagen: Reitzel.

Hansen, Mogens H. 2006. "*Emporion*: A Study in the Use and Meaning of the Term in the Archaic and Classical Periods." In *Greek Colonisation, I*, edited by Gocha R. Tsetskhladze, 1–39. Leiden: Brill.

Hansen, Mogens H., and Thomas H. Nielsen, eds. 2004. *An Inventory of Archaic and Classical Poleis*. Oxford: Oxford University Press.

Hawkins, John D. 2000. *Corpus of Hieroglyphic Luwian Inscriptions*, I. Berlin: de Gruyter.

Hodos, Tamar. 2006. *Local Responses to Colonization in the Iron Age Mediterranean*. London: Routledge.

Hodos, Tamar. 2009. "Colonial Engagements in the Global Mediterranean Iron Age." *Cambridge Archaeological Journal*, 19: 221–241.

Hodos, Tamar. 2010. "Globalization and Colonization." *Journal of Mediterranean Archaeology*, 23(1): 81–106.

Hoftijzer, Jacob, and Karel Jongeling. 1995. *Dictionary of the North-West Semitic Inscriptions*. Leiden: Brill.
Huss, Werner. 1994. *Die Karthager*. Munich: Beck.
Kaplan, Philip. 2003. "Cross-Cultural Contacts among Mercenary Communities in Saite and Persian Egypt." *Mediterranean Historical Review*, 18: 1–31.
Kaufman, Brett. 2009. "A Citizen of Tyre in Sabratha." *MAARAV*, 16(1): 39–48, 143–148.
Kaufman, Stephen A. 2007. "The Phoenician Inscription of the Incirli Trilingual." *MAARAV*, 14(2): 7–26.
Kestemont, Guy. 1983. "Tyr et les Assyriens." In *Sauvons Tyr – Histoire phénicienne*, edited by Eric Gubel, Edward Lipiński, and Brigitte Servais-Soyez, 53–78. Leuven: Peeters.
Kestemont, Guy. 1985. "Les Phéniciens en Syrie du nord." In *Phoenicia and its Neighbors*, edited by Eric Gubel and Edward Lipiński, 135–149. Leuven: Peeters.
Kuhrt, Amélie. 2002. "Greek Contact with the Levant and Mesopotamia in the First Half of the First Millennium BC: A View from the East." In *Greek Settlements in the Eastern Mediterranean and the Black Sea*, edited by Gocha R. Tsetskhladze and Anthony M. Snodgrass, 17–25. Oxford: Archaeopress.
Lanfranchi, Giovanni B. 2009. "A Happy Son of the King of Assyria." In *Of God(s), Trees, Kings, and Scholars*, edited by Mikko Lukko, Saana Svärd, and Raija Mattila, 127–150. Helsinki: Finnish Oriental Society.
Larsen, Mogens T. 1976. *The Old Assyrian City-State and its Colonies*. Copenhagen: Akademisk Forlag.
Larsen, Mogens T. 2000. "The Old Assyrian City-State." In *A Comparative Study of Thirty City-State Cultures*, edited by Mogens H. Hansen, 89–115. Copenhagen: Reitzel.
Lehmann, Gunnar. 2005. "Al Mina and the East." In *The Greeks in the East*, edited by Alexandra Villing, 61–92. London: British Museum.
Lehmann, Gunnar. 2008. "North Syria and Cilicia c.1200–300 BCE." In *Beyond the Homeland*, edited by Claudia Sagona, 179–191. Leuven: Peeters.
Lemaire, André. 2000. "Tarshish-Tarsisi." In *Studies in Historical Geography and Biblical Historiography*, edited by Gershon Galil and Moshe Weinfeld, 44–62. Leiden: Brill.
Lichtheim, Miriam. 1976–*1980*. *Ancient Egyptian Literature, II–III*. Berkeley: University of California Press.
Lipiński, Edward. 2004. *Itineraria Phoenicia*. Leuven: Peeters.
Lopez-Ruiz, Carolina, and Brian Doak, eds. 2019. *The Oxford Handbook of the Phoenician and Punic Mediterranean*. Oxford: Oxford University Press.
Lowe, Benedict. 2000. "Between Colonies and Emporia." In *Hellenistic Economies*, edited by Zosia H. Archibald, John Davies, Vincent Gabrielsen, and Graham J. Olive r, 133–151. London: Routledge.
Lutz, R. Theodore. 2001. "Phoenician Inscriptions from Tell el-Maskhuta." In *The World of the Aramaeans*, edited by P.M. Michèlle Daviau, John W. Wevers, and Michael Weigl, 190–212. Sheffield: Sheffield Academic Press.
Maier, Franz-Georg. 1985. "Factoids in Ancient History." *JHS*, 105: 32–39.
Malkin, Irad. 1994. *Myth and Territory in the Spartan Mediterranean*. Cambridge: Cambridge University Press.

Malkin, Irad. 2011. *A Small Greek World*. Oxford: Oxford University Press.
Markoe, Glenn. 2000. *The Phoenicians*. London: British Museum.
Modrall, Emily, Emma Blake, and Robert Schoen. 2012. "Phoenicio-Punic Pottery in the Hinterland of Motya and Marsala." In *L'Africa romana XIX*, edited by Maria Bastiana Cocco, Alberto Gavini, and Antonio Ibba, 1597–1610. Rome: Carocci.
Moran, William L. 1992. *The Amarna Letters*. Baltimore: Johns Hopkins University Press.
Morris, Ian. 1996. "The Absolute Chronology of the Greek Colonies in Sicily." *Acta Archaeologica*, 67: 51–59.
Niemeyer, Hans-Georg. 1990. "The Phoenicians in the Mediterranean." In *Greek Colonists and Native Populations*, edited by Jean-Paul Descoeudres, 469–489. Oxford: Clarendon Press.
Niemeyer, Hans-Georg. 1993. "Trade Before the Flag?" In *Biblical Archaeology Today, 1990*, edited by Avraham Biran and Joseph Aviram, 335–344. Jerusalem: Israel Exploration Society.
Niemeyer, Hans-Georg. 2000. "The Early Phoenician City-States on the Mediterranean." In *A Comparative Study of Thirty City-State Cultures*, edited by Mogens H. Hansen, 89–115. Copenhagen: Reitzel.
Niemeyer, Hans-Georg. 2006. "The Phoenicians in the Mediterranean, Between Expansion and Colonisation." In *Greek Colonisation, I*, edited by Gocha R. Tsetskhladze, 143–168. Leiden: Brill.
Nijboer, Albert J. 2004. "La cronologia assoluta dell'età del ferro nel Mediterraneo, dibattito sui metodi e sui risultati." In *Oriente e Occidente*, edited by Gilda Bartolini and Filippo Delpino, 527–556. Pisa: Istituti Editoriali Poligrafici Internazionali.
Nijboer, Albert J., and Johannes van der Plicht. 2006. "An Interpretation of the Radiocarbon Determination of the Oldest Indigenous-Phoenician Stratum thus far Excavated at Huelva, Tartessos (South-West Spain)." *BABesch*, 81: 31–36.
Oggiano, Ida. 2012. "Architectural Points to Ponder under the Porch of Amrit." *Rivista di studi fenici*, 40(2): 191–210.
Pappa, Eleftheria. 2012. "Framing Some Aspects of the Early Iron Age 'Chronological Mess'." *Kubaba*, 3: 1–38.
Parpola, Simo, and Kazuko Watanabe. 1988. *Neo-Assyrian Treaties and Loyalty Oaths*. Helsinki: Helsinki University Press.
Pingel, Volker. 2002. "Sobre las muestras radiocarbónicas procedentes de los yacimientos fenicios del tramo inferior del Río Vélez junto a Torre del Mar (Málaga)." In *Toscanos y Alarcón*, edited by Hermanfrid Schubart, 245–252. Barcelona: Universitat Pompeu Fabra.
Pingel, Volker. 2006. "Comentarios a las dataciones por radiocarbono del Morro de Mezquitilla (Málaga)." In *Morro de Mezquitilla*, edited by Hermanfrid Schubart, 147–151. Malaga: Diputación Provincial.
Plácido Suárez, Domingo. 1993. "Le vie di Ercole nell'estremo Occidente." In *Ercole in Occidente*, edited by Attilo Mastrocinque, 63–80. Trento: Università degli Studi di Trento.
Polanyi, Karl. 1963. "Ports of Trade in Early Societies." *The Journal of Economic History*, 23(1): 30–45.
Quinn, Josephine. 2018. *In Search of the Phoenicians*. Princeton: Princeton University Press.

Quinn, Josephine C., and Nicholas Vella, eds. 2014. *The Punic Mediterranean*. Cambridge: Cambridge University Press.
Raaflaub, Kurt. 2004a. "Zwischen Ost und West: Phönizische Einflüsse auf die griechische Polisbildung?" In *Griechische Archaik und der Orient*, edited by Robert Rollinger and Christoph Ulf, 271–289. Berlin: Akademie Verlag.
Raaflaub, Kurt. 2004b. "Archaic Greek Aristocrats as Carriers of Cultural Interaction." In *Commerce and Monetary Systems in the Ancient World*, edited by Robert Rollinger and Christoph Ulf, 197–217. Stuttgart: Steiner.
Rendeli, Marco. 2005. "La Sardegna e gli Eubei." In *Il Mediterraneo di Herakles*, edited by Paolo Bernardini and Raimondo Zucca, 91–124. Rome: Carocci.
Ridgway, David. 1992. *The First Western Greeks*. Cambridge: Cambridge University Press.
Ridgway, David. 1999. "The Carthaginian Connection." In *Archäologische Studien in Kontaktzonen der antiken Welt*, edited by Renata Rolle, Karin Schmidt, and Roald Docter, 301–318. Göttingen: Vandenhoeck & Ruprecht.
Riis, Poul J. 1970. *Sukas, I*. Copenhagen: Munksgaard.
Ruiz Mata, Diego. 1999. "La fundación de Gádir y el castillo de Doña Blanca." *Complutum*, 10: 279–317.
Sagona, Claudia, ed. 2008. *Beyond the Homeland*. Leuven: Peeters.
Sagona, Claudia. 2013. "Phoenician and Carthaginian Migrations." In *The Encyclopedia of Global Human Migration*, edited by Immanuel Ness, 2411–2415. Chichester: Wiley Blackwell.
Scheid, John, and Jesper Svenbro. 1985. "Byrsa: La ruse d'Élissa et la foundation de Carthage." *Annales*, 40(2): 328–342.
Schmitz, Philip. 2012. *The Phoenician Diaspora*. Winona Lake: Eisenbrauns.
Sherratt, Susan, and Andrew Sherratt. 1993. "The Growth of the Mediterranean Economy in the Early First Millennium BC." *World Archaeology*, 24(3): 361–378.
Snodgrass, Anthony. 1980. *Archaic Greece*. Berkeley: University of California Press.
Sommer, Michael. 2009. "Networks of Commerce and Knowledge in the Iron Age." In *Greek and Roman Networks in the Mediterranean*, edited by Irad Malkin, Christy Constantakopoulou, and Katarina Panagopoulou, 97–111. London: Routledge.
Sommer, Michael. 2010. "Shaping Mediterranean Economy and Trade." In *Material Culture and Social Identities in the Ancient World*, edited by Shelley Hales and Tamar Hodos, 114–137. Cambridge: Cambridge University Press.
Spagnoli, Federico. 2013. "Phoenician Cities and Water." In *A History of Water, I*, edited by Terje Tvedt and Terje Oestigaard, 89–106. London: I.B. Tauris.
Stager, Jennifer M.S. 2005. "'Let No One Wonder at This Image'." *Hesperia*, 74(3): 427–449.
Stockhammer, Philipp. 2013. "From Hybridity to Entanglement." *Archaeological Review from Cambridge*, 28(1): 11–28.
Sznycer, Maurice. 1975. "'L'assemblée du peuple' dans les cités puniques d'après le témoinage épigraphiques." *Semitica*, 25: 47–68.
Teixidor, Javier. 1979. "Les fonctions de *rab* et de suffète en Phénicie." *Semitica*, 29: 9–17.
Tekoğlu, Recai, and André Lemaire. 2000. "La bilingue royale louvito-phénicienne de Çineköy." *CRAIBL*, 144(3): 961–1007.

Thompson, Christine M., and Sheldon Skaggs. 2013. "King Solomon's Silver?" *Internet Archaeology*, 35. doi:10.11141/ia.35.6.

Tsetskhladze, Gocha R., ed. 2006. *Greek Colonisation, I*. Leiden: Brill.

Vives-Ferrándiz Sánchez, Jaime. 2008. "Negotiating Colonial Encounters." *Journal of Mediterranean Archaeology*, 21(2): 241–272.

Wagner, Carlos G. 2007. "El barco negro en la costa." *Gerión*, 25 (Extra 1): 121–131.

Waldbaum, Jane C. 1997. "Greeks *in* the East or Greeks *and* the East?" *BASOR*, 305: 1–17.

Whittaker, Charles Richard. 1974. "The Western Phoenicians: Colonisation and Assimilation." *PCPS*, 20: 58–79.

Xella, Paolo, ed. 2013. *The Tophet in the Phoenician Mediterranean (SEL 29–30)*. Verona: Essedue.

FURTHER READING

There are useful summaries of Phoenician colonization by Niemeyer (2000), Culican (*CAH* 3.3, 461–546), and Sagona (2013). Markoe (2000) and Aubet (2001) have provided comprehensive surveys; note also various pertinent chapters in Lopez-Ruiz and Doak (2019). For treatment of Phoenician and Greek colonization as linked within Mediterranean-wide systems, see Hodos (2006) and Malkin (2011); for culturally mixed settlements, including indigenes, see van Dommelen (2006), Hodos (2010), and Celestino and López-Ruiz (2016). Archaeological surveys have demonstrated how Phoenicians exploited their hinterlands, see van Dommelen and Gómez Bellard (2008) and Modrall, Blake, and Schoen (2012).

CHAPTER NINE

Neo-Assyrian through Persian Empires

Robert Rollinger

Dimensions of Encounter

There is vast documentation for Greeks within ancient Near Eastern empires. This applies also to the Neo-Assyrian, Neo-Babylonian, and Persian Empires (Map 3). In cuneiform texts of these periods Greeks appear from the eighth century BC. The languages concerned are Akkadian (Assyrian and Babylonian), Old-Persian, Elamite, and Aramean. Besides indications in archival texts, it is references in Royal inscriptions where Greeks are attested. There the ancient Near Eastern texts refer to these "Westerners" as Yamanāya/Yamnāya, and with Yaman they also mention a land of origin for these people. Yet there is some disagreement in recent scholarship which Greek population is meant exactly by these designations and where Yaman has to be precisely located. Frequently the term is just equated with "Ionians," yet this conveys considerable problems. Both terms, "Ionian" in Greek sources, as well as Yamanāya/Yamnāya in ancient Near Eastern ones, are mutable and indeed do take on different meanings over time. They are subject to developments and dynamics of meaning, independent of the etymologically common origins of the term or the question as to who adapted and further developed it (cf. Rollinger 2007a, 260–261 n. 7). The veracity of this caveat is immediately evident if one considers sources from Achaemenid times. The inscriptions of Darius I not only mention the Babylonian Yamanāya, but also provide an Old Persian (sing. Yauna, plur. Yaunā) and Elamite (Yauna-ip/-ap) equivalent. There is also a noticeable attempt to differentiate further within the terms used, and thus to arrive at a greater precision and distinctiveness. There is almost a taxonomy at play here, and newly coined terms such as Yaunā takabarā = ("Greeks" *takabarā*), Yaunā tayai uškahyā = ("Greeks" of the mainland), [Yaunā] tayai drayahyā (dārayanti) = (["Greeks"] [living] close to the sea), [Yaunā] tayā para draya (dārayanti) = (["Greeks")] [living] beyond the sea) are still disputed (Calmeyer 1982; 1983a; 1983b; 1987; Klinkott 2001; Sancisi-Weerdenburg

---

A Companion to Greeks Across the Ancient World, First Edition. Edited by Franco De Angelis.
© 2020 John Wiley & Sons, Inc. Published 2020 by John Wiley & Sons, Inc.

2001a; 2001b; Rollinger 2006a; 2006b), as far as their specific meaning goes, but they nevertheless serve to show the scope of possible meanings. The same can be said for evidence from Hellenistic times, such as the new toponym Makkadūnu in Babylonian texts, or the defamation of troops led by Alexander and the Diadochi as Hanî, an older, distinctively pejorative term for Western foreigners. At the same time, Yamanāya remains in use for the conquerors from the West (Joannès 1997, 150–151).

What can we learn from this that helps us to understand the usage of toponyms such as Yaman or ethnonyms like Yamnāya (Assyrian) or Yamanāya (Babylonian)? For one, we may see that these terms were subject to changing use. Second, we must assume that its usage in Neo-Assyrian times was not the same as in the Neo-Babylonian time, and that, even later in the past, Achaemenid uses were different still. It is at least possible that the divergent use of the ethnonym in Babylonian and Assyrian times is an indication for different points of reference, though this must remain a hypothesis and is, perhaps, unlikely (Rollinger 1997, 168–170). The whole matter is complicated by idiosyncrasies in the source material. The evidence for both periods belongs to different genres: Neo-Assyrian material mostly (with only some exceptions) stems from royal annals, while the Neo-Babylonian sources are almost universally of a documentary nature. This difference in genres has to be taken into account, as the specific point of view of our sources may skew our general image.

These constraints notwithstanding, and considering the change that may very well have happened over time, we shall take our first cue from the source material dating to the Achaemenid period. It is only thus that we can lay the foundations for analyzing earlier periods. While there is now an almost unmanageable amount of scholarship dealing with "Ionians" in Archaemenid inscriptions, no consensus has been reached as concerns the geographical allocation of the different terms, so that individual points continue to be argued vehemently. But maybe some degree of certainty can be reached for aspects that are relevant to our purposes. There is consensus that, among others, "Greeks" from Asia Minor are addressed in these inscriptions. The Yaunā tayai uškahyā = "Greeks" of the mainland can hardly be interpreted otherwise. There is a high likelihood that an analogous interpretation for the [Yaunā] tayai drayahyā (dārayanti) = ["Greeks"] [living] near the sea is also correct, as it seems that this group belongs in the northwestern regions of Asia Minor (Schmitt 1972; Klinkott 2001, 111–112). There is, however, an even chance that none of these groups in fact matches the population defined as Ionians by modern scholars, either as a group of peoples sharing the same dialect or as a network of individual *poleis* that together saw the sacred area dedicated to Poseidon Helikonios known as the Panionion as a religious and cultic center (Smarczyk 2000; Ehrhardt 2005; Kerschner 2005; Lohmann 2005). Compared to this, we can be much less certain of the identification of the [Yaunā] tayā para draya (dārayanti) = ["Greeks"] [living] beyond the sea as inhabitants of the Greek islands or even of mainland Greece. There can be no doubt, however, that these distant Greeks are included in one of the designations found in the inscriptions, or, indeed, in the general designation Yauna, even if there is less certainty today than there used to be about the identity of the Yaunā takabarā as peoples inhabiting Thessaly or Macedonia (Rollinger 2006b).

In a widely received analysis, Hilmar Klinkott has pointed out that "Greeks" as well as non-Greek populations must be included in these Near Eastern descriptions (Klinkott 2001, 137–138). This can be shown for the Neo-Babylonian time (see below) and the possibility should at least not be excluded for the Achaemenid period. The assumption that Achaemined texts not only refer to "Ionians" as "Greeks" of Asia Minor, even less to (eastern) Ionians in a modern sense, but included in their description also island Greeks and maybe even "Greeks from the mainland" is further backed up by the testimony of a source seldom considered in this respect. This is the Persian embassy mentioned in *The Acharnians* by Aristophanes, led by a certain Pseudartabas. It is irrelevant to our purposes whether, in the confines of the play, the embassy is meant to be genuine or understood as Athenian impostors clad in Persian garments (Hutzfeld 1999, 154–159). What is important is that Pseudartabas displays a pointedly Persian point of view, much to the delight of the audience regaled with his incomprehensible Persian language (l. 100) (Schmitt 1984). In pidgin-Greek, Pseudartabas dashes Athenian hopes of Persian subsidies by explaining: "Thou shalt not have gold, thou gaping-arsed Ionian" (l. 104). Since the term "Ionian" (Iaonau) (l. 104) no doubt corresponds to the Yauna mentioned in Persian inscriptions, the latter must perforce also have included "Greeks" as such and have been attributable also to "mainland Greeks," as shown by Aristophanes. There is no certainty as to the breadth of the term, though: should it be exclusively applied to "Athenians" (Burkert 1992, 160 ad 18), to Athenians and Aegean Greeks, to "peoples speaking Greek" (Heubeck 1987, 147 ad 18), or, widest of all, generally to "Westerners"? Still, the passage from Aristophanes, which may well reflect Athenian views and usages of the term "Ionians" specific to the second half of the fifth century, mirrors Achaemenid usage and opens our vista from Asia Minor to the Aegean and on to the Greek mainland.

If, building on these foundations, we now open our investigation up further and look to the usage of the term "Ionian" in Near Eastern sources pre-dating the Achaemenid period, we may arrive at a clearer picture. For here, too, it can be shown that while populations from Asia Minor are no doubt meant by this designation, the term is also applied to more western peoples.

Our first point of reference must be a tangle of documents partially published by Ernst Weidner in 1939. These documents were found in the archives of the so-called Südburg in Babylon, and the dossier published by Weidner was dated to the eleventh and thirteenth regal year of Nebuchadnezzar II (594/592) (Pedersén 2005a; 2005b, 117–118). They deal with the monthly rationing of sesame oil, with recipients including Babylonians as well as foreigners. Ever since Weidner, modern scholarship has concerned itself primarily with the latter and assumed that they must have been exiles or prisoners deported to Babylonia. But mentioned among the foreigners are a large number of specialists of a wide variety of professions, and the question must be asked whether many of these foreigners were not more likely to have been volunteers, migrant workers who made a living in foreign parts of the world. In this context, not only are the Yamanāya mentioned, but individual persons are listed by name. Remarkably, none of the surviving personal names could be interpreted as being Greek; instead they point toward a non-Greek milieu in Asia Minor. Though, of course, the remaining three (!) names are hardly representative, and care should be taken not to mistake the linguistic horizon of personal names with the language spoken by or the identity of its bearer. These Neo-Babylonian documents are nevertheless evidence the designated of Yamanāya did not exclusively mean "Greeks," but also included inhabitants of western Asia Minor.

An additional Neo-Babylonian document, not previously mentioned or considered in this context, may open up a new perspective. This is document YOS 17 253, issued on the second of Aiaru in the fourth regal year of Nebuchadnezzar (April 29, 601 BC) in an unknown place. It documents a consignment of 4½ minas (2¼ kg) of "blue purple wool" from Yaman to two weavers (lúUŠ.BAR^mc/išparū), identified by name. One of them, Kudurru, sets aside 83⅓ g of the textile for a festive garment (túgNÌ.LÁM/lamaḫuššú). The logographic characters SÍG.ZA.GÌN.KUR.[RA] must be translated as *takiltu* (Akkadian), meaning blue purple, or, rather, wool dyed that color (Rollinger 2007a, 267–269). One may reasonably be surprised at why purple-dyed wool should be imported to Babylonia from Yaman. Amélie Kuhrt has questioned this (Kuhrt 2002, 12), but this source should not be dismissed easily. There is further evidence for SÍG.ZA.GÌN.KUR.[RA]/*takiltu* being imported from the far west into the Near East. Three documents extensively discussed by A. Leo Oppenheim and dated to November 14, 551 (TCL 12 84) and October 15, 550 (YOS 6 168 l. 5 and the "copy" PTS 2098 l. 6), respectively, mention two further occasions where this seems to have occurred, one mentioning 16 mina and 15 shekels, the other 11 minas and 20 shekels (TCL 12 84, l. 12) worth of purple-dyed wool (Oppenheim 1967; Joannès 1999, 192–194). Even though these documents mention no specific point of origin for the wool, the complete register of goods mentions Yaman/"Ionia," Labnānu/Lebanon, and Miṣir/Egypt, and generally points to the West. There is an analogous picture found in the Old Testament, where particular attention must be paid to the "Lament on the Fall of Tyre" (Ez. 27), convincingly situated by Mario Liverani in the period between 612 and 585 BC (Liverani 1991, 71–72, 79). Verse 7 mentions Tyre importing blue-purple wool, that is, *t^ekēlät* (תכלת), and red-purple wool, that is, *argāmān* (ארגמן), from Elîšā (אלישה). This is not only the exact same terminology as in the Akkadian tablets, what is more, by way of Tyre, the way to the extreme west is open. Even if the exact localization of Elîšā remains controversial, there is no doubt among scholars as to the general geographical direction (cf. Diakonoff 1992, 175–176). It should also be pointed out that the register of peoples in Genesis 10 describes Elîšā (אלישה) as well as Taršîš, Kittîm, and Rōdānîm as belonging to the "Sons of Jawan" (בני יון) (v. 4). The following verse (5) gives further information: "By these were the lands of the Gentiles divided in their lands; every one after his tongue, after their families, in their nations."

Thus there is a remarkably similar picture, geographically as well as regarding content, drawn in Babylonian documents and in the Book of Ezekiel. But in both cases, there is no basis for a geographically precise location for Yaman/Jāwān. Some measure of precision can be adduced from consulting a fragment of Democritus of Ephesus that is transmitted in the works of Athenaios (12.29/525c-d = *FGrH* 267 F1). He mentions different kinds of luxurious robes the Ephesians used to wear. These are dyed in various colors with beautiful designs woven into them. He also adds specific terms for these garments: *sarapeis*, *kalasireis* "made in Corinth," Persian *kalasireis* "the most beautiful of all," and *aktaiai* "the most expensive type of Persian garment."

Although Democritus's notice was probably written in the third century BC, it appears to reflect circumstances of a much older date (Blum 1998, 144). This is hinted at by the unusual terminology for luxury garments. It is remarkable that, while the terminology points to an Anatolian-Near Eastern origin of the products, these garments were apparently manufactured in Greek workshops. This is emphasized particularly for the Persian *kalasireis* manufactured in Corinth. Furthermore, three choices of dye color are mentioned: purple, violet, and dark blue. Though one should not take the similarities too far, it is striking that, taking into account the Babylonian cuneiform tablets mentioned above, the color designations match the complementary pairing mentioned in the Hebrew bible as *tᵉkēlät* (תכלת)/*argāmān* (ארגמן) and in the Septuagint as (Blum 1998, 36–37; Steigerwald 1986, 42–45).

The vague historical context transmitted by the notice of Democritus of Ephesus is filled out by a passage from Plutarch's Life of Alexander (Plut., *Alex.* 36). Upon the conquest of Susa, Alexander came into possession of "five thousand talents' weight of purple from Hermione, which, although it had been stored there for a hundred and ninety years, still kept its colors fresh and lively. The reason for this, they say, is that honey was used in the purple dyes, and white olive oil in the white dyes; for these substances, after the like space of time, are seen to have a brilliancy that is pure and lustrous" (after Bernadotte Perrin). This is remarkable not only for the reference to enormous quantities of purple-dyed textiles in the royal depots of Susa, but also for the addendum mentioned in passing, that this cloth has been in storage for almost 200 years and originally hailed from Hermione in the Argolid. As far as the chronology of textile production goes, this would bring us back to the last third of the sixth century BC and add further credence to Achaemenid processes of production as described by Democritus of Ephesus. The cloth known as "purple from Hermione" respectively must have been prepared using a special technique to guarantee its longevity. From this we may conclude that Hermione was indeed a highly specialized center of production for high-quality purple cloth and textiles in late Archaic times. Furthermore, Hermione was not part of the Persian Empire, but was rather, like Corinth, a place of production outside the boundaries of Achaemenid Persia that produced wares and goods for its consumption.

We may add further proof for this hypothesis that also strengthens the connection to the situation mentioned in Babylonian documents. It is indeed astounding that, as far as I can see, this particular piece of evidence has never been used in this context, even though it fits remarkably well. I mean the visual representation of the gift-bearing delegation XII on the eastern and northern Apadāna staircase in Persepolis, both dating to the reign of Darius I (Figures 9.1 and 9.2). Even though neither of these delegations is clearly identified by an accompanying inscription, and although there has been some considerable dispute within scholarly circles as to their identity, there exists now something of a consensus in interpreting delegation XII as "Greek" gift-bearers (Calmeyer 1982, 154–155; 1983b, 154; Hachmann 1995; Curtis and Tallis 2005, 67; but cf. also Root 2007). What is remarkable, however, is the nature of the gifts they bear: two figures carry balls of wool, two others present folded lengths of cloth of different quality. Only the sole preceding figure is carrying two empty bowls and thus differs from his companions. Naturally, these depictions do not in any way convey information as to the point of origin of the gifts. But it does confirm the notion that those peoples described as Yamanāya have been known for the production and sale of dyed wools and cloths as early as the sixth century BC. The Achaemenid Apadāna bas-relief was no doubt also meant to express political claims to the regions depicted. But in a way akin to the Achaemenid royal inscriptions, it does leave room to speculate as to the precise geographic identity of the peoples depicted. In other words, it is by no means clear which Yamanāya are meant to be visually represented, and there is no conclusive evidence for an exclusively Anatolian focus.

Let us now reconsider the Neo-Babylonian evidence, firstly the documents published and discussed by A. Leo Oppenheim almost 50 years ago as mentioned earlier (Oppenheim

Figure 9.1 "Greek" gift-bearers (Delegation XII) on the eastern Apadāna staircase in Persepolis carrying balls of wool and folded lengths of cloth.

1967). Both YOS 6 168 (resp. PTS 2098) and TCL 12 84 probably hail from Uruk and both give a glimpse of a standardized yearly delivery processes. Apart from the deliveries of wools, Yaman is also mentioned as the point of origin for metals imported into Babylonia. In both cases, 295 minas (approximately 147.5 kg) of copper (UD.KA.BAR = ZABAR) and 130 minas (approximately 65 kg) of iron ore from Yaman (^{kur}ia-a-ma-na) are registered using the same formula for denoting their origins (^{kur}ia-a-ma-na/^{kur}ia-a-ma-nu). YOS 6 168 records a further delivery of 600 minas, or approximately 300 kg, of copper from Yaman (^{kur}ia-a-ma-na). Both texts mention only one other origin for imported metal, namely Lebanon (Labnānu), from where 257 minas of iron ore were imported. The origin of a further 37 minas of tin is not recorded and remains unknown. It is also possible that the Lebanese iron ore was of lower quality, since 42⅔ shekels were paid over for 257 minas (1 shekels/6 minas), while the ore delivered by the mines of Yaman was worth 32½ shekels, or 4 minas per silver shekel (Rollinger 2007a, 274–275). While there is no certainty that the indication of origin recorded in these documents was indeed meant as a geographical indication, it is nevertheless probable that, even if they were meant as a form of quality description, the terms most likely reflect those regions from which similar products were usually imported.

It is difficult to determine which regions those were. Oppenheim suspected Cyprus and "any other locality in western Asia colonized by Greeks" as a point of origin for copper,

Figure 9.2 "Greek" gift-bearers (Delegation XII) on the northern Apadāna staircase in Persepolis carrying balls of wool and folded lengths of cloth.

while casting his net wider for iron ore: "The 'Greek' iron was certainly brought from some region in the islands or the western coast of Asia Minor" (Oppenheim 1967, 241; cf. also Joannès 1991, 266; Dandamayev 1993, 68). If we take a closer look at possible mining sites, we may suppose two centrally important geographical regions: in the west, an area bordered by Anatolia in the northwest and northern Syria in the southeast, and, further to the east, the territories between the Black Sea and the Caspian Sea (Wäfler 1980-81, 79–80). This is confirmed, for example, by Assyrian royal annals that show metal tributes predominantly being drawn from these two areas (Lipiński 2000, 535–538). Neo-Babylonian documents, as we have seen, also point largely to the Syrian-Cilician region.

But where shall we find the considerably more western Yaman? Iron and copper ore deposits are not restricted only to western Anatolia, a region stretching from the Troad to Caria-Lycia (Wäfler 1980–1981, 80). Such deposits may also be found in the Aegean, in a territory stretching from Chalcidice in the north to Crete in the south, and including Euboea and the Cyclades as far as the Dodecanese (Rhodes) (Tichy 1997, 715–716). Importantly, for each of these regions, with the exception of Crete and Euboea, ore mining is attested for the first part of the first millennium BC.

Here, too, the register of trading partners in Ezekiel 27 supplements the information gleaned from Babylonian texts. Of special importance is verse 13: "Merchants from Jawan,

Tubal, and Meshech brought slaves and articles of copper to trade with you" (cf. Zaccagnini 1996, 456; Corral 2002, 151–152 n. 39). While Tūbal (תבל) and Mäšäk (משך) point to Cappadocia and Phrygia, Jāwān is to be sought in the bordering regions to the west (Liverani 1991, 70). The ores imported from these regions are interesting too: copper ore (נחשת) is also mentioned in both Neo-Babylonian texts. The slave trade cited is also known to us from other sources. The oldest Near Eastern source that mentions Yamnāya, the letter of Qurdi-Aššur-lāmur, dating back to the time of Tiglatpilesar III, describes a similar arrangement (Rollinger 2001, 237–238). The *Odyssey* also mentions this form of economic behavior as characteristic of the Taphians, a people equally renowned for their skills in rowing and for their preference of engaging in slave trade. Eumaios's nurse, a woman originally from Sidon, recounts her abduction by Taphians: "But Taphian pirates seized me, as I was coming from the fields, and brought me here, and sold me to the house of yonder man, and he paid for me a goodly price" (*Od*. 15.427–429, after Augustus T. Murray). Moreover, the *Odyssey* also connects the same Taphians to the trade in iron and ore (*Od*. 1.180–185). If we now try to reconcile this pattern with the information gained from analyzing YOS 6 168 and TCL 12 84 and to embed all of this into the wider historical context as described in Ezekiel 27: 12–24, we arrive at a scenario clearly reminiscent of the reconstruction of the Tyrrhenian trade network as established by Mario Liverani (1991, 68–74 with figure 2). This reconstruction is based on four trading "belts" in the form of concentric circles centering on Tyre itself. The first and second zones supply agrarian and "animal products," respectively. Jāwān is located at the intersection of zones III and IV, with the former being responsible for "manufactured products" and the latter for "metals and exotic products."

To summarize, we have arrived at a more geographically precise definition of Yaman that is not restricted to that part of western Asia Minor later known as "Ionia," and, indeed not at all restricted to the coastal zones belonging to it. Rather, it is necessary to understand Yaman in a wider sense, encompassing, at the least, the whole Aegean. If we combine this conclusion with established knowledge, we gain a rounder picture of the situation as a whole. Furthermore, if we take into account the dispersion of ceramic remains in the Levant between the eighth and sixth centuries BC, we find that a disproportionally large part of those remains originated from the Aegean, with Euboea, "Dorian" Rhodes, and, somewhat later, Corinth being particularly well represented (Haider 1996; Waldbaum 1994; 1997). This is almost identical to the region defined by Ian Morris as "Central Greece" (Morris 1998), where, to a high degree, revolutionary changes have been traced that are commonly associated with a stimulating influence from Near Eastern cultures.

We should remember that in the earliest piece of Greek literature (if one accepts *Il*. 13.685 as a later interpolation), the *Iaones* gather for a common festival on Delos (*Hom. Hymn*. 3, 146–155). Here, too, it becomes evident that an equation of the Yamanāya or *Iaones* with the "Ionians" of Asia Minor, or even with speakers of a dialect that could be classified as "Ionian," would be misleading. It has already been indicated that Yamanāya would not only have denoted "Greeks" in a linguistic sense, but also speakers of different dialects or languages. But there exists circumstantial evidence that Yamanāya was a term applied primarily to inhabitants of that cultural and language area that arose from the Aegean region. This evidence has, surprisingly, not yet been taken into account in this context and consists of a fragmentary text, probably part of a larger chronicle, describing the failed invasion of Egypt by Nebuchadnezzar in 568 BC. Herein is mentioned a place or a region of the earth known as ᵘʳᵘpu-ṭu-ia-a-man-[x] (Brinkman 1989, 60). Pūṭu-Yaman can be most plausibly equated with the Libya of the Yamanāya, probably meaning Cyrene or Cyrenaica (cf. Edel 1978; Zadok 1985, 252; Haider 1996, 71; Niemeier 2001, 19; Kuhrt 2002, 12 n. 24). If this assumption is correct, it would mean two things. First, Yaman was associated with the Aegean area to such a high degree that a foundation originating from there was still, to Levantines, associated with Yaman. Second, we see here a first attempt in pre-Achaemenid times, by adding epithets, to categorize and put in order the territory inhabited by the Yamanāya.

To recapitulate, even though the information provided by ancient Near Eastern sources is sparse and heterogeneous, we can glean from the Neo-Babylonian-Chaldean documents the contours of a geographic horizon that permits us to locate the Yamanāya with at least a degree of precision. While Neo-Assyrian sources describe them as "being from the centre of the sea," meaning from the far west (Rollinger and Ruffing 2014, 98–134), this can be stated more precisely by using Neo-Babylonian documentary evidence. This evidence clearly points beyond the Anatolian region and encompasses the whole Aegean and parts of the Greek mainland. Clearly, until the middle of the sixth century BC, the term was still being employed in a decidedly vague fashion. This is also the case with sources from the Achaemenid period, even if here we can observe for the first time – and building on Neo-Babylonian precursors – an effort to diversify the general usage of the term Yaman, and here, also, we find that the scope of that term clearly goes beyond "Ionia" in a strict sense and also beyond Asia Minor itself. These findings are confirmed by the testimony of the earliest Greek literary sources, the Homeric Hymn to Apollo, where the *Iaones* are mentioned, but also by the fragment of the writings of Democritus of Ephesus. The latter, together with the Babylonian term of Pūṭu-Yaman, is particularly important for locating Yaman. While Pūṭu-Yaman refers to "Greeks" in Pūṭu (Libya) who originated from the Aegean islands (Yaman), Democritus describes Corinth as a place of production for the very same goods referenced in a Neo-Babylonian document as being from "Yaman." The importation of metals from the same region is more difficult to interpret. It is probable that "Yaman" in this context must also be understood as referring to a specific point of origin, but there is another hypothesis that has gained traction in recent years and that must be discussed.

In recent scholarship, a controversy has developed over the question of Greek ceramics in closed find deposits in the Levant on the one hand, and the presence of large quantities of *orientalia* in Aegean-Greek deposits on the other (Popham 1994, 28–29; Boardman 1996; 2002; Papadopoulos 1996; Boardman and Popham 1997; Fletcher 2004; Niemeyer 2003; 2004). Can we assume the presence of Greek merchant vessels or must we think this a secondary process, following the opening of the Aegean and the western Mediterranean to international trade by Levantine merchants? There is some evidence for a trailblazing role played by Levantine traders and for attributing revolutionary pioneer work to the "Phoenician" city-states as trans-shipment sites (Aruz 2014). And it is not by chance that, in one of his inscriptions, the Neo-Assyrian king Esarhaddon (680–669 BC) mentions Taršîš and thus refers to southern Spain (Rollinger and Ruffing 2014, 112–115).

If one subscribes to such a scenario, considers changes, often qualified as revolutionary, that happened in individual societies of the Aegean-Greek region during the eighth and seventh centuries BC (Morris 1997, 548; 1999), and ascribes both developments to intensifying contacts with the Levantine-Oriental world (Rollinger 2014; 2015), the obvious conclusion must be that Aegean seamen slowly infiltrated those regions indicated by their Levantine predecessors. Not only was intermediary trade essential to this evolution, but even more so was the production of wares that were in demand in international trade and which could be sold with a profit. This would explain Aegean ceramics turning up in ever-increasing numbers in the eighth century, and also the purple-dyed high-quality fabrics that we encounter in Neo-Babylonian documents at the turn of the seventh century.

How does this relate to the trade in metal ores? Here too, it is likely that we are dealing with new mining sites being developed, though the possibility should not be excluded that Aegean seaman successfully established themselves as intermediary tradesmen in this area, and that the real mining sites lay even further to the west. Such prospects force us to open our gaze to the whole breadth of the Mediterranean, which from this point onward lay open to Aegean traders and colonists. The western Mediterranean also played a pivotal role in the procuring of metal ore. In this context, much has been made recently of the significance of, for example, Pithekoussai as an international trading hub, where cultural contacts were groomed between East and West, and where international trading goods and resources were exchanged (Ridgway 1994, 2004). It is therefore not absolutely clear from which sources the Yamanāya obtained their copper and iron. What is certain, however, is that they engaged in trading these resources and that, from the point of view of the Levantines, the Yamanāya were firmly situated in the Aegean.

Contacts and Perceptions Through Time

Neo-Assyrian Times (Eighth–Seventh Centuries)

The oldest cuneiform documents referring to the Yam(a)nāya are two letters that the Assyrian governor Qurdi-Aššur-lāmur, residing somewhere at the Levantine coast, sent to his king Tiglath-pileser III. (Nimrud Letter 69 = ND 2370 = Saggs 2001, 164–166, and ND 2737 = Saggs 2001, 166–167). The tasks and duties of this official can be coined in the following way: "An important part of his role was to protect the trading activities of Phoenician merchants, while exacting tax from them, and by placing tax inspectors at trade centers (*kāru, bīt kāri*)" (Yamada 2008, 309). It is difficult to understand what these facilities exactly were, but an inscription of Tiglath-pileser III, established in Iran in 737 BC, conveys important information on this issue (RINAP 1, Tiglath-pileser III 35 ii 10'–16'). The text mentions, among several Levantine cities, an institution called *bīt kāri* that is located at the coast. The term has been interpreted either as "emporium" (Tadmor 1994, 102–105; Tadmor and Yamada 2011, 85), or more generally as "a place of trade" (Yamada 2005, 68). It is also referred to as *bīt ṣabūtāte šarrūte*, which appears to define a "royal storehouse" (Tadmor 1994, 102–105; Tadmor and Yamada 2011, 86), or a facility "which supplies the royal needs" (Yamada 2005, 68). It remains a matter of discussion whether the text refers to a single institution attached to a single place, that is, Aḫtâ, or whether such facilities existed at all coastal cities mentioned in the inscription (Siannu, Ellišu, Ṣimirra, Rēši-ṣūri, Aḫtâ). In any case, it can hardly be doubted that this emporium/trading place served as Assyrian trading center, supplying royal needs with the revenue from trade and taxation on the goods imported by local sea-faring traders, Phoenician, Philistine, or Greek (Yamada 2005, 68).

Another letter of Qurdi-Aššur-lāmur to the king (ND 2715) mentions several such emporia/trading places (*bīt kārāni*) in the region of Tyre. Officially, these institutions are under the authority of the king of Tyre but are nevertheless controlled by Assyrian officials. When the inhabitants of Sidon expelled one of these officials, the Assyrians reintroduced him by force. Subsequently, they imposed a trade ban on the export of wool originating from Lebanon to Egypt and Pilistu (Saggs 2001, 155–158, plate 31; Yamada 2005, 59; 2008, 301–302). Eventually, after the conquest of Pilistu in 734 BC, an emporium of the land Assur (*bīt kāri ša māt Aššūr*) was also established in the city of Gaza (RINAP 1 Tiglath-pileser III 49 rev. 16; cf. Tadmor 1994, 188–189 with n. 16; Yamada 2005, 69).

These institutions, established by the Assyrian administration, had considerable influence on the Assyrian contacts with the West. The Assyrian bureaucracy was eager to foster and control commercial activities and to extract taxes from maritime trade. Assyrian power and influence reached far beyond the seashore and it affected the Levantine trading activities to the west (Broodbank 2013). Even though the Assyrian sources do not mention Greeks in this context, the Yamnāya must also have been touched by this kind of administrative control. In any case, it pertained to those Greeks who settled in cities that were under Assyrian control. Although our sources are also fairly mute on this phenomenon, there is one further letter of Qurdi-Aššur-lāmur that offers more information on this.

According to Yamada, the letter ND 2737 dates between 748 and 734 BC and is the earliest cuneiform document that mentions Greeks (Saggs 2001, 166–167, plate 33; Yamada 2008, 305–306, 309). Unfortunately, the letter is damaged considerably and it is not easy to fully understand its content. Qurdi-Aššur-lāmur reports about the work performed on a town moat when a marauding gang appears on the scene. The attackers escape to the mountains. In the next episode of the text, two cities are mentioned by name. Whether this happens in the course of the pursuit (Na'aman 2004, 70), is not clear. The first one can be read as ^{uru}*ia-ú-na* (obv. l. 14'), the second one probably is ^{uru}*r[e-š]i-ṣu-ri*, that is, Rēši-ṣūri (obv. l. 14'). It is highly plausible that ^{uru}Iauna is related to Yaman and means something like "Yaman-city," that is, "Greek-city" (*pace* Bagg 2007, 129–130; cf. Rollinger 2011b, 271). If this is true, we have the first attestation for the settlement of Greeks on Assyrian territory in our cuneiform documentation. That the city was under firm Assyrian control becomes evident from the fact Qurdi-Aššur-lāmur levies in total 200 persons from the two cities mentioned in the letter and transfers the command of them to a military commander (*turtānu*) (obv. 16'–18'). The text ends abruptly with the return to work on the moat. Unfortunately, we do not know where exactly ^{uru}*ia-ú-na* has to be situated. In any case, it must be close to the coast and it is highly probable that the events referred to in the letter have to be located to the south of the Gabal al-Aqra' (Na'aman 2004, 70). This means that it cannot be identified with al-Mīnā'. It is attractive to equate it with Ra's al-Basīṭ, but this remains speculation. The same applies for identifying Rēši-ṣūri with Ra's Ibn Hāni' (cf. Bagg 2007, 203). The testimony is also important because it reopens the debate on the role al-Mīnā' played and the character of the site. The site was interpreted as a Greek colony or even as a Greek mercenary camp (for an overview of the discussion see Hodos 2006, 37–40). The material in its earliest stratum X appears to have been almost exclusively Greek and is dated between 770 and ca. 750 BC. But since the earliest Cypriot and Phoenician pottery of the younger stratum IX has been dated to the end of the ninth century BC, the chronology and foundation of the site remain opaque. In any case, the material remains of the earlier strata look very much similar to other contemporary North Syrian sites like Ra's al-Basīṭ and Tell Sukas. Most likely all these cities shared a multicultural milieu where Greeks played a certain role. This is also true for al-Mīnā', which served as port for Tell Tayinat and where trade with the West obviously loomed large. As we have seen, al-Mīnā' cannot be equated with "Yaman-city" of ND 2737 and, so far, the identification of the latter site remains open for discussion. Maybe the designation "Yaman-city" is due to the perspective of the text, the setting of which is the incursion of a marauding gang. Since, as we have also seen, the Yamnāya were referred to by Qurdi-Aššur-lāmur as pirates and buccaneers (Yamada 2008, 310), the Assyrian official may have labeled a site as "Yaman-city" where at that specific moment there was a considerable presence of such "Greeks." Be that as it may, starting with Qurdi-Aššur-lāmur's famous letter ND 2370 dating around 732/730 BC, the ethnonym Yamnāya is connected with marauding gangs. This perspective reappears in most of the Neo-Assyrian sources focusing on these "Westerners" excluding other fields of employment and activities. By contrast, the typically Greek mercenary activity, so readily accepted by modern scholarship, is hardly in evidence, or at least only in beginning stages (Rollinger 2001, 256–257 Rollinger and Korenjak 2001; Luraghi 2006). Admittedly, one must question to what degree this picture, informed by royal inscriptions, for the most part, is really accurate and how much distortion is caused by the firm embedment of our source material in traditional royal ideology and the world-view connected to it.

Barbara Patzek has described the Aegean–Levantine relationship of this time as a "relationship of distance" (*Fernverhältnis*) (Patzek 1996, 2–3). This is accurate, insofar as our sources mentioning contacts primarily for the coastal region between Cilicia and Egypt are concerned. On the whole, however, this appraisal is only partially correct. On closer examination, it turns out that there is some evidence for the presence of "Greeks" within the Neo-Assyrian Empire and such a presence must indeed be assumed (Boardman 1997; Rollinger 2001, 243–244). This, in turn, supports the notion that the Yamnāya could not only have appeared in the guise of corsairs. Reference has already been made to the developing mercenary trade. Other sources belong in this context as well, such as for instance the inscriptions of Sennacherib that mention the employment of "Greek" shipwrights in the Assyrian navy, even if they are, indeed, deported people (Rollinger 2007b). The notion of the Yamnāya as "Westerners" is, of course, due to the Assyrian perspective and the world-view inherent in Assyrian sources. But the provenance of ceramics found in Levantine coastal settlements clearly points to central Aegean origins, which are also referenced in cuneiform inscriptions of later periods.

Neo-Babylonian Times (Sixth Century)

This picture changed fundamentally with the appearance of Neo-Babylonian-Chaldean sources. Not only can Yaman now be identified as the central Aegean-Anatolian area, but there are also important differences in the characterization of the peoples described as Yamanāya. No more mention is made of pirates or buccaneers. Instead, either Yaman is depicted as the region of origin for important resources imported into Asia Minor, or individuals hailing from Yaman are described as intermediary traders to eastern markets. In all likelihood, these shifting views reflect important social and economic changes within the Aegean, and the demand for specialists from these areas seems to have risen considerably.

We can also trace a steadily rising demand for mercenaries to the accession of the Saite dynasty in Egypt. This demand will have led ever more Greeks to the Levant, with Antimenidas, the brother of Alkaios, being only the most prominent example (but see now also Fantalkin/Lytle 2016). It is probably no coincidence that there is an abundance of archaeological evidence for the presence of Greek mercenaries in individual fortresses in Phoenicia and Palestine (Haider 1996, 69–79), such as Tell Kabri and Meẓad Ḥashavjāhû (Fantalkin 2001).

This picture may be completed with early Arab graffiti from the Oasis of Taymā'. Part of these inscriptions, written in the Taymanian language, was supplemented by visual representations and may be traced to the entourage of the Babylonian king Nabonidus, who spent 10 years there (Hayajneh 2001a; 2001b). It is remarkable that the names of the scribes are obviously not Arab. Indeed, the terminology indicates an Aramaic-Babylonian milieu. For a few personal names, a Greek etymology is not impossible, such as for the inscriptions Taymā' 3 and 4 (numbers according to Müller and al-Said 2001). Taymā' 3 proclaims: "I am 'nds, overseer (or bodyguard) of the king of Babel; I was in charge of the vanguard." (Müller and al-Said 2001, 114; Hayajneh 2001a, 87; 2001b, 49–50). The proper name is not Arab in origin. Hani Hayajneh thought it Elamite. Walter Müller assumed a possibly Greek origin and proposed Endios, Enodios, or even Oineidēs or Oiniadēs. The same name – maybe even the same person – is also mentioned in Taymā' 4: "I am 'nds, the servant of Nabonidus, king of Babel" (Müller and al-Said 2001, 117; Hayajneh 2001a, 89; 2001b, 32–35, 53). Both persons seem to have been close to the Babylonian king, probably in military roles. A similar indication is found in Taymā' 2: "*sktrsl*, son of *srtn*, came with the military commander" (Müller and al-Said 2001, 113; Hayajneh 2001a, 86–87; 2001b, 43–45). Hayajneh makes the connection to a Babylonian personal name, Sakkut-rîsi-ili, and does not resolve the patronymic. Müller and al-Said discuss the possibility of an ancient Anatolian personal name, and think a Carian origin most likely. As far as the patronymic is concerned, they accept the possibility of a Greek name-form S(t)ratōn, S(t)rotōn. In this case, too, we are certainly dealing with a high-ranking military background, since *sktrsl* belonged to the inner circle of the *rbsrs*, a term that may be interpreted as an Aramaic variant of the Akkadian *rab ša rēši* (Hayajneh 2001b, 35–37). This official is known to us, at least from Assyrian times, as a court official who could also on occasion be entrusted with high-ranking military commands. This is probably the case here (Mattila 2000).

If these persons were indeed Greeks, we have here the first authentic Near Eastern testimony for Greek soldiers within the Babylonian army. Furthermore, these soldiers, most likely mercenaries, seem to have occupied high-ranking command posts, and at least some of them would even have had access to the king. Their long residence in Taymā' apparently also led to the adaption of the local language and writing system, at least for commemorative graffiti. This is of particular importance, even if the persons mentioned were not, in fact, Greeks. They were not, in any case, bearers of Arab names and must have entered Taymā' from outside, in the train of the Babylonian army. At the very least, these graffiti produced by officers and high-ranking commanders who enjoyed royal trust are a clear indication that people of non-Babylonian descent could rise to prominence in the royal army.

The Taymā' graffiti neatly fit into the scenario of a steadily growing participation of "Greeks" in Near Eastern societies. The same goes for the Yamanāya mentioned in rationing lists from the reign of Nebuchadnezzar (see above). Even if we cannot conclusively prove the exact status of the recipients, the terminology of occupations shows that they must have been specialists of one form or another. Two separate terms are attested for persons subsumed under the heading of Yamanāya. A number of "Greeks" are described as ˡúNAGARᵐᵉˢ/*nagārū*, a term that describes artisans, including carpenters, joiners, and cabinet makers. They are further divided into two groups of seven or eight individuals. What is remarkable is that some of these craftsmen were apparently also employed in shipbuilding. Some of them are recorded as being assigned to a *bīt sapīnati*, probably meaning a boathouse or shipyard, with five Egyptians being deputized to stand guard (ˡúEN.NUN). A further occupational title is mentioned, but poses some problems. We do not know with any certainty what is meant by the term ˡúEDIN-*ú*. Some of those people for whom the term is used originally hailed from Yaman, from Lydia, Pirindu, Ḫume, and Parsu. Pedersén conjectured "some kind of official messengers from these countries," reasoning that "only the two (scil. *ṣērú*) from Pirindu were together at the same time in Babylon. When more than one person is attested for the other areas, they seem to have been there one after the other" (Pedersén 2005a, 270). If this assumption is correct, we have the first surviving evidence of diplomatic contacts between "Greek" *poleis* and the Babylonian royal court.

The impression we gain from the rationing lists is that of a multicultural milieu. Apart from the Yamanāya, we read about Carians, Lydians, Cilicians and Syrians, Phoenicians, meaning inhabitants of Tyre, Byblos, and Arwad, Philistines (Askalon), Arabs, Egyptians, Elamites, Medes and Persians, and also natives from Iuda, including their King Jeconiah. The steadily growing influence and presence of "Greek" specialists is further confirmed by the Old Testament, and an analogous picture is transmitted by contemporary Egyptian sources (Vittmann 2003, 194–235).

Further evidence for the broad spectrum of Greek "immigrants" can be adduced in the guise of a remarkable cuneiform document. FLP 1574, a private business deed dating to 1.IX.549/548 and issued in Elammu, near Uruk, records the sale of a slave (*qallu*) bearing the fine Babylonian name of Mušēzib-Nabû (Dillard 1975, 128–129; Jursa 2015, 376). He is described in line 5 as ᵘʳᵘi-ma?-na-a-a, which we may interpret as Yamanāya, "Greek" (Zadok quoted in Fantalkin 2001, 131 n. 59). But this reading, particularly that of the syllable "ma," is by no means certain, and in this context we might rather expect ᵘʳᵘia-(a-)ma-na-a-a. A similarly idiosyncratic spelling can be observed in the case of ˡi-ma?-na-a-a ˡúENGAR. He appears in a document of uncertain date (CT 56, 506) that probably belongs to the Neo-Babylonian period, and might have been an unfree person, since the text mentions him being captured by the *rab bīti* (major-domo) of Nabû-ereš. Either a certain Nabû-uṣalli (l. 3) or Aplāja (l. 4) stand surety for him. Here too, we cannot be certain that we are dealing with a peasant bearer of a hypocorism, which would point to a "Greek" origin. Even less certainty is to be had in the case of an ˡi-man-na-a-a who allegedly appears in an administrative document from Ebabbar in Sippar dating to the year

573/572 (Van Soldt 1983, 145 no. 6, l. 5). The reading ⁱi-sin-na-a-a should probably be preferred and thus this particular piece of evidence cannot be adduced for proving "Greeks" in a cuneiform context.

Be that as it may, buyer and both sellers of Mušēzib-Nabû have Babylonian names, though one of the sellers also has a western-semitic patronymic (ra-ṣi-pa), as does one of the witnesses (Zadok 2003, 521 (sub 3.1.1.1.1.3, 4)). It is far from certain that this should indicate Syrian agency in the sale of Mušēzib-Nabû, but the Babylonian names as such are noteworthy, as is the fact that we have here the first record of a privately owned (and sold) "Greek" slave in a Babylonian context – if the interpretation as Yamanāya is indeed correct.

An undated document probably belongs to the Neo-Babylonian period and mentions a ᵐᶠia-man-na-[...] (CT 56, 813, rev. i l. 5'; cf. Zadok 1985, 187). She is further described rev. i line 6' as the daughter (DUMU.MÍ-su) of a previously named person probably mentioned in line 5 (which is incomplete). The presence of a large number of personal names, including filiations, divided into several individual registers that include the respective totals of peoples, might well indicate that we are dealing here with a form of census and that the persons named were probably slaves (*širku*). If we are right in assuming a female "Greek," she was probably part of a larger family group that consisted of unfree persons.

On the whole, we may assume a steadily increasing intensity of cultural contacts for Babylonian-Chaldean times, which will have led to ever-increasing numbers of "Greeks" finding their way to Babylonia itself. The world-view presented in Greek sources may be a reflection of this. Here, the great seats of power of the Assyrian Empire are only vaguely referred to, while Babylon has a conspicuous place in Greek tradition (cf. Rollinger 2011a; Rollinger 2013).

Persian Times (Sixth to Fourth Centuries)

Achaemenid sources again point to processes of change. The source material itself is relatively comprehensive and mentions "Greeks" in royal inscriptions and in the context of archival material. We have already indicated attempts to render the vague term Yaman/Yauna more precisely and this is, in fact, an indication of a vastly extended geographical horizon. But still, "Greeks" remained, to the world-view presented in royal inscriptions, a marginal group, just as they had been in Neo-Assyrian annals. Special emphasis is laid on their role as royal subjects, as throne-bearers, and as gift-bearers, one among many such groups in the loyal and obedient subjects of the empire.

Archival remains paint a decidedly more nuanced picture. Here, we can recognize a "Greek" population employed in the centers of empire and performing a wide variety of activities, ranging from middle-ranking leadership positions to employment as a dependent working force, as, for instance, in the Elamite archival tablets of Persepolis (Rollinger 2006a). We may add four further documents that have only recently become known. The first is part of the archive of Murašû in Nippur and dates back to the reign of Darius II (Donbaz and Stolper 1997, 104–105 no. 32 = Ni. 2834+2846). Line 2 of this document mentions a field (ŠE.NUMUN) belonging to a certain Uštāna (ⁱuš-ta-na-'), undoubtedly an Iranian name. In line 3, we find a [x]ia-a-ma-na-[x ...]. When this tablet was first published, the editors amended this to mean [ᵐ]ia-a-ma-na-['] and remarked: "Jāmana', occurring beside the well-attested Iranian Uštāna, is perhaps a hypocoristic of an Iranian name formed on the Ir. *yauna-, rather than a gentilic, 'the Greek.'" By contrast, Ran Zadok proposed a different emendation and understood [lúia-a-ma-na-[A+<A>] to be a gentilic epithet of Uštāna (Zadok 2005, 80). But no matter whether we understand this passage to mean a "field of Uštāna and Jāmana" or the "field of Uštāna, the 'Greek,'" it is certain that a "Greek" appears here as (co-)owner of this field. In addition, if we agree with Zadok, we have here a telling example of the complexity of "ethnic" distinctiveness: a "Greek," bearing an Iranian name, owns a field in distant Babylonia. On the other hand, if we agree with the interpretation of Donbaz and Stolper, we are dealing with an interesting parallel to those persons named Yauna that we encounter in the Elamite archival records of Persepolis and who obviously belonged to the middle ranks of the bureaucracy.

The second document, BM 32891, belongs to the group of business deeds attributable to the trading house of Egibi (Abraham 2004, 328–329; Zadok 2005, 80). It dates from the reign of Darius I and was issued in Babylon. It served as proof of receipt for an unknown quantity of grain that was delivered to a certain Bazbaka by Marduk-nāṣir-apli, a representative of the trading house of Egibi, on the order of Gūzānu, the city prefect (šakin ṭēmi) of Babylon. This Bazbaka is described in obverse line 4–5 as [lús]i-pi-ri / šá um-ma-nu u lú[x x] lúia-ma-⌈na⌉-a-a. The first part of this titulature can be interpreted in different ways. Either we can understand this office as *lúsepīru ša ummâni*, in which case Bazbaka was "scribe of the artisans," or, alternatively, it may be interpreted as *lúsepīru ša ummāni*, meaning "scribe of the soldiers." The final part of his title may help us here, since, as Karlheinz Kessler has persuasively argued, it must likely be emended as lú[GAR (šá)] lúia-ma-⌈na⌉-a-a (Kessler 2006). Bazbaka, incidentally in all probability an Iranian name, was thus "scribe of the soldiers and supervisor (šaknu) of the 'Greeks.'" If *sepīru* denotes a scribe used to working with documents written in alphabetic scripts (Jursa 2012), the area of responsibility of the *šaknu ša* lú*Yamanāya*, meaning the supervision of groups of foreigners, is probably indicative of the *ḫadru*-organization characteristic for the Achaemenid period (Wiesehöfer 1999). This form of organization typically encompassed a number of "fiefdoms" called bow-land (*bīt qašti*), whose award was tied to appropriate forms of tribute and service. The latter was almost certainly of a usually military nature, though there is nothing to preclude us from assuming certain civilian services being required of them in peacetime. In fact, we might go as far as to posit a certain similarity between these Yamanāya and the *nagārū* of Neo-Babylonian-Chaldean times, and maybe even with those laborers that Darius I mentions in his famous inscription in from Susa (DSf). Here, he proudly boasts of the participation of laborers from all corners of his empire in the construction of his palace in Susa, including "Greeks" (Rollinger 2006a). But a military role was probably the main function of these administrative units, though we know nothing of the recruitment of these Yamanāya. Were they deported populations forced into military service? Or were they regular troops of Anatolian "Greek" provenance, or, equally possible, were they hired mercenary units that hailed from beyond the confines of the empire? If the latter should be the case, this would be the first mention in cuneiform texts of "Greek" mercenaries in Achaemenid Babylon. In any case, these "Greeks" were organized along "national" or, rather, ethnic lines within larger units that the local administration of Babylon, indeed, a specific department, was responsible for.

But our document holds more information still. Besides the scribes, it also mentions a total of five witnesses, of whom the first four are referenced with patronymic and "family names." The fifth witness, however, is a certain [Iddin]-Nabû, referred to as "the Greek" (rev. l. 15). We are obviously dealing here with a Yamanāya that can act as witness on official business. The missing patronymic and the equally missing "family name" mark him as a foreigner, just as the gentilic Yamanāya points to his origins. But this should not lead us to conclude that he cannot have been born in Babylonia and that we must see in him a first-generation migrant. On the contrary, a comparison with the Egyptian diaspora in Babylonia tells us that Babylonian names appear increasingly often in the second generation, while the gentilic Miṣrāya is often also kept (cf. Bongenaar and Haring 1994, 64 with n. 9). We can posit a similar process in the case of Iddin-Nabû, who was probably a member of those Yamanāya that Bazbaka was responsible for. What is remarkable is that "the Greek" bears a Babylonian name, which by necessity reminds us of Mušēzib-Nabû, whom we encountered in the middle of the sixth century BC. But he enjoyed a considerably different social status. This must not necessarily be laid at the door of a vastly different potential for the integration of "Greeks" in Achaemenid Babylonia. It is more likely that this is simply a reflection of the many different forms that life in foreign countries could take, ranging from dependent or unfree labor conditions, to the freeholding possession of land, and up to the faculty of independently conducting business. This complements our evidence from Persepolis, just as the Babylonian name reminds us of the potential for peaceful assimilation in Babylonian society, and, indeed, of the willingness of foreigners from Yaman to adapt.

The third and the fourth documents both originate from the Achaemenid archives in Persepolis (for details see Rollinger and Henkelman 2009). NN 2108 mentions a certain quantity of *kudagina* allocated to a group of Greeks (Greeks (⌈HAL*i*⌉-*u-nu*-⌈*ia*⌉-*ip*)). The document is authorized by the satrap of Sardis Irdaparna. Although we do not know exactly what the Elamite term *kudagina* refers to, it appears to be a kind of "candied dried peaches/plums/damson." Obviously these Greeks receive a special and extraordinary allocation from the Achaemenid administration. This points at the fact that the Greeks of this document do not represent a common working force, as they do in most of the other documents, but a group of hired specialists that is treated accordingly. Apparently, they have been recruited in the west, whether from inside or from outside the empire we do not know. NN 2261: 33–4 (journal entry) refers to one sheep/goat a certain Bakambama has received for another group of Greeks (HAL*uk-ku* HAL*ia-u-na-ip*) that was on its way to Persepolis. Of special interest is the place from where this group set forth. Since the document is a travel authorization of Bakabaduš, who is the Persian satrap in Arachosia, the gang must have been sent there to perform some kind of work. It is noteworthy that the presence of Greeks can already be testified to at the very eastern fringes of the Achaemenid Empire around 500 BC.

But it is not only the direct testimony of our sources that allows us to assess the increasing presence of Greek specialists at the periphery and at the very core of the Achaemenid Empire. Some indirect evidence must also be considered. Of this evidence, we have already mentioned the inscription of Darius at Susa (DSf). Indeed, we might see in the palace in Susa a reflection of the empire itself, as it had been constructed by laborers and resources gathered from every part of the great king's dominions. This included "Greeks" from the far west. Apart from written sources, the archaeological remains of royal palaces in Pasargadai, Persepolis, and Susa also contain clear indications of Greek craftsmanship (Boucharlat 2002). This craftsmanship is present, too, at the western periphery of the empire, in the form of the sarcophagi of the royal *necropolis* of Sidon or in the offering of the temple boys of Bostan eš-Šeiḫ (Stucky 1993), both of which are influenced by Greek tradition. It is also noticeably in the eastern frontier regions of central Asia, if we give credence to David Stronach's conjecture that parts of the Oxus Treasure recall Greek artisanship (Stronach 1998, 236–238, 243b).

An Aramaic report on customs dating to the beginning of the fifth century completes this picture (Porten and Yardeni 1993, 82–193: C3.7). This singular document allows us a wholly unexpected peek into the trade relationships of the Egyptian satrapy. "Sidonian" and "Greek" merchantmen seem to have dominated the market (Briant and Descat 1998, 62–69). They imported wine, oil, perfumes, metal ores such as iron, copper, and tin, but also timber, wool, and a host of convenience products. The points of origin of some of these goods are clearly indicated, such as for the "Greek" (*ḫmr Ywn*) and Sidonian wine (Porten and Yardeni 1993: GV2, 5f.; DV2, 5f.), or for Samian clay (Porten and Yardeni 1993: GV2, 19; DV2, 16). One primary export article was Egyptian natron, which was used in a variety of ways (Bresciani 1996). It is worth pointing out that this document clearly indicates trade agreements not only with "Greek" regions under Achaemenid domination, but also with the Aegean world and beyond that lay outside the dominions of the Great King (Carlson 2013, 18–19).

The conquests of Alexander the Great opened up the next chapter of cultural interaction and led to a further intensification of contacts and a growing body of knowledge (see Chapters 17 and 21, this volume). Evidence for the preliminary stages that were of particular importance for the development of Aegean society in Homeric and Archaic times, however, can be looked for and found in older source material!

LIST OF ABBREVIATIONS

CT 56 = Pinches, Theophilus G. 1982. *Neo-Babylonian and Achaemenid Economic Texts*, Cuneiform Texts from Babylonian Tablets 56. London: Published for the Trustees of the British Museum by British Museum Publications.

CTN 3 = Dalley, Stephanie, and J. Nicholas Postgate. 1984. *The Tablets from Fort Shalmaneser*, Cuneiform Texts from Nimrud 3. Oxford: British School of Archaeology in Iraq.

FGrH = Jacoby, Felix. 1954. *Die Fragmente der griechischen Historiker: Dritter Teil A and a (Kommentar)*. Leiden: Brill.

FLP = Frederick Lewis Collection of the Free Library of Philadelphia (see Dillard, Raymond B. 1975. *Neo-Babylonian Texts from the Frederick Lewis Collection of the Free Library of Philadelphia*. PhD dissertation, Dropsie University).

PTS = Princeton Theological Seminary (Signature of a Tablet).

RINAP = The Royal Inscriptions of the Neo-Assyrian Period (1 = Tadmor, Hayim, and Shiego Yamada. 2011. *The Royal Inscriptions of Tiglath-Pilser III (744–727 BC), and Shalmaneser V (726–722 BC), Kings of Assyria*, Royal Inscriptions of the Neo-Assyrian Period 1. Winona Lake: Eisenbrauns).

TCL 12 =   Contenau, Georges. 1927. *Contrats néo-babyloniens I de Téglath-phalasar III à Nabonide*, Textes Cunéiformes: Musée de Louvre 12. Paris: P. Geuthner.
YOS 6 =   Dougherty, Raymond Philip. 1920. *Records from Erech: Time of Nabonidus (555–538 BC)*, Yale Oriental Series: Babylonian Texts 6. New Haven: AMS Press.
YOS 17 =   Weisberg, David B. 1980. *Texts from the Time of Nebuchadnezzar*, Yale Oriental Series: Babylonian Texts 17. New Haven: Yale University Press.

REFERENCES

Abraham, Kathleen. 2004. *Business and Politics under the Persian Empire: The Financial Dealings of Marduk-nāṣir-apli of the House Egibi (521–487 BCE)*. Bethesda: CDL Press.

Alexander, Fantalkin and Lytle, Ephraim. 2016. *Alcaeus and Antimenidas: Reassessing the Evidence for Greek Mercenaries in the Neo-Babylonian Army*. In: Klio, 98 (1): S. 90–117.

Aruz, Joan. 2014. "Art and Network Interaction Across the Mediterranean." In *Assyria to Iberia at the Dawn of the Classical Age*, edited by Joan Aruz, Sarah B. Graff, and Yelena Rakic, 112–124. New York: Metropolitan Museum of Art.

Aruz, Joan, Sarah B. Graff, and Yelena Rakic, eds. 2014. *Assyria to Iberia at the Dawn of the Classical Age*. New York: Metropolitan Museum of Art.

Bagg, Ariel M. 2007. *Die Orts- und Gewässernamen der neuassyrischen Zeit. Teil 1: Die Levante*, Répertoire Géographique des Textes Cunéiformes 7/1, Tübinger Atlas des Vorderen Orients Beihefte 7/7/1. Wiesbaden: Reichert Verlag.

Blum, Hartmut. 1998. *Purpur als Statussymbol in der griechischen Welt*, Antiquitas Reihe 1: Abhandlungen zur alten Geschichte 47. Bonn: R. Habelt.

Boardman, John. 1996. "Euboean Overseas: A Question of Identity." In *Minotaur and Centaur: Studies in the Archaeology of Crete and Euboea Presented to Mervyn Popham*, edited by Doniert Evely, Irene S. Lemos, and Susan Sherratt, 155–160. Oxford: Tempus Reparatum.

Boardman, John. 1997. "An Early Greek Sherd at Nineveh." *Oxford Journal of Archaeology*, 16: 375.

Boardman, John. 2002. "Al Mina: The Study of a Site." *Ancient West & East*, 1(2): 315–331.

Boardman, John, and Mervyn Popham. 1997. "Euboean Pottery, East and West." *Pact: Revue du Groupe européen d'études pour les techniques physiques, chimiques et mathématiques appliquées à l'archéologie, Conseil de l'Europe, Assemblée parlementaire*, 40: 15–25.

Bongenaar, Arminius C.V.M., and Ben J.J. Haring. 1994. "Egyptians in Neo-Babylonian Sippar." *Journal of Cuneiform Studies*, 46: 59–71.

Boucharlat, Rémy. 2002. "Greece: Relations with Persian Empire VII: Greek Art and Architecture in Iran." *Encyclopaedia Iranica*, 11: 329–333.

Bresciani, Edda. 1996. "Plinio, il natron e le navi del Mediterraneo." In *Alla soglie della classicità: Il Mediterraneo tra tradizione e innovazione: Studi in onore di Sabatino Moscati*, edited by Enrico Acquaro, 59–61. Pisa: Istituti editoriali e poligrafici internazionali.

Briant, Pierre, and Raymond Descat. 1998. "Un register douanier de la satrapie d'Egypte à l'époque achéménide." In *La commerce en Egypte ancienne*, Bibliothèque d'étude 121, edited by Nicolas Grimal, and Bernadette Menu, 59–104. Cairo: Institut français d'archéologie orientale.

Brinkman, John A. 1989. "The Akkadian Words for 'Ionia' and 'Ionian'." In *Daidalikon: Studies in Memory of Raymond V. Schoder*, edited by Robert F. Sutton, 53–71. Wauconda: Bolchazy Carducci.

Broodbank, Cyprian. 2013. *The Making of the Middle Sea: A History of the Mediterranean from the Beginning to the Emergence of the Classical World*. London: Oxford University Press.

Burkert, Walter. 1992. *The Orientalizing Revolution: Near Eastern Influence on Greek Culture in the Early Archaic Age*. Cambridge: Harvard University Press.

Calmeyer, Peter. 1982. "Zur Genese Altiranischer Motive 1: Die 'Statistische Landcharte des Perserreiches'." *Archäologische Mitteilungen aus Iran*, 15: 105–187.

Calmeyer, Peter. 1983a. "Zur Genese Altiranischer Motive 2: Die 'Statistische Landcharte des Perserreiches'." *Archäologische Mitteilungen aus Iran*, 16: 109–263.

Calmeyer, Peter. 1983b. "Zur Rechtfertigung einiger großköniglicher Inschriften und Darstellungen: Die Yauna." In *Kunst und Kultur der Achämenidenzeit und ihr Fortleben*, edited by Heidemarie Koch and David N. Mackenzie, 153–169. Berlin: Reimer Verlag.

Calmeyer, Peter. 1987. "Zur Genese Altiranischer Motive: Die 'Statistische Landcharte des Perserreiches'. Nachträge und Korrekturen." *Archäologische Mitteilungen aus Iran*, 20: 129–46.

Carlson, Deborah. 2013. "A View from the Sea: The Archaeology of Maritime Trade in the 5th Century BC Aegean." In *Handels- und Finanzgebaren in der Ägäis im 5. Jh. v. Chr.*, BYZAS 18, edited by Anja Slawisch, 1–23. Istanbul: Ege Yayinlari.

Corral, Martin Alonso. 2002. *Ezekiel's Oracles Against Tyre: Historical Reality and Motivations*, Biblica et Orientalia 46. Rome: Gregorian and Biblical Press.

Curtis, John, and Nigel Tallis, eds. 2005. *Forgotten Empire: The World of Ancient Persia*. Berkeley: California University Press.

Dandamayev, Muhammad A. 1993. "Textual Evidence for Iron in Babylonia in the Sixth Century BC." In *Šulmu IV: Everyday Life in the Ancient Near East: Papers Presented at the International Conference, Poznań 19–22 September 1989*, edited by Julia Zabłocka and Stefan Zawadzki, 67–72. Poznań: UAM.

Diakonoff, Igor M. 1992. "Proto-Afrasian and Old Akkadian: A Study in Historical Phoenitics." *Journal of Afroasiatic Languages*, 4(1–2): 1–133.

Dillard, Raymond B. 1975. *Neo-Babylonian Texts from the Frederick Lewis Collection of the Free Library of Philadelphia*. PhD dissertation, Dropsie University.

Donbaz, Veysel, and Matthew Stolper. 1997. *Istanbul Murašû Texts*, Uitgaven van het Nederlands Historisch-Archaeologisch Instituut te Istanbul 79. Istanbul: Nederlands Historisch-Archaeologisch Instituut te Istanbul.

Edel, Elmar. 1978. "Amasis und Nebukadrezar II." *Göttinger Miszellen*, 29: 13–20.

Ehrhardt, Norbert. 2005. "Die Ionier und ihr Verhältnis zu den Phrygern und Lydern. Analyse der literarischen, epigraphischen und numismatischen Zeugnisse." In *Neue Forschungen zu Ionien*, Asia Minor Studien 54, edited by Elmar Schwertheim and Engelbert Winter, 93–111. Bonn: Habelt.

Fantalkin, Alexander. 2001. "Meẓad Ḥashavyahu: Its Material Culture and Historical Background." *Tel Aviv*, 28(1): 3–165.

Fletcher, Richard. 2004. "Sidonians, Tyrians and Greeks in the Mediterranean: The Evidence from Egyptianising Amulets." *Ancient West & East*, 3(1): 51–77.

Hachmann, Ralf. 1995. "Völkerschaften auf den Bildwerken von Persepolis." In *Beiträge zur Kulturgeschichte Vorderasiens: Festschrift für Rainer Michael Boehmer*, edited by Uwe Finkbeiner, Reinhard Dittmann, and Harald Hauptmann, 195–223. Mainz: Verlag Philipp von Zabern.

Haider, Peter W. 1996. "Griechen im Vorderen Orient und in Ägypten bis ca. 590 v. Chr." In *Wege zur Genese griechischer Identität: Die Bedeutung der früharchaischen Zeit*, edited by Christoph Ulf, 59–115. Berlin: Wiley-VCH Verlag.

Hayajneh, Hani. 2001a. "First Evidence of Nabonidus in Ancient North Arabian Inscriptions from the Region of Taymā'." *Proceedings of the Seminar of Arabian Studies*, 31: 81–95.

Hayajneh, Hani. 2001b. "Der babylonische König Nabonid und der *RBSRS* in einigen neu publizierten frühnordarabischen Inschriften aus Taymā'." *Acta Orientalia*, 62: 22–64.

Heubeck, Alfred. 1987. "Zum Namen der Ἰώνες." *Münchner Studien zur Sprachwissenschaft*, 48: 139–148.

Hodos, Tamar. 2006. *Local Responses to Colonization in the Iron Age Mediterranean*. London: Routledge.

Hutzfeldt, Birger. 1999. *Das Bild der Perser in der griechischen Dichtung des 5. vorchristlichen Jahrhunderts*, Serta Graeca: Beiträge zur Erforschung griechischer Texte 8. Wiesbaden: Reichert Verlag.

Joannès, Francis. 1991. "L'Asie Mineure méridionale d'après la documentation cunéiforme d'époque néo-babylonienne." *Anatolia Antiqua*, 1: 261–266.

Joannès, Francis. 1997. "Le monde occidental vu de Mésopotamie, de l'époque néo-babylonienne à l'époque hellénistique." *Transeuphratène*, 13: 141–153.

Joannès, Francis. 1999. "Structures et opérations commerciales en Babylonie à l'époque néo-babylonienne." In *Trade and Finance in Ancient Mesopotamia*, edited by Jan Gerrit Dercksen, 175–194. Istanbul: Het Nederlands Inst Vh Nabije.

Jursa, Michael. 2012. "Ein Beamter flucht auf Aramäisch: Alphabetschreiber in der spätbabylnischen Epistolographie und die Rolle des Aramäischen in der babylonischen Verwaltung des sechsten Jahrhundert v. Chr." In *LEGGO! Studies Presented to Prof. Frederick Mario Fales on the Occasion of his 65th Birthday*, edited by Giovanni B. Lanfranchi, Daniele Morandi Bonacossi, Cinzia Pappi, and Simonetta Ponchia, 379–397. Wiesbaden: Harrassowitz.

Jursa, Michael. 2015. "Labor in Babylonia in the First Millennium BC." In *Labor in the Ancient World*, edited by Piotr Steinkeller and Michael Hudson, 345–396. Dresden: ISLET.

Kerschner, Michael. 2005. "Die Ionier und ihr Verhältnis zu den Phrygern und Lydern. Beobachtungen zur archäologischen Evidenz." In *Neue Forschungen zu Ionien*, edited by Elmar Schwertheim and Engelbert Winter, 113–146. Bonn: Habelt.

Kessler, Karlheinz. 2006. "Neue Informationen zu Ioniern und Karern aus Babylonien." In *Hayat Erkana'a Armağan: Kültürlerin Yansıması / Studies in Honor of H. Erkanal: Cultural Reflections*, edited by Betül Avunç, 487–490. Istanbul: Homer Kitabevi.

Klinkott, Hilmar. 2001. "Yauna: Die Griechen aus persischer Sicht?" In *Anatolien im Lichte kultureller Wechselwirkungen: Akkulturations-phänomene in Kleinasien und seinen Nachbarregionen während des 2. und 1. Jahrtausends v. Chr.*, edited by Hilmar Klinkott, 107–148. Tübingen: Attempto.

Kuhrt, Amélie. 2002. *"Greeks" and "Greece" in Mesopotamian and Persian Perspectives: A Lecture Delivered at New College, Oxford, on 7th May, 2001*. Oxford: Leopard's Head Press.

Lipiński, Edward. 2000. *The Aramaeans: Their Ancient History, Culture, Religion*. Leuven: Peeters.

Liverani, Mario. 1991. "The Trade Network of Tyre According to Ez. 27." In *Ah, Assyria... Studies in Assyrian History and Ancient Near Eastern Historiography Presented to Hayim Tadmor*, edited by Mordechai Cogan and Israel Eph'al, 65–79. Jerusalem: Magnes Press.

Lohmann, Hans. 2005. "Melia, das Panionion und der Kult des Poseidon Helikonios." In *Neue Forschungen zu Ionien*, Asia Minor Studien 54, edited by Elmar Schwertheim and Engelbert Winter, 57–91. Bonn: Habelt.

Nino, Luraghi. 2006. "Traders, Pirates, Warriors: The Proto-History of Greek Mercenary Soldiers in the Eastern Mediterranean." *Phoenix*, 60(1–2): 21–47.

Mattila, Raija. 2000. *The King's Magnates: A Study of the Highest Officials of the Neo-Assyrian Empire*, State Archives of Assyria Studies 11. Helsinki: The Neo-Assyrian Text Corpus Project.

Morris, Ian. 1997. "Homer and the Iron Age." In *A New Companion to Homer*, Mnemosyne Supplementum 163, edited by Ian Morris and Barry Powell, 535–559. Leiden: Brill.

Morris, Ian. 1998. "Archaeology and Archaic Greek History." In *Archaic Greece: New Approaches and New Evidence*, edited by Nick Fisher and Hans van Wees, 1–91. London: The Classical Press of Wales.

Morris, Ian. 1999. "Negotiated Peripherality in Iron Age Greece: Accepting and Resisting the East." In *World-Systems Theory in Practice: Leadership, Production, and Exchange*, edited by P. Nick Kardulias, 63–84. Lanham: Rowman & Littlefield.

Müller, Walter W., and Said F. al-Said. 2001. "Der babylonische König Nabonid in taymanischen Inschriften." *Biblische Notizen*, 107/108: 109–119.

Na'aman, Nadav. 2004. "Re'ṣuri and Yauna in a Neo-Assyrian Letter (ND 2737)." *N.A.B.U.*, 68: 69–70.

Niemeier, Wolf-Dietrich. 2001. "Archaic Greeks in the Orient: Textual and Archaeological Evidence." *Bulletin of the American Schools of Oriental Research*, 322: 11–32.

Niemeyer, Hans Georg. 2003. "On Phoenician Art and its Role in Trans-Mediterranean Interconnections ca. 1100–600 BC." In *ΠΛΟΕΣ: Sea Routes: Interconnections in the Mediterranean 16th–6th c. BC: Proceedings of the International Symposium Held at Rethymnon/Crete, September 29th–October 2nd 2002*, edited by Nicholas Chr. Stampolidis and Vassos Karageorghis, 201–207. Athens: University of Crete and the A.G. Leventis Foundation.

Niemeyer, Hans Georg. 2004. "Phoenician or Greek: Is there a Reasonable Way out of the Al Mina Debate?" *Ancient West & East*, 3(1): 38–50.

Oppenheim, Leo A. 1967. "Essay on Overland Trade in the First Millennium BC." *Journal of Cuneiform Studies*, 21: 236–254.

Papadopoulos, John K. 1996. "Phantom Euboeans." *Journal of Mediterranean Archaeology*, 10: 191–206.

Patzek, Barbara. 1996. "Griechen und Phöniker in homerischer Zeit: Fernhandel und der orientalische Einfluß auf die frühgriechische Kultur." *Münstersche Beiträge zur antiken Handelsgeschichte*, 15(2): 1–32.

Pedersén, Olof. 2005a. "Foreign Professionals in Babylon: Evidence from the Archive in the Palace of Nebuchadnezzar II." In *Ethnicity in Ancient Mesopotamia: Papers Read at the 48th Rencontre Assyriologique Internationale Leiden, 1–4 July 2002*, CRRAI 48, Publications de l'Institut historique-archéologique néerlandais de Stamboul 102, edited by Wilfred H. Van Soldt, 267–272. Leiden: Nederlands Instituut voor het Nabije Oosten.

Pedersén, Olof. 2005b. *Archive und Bibliotheken in Babylon: Die Tontafeln der Grabung Robert Koldeweys 1899–1917*, Abhandlungen der Deutschen Orient-Gesellschaft 25. Wiesbaden: Harrassowitz.

Popham, Mervyn. 1994. "Precolonization: Early Greek Contact with the East." In *The Archaeology of Greek Colonisation: Essays Dedicated to Sir John Boardman*, Oxford Monograph 40, edited by Gocha R. Tsetskhladze and Franco De Angelis, 11–34. Oxford: University School of Archaeology.

Porten, Bezalel, and Ada Yardeni, eds. 1993. *Textbook of Aramaic Documents from Ancient Egypt*. Jerusalem: Hebrew University, Department of the History of the Jewish People.

Ridgway, David. 1994. "Phoenicians and Greeks in the West: A View from Pithekoussai." In *The Archaeology of Greek Colonisation: Essays Dedicated to Sir John Boardman*, Oxford Monograph 40, edited by Gocha R. Tsetskhladze and Franco De Angelis, 35–46. Oxford: University School of Archaeology.

Ridgway, David. 2004. "Euboeans and Others along the Tyrrhenian Seaboard in the 8th Century BC." In *Greek Identity in the Western Mediterranean: Papers in Honour of Brian Shefton*, edited by Kathryn Lomas, 15–33. Leiden: Brill.

Rollinger, Robert. 1997. "Zur Bezeichnung von 'Griechen' in Keilschrifttexten." *Revue d'Assyriologie et d'Archéologie Orientale*, 91: 167–172.

Rollinger, Robert. 2001. "The Ancient Greeks and the Impact of the Ancient Near East: Textual Evidence and Historical Perspective." In *Mythology and Mythologies: Methodological Approaches to Intercultural Influences: Proceedings of the Second Annual Symposium of the Assyrian and Babylonian Intellectual Heritage Project Held in Paris/France, October 4–7 1999*, Melammu Symposia 2, edited by Robert M. Whiting, 233–264. Helsinki: Neo-Assyrian Text Corpus Project.

Rollinger, Robert. 2006a. "The Eastern Mediterranean and Beyond: The Relations between the Worlds of the 'Greek' and 'Non-Greek' Civilizations." In *A Companion to the Classical Greek World*, edited by Konrad Kinzl, 197–226. Chichester: Wiley Blackwell.

Rollinger, Robert. 2006b. "*Yaunā takabarā* und *maginnāta* tragende 'Ionier': Zum Problem der 'griechischen' Thronträgerfiguren in Naqsch-i Rustam und Persepolis." In *Altertum und Mittelmeerraum: Die antike Welt diesseits und jenseits der Levante: Festschrift für Peter W. Haider zum 60. Geburtstag*, Oriens et Occidens 12, edited by Robert Rollinger and Brigitte Truschnegg, 365–400. Stuttgart: Steiner Verlag.

Rollinger, Robert. 2007a. "Zu Herkunft und Hintergrund der in altorientalischen Texten genannten 'Griechen'." In *Getrennte Wege? Kommunikation, Raum und Wahrnehmung in der Alten Welt*, Oikumene 2, edited by Robert Rollinger, Andreas Luther, and Josef Wiesehöfer, 259–330. Frankfurt: Verlag Antike.

Rollinger, Robert. 2007b. "Überlegungen zur Frage der Lokalisation von Jawan in neuassyrischer Zeit." *State Archives of Assyria Bulletin*, 16: 63–90.

Rollinger, Robert. 2011a. "Assur, Assyrien und die klassische Überlieferung: Nachwirken, Deutungsmuster und historische Reflexion." In *Assur: Gott, Stadt und Land*, Colloquien der Deutschen Orient-Gesellschaft 5, edited by Johannes Renger, 311–345. Wiesbaden: Harrassowitz.

Rollinger, Robert. 2011b. "Der Blick aus dem Osten: 'Griechen' in vorderasiatischen Quellen des 8. und 7. Jahrhunderts v. Chr.: Eine Zusammenschau." In *Der Orient und die Anfänge Europas: Kulturelle Beziehungen von der Späten Bronzezeit bis zur Frühen Eisenzeit*, Philippika 42, edited by Hartmut Matthäus, Norbert Oettinger, and Stephan Schröder, 267–282. Wiesbaden: Harrassowitz.

Rollinger, Robert. 2013. "s.v. Assur." In *Wörterbuch alttestamentlicher Motive*, edited by Michael Fieger, Jutta Krispenz, and Jörg Lanckau, 35–39. Darmstadt: Wissenschaftliche Buchgesellschaft.

Rollinger, Robert. 2014. "Homer and the Ancient Near East: Some Considerations on Intercultural Affairs." In *The Intellectual Heritage of the Ancient Near East*, edited by Ilkka Lindstedt, Jaakko Hämenn-Anttila, Raija Mattila and Robert Rollinger, 131–142. Münster: Ugarit-Verlag.

Rollinger, Robert. 2015. "Old Battles, New Horizons: Ancient Near-Eastern Influences on the Homeric Epics." In *Mesopotamia in the Ancient World: Impact, Continuity, Parallels: Proceedings of the 7th Symposium of the Melammu Project Held in Obergurgl/ Austria, November 4–8 2013*, Melammu Symposia 7, edited by Robert Rollinger and Erik van Dongen, 5–32. Münster: Ugarit Verlag.

Rollinger, Robert. 2018. "Between Deportation and Recruitment: Craftsmen and Specialists from the West in Ancient Near Eastern Empires (from Neo-Assyrian times through Alexander III)." In *Infrastructure and Distribution in Ancient Economies*, edited by Bernhard Woytek, 425–444. Vienna: Austrian Academy of Sciences.

Rollinger, Robert, and Wouter Henkelman. 2009. "New Observations on 'Greeks' in the Achaemenid Empire According to Cuneiform Texts from Babylonia and Persepolis." In *Organisation des pouvoirs et contacts culturels dans les pays de l'empire achéménide*, Persika 14, edited by Pierre Briant and Michel Chauveau, 331–351. Paris: de Boccard.

Rollinger, Robert, and Martin Korenjak. 2001. "Addikritušu: Ein namentlich genannter Grieche aus der Zeit Asarhaddons (680–669 v. Chr.): Überlegungen zu ABL 140." *Altorientalische Forschungen*, 28: 372–384.

Rollinger, Robert, and Kai Ruffing. 2014. "World View and Perception of Space." In *Aneignung und Abgrenzung: Wechselnde Perspektive auf die Antithese 'Ost' und 'West' in der griechischen Antike*, Oikumene 10, edited by Nicolas Zenezen, Tonio Hölscher, and Kai Trampedach, 93–161. Heidelberg: Verlag Antike.

Root, Margret C. 2007. "Reading Persepolis in Greek: Gifts of the Yauna." In *Persian Responses: Political and Cultural Interaction with(in) the Achaemenid Empire*, edited by Christopher Tuplin, 177–224. Swansea: The Classical Press of Wales.

Saggs, H.W.F. 2001. *The Nimrud Letters: 1952*, Cuneiform Texts from Nimrud 5. Trowbridge: British School of Archaeology in Iraq.

Sancisi-Weerdenburg, Heleen. 2001a. "*Yaunā* by the Sea and Across the Sea." In *Ancient Perceptions of Greek Ethnicity*, Center for Hellenic Studies Colloquia 5, edited by Irad Malkin, 323–346. Cambridge: Center for Hellenic Studies, Trustees for Harvard University.

Sancisi-Weerdenburg, Heleen. 2011b. "The Problem of the Yauna." In *Achaemenid Anatolia: Proceedings of the First International Symposium on Anatolia in the Achaemenid Period, Bandirma 15–18 August 1997*, Uitgaven van het Nederlands Historisch-Archaeologisch Instituut te Istanbul 92, edited by Tomris Bakır, 1–11. Leiden: Nederlands Instituut voor het Nabije Oosten.

Schmitt, Rüdiger. 1972. "Die achaimenidische Satrapie tyaiy drayahya." *Historia*, 21: 522–527.

Schmitt, Rüdiger. 1984. "Perser und Persisches in der alten attischen Komödie." In *Orientalia J. Duchesne-Guillemin Emerito Oblata*, Acta Iranica 23, edited by Jacques Duchesne-Guillemin, 459–472. Leiden: Brill.

Smarczyk, Bernhard. 2000. "Die Ionier Kleinasiens: Der Beitrag kultisch-religiöser und mythischer Traditionen zur Entwicklung ihres Identitätsgefühls." In *Antike Randgesellschaften und Randgruppen im östlichen Mittelmeerraum: Ringvorlesung an der Westfälischen Wilhelms-Universität Münster*, edited by Hans-Peter Müller and Volker Siegert, 46–74. Münster: LIT.

Steigerwald, Gerhard. 1986. "Die antike Purpurfärberei nach dem Bericht Plinius' des Älteren in seiner 'Naturalis Historia'." *Traditio*, 42: 1–57.

Stronach, David. 1998. "On the Date of the Oxus Gold Scabbard and other Achaemenid Matters." *Bulletin of the Asia Institute*, N.S. 12: 231–248.

Stucky, Rolf. 1993. *Die Skulpturen aus dem Eschmun-Heiligtum von Sidon: Griechische, römische, kyprische und phönizische Statuen und Reliefs vom 6. Jahrhundert v. Chr. bis zum 3. Jahrhundert v. Chr.*, Beiheft zur Halbjahresschrift Antike Kunst 17. Basel: Vereinigung der Freunde antiker Kunst.

Tadmor, Hayim. 1994. *The Inscriptions of Tiglath-Pileser III, King of Assyria*. Jerusalem: Israel Academy of Sciences and Humanities.

Tadmor, Hayim, and Shiego Yamada. 2011. *The Royal Inscriptions of Tiglath-Pilser III (744–727 BC), and Shalmaneser V (726–722 BC), Kings of Assyria*, Royal Inscriptions of the Neo-Assyrian Period 1. Winona Lake: Eisenbrauns.

Tichy, Franz. 1997. "s.v. Bodenschätze. I: Geographie." *Der Neue Pauly*, 2: 713–717.

Van Soldt, Wilfred H. 1983. "The Cuneiform Texts in the Rijksmuseum van Oudheden, Leiden (II)." *Oudheidkundige Mededelingen uit het Rijksmuseum van Oudheden te Leiden*, 64: 143–162.

Vittmann, Günter. 2003. *Ägypten und die Fremden im ersten vorchristlichen Jahrtausend*. Mainz: Verlag Phillip von Zabern.

Wäfler, Markus. 1980–1981. "Zum assyrisch-urartäischen Westkonflikt." *Acta Praehistorica et Archaeologica*, 11/12: 79–98.

Waldbaum, Jane C. 1994. "Early Greek Contacts with Southern Levant, ca. 1000–600 B.C.: The Eastern Perspective." *Bulletin of the American Schools of Oriental Research*, 293: 53–66.

Waldbaum, Jane C. 1997. "Greeks in the East or Greeks and the East? Problems in the Definition and Recognition of Presence." *Bulletin of the American Schools of Oriental Research*, 305: 1–17.

Weidner, Ernst F. 1939. "Jojachin, König von Juda, in babylonischen Keilschrifttexten." In *Mélanges Syriens offerts à Monsieur René Dussaud: Second Volume*, Bibliothèque archéologique et historique 30, edited by Académie des inscriptions et belles-lettres, 923–935. Paris: P. Geuthner.

Wiesehöfer, Josef. 1999. "Kontinuität oder Zäsur? Babylon unter den Achaimeniden." In *Babylon: Focus mesopotamischer Geschichte, Wiege früher Gelehrsamkeit, Mythos in der Moderne*, Colloquien der Deutschen Orient-Gesellschaft 2, edited by Johannes Renger, 167–188. Saarbrücken: Saarbrücker Druckerei und Verlag.

Yamada, Shigeo. 2005. "*Kārus* on the Frontiers of the Neo-Assyrian State." *Orient: Reports of the Society for Near Eastern Studies in Japan*, 40: 56–89.

Yamada, Shigeo. 2008. "Qurdi-Aššur-lāmur: His Letters and Career." In *Treasures on Camel's Humps: Historical and Literary Studies from the Ancient Near East Presented to Israel Eph'al*, edited by Mordechai Cogan and Dan'el Kahn, 296–311. Jerusalem: Magnes Press.

Zaccagnini, Carlo. 1996. "Tyre and the Cedars of Lebanon." In *Alla soglie della classicità: Il Mediterraneo tra tradizione e innovazione: Studi in onore di Sabatino Moscati*, edited by Enrico Acquaro, 451–466. Pisa: Istituti editoriali e poligrafici internazionali.

Zadok, Ran. 1985. *Geographical Names According to New- and Late-Babylonian Texts*, Répertoire géographique des textes cunéiformes 8. Wiesbaden: Reichert Verlag.

Zadok, Ran. 2003. "The Representation of Foreigners in Neo- and Late-Babylonian Documents Eighth through Second Centuries BCE." In *Judah and the Judeans in the Neo-Babylonian Period*, edited by Oded Lipschits and Joseph Blenkinsopp, 471–589. Winona Lake: Eisenbrauns.

Zadok, Ran. 2005. "On Anatolians, Greeks and Egyptians in 'Chaldean' and Achaemenid Babylonia." *Tel Aviv*, 32(1): 76–106.

FURTHER READING

Aruz, Graff, and Rakic (2014) is an up-to-date and multiperspective approach on transcultural affairs from Iran to the Strait of Gibraltar. Hodos (2006) offers an excellent overview on transcultural contacts in the Mediterranean from the archaeological point of view. Rollinger (2018) is a comprehensive perspective on East–West contacts.

CHAPTER TEN

Greeks in Iron Age Central Europe: Patterns of Interaction and Change

Peter S. Wells

The Setting: Early Iron Age Central Europe

The focus of this chapter is on the central region of the European continent, from northwestern Switzerland in the southwest to southern Poland in the northeast, and including parts of Germany, Austria, and the Czech Republic (Map 10.1). This part of Europe is known as the hilly uplands, with a topography dominated by the Alps in the south, the Rhine River flowing north and the Danube flowing east, and low hills, tributary rivers and streams, and fertile river terraces and valleys. Since Neolithic times, the land has been farmed relatively intensively, and the soils are highly productive for crops. By the Early Iron Age, much of the land had been cleared of forest for agriculture and the raising of livestock, but stands of trees remained throughout the region and were exploited for wood for building and for fuel, both for cooking and for smelting iron. The climate during the Early Iron Age was similar to that of today. Summers were moderately hot, winters could be cold, especially in the southern parts of the region in the foothills of the Alps.

The beginnings of evidence for regular interactions between communities in central Europe and those in Greece and its colonies lie around the start of the sixth century BC. In order to situate the topic of this chapter, I include a summary discussion of the societies of central Europe prior to the appearance of the first evidence for these interactions (for more complete discussion, see Wells 2011).

The eighth century BC was a time of substantial change in economic and social patterns throughout central Europe. In the standard chronological system, developed at the end of the nineteenth and beginning of the twentieth century, the final phase of the Bronze Age, commonly known as the Urnfield period, dates 1200–800 BC, and the Early Iron Age begins at 800 BC. It is during the Early Iron Age that evidence for regular interaction between central Europeans and Greeks first appears.

A Companion to Greeks Across the Ancient World, First Edition. Edited by Franco De Angelis.
© 2020 John Wiley & Sons, Inc. Published 2020 by John Wiley & Sons, Inc.

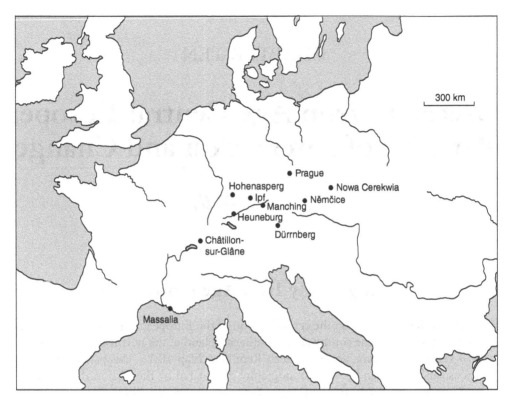

Map 10.1 Greek-Iron Age Central Europe.

The Early Iron Age is defined as the time when iron first began to come into general use as the principal material for making tools and weapons. During the first couple of centuries of the Iron Age, bronze continued to be used for many purposes, and that metal remained in general use for personal ornaments (such as bracelets, neck rings, pendants, and fibulae), vessels (cauldrons, bowls, plates, cups), and defensive weapons (helmets, shields, breastplates).

Most settlements of Early Iron Age Europe were small, consisting of a few houses and rarely exceeding 100 persons in population. Houses were solidly built, rectangular in shape and usually with substantial vertical posts sunk into the ground supporting walls of wattle-and-daub and thatched roofs. Settlements were often enclosed by ditches or palisades.

The agricultural economy was based on the cultivation of cereals, especially millet, wheat, and barley, supplemented by garden crops such as lentils. Livestock raised included pigs, cattle, sheep, and goats.

Most villages had a kiln in which to fire pottery. We do not know much about how pottery production was organized; probably one or two individuals served as the potters for each community. By the latter part of the Early Iron Age, most village communities included a blacksmith who forged tools and weapons. Iron ore is abundant in central Europe, and most communities had access to it. Copper and tin are much more restricted in their distributions in nature, and to make the alloy bronze, most communities needed to participate in exchange systems to acquire the metal. Bronze casting to make jewelry and other ornaments was done in many village communities. A variety of other crafts were carried out in the settlements, including textile weaving, leather processing, and the carving of materials such as wood, bone, antler, lignite, and jet (the latter two substances for beads and rings).

Trade between communities is well attested by the presence of substances and finished products that originated beyond the vicinity of the individual settlements. Copper and tin had to be mined and the ores smelted in the mountainous areas where the ores occurred, the metals had to be brought together to be alloyed, and ingots of the metal, or finished products, had to be transported to communities that wanted them. Bronze is well represented at settlements throughout central Europe; hence it is clear that communities were linked in vast trade networks. Other goods that circulated regularly included amber for ornaments, glass beads, and graphite for decorating pottery.

Among the richest sources of information about the central European Early Iron Age are the burials. At the beginning of the Early Iron Age, common burial practice was cremation of the body, then burial of the cremated remains, often with an earth mound placed over the grave. In the course of the Early Iron Age, burial practice changed gradually to inhumation. By the sixth century BC, many burials of both men and women were outfitted with substantial quantities of grave goods and covered with mounds. Grave goods consisted mainly of personal ornaments and pottery in the case of women; the more richly outfitted men's graves had in them sets of weapons and bronze vessels associated with feasting. The great majority of graves had very few or no grave goods. The differentiation between the well outfitted graves with the biggest mounds over them and poorly equipped graves with small mounds or no mounds suggests that society was becoming increasingly stratified during the course of the Early Iron Age (for recent discussions of Iron Age social organization, see Hill 2006 and Schier 2010).

In the discussion that follows, I treat Greek activity in central Europe in three phases, since the patterns evident in the archaeological evidence are different at different times and indicate changes in the character and results of interactions.

Greek Activity in Central Europe, Sixth and Fifth Centuries BC

It is important to examine the evidence for Greek interaction with communities in central Europe in the context of the profound economic and political changes that were taking place in the greater Mediterranean region during the final millennium BC, which have been explored in a number of recent studies (e.g., Hodos 2009; Fletcher 2012; Osborne 2018).

The evidence for interaction between communities in central Europe and the Greek world can be considered in terms of four categories – imports, architecture, sculpture, and cultural practices. The presentation here is selective, not comprehensive.

Imports

Attic pottery – pottery made at Athens and in its immediate vicinity – has been identified from more than 20 sites in central Europe – in Germany, Switzerland, Austria, and the Czech Republic (Pape 2004; Hansen and Böhr 2011, 219, figure 6). Attic pottery is of special importance to archaeologists studying interactions between communities in central Europe and the Greek world, because its place of origin is clear and because it often provides the best evidence for establishing the date of assemblages in which it is recovered. Black-figure Attic pottery began to arrive into central Europe during the third quarter of the sixth century BC, and red-figure pottery arrived during the latter part of the fifth century BC. As Hansen and Böhr's recent map (2011, 219, figure 6) shows, Attic pottery is not evenly distributed throughout the region, but tends to be concentrated at a number of locations. In the western part of the distribution, these are associated with major fortified hilltop settlements that are surrounded by richly outfitted burials. These include the much-studied complexes at the Heuneburg on the upper Danube River in southwest Germany (Pape 2000), the Hohenasperg in the Neckar River valley (Biel and Balzer 2012), Breisach in the upper Rhine valley (Balzer, Bräuning, and Dehn 2012), the Ipf in eastern Württemberg (Krause, Euler, and Fuhrmann 2008), the Marienberg on the middle Main River (van Endert 1997), the Üetliberg in Zurich (Siegfried 1997), and Châtillon-sur-Glâne in western Switzerland (Dietrich-Weibel, Lüscher, and Kilka 1998). In the eastern part of the distribution, Attic pottery occurs at a series of lowland settlements in Bohemia (Bouzek and Koutecký 1975; Bouzek and Smrž 1994; Trefný 2008), with a notable concentration in the region around the city of Prague. Local imitations of Attic pottery have been recovered at a number of sites in Bohemia as well (Bašta, Baštová, and Bouzek 1989; Chytráček 2008).

Attic pottery occurs in two types of contexts – on settlement sites and in graves. From the sherds recovered on the settlement at the Heuneburg, it is possible to identify different categories of vessels, including kraters and cups. In graves, vessels of Attic pottery are almost exclusively cups, as at Kleinaspergle at the Hohenasperg (Böhr 1988) and at Rodenbach in the Rhineland (Sperber 2002).

Sherds of ceramic amphorae, most of them from Massalia and its region situated on the Mediterranean coast at the mouth of the Rhône River in southern France, have been recovered at a number of sites, notably at the Heuneburg (van den Boom and Pape 2000) and at Châtillon-sur-Glâne (Lüscher 1996), and they have played a major role in discussions of the wine trade from the Mediterranean world into temperate Europe. The dates of the amphorae correspond closely to those of the Attic pottery.

Bronze vessels manufactured in Greek workshops are less well represented in central Europe than are Attic pottery and amphorae, but they are no less important in terms of the information we can derive from them. Early in the sixth century BC, bronze jugs believed to have arrived via Greek traders ended up in graves at Kappel and Vilsingen in southwestern Germany (Shefton 1979). A bronze hydria with an elaborate ornament of a female figure surrounded by animals was recovered in a burial at Grächwil in Switzerland (Guggisberg 2004). That vessel is believed to have been made in a Greek colonial workshop in southern Italy about 580 BC. Late in that century, the great bronze cauldron found in the grave at Hochdorf (see below), with a diameter of 1.04 m, was manufactured in a Greek colony in southern Italy around 540–530 BC (Biel 1985, 120; Bieg 2002). Comparable in scale is the most spectacular Greek bronze vessel recovered in an Iron Age grave, the krater in the burial at Vix at Châtillon-sur-Seine in France, where it is associated with two Attic kylikes and Etruscan bronze vessels, all part of an elaborate set of vessels for feasting (Rolley 2003; see the chapter by Sanmartí, this volume). In the grave at Grafenbühl, to be discussed below, were found the remains of a Greek bronze tripod (Herrmann 1970) and fragments of two bronze vessels.

Excavators at the Ehrenbürg in northern Bavaria recovered remains of a small polychrome glass vessel, perhaps an ointment jar, believed to have been manufactured in a Greek workshop (Abels 1989). A similar glass vessel is represented by a fragment found at the settlement of Strakowice in southern Bohemia (Michálek 1992).

Other imports include two ornamental figurines of sphinxes found in the Grafenbühl grave, one of ivory, the other of bone with a face carved of amber (Zürn 1970, 17 and plate 66, 1.2). In the same grave were carved pieces of bone and ivory, probably parts of a couch (or possible a throne, according to Jung's [2007] interpretation), together with many plaquettes carved from bone, ivory, and amber, thought to have been parts of the same piece of furniture imported from Greece (Zürn 1970, 16–20, plates 3, 6–9). Similar pieces have been identified from a burial in a mound known as Römerhügel, not far from Grafenbühl and also part of the Hohenasperg complex, and from a burial at Giessübel-Talhau near the Heuneburg. (For general overviews of Greek imports in this period, see Frey 1999 and Mac Sweeney and Wells 2018.)

Architecture

During excavations at the Heuneburg in the early 1950s, archaeologists uncovered remains of a wall built of clay bricks resting on a 3m-wide foundation of cut stone blocks (Burkhardt 2010). Together, the foundation and the clay brick wall reached a height of 3.5m in places. The wall was built around the entire plateau on which the Heuneburg is situated, surrounding a space about 3.5 ha in area, and it includes at least 11 towers projecting outward from the wall toward the west. The wall was constructed during the phase Hallstatt D1 at the Heuneburg, sometime in the first quarter of the sixth century BC. It was rebuilt at least once and finally destroyed around the middle of the second half of the sixth century BC.

The wall at the Heuneburg is the only wall built of clay bricks known in temperate Europe. Archaeologists seek parallels in the Mediterranean world, where clay brick architecture is well documented from the Bronze Age on, and close comparisons have been noted with walls surrounding Greek cities.

Since there was no earlier tradition of clay brick architecture in temperate Europe, the conception, design, and construction of the wall must have involved architects skilled in the technique of clay brick architecture from the Mediterranean world. The wall is intriguing evidence pertaining to Greek activity in central Europe. Imports, such as the pottery and bronze vessels mentioned above, could have arrived indirectly, via communities inhabiting lands between the Greek Mediterranean and the centers of temperate Europe. But the construction of the clay brick wall required the direct transmission of technical knowledge by persons who knew how to build such structures. As yet, we lack the evidence to suggest whether a Greek architect, or team of architects, came to the Heuneburg to plan and oversee construction of the wall; or whether individuals from the Heuneburg area learned the techniques somewhere in the Mediterranean world. The wall required a large amount of labor on the part of the builders. A political structure must have been in place at the Heuneburg to command that effort under the direction and supervision of the architects.

Excavations conducted between 2004 and 2006 at the site of Bugfeld situated east-southeast of the hilltop settlement on the Ipf in central southern Germany revealed a rectangular structure 266 m² in area paved with stone, mostly white limestone quarried over a kilometer away (Krause 2012). Just east of this structure were found large postholes that formed the foundation of a rectangular building about 15 by 15 m in size. The excavators suggest that this pair of structures, unusual for temperate Europe, has its closest parallels in sanctuary sites associated with Greek colonies in southern Italy and Sicily. The sherds of Attic pottery recovered on the nearby Ipf indicate that indeed the community here was in contact with the Greek world.

Sculpture

At Hirschlanden near the Hohenasperg and at the Glauberg north of Frankfurt, life-size stone statues of men equipped with weapons have been found, the former dating to around 530 BC, the latter to around 400 BC. Both are associated with burial mounds. The form and posture of both statues have been compared with those of Greek *kouroi* (Steuernagel 2002), but some argue that closer parallels are to be found in the Etruscan sculptural traditions of Italy (Frey 2002; Müller 2009, 180). Whether the closest connections are to be identified with Greece or with Etruscan Italy, the important point is that, like the clay brick wall at the Heuneburg, these sculptures demonstrate the transmission of technical knowledge from societies of the Mediterranean world to communities in temperate Europe. Both statues were sculpted from local stone. These two specimens are the most "Mediterranean-like" of a larger series of stone sculptures in temperate Europe dating from the late sixth century BC on (Frey 2002).

Cultural Practices

As will be seen below, there is strong evidence that the practice of the Greek *symposion* was adopted by Iron Age elites during the latter part of the sixth and beginning of the fifth centuries BC, at least in the regions of eastern France and southwest Germany. In Greece, the *symposion* played an important cultural, social, and political role in fostering common identities and social competition among the aristocratic groups in late seventh- and early sixth-century BC Athens (Murray 1990; Wehgartner 1995). Descriptions of specific events by Plato and Xenophon inform us about the process of these feasting and entertainment events, and representations of them on Attic pottery provide links between the behaviors of the participants and the material culture they used.

In richly outfitted graves of the late sixth century BC in temperate Europe, full sets of the same categories of feasting equipment as those documented from the Greek world were arranged in the tombs, notably those of Hochdorf and Grafenbühl. Such arrangements have been interpreted as indications that the practice of the Greek ritual was adopted along with the imported Attic cups, bronze vessels, and other paraphernalia.

If this interpretation is correct, then the adoption of Greek practices had significance similar to that of the clay brick wall at the Heuneburg. Only through personal contact – whether by a central European participating in a *symposion* in the Greek world or a Greek (or someone knowledgeable in Greek practices) instructing elites in central Europe in the appropriate practices involved with the arriving imports – could a ritual such as the Greek *symposion* be replicated so far from the shores of the Mediterranean.

The Impact of Greek Interaction: The Heuneburg and the Hohenasperg

The richest evidence for interaction between the Greek world and communities in central Europe is concentrated at two locations that have been the objects of study for well over a century: the Heuneburg on the upper Danube in southwest Germany, near the modern town of Herbertingen; and the Hohenasperg on the middle Neckar River near Ludwigsburg, north of Stuttgart. The evidence from the settlements and from the numerous graves around them provides the most detailed view into the character of interactions with the Greek world, and of the causes, results, and effects of those interactions on the societies of temperate Europe. Comparable evidence is available from the site of Mont Lassois in eastern France and the associated burials there, including the Vix tomb (Chaume and Mordant 2011; Sanmartí, this volume). Similar evidence is emerging at other sites throughout temperate Europe, and as ongoing research progresses, we shall gain a much more detailed picture of the questions addressed here. At the present time, the Heuneburg and the Hohenasperg and their associated burials provide the most comprehensive evidence.

The Heuneburg and its Region

The Heuneburg is the most thoroughly excavated Early Iron Age hilltop settlement in temperate Europe, and the results of the investigations provide rich and detailed information about the local community and its interactions with the Greek world (Krausse et al. 2016). The hilltop settlement covers a plateau about 3.5 ha in area above the upper Danube River in a fertile region of southwest Germany. The site was settled around 600 BC, at which time construction of the wall surrounding the plateau was begun, and it was densely occupied until the early decades of the fifth century BC. In the landscape around the plateau, at distances ranging from 0.5 to 5 km, are 11 exceptionally large burials mounds, as well as numerous smaller mounds of more typical size.

Research on the imposing mounds began in 1876–1877, and those investigations resulted in the discovery of gold neck rings, bronze vessels, and other grave goods indicating that the Heuneburg and its surrounding graves were parts of a complex and important center. Settlement excavations began in 1950 and soon uncovered the clay brick wall discussed above and recovered sherds of Attic pottery. As excavations have continued throughout much of the latter half of the twentieth and beginning of the twenty-first century, more sherds of Attic pottery have been recovered, along with other imports from the Greek world, including sherds of transport amphorae and of other categories of pottery. The excavations have shown the Heuneburg to have been the site of workshops processing a wide range of materials, including iron, bronze, gold, lignite, jet, and coral imported from the Mediterranean coast (Gersbach 1999).

The early excavations focused on the top of the plateau – the "hillfort." More recently, archaeologists have begun exploring the surrounding landscape and in the process have begun to uncover what can only be described as a huge settlement surrounding the plateau. The outer settlement complex is thought to cover some 50 ha of land and to represent a large suburban population. Krausse et al. (2016, 85) estimate a total population of around 5000 for the hilltop site and the surrounding suburbs, a very large number for Early Iron Age temperate Europe.

The Hohenasperg and its Region

Like the Heuneburg, the Hohenasperg is a plateau extending above fertile agricultural land. It is situated near Ludwigsburg north of Stuttgart, about 90 km north of the Heuneburg. Unlike the Heuneburg, whose surface had been largely undisturbed when archaeologists began fieldwork, the top of the Hohenasperg has been severely disturbed in historical times. In the early part of the sixteenth century a fortress was built on the site. As a result of that and later construction activity, it is unlikely that any archaeological layers remain undisturbed (Biel and Balzer 2012). Even without the direct evidence of imported materials in settlement deposits on the Hohenasperg, its topographical situation and archaeological materials from the surrounding lands make clear that this site must have been occupied by a settlement of similar character to that at the Heuneburg.

The chronological evidence from the burials in the large mounds around the Hohenasperg indicate that the Hohenasperg and the Heuneburg were active centers at the same time during the sixth and early fifth centuries BC, but there is much more evidence at the Hohenasperg for later activity than there is at the Heuneburg.

As is the case with the large burial mounds at the Heuneburg, the mounds at the Hohenasperg attracted attention early. Excavations were carried out during the late nineteenth century at the sites of Römerhügel (1877) and Kleinaspergle (1879), and the wealth of finds from the graves in these mounds made clear that this was another special region. For understanding how Greek imports and practices were adopted and transformed to serve the local cultural needs, three graves at the Hohenasperg complex are especially informative. The grave at Hochdorf, 9.9 km west of the Hohenasperg, dates to about 525 BC. The burial at Grafenbühl, situated just 650 m east of the Hohenasperg, to about 500 BC. And the second grave at Kleinaspergle, just south of the Hohenasperg, dates to around 410 BC. All three graves were contained in substantial wooden chambers, which were covered with large mounds of earth.

The earliest of the rich graves and in many ways the most informative burial is that at Hochdorf (Biel 1985). It was discovered in 1978 and meticulously excavated in 1979. It provides us with an extraordinarily detailed view into the character of elite burial during the latter half of the sixth century BC. Whereas many of the rich graves of this period were looted in antiquity, the Hochdorf burial was not, perhaps because of the massive stone layer, estimated at 50 tons, covering the wooden burial chamber. The excavators found everything intact in the grave. The preservation of organic materials, including textiles, animal fur, and plant parts, was exceptionally good, because much of the grave was waterlogged. The excavations, conducted by Jörg Biel, were of unusually high quality, and they included removing part of the grave in a block for precise investigation under laboratory conditions.

The grave contained the remains of an adult man about 40 years of age. He had been laid on a bronze couch 2.75 m long, made of sheet bronze with solid bronze rods as supports. It rested on eight cast bronze figurines of women, which stood on axles on which wheels were mounted. The back of the couch was decorated with repoussé scenes of pairs of men wielding swords and charioteers holding swords and shields.

The man's body was decorated with a variety of gold ornaments. Around his neck was a large neck ring of sheet gold, ornamented with tiny horse-and-rider motifs pressed from the back. On his chest were two gold serpentine fibulae. On his right wrist was a broad gold bracelet, and a wide gold belt plaque covered the front of his torso. The bronze sheath of the dagger that he wore at his waist was coated with gold, as was the hilt. Even his shoes were covered with ornate gold pieces.

The objects in the Hochdorf burial chamber inform us about feasting practices and their connection with the Greek *symposion*. In the northwest corner of the chamber was a bronze cauldron with a capacity of some 400 liters, believed to have been manufactured in a Greek workshop in southern Italy sometime around 530 BC, as noted above. With the cauldron was a small decorated gold bowl, apparently to serve as a ladle for extracting liquid from the cauldron. Inside the cauldron remains of pollen indicate the presence of a substance similar to mead of later times.

On the south wall of the chamber hung nine drinking horns. One, located closest to the man's head, was of iron and of immense size – 1.23 m long, with a mouth diameter of 14.5 cm and a capacity of 5.5 liters. It was decorated with gold bands around it. The other eight were natural horns from wild cattle – aurochs – which were not preserved. The gold bands that had been attached to their openings indicate that the mouth of each horn was between 10.5 and 13.5 cm in diameter.

Along the east wall of the chamber was a four-wheeled wagon, arranged with its front toward the south. On the bed of the wagon was a set of nine bronze plates, matching in number the drinking horns on the south wall.

In his analysis of these vessels – the Greek imported cauldron, the gold bowl, the drinking horns, and the plates – Dirk Krausse (1996) has argued that the objects and their arrangement in the grave indicate the adoption, and the transformation into the local medium, of the Greek practice of the *symposion*. Even the bronze couch, a unique object in Early Iron Age temperate Europe, is likely to have been used in the context of a local version of the Greek *symposion* (Boardman 1990).

In contrast to Hochdorf, the Grafenbühl grave, excavated in 1964 and 1965, was found to have been looted in antiquity (Zürn 1970). Materials had been scattered throughout the grave, including fragmentary remains of lavish objects. Skeletal parts of a 30-year-old man were found in the southwest corner of the burial chamber.

The objects recovered included remains of a tripod from the Greek world, with iron supports and bronze bases in the form of a lion's feet, and carved pieces of ivory, amber, and bone believed to belong to a couch made in a Greek workshop and transported to this location in southwest Germany (Fischer 1990). Associated with the tripod were fragments of two bronze basins and a drinking horn made of iron (Baitinger 1996). The couch, tripod, basins, and drinking horn indicate a set of equipment for feasting very much like the larger set in the Hochdorf grave. Objects similar to those associated with the couch in the Grafenbühl grave have been identified among the remains from two graves excavated during the nineteenth century, one at Römerhügel and one in the Giessübel-Talhau group at the Heuneburg (Krausse 1996, 327). Couches may have been much more common in the richly outfitted burials than the evidence from the recently excavated burials at Hochdorf and Grafenbühl indicates.

Other objects in the grave included the two small sphinx figurines mentioned above and an ivory lion's foot, perhaps originally attached to a chest, all three items believed to have been made in Greek workshops. Numerous small and fragmentary pieces of gold suggest that the grave must have contained considerable amounts of that metal before it was looted.

Of special note is the presence of an object consisting of two roughly rectangular pieces of sheet bronze, attached to a handle at one end, interpreted by Krausse (1996, 328) as a musical instrument, a castanet. Krausse notes that representations of similar objects in the Greek and Etruscan worlds show them in the hands of dancers. Perhaps this object played a part in the ritual of burial. It may have been part of the feasting activity represented by the couch, tripod, and bronze vessels. Music was an important element in the Greek *symposion*, and this object may represent its practice here in central Europe.

When investigators tunneled into the imposing mound of Kleinaspergle in 1879, they found that the central chamber had been looted, as was the case at Grafenbühl, but they came upon a chamber off to the side that contained a wealth of grave goods. We do not have a precise plan of that grave, such as we have for those of Hochdorf and Grafenbühl, but at least a rough sketch was made in 1879 (Krausse 2004, 199, figure 4). It shows bronze vessels, gold-covered drinking horn mounts, and two Attic kylikes arranged along the north wall of the chamber; cremated remains just east of the center; and otherwise open space within the chamber. The objects included a bronze cauldron 93 cm in diameter, with a wooden bowl inside; a bronze jug; a ribbed bucket; an Etruscan stamnos; two gold-covered mounts for drinking horns; an Attic red-figure kylix; and an Attic firnis kylix (Kimmig 1988).

In recent years, a number of small settlements in the vicinity of the Hohenasperg have yielded Attic red-figure pottery (Balzer 2010, 227), showing that these Greek imports were being used by a number of communities in the region, not restricted to the elites represented in the richest burials. One of these settlements is at Hochdorf, 400 m west of the burial discussed above (Biel 1997). Sherds of amphorae from the region of Greek Massalia have also been found in the area, as for example in a pit at the small settlement of Sersheim "Reutwälde," 10 km northwest of the Hohenasperg (Balzer 2010, 227, figure 21).

Display, Performance, Meanings: The Significance of the Greek Contacts

The evidence from settlement sites at which sherds of Greek imported pottery and amphorae have been found, such as the Heuneburg, does not allow us to say much about how the imported objects were used. But the arrangements of the objects in graves provide much more information.

As John Bender and Michael Marrinan (2010) argue in their recent book *The Culture of Diagram*, the way that a society arranges things, whether decoration on pottery, subjects in paintings, or displays of objects in burials, can tell us important things about how the members of that society thought about the world they lived in. I have argued elsewhere (Wells 2012, chapter 8) that changing patterns of arrangement of objects in graves indicate important themes about the societies of Bronze and Iron Age Europe, and these ideas lend themselves well to close examination of the burials outfitted with Greek imports.

We are fortunate to have very well documented plans of the graves at Hochdorf and Grafenbühl and at least a rough sketch of the situation of the objects at Kleinaspergle. Other richly outfitted graves of this period, such as that at Vix in eastern France and grave 44/2 at the Dürrnberg in Austria (Penninger and Pauli 1972, 76–80) show very similar patterns.

The plan of the grave at Hochdorf (Biel 1985, 47, figure 32; Krausse 1996, 27, figure 3) illustrates the point. We need to remind ourselves that what we as archaeologists find when we excavate is a static representation of only a part of a funerary ceremony. Most funerals, especially those of elite individuals such as those buried with Greek imports in Early Iron Age central Europe, are accompanied by ritual performances that could include instrumental music, songs, dances, and speeches. The character and content of much of those performances are lost to us, but we can reconstruct to some extent the part of the performance that resulted in the arrangement of objects that we find in graves that we excavate.

Funerary rituals, especially those for elite individuals, are community events in which many people participate. The purpose of such rituals is not only to lay someone to rest, but also to make assertions about the social organization of the community and to shape participants' memories of the event in ways that favor the performers' representations.

The arrangement of grave goods, including the Greek imports and objects associated with them, was part of the performance.

The Hochdorf grave included an unusually elaborate set of objects associated with feasting (probably for the simple reason that it was not looted, as many of its type were). These objects were not piled in the middle of the grave, but purposefully arranged around the outer edge of the grave space. The couch with the deceased man on it was flush with the west wall of the chamber. The Greek bronze cauldron occupied the northwest corner, and the gold bowl was placed with it. The wagon, with the nine bronze plates arranged on its bed, was placed flush with the east wall and filled most of the eastern third of the grave. Hanging on the south wall, from the head end of the couch to the end of the wagon pole, were the nine drinking horns. The open space in the center of the grave was almost entirely enclosed by objects associated with feasting. Even at the north end, where there was a space between the great bulbous cauldron and the back right wheel of the wagon, the passage into the center of the grave was narrowed by the two large and projecting objects on either side.

Within the visual frame formed by the couch, cauldron, wagon, and drinking horns, the open space in the center was important. It clearly was intentionally left uncovered by grave goods. Perhaps those performing the funerary ceremony stood in this central space as they arranged the objects in the grave, speaking about each one as it was set into place. Perhaps some participants could walk into this space for a close view of the objects around them. Perhaps the principal purpose of this open space was to stimulate memories of the feasts in which the deceased individual and his eight followers used the objects now laid out during the ceremony. Investigators from fields such as cognitive psychology (Gibson 1979) and design theory (Brett 2005) emphasize the importance of open spaces within fields intented for visual reception. Gibson calls these "affordances," and they are powerful visual devices that stimulate responses in viewers. I would argue that the response stimulated in the course of the funerary ceremony at Hochdorf was visualizing or reimagining the festive, and socially and politically significant, events that the deceased individual had hosted in the past.

The enormous Greek cauldron was the central piece in this display. It is the most massive, most visually striking of all of the objects, still breathtakingly large and imposing even to the modern visitor to the Württembergisches Landesmuseum in Stuttgart where it is displayed. In the much smaller-scale life of Early Iron Age Europe, where not many things were that size, it must have been striking indeed. In addition to its special visual qualities, this was the object that held that which was most essential to the feast – the alcoholic beverage (Dietler and Hayden 2001; Arnold 2004). It would have been the center of attention at any celebratory event. Especially significant for our understanding of the role of interactions with the Greek world for the peoples of central Europe is the fact that the Greek cauldron was fully integrated into the local set of drinking and eating paraphernalia.

Just as at Hochdorf, in the Grafenbühl burial chamber, the deceased individual had been placed in the southwest corner of the grave (Zürn 1970, 12–13). Other than the situation of the skeletal remains, the two feet of the Greek bronze tripod, and the ornamental parts of the couch, everything else in the grave was in disarray when the archaeologists excavated. But the noted positions of these few objects, and the arrangement of the vessels along the north wall of the chamber at Kleinaspergle, make apparent that, as in the Hochdorf burial, the Greek imports in these other two graves had been positioned precisely, with respect to the other objects in the graves and to the spaces left open, to convey their importance in the ritual life of Early Iron Age society. The display of the imports in the performance of the funerary ceremonies illustrates the significance of these highly visible connections with the Greek world.

Mechanisms and Effects

Two topics remain to be addressed, the mechanisms through which the Greek imports reached central Europe, and the effects of the interactions on the societies involved. Both of these issues have been discussed at great length over the past half century, and here I shall only present the essence of the arguments.

Eggert (2010) recently has reviewed the principal mechanisms suggested for the arrival of the imports. One is as political gifts. In an influential paper, Franz Fischer (1973) argued that the large and costly imports, such as the Hochdorf cauldron, the Vix krater, and the Grafenbühl couch, most likely were political gifts presented by representatives of Greek interests, perhaps economic, perhaps political, to potentates in temperate Europe. As Fischer shows, this mechanism of transmission is well documented in the ancient Mediterranean world.

A second possible mechanism is gifts associated with marriage between members of the different societies. Here again, textual sources indicate that special objects were often transferred between societies in connection with marriages between elite individuals from the different groups.

A third mechanism is raiding and looting. Numerous written sources from the Mediterranean world describe invasions by peoples from temperate Europe into Italy and Greece, especially after 400 BC, but the pattern may well have been established earlier. Such incursions may have resulted in the bringing back of attractive goods as booty to central Europe, where some ultimately ended up in burials.

A fourth mechanism is the exchange of goods – trade. For bulk goods such as wine, barter trade may have been involved. As Attic pottery is found on increasing numbers of sites throughout central Europe, some form of exchange seems increasingly likely for these "everyday luxuries."

The ever-increasing quantity of Greek objects being recovered in central Europe, their relatively wide distribution on settlements and in graves, and the variety of objects involved should encourage us to explore all of these mechanisms as means through which the imports may have reached communities in temperate Europe. No doubt a variety of different mechanisms was involved. As more discoveries of Greek imports are made, especially in well documented contexts such as the grave at Hochdorf, we shall gain better understanding of the processes involved in their transmission and integration into local practices. It is important to bear in mind that while Attic pottery, transport amphorae, and Greek bronze vessels are being recovered at increasing numbers of sites throughout the central regions of the European continent, their total numbers are small relative to the local pottery and metal vessels. The Greek imports turn up consistently at the large hillforts, such as the Heuneburg, and in the richest burials, but rarely occur on smaller settlements or in graves of modest wealth.

The principal debate regarding the effects of the Greek interactions on communities in central Europe revolves around the extent to which the interactions with the Greek world in any way "caused" the rise of the centers such as the Heuneburg and the Hohenasperg and the development of the stratified society that seems to be represented by the contrast between the rich graves containing imports and gold on the one hand, and the much more typical, less well outfitted burials on the other (Wells 2015). When serious discussion of this issue began in the 1950s and 1960s, many scholars believed that the outside contact, in this case with the Greek and Etruscan worlds, was an active force in generating economic and political change in temperate Europe. More recently, investigators tend to explain cultural change more in terms of internal social dynamics rather than as the result of outside forces. Jörg Biel (1988, 208) argues that the stratified social structure evident in graves such as Hochdorf and Grafenbühl developed before the intensive contacts with the Greek world began, and that it was the existence of that stratified society that made possible the development of those interactions on the part of the European elites.

Greek Activity in Central Europe: Fourth and Third Centuries BC

The centers of the sixth and early fifth centuries BC, including the Heuneburg and the Hohenasperg, declined in economic activity during the fifth century BC (see Krausse 2006; Beilharz and Krausse 2012; Wells 2012, 193–196). The Kleinaspergle grave at the Hohenasperg stands out as the only richly outfitted burial containing Greek imports and objects characteristic of the new, La Tène style, in the vicinity of either of these centers (on Early La Tène style, see Megaw and Megaw 2001). The same decline in manufacturing and commercial activity is apparent at other major sites throughout temperate Europe. The decline in the numbers and in the richness of lavishly outfitted burials after 400 BC was also a Europe-wide phenomenon (Schönfelder 2007a). Greek imports are much rarer during the fourth and third centuries BC than during the sixth and fifth, but there are a few. For example, in the latter half of the fifth century BC, an Attic red-figure kantharos was placed in a burial at Rodenbach in the middle Rhineland as part of a small set of feasting vessels (Sperber 2002). The bronze bucket in the grave at Waldalgesheim, also in the middle Rhineland and also dated to the latter part of the fourth century BC, may have been made in a Greek colonial workshop in southern Italy (Shefton 1994; Joachim 1995, 59).

Mercenary Soldiers

During the fourth and third centuries BC, texts written by authors in the literate societies of the Mediterranean Basin mention the presence of Celtic mercenaries serving in the armies of potentates active in the eastern Mediterranean region (Szabó 1995). The geographical origins of these soldiers are not specified, but from other references to "Celts," it is most likely that at least a substantial proportion of these mercenary troops came from central Europe. Their experiences serving in lands of the eastern Mediterranean region exposed them to cultures and lifestyles very different from their own. Martin Schönfelder (2007b) has examined archaeological evidence in central Europe that may pertain to the return of soldiers to their homelands, but the evidence available at present is sparse. Aurel Rustoiu (2006, 56) suggests that military recruiters for the armies of the Greek potentates may have traveled into central Europe to recruit men to serve as mercenaries. Such recruitment efforts would help to explain how so many "Celtic" soldiers came to fight on behalf of Greek military commanders during this period.

Coins and Coinage

A number of Greek coins minted during the latter half of the fourth century BC have been recovered in central Europe, including especially gold staters of the Macedonian kings Philip II (359–336 BC) and his son Alexander the Great (336–323 BC). These coins, which served as models for the development of local coinage, had the head of Apollo or of Athena on one side and either a winged goddess or a two-wheeled chariot on the other (Mannsperger 1981, 228). Mannsperger (1981, 242) argues that these gold coins represent earnings that returning mercenaries brought back with them to their homes in central Europe.

Actual Greek coins that have been found in central Europe are relatively few, perhaps because they were ordinarily melted down to make the gold into jewelry. A coin minted in the Greek colony of Massalia shortly after 400 BC was found at the site of Aubstadt in northern Bavaria (Overbeck 1988), and another from Massalia of about the same date was recovered at the Dürrnberg bei Hallein in Austria (Stöllner and Tadic 1998). Mannsperger (1981, 242) reports just four Greek gold coins found in the German state of Baden-Württemberg. But in some places, the numbers of Greek coins are larger. At Němčice in

Moravia in the Czech Republic, among a total of 424 reported coins recovered in the course of archaeological excavations, 384 are "Celtic" coins minted in temperate Europe, and 40 are from different regions of the Mediterranean, many of them minted in Greek cities (Čižmář, Kolníková, and Noeske 2008). The series of local coins at the site begins with gold copies of the staters of Alexander the Great (Kolníková 2007, 24). Recent excavations at the settlement of Nowa Cerekwia in southern Poland have yielded five Greek coins along with larger numbers of local Celtic coins (Mielczarek 2008, 13).

While the idea that the early Greek coins in central Europe arrived via returning Celtic mercenaries has been much discussed (Mannsperger 1981; Kellner 1991), it is likely that a variety of different mechanisms were involved. Mielczarek (2008, 14) suggests that Greek coins may have been part of the commercial networks along which amber was transported from the shores of the Baltic Sea southward to the shores of the Mediterranean. During these centuries of the Late Iron Age, commerce was growing throughout the greater Mediterranean region, including temperate Europe, the Near East, and North Africa, as well as in the lands immediately adjacent to the Mediterranean Sea, and there is every reason to think that Greek coins were circulating widely.

For our understanding of cultural change in central Europe during the fourth and third centuries BC, the importance of Greek coins is twofold. On the one hand, their presence at sites in central Europe indicates contact and interaction between communities in central Europe and the Greek world during this period. That contact probably took many different forms, some direct, such as payment for mercenary service, and some indirect, such as down-the-line trade between the Greek Mediterranean and central European communities. On the other hand, Greek coins served as models for the development of local systems of coinage within central Europe.

The first groups of coins minted in central Europe after Greek prototypes were of gold and would not have been part of a monetary system. Gold coins served as treasure or bullion, to be used for special purposes, such as marriage presents or diplomatic gifts, or melted down to make other objects. Significantly, these early coins, as well as the later silver and bronze coins, were the first medium in central Europe that displayed images on a widespread basis. I have discussed some of the implications of this change elsewhere (Wells 2012, 178–180).

In contrast to coin usage in the Mediterranean world at this time, the contexts in which Iron Age ("Celtic") coins occur indicates that they were used largely for ceremonial and ritual purposes, rather than as currency (Haselgrove and Wigg-Wolf 2005). Coins minted in temperate Europe often bear images of objects that played special roles in ritual activity among the Iron Age peoples, such as neck rings, fibulae, and swords (see e.g., Wells 2012, 180, figure 43, and 181, figure 44).

Greek Activity in Central Europe: Second and First Centuries BC

During the second century BC, some coins minted in central Europe included legends cut into their dies, sometimes in Greek letters, sometimes in Latin. Early copies of Greek prototypes imitated the writing on the Greek originals, but later, Celtic names were written on coins. Allen and Nash (1980, 109) estimate that some 500–600 different names have been identified in coin legends, which generally consist of only the one word.

Coin legends constitute the earliest widespread use of writing in temperate Europe and thus signal the beginning of a profound shift in systems of symbolizing meaning. Given the evidence for increased commercial interaction between the Greek world and temperate Europe, as well as the historical texts concerning mercenary service by central Europeans in armies of the Mediterranean world, the adoption of this incipient usage of writing at this time is not surprising. But it indicates the depth of the cultural changes that were taking place in temperate Europe as a result of interactions with Greece and other societies of the Mediterranean world.

Early writing in central Europe using Greek letters was not restricted to coin legends, though those are by far the most abundant examples (Steuer 1999). In a grave at Münsingen in Switzerland, a glass bead dating to about 300 BC has Greek letters incised into its surface (Gambari and Kaenel 2001). An iron sword recovered at Port, also in Switzerland, has the name Korisios, in Greek letters, stamped into the top of the blade (Wyss 1956). Linguistic analysis informs us that Korisios is a Celtic name, though the letters with which it was written are Greek. We do not know who Korisios was – whether the smith who made the blade or the owner of the sword. At the Late La Tène *oppidum* settlement of Manching in southern Bavaria, two sherds of pottery have Greek letters incised into their surfaces, one with the complete name BOIOS, the other fragmentary (Krämer 1982). Among discoveries from the final two centuries BC, many ceramic vessels of the type known as "cooking pots" (*Kochtöpfe*) have incised linear patterns on the exterior of their bases, a system that Zeidler (2003) suggests may represent a form of writing. If this suggestion proves to be correct, it is possible that these linear signs borrowed design elements of Greek letters, just as Greek coins served as models for Celtic coins.

Conclusion: Lasting Effects

Interactions with the Greek world had profound and lasting effects on the peoples of central Europe. The development of the La Tène style of art and decoration was stimulated in large measure by the introduction of motifs and design elements on Greek manufactured goods (Echt 2004; Krausse 2006). The style spread throughout Europe and remained central to decorative traditions throughout the Iron Age and the first millennium AD (Megaw and Megaw 2001; Müller 2009).

Contact and exchange with Greek communities, and later with Etruscan and Roman Italy, opened the societies of temperate Europe to the wider world beyond the geographical limits of that continent (Wells 2012, chapters 11 and 12). Coinage, introduced through interaction with Greek military and commercial spheres, brought a new medium of imagery, a new form of stored wealth, and a new technology of communication – writing – into temperate Europe.

The effects of the interactions on Greek society have not yet been explored in detail but would richly reward investigation.

REFERENCES

Abels, Björn-Uwe. 1989. "Eine mediterrane Glasscherbe von der Ehrenbürg bei Forchheim." *Das archäologische Jahr in Bayern 1988*: 81–83.

Allen, Derek F., and Daphne Nash. 1980. *The Coins of the Ancient Celts*. Edinburgh: Edinburgh University Press.

Arnold, Bettina. 2004. "Iron Age Feasting." In *Ancient Europe 8000 B.C.–A.D. 1000: Encyclopedia of the Barbarian World*, vol. 2, edited by Peter Bogucki and Pam Crabtree, 179–183. New York: Thompson/Gale.

Baitinger, Holger. 1996. "Ein Trinkhorn aus dem späthallstattzeitlichen Prunkgrab Asperg 'Grafenbühl,' Kr. Ludwigsburg?" *Archäologisches Korrespondenzblatt*, 26: 173–177.

Balzer, Ines. 2010. "Neue Forschungen zu alten Fragen: Der früheisenzeitliche 'Fürstensitz' Hohenasperg (Kr. Ludwigsburg) und sein Umland." In *"Fürstensitze" und Zentralorte der frühen Kelten*, part I, edited by Dirk Krausse and Denise Beilharz, 209–238. Stuttgart: Konrad Theiss Verlag.

Balzer, Ines, Andrea Bräuning, and Rolf Dehn. 2012. "Der Breisacher Münsterberg und sein Umfeld." In *Die Welt der Kelten: Zentren der Macht – Kostbarkeiten der Kunst*, edited by Denise Beilharz, Ralph Röber, Katja Hald, and Thomas Hoppe, 165–170. Ostfildern: Jan Thorbecke Verlag.

Bašta, Jaroslav, Dara Baštová, and Jan Bouzek. 1989. "Die Nachahmung einer attisch rotfigurigen Kylix aus Pilsen-Roudná." *Germania*, 67: 463–476.

Beilharz, Denise, and Dirk Krausse. 2012. "Prunkvoll bis in den Tod – Leben und Sterben der frühkeltischen Elite." *Archäologie in Deutschland*, 2012(5): 20–22.

Bender, John, and Michael Marrinan. 2010. *The Culture of Diagram*. Stanford: Stanford University Press.

Bieg, Gebhard. 2002. *Hochdorf V: Der Bronzekessel aus dem späthallstattzeitlichen Fürstengrab von Eberdingen-Hochdorf (Kr. Ludwigsburg). Griechische Stabdreifüsse und Bronzekessel der archaischen Zeit mit figürlichem Schmuck*. Stuttgart: Konrad Theiss Verlag.

Biel, Jörg. 1985. *Der Keltenfürst von Hochdorf*. Stuttgart: Konrad Theiss Verlag.

Biel, Jörg. 1988. "Die Hallstattkultur in Württemberg." In *Archäologie in Württemberg: Ergebnisse und Perspektiven archäologischer Forschung von der Altsteinzeit bis zur Neuzeit*, edited by Dieter Planck, 199–214. Stuttgart: Konrad Theiss Verlag.

Biel, Jörg. 1997. "Le Hohenasperg et l'habitat de Hochdorf." In *Vix et les éphémères principautés celtiques: Les VIe-Ve siècle avant J.-C. en Europe centre-occidentale*, edited by Patrice Brun and Bruno Chaume, 17–22. Paris: Editions Errance.

Biel, Jörg, and Ines Balzer. 2012. "Der Hohenasperg." In *Die Welt der Kelten: Zentren der Macht – Kostbarkeiten der Kunst*, edited by Denise Beilharz, Ralph Röber, Katja Hald, and Thomas Hoppe, 139–144. Ostfildern: Jan Thorbecke Verlag.

Boardman, John. 1990. "Symposium Furniture." In *Sympotica: A Symposium of the Symposium*, edited by Oswyn Murray, 122–131. Oxford: Clarendon Press.

Böhr, Elke. 1988. "Die griechischen Schalen." In *Das Kleinaspergle: Studien zu einem Fürstengrabhügel der frühen Latènezeit bei Stuttgart*, edited by Wolfgang Kimmig, 176–190. Stuttgart: Konrad Theiss Verlag.

Bouzek Jan, and Drahomír Koutecký. 1975. "Ein attisches Gefässfragment aus Böhmen." *Germania*, 53: 157–160.

Bouzek, Jan, and Zdenek Smrž. 1994. "Drei Fragmente attischer Keramik aus Droužkovice in Nordwestböhmen." *Germania*, 72: 581–586.

Brett, David. 2005. *Rethinking Decoration: Pleasure and Ideology in the Visual Arts.* Cambridge: Cambridge University Press.

Burkhardt, Nadin. 2010. "Die Lehmziegelmauer der Heuneburg im mediterranen Vergleich." In *"Fürstensitze" und Zentralorte der frühen Kelten*, part II, edited by Dirk Krausse and Denise Beilharz, 29–50. Stuttgart: Konrad Theiss Verlag.

Chaume, Bruno, and Claude Mordant, eds. 2011. *Le complexe aristocratique de Vix: Nouvelles recherches sur l'habitat, le système de fortification et l'environnement du mont Lassois.* 2 vols. Dijon: Éditions Universitaires de Dijon.

Chytráček, Miloslav. 2008. "Die Nachahmung einer rotfigurigen Trinkschale aus der frühlatènezeitlichen Flachlandsiedlung von Chržín (Mittelböhmen) und das überregionale Verkehrsnetz der Hallstatt- und Frühlatènezeit in Böhmen." *Germania*, 86: 47–101.

Čižmář, Miloš, Eva Kolníková, and Hans-Christoph Noeske. 2008. "Němčice-Víceměřice – ein neues Handels- und Industriezentrum der Latènezeit in Mähren." *Germania*, 86: 655–700.

Dietler, Michael, and Brian Hayden, eds. 2001. *Feasts: Archaeological and Ethnographic Perspectives on Food, Politics, and Power.* Washington, DC: Smithsonian Institution Press.

Dietrich-Weibel, Barbara, Geneviève Lüscher, and Thierry Kilka. 1998. *Posieux/Châtillon-sur-Glâne. Keramik (6.-5. Jr.v.Chr.)/Céramiques (VIe-Ve siècles av. J.-C.).* Fribourg: Editions Universitaires.

Echt, Rudolf. 2004. "Äusserer Anstoss und innerer Wandel – drei Thesen zur Entstehung der Latènekunst." In *Die Hydria von Grächwil: Zur Funktion und Rezeption mediterraner Importe in Mitteleuropa im 6. und 5. Jahrhundert v. Chr.*, edited by Martin Guggisberg, 203–215. Bern: Bernisches Historisches Museum.

Eggert, Manfred K.H. 2010. "Früheisenzeitlicher 'Handel' aus kulturanthropologischer Sicht." In *"Fürstensitze" und Zentralorte der frühen Kelten*, part I, edited by Dirk Krausse and Denise Beilharz, 40–45. Stuttgart: Konrad Theiss Verlag.

Fischer, Franz. 1973. "ΚΕΙΜΕΛΙΑ: Bemerkungen zur kulturgeschichtlichen Interpretation des sogenannten Südimports in der späten Hallstatt- und frühen Latène-Kultur des westlichen Mitteleuropa." *Germania*, 51: 436–459.

Fischer, Jutta. 1990. "Zu einer griechischen Kline und weiteren Südimporten aus dem Fürstengrabhügel Grafenbühl, Asperg, Kr. Ludwigsburg." *Germania*, 68: 115–127.

Fletcher, Richard Nathan. 2012. "Opening the Mediterranean: Assyria, the Levant and the Transformation of Early Iron Age Trade." *Antiquity*, 86: 211–220.

Frey, Otto-Herman. 1999. "Griechisch-etruskischer Import." In *Reallexikon der germanischen Altertumskunde*, vol. 13, edited by Dieter Geuenich, 29–38. Berlin: de Gruyter.

Frey, Otto-Herman. 2002. "Menschen oder Heroen? Die Statueten vom Glauberg und die frühe keltische Grossplastik." In *Das Rätsel der Kelten vom Glauberg: Glaube, Mythos, Wirklichkeit*, edited by Holger Baitinger and Bernhard Pinsker, 208–218. Stuttgart: Konrad Theiss Verlag.

Gambari, Filippo M., and Gilbert Kaenel. 2001. "L'iscrizioni celtica sulla perla da Münsingen: una nuova lettura." *Archäologie der Schweiz*, 24(4): 34–37.

Gersbach, Egon. 1999. "Heuneburg." In *Reallexikon der germanischen Altertumskunde*, vol. 14, edited by Dieter Geuenich, 526–531. Berlin: de Gruyter.

Gibson, James J. 1979. *The Ecological Approach to Visual Perception*. Hillsdale NJ: Lawrence Erlbaum Associates.

Green, Miranda J., ed. 1995. *The Celtic World*. New York: Routledge.

Guggisberg, Martin A. ed. 2004. *Die Hydria von Grächwil: Zur Funktion und Rezeption mediterraner Importe in Mitteleuropa im 6. und 5. Jahrhundert v. Chr*. Bern: Bernisches Historisches Museum.

Hansen, Leif, and Elke Böhr. 2011. "Ein seltener Fund aus Westhofen (Lkr. Alzey-Worms): Fragment einer attischen Trinkschale." *Archäologisches Korrespondenzblatt*, 41: 213–230.

Haselgrove, Colin, and David Wigg-Wolf, eds. 2005. *Iron Age Coinage and Ritual Practices*. Mainz: Philipp von Zabern.

Herrmann, Hans-Volkmar. 1970. "Die südländischen Importstücke." In "Der 'Grafenbühl' bei Aperg, Kr. Ludwigsburg," by Hartwig Zürn, 25–34. In *Hallstattforschungen in Nordwürttemberg*, edited by Hartwig Zürn, 7–51. Stuttgart: Verlag Müller & Gräff.

Hill, Jeremy D. 2006. "Are We Any Closer to Understanding How Later Iron Age Societies Worked (or Did not Work)?" In *Celtes et Gaulois, l'Archéologie face à l'Histoire, 4: les mutations de la fin de l'âge du Fer*, edited by Colin Haselgrove, 169–179. Glux-en-Glenne: Bibracte, Centre archéologique européen.

Hodos, Tamar. 2009. "Colonial Engagements in the Global Mediterranean Iron Age." *Cambridge Archaeological Journal*, 19: 221–241.

Joachim, Hans-Eckart. 1995. *Waldalgesheim: Das Grab einer keltischen Fürstin*. Cologne: Rheinland-Verlag.

Jung, Matthias. 2007. "Kline oder Thron? Zu den Fragmenten eines griechischen Möbelpfostens aus dem späthallstattzeitlichen 'Fürstengrab' Grafenbühl in Asperg (Kr. Ludwigsburg)." *Germania*, 85: 95–107.

Kellner, Hans-Jörg. 1991. "Coinage." In *The Celts*, edited by Sabatino Moscati, Otto H. Frey, Venceslas Kruta, et al., 451–459. New York: Rizzoli International Publications.

Kimmig, Wolfgang. 1988. *Das Kleinaspergle: Studien zu einem Fürstengrabhügel der frühen Latènezeit bei Stuttgart*. Stuttgart: Konrad Theiss Verlag.

Kolníková, Eva. 2007. "Fundmünzen vom Keltenzentrum Němčice (Mähren) – Beitrag zum keltischen Münzumlauf im Mitteldonaugebiet." *In Money Circulation in Antiquity, the Middle Ages and Modern Times: Time, Range, Intensity*, edited by Stanislaw Suchodolski, 21–32. Warsaw: Institute of Archeology and Ethnology Polish Academy of Sciences, Avalon.

Krämer, Werner. 1982. "Graffiti auf Spätlatènekeramik aus Manching." *Germania*, 60: 489–499.

Krause, Rüdiger. 2012. "Der Ipf im Nördlinger Ries." In *Die Welt der Kelten: Zentren der Macht – Kostbarkeiten der Kunst*, edited by Denise Beilharz, Ralph Röber, Katja Hald, and Thomas Hoppe, 146–154. Ostfildern: Jan Thorbecke Verlag.

Krause, Rüdiger, Daniela Euler, and Katharina Fuhrmann. 2008. "Der frühkeltische Fürstensitz auf dem Ipf bei Bopfingen im Nördlinger Ries (Ostalbkreis, Baden-Württemberg): Neue Forschungen zur Burg und deren Siedlungsumfeld." In *Frühe Zentralisierungs- und Urbanisierungsprozesse*, edited by Dirk Krausse and Christoph Steffen, 249–279. Stuttgart: Konrad Theiss Verlag.

Krause, Dirk. 1996. *Hochdorf III: Das Trink- und Speiseservice aus dem späthallstattzeitlichen Fürstengrab von Eberdingen-Hochdorf (Kr. Ludwigsburg)*. Stuttgart: Konrad Theiss Verlag.

Krause, Dirk. 2004. "Komos und Kottabos am Hohenasperg? Überlegungen zur Funktion mediterraner Importgefässe des 6. und 5. Jahrhunderts aus Südwestdeutschland." In *Die Hydria von Grächwil: Zur Funktion und Rezeption mediterraner Importe in Mitteleuropa im 6. und 5. Jahrhundert v. Chr.*, edited by Martin A. Guggisberg, 193–201. Bern: Bernisches Historisches Museum.

Krause, Dirk. 2006. "The Prehistory of the Celts in South-West Germany: Centralisation Processes and Celtic Ethnogenesis in the Heart of Europe." In *Celtes et Gaulois: L'Archéologie face à l'Histoire: La Préhistoire des Celtes*, edited by Daniele Vitali, 131–142. Glux-en-Glenne: Bibracte.

Krause, Dirk, Manuel Fernández-Götz, Leif Hansen, and Inga Kretschmer. 2016. *The Heuneburg and the Early Iron Age Princely Seats: First Towns North of the Alps*. Budapest: Archaeolingua.

Lüscher, Geneviève. 1996. "Der Amphorenimport in Châtillon-sur-Glâne (Kanton Freiburg/Schweiz)." *Germania*, 74: 337–360.

Mac Sweeney, Naoíse, and Peter S. Wells. 2018. "Edges and Interactions beyond Europe." In *The Oxford Handbook of the European Iron Age*, edited by Colin Haselgrove, Katharina Rebay-Salisbury, and Peter S. Wells. Oxford: Oxford University Press. Online.

Mannsperger, Dietrich. 1981. "Münzen und Münzfunde." In *Die Kelten in Baden-Württemberg*, edited by Kurt Bittel, Wolfgang Kimmig, and Siegwalt Schiek, 228–247. Stuttgart: Konrad Theiss Verlag.

Megaw, Ruth, and Vincent Megaw. 2001. *Celtic Art: From its Beginnings to the Book of Kells*. New York: Thames & Hudson.

Michálek, Jan. 1992. "Eine mediterrane Glasscherbe aus Südböhmen." *Germania*, 70: 123–126.

Mielczarek, Mariusz. 2008. "On Greek Coin Finds from the Central European *Barbaricum*." In *Roman Coins Outside the Empire: Ways and Phases, Contexts and Functions*, edited by Aleksander Bursche, Renate Ciolek, and Reinhard Wolters, 11–34. Wetteren: Moneta.

Moscati, Sabatino, Otto H. Frey, Venceslas Kruta, et al., eds. 1991. *The Celts*. New York: Rizzoli International Publications.

Müller, Felix, ed. 2009. *Art of the Celts 700 BC to AD 700*. Bern: Historisches Museum.

Murray, Oswyn, ed. 1990. *Sympotica: A Symposium on the Symposion*. New York: Oxford University Press.

Osborne, Robin. 2018. *The Transformation of Athens: Painted Pottery and the Creation of Classical Greece*. Princeton: Princeton University Press.

Overbeck, Bernhard. 1988. "Ein massiliotischer Obol aus Aubstadt." *Das archäologische Jahr in Bayern*, 1987: 84.

Pape, Joëlle. 2000. "Die attische Keramik der Heuneburg und der keramische Südimport in der Zone nördlich der Alpen während der Hallstattzeit." In *Importe und mediterrane Einflüsse auf der Heuneburg*, edited by Wolfgang Kimmig, 71–175. Mainz: Verlag Philipp von Zabern.

Pape, Joëlle. 2004. "Importierte mediterrane Keramik in der Zone nördlich und nordwestlich der Alpen während der Hallstattzeit: Zur Frage des Weinhandels." In *Die*

Hydria von Grächwil: Zur Funktion und Rezeption mediterraner Importe in Mitteleuropa im 6. und 5. Jahrhundert v. Chr., edited by Martin Guggisberg, 107–120. Bern: Verlag Bernisches Historisches Museum.

Penninger, Ernst, and Ludwig Pauli. 1972. *Der Dürrnberg bei Hallein I: Katalog der Grabfunde aus der Hallstatt- und Latènezeit*, part 1. Munich: Beck.

Rolley, Claude, ed. 2003. *La tombe princière de Vix.* 2 vols. Paris: Picard.

Rustoiu, Aurel. 2006. "A Journey to Mediterranean: Peregrinations of a Celtic Warrior from Transylvania." In *Studia Universitatis "Babeş-Bolyai" Historia*, 51(1): 42–85.

Schier, Wolfram. 2010. "Soziale und politische Strukturen der Hallstattzeit: Ein Diskussionsbeitrag." In *"Fürstensitze" und Zentralorte der frühen Kelten*, part II, edited by Dirk Krausse and Denise Beilharz, 375–405. Stuttgart: Konrad Theiss Verlag.

Schönfelder, Martin. 2007a. "Considérations sur les élites celtiques des IVe-IIIe s. av. J.-C." In *La Gaule dans son context européen aux IVe et IIIe siècles avant notre ère*, edited by Christine Mennessier-Jounnet, Anne-Marie Adam, and Pierre-Yves Milcent, 291–299. Lattes: Association pour le Développement de l'Archéologie en Languedoc-Roussillon.

Schönfelder, Martin. 2007b. "Zurück aus Griechenland – Spuren keltischer Söldner in Mitteleuropa." *Germania*, 85: 307–328.

Shefton, Brian B. 1979. *Die "Rhodischen" Bronzekannen.* Mainz: Verlag Philipp von Zabern.

Shefton, Brian B. 1994. "The Waldalgesheim Situla: Where was it Made?" *Marburger Studien zur Vor- und Frühgeschichte*, 16: 583–593.

Siegfried, Anita. 1997. "Le site du 'Üetliberg, Uto-Kulm' près de Zurich." In *Vix et les éphémères principautés celtiques: Les VIe-Ve siècle avant J.-C. en Europe centre-occidentale*, edited by Patrice Brun and Bruno Chaume, 27–35. Paris: Editions Errance.

Sperber, Lothar. 2002. "Ausstattung eines Fürstengrabes in der Pfalz." In *Das Rätsel der Kelten vom Glauberg: Glaube, Mythos, Wirklichkeit*, edited by Holger Baitinger and Bernhard Pinsker, 302–304. Stuttgart: Konrad Theiss Verlag.

Steuer, Heiko. 1999. "Griech. Schrift bei den Kelten." *Reallexikon der germanischen Altertumskunde*, vol. 13, edited by Dieter Geuenich, 28–29. Berlin: de Gruyter.

Steuernagel, Dirk. 2002. "Der griechische Kouros – Ein Vorbild?" In *Das Rätsel der Kelten vom Glauberg: Glaube, Mythos, Wirklichkeit*, edited by Holger Baitinger and Bernhard Pinsker, 219–220. Stuttgart: Konrad Theiss Verlag.

Stöllner, Thomas, and Antonio Tadic. 1998. "Eine griechische Münze vom Dürrnberg bei Hallein, Land Salzburg." *Germania*, 76: 304–310.

Szabó, Miklós. 1995. "Guerriers celtiques avant et après Delphes: Contribution à une période critique de monde celtique." In *L'Europe celtique du Ve au IIIe siècle avant J.-C.: Contacts, Echanges et mouvements de populations*, edited by Jean-Jacques Charpy, 49–67. Sceaux: Kronos B.Y. Editions.

Trefný, Martin. 2008. "Attická červenofigurová keramika z laténského sidliště v Praze-Ruzyni, poloha Jiviny" ("Attic red-figure ceramics from the La Tène settlement at the Jiviny site at Prague-Ruzyně"). *Archeologické rozhledy*, 60: 114–126.

van den Boom, Helga, and Joëlle Pape. 2000. "Die massaliotischen Amphoren." In *Importe und mediterrane Einflüsse auf der Heuneburg*, edited by Wolfgang Kimmig, 43–70. Mainz: Verlag Philipp von Zabern.

van Endert, Dorothea. 1997. "Le Marienberg à Würzburg (Bavière) pendant la période du Hallstatt D2/3 et son environment naturel et archéologique." In *Vix et les éphémères principautés celtiques: Les VIe-Ve siècle avant J.-C. en Europe centre-occidentale*, edited by Patrice Brun and Bruno Chaume, 23–26. Paris: Editions Errance.

Wehgartner, Irma. 1995. "Das Symposion." In *Luxusgeschirr keltischer Fürsten – Griechische Keramik nördlich der Alpen*, edited by Irma Wehgartner and Helge Zöller, 25–31. Würzburg: Mainfränkisches Museum.

Wells, Peter S. 2011. "The Iron Age." In *European Prehistory*, 2nd ed., edited by Sarunas Milisauskas, 405–460. New York: Springer.

Wells, Peter S. 2012. *How Ancient Europeans Saw the World: Vision, Patterns, and the Shaping of the Mind in Prehistoric Times*. Princeton: Princeton University Press.

Wells, Peter S. 2015. "Cultural Colonization without Colonial Settlements: A Case Study in Early Iron Age Temperate Europe." In *Rethinking Colonialism: Comparative Archaeological Approaches*, edited by Craig N. Cipolla and Katherine H. Hayes, 76–98. Gainesville: University Press of Florida.

Wyss, René. 1956. "The Sword of Korisios." *Antiquity*, 30: 27–28.

Zeidler, Jürgen B. 2003. "A Celtic Script in the Eastern La Tène Culture?" *Études Celtiques*, 35: 69–132.

Zürn, Hartwig. 1970. "Der 'Grafenbühl' bei Asperg, Kr. Ludwigsburg." In *Hallstattforschungen in Nordwürttemberg: Die Grabhügel von Asperg (Kr. Ludwigsburg), Hirschlanden (Kr. Leonberg) und Mühlacker (Kr. Vaihingen)*, edited by Hartwig Zürn, 7–51. Stuttgart: Verlag Müller & Gräff.

FURTHER READING

Allen and Nash (1980) is an excellent introduction to Iron Age European coinage. Jörg Biel (1985) is the main site report on the Hochdorf grave, with excellent color photographs. Green (1995) includes chapters by experts on all different aspects of the Celts, including archaeology, history, language, religion. Megaw and Megaw (2001) is the best overview of Celtic art with good discussion of other aspects of Iron Age societies. Moscati et al. (1991) includes chapters by experts from all over Europe about specific sites and general issues regarding the Celts. Excellent color illustrations. Müller (2009) is an excellent overview of our understanding of the Celts with stunning color photographs of important objects. Wells (2012) is a new perspective on the material culture, including art and decoration, of Bronze and Iron Age Europe.

CHAPTER ELEVEN

Anatolia

Andrew Brown

Anadolu, Anatolia, or Asia Minor has been a focus of cultural engagement and development for millennia. Its long and varied history has encompassed dead empires and great battles, but in all periods it has provided stimulus, inspiration, and natural resources for its incumbent populations. For the Greeks of the Iron Age and Archaic periods, this was no less the case. Greek-speaking populations had already been attracted to the region by the end of the Bronze Age, and their partial annexation of the west coast between the twelfth century and the end of the Archaic period, reasonably fixed in Anatolia by the Battle of Lade in ca. 494 BC (Greaves 2010, xii), provided new direction and yet at once the potential threat of dangerous neighbors.

What defines "Greek" settlement here, particularly by the seventh century BC, is the landscape's location as both geographic and intellectual middle grounds. It is from this position that the developing *poleis* of Anatolia had freedom to experiment with new ideas and influences stimulated by direct contact with the Anatolian populations of Phrygia, Lydia, Lycia, and Caria, as well as increasing interaction with the Near East and Egypt. The period is characterized by fluidity and agency amongst its diverse peoples, of whom "Greeks" were just one. By the end of the Archaic period, this cultural engagement zone enabled Ionia, especially, and Miletos, in particular, to develop into a cultural powerhouse within the Aegean region, bringing with it new material assemblages, ideas, and wealth.

Geography

The Anatolian peninsula extends as the westernmost projection of Asia, bounded on the north by the Black Sea, on the west by the Aegean, and on the south by the Mediterranean (Map 11.1). The Hellespont and Sea of Marmara separate Anatolia from European

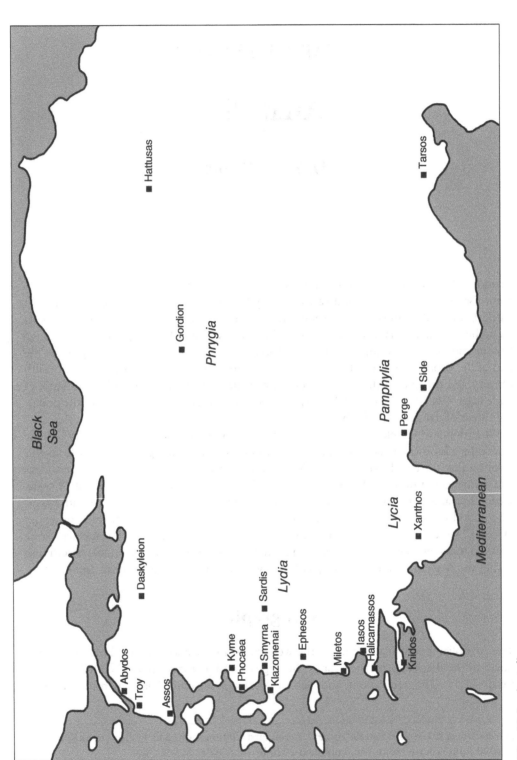

Map 11.1 Anatolia.

Thrace, and in the east the region is nominally defined by the eastern extension of the modern Turkish state. A central plateau that attains average altitudes of over 1000 m dominates the peninsula, rising toward steppe and mountainous regions in the east, where its highest peak, Ağrı Dağ (Mt. Ararat), reaches 5137 m. The narrow coastal strips, particularly in the west, provide the only real lowlands punctuated by fertile river deltas that offer natural and mineral wealth.

The central plateau is characterized by hot summers and cold winters, with a Mediterranean climate on the western and southern coastlines, and a more temperate zone in the Black Sea regions. Access to the central plateau from the south is restricted by the Taurus mountain range; thus, Iron Age Greek settlement focused largely on the western and southwestern coastlines (although see Guldager Bilde, Handberg, and Petersen, Chapter 20, this volume, for the Black Sea region). Anatolia's many watercourses were exploited in antiquity both as sources of natural wealth and as arterial routes into the wider landscape, most evident via the Hellespont (Dardanelles), which creates a direct link between the Aegean and the Black Sea. Key settlements profited from good natural harbors, although in later periods suffered forcible relocation(s) due to the alluvial processes of many river systems.

Late Bronze Age

The latter stages of the Bronze Age in Anatolia are shaped by interactions between the central Anatolian Hittite Empire, its allied states, and neighboring foreign powers. Hatti, the heartland of the empire, exerted varying degrees of political and cultural influence from its capital at Hattušaš/Boğazköy as far west as the Aegean coastline, resulting in direct contact between the Anatolian and Aegean worlds. Anatolia's Late Bronze Age political geography, based on surviving second millennium BC texts, suggests the west coast was home to the *Arzawa* kingdoms. *Millawanda* (= Miletos) lay between the *Lukka* lands (Lycia) to the southeast and *Mira-Kuwaliya*, the latter focused on the Maeander valley with *Apaša* (= Ephesos) as its regional center. To the east was *Hapalla*, while the *Seha River Land* lay beyond the Karabel Pass at *Mira*'s northern border. The northwestern corner of Anatolia was home to *Wilusa* with its regional capital at Troy (Easton et al. 2002, 94–101; Bryce 2005). Significantly, this placed them geographically between, and brought interaction with, Hatti and her peer, the Kingdom of *Ahhiyawa*.

Discussion over the location of *Ahhiyawa* has been extensive, but with growing acceptance that *Ahhiyawa* = Mycenaean Greece (Mac Sweeney 2013, 58; Bryce 2005; Vaessen 2016). The significance for later Greek settlement in Anatolia is twofold. Primarily, it demonstrates early interaction between western Anatolia and Aegean Greece. Archaeologically, Mycenaean influence and emulation are evident along the coastline from the thirteenth to twelfth centuries BC, notably through the appearance of imported and locally produced Mycenaean ceramics at Ephesos, Iasos, Limantepe, and elsewhere. By the end of the Bronze Age, these local products form one aspect of hybrid Mycenaean-Anatolian material and burial traditions at sites like Miletos, Müsgebi, Panaztepe, and Troy (Mountjoy 1998; Vaessen 2016).

Some have argued (Niemeier 2005) that Miletos demonstrates prerequisites of a Mycenaean colony, notably through its production of Mycenaean ceramics, burial forms, and the possible use of Linear B. This conclusion is partially supported by Hittite sources, which suggest *Millawanda* was under *Ahhiyawan* control and subject to Hittite raiding (Mountjoy 1998; Greaves 2002, 69–71; Niemeier 2005). This highlights the second feature key to Anatolia's later development: the western Anatolian settlements were not only geographically positioned at the interface of Aegean and Anatolian worlds, but also culturally so, and profited from the intellectual freedom this engendered. The ability to exploit east–west information flows and the receptiveness of Anatolian populations are evident in the hybrid Late Bronze Age assemblages noted above and continue as a feature of the Iron Age. Furthermore, a degree of political freedom, evident in Miletos's conflict with, and revolt by various *Arzawa* kingdoms from (Niemeier 2005), Hatti is a characteristic that defines what is to come.

The collapse of the Mycenaean and Hittite Empires in the twelfth century ushered in the Iron Age. This transitional period is poorly understood on the west coast, with the latest Bronze Age stages represented by limited ceramic finds, and perhaps burials at Müsgebi (Mountjoy 1998). That occupation persisted is apparent from sites like Miletos and Troy, which demonstrate potential, albeit often tenuous, settlement continuity despite significant destruction events (Becks 2003; Greaves 2002). The absence of well-defined archaeology points to a period of change and upheaval, from which the region did not fully recover until later in the Iron Age.

Migration and the Early Iron Age

What happens next is harder to define and has often stimulated polarized debate. By the end of the Archaic period, "Greek" settlement in Anatolia is explained as an extensive series of migration traditions, in which complex narratives and mythical genealogies provided a link with Mycenaean ancestry to legitimate Greek presence. Traditional narratives suggest that, following the collapse of Mycenae, migrant Aegean populations founded new settlements along the Anatolian coastline. This was confined almost exclusively to the west and southwest, with three distinct migrant groups recognized: Aeolians in the north, Ionians to their south, and Dorians further south again. Each had their own defined dialect (Aeolic, Ionic, and Doric) and migration traditions. For the Aeolians (Rose 2008), populations from Thessaly, Boeotia, and Locris under the leadership of Orestes, son of Agamemnon, and his descendants settled the coast between the Troad and Smyrna (Bayraklı), including the islands of Lesbos and Tenedos. In the Ionian tradition, Athens plays a central role as progenitor of a migrant population led by Neleus and Androcles, sons of the last King of Athens, Codrus. They occupy the coast between Phocaea and Miletos, founding new settlements and ousting, often forcibly, local Anatolian populations (Greaves 2010; Mac Sweeney 2017). While in the Dorian tradition, populations from the Peloponnese found a hexapolis of six cities incorporating the Anatolian settlements of Halicarnassos and Knidos with those of Rhodes and Kos. The result is that by the seventh century the western coast of Anatolia is home to Greek-speaking populations living in *polis*-type settlements.

For some, the migration represents historical fact upon which the archaeological data can be hung (Vanschoonwinkel 2006). In support of this, the correlation between the literary evidence, the spread of the dialectical groups, and the appearance of Protogeometric Greek ceramics in western Anatolia is highlighted. The linguistic transmission of Homeric epic, first through Lesbos, Aeolia, and finally to Ionia, is also noted. Indeed, it is striking how closely the three dialectical groups correlate with later ethnic and cultural divisions. However, there is also evidence of linguistic divergence. Herodotus (1.142) recognized four distinct Ionian dialects, and non-Greek loan words populate the work of Ephesian poet Hipponax. Similarly, both Greek and Carian populations of Halicarnassos adopt the Ionian language, yet it is clear that Carian onomastics survive into the Classical period on a par with those of Greek. This lack of coherence might argue against the dialectical groups as markers for ethnic or group identity, and a counter-argument suggests the spread may result from prolonged periods of interaction, with diffusion of similar linguistic traits (Hall 2007; Mac Sweeney 2013; Greaves 2011). Arguments against the historical utility of the literary tradition lie in their late appearance. Although the Ionian tradition provided Athenian and Ionian populations with a sense of collective identity, this was influenced by contemporary fifth-century BC politics and sentiment when these narratives developed (Mac Sweeney 2013, 2017; Greaves 2010). Indeed, this shared Athenian-Ionian identity was at times exploited by both sides for political gain, as in Miletos's attempts to garner Athenian support during the Ionian Revolt by appealing to her mother-city role (Greaves 2010, 11). Analysis of the literary traditions demonstrates a lack of coherence in terms of collective group identity, ancestry, and in some cases consensus as to the leadership of migrant groups. These narratives were shaped not by the historicity of Early Iron Age migration but rather by contemporary rationalizations of kinship and power within the sociopolitical contexts of their development (Mac Sweeney 2013; Vaessen 2014). On the other hand, what they do demonstrate is the mixed nature of Anatolia during the Early Iron Age. The Carian element at Halicarnassos has already been noted, but it is clear that "Greeks," whether Aeolian, Ionian, or Dorian, lived in a multi-ethnic landscape that included Lydians, Lelegians, Thebans, "Amazons," and others. In the case of Ionian Colophon, it is unclear whether the initial foundation even included Ionian elements at all (Mac Sweeney 2013, 169).

That people could and did move around the Aegean in the Early Iron Age is highly probable. That some "Greek" populations made their way to Anatolia is equally plausible, although it seems unlikely this was as part of an organized migration wave. More probable is a gradual, protracted process that involved interaction between various different population groups, resulting in later Iron Age periods in emergent new identities. An alternative approach to the migration traditions, therefore, suggests they contain kernels of truth that can be tested archaeologically. In part, this is complicated by the paucity of published archaeological data, particularly for earlier phases of the Iron Age. Nevertheless, it is apparent that the focus of early Greek activity is on the west coast.

Continuity of occupation from the Late Bronze Age and into the Early Iron Age is hinted at through the presence of twelfth-century BC ceramics, notably from Ephesos, Miletos, and the Dorian region (Mountjoy 1998), and sparse evidence for maintained domestic, cult, and burial activity. These are scarce finds, often associated with areas that experienced prolonged contact with Mycenaean Greece, perhaps suggestive of maintained and complex east–west exchanges (Mac Sweeney 2017).

The nature and extent of occupation is no less clear with the emergence of Protogeometric ceramics of Greek style in the eleventh to tenth centuries BC, since they remain our primary source of data and yet are found in very limited quantity and often as unstratified site finds. Small assemblages occur at a number of western Anatolian sites, notably in Ionia at Phocaea, Klazomenai, and Teos, with excavated material also evident at the later temples of Artemis at Ephesos and Athena at Miletos, all with demonstrable Attic, Thessalian, or Euboean influence (Lemos 2002; Mac Sweeney 2017; Vaessen 2014). Significantly, many appear to be locally produced (Lemos 2002) and are indicative of the receptiveness of Anatolian populations to new influences rather than markers of migrant populations. As important for later regional development is the transmission of these ceramics to non-Greek neighbors, with assemblages noted at Sardis and Carian Iasos, perhaps at Kaunos, and in burial contexts at Asarlık, Dirmil, and Çömlekçi (Halicarnassos) (Lemos 2002). What the Protogeometric wares demonstrate are the maintenance of long-distance information flows alongside complex cultural exchanges with and between Greek and non-Greek populations alike (Vaessen 2014). At sites like Miletos, where the literary sources suggest mixed Greek-Carian populations (Hdt. 1.146), these may have occurred at varying social levels, resulting in material assemblages defined by the local setting of such interactions.

The Aeolian and Troadic settlements present a different picture. Here, gray ware ceramics are characteristic, in some cases almost to the exclusion of imported or decorated ceramics. These were originally termed "Aeolian" gray wares and used as cultural markers for the Aeolian migration, particularly given that their distribution correlates largely with the landscape and dialectical groups defined by the migration traditions. Yet, analysis indicates a probable local origin ultimately derived from Bronze Age traditions (Mommsen, Hertel, and Mountjoy 2001; Chabot Aslan 2002). Their presence gives the northern coastline a distinct regional identity that differs from Ionia, and gray ware assemblages are prolific at sites including Kyme, Gryneion, Phocaea, Smyrna, Neandria, Tenedos, and Troy, as well as on Lesbos. Smyrna provides an example for the evolving nature of settlement and the difficulties of ascribing ethnic identity with material culture. In its earliest levels, ca. 1000 BC, gray wares proliferate while square and oval houses characterize what architecture survives. The latter find parallels in structures at Troy, Miletos, and perhaps Ephesos (Akurgal 1983; Greaves 2002, 76; Cook 1958–1959; Rose 2008), while at Phocaea hints of more substantial architecture are present in similar oval buildings and an oval tower, which point to the general expansion of settlement toward the Archaic period (Özyiğit 2003). By the ninth to eighth centuries Smyrna has fortifications, public and private spaces, and begins to resemble the urban *poleis* that define Archaic Anatolia (Akurgal 1983; Cook 1958–1959). This is accompanied by a change in material culture that sees the displacement of gray wares by locally produced Protogeometric ceramics of Thessalian and Euboean influence (Cook 1958–1959, 10–17). Literary sources suggest Smyrna was initially an Aeolian foundation that became Ionian following its capture by refugees from Colophon. This has often been used as an explanation for the ceramic change, although clearly the process was a gradual one. Another perspective might be considered. The literary sources are post-fifth-century BC in date, affected by contemporary politics, as well as by inter-*poleis* rivalries within Anatolia. While they may provide an explanation for Smyrna's shift in allegiance, they do not necessarily reflect Early Iron Age realities. Instead, Smryna's development may be indicative of an independent settlement within a fluid landscape that sought to adapt to new social, political, and cultural directions. In this regard, the hybrid material assemblages apparent by the eighth century perhaps reveal her population's attempts to realign with emergent, powerful neighbors in Ionia rather than any deliberate switch between perceived Aeolian and Ionian identities (Mac Sweeney 2011). A similar scenario is evident at Troy. Here, the earliest Iron Age levels contain new handmade ceramics and architectural styles influenced by the Balkans and Thrace (Becks 2003). In the succeeding tenth-century phase this influence disappears, replaced by assemblages reminiscent of the Late Bronze Age but punctuated by Protogeometric Greek ceramics demonstrative of maintained long-distance trade routes. As with Smyrna, these shifts in cultural assemblages perhaps represent changing social and political influence at the site (Becks 2003, 45–50).

There is slight evidence for stratigraphical continuity into the eighth century at Troy. The survival of structures of Geometric date (Rose 2014, 50–51) parallel examples at Miletos, Lesbos, as well as the earlier structures noted at Smyrna. Yet, architecture of this period remains ambiguous in western Anatolia, and indeed, Smyrna's early fortifications demonstrate closer affinity with the East than with Greece. Geometric ceramics are more readily abundant, and are well known from Smyrna, Klazomenai, Ephesos, Miletos, and the Ionian islands. Their numerous idiosyncrasies reflect local production nuances and cultural development, but they are essentially East Greek in form and decoration (Cook and Dupont 2003; Kerschner and Schlotzhauer 2005; Ersoy 2004). Gray wares continue to dominate in the north but evolve with the introduction of the Aegean *skyphos* and other vessel forms (Chabot Aslan 2002). Perhaps more revealing is the transmission of Geometric assemblages to Anatolian neighbors. Imitation Geometric wares have been noted at Sardis, while at Iasos and Kaunos specific elements of the Ionian Geometric are integrated to produce an essentially hybrid ware (Cook and Dupont 2003; Özgünel 2006). No doubt resident "Greeks" hastened these developments, but the situation was far from a simple transplantation of Greek populations into an empty landscape. Rather, early residential and commercial exchanges between diverse Aegean and Anatolian populations stimulated fluid cultural engagement within which ideas and influences were transmitted, adopted, and reproduced.

The Eighth to Seventh Centuries BC

The Anatolian settlements of the late Early Iron Age and Archaic periods experienced extensive growth affected by new internal and external influences, and emergent regional identities. This period witnessed the rise of Ionia, and especially Miletos, as a key regional power, combined with the movement of Greek-speaking populations that brought direct contact with the non-Greek world. For the Greeks in Anatolia, interaction with Anatolian neighbors and the East provided new impetuses resulting in cultural assemblages that defined Anatolia but also impacted Archaic Greece.

Western Anatolia from the eighth century is typically viewed in terms of its Aeolian, Ionian, and Dorian landscapes. It maintained direct links with Aegean Greece, most notably through nearby Aegean islands, but benefited from its physical and intellectual middle ground between East and West. The settlements of the coastline were in many respects typical of other Greek *poleis*, with those distinctive features that defined citizen and city-state. By the seventh century, the majority exhibit the beginnings of defined settlements with public, private, and cult places, urban fortifications, rural *chorai*, and the separation of the living and dead. But there are also clear differences with their Aegean counterparts. Political rule was by "tyranny" and later oligarchy or timocracy, which reflected the adoption of political structures that characterized contemporary Anatolia seen, for example, in Archilochus's description of Lydian King Gyges (ca. 680–644 BC) or the ruling dynasts in neighboring Caria and Lycia (Harl 2011, 755). This was not imposition of power by ruthless elites, but rather the reception of local mechanisms of governance that differed from those of other Greek *poleis*.

As these settlements developed new political and cultural direction, the first indications of regional identities began to emerge. In the north, an Aeolian League of 12 cities centered on Kyme with a shared cult center at Gryneion by the seventh century, although it probably had earlier roots (Rose 2008). It stood as a loose political and cult alliance, and signaled a growing sense of belonging, heightened perhaps by Smyrna's switch to Ionia. The development of a broadly contemporary Ionian League may have added to this emergent sense of identity. The Ionian League was also formed of 12 *poleis*, with shared cult rites at the *Panionion* on Mt. Mycale. Its longevity, at least as late as the second century AD (Mac Sweeney 2013, 158), highlights the maintenance of an Ionian identity, although this may not have been as concerted as might be expected. Indeed, while the shared Ionian festival of *Apatauria* points to Ionian self-identity, non-observance by Colophon and Ephesos is indicative of, at best, loose political affiliation exploited as and when required (Mac Sweeney 2011, 77; Mac Sweeney 2013, 156).

Prosperity stimulated population growth and expansion of the urban core. Smyrna witnessed extensive redevelopment following an earthquake and by the seventh century exhibits houses with stone foundations on a well-defined street plan, a Temple to Athena, defined necropoleis, and city walls (Cook and Nicholls 1998; Akurgal 1983; Cook 1958–1959). The later appearance of a sixth-century fortification at Phocaea (Figure 11.1), preserved within the later Maltepe tumulus, demonstrates both settlement development and receptivity to Anatolian influence, its glacis and carved masonry reflecting Anatolian traditions seen at sites like Sardis and Kerkenes Dağ (Greaves 2010, 117). Miletos arguably provides the clearest demonstration of Anatolian Greek development. The settlement, positioned on a broad bay at the mouth of the Büyük Menderes (Maeander) River, provided perhaps the best natural harbor in western Anatolia. Her resultant ability to tap into local and long-distance trade by the seventh century saw Miletos rivaled only by Samos and Mitylene. This on occasion brought with it conflict, notably with Samos during the Lelantine War (ca. 710–650 BC), but also the expansion of Milesian territory to encompass a series of harbors, settlements at Kaletepe, Assessos, and Kalabaktepe, and the sanctuary of Branchidae-Didyma (Greaves 2002). By the time of the Ionian Revolt in 499 BC, Miletos was able to launch a naval fleet on a par with any in the eastern Aegean and had seen her population expand exponentially. During the Archaic period she was unrivaled amongst the Anatolian *poleis*, her growth stimulating expansion outside the immediate *chora* that prompted colonial activity and direct interaction with new, foreign powers.

Figure 11.1 The city wall at Phocaea preserved in the Maltepe tumulus. Source: courtesy D. Diffendale.

By the ninth century, Gordion had emerged as the capital of a Phyrgian Kingdom with influence over large areas of the post-Hittite landscape. In the west this extended at least as far as Daskyleion, although direct evidence for Phrygian presence in the west has so far only been substantiated through ceramics at Sardis and Beycesultan (Mac Sweeney 2011, 73–74). The Phrygian citadel provides a monumental display of Anatolian culture, with stone gates, city walls, and public spaces. The New Chronology at Gordion suggests it experienced destruction ca. 800 BC (Sams and Voigt 2011, 155–156), the rebuilt Middle Phrygian citadel contemporary with many of the large tumulus burials that are distinctive of its necropoleis. This is the home of King Midas, mentioned in Assyrian sources as Mita of Mushki and still living in 709 BC. Gordion survived into the mid-sixth century when it was destroyed by the Persian advance through Anatolia, although by this time it had already passed into the control of Lydian Sardis.

Proximity to Phrygia must surely have impacted the developing *poleis* and, while direct political influence is difficult to substantiate, resulted in new influences for the populations of western Anatolia. Literary references suggest closeness at an elite level, and arguably political alliances, through Homeric allusion to the Phrygian origin of Hecube, Priam's wife, as well as Midas's reported marriage to a Greek princess at Kyme (Morris 2006, 70). But this was not a one-way process. Phrygia was equally affected by her proximity to the *poleis*, perhaps most overtly through Midas's supposed dedication of a royal throne at Delphi (Hdt. 1.14) and the appearance of Greek ceramics at Gordion and Daskyleion. These early cultural exchanges between the *poleis* and Phrygia, into the seventh century, affected the development of both, and perhaps more so following increased movement of Greek populations.

Expansion

Contemporary with Phrygian growth, Anatolia witnessed an increase in its number of emergent Greek *poleis*. In southern Anatolia, Rhodian foundations appear at Phaselis and Soli/Pompeiopolis, with possible Samian colonists at nearby Kelenderis (Grainger 2009). In Pamphylia, a Greek presence is possible at Aspendos, Magydos, Perge, and Side, although here there are mixed populations. Indeed, Aspendos's silver coinage after ca. 500 BC preserves the city-ethnic, ΕΣΤΓΕΔΙΙΥΕ, in the local Pamphylian language. Similarly, sixth-century BC graffiti at Perge are found in both Greek and Pamphylian script (Grainger 2009, 57, 59). Surviving evidence for early occupation along this coastline is sparse. However, Late Geometric and East Greek ceramics at Soli/Pompeiopolis, Perge, and Kelenderis at least demonstrate developing trade routes, hinted at again by similar ceramics at Tarsos and Mersin. In the case of Tarsos, revolt against Assyrian authority, involving Greek population elements and the Assyrian governor of Cilicia, resulted in its destruction by Sennacherib in 696 BC (Hall 2007, 38). It is unlikely that this represents revolt by a truly Greek foundation since the population was at best mixed, but it highlights the movement of objects and people along the south coast.

More concerted expansion is apparent in the north and west, with the Hellespont a notable focal point through Miletos's attempts to tap into the potential wealth of the Black Sea region (see Guldager Bilde, Handberg, and Petersen, Chapter 20, this volume). But she was by no means alone. Phocaean colonists are noted at Lampsakos, with Megarians at Astacus, Selymbria, Byzantium, and Chalcedon by the seventh to sixth centuries BC. The foundation of Abydos on the Hellespont affords a different perspective to Milesian colonial enterprise since it was only through permission from Gyges that settlement here was possible, indicative of maintained Anatolian control over a landscape where the *poleis* by no means held the dominant position (Cook 1999).

Mixed populations are perhaps also evident in the Troad at sites like Assos, Antandros, and Skepsis, with the remnants of the local *Gergithoi* in the hinterland. Proximity to Lesbos undoubtedly played a role here, and at an early stage Mitylene exerted influence over the coastline to Sigeion on the Hellespont, stimulating protracted conflict with Athens during the late seventh century. Under the arbitration of Corinthian tyrant Periander, Athens was awarded the landscape around Sigeion, founding a second colony at Elaeus on the opposite shore of the Hellespont and effectively opening up the straits to Athenian trade. Both colonies exhibit Attic influence, most evident in their burial and ceramic assemblages, which, unlike neighboring settlements, are largely devoid of locally produced gray wares in favor of Attic imports (Cook 1999). Sigeion's maintained contact with Athens is demonstrable through two Attic inscriptions and the adoption of coinage in imitation of Attic "owls" but carrying the Sigeion city-ethnic, ΣΙΓΕ. Athenian influence is apparent more broadly, notably in the selective adoption and reproduction of Attic ceramics at a number of Troadic sites, as well as changes, from the sixth century, in burial with the displacement of local wares by Greek and Attic influenced assemblages on nearby Tenedos (Arslan and Sevinç 2003). This perhaps simply reflects the adoption of new material forms, but it may also hint at realignment with a new regional power.

Anatolian influence in the Aegean and western Mediterranean was more restricted, although Aeolians, Carians, Klazomenaians, and Milesians are apparent in the northern Aegean and Thrace. Movement to the western Mediterranean was a later development and perhaps motivated by increased pressures within Anatolia resultant from Lydian empire building (see Adornato, Chapter 13, and Sanmartí, Chapter 18, this volume). By the sixth century, Anatolian populations had reached Italy, France, and Spain, most evident in the Phocaean foundation of Massalia (Marseille) with its strong ties to the mother city and the maintained shared cults of Apollo Delphinios and Artemis Ephesos (Malkin 2011, 171–204).

Arguably the most significant overseas interactions by the Anatolian Greeks lie in their contact with the Near East and Egypt (see Rollinger, Chapter 9, and Manning, Chapter 17, this volume). The cultural borrowings and reinterpretations of Eastern ideas and objects, often couched in terms of the *Orientalizing phenomenon*, brought new intellectual and material development that defined western Anatolia, and in turn the wider Greek world. Ionian and Carian populations were evidently already in direct contact with the Near East by the eighth century BC. Indeed, Assyrian records highlight the presence of Ionian mercenaries in Phoenicia and Milesians aiding Pharaoh Psammetichos I in his campaigns against Assyria. Graffiti at Abu Simbel and Abusir are illustrative of Carian and Ionian activity into the 590s BC (Morris 2006, 67–68; Mac Sweeney 2011, 79; Adiego 2007). But the evidence is not restricted to the Near East. Following his campaign of 608 BC, Pharaoh Necho dedicated armor at the sanctuary of Branchidae-Didyma, and Carian mercenary activity is probably attested in a seventh-century basalt head of Osiris at Iasos (Berti 1992, 95–96). Similarly, Pedon, son of Amphithetos, dedicated an Egyptian statue in Caria, while the lyric poet Alcaeus writes of his brother, Antimenidas, working as a mercenary in Babylon (Morris 2006, 75).

These early exchanges resulted in the movement of people, objects, and almost certainly ideas. However, it is the colonial enclave at Naukratis, under initial Pharonic restriction, where real change occurs. Naukratis was essentially a joint mercantile venture, its shared sanctuary founded by nine East Greek *poleis*, the *Hellenion*, arguably the clearest indicator for shared identity outside Anatolia. Recognizable East Greek ceramics reach the site by the seventh century and in return Naukratite faïence, alabaster, and tridacna shell products find their way back to Anatolia, most notably at Smyrna and Miletos (Boardman 1999). Significantly for Anatolia, this created new markets (economic) and influences (cultural) so that by the end of the seventh century, expanding trade routes are evident in the distribution of East Greek ceramics to Cilicia, Al Mina, Naukratis, Daphnae, and the western Mediterranean. These periods of expansion and trade fostered inspiration and the redefinition of ideas and materials amongst the Greek populations of Anatolia, most evident in the gradual emergence of distinct cultural assemblages that defined the region.

The Seventh Century and Lydia

A change in Anatolian political orientation is witnessed in the seventh century. Phrygian power waned, partly due to possible invasion and the destruction of Gordian, to be replaced by the Lydian Mermnad dynasty established by Gyges (ca. 680–644 BC) with his capital at Sardis. Lydia herself was not immune to outside threat, especially from the Kimmerians, and Gyges appears in Assyrian records asking for help from Ashurbanipal. It was not until the reign of Alyattes (ca. 609–560 BC), following Kimmerian raids on the west coast and the destruction of Sardis, that Lydian order was fully imposed and the threat removed (Sagona and Zimansky 2009, 363; Mac Sweeney 2011, 79). The new Lydian dynasty established close links with the Anatolian *poleis* until the mid-sixth-century Persian annexation of Anatolia by Cyrus II. Initially, there is evidence for elite political interaction, notably the marriage of Alyattes's daughter to the Ephesian ruler Melas, which no doubt helped to cement state-level exchanges between the two (Roosevelt 2012, 902; Mac Sweeney 2013, 151). But, as with Phrygia, the *poleis*' position in the hinterland of the Anatolian power engendered east–west exchanges. Gyges became the first non-Greek after Midas to dedicate at Delphi and is followed by Alyattes and Croesus (Hdt. 1.14, 1.92). For Croesus this was something of a double-edged sword since his misinterpretation of an ambiguous oracular reading ultimately led to Lydian collapse at Persian hands (Hdt. 1.53).

It is clear from Greek sources that Lydian political control extended to cover large areas of western Anatolia and the Lydian Kings were not averse to reinforcing their position through force when needed. Gyges campaigned against Miletos, Smyrna, and Colophon, while his son, Adys, continued offensives against Miletos and took Priene (Roosevelt 2012, 901). Subsequent campaigns by Sadyattes and Alyattes against Miletos occurred in tandem with those against Klazomenai and, notably, Alyattes's sack of Smyrna in ca. 600 BC (Hdt. 1.16–19). This latter event is attested archaeologically in a huge siege mound that enabled Lydian forces to breach Smyrna's fortifications, alongside widespread destruction of seventh-century BC houses (Cook 1958–1959). This was a period of Lydian empire building that finally stabilized under Croesus, who brought the majority of western Anatolia under Sardis's control and exacted annual tribute from its populations (Roosevelt 2012, 902). While this meant subservience for the *poleis*, Lydian control was not restrictive, and they experienced a degree of freedom for experimentation and independent development (Mac Sweeney 2011, 80).

Sardis demonstrates the trappings of a large regional center, with fortified citadel, lower town, large terraces, and retaining walls that parallel examples at Pasargadae in Persia (Roosevelt 2012; Sagona and Zimansky 2009). Greek influence is evident too and encouraged Greeks like Solon and Alcaemon to visit Sardis, while prompting Lydian offerings at Branchidae-Didyma. Ceramics from western Anatolia appear in increasing volume from the seventh century, and the possible involvement of Ionian craftsmen is apparent in Croesus's building projects. While no temple structures of this period remain, surviving models found during excavation suggest the use of Ionic architecture (Roosevelt 2012, 904). To some extent this might reflect Sardis's close association with Archaic Ephesos. Surviving inscriptions on the columns of the Artemision at Ephesos indicate Croesus's patronage, and it is evident that Ephesian Artemis was venerated at Sardis alongside the Anatolian goddess Kybele (Morris 2006, 70–73; Hdt. 1.92). Artemis was not the sole

"Greek" deity recognized at Sardis, and she appears in conjunction with a mixture of Greek and Anatolian cult practice that included ritual meals and the burial of dogs (Roosevelt 2012). This demonstration of religious syncretism certainly resulted in close links between Sardis and Ephesos, and possibly saved the latter from destruction at Lydian hands.

Perhaps the most overt development of this period lies in the re-emergence of monumental architecture and the need of the *poleis* to house their patron deities. The Aeolic order develops during the seventh century around Smyrna and the Hellespont, with notable examples of Aeolian temple structures at Larisa, Neandria, and Smyrna. The influence here is from Egypt, and the adaptation of Eastern motifs, in this case the lotus, on column capitals is characteristic (Akurgal 1983; Cook and Nicholls 1998). By the sixth to fifth centuries an Ionic order had emerged in the south and coincided with the spread of temple building around western Anatolia, notably at sites like Priene. What sets the region apart is the sheer scale of the structures involved, and this owes much to the influence and emulation of Near Eastern prototypes both in form and in concept. The earliest examples perhaps date to the eighth century, but by the sixth century the temples of Artemis at Ephesos, Apollo at Didyma, and Hera on Samos represent the largest displays of "Greek" architecture in the Mediterranean.

Although indicative of the region's receptiveness to new stimuli, architectural development perhaps also reflects the nature of contemporary Anatolia. Structures like this would have served as overt markers of *polis* identity, status, and position, and there are clear divergences throughout the region that demonstrate this in action. Thus, while the Artemision and the temples of Branchidae-Didyma outwardly display the Ionic order, the temple of Apollo Didyma, for example, reveals potential Anatolian (Urartian?) influence through its hypaethral form (Greaves 2002, 111–114). Similarly, the sixth-century Ionic capitals from Phocaea, with griffin and horse protomes, mirror influences found, for example, on *Orientalizing* bronze work at Samos and Olympia (Özyiğit 2006). Perhaps the clearest example is found in the sixth-century Temple of Athena at Assos (Figure 11.2) (Wescoat 2012). This is unique in Anatolia through the incorporation of an Ionic frieze within a Doric temple, its depictions of Herakles recalling sculptural elements from the Parthenon. A truly hybrid structure, the Temple of Athena reflects the various influences felt at Assos by the sixth century, and perhaps points to influence from a wider Athenian-Ionian diaspora. While this may simply be a result of proximity to Lesbos or Athenian interests in the Troad, it must be wondered whether the shift in contemporary Anatolian politics, and the appearance of Persia, also played their part.

These architectural developments were not confined to the "Greek" *poleis*, but are also a feature of their non-Greek neighbors. Elements of Ionian architecture and influence are apparent at Sardis and the Archaic and later remains of the Temple of Zeus at Labraunda, which draw parallels to other western Anatolian sites like Priene and Halicarnassos. At Phrygian Daskyleion a mid-seventh-century temple model also displays the Ionic order (Bakır et al. 2004), while later in Carian Iasos, Doric architecture is found at the Sanctuary of Zeus Megistos. Similarly, the Harpy Tomb and Nereid monuments of Xanthos, and the funerary monuments of Telmessos (Fethiye), incorporate elements of Anatolian and Ionic Greek architecture to produce cult monuments whose hybrid forms typify the nature of cross-cultural exchanges in Anatolia at this time (Draycott 2007). This influence extends

Figure 11.2 Reconstruction of the east façade of the Temple of Athena at Assos. Source: Clarke 1898: figure 62.

well into the sixth century. Indeed, following Persian annexation of Anatolia, Ionian architectural elements appear in the East, most evident in Cyrus's mausoleum at Pasargadae and the use of Greek craftsmen and columns at Persepolis, where Telephanes of Phocaea is reported to have worked for both Darius and Xerxes (Curtis 2005).

The preservation of Phocaea's city wall (Figure 11.1) in the later Maltepe tumulus (Greaves 2011, 505) highlights another distinctive element of Anatolian-Greek identity through the adoption of Anatolian burial forms. The tumulus belies Lydian influence, which inspired specifically elite burial that was not restricted to Phocaea but adapted by a number of *poleis*, notably Ephesos, Klazomenai, and Smyrna, during the period of Lydian hegemony. While this may in part simply reflect the use of burial forms typical of the Anatolian landscape, it plausibly also reflects changing sociopolitical affiliations, at least at an elite level, between individual *poleis* and regional Anatolian powers. At Phocaea, for example, the use of tumuli, combined with a rock-cut chamber tomb at Şeytan Hamamı, is distinctive of affiliation with the Lydian world (Greaves 2010, 97; Greaves 2011, 506). Yet, the sixth-century Taş Kule tomb (Figure 11.3) finds its closest parallel in the tomb of Cyrus the Great in Iran, and may reflect alignment with, or control by, a new, Persian, authority (Cahill 1988). This is more evident in later periods, particularly around the Troad and Granicus river valley. Here, Anatolian style tumuli by the fourth century are punctuated by elaborately carved sarcophagi, notably at Çan, that draw on western Anatolian and Persian influences (Rose 2014). This mixing of cultural elements, evident in hybrid Achaemenid/Anatolian stelae and burial contexts like Taş Kule, arguably demonstrates the reaction and outward affiliation of local elites to new regional authority.

Figure 11.3 The Taş Kule tomb with false door. Source: courtesy D. Diffendale.

The use of burial for political display and demonstrations of power and prestige is evident too in Miletos's Lion Tomb (Greaves 2002, 87–89) and extended to neighboring Lydian and Lycian landscapes. Indeed, a number of tombs preserve *klinai* and painted interiors that reveal Greek influence. Those of Elmalı and Güre (Uşak), for example, combine East Greek, Anatolian, and Persian elements, and may go some way to demonstrate the adoption of Persian influence and costume in western Anatolia (Harl 2011, 760). This is reflected, too, in a series of wall paintings from Gordion and Düver that have clear Ionic influence, which can perhaps also be detected in the contemporary development of Etruscan tomb painting (Boardman 1999, 206; Harl 2011, 757).

Of course, burial was not just an elite process, and from the seventh century the Anatolian *poleis* develop large necropoleis that are in many respects typically "Greek," albeit with their own idiosyncrasies. Thus, gray ware amphorae, combined with occasional decorated ceramics and metalwork, typify eighth- to seventh-century burials in the Troad and are striking in their similarities to Late Bronze Age traditions, while Elaeus's necropolis is conspicuous in its Attic influence (Cook 1999). At Klazomenai, painted terracotta sarcophagi create distinct, hybrid burial assemblages that are only occasionally found in neighboring landscapes, such as at Phocaea (Cook and Dupont 2003). It is within burial contexts, too, that some of the clearest indicators for local experimentation are apparent, for example, through the imitation of imported ceramics at sites like Assos and Antandros, and the adaptation of Ionian ceramics in Caria.

Alongside increasing imports of Greek ceramics (Geometric, Corinthian, and Attic), the assemblages of the seventh and sixth centuries offer an extensive source of data for local interaction between *poleis* and Anatolian populations. Gray wares continue in Aeolia and the Troad, but there is evidence for experimentation in form and style, most notably in the emulation of Phrygian metalwork. This period also sees the development of decorated ceramics with their origins in the multiple influences of the Anatolian coastline. A sub-Geometric ware of probable Troadic origin, termed G2-3, emerges with a distribution confined to the northeastern Aegean. It forms a distinct counterpart to local gray wares not apparent elsewhere in Anatolia and perhaps signals the Troad's cultural engagement with Samothrace in particular (Rose 2014). In Ionia and Aeolia, so-called *Orientalizing* or *East Greek* ceramics emerge that are distinctly western Anatolian but incorporate elements of Greek, Anatolian, and Near Eastern styles and motifs. Key amongst them are Wild Goat wares (Figure 11.4), characterized by stylized animals or birds in running

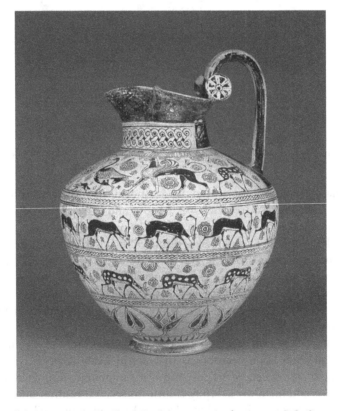

Figure 11.4 Wild Goat ware oenochoe, Ionian, ca. seventh century BC. Source: Digital image courtesy of the Getty's Open Content Program. http://www.getty.edu/art/collection/objects/9694/unknown-maker-oinochoe-east-greek-milesian-about-625-bc/?dz=#b3db43215e0d0d34262b91ab6e8cb573761827cb

friezes, often with the addition of Eastern motifs such as sphinxes, griffins, and lotuses (Cook and Dupont 2003; Kerschner and Schlotzhauer 2005). A developed form of Wild Goat, termed *Fikellura*, is distinctively Ionian and provides a key chronological marker since its production spans the last half of the sixth century through to Miletos's destruction in 494 BC. Perhaps initially Ionian (Milesian?), locally produced Wild Goat is evident throughout Ionia and Aeolia, with clear regional variation. Yet, it was not confined solely to the Greek *poleis* of Anatolia. Local workshops appeared in Caria, possibly Lycia, and with a Lydian version at Sardis (Cook and Dupont 2003; Özgünel 2006). Elsewhere, a form of Wild Goat not seen in Anatolia developed at Naukratis, while Wild Goat by the Swallow Painter at Vulci (Etruria) highlights the extent of Ionian influence during the Archaic period, even if this is a somewhat exceptional case (Cook and Dupont 2003).

Although the evidence remains slight, interaction with Lydia occasionally directly affected Greek ceramic traditions. At Smyrna and Pitane, seventh-century vessels have been identified depicting a seven-stringed lyre of Lydian origin, and Lydian *Marbled Wares* find their way into the assemblages of the west coast (Boardman 1999, 97). Perhaps more obvious is the adoption into the Greek ceramic repertoire of the distinctive *Lydion* vessel form, which, while characteristically Lydian, represents the only clear demonstration of Greek adaptation of Lydian prototypes.

One of the key elements to emerge from Greek–Lydian interactions is the development of coinage. Possibly stimulated by the need for Lydian payment of Ionian and Carian mercenaries, or to redistribute accumulated bullion, this was almost certainly aided by the mineral wealth of Sardis's position on the River Pactolus (Greaves 2010, 86–89; Balcer 1991). The earliest hoard, from the Artemision, dates to ca. 600 BC and comprises electrum coins and blanks of probable Lydian production. Some early issues carry legends or merchant's marks, including one reading "I am the badge of Phanes," while others begin to use distinctive devices. A seal's head on the early coinage at Phocaea might be seen as a marker of self-identity, serving as a pun on the city name (*phoke* (Greek) = "seal"), but becoming a badge that identified the *polis* to the wider Greek world (Howgego 1995). With the development of bimetallic gold and silver coinage during the sixth century, this link with individual *polis* identity and political position was often exploited. The use of Athenian coin types noted at Sigeion provided a marker of political affiliation and maintained ties as daughter colony. Similarly, the use of the Pamphylian city-ethnic on the coinage of Aspendos represents the deliberate perpetuation of a local, non-Greek identity (Grainger 2009). A similar scenario might be seen at Skepsis, whose Aeolic city-ethnic changes to the Ionic during the fifth century, perhaps reflecting an influx of refugees following Miletos's destruction in 494 BC noted in literary sources that may have resulted in a shift in the composition or affiliation of her populace (Cook 1999). The use of coinage in the expression of political or local identity equally expanded to non-Greek Anatolian populations, most notably in dynastic Lycia where local elites were able to demonstrate political status by placing their names on new coin issues.

The exposure of the Anatolian *poleis* to multiple exchanges of information and ideas often stimulated the emergence of distinct regional styles. Most notable is the development of free-standing sculpture, particularly in the *kouroi* (*kouros* (m) and *kore* (f)) that represent an adaptation of Egyptian funerary statues. Early *kouroi* demonstrate many characteristics of their Egyptian antecedents, but a number of local schools emerged, such as on Samos, whose products were recognizable and transmitted within and without Anatolia. Contact with the Near East brought further material stimuli, and the preserved 494 BC destruction levels of the Temple of Athena at Miletos revealed at least eight bronze cauldrons with griffin heads and Near Eastern horse trappings of seventh- to sixth-century date. This represents the largest number of such cauldrons outside the sanctuaries of Olympia and Samos, their importation and local imitation indicative of the receptiveness of Anatolian craftsmen (Morris 2006, 76). Indeed, Ionian bronze work has a relatively wide distribution within the Mediterranean, finding its way as far west as Etruria and the south of France. Early examples of Near Eastern ivory also appear at sites like Smyrna, Erythrae, and Ephesos, where elements of Eastern influence are incorporated into local Anatolian ivory production. At Ephesos, a series of couchant animals demonstrate emulation of Eastern prototypes, while local ivory workshops are evident in Ionia and Lydia, their products found both within and without Anatolia at sites like Delphi (Greaves 2010; Boardman 1999).

By the sixth century, Ionian workshops are producing gems that are found from Sardis to Etruria, where a potential workshop with Ionian artisans or their apprentices has been recognized (Spier 2010). Contemporary with these workshops is the appearance, for example, of small lead medallions depicting a goddess astride a lion's back (Körpe and Körpe 2001). Examples have been identified at Samos, Ephesos, Chios, and Skepsis, with a silver parallel in the east at Zincirli. The importance of these small medallions extends beyond obvious demonstrations of Ionian metalwork and their Eastern inspiration. More significantly, they potentially highlight the religious syncretisms apparent in Anatolia during the Archaic period. In this instance can arguably be seen the adoption of the Anatolian mother goddess, Kybele, who experiences increasing veneration and transmission into the broader Greek pantheon. Altar B at Troy, Windmill Hill and the rock-cut niches below the Temple of Athena at Phocaea, and a rock-cut niche at Samos, all point to her worship, but this extended to encompass wider areas of the Anatolian landscape (Greaves 2011, 506; Greaves 2010, 216). A correlation between Kybele and Ephesian Artemis may well also be possible, since the two share many characteristics, albeit Artemis was specifically Ephesian in this form. In this regard, the Artemision provided a key milieu for interaction between Sardis and Ephesos, evident not least in Lydian patronage, which, combined with the worship of Ephesian Artemis at Sardis, suggests the relationship between the two may have gone much deeper (Roosevelt 2012; Morris 2006). At the very least, Ephesos was afforded a unique identity within Anatolia founded on close interaction, and even shared cult development, with a potentially aggressive regional power and all the political and social engagement this engendered.

The Greek migration tradition is inherently associated with the development of Greek language, both written and spoken. The dialectical groups that define Aeolian, Ionian, and Dorian provide the basis for regional variation and the (late) construction of ethnic groupings. In part, too, a link is found with Homeric epic, which, although Ionic, contains elements of Aeolic explained as a result of its transmission through Aeolia and Ionia. The Aeolic dialects, spoken in Boeotia, Thessaly, and on Lesbos, formed the basis of the lyric poetry of Sappho and Alcaeus, while divergences in the isoglosses of surviving language enable the identification of dialects with mixed origin, such as those of Pamphylia (Panayotou 2007), or compensation for local linguistic variation. There is evidence, however, that the Greek languages were not always adopted by Anatolian populations or indeed withstood the influence of non-Greek languages. At Side, migrant populations from Kyme are reported to have almost immediately adopted the Sidetan tongue that appears on her coinage, the mixed populations here favoring the local language, with Greek only appearing in later, Hellenistic, bilingual inscriptions (Hawkins 2010).

In tandem with the spread of language came the development of writing and the use of the alphabet. Writing is not abundant in western Anatolia until at least the seventh century with graffiti at Aeolian and Ionian sites like Smyrna (Greaves 2010, 14–20), more complete inscriptions only appearing during the sixth with writing also seen on contemporary coinage. Often regarded as a marker for Greek presence, within an Anatolian context it had more wide-ranging implications for Greek–non-Greek interactions. The adoption of a similar alphabetic script by Phrygian populations was used to express their own language with its clear Phrygian onomastics. It is notable that the New Chronology at Gordion suggests at least an eighth-century BC date for the earliest Phrygian examples, raising the question of how and when the various alphabetic scripts developed and were transmitted within Anatolia (Brixhe 2004). Other Anatolian populations, most notably the Lydians, Lycians, and Carians, adopt similar alphabetic scripts to represent their own distinct language sets. In some instances, loan words in Greek hint at the complexities of early interactions, while bilingual Lydian-Greek inscriptions at both the Temple of Athena at Smyrna and the Artemision are demonstrative of the close links with Sardis and the potential use of multiple languages within the Anatolian milieu (Greaves 2010, 16–20). Contrastingly, the already noted survival of Carian onomastics indicates that the use of "Greek" scripts, or even language, did not necessarily subvert local Anatolian traditions or identities (Adiego 2007; Hall 2002, 104–111). In this regard, what is perhaps most evident through surviving inscriptions and references to language in western Anatolia is the demonstrable mixed populations that would have been readily apparent to those occupying the landscape. In addition to Greek dialects, Phrygian, Lydian, Carian, Lycian, and following Persian annexation, Aramaic are all attested singularly and in bi- or trilingual inscriptions, and would have formed components of a cultural milieu where "Greeks" were by no means the only, or indeed the most significant, element.

Persia and Revolt

The mid-sixth century brought political and social change for the Anatolian *poleis*. Croesus's defeat at Sardis by Cyrus the Great led to Persian annexation and the displacement of Lydian influence. Under Persian rule, the entire western Anatolian region was incorporated into a new satrapy administered from a regional capital at Sardis. In each *polis* Persian authorities installed their own tyrants in place of local elites, often to the dissatisfaction of the populace. The emergence of Aramaic script, evident in a bronze talent lion weight from Abydos (Cook 1999, 57), highlights the spread of Persian administration, and burials like the Çan sarcophagus at least point to the presence of increasingly "*Persianized*" elites, if not a direct Persian presence if Xerxes's activities on the Hellespont are anything to go by (Hdt. 7.106, 9.115–116). However, control over the Hellespont remained Greek, and particularly Athenian, so that by 478 BC the Delian League exacted tribute from many of the Anatolian *poleis*.

It is notable that in this period the flows of objects between Greece, Anatolia, and Persia did not diminish. On the contrary, increased circulation of Anatolian ceramics is evident in Persia alongside an influx of Attic at sites like Daskyleion. Equally, the sixth century sees an increase in coinage, based on both pre-existing weight standards and those linked with Persia, and later increased contributions to the Delian League. This reflects a degree of economic stability, but it is also clear that Persian hegemony brought with it political and social change that stifled local development (Balcer 1991). It was probably in part the removal of the relative freedoms experienced by the Anatolian *poleis* in earlier stages of the Archaic period that led to attempts to overthrow Persian rule, first in 511 BC and then more decisively in full Revolt in 499 BC. Significantly, too, the stifling of Milesian development during the sixth century, and corresponding growth of Athens, saw Miletos gradually lose her pre-eminent position within the Aegean. Miletos, and her tyrant Aristagoras, was the driving force in the revolt, and in 498 BC an Ionian army gathered at Ephesos set out to take Sardis. The Persian satrap, Artaphernes, held the citadel but Sardis was destroyed by fire, inciting the wrath of Persian King Darius. There followed an uneasy period of revolt and conflict before a final battle at Lade in 494 BC resulted in the eventual destruction of Miletos and victory for Persia. In many respects, the Battle of Lade represents a fitting end point for the Archaic period in Anatolia (Greaves 2010, xii). Not only did it signal the end of the region's most successful and powerful *polis*, Miletos, but it also witnessed the end of experimentation and growth that are the defining features of what it meant to be "Greek" in Anatolia.

The Influence of Anatolia

The visible achievements of the Anatolian Greeks, particularly in Ionia, are striking and evident both archaeologically and historically. Key elements that define the Archaic Greek world, monumental architecture, free-standing sculpture, and coinage, evolved within the Anatolian milieu and impacted upon the wider Mediterranean. However, arguably the greatest contribution lay in those less visible features that were central to the development of Archaic Greece, and, indeed, are still relevant today. Anatolia provided an intellectual breeding ground within which ideas and ideologies could easily flow, to be adapted and redefined by incumbent populations. The earliest examples lie in the development of dactylic hexameter epic poetry by the eighth century with the Homeric *Iliad* and *Odyssey*, the focus of the former on events in Anatolia perhaps a reflection of its Anatolian context when committed to paper (Mac Sweeney 2011, 76; Hall 2002, 118). Evidence of this emergent intellectualism is apparent in the works of a number of now lost poets as well as Hesiod's various contributions, most notably his *Theogony*, which, in drawing on Hittite-Hurrian myth, is significant in its demonstration of Eastern influence. This continues into the sixth century with the appearance of Ionic meter in the poetry of Alcaeus and Sappho, and is representative of the intellectual developments witnessed in the Anatolian milieu during the Archaic period.

Within Ionia, notably around Miletos and Ephesos, the Eastern influences apparent in Hesiod developed further and were no doubt stimulated by the *poleis*' increased external contacts. It is here that the Archaic period witnesses the emergence of logical reasoning, geography, historical method, mathematics, and philosophy. Miletos was home to the first pre-Socratic philosophers in Thales of Miletos (ca. 620–546 BC) and his followers Anaximander (ca. 610–545 BC) and Anaximenes (ca. 585–528 BC), all of whom were influenced by ideas from Babylon to Egypt. Similarly, Heraclitus of Ephesos (late sixth century BC) drew inspiration from the East as did Pythagoras of Samos (ca. 570–495 BC) in both his philosophical and his mathematical thinking (Morris 2006, 74; Mac Sweeney 2011, 80). While in the fifth-century works of Hecataeus of Miletos and Herodotus of Halicarnassos (ca. 490–425 BC) can be seen the first geography, world map, and historical analysis of the Greek world.

Although the surviving archaeological and material remains of Archaic Anatolia certainly contributed to Archaic Greece, not least in architectural style and the reception of Eastern influence, arguably the greatest contributions were intellectual and ideological. The intellectualism generated through the cultural and political interactions of settlement in Anatolia formed the cornerstone of later Greek scholarship, and it is perhaps to this that the *poleis* of Anatolia made their greatest contribution.

Conclusions

In its *longue durée* development, Anatolia, and its western coastline in particular, offered Greek populations the potential for extensive and often rapid cultural advancement. In the Early Iron Age the evidence for this is slight, but in the gradual emergence of the Anatolian *poleis* can be seen a demonstration of localized development and receptivity of populations to new stimuli. Although the migration traditions are suggestive of more clearly defined group identity, the archaeological evidence instead points more toward discrete local divergences and the ability of populations to adapt to external change, as perhaps is evident at Smyrna and Troy.

From the eighth century the region flourishes and indications of evolving identities are apparent. Ionia takes the lead, and, although there is limited Greek settlement of the southern coastline, the focus remains in the west. Here, the narrow coastal strip between the Aegean and the Anatolian hinterland served as a middle ground within which the Greek *poleis* capitalized. In turn, this fostered direct contact and cross-cultural exchanges with Anatolian neighbors in the Phrygians, Lydians, Lycians, and Carians. Increasing overseas contacts saw the emergence of distinct ceramic assemblages that typify western Anatolia, monumental architecture, free-standing sculpture, coinage, not to mention new intellectual stimuli. This active milieu of emulation and reciprocity depended to a degree on the political and social freedoms afforded under both Phrygian and Lydian regional control.

What defined Greek identity within Anatolia was not necessarily association with a broader regional sense of being "Greek," although this can perhaps be seen emergent in the Aeolian and Ionian Leagues. Rather, it was the ability to adapt and to experiment within a landscape of multiple populations in which those who spoke "Greek" were but a small part. This was as much defined by the presence of the Anatolian hinterland as it was by that of Aegean Greece. In this regard, the term "East Greece" represents something of a misnomer. Rather, the region, while certainly influenced by and influencing the Greek world, should perhaps be seen as a multi-influenced, multiethnic, even multicultural, landscape dependent on its own unique local development that acted as a middle ground between East and West.

REFERENCES

Adiego, Ignacio-Javier. 2007. *The Carian Language. Handbook of Oriental Studies Section 1, The Near and Middle East, vol. 86*. Brill: Leiden.

Akurgal, Ekrem. 1983. *Alt-Smyrna I: Wohnschichten und Athenatempel*. Ankara: Türk Tarih Kurumu Basımevi.

Arslan, Nurettin, and Nurten Sevinç. 2003. "Die eisenzeitliche Graber von Tenedos." *Istanbuler Mitteilungen*, 53: 223–250.

Bakır, Tomris, Aytekin Erdoğan, H. Bulut, and Handan Yildizhan. 2004. "Daskyleion 2002 Yılı Kazı Çalişmaları." *25 Kazı Sonuçları Toplantısı*, 1: 311–318.

Balcer, Jack M. 1991. "The East Greeks under Persian Rule: A Reassessment." In *Asia Minor and Egypt: Old Cultures in a New Empire: Proceedings of the Gröningen 1998 Achaemenid History workshop*, edited by Heleen Sancisi-Weerdenberg and Amelie Kuhrt, 57–65. Leiden: Neederlands Instituut voor het Nahije Oosten.

Becks, Ralf. 2003. "Troia VII: The Transition from the Late Bronze Age to the Early Iron Age." In *Identifying Changes: The Transition from Bronze to Iron Ages in Anatolia and its Neighbouring Regions*, edited by Bettina Fischer, Hermann Genz, Eric Jean, and Kemalettin Koroğlu, 41–53. Istanbul: Türk Eskiçağ Bilimleri Enstitüsü.

Berti, Fede. 1992. "Mission Archéologique Italienne de Iasos: Compte rendu des travaux de 1991." *14 Kazı Sonuçları Toplantısı*, II: 91–116.

Boardman, John. 1999. *The Greeks Overseas: Their Early Colonies and Trade*. 4th ed. London: Thames & Hudson.

Brixhe, Claude. 2004. "Phrygian." In *The Cambridge Encyclopedia of the World's Ancient Languages*, edited by Roger D. Woodward, 777–788. Cambridge: Cambridge University Press.

Bryce, Trevor. 2005. *The Trojans and their Neighbours*. London: Routledge.

Cahill, Nicholas. 1988. "Taş Kule: A Persian-Period Tomb near Phokaia." *American Journal of Archaeology*, 92(4): 481–501.

Chabot Aslan, Carolyn. 2002. "Ilion before Alexander: Protogeometric, Geometric and Archaic Pottery from D9." *Studia Troica*, 12: 81–130.

Clarke, Joseph T. 1898. "Report on the Investigations at Assos, 1882, 1883, Part I." *Papers of the Archaeological Institute of America, Classical Series II*. New York: The Macmillan Company.

Cobet, Justus, Volkmar von Graeve, Wolf-Dietrich Niemeier, and Konrad Zimmermann, eds. 2007. *Frühes Ionien: Eine bestandsaufnahme. Akten des symposions: 100 Jahre Milet, 1999*. Mainz: Philip von Zabern.

Cook, John M. 1958–1959. "Old Smyrna, 1948–1951." *Annual of the British School at Athens*, 53–54: 1–34.

Cook, John M. 1999. *The Troad: An Archaeological and Topographical Study*. Oxford: Oxford University Press.

Cook, John M. 1962. *The Greeks in Ionia and the East*. London: Thames & Hudson.
Cook, John M., and Richard V. Nicholls. 1998. *Old Smyrna Excavations: The Temples of Athena*. London: British School at Athens.
Cook, Robert M., and Pierre Dupont. 2003. *East Greek Pottery*. London: Routledge.
Crielaard, Jan Paul. 2009. "The Ionians in the Archaic Period. Shifting Identities in a Changing World." In *Ethnic Constructs in Antiquity: The Role of Power and Tradition*, edited by Ton Derks and Nico Roymans, 37–84. Amsterdam: University Press.
Curtis, John. 2005. "Greek Influence on Achaemenid Art and Architecture." In *The Greeks in the East*, edited by Alexandra Villing, 115–123. London: The British Museum.
Draycott, Catherine. 2007. "Dynastic Differences: Differentiating Status Claims in the Archaic Pillar Tomb Reliefs of Lycia." In *Anatolian Iron Ages 6: The Proceedings of the Sixth Anatolian Iron Ages Colloquium Held at Eskişehir, 16–20 August 2004*, edited by Antonio Sagona and Altan Çilingiroğlu, 103–134. Louvain: Peeters.
Easton, Donald F., John D. Hawkins, Andrew G. Sherratt, and E. Susan Sherratt. 2002. "Troy in Recent Perspective." *Anatolian Studies*, 52: 75–109.
Ersoy, Yasar E. 2004. "Klazomenai: 900–500 BC: History and Settlement Evidence." In *Klazomenai, Teos, and Abdera: Metropoleis and Colony. Proceedings of the International Symposium Held at the Archaeological Museum of Abdera, Abdera, 20–21 October 2001*, edited by Aliki Moustaka, Eudokia Skarlatidou, Maria-Christina Tzannes, and Yasar E. Ersoy, 43–76. Thessaloniki: University Studio Press.
Grainger, John D. 2009. *The Cities of Pamphylia*. Oxford: Oxbow.
Greaves, Alan M. 2002. *Miletos: A History*. London: Routledge.
Greaves, Alan M. 2010. *The Land of Ionia: Society and Economy in the Archaic Period*. Chichester: Wiley Blackwell.
Greaves, Alan M. 2011. "The Greeks in Western Anatolia." In *The Oxford Handbook of Ancient Anatolia (10,000–323 B.C.E.)*, edited by Sharon R. Steadman and Gregory McMahon, 500–514. Oxford: Oxford University Press.
Hall, Jonathan M. 2002. *Hellenicity: Between Ethnicity and Culture*. Chicago: Chicago University Press.
Hall, Jonathan M. 2007. *A History of the Archaic Greek World ca. 1200–479 BCE*. Chichester: Blackwell.
Harl, Kenneth W. 2011. "The Greeks in Anatolia: From the Migrations to Alexander the Great." In *The Oxford Handbook of Ancient Anatolia (10,000–323 B.C.E.)*, edited by Sharon R. Steadman and Gregory McMahon, 752–774. Oxford: Oxford University Press.
Hawkins, Shane. 2010. "Greek and the Languages of Asia Minor to the Classical Period." In *A Companion to the Ancient Greek Language*, edited by Egbert J. Bakker, 213–227. Chichester: Blackwell.
Howgego, Chris. 1995. *Ancient History from Coins*. London: Routledge.
Kealhofer, Lisa, ed. 2005. *The Archaeology of Midas and the Phrygians: Recent Work at Gordion*. Philadelphia: University of Pennsylvania Museum of Archaeology and Anthropology.
Kerschner, Michael, and Udo Schlotzhauer. 2005. "A New Classification System for East Greek Pottery." *Ancient West & East*, 4(1): 1–56.
Körpe, Reyhan, and Funda Körpe. 2001. "A Lead Medallion from Skepsis in the Troad." *Studia Troica*, 11: 421–426.

Lemos, Irene S. 2002. *The Protogeometric Aegean: The Archaeology of the Late Eleventh and Tenth Centuries BC*. Oxford: Oxford University Press.

Mac Sweeney, Naíose. 2011. *Community Identity and Archaeology: Dynamic Communities at Aphrodisias and Beycesultan*. Michigan: Michigan University Press.

Mac Sweeney, Naíose. 2013. *Foundation Myths and Politics in Ancient Ionia*. Cambridge: Cambridge University Press.

Mac Sweeney, Naíose. 2017. "Separating Fact from Fiction in the Ionian Migration." *Hesperia*, 86(3): 379–421.

Malkin, Irad. 2011. *A Small Greek World: Networks in the Ancient Mediterranean*. New York: Oxford University Press.

Mommsen, Hanns, Dieter Hertel, and Penelope Mountjoy. 2001. "Neutron Activation Analysis of the Pottery from Troia in the Berlin Schliemann Collection." *Archäologischer Anzeiger*, 2001: 169–211.

Morris, Sarah P. 2006. "The View from East Greece: Miletus, Samos and Ephesus." In *Debating Orientlization: Multidisciplinary Approaches to Change in the Ancient Mediterranean*, edited by Corinna Riva and Nicholas C. Vella, 66–84. London: Equinox.

Mountjoy, Penelope A. 1998. "The East Aegean-West Anatolian Interface in the Late Bronze Age: Mycenaeans and the Kingdom of Ahhiyawa." *Anatolian Studies*, 48: 33–68.

Niemeier, Wold-Dietrich. 2005. "Minoans, Mycenaeans, Hittites and Ionians in Western Asia Minor: New Excavations in Bronze Age Miletos-Millawanda." In *The Greeks in the East*, edited by Alexandra Villing, 1–36. London: The British Museum.

Özgünel, Coskun. 2006. *Karia Geometrik Seramiği*. Istanbul: Homer Kitabevi.

Özyiğit, Ömer. 2003. "Recent Work at Phokaia in Light of Akurgal's Excavations." *Anadolu/Anatolia*, 25: 109–127.

Özyiğit, Ömer. 2006. "2005 Yılı Phokaia Kazı Çalişmaları" *28 Kazı Sonuçları Toplantısı*, 2: 341–54.

Panayotou, Anna. 2007. "Pamphylian." In *A History of Ancient Greek: From the Beginnings to Late Antiquity*, edited by Anastasios-Foivos Christidis, 427–432. Cambridge: Cambridge University Press.

Roosevelt, Christopher. 2009. *The Archaeology of Lydia, from Gyges to Alexander*. Cambridge: Cambridge University Press.

Roosevelt, Christopher H. 2012. "Iron Age Western Anatolia: The Lydian Empire and Dynastic Lycia." In *A Companion to the Archaeology of the Ancient Near East*, edited by Daniel T. Potts, 896–913. Chichester: Blackwell.

Rose, C. Brian. 2008. "Separating Fact from Fiction in the Aiolian Migration." *Hesperia*, 77(2): 399–430.

Rose, C. Brian. 2014. *The Archaeology of Greek and Roman Troy*. New York: Cambridge University Press.

Sagona, Antonio, and Paul Zimansky. 2009. *Ancient Turkey*. Abingdon: Routledge.

Sams, Kenneth, and Mary Voigt. 2011. "In Conclusion." In *The New Chronology of Iron Age Gordion*, edited by C. Brian Rose and Gareth Darbyshire, 155–168. Philadelphia: University of Pennsylvania Press.

Spier, Jeffrey. 2000. "From East Greece to Etruria: A Late Sixth-century BC Gem Workshop." In *Periplous: Papers on Classical Art and Archaeology Presented to Sir John*

Boardman, edited by Gocha R. Tsetskhladze, A. John N.W. Prag, and Anthony M. Snodgrass, 330–335. London: Thames & Hudson.
Stampolidis, Nicholas, Çiğdem Maner, and Konstantinos Kopanias, eds. 2015. *NOSTOI: Indigenous Culture, Migration and Integration in the Aegean Islands and Western Anatolia during the Late Bronze and Early Iron Age*. Istanbul: Koç University Press.
Vaessen, Rik. 2014. "Ceramic Developments in Coastal Western Anatolia at the Dawn of the Early Iron Age." In ΑΘΥΡΜΑΤΑ: *Critical Essays on the Archaeology of the Eastern Mediterranean in Honour of E. Susan Sherratt*, edited by Yannis Galanakis, Toby Wilkinson, and John Bennet, 223–232. Oxford: Archaeopress.
Vaessen, Rik. 2016. "Cosmopolitanism, Communality and the Appropriation of Mycenaean Pottery in Western Anatolia." *Anatolian Studies*, 66: 43–65.
Vanschoonwinkel, Jacques. 2006. "Greek Migrations to Aegean Anatolia in the Dark Age." In *Greek Colonisation: An Account of Greek Colonies and Other Settlements Overseas*, vol. 1, edited by Gocha R. Tsetskhladze, 115–142. Leiden: Brill.
Wescoat, Bonna D. 2012. *The Temple of Athena at Assos*. Oxford: Oxford University Press.

FURTHER READING

Cook (1962) remains a useful, albeit dated, introduction. Significant recent contributions include Sagona and Zimansky (2009) and Stampolidis, Maner, and Kopanias (2015). Greaves (2010) provides a thorough synthesis of the archaeology and history of Ionia, its achievements and study, while Mac Sweeney (2013) and Crielaard (2009) offer detailed accounts of Ionian origins, foundation myths, and developing identities. For Ionia and the Ionian Migration, with both sides of the historical debate well presented, key texts are Cobet, von Graeve, Niemeier, and Zimmermann (2007) and Mac Sweeney (2017). A useful counterpoint, dealing with the Aeolian migration, is provided by Rose (2008). In their interactions with neighboring non-Anatolian populations, good introductions to the Phrygians can be found in Kealhofer (2005). Similarly, for the Lydians and Sardis see Roosevelt (2009).

CHAPTER TWELVE

Greeks on the Island of Cyprus: "At home" on the Frontiers

Maria Iacovou

At least we're sailing our seas,
the waters of Cyprus, Syria, and Egypt,
the beloved waters of our home countries.
Konstantinos Kavafys,

"Going back home from Greece" (1914)

"Going Back Home from Greece"

The chapter begins with a stance from the "cultural anthem" (Iacovou 2008a, 279) of those Greeks whose homelands were, and in the case of Cyprus still are, on the frontiers of the eastern Mediterranean. Of them all, the living Hellenism of Cyprus presents a stubborn historical continuity, which dates back to the penultimate century of the second millennium BC. "Kavafis encapsulates the diachronic identity of this Eastern Mediterranean frontier Hellenism in 'Going back home from Greece,' a poem written in 1914 that no Greek historian/archaeologist can afford to disregard" (Iacovou 2008a, 278). This view is endorsed by Arnaldo Momigliano's emphasis on "the importance of historians understanding both ancient and modern contexts in order to obtain an effective appreciation of any piece of historical scholarship" (Moore and Macgregor Morris 2008, 4).

Since "the Greeks … were ever in process of becoming" (Myres 1930, 538), knowledge of the ancient literary corpus should not be considered sufficient for a Greek historian. Greek is a living culture in perpetual development; it is expressed in the same language from at least as early as the late second millennium BC, and in this language it continues to produce classics, hardly less relevant to the historian than the epics of Homer or

---

A Companion to Greeks Across the Ancient World, First Edition. Edited by Franco De Angelis.
© 2020 John Wiley & Sons, Inc. Published 2020 by John Wiley & Sons, Inc.

Herodotus's *Histories*. The authors of these classics are not always from Athens or Greece "proper"; they are, like Kavafys (cf. Savidis 1992), children of the Greek *diaspora* or, like the Nobel Laureate George Seferis (cf. Beaton 2003), refugees displaced from the constantly embattled, and in the first half of the twentieth century dramatically shrunken, frontier territories of a Greek-speaking universe, who were forced to seek refuge in the state of modern Greece.

Greekness: A Shared Language

The regions that are today within the state boundaries of the Hellenic Republic did not represent in antiquity, or in later periods, the established cultural or political center of the Greek universe. Greekness was not a privilege to be granted, like honorary citizenship, by whichever city-state or region had a cultural or political predominance at the time. Communities that have been identified as Greek had one common denominator: their language. It is primarily this shared language – one of "the central pillars of ancient Greek identity" (Sherratt 2003, 231–232) – that defines Greekness. Almost everything else is shaped by immutable regional factors: the landscape and its natural resources. Neither mortuary nor cultic traditions or sacred space were the same in the hundreds of communities spread across the ancient world, whose language was Greek. Hence, there is no distinct material package by which we can trace the movements of Greek-speaking populations across the ancient world.

Immutable Properties

Cyprus, the easternmost of the Mediterranean islands, has an area of 9251 km^2 (Map 12.1). Despite its proximity to southern Anatolia (80 km from the tip of the Karpasia peninsula) and the Levant (175 km from Salamis to the Syrian coast), the island "cannot be treated as simply a provincial appendage" (Peltenburg 2013, 4): since early prehistory, it fostered independent cultures quite distinct from those of the Near East. The geological "heart" of the island is the igneous zone of the Troodos massif, which covers a third of the island's total area and is richly forested, especially with pine. All the rivers flow from the Troodos; rainwater cannot penetrate the pillow lavas, which are rich in copper ore. Substantial plains are formed between the Troodos and the limestone formation of the narrow Kyrenia or Pentadaktylos range to the north; they are the central lowlands, which extend from the bay of Salamis to the east to the bay of Morphou to the west (Peltenburg 2013, 6).

Cyprus is hostage to a semi-arid climate zone. "On account of its position ... Cyprus receives fewer lows and the air masses are not prodigious in their rainfall potentialities" (Christodoulou 1959, 19). Consequently, "[t]he most serious problem in land use in Cyprus and the most fundamental in the economy of Cyprus is the intractable problem of rainfall variability" (Christodoulou 1959, 28). Coupled with the fact that Cyprus's soil productivity is limited and regionally divergent, it is unlikely that the island's Late Bronze Age pre-Greek state formation model (Iacovou 2013a, 19–20) could have relied on a

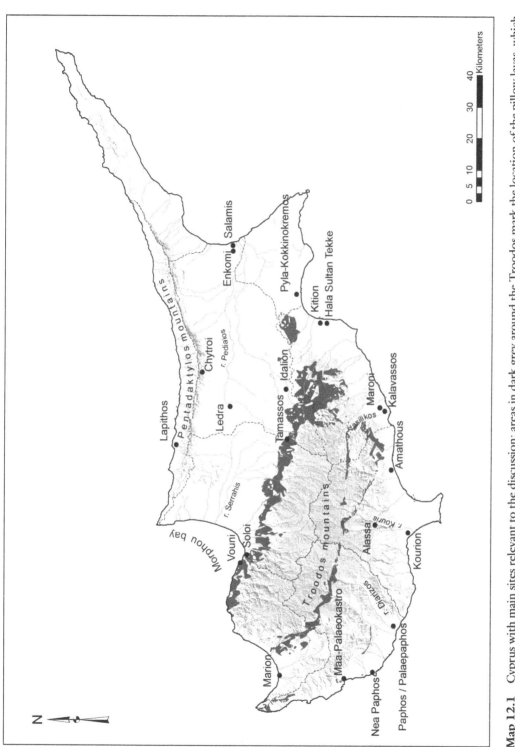

Map 12.1 Cyprus with main sites relevant to the discussion; areas in dark grey around the Troodos mark the location of the pillow lavas, which contain rich copper deposits. Source: Digital geological data from the Cyprus Geological Survey. Map drafted by Athos Agapiou for the Palaepaphos Urban Landscape Project. © PULP.

regular annual bulk export of staples. Cyprus is not Sicily when it comes to grain, and it is not Crete as regards olive oil. No colonial enterprise took place in Cyprus in the name of occupying agriculturally rich territories from where surpluses could be produced (Iacovou 2012, 211). But the island's name did become synonymous in Roman times with good quality copper (cf. Kassianidou 2013, 36).

Cyprus had a literate pre-Greek population in the Late Bronze Age (cf. Steele 2019, 11). Yet, inscriptions issued by Cypriot *basileis* since the Archaic period suggest that the majority of *polis*-states (Iacovou 2013a, 15–16) used Greek as their official language. Textual evidence, therefore, and not any other type of material evidence, such as monumental sacred landmarks (e.g., Greek-style temples in Sicily), discloses the establishment of people who spoke Greek on Cyprus, and also the growth of *polis*-states (Hatzopoulos 2014), whose political authorities used Greek as their official language. The former event, which we define as migration (Iacovou 2014), did not necessarily have to develop into the latter, that is, state formation. Human migrations can remain undocumented; as far as history is concerned, they can be as invisible as if they had never taken place. In the absence of records in the Greek language, a Greek migration to Philistia at the end of the Late Bronze Age remains a claim that lacks historicity (cf. Iacovou 2013b, 613, 617–618). On Cyprus, on the other hand, "the migration acquired a linguistically and epigraphically supported physical presence" (Iacovou 2008b, 627). Greek persisted irrespective of the termination of the city-state system. The political unification of Cyprus by the Ptolemies in the third century BC silenced the other languages (Eteocypriot and Phoenician) that were in use during the first millennium BC. Since then, Greek has been the language in which the people of Cyprus express their rich intangible traditions; it has become one with the islanders' identity.

Cyprus in the Late Bronze Age

That which stands out and encapsulates the essence of the bond that was forged between Cyprus and the Greek language is the manner by which the Greeks make their presence on the island known to us. They adopted the local Late Cypriot (LC) script, the Cypro-Minoan, which preserves the unknown and indecipherable language(s) of Bronze Age Cyprus (Olivier 2007; Steele 2019, 95). The windows that this gesture opens provide impressive visibility to the protohistory of Cyprus. The "marriage" between the local script (Cypro-Minoan) and the immigrant language (Greek) was consummated from as early as the tenth century BC, to judge from the context of the earliest known inscribed item, the *obelos* (spit) of Opheltas, found in a tomb at Palaepaphos (Karageorghis 1983, 60–61, plate 88). This inscription provides the missing link, which justifies "[t]he process of adaptation of the earlier script to the writing of Greek" (Morpurgo-Davies and Olivier 2012, 112). Morpurgo-Davies adds: "The simplest hypothesis is that [..] a Greek speaker used the Cypro-Minoan script to write down a name (his name?) in the genitive using the forms of his dialect." The name is attested in Linear B and alphabetic Greek; the dialect is the Arcado-Cypriot, "a descendant of a dialect very close to the Mycenaean written in Linear B, which also counts as the ancestor of Arcadian" (Morpurgo-Davies and Olivier 2012, 113). *Obeloi* were introduced in the material culture in the eleventh century and are considered a Cypriot invention (Coldstream 1977, 146). In the Archaic period, they accompanied warrior burials, often together with a pair of fire-dogs, and were also found in built tombs (Matthäus 2007). Although they occur in fractions or multiples of six (Iacovou 2013c, 140), the fact that they are not made of pure metals suggests that they were not exchange units for copper (Charalambous et al. 2014, 212–213). However, they convey high status in the context of the Early Iron Age, and mark the transition to a new social landscape, and a new system of values, which had abandoned the oxhide ingot, now probably too heavy a unit of pure copper to continue to be traded after the collapse of the palace-based organizations (about 28 kg: Knapp 2008, 310).

The late thirteenth century BC experienced the collapse of the economic system of the age of internationalism, which generated unrest and population movements. We assume that the main impact of the move of Greek-speaking populations to Cyprus took place in the post-palatial Mycenaean era. But why would people in the course of a generalized crisis choose to seek their fortunes on the easternmost Mediterranean island? Cyprus/*Alashiya* was a significant commercial partner of the dying system and the most important supplier of raw copper in the Mediterranean (cf. Knapp 1996; Muhly 2009, 31–33). *Alashiya* was a decentralized polity (Peltenburg 2012, 14); it did not have a central state organization to lose. Its writing system survived long enough for the Greek immigrants to experience because it was not guarded by palace or temple scribes (cf. Snodgrass 1994).

In the absence of a centrally controlled economy, the Late Cypriot polities responded in vastly different ways to the crisis. Some collapsed causing the depletion of their economic territories; these were mainly (from east to west) the settlement systems of the Maroni, the Vasilikos, and the Kouris river valleys on the south (Iacovou 2012, 216). The closure of major urban centers, such as Kalavasos-*Ayios Dhimitrios*, Alassa-*Paliotaverna*, and *Pano Mandilaris*, which were thoroughly deserted (South-Todd 2002), suggests that the residents of the affected regions were on the move. The polities which did survive (e.g., Enkomi and Hala Sultan Tekke), and even profited from the crisis (e.g., Kition and Palaepaphos), were all major coastal emporia, where material evidence suggests that the infrastructure for mining, processing, and distribution of metals carried on in the twelfth century.

The enhanced role of port authorities in the trading pattern of this critical period becomes all the more evident if we follow the fate of Hala Sultan Tekke and Enkomi. The leading polity of the island's southeastern region since the beginning of the Late Bronze Age, Hala Sultan Tekke was abandoned when its port basin silted up: by 1000 BC its anchorage had become the Larnaca salt lake (Gifford 1978; Devillers, Brown, and Morhange 2015). Similarly, when the original anchorage of Enkomi-Old Salamis (Yon 1980, 79) turned into a lagoon (Devillers 2008), the settlement moved closer to the coast. This resulted in the foundation of (New) Salamis in the eleventh century BC. The abandonment of a 500-year-old urban metropolis in the name of relocating 2 km away from its original position underlines the spatial and visual proximity that authorities needed to have with their commercial port (Iacovou 2013a, 31). Moreover, the evidence from Enkomi, Kition, and Palaepaphos suggests that these authorities were associated with sanctuaries. Monumentality in ritual architecture occurs for the first time in relation to the sanctuaries of Kition and Palaepaphos (Webb 1999, 289). The material evidence from the Kition temples shows that the relationship between cult and maritime trade was "of at least equal importance to that between cult and metallurgy" (Webb 1999, 302).

Hence, in the twelfth century, when immigrants began infiltrating Cyprus's urban emporia, sanctuary and port functioned as an inseparable unit. It is not unlikely that the industrial intensification, which includes the production and export of the first carburized iron objects (Sherratt 1994), resulted from the availability of extra labor forces from within the island and economic migrants from overseas. The thirteenth-century precursors of the latter may have been craftsmen skilled in the arts of elite bronze work and ivory- and seal-carving, who were established in the LC IIC urban centers and introduced their clientele to Aegean-style iconographic traits and pictorial agendas (Georgiou 2012).

Immigrants experienced the island's politico-economic system and contributed to its long-term success. This, and the fact that the Greeks did not come as culturally superior colonists, should explain why the open-air *temenos* of Cyprus was never replaced with Greek-style temples in the first millennium BC. Constructed in the midst of a Mediterranean-wide crisis, with megalithic worked blocks, the *temenos* walls of Paphos and Kition served in the first millennium as the urban "cathedrals" of a Greek (at Paphos) and a Phoenician (at Kition) royal dynasty. The Greeks addressed the Goddess as *wanassa* and *theos* and, from the fourth century, as Aphrodite; the Phoenicians called her Astarte (Yon 2006, 106–107), but never did a distinctly Greek or Phoenician set of cults develop in Cyprus (Papantoniou 2012, 100).

The long-term survival of the script and the open-air sanctuary model, and their adoption by new linguistic groups in the first millennium BC, emphasizes their association with the economic system. The Greek immigrants' unwarranted early interest in the technology of writing (Steele 2019, 47–48) seems less curious when one is reminded that the Cypro-Minoan script first appeared in the sixteenth century BC in association with the copper industry: the earliest known Cypro-Minoan tablet comes from Enkomi's metallurgical complex (Peltenburg 1996, 26). Since "it was a common practice to inscribe both the oxhide ingots and the miniature ones" (Papasavvas 2009, 101–102) with Cypro-Minoan signs as late as the twelfth century, it should not come as a surprise that the Cypriot script and the Greek language signed and sealed their union on an *obelos*, a prestigious metal object made from the island's primary industrial product.

Early Iron Age

Before the Ptolemaic takeover, Iron Age Cyprus was home to three linguistic groups: Greek, Phoenician, and Eteocypriot (cf. Steele 2019, 128, 146). This multilingual demography does not have a material culture equivalent: like the cult system, the three languages did not match three distinct ethnic cultures. In order to account for the distribution of the three groups around the island, we should try to establish how each one became the official, or preponderant, language per political unit. During an era of human diasporas, as was the twelfth century, immigrants could have reached the island from east and west. Semitic people from the land of Canaan, whom scholars call Phoenicians, would have been attracted to Cyprus as early as the Greek people, and for the same reason: the island's huge potential in the metals' trade. But the notion that people from overseas overran Cyprus and were established in a perfect mix with the locals all over the island is misleading: economic migrants leaving behind collapsed economies and destruction horizons – of which plentiful evidence exists in the Aegean and on the Syro-Palestinian coast (cf. Bell 2012, 186) – would not have gone to look for new opportunities in the depleted regions of Cyprus. They would have targeted the active emporia on the southern and eastern coasts, where they also knew better than to expect that they would encounter an inferior local stock.

The distinct politico-linguistic identities, which the polities of Kition, Amathous, Kourion, and Paphos on the southern coast had developed in the Archaic and Classical periods, were the result of events and processes initiated no later than the critical years of the twelfth century. The presence of Greeks speaking a form of dialect that continued in the first millennium and the continuity of literacy in the Cypriot script from the second to the first millennium (Morpurgo-Davies and Olivier 2012, 113), which is strongly evident at Paphos and Kourion, is absent from Kition. Here the Cypriot script all but disappears after the Late Bronze Age. For a period of five centuries, from the ninth to the end of the fourth century, the epigraphic material is in the Phoenician alphabet (about 150 inscriptions as opposed to a dozen in the syllabary: Yon 2004, 159, 337). Apparently, the people established in the territory of Kition had no need of the local script: the Cypro-Minoan was replaced by an imported alphabetic scribal tool that served an imported language.

Between Kition and Kourion lies Amathous, the polity of the Eteocypriot linguistic group. Founded from scratch in the eleventh century BC, this new coastal emporium transformed the settlement pattern in the Vasilikos and Maroni Valleys "out of all recognition" (South-Todd 2002, 68). The revival of the economy of this vast region was evidently affected by a regrouping of the autochthonous populations (Iacovou 2012, 220). The Amathousians and their royal dynasties wrote the indecipherable Eteocypriot language in the Cypriot syllabary until the end of the fourth century BC (Satraki 2012, 389, nos. 23–26). Eteocypriot is a modern term used by linguists to differentiate between the readable (Greek) and the unreadable (Eteocypriot) syllabic inscriptions of Cyprus. Although there is as yet no confirmed association with the prehistoric Cypriot language(s), it is justifiably believed to represent a language spoken by indigenous people. The term was created by analogy to the ancient term Eteocretan, which is used for the non-Greek language that survived in a few Iron Age Cretan cities; but Eteocretan inscriptions were written in the Greek alphabet (Whitley 1998, 38). The territory of Amathous is believed to have reached all the way to the east side of the Kouris River (Fourrier 2007, 117). West of the river, the predominant language in the polity of Kourion was Greek written in the Paphian syllabary (Mitford 1971; Satraki 2012, 401).

The long-term, and side-by-side, survival of three languages on an island where one should have silenced the others, suggests that within a region-bound politico-economic system, linguistic identities were also region-bound (Iacovou 2008b, 640), and contained within political boundaries. Phoenician and Eteocypriot were majority languages as well as state languages only within their micro-regions. Both of them disappeared from the written record of the island in the third century, shortly after Ptolemy Lagos had abolished the Cypriot states (Iacovou 2014, 108).

Archaic and Classical Cyprus

"The fifth-century Greek perception of the beginning of history gave the *nostoi* a special role. History began with the returns from Troy" (Malkin 1998, 3). Teucer and Agapenor, the legendary founders of Salamis and Paphos respectively, were *nostoi* heroes, and Malkin (1998, 210) claims that at least by the eighth century the origins of some Greek cities in Asia Minor and Cyprus had begun to be explained in terms of the *nostoi*. The earliest epigraphical evidence concerning non-legendary Greek leaders in Cyprus belongs to this chronological milieu. In the seventh century, two of Opheltas's Greek-speaking kin from Paphos inscribed precious objects, a silver bowl and a pair of golden arm-bracelets (Mitford 1971, 373–376; 7–11; Satraki 2012, 391), with their name and official title: Akestor and Eteandros identified themselves as *basileis* of Paphos. Two seventh-century silver bowls (albeit fragmentary) from the "Kourion treasure" also bear syllabic inscriptions by *basileis* (Satraki 2012, 416). A total of 22 of these precious vessels are known from Archaic Cyprus (Markoe 1985; Karageorghis 2000, 180 nos. 297–307), and despite the fact that they are described as "Cypro-Phoenician," none bears a Phoenician inscription (Satraki 2013, 127). Consequently, in the seventh century, the first eponymous state rulers of the island are introduced in Greek syllabic inscriptions on precious metal objects; their names are Greek and their office is defined by the term *basileus*. The history of this term charts the route of the migration from the Aegean to Cyprus (Iacovou 2014, 109). The study of the Linear B tablets has shown that Mycenaean officials known as *qa-si-re-we* were provincial dignitaries who had an intimate and structured relation with metals; they were, for example, responsible for the palaces' metal stores and for the allocation of bronze to metal workers (Weingarten 1997, 531). When the palace and its *wanax* (see below) were removed, these local administrators became "the chief power figures in the regional socio-political systems that developed in post-palatial Greece" (Palaima 1995, 124–125). The term *basileus* was evidently introduced to Cyprus, and specifically to Paphos, by Greek migrants but, at that time, the term would have signified a less exalted office.

The institutional role of the *basileus* in the Cypriot *polis*-states proves that the office was politically upgraded after the migration (Iacovou 2006): from the seventh century to the end of the fourth, all Greek monarchs in Cyprus were identified by this one Mycenaean term, written *pa-si-le-wo-se* in the syllabic inscriptions and often *pa-* for short on their coin issues. Numismatic economy was introduced in the second half of the sixth century, with the silver coins of Salamis and Paphos, and by the end of the century with those of Idalion (Destrooper-Georghiades 1993, 88–89, no. 7; 2002; Satraki 2012, 285–287) (Figures 12.1 and 12.2). The legends on them are exclusively syllabic. Iron Age Cypriot literacy in its earliest direct association with state economy is expressed in the syllabary (Iacovou 2013c, 146). In the fourth century, following the official introduction of the Greek alphabet by Evagoras of Salamis, the term *basileus* began to be inscribed alphabetically (Masson, 1983, 79, 218 no. 212), though almost never at the exclusion of the syllabary, which since the seventh century had become the "signature" of the Cypriot *basileis* (Iacovou 2013c) (Figure 12.3). The term *wanax*, on the other hand, the head of a Mycenaean palatial state in Linear B, was reserved in Cyprus for the sons and brothers of a *basileus*, and *wanassa* for the sister or wife (Satraki 2013, 135).

Figure 12.1 Salamis. Silver siglos (10.59 g), Evelthon (ca. 530/520 BC). Obverse with reclining Ram; syllabic inscription with the king's name. Source: BCCF 2000-01-01. Courtesy Bank of Cyprus Cultural Foundation.

Figure 12.2 Idalion. 1/3 of silver siglos (3.51 g), Stasikypros (ca. 460–450 BC). Obverse with Sphinx seated to left; syllabic inscription with the king's name in shorthand. Source: BCCF 1994-01-01. Courtesy Bank of Cyprus Cultural Foundation.

Figure 12.3 Paphos. Cypro-syllabic inscription of the royal family of Onasicharis, king of Paphos, son of King Stasis of Paphos (late sixth century BC). 98 cm. Source: Courtesy Department of Antiquities, Republic of Cyprus.

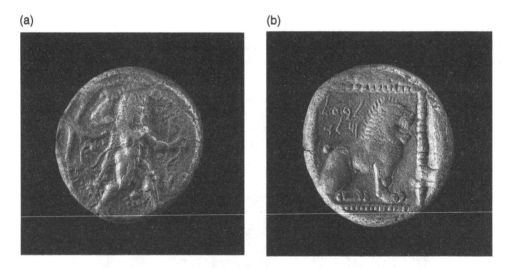

Figure 12.4 Kition. Silver siglos (10.70 g), Baalmilk I (ca. 479–449 BC). (a) Obverse with Herakles striding and Phoenician inscription right; (b) reverse with seated lion and Phoenician inscription. Source: BCCF 1987-02-01. Courtesy Bank of Cyprus Cultural Foundation.

Despite the wide, but thin, distribution of the Phoenician alphabet around the island (Lipinski 2004, 42–46), the Phoenician term for king (*mlk*) is not recorded before the fifth century. Most of the pre-Classical Phoenician inscriptions of Cyprus (Masson and Sznycer 1972) occur on earthen pots, including the much-cited pilgrim inscription on an imported Red Slip bowl from the sanctuary of Kition (Yon 2004, 169). Thus, the silver coins of Baalmilk I (Figure 12.4), founder of the Kitian dynasty (ca. 479–450), carry the first declaration of Phoenician kingship (Satraki 2012, 298). The terms *mlk* and *adn* (i.e., Adonis, prince, the equivalent of the *wanax*) are confined to fifth- and fourth-century inscriptions from Kition and Idalion (the latter was conquered by Kition around the middle of the fifth century). Tamassos also came under the rule of Kition for about three decades in the fourth century, during the reign of the last king, Pumayaton (Satraki 2012, 328–329).

What of the term *sharru*, which, in the Near Eastern world, "was used for rulers of many entities, ranging from large territorial states to towns, fortified, ritual and administrative centres" (Peltenburg 2012, 9)? In Cyprus it occurs once on the stele of Sargon II: the only royal Assyrian monument that has ever been found west of the continent. Set up at Kition (Yon 2004, 345), it declared that "seven sharru of the land of Ia', a district if Iadnana, whose distant abodes are situated a seven days' journey in the sea of the setting sun," had offered their submission to Sargon II (722–705). Under Sargon II the Assyrian Empire had acquired its greatest expansion. When the Cypriot leaders saw that the Assyrians were in control of the Levantine trading ports, they hastened to submit voluntarily out of "fear of being excluded from the Assyrian economic sphere" (Stylianou 1989, 390). Thus, Cyprus appears anew in the Near Eastern records, not as *Alashiya* (cf. Amadasi Guzzo and Zamora 2018), but as "Ia," an island (according to Lipinski 1991, 64) divided into many political units (for the etymology of Iadnana, Muhly 2009). The Assyrians never crossed the sea to occupy Cyprus. The treaty, which rendered the Cypriot polities client kingdoms, was negotiated in 707 BC (Saporetti 1976, 83–88) by a group of Cypriot representatives, whom the Assyrians addressed as *sharru*. It was the title also borne by their own emperors but not the title chosen by Akestor and Eteandros, who, shortly afterwards, called themselves *basileis*.

A generation later (673/672 BC), Esarhaddon (680–669) acknowledged the receipt of gifts from the 10 *sharru* of *Iatnana* for the rebuilding of his palace at Nineveh. In this instance, the royal scribes recorded the island's 10 polities and the ruler of each one by name (cf. Satraki 2013, 126): Akestor of Edial (Idalion), Pylagoras (or Phylagoras) of Kitrusi (Chytroi), Kisu of Sillua (Salamis), Eteandros of Pappa (Paphos), Eresu (Aratos?) of Sillu (Soloi), Damasos of Kuri (Kourion), Admesu (Admitos?) of Tamesu (Tamassos), Damusi of Qartihadasti, Onasagoras of Lidir (Ledra), and Bususu of Nouria. Unique in the textual history of Cyprus, the kings' list, reveals the two main processes that were at work in the course of the Early Iron Age: (i) by the first quarter of the seventh century more than half of the 10 Cypriot polities had been claimed by rulers that were Greek, or had become Greek; (ii) while in the twelfth and eleventh centuries the territorial restructuring appeared to be centered upon coastal polities, in the next three centuries at least four inland polities had been founded. All four were close to copper ore bodies and appear to have had Greek-named rulers: Akestor of Idalion, Pylagoras/Phylagoras of Chytroi, Admitos(?) of Tamassos, and Onasagoras of Ledra. Of the remaining six toponyms on the list, four – Salamis, Paphos, Soloi, and Kourion – are coastal capitals, well attested in the textual records, and always in association with Greek *basileis*. For Qartihadasti and Nouria, different propositions have been made to associate them with one of the four Cypriot polities, which are missing from Esarhaddon's list, that is, Kition, Amathous, Marion, and Lapithos (Baurain 1981; Hermary 1987; Lipinski 2004, 74; Masson 1985, 1992), but no consensus has been reached. It is more important to recognize that neither Qartihadasti nor Nouria had been adopted as toponyms by any of the island's linguistic groups. Despite the political supremacy that Greek had gained, the island's political geography remained fluid: "there were hardly ever long periods of respite from the readjustment of economic regions, in the course of which sites gained and lost their primary status" (Iacovou 2013a, 37). At the end of the fourth century, when Ptolemy proceeded to abolish the segregated state system, the Cypriot polities were no longer 10 but seven (Iacovou 2013a, 27): Salamis, Paphos, Soloi, Marion, Amathous, Kition, and Lapithos were all managed from coastal capitals, and all but Kition had Greek-named *basileis*; even the Amathousian ruler was named Androkles and his sons Orestheus and Andragoras (Hellmann and Hermary 1980: 259–266; Masson and Hermary 1982).

With the reappearance of Eastern empires on the Mediterranean scene, territorial fragmentation was put into reverse gear and, in the long run, land-locked polities were gradually absorbed by, or appended to, coastal polities (Iacovou 2018, 27–28). The latter were in charge of harbor facilities and in possession of commercial fleets and men of war (Yon 2006, 48, figure 27, on the fourth-century ship yards of Kition). How did the island manage to sustain that many micro-states to the end of the fourth century BC? "The geography of the new cities of the Greeks and Phoenicians in the early first millennium," observe Horden and Purcell, "is clearly related to the distribution of sources of metal ores" (2000, 348). In the case of Cyprus, the factor that gave long-term success to the decentralized polity system is the distribution of the copper ores around the Troodos mountains, "one of the five richest areas in copper deposits in the world per unit of surface area" (Constantinou 2010, 23). The ore bodies, inexhaustible to this day, ring the mountains and are relatively close to the surface and to the source of fuel. This particular copper geography made it possible for a multitude of Cypriot polities to develop complex industrial economies. State formation did not require the island's economic and political unification, but it did require the establishment of authority over a geographically unified territory that incorporated ore bodies, land for the production of foodstuffs, and a gateway on the coast ("The tripartite model": Iacovou 2013a, 31–32).

Sacred legitimation was an integral characteristic of Cypriot kingship. The Cypriot *basileus* had undivided authority over the secular and the sacred landscape of his territorial state (cf. Hermary 2014): hence the Paphian kings' self-definition as *basileis* and priests of the goddess (Masson 1983, nos. 6–7, 16–17). The proliferation and enhancement of extra-urban sanctuaries, since the beginning of the seventh century BC, provides material expression concerning the protection of state boundaries, mining areas, and routes that brought ore and other resources to the coast (Fourrier 2002, 2007). Anna Satraki (2012, 361) has observed that *basileis* inscriptions, built tombs, and colossal statues, which were dedicated at "rural" sanctuaries, appear together at the beginning of the seventh century; they are constituent elements in the development of a royal ideology. Some of the most impressive statuary (e.g., the Ayios Photios stone sculpture in the Cesnola collection: Hermary and Mertens 2014) were dedicated at frontier sanctuaries in the eastern lowlands (Counts 2004), where the routes that brought metallic resources to Salamis's harbor were exposed to constant threat by neighboring polities (Satraki 2012, 354).

Secular palaces also began to be established in the Cypro-Archaic period. The evidence from the palatial complexes of Amathous, Vouni, and Idalion shows that, besides storage and industrial areas, they contained palace sanctuaries and administrative archives (Hadjicosti 1997; Petit 2002). The image of Hathor, the Egyptian goddess, who protects mines and miners (Papantoniou 2013, 174), was adopted in the Archaic period as a component of the royal iconography and received pride of place in the Cypriot palaces (Carbillet 2011; Satraki 2013, 134). The dependency of Cypriot kingship on the procurement of metallic wealth should explain why, in the end, the legendary Arcadian king

Agapenor lost his title as founder of the Paphian royal house to Kinyras: the Greek *basileis* of Paphos opted to become *Kinyradae* in order to claim descent from the proverbially wealthy (Plato, *Laws* 2.260), pre-Greek "copper king" of the island, who was also the beloved priest of the Cypriot goddess (Iacovou 2008b, 649).

In the Cypro-Archaic era the "manifestations of royal power in the visual record" (Satraki 2013, 123) had Eastern, and in particular Egyptian, prototypes. Curiously, however, not long after the Cypriots had pledged allegiance to the Persians (last quarter of the sixth century), the Cypriot royal model and its iconographic vocabulary underwent a process of Hellenization (Satraki 2013, 139; Papantoniou 2013, 174). The stylistic development of Archaic Cypriot sculpture, which begins with Egyptianizing and ends with Ionian "flavors" (Satraki 2013, 126, 132), and its distribution in East Greece (Hermary 2009) point to the trade relations that were built between the Ionian region and the Cypriot polities. The growing visibility of East Greek and Attic pottery in sanctuaries (Fourrier and Hermary 2006, 114) and palaces (e.g., Amathous and Vouni: Hermary 2013), and the inception of dedications to Panhellenic sanctuaries by Cypriots (e.g., Evelthon, the renowned sixth-century ruler of Salamis, offered a *thymiaterion* to Delphi: Herodotus 4.162; Pouilloux 1976) are suggestive of economic alliances, which led some of the Cypriot *basileis*, like Onesilos of Salamis and Aristokypros of Soloi, to join the Ionian Revolt. For a long time since the late eighth century, the Cypriot leaders had only one Near Eastern superpower with which to negotiate, and they did so with the adroitness of seasoned diplomats. Now, however, Cypriot statesmen opted to join a geopolitical league that did not have an empire at its head; it consisted of *poleis*-states that were soon to have Athens at the helm of a new economic sphere:

> the Ionian states – proactive in trade at an early date and long involved in close interaction with other major Aegean trading groups at home and abroad – became strongly aligned with Athenian political and military initiatives during and after the period of conflict with Persia, in the late sixth through fifth centuries. (Wallace 2010, 392)

The first time that a Persian military force had reason to land in Cyprus was in order to punish Evelthon's grandson and his Solian ally: Onesilos and Aristokypros lost the battle and their lives, but the Ionian/Athenian coalition won the day. In the long run, it also won Cyprus, despite the fact that in the battle of Salamis (in Greece), the impressive naval force of the Cypriot polities, altogether 150 warships, had to fight on the side of the Persians (Hdt. 7.90). It was after the failure of Onesilos's uprising that Kition acquired its Phoenician royal dynasty and initiated, without delay, military aggression against the most resilient of the inland capitals, Idalion. Assigned to the first half of the fifth century, the confrontation and its evident conclusion in favor of Kition are documented by Phoenician royal inscriptions: the successors of Baalmilk I all bear the title of kings of Kition and Idalion (Yon 2004). The takeover has also been confirmed by the recent discovery of a Phoenician economic archive within the palace of Idalion (Amadasi Guzzo 2017).

One of the dramatic episodes of the Idalion–Kition clash is vividly described on the Idalion tablet. Inscribed with the longest surviving Greek syllabic text, the bronze tablet preserves in its entirety a decree that was jointly issued by *basileus* Stasikypros and the *polis* of the Idaliots, and is dated to the year of the archonship of Philokypros (Masson

1983, no. 217). It provides a detailed account of the compensation received by a family of doctors who had treated the defenders of Idalion injured during the siege of the *polis* by the Medes and the Kitians. The Idalion tablet is by far the most important document on the development of political and civic institutions in a Cypriot *polis* at the end of the Archaic period (Hatzopoulos 2011; Hatzopoulos and Georgiadou 2013).

From the fifth century, "strong 'hellenising' processes in the Cypriot culture, were both politically supervised *and* culturally motivated" (Papantoniou 2011, 44). They are most apparent in the transformations of the religious iconography, as in the Hellenization of the Phoenician Melqart, who was dressed in the lion skin of the Greek Herakles, and in "the decline of Hathor and the emergence of Aphrodite" (Papantoniou 2013, 171, 174). The iconographic expressions of the indigenous Cypriot deity, with whom both Phoenician Astarte and Greek Aphrodite were associated (Budin 2003; Papantoniou 2012, 230), began to change when the local rulers reoriented their royal ideologies to relate to Greek prototypes. They even began to associate their lineage with Greek deities (e.g., Apollo and Zeus). The Greek gods prominently featured on Cypriot coinage in the fourth century are an eloquent pictorial statement of the reorientation process (Satraki 2013, 139; Papantoniou 2013, 171 with references).

Irrespective of Kition's territorial expansion within the island, the politico-economic alignment of the Cypriot polities with the Athenian league, and in particular with the economic-cultural sphere of Athens, reached a climax in the reign of Evagoras of Salamis who, besides being credited for the introduction of the Greek alphabet (attested on his coinage; Figure 12.5), was made honorary Athenian citizen in 410 and whose statue was erected in the Agora (Isocrates, *Evagoras*, 57). More than 500 years since the permanent establishment of Greek populations on the island, a Greek Cypriot *basileus* at the far end of the eastern Mediterranean, and still under Persian rule, was promoted in Athens, via the influential orator Isocrates, as the ideal Greek statesman who could have united the Hellenes. The fifth- and fourth-century cultural transformations observed in all the Cypriote *poleis* have been eloquently described as "'Hellenisation' before 'Hellenisation'" (Papantoniou 2011, 43). The adoption of Greek attitudes and Greek cultural prototypes by Kition occurred as it continued to be at war with its Salaminian neighbors. The funerary stelae of Classical Kition are stylistically Greek, but inscribed with Phoenician names (Yon 2004, 165, figure 18). Imported Cycladic marble was regularly employed for the stelae and the sarcophagi of Kition; some have an anthropomorphic lid, others are decorated with Greek iconographic themes and their roof-shaped lid imitates the architecture of a Greek temple (Yon 2006, 127; Georgiou 2009; Michaelides and Papantoniou 2018, 276). Greek influence extended to the language: Melkiathon (392–362), the greatest of the Kitian rulers, celebrated his victory against Evagoras and Salamis's Paphian allies with the dedication of a trophy on which the surviving Phoenician inscription uses the Greek word *tropaeon* written in the Semitic alphabet (Yon 2006, 60). The economic impetus behind the Hellenizing trends is also made evident when Kitian merchants sought from Athens, and were granted, a special right confirmed in 333 BC: to erect a temple to their goddess in Piraeus. Although in Kition the goddess is named Astarte, in Piraeus she is Aphrodite (Yon 2004, 132; Papantoniou 2013, 177).

Of all the Cypriot *poleis*, the first to make frequent use of the Greek alphabet was Eteocypriot Amathous. It has also been suggested that the Amathousian rulers promoted

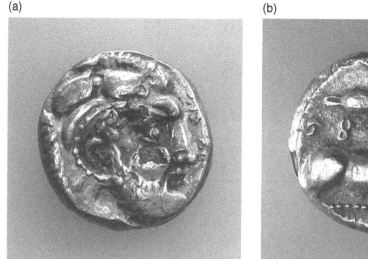 

Figure 12.5 Salamis. Silver-plated siglos (8.28 g.), Evagoras I (ca. 411–374 BC). (a) Obverse with bearded Herakles and syllabic inscription with king's name; (b) reverse with he-goat, syllabic inscription with royal title [pa] and alphabetic E, the initial of Evagoras. Source: BCCF 2000-10-02. Courtesy Bank of Cyprus Cultural Foundation.

the myth of their autochthonism to appeal to the Athenians, who also prided themselves on being autochthonous (Petit 1995). Two fourth-century dedications by the last king, Androkles, to the sanctuary of the Amathousian goddess on the summit of the citadel, were inscribed bilingually in syllabic Eteocypriot and alphabetic Greek. In both inscriptions the alphabetic text addresses the goddess as *Kypria*; in addition we also read (in one of the two) the first spelling of the name Aphrodite in the alphabet (Masson and Hermary 1982; Satraki 2012, 280 nos. 25–26). Papantoniou ingeniously termed this process "Hellenising the Cypriot Goddess" (2011). At about the same time, Nikokles, the last ruler of Paphos, dedicated sanctuaries to Hera and Artemis but, faithful to the antiquity of the royal syllabic formula, which identified him and his father Timarchos before him, as *basileus* and priest of the *wanassa*, had their names written in the syllabary (Satraki 2012, 232 nos. 10–12, 15–17). In Paphos, the region where the Greeks adopted and "Hellenized" the Cypriot script, the Greek alphabet was hardly ever used by the local *basileis* (except in digraphic inscriptions; Figure 12.6).

By 332 BC, exercising the same diplomatic shrewdness with which their predecessors had gone to offer gifts and allegiance to Sargon II in 707 BC, the *basileis* of Cyprus joined the rising star of Alexander in the waters of Tyre with 120 warships (Arrian, *Anabasis* 2.20). In this manner, they pledged allegiance to the first Hellenic empire-to-be. Whether the new empire was to have an eastern or a western continental center, the ulterior motive behind the timely moves of the Cypriot monarchs was the same: the preservation of their autonomous rule and the maintenance of their Mediterranean-wide trading base under the aegis of whichever empire ran the economic system. Access to metallic wealth and possession and maintenance of commercial fleets and men of war were the key assets through which the seven coastal polities had safeguarded their political autonomy to the

Figure 12.6 Paphos. Cypro-syllabic inscription of Nikokles, king of Paphos and priest of *wanassa*, and son of Timarchos, king of Paphos (last quarter of fourth century BC). 113 cm high × 37 cm wide. Source: Courtesy Department of Antiquities, Republic of Cyprus.

end of the fourth century BC. Even the easternmost capital of Salamis had one long leg planted in the copper ores, some 100 km away into the heart of the island (around Tamassos), and the other in the sea. The long-term success of this political economy is vividly encapsulated in the epigram in honor of Nikokreon, the last of the *Teukridae basileis* of Salamis. The epigram survives on the base of a lost statue of the Salaminian ruler erected by the Argives (after 331 BC), who wished to thank him for having sent to Argos raw copper to be cast into prizes for the young athletes in the games of Hera (Chavane and Yon 1978, 147, 309; Christodoulou 2009).

Hellenistic Cyprus

Granted that the development of naval power was a pressing concern for the early Ptolemies, Cyprus's shipbuilding and sailing expertise and copper reserves were among the principle assets for which Ptolemy fought bitterly against Antigonos to acquire Cyprus.

Ptolemy succeeded in annexing Cyprus in 294 BC, and it stayed in Ptolemaic hands until it became a Roman province in 58 BC. Copper and the sea remained the prevalent ingredients of the politico-economic model during the Ptolemaic period ("Cyprus' permanent values": Gordon 2012, 30–39). That the copper trade became an imperial monopoly is made evident by two inscriptions dedicated at the sanctuary of Palaepaphos: one honors Potamon as officer in charge of the metals (Mitford 1961, 39 no. 107; Nicolaou 1971, 26), and the other underlines the high esteem in which shipbuilders were held: apparently, Ptolemy II dedicated a statue to the naval architect Pyrgoteles, who had built him a 30-oared and a 20-oared warship (Mitford 1961, 9 no. 17; Nicolaou 1971, 20). As late as the fourth century AD, when Ammianus Marcellinus was composing his *History* (14.8.4), it was regarded a wonder that Cyprus could build ships entirely from its own island resources, a fact that also underlines the significance of the local timber sources.

The Ptolemies established a Cyprus-wide administration, which was entirely in the hands of foreign, though Greek-speaking, rulers. The termination of Cyprus's indigenous political geography consisted of a series of dramatic episodes that were directed against the living representatives of the segmented polity system. The extermination of the local kings marked the end of the Cypriot *polis* as political center of a territorial state. Hence, the first time that boundaries were lifted between politico-economic territories was in the name of the establishment of a colonial regime that put an end to the *polis*-states of the island, though not to the *polis* as a civic center. It is ironic that democratic institutions, such as the *boule* and the *demos*, acquire prominence in the epigraphical sources only after the Cypriot *poleis* had lost their political autonomy (Iacovou 2014, 103–104). Emblematic urban landscape markers, such as the agora and the gymnasium – "the Hellenistic civic institution *par excellence*" (Gordon 2012, 105) – with which we tend to associate citizen life in the Hellenistic *polis* were constructed in the urban centers of Cyprus after the first *per force* colonization of the island by an imperial system that projected its military and political superiority over the island's population.

Cyprus was governed (at least from the end of the third century) by a governor-general, the *strategos*, who was appointed by the Ptolemaic king in Alexandria (cf. Michaelides and Papantoniou 2018, 268). Before long, the *strategos* also assumed the title of *archiereus* ("high priest") and later that of *nauarchos* ("naval commander"). This powerful colonial administrator governed the island, which was the all-important naval base and buffer zone of the Ptolemaic Kingdom (Papantoniou 2013, 182), with the iron grip of a military commander. Although the Cypriots were denied access to military offices, considerable numbers of mercenaries were established and given land in Cyprus (Bagnall 1976, 57), and garrisons were positioned in the urban centers. Still, there is no record of rebellious acts on behalf of the local population. Other than the ruthless extermination of the local kings, with which Ptolemaic rule was initiated, the sociocultural traditions of the Cypriots were not actively suppressed (Hatzopoulos 2009). The Ptolemies saw no need to disturb civic structures related to the *poleis*, which apparently were able to maintain a degree of autonomy, especially in relation to the control of their countryside (Bagnall 1976, 79).

"[T]he Ptolemies mollified those who still had political aspirations by allowing them to participate in civic politics" (Gordon 2012, 104). Thus, Ptolemaic rule succeeded in legitimizing its power through the integration of Cypriot elites in innocuous civic (e.g., gymnasiarchs) as well as religious (e.g., *Kinyrades* priests) positions. In reality, as high priest, the Ptolemaic *strategos*, who was responsible for collecting revenues from the sanctuaries, oversaw all religious practices on the island, but it was "a well-organized practice aimed at limiting resistance" (Papantoniou 2013, 190). Thus, under the political aegis of Ptolemaic colonization, "'Hellenistic' 'Hellenisation'" (Papantoniou 2011, 36) had a long-term impact upon Cypriot religion and, also, it decisively transformed the island's linguistic landscape.

When the territorial boundaries between the Cypriot polities were lifted and the island became a political unity, the Eteocypriot syllabary and the Phoenician alphabet died out quite rapidly. In Kition, where to the end of the fourth century the epigraphic record was in the Phoenician alphabet, soon after the Ptolemaic takeover, Phoenician was replaced by alphabetic Greek (Yon 2004, 161). We know that Greek mercenaries were established in the area but, more importantly, Kition, despite its becoming a secondary city (with a gymnasium), was one of the three *poleis* – along with Salamis and Nea Paphos – where Ptolemaic coins were minted. This could help explain the rapid withdrawal of the Phoenician script, though onomastics confirm the continued presence of Semites.

The Greek syllabary, though no longer sustained by a political authority, survived beyond the third century, at least in the region of Paphos, where it is attested as late as the first century BC on clay sealings in the Roman archive of Nea Paphos (Michaelidou-Nicolaou 1993). When the Greek alphabet was established as the official scribal tool of the Ptolemaic administration, Greek was made the language of power and authority across the island for the first time. This, however, was the Greek *koine* and, though it "killed" Phoenician and Eteocypriot, it did not eliminate the ancient Greek dialect of the Cypriots, which survived as an oral language long after its exclusive scribal system, the syllabary, had become obsolete. Thus, Cyprus became monolingual in the Ptolemaic period but bi-dialectal, as it is to this day. Today, the modern versions of common Greek and the Cypriot dialect are inseparably linked to the cultural identity of the Cypriot Greeks.

The introduction of the Ptolemaic ruler cult, which in Cyprus was promoted by Ptolemy II Philadelphos (284–246) in the context of an empire-wide program that led to the deification of his sister Arsinoe, generated a whole range of assimilating processes, in which urban and rural sanctuaries, elites and non-elites were involved. In Cyprus, where at least three port cities were named Arsinoe, the worship of Arsinoe II was linked to that of the Cypriot Aphrodite (Anastassiades 1998), who as *Euploia* incorporated attributes related to the protection of the Ptolemaic navy. The *temenos* of *Kypris* at Palaepaphos, which was chosen as the center for the ruler cult, lost the regional identity it had since the Late Bronze Age (as the politico-religious center of the polity of Paphos) and became the island's first pan-Cypriot sanctuary (cf. Iacovou 2019). Yet, the open-air sanctuary type and the aniconic cult image of the goddess (the baetyl) were respected. Though the construction of temples in the Ptolemaic period is recorded in inscriptions and is confirmed by a number of surviving examples (e.g., the temple of Zeus at Salamis from the end of the second century), neither the Ptolemies, nor the Romans later, constructed a Greek-style temple in Palaepaphos.

The ruler cult was incorporated "voluntarily" within Cypriot traditional sanctuaries, which were nowhere close to the coast (e.g., the *Arsinoeion* at Idalion: Anastassiades 1998, 2003), but it was also introduced in sanctuaries founded *ex novo* in the Ptolemaic period (e.g., Soloi-*Cholades*) according to the Cypriot open-air type (Anastassiades 2009, 145).

With the introduction of the cults of Greco-Egyptian deities, an already complex sacred landscape developed an intimidating syncretistic character. Religion, however, became a key element in the construction of the Cypro-Greek identity in the context of Ptolemaic rule, and this is directly related to the loss of political autonomy. A response to what it was to be Greek in Cyprus from the third century BC to AD 1960 (the island did not regain independence after the Ptolemaic takeover, but persevered under foreign overlords and colonial empires for more than two millennia) is encapsulated by Mario Vitti in a book where he records memories from growing up in Constantinople in the twentieth century. Religion, Vitti observes (2013, 108), was of seminal significance for the minorities living there, because without political identity and without the right to enter public offices, since all power was exclusively in the hands of the Turks, religion was the only area open to them where they could develop a social identity. Similarly, in the colonial environment of Hellenistic Cyprus, the Greek-speaking autochthonous people employed religion and priesthood (Papantoniou 2013, 190) in connection with their steadily growing participation in civic offices – for example, the prestigious "quasi-political" institution of the *Koinon Kyprion* (Gordon 2012, 106) – as the main vehicles through which they could define their cultural identity. After adopting Christianity (in the Roman period) it was again through religion that they defined their Cypriot Greekness and defended their frontier position within the Greek *oikoumene*.

REFERENCES

Amadasi Guzzo, M.G. 2017. "The Idalion Archive 2. The Phoenician inscriptions." In Αρχαία Κύπρος. Πρόσφατες εξελίξεις στην αρχαιολογία της ανατολικής Μεσογείου, edited by Nikos Papademetriou and Maria Toli, 275–284. Athens: Museum of Cycladic Art.

Amadasi Guzzo, M.G., and J.A. Zamora. 2018. "The Phoenician name of Cyprus: New Evidence from Early Hellenistic Times." *Journal of Semitic Studies*, 63: 77–97.

Anastassiades, Aristodemos. 1998. "*Arsinoes Philadelphou [Greek]. Aspects of a Specific Cult in Cyprus.*" *Report of the Department of Antiquities*, Cyprus: 129–140.

Anastassiades, Aristodemos. 2003. "Egypt in Cyprus: The Ptolemaic Ruler Cult." *Kypriakai Spoudai*, 64–65: 41–52.

Anastassiades, Aristodemos. 2009. "Fusion and Diffusion. Isiac Cults in Hellenistic and Roman Cyprus." In *Egypt and Cyprus in Antiquity*, edited by Demetrios Michaelides, Vasiliki Kasianidou, and Robert Merrillees, 144–150. Oxford: Oxbow.

Bagnall, Roger S. 1976. *The Administration of the Ptolemaic Possessions Outside Egypt*. Leiden: Brill.

Baurain, Claude. 1981. "Un autre nom pour Amathonte de Chypre?" *Bulletin de correspondance hellénique*, 105: 361–372.

Beaton, Roderick. 2003. *George Seferi: Waiting for the Angel. A Biography*. New Haven: Yale University Press.

Bell, Carol. 2012. "The Merchants of Ugarit: Oligarchs of the Late Bronze Age Trade in Metals?" In *Eastern Mediterranean Metallurgy and Metalwork in the Second Millennium BC*, edited by Vasiliki Kassianidou and George Papasavvas, 180–187. Oxford: Oxbow.

Budin, Stephanie L. 2003. *The Origin of Aphrodite*. Bethesda: CDL Press.
Carbillet, Aurelie. 2011. *La figure hathorique à Chypre (IIe–Ier mill. av. J.-C.)*. Münster: Ugarit-Verlag.
Charalambous, Andreas, Vasiliki Kassianidou, and George Papasavvas. 2014. "A Compositional Study of Cypriot Bronzes Dating to the Early Iron Age Using pPortable X-ray Fluorescence Spectrometry (pXRF)." *Journal of Archaeological Science*, 46: 205–216.
Chavane, Marie-José, and Marguerite Yon. 1978. *Testimonia Salaminia 1. Salamine de Chypre X*. Paris: de Boccard.
Christodoulou, Demetrios. 1959. *The Evolution of the Rural Land Use Pattern in Cyprus*. London: Geographical.
Christodoulou, Panos. 2009. "Nicokréon: le dernier roi de Salamine de Chypre. Discours idéologique et pouvoir politique." *Cahier du centre d'études chypriotes*, 39: 235–258.
Coldstream J. Nicolas. 1977. *Geometric Greece*. New York: St Martin's Press.
Constantinou George. 2010. "The Birth of an Island." In *Cyprus: Crossroads of Civilizations*, edited by Sophocles Hadjisavvas, 21–27. Nicosia: The Government of the Republic of Cyprus.
Counts, Derek. 2004. "Art and Religion in the Cypriote Mesaoria: The View from Athienou-*Malloura*." *Cahier du centre d'études chypriotes*, 34: 173–190.
Destrooper-Georghiades, Anne. 1993. "Continuités et ruptures dans le monnayage chypriote à l'époque achéménide." *Transeuphratène*, 6: 87–101.
Destrooper-Georghiades, Anne. 2002. "Les royaumes de Kition et d'Idalion aux Ve et IVe siècles à la lumière des témoignages numismatiques." *Cahier du centre d'études chypriotes*, 32: 351–368.
Devillers, Benoit. 2008. *Holocene, Morphogenesis and Anthropisation of a Semi-Arid Watershed, Gialias River, Cyprus*. Oxford: Archaeopress. BAR Series 1775.
Devillers, B., Brown, M., & Morhange, C. 2015. "Paleo-Environmental Evolution of the Larnaca Salt Lakes (Cyprus) and the Relationship to Second Millennium BC Settlement." *Journal of Archaeological Science: Reports*, 1: 73–80.
Fourrier, Sabine. 2002. "Les territoires des royaumes Chypriotes archaiques: une esquisse de géographie historique." *Cahier du centre d'études chypriotes*, 32: 135–146.
Fourrier, Sabine. 2007. *La Coroplastie Chypriote Archaïque. Identités culturelles et politiques à l'époque des royaumes*. Paris: de Boccard.
Fourrier, Sabine, and Antoine Hermary. 2006. *Le Sanctuaire d'Aphrodite des origines au début de l'époque impériale. Études Chypriotes XVII*. Paris: de Boccard.
Georgiou, Artemis. 2012. *Pyla-Kokkinokremos, Maa-Palaeokastro and the Settlement Histories of Cyprus in the Twelfth Century BC*. PhD dissertation, Merton College, University of Oxford.
Georgiou, Giorgos. 2009. "Three Stone Sarcophagi from a Cypro-Classical Tomb at Kition." *Cahier du centre d'études chypriotes*, 39: 113–139.
Gifford, John A. 1978. *Paleogeography of Archaeological Sites of the Larnaca Lowlands, Southeastern Cyprus*. PhD dissertation, University of Minnesota.
Gordon, Jody M. 2012. *Between Alexandria and Rome: A Postcolonial Archaeology of Cultural Identity in Hellenistic and Roman Cyprus*. PhD dissertation, University of Cincinnati.

Hadjicosti, Maria. 1997. "The Kingdom of Idalion in the Light of New Evidence." *Bulletin of the American Schools of Oriental Research*, 308: 49–63.

Hatzopoulos, Miltiades. 2009. "Chypre, de la multiplicité des royaumes a l'unité de la province lagide: Transition et adaptation." *Cahier du centre d'études chypriotes*, 39: 227–234.

Hatzopoulos, Miltiades. 2011. "'Factoides'" et la date du Bronze d'Idalion." In *Proceedings of the IV International Cyprological Congress*, edited by Andreas Demetriou, 499–507. Nicosia: Society of Cypriot Studies.

Hatzopoulos, Miltiades. 2014. "Cypriote Kingships in Context." *Cahiers du centre d'études chypriotes*, 44: 217–233.

Hatzopoulos, Miltiades, and Anna Georgiadou. 2013. "Donations de Macédoine et de Chypre." In *Epigraphy, Numismatics, Prosopography and History of Ancient Cyprus. Papers in Honour of Ino Nicolaou*, edited by Demetios Michaelides, 203–210. Uppsala: Åströms förlag.

Hellmann, Marie-Christine, and Antoine Hermary. 1980. "Inscriptions d'Amathonte, III." *Bulletin de correspondance hellénique*, 104: 259–275.

Hermary, Antoine. 1987. "Amathonte de Chypre et les Phéniciens." In *Studia Phoenicia V. Phoenicia and the East Mediterranean in the First Millennium B.C.*, edited by Edward Lipinski, 375–388. Leuven: Orientalia Lovaniensia Analecta.

Hermary, Antoine. 2009. "Ionian Styles in Cypriote Sculpture of the Sixth Century BC." In *Cyprus and the East Aegean. Intercultural Contacts from 3000 to 500 BC*, edited by Vassos Karageorghis and Ourania Kouka, 244–251. Nicosia: Leventis Foundation.

Hermary, Antoine. 2013. "Building Power: Palaces and the Built Environment in Cyprus in the Archaic and Classical Periods." *Bulletin of the American Schools of Oriental Research*, 370: 83–101.

Hermary, Antoine. 2014. Les foncions sacerdotales des souverains chypriotes. *Cahiers du centre d'études chypriotes*, 44: 137–152.

Hermary, Antoine, and Joan Mertens 2014. *The Cesnola Collection of Cypriot Art: The Stone Sculpture*. New York: The Metropolitan Museum of Art.

Horden, Peregrine, and Nicholas Purcell. 2000. *The Corrupting Sea: A Study of Mediterranean History*. Oxford: Blackwell.

Iacovou, Maria. 2006. "The *Basileus* in the Kingdoms of Cyprus." In *Ancient Greece from the Mycenaean Palaces to the Age of Homer*, edited by Sigrid Deger-Jalkotzy and Irene S. Lemos, 315–335. Edinburgh: Edinburgh University Press.

Iacovou, Maria. 2008a. "Cyprus from Migration to Hellenisation." In *Greek Colonisation: An Account of Greek Colonies and Other Settlements Overseas*, edited by Gocha R. Tsetskhladze, 219–288. Leiden: Brill.

Iacovou, Maria. 2008b. "Cultural and political configurations in Iron Age Cyprus: The Sequel to a Protohistoric Episode." *American Journal of Archaeology*, 112: 625–657.

Iacovou, Maria. 2012. "External and Internal Migrations during the 12th Century BC: Setting the Stage for an Economically Successful Early Iron Age in Cyprus." In *Cyprus and the Aegean in the Early Iron Age. The Legacy of Nicolas Coldstream*, edited by Maria Iacovou, 207–222. Nicosia: Bank of Cyprus Cultural Foundation.

Iacovou, Maria. 2013a. "Historically Elusive and Internally Fragile Island Polities: The Intricacies of Cyprus's Political Geography in the Iron Age." *Bulletin of the American Schools of Oriental Research*, 370: 15–47.

Iacovou, Maria. 2013b. "Aegean-Style Material Culture in Late Cypriote III: Minimal Evidence, Maximal Interpretation." In *The Philistines and Other "Sea Peoples" in Text and Archaeology*, edited by Ann Killebrew and Gunnar Lehmann, 585–618. Atlanta: Society of Biblical Literature.

Iacovou, Maria. 2013c. "The Cypriot Syllabary as a Royal Signature: The Political Context of the Syllabic Script in the Iron Age." In *Syllabic Writing on Cyprus and its Context*, edited by Philippa Steele, 133–152. Cambridge: Cambridge University Press

Iacovou, Maria 2014. "Beyond the Athenocentric misconceptions. The Cypriote polities in their economic context." *Cahiers du centre d'études chypriotes*, 44: 95–117.

Iacovou, M. 2018. "From the Late Cypriot polities to the Iron Age 'kingdoms'. Understanding the political landscape of Cyprus from within." In *Les royaumes de Chypre à l'épreuve de l'histoire: Transitions et ruptures de la fin de l'âge du Bronze au début de l'époque hellénistique*, edited by Anna Cannavò and Ludovic Thély, 7–28. Paris: de Boccard.

Iacovou, Maria. 2019. "Palaepaphos: Unlocking the landscape context of the sanctuary of the Cypriot goddess." *Open Archaeology*, 5: 204–234.

Karageorghis, Vassos. 1983. *Palaepaphos-Skales: An Iron Age Cemetery in Cyprus. Ausgrabungen in Alt-Paphos auf Cypern 3*. Constance: Universitätsverlag.

Karageorghis, Vassos. 2000. *Ancient Art from Cyprus: The Cesnola Collection*. New York: Metropolitan Museum of Art.

Kassianidou, Vasiliki. 2013. "Mining Landscapes of Prehistoric Cyprus." *Metalla*, 20(2): 36–45.

Knapp, A. Bernard. 1996. *Near Eastern and Aegean Texts from the Third to the First Millennia BC: Sources for the History of Cyprus*, vol. 2. Altamont, NY: Greece and Cyprus Research Center.

Knapp, A. Bernard. 2008. *Prehistoric and Protohistoric Cyprus: Identity, Insularity, and Connectivity*. Oxford: Oxford University Press

Lipinski, Edward. 1991. "The Cypriot Vassals of Esarhaddon." In *Ah, Assyria… Studies in Assyrian History and Ancient Near Eastern Historiography presented to Hayim Tadmor*, edited by Mordechai Cogan and Israel Eph'al, 58–64. Jerusalem: Magnes Press.

Lipinski, Edward. 2004. *Itineraria Phoenicia, Studia Phoenicia XVIII*. Leuven: Peeters.

Malkin, Irad. 1998. *The Returns of Odysseus: Colonization and Ethnicity*. Los Angeles: University of California Press.

Markoe, Glenn. 1985. *Phoenician Bronze and Silver Bowls from Cyprus and the Mediterranean*. Berkeley: University of California Press.

Masson, Olivier. 1983. *Les inscriptions chypriotes syllabiques. Recueil Critique et Commenté*, 2nd supplement. Paris: de Boccard.

Masson, Olivier. 1985. "La dédicase à Ba'al du Liban (CIS, I,5) et sa provenance probable de la région de Limassol." *Semitica*, 35: 33–46.

Masson, Olivier. 1992, "Encore les royaumes chypriotes dans la liste d'Esarhaddon." *Cahier du centre d'études chypriotes*, 18: 27–30.

Masson, Olivier, and Antoine Hermary. 1982. "Inscriptions d'Amathonte, IV." *Bulletin de correspondance hellénique*, 106: 235–244.

Masson, Olivier and Maurice Sznycer. 1972. *Recherches sur les Phéniciens à Chypre*. Geneva: Droz.

Matthäus, Hartmut. 2007. "The Royal Tombs of Tamassos: Burial Gifts, Funerary Architecture and Ideology." *Cahier du centre d'études chypriotes*, 37: 211–230.

Michaelides, Demetrios and Giorgos Papantoniou. 2018. "The Advent of Hellenistic Cyprus." In *Les royaumes de Chypre à l'épreuve de l'histoire: Transitions et ruptures de la fin de l'âge du Bronze au début de l'époque hellénistique*, edited by Anna Cannavo and Ludovic Thély, 267–290. Paris: de Boccard.

Michaelidou-Nicolaou, Ino. 1993. "Nouveaux documents pour le syllabaire chypriote." *Bulletin de correspondance hellénique*, 117: 346–347.

Mitford, Terence B. 1961. "The Hellenistic Inscriptions of Old Paphos," *Annual of the British School at Athens*, 56: 1–41.

Mitford, Terrence B. 1971. *The Inscriptions of Kourion*. Philadelphia: American Philosophical Society.

Moore, James, and Ian Macgregor Morris. 2008. "History in Revolution? Approaches to the Ancient World in the Long Eighteenth Century." In *Reinventing History: The Enlightenment Origins of Ancient History*, edited by James Moore, Ian Macgregor Morris, and Andrew Bayliss, 3–29. London: University of London Institute of Historical Research.

Morpurgo-Davies, Anna and Jean-Pierre Olivier. 2012. "Syllabic Scripts and Languages in the Second and First Millennia BC." In *Parallel Lives: Ancient Island Societies in Crete and Cyprus*, edited by Gerald Cadogan, Maria Iacovou, Katerina Kopaka, and James Whitley, 105–118. London: British School at Athens.

Muhly, James D. 2009. "The Origin of the Name 'Ionian'." In *Cyprus and the East Aegean. Intercultural Contacts from 3000 to 500 BC*, edited by Vassos Karageorghis and Ourania Kouka, 23–30. Nicosia: Leventis Foundation.

Myres, John L. 1930. *Who Were the Greeks?* Berkeley: University of California Press.

Nicolaou, Ino. 1971. *Cypriot Inscribed Stones*. Nicosia: Department of Antiquities.

Olivier, Jean-Pierre. 2007. *Édition holistique des textes chyprominoens*. Pisa: Fabrizio Serra.

Palaima, Thomas. 1995. "The Nature of the Mycenaean *Wanax*: Non-Indo-European Origins and Priestly Functions." In *The Role of the Ruler in the Prehistoric Aegean*, edited by Paul Rehak, 119–139. Aegaeum 11. Liège: Peeters.

Papantoniou, Giorgos. 2011. "'Hellenising' the 'Cypriot Goddess': 'Reading' the Amathousian Terracotta Figurines." In *From Pella to Gandhara: Hybridisation and Identity in the Art and Architecture of the Hellenistic East*, edited by Anna Kouremenos, Sujatha Chandrasekaran, and Roberto Rossi, 35–48. British Archaeological Reports International Series 2221. Oxford: Archaeopress.

Papantoniou, Giorgos. 2012. *Religion and Social Transformations in Cyprus: From the Cypriot Basileis to the Hellenistic Strategos*. Leiden: Brill.

Papantoniou, Giorgos. 2013. "Cypriot Autonomous Polities at the Crossroads of Empire: The Imprint of a Transformed Islandscape in the Classical and Hellenistic Periods." *Bulletin of the American Schools of Oriental Research*, 370: 169–205.

Papasavvas, George. 2009. "The Iconography of the Oxhide Ingots". In *Oxhide Ingots in the Central Mediterranean*, edited by Fulvia Lo Schiavo, James D. Muhly, Robert Maddin, and Alessandra Giumlia-Mair, 41–81. Rome: CNR-Istituto di studi sulle civilitá dell-Egeo e del Vicino Oriente.

Peltenburg, Edgar. 1996. "From Isolation to State Formation in Cyprus, c. 3500–1500 B.C." In *The Development of the Cypriot Economy from the Prehistoric Period to the*

Present Day, edited by Vassos Karageorghis and Demetrios Michaelides, 17–44. Nicosia: University of Cyprus.

Peltenburg, Edgar. 2012. "Text Meets Material in Late Bronze Age Cyprus." In *Cyprus: An Island Culture: Society and Social Relations from the Bronze Age to the Venetian Period*, edited by Artemis Georgiou, 1–23. Oxford: Oxbow.

Peltenburg, Edgar. ed. 2013. *Associated Regional Chronologies for the Ancient Near East and Eastern Mediterranean: Cyprus*. Turnhout: Brepols.

Petit, Thierry. 1995. "Amathous (Autochthones eisin). De l'identité amathousienne à l'époque des royaumes (VIII–IV siècles av. J.-C.)." *Sources Travaux Historiques*, 43–44: 51–64.

Petit, Thierry. 2002. "Sanctuaires palatiaux d'Amathonte." *Cahier du centre d'études chypriotes*, 32: 289–326.

Pouilloux, Jean. 1976. "Chypriotes à Delphes." *Report of the Department of Antiquities*, 158–167. Nicosia: Department of Antiquities.

Saporetti, Claudio. 1976. "Cipro nei testi neoassiri." *Studi Ciprioti e Rapporti di Scavo*, 2: 83–88.

Satraki, Anna. 2012. *Kyprioi Basileis apo ton Kosmaso mechri to Nikokreonta*. Athens: University of Athens.

Satraki, Anna. 2013. "The Iconography of *Basileis* in Archaic and Classical Cyprus: Manifestations of Royal Power in the Visual Record." *Bulletin of the American Schools of Oriental Research*, 370: 123–144.

Savidis, George, ed., 1992. *C.P. Cavafy. Collected Poems*. Trans. Edward Keeley and Philip Sherrard. Princeton: Princeton University Press

Sherratt, E. Susan. 1994. "Commerce, Iron and Ideology: Metallurgical Innovation in 12th–11th Century Cyprus." In *Cyprus in the 11th Century BC*, edited by Vassos Karageorghis, 59–107. Nicosia: A.G. Leventis Foundation.

Sherratt, E. Susan. 2003. "Visible Writing: Questions of Script and Identity in Early Iron Age Greece and Cyprus." *Oxford Journal of Archaeology*, 22: 225–242.

Snodgrass, Anthony M. 1994. "Gains, Losses and Survivals: What We Infer for the 11th Century BC." In *Cyprus in the 11th Century BC*, edited by Vassos Karageorghis, 167–173. Nicosia: A.G. Leventis Foundation.

South-Todd, Alison. 2002. "Late Bronze Age Settlement Patterns in Southern Cyprus." *Cahiers du centre d'études chypriotes*, 32: 59–72.

Steele, Philippa. 2019. *Writing and Society in Ancient Cyprus*. Cambridge: Cambridge University Press

Stylianou, Petros J. 1989. *The Age of the Kingdoms: A Political History of Cyprus in the Archaic and Classical Periods*. Nicosia: Archbishop Makarios III Foundation.

Vitti, Mario. 2013. *Η πόλη όπου γεννήθηκα. Ισταμπούλ 1926–1946*. Athens: Gavrielides Books.

Wallace, Saro. 2010. *Ancient Crete: From Successful Collapse to Democracy's Alternatives, Twelfth to Fifth Centuries BC*. Cambridge: Cambridge University Press

Webb, Jennifer. 1999. *Ritual Architecture, Iconography and Practice in the Late Cypriot Bronze Age*. Jonsered: Paul Åströms förlag.

Weingarten, Judith. 1997. "Sealing Bureaucracy of Mycenaean Knossos." *In La Crète Mycénienne*, edited by Jan Driessen and Aleaxandre Farnoux, 517–535. Bulletin de correspondance hellénique, supplément 30. Paris: de Boccard.

Whitley, James. 1998. "From Minoans to Eteocretans: The Praisos Region, 1200–500 B.C." In *Post-Minoan Crete*, edited by William G. Cavanagh, Mike Curtis, J. Nicolas Coldstream, and Alan W. Johnston, 27–39. London: British School at Athens.

Yon, Marguerite. 1980. "La fondation de Salamine." In *Colloques Internationaux du CNRS Salamine de Chypre: Histoire et Archeologie*, edited by Marguerite Yon, 71–80. Paris: Éditions du CNRS.

Yon, Marguerite. 2004. *Kition dans les textes. Testimonia littéraires et épigraphiques et Corpus des inscriptions. Kition-Bamboula V*. Paris: Éditions Recherche sur les civilisations.

Yon, Marguerite. 2006. *Kition de Chypre. Guides archéologiques de l'institut français du Proche-Orient 4*. Paris: Éditions Recherche sur les Civilisations.

FURTHER READING

The following works can be recommended on Cypriot language, writing, archaeology, history, and culture.

On the Iron Age, see:

Counts, Derek, and Maria Iacovou. 2013. "New Approaches to the Elusive Iron Age Polities of Ancient Cyprus: An Introduction." *Bulletin of the American Schools of Oriental Research*, 370: 1–13.

Hatzopoulos, Miltiades, and Maria Iacovou, eds. 2014. *Basileis and Poleis on the Island of Cyprus: The Cypriote Polities in Their Mediterranean Context. Cahiers du centre d'études chypriotes*, 44.

For language and writing, see the following works:

Egetmeyer, Markus. 2010. *Le dialecte grec ancien de Chypre, vol. I, Grammaire; vol. II, Répertoire des inscriptions en syllabaire chypro-grec*. Berlin: de Gruyter.

Masson, Olivier, and Terrence B. Mitford. 1986. *Les inscriptions syllabiques de Kouklia-Paphos. Ausgrabungen in Alt-Paphos auf Cypern 4*. Constance: Universitätsverlag.

Steele, Philippa. 2013. *A Linguistic History of Ancient Cyprus: The Non-Greek Languages, and their Relations with Greek, c.1600–300 BC*. Cambridge: Cambridge University Press.

On Cypriot sanctuaries and statuary, including the role of female divinities, see the following works:

Ulbrich, Anja. 2008. *Kypris: Heiligtümer und Kulte weiblicher Gottheiten auf Zypern in der kyproarchaischen und kyproklassischen Epoche (Königszeit)*. Münster: Ugarit-Verlag.

Faegersten, Fanni. 2003. *The Egyptianizing Male Limestone Statuary from Cyprus: A Study of a Cross-Cultural Eastern Mediterranean Votive Type*. Lund: Lund University.

On Classical coinage, see:

Markou, Evangéline. 2011. *L'or des rois de Chypre. Numismatique et histoire à l'époque classique*. Athens: Centre de Recherches de l'antiquité grecque et romaine.

On the Ptolemaic period, see:

Keen, Paul W. 2012. *Land of Experiment: The Ptolemies and the Development of Hellenistic Cyprus 312–58 BC*. PhD dissertation, University of Chicago.

CHAPTER THIRTEEN

Southern Italy

Gianfranco Adornato

Boundaries and Toponyms

The geography, foundation myths, *ethne*, cities, and boundaries relating to the notion of *Italía*, *Megale Hellas*, and *Magna Graecia* underwent changes and transformations over the course of the centuries, as literary sources testify (Map 2). These topics were discussed and fiercely debated even in ancient times: to Strabo (6.1.4), for example, Antiochus's ethnography seemed overly simplistic and outdated. In fact, according to Antiochus,[1] the region inhabited by Oinotrians (*Oinotria*) lay on the isthmus between the Scylletic and Napetine Gulfs, which stretched to the Strait of Messina. Later, the territory extended north to comprise Metapontion and the Sirites, places inhabited by *Chones*; in Antiochus's day, the boundaries of *Italía* were the Laos River on the Tyrrhenian side and Metapontion on the Sea of Sicily, with the exclusion of Taras, the inhabitants of which were called Iapygians.

A perspective from the sea, with a sequence of toponyms, populations, and navigation distances (the *paraplos*, a coastal unit of measurement), can be found in the *Periplus* by Pseudo-Scylax:

> And after the Volscians there adjoin Campanians. And there are the following Hellenic cities in Campania: Kyme and Neapolis. By these are the island and the Hellenic city of Pithekoussai. And the coastal voyage of Campania is of one day. And after Campanians there adjoin Samnites, and the coastal voyage of the Samnites is a day's half. And to Samnites there adjoin Leukanoi as far as Thurii. And the voyage beside Leukania is of 6 days and 6 nights… In this are the following Hellenic cities: Poseidonia, Helea, Laos, a colony of Thurians, Pandosia, Plateeis, Terina, Hipponion, Medma, and Rhegion, a promontory with a city… from Rhegion the cities are the following: Lokroi, Kaulonia, Kroton, Lakinion, sacred to Hera, and the island Kalypso,

---

A Companion to Greeks Across the Ancient World, First Edition. Edited by Franco De Angelis.
© 2020 John Wiley & Sons, Inc. Published 2020 by John Wiley & Sons, Inc.

in which Odysseus dwelt beside Kalypso, and river Krathis and Sybaris and Thurii. These are the Hellenes in Leukania. And after Leukania are the Iapygians, as far as Orion Mountain in the Adriatic Gulf. The coastal voyage beside Iapygia is of 6 days and 6 nights. And in Iapygia live Hellenes, and the cities are the following: Herakleion, Metapontion, Taras and a harbor, Hydrous, up to the mouth of the Adriatic or of the Ionian gulf.[2]

The conformation of the territory had already been the subject of debate among ancient authors as well. Pliny (*HN* 3.43) noted that the territory of *Magna Graecia* bent to the left at a certain point (the Sorrentine peninsula), and ended in the shape of an Amazonian shield: the central protuberance would be Cape Cocynthum, from which two crescent-shaped gulfs stretch, the Leucopetra to the right, and the Lakinion to the left. In a later passage (3.95), Pliny mentions Lokroi as the beginning of

> the fore-part of Italy, called Magna Graecia, whose coast falls back in three bays formed by the Ausonian sea, so called after the Ausones, who were the first inhabitants of the country. According to Varro it is 86 miles in extent; but most writers have made it only 75. Along this coast there are rivers innumerable, but we shall mention those only that are worthy of remark. After leaving Lokroi we come to the Sagra.

In this latter context, the geopolitical appellation *Magna Graecia* has a well-defined territorial meaning. In earlier times, the term *Megale Hellas* (in Latin, *Magna Graecia*) was linked to the importance and opulence of Western Greek cities: this use was chronologically tied to the political and philosophical action of Pythagoras in southern Italy.[3] It is a late hermeneutic vein, often adopted and attested to by Latin authors: Cicero,[4] for example, stated that "that part of Italy called *Magna Graecia* flourished with strong and great cities."[5]

A reading of the literary sources suggests that the toponym *Italia* was known and utilized as early as the Archaic age to indicate cities, territories, and *ethne* of what is today southern Italy, the ancient boundaries of which were particularly fluid. With *Megale Hellas*, the geographical reference seems to be limited to the Greek cities of the Ionian coast, in connection with events linked to Pythagoras and Pythagoreans. Later, the Latin term *Magna Graecia* came to indicate the rich and powerful Western Greek cities (Cicero), and successively to comprise the territory between the Salentine peninsula and Rhegion (Pliny), from a point of view that was by then completely Roman.

Routes, Contacts, and Local Populations

Recollections of Bronze Age trade, the need for raw materials, and an awareness of the routes and territories frequented by Cypriots and Levantines – heirs to Mycenaean maritime culture – may have contributed to the resumption of contacts with Italy in the first half of the eighth century BCE by Phoenicians and then Greeks. Relations between the Aegean-Mycenaean area and Proto-Apennine cultures had been interrupted during the eleventh century BCE (on earlier contacts: Vagnetti 1996; Peroni and Vagnetti 1998), but there is evidence of contacts with local populations in Italy around the beginning of the eighth century BCE as attested by Euboean-Cycladic or pendent-semicircle and Corinthian-made chevron-motif bowls.[6] Dealings took place between local communities and Aegean sailors prior to any presupposition of settlements; there were probably intermediate stops along the coast of Puglia, the Metapontine area, and Calabria all the way to Sicily and back up through the Strait of Messina to zones where raw materials could be found in Etruria and Sardinia. Corinthian sailors are considered to have been the first "prospectors" to reach the coasts of the Italian peninsula, as pottery from the Messapic settlement of Otranto attests (D'Andria 1982; Coldstream 2003, 221–245, 394–396: in general: Domínguez 2007; D'Andria 2012).

When the Greeks arrived, Iron Age protohistoric communities in Italy presented three distinct cultural *facies*: (i) individual inhumation burial in pits (*Fossakultur*); (ii) secondary cremation in vases, typical of Villanovan culture in northern Campania, the Salernitan area, and the Diano Valley; and (iii) group inhumation in small caves (*facies sicula*), widespread in southern Calabria (La Torre 2011). Around the mid-eighth century BCE, in Ionian Basilicata dynamics of attraction toward the coast are attested, probably stimulated by the presence of trade and craft-manufacturing outposts at the mouths of rivers. It determines the fragmentation of local settlement systems and the beginning of proto-urban types of situations (Giardino and De Siena 1999; De Siena 2005). An exemplary case was the Oinotrian settlement at Incoronata, with its scattered organization of residential and burial clusters. Later, the settlement shrank in size, a transformation that coincided with the appearance of imported Greek and oriental materials in residential areas and the necropolis. Such exchanges gave rise to a progressive substitution of earlier Oinotrian material culture around the end of the eighth/beginning of the seventh century BCE, as evidenced by vases and pottery materials from the site and from local workshops (Denoyelle and Iozzo 2009).

Some scholars have hypothesized that the Incoronata site was Greek in this "second" phase, having developed on the site of an earlier Oinotrian village as an expression of the trading ambitions of the Ionians of Siris. The organizational structure, however, remained local, as demonstrated by construction techniques like those in contemporary housing structures found beneath the Archaic levels of the *polis* of Metapontion (Andrisani locality), while the settlement underwent a gradual internal evolution. Hence we can deduce that around trading posts near the mouths of the Sinni and Basento Rivers, areas set up for artisanal production and trade with inland communities began to appear. Recent excavations at Incoronata have allowed for definition of a few aspects of the site, which was characterized by manufacturing activities common among both Greeks and non-Greeks during the seventh century BCE: in fact, an area designated as a *kerameikos* has been identified, while material storage areas have been linked to a sacred place that has not yet been individuated on the plateau (Denti 2013).

The Ionian coast hosted no real *apoikiai* during this period, but offered favorable conditions for the creation of a dynamic milieu that was open to trade and exchange and willing to accept heterogeneous cultural elements. In the second half of the seventh century BCE, the *apoikia* of Metapontion is archaeologically attested, contemporaneously with the violent destruction, perhaps by the Achaean *apoikoi* themselves, of the small settlements on the plateau of Incoronata and at Andrisani.

New data have emerged from surveys and excavations carried out in the area of the Achaean settlement of Kaulonia, providing a clearer understanding of the role played by this part of southern Calabria in protohistorical and historical times (Facella 2011). Of particular significance is the discovery of two areas of secondary-cremation pit or well tombs, a funerary rite rarely attested to in Iron Age Calabria, where inhumation was practiced. Funerary contexts on the Franchi plateau have turned up imported Greek pottery datable to the last decades of the eighth century BCE, contemporary with older material found at Kaulonia.[7] Such contacts prior to the settlement of the *apoikiai* must have resulted from the Greek prospectors' interest in metal resources: the mining district of Stilo was the most important iron deposit in southern Italy, and also offered veins of copper and silver. Unlike other Achaean *apoikiai*, which had large inland areas dedicated to agriculture, Kaulonia did not have an agricultural vocation, due in part to its location among clayey-soil hills poorly suited to cultivation. Here, other factors determined the choice of the site for the future *apoikia*, such as outcroppings of sandstone for construction, mining resources, and the exploitation of forest resources (tar and wood) (on the latter: Adornato 2004; Facella 2011).

Interferences and "contaminations" in southern Calabrian vase production can be noted following these contacts, which preceded the settlement of the main *poleis*. At Ianchina near Locri, a settlement arose beginning in the ninth century BCE, made up of various nuclei of huts. Funerary accessories from the last quarter of the eighth century BCE include vases of local or colonial production imitating Geometric pottery shapes and patterns produced in Greece. The Canale necropolis, not far from the site of Lokroi Epizephyrioi, produced some small amphorae of typically local production, but with a typically Euboean repertoire: quadrifoils, rhombuses, and birds are the recurring decorative motifs on these materials created by local communities (Mercuri 2012). Along with these imitations, the discovery at Lokroi – unfortunately outside an archaeological context – of an imported Attic oenochoe should be mentioned: it dates to around the first quarter of the seventh century BCE, thus prior to the founding of Lokroi, according to what literary sources indicate. The founding of the *apoikia*, which is set generically after that of Kroton and Syracuse (Strabo), and around 679/678 BCE (Eusebius), corresponds to the abandonment of the Ianchina settlement from an archaeological point of view, since the presence of Protocorinthian pottery is not attested, unlike at Lokroi. All this pottery also helps to establish the correct framework for understanding the well-known little bronze horse of Aetolian production, long the subject of debate with regard to its chronology and area of production (Parra 2012). In light of this broader framework, the foundation of Lokroi should be chronologically set around the end of the eighth century BCE, in accordance with the generic information offered by Strabo (Sabbione 1982; Adornato et al. 2018).

Apoikiai: Far from Home

The dawn of Magna Graecia is manifested in all its true ruthlessness in a shipwreck scene: a local Late Geometric (LG) krater depicts an overturned ship surrounded by fish and human beings, apparently all males.[8] One of the sailors has already become a meal for a voracious fish. The scene effectively encapsulates the dangers of sailing the Mediterranean, not the least of which are those linked to the experience of the *apoikia*, literally "far from home." It hardly seems insignificant that the oldest visual representation from Magna Graecia comes from its most ancient city, Pithekoussai, founded by Eretrians and Chalcidians (Strab. 5.4.9), or by Chalcidians alone, according to Livy's account (8.22). The settlement's necropolis in the San Montano valley is known, having been investigated since 1952 and published with great expertise (Buchner and Ridgway 1993); its most ancient archaeological materials, Aetos 666 *skyphoi*, can be dated to around LG I. According to the archaeological evidence, the settlers must have been Euboeans for the most part, with other individuals of Levantine, Aramaic, and Phoenician provenance, alongside a nucleus of local peoples. Little is known of the inhabited area, despite the discovery of material from the Gosetti dump site on the Monte Vico acropolis and the "metallurgical zone" at Mazzola. Due to this knowledge gap, much debate has occurred on the site's nature and function (*emporion* or *apoikia*). The recent discovery of an oval-plan rural dwelling at Punta Chiarito, however, allows the reconstruction of a settlement nucleus (Monte Vico-Mezzavia) with necropolis (San Montano) and a few rural nuclei for the management of agricultural resources (grape vines in particular), shedding light on the nature of the settlement as a permanent settlement, rather than a trade enclave. In fact, archaeological investigations indicate that there must have been a small rural village arranged on terraces in the Punta Chiarito zone, beginning in the second half of the eighth century BCE. This community was involved in agriculture, livestock, and fishing, and was abandoned after a volcanic event (Gialanella 1996).

Trade contacts between Euboeans and Phoenicians and the presence of Euboean peoples in the West help us to understand the appearance of the Euboean alphabet and the rapid development of literacy in Pithekoussai and Kyme. In Pithekoussai, more than 40 inscriptions on vases have been found dating to between the second half of the eighth century BCE and the first decades of the seventh century BCE; in Kyme, the earliest attestations date to the end of the eighth century BCE. The burial of an adolescent[9] was the source of longest eighth-century inscription: on a Rhodian cup, three lines of retrograde script are etched, reading: "Nestor… had a fine drinking cup, but whoever drinks from this cup will soon be taken with desire for fair-crowned Aphrodite" (Dubois, *IGDGG* I.2). The shape, the verses, and the mention of an epic hero suggest an aristocratic and cultured sphere, in which the rules of the symposium and oral epic tradition were known.[10] A fragment of a local krater dating to the last quarter of the eighth century BCE found at Mazzola bears the painted retrograde inscription "[…]*inos m'epoiese*," the oldest potter's signature.[11]

According to the chronology of the beginning of local vase production and imitation, we can infer that Pithekoussai must have been structured around the last quarter of the eighth century BCE. That date is supported by DeVries's (2003, 154) meticulous analysis of the chronology of Corinthian pottery, calibrated on Attic and Argive productions and on archaeological context in Corinthian and Western *apoikiai*. The scholar concludes by proposing a late date for the settlement of Pithekoussai, around 730 BCE, based on the oldest attestations of imported pottery:

> the foundation of Pithekoussai was not an utterly precocious, isolated early event but should rather be understood as an integral part of a broadly based colonial movement away from the Aegean that saw the foundation of settlements in a quite closely packed sequence.[12]

The chronological sequence of the settlement of Pithekoussai should be read in light of literary sources as well as archaeological evidence from Kyme, since Strabo (5.4.4) recounts that Kyme was the oldest Greek *apoikia* in the West, founded by Megasthenes of Chalcis and Hippocles of Kyme. With regard to its foundation, a later literary source notes that the Chalcidians founded Kyme after disembarking at *Aenaria* (Pithekoussai), but we do not know how much time passed between the two events.[13] Phlegon of Tralles mentions the Euboean *apoikoi*'s aggression against local populations at the time of the settlement of the city of Kyme (*FGrH* 257 F36 X B 53–56). I would like to probe further these two literary sources, neglected in the debate and in the recent revision of the methodological approach to questions regarding *apoikiai* in the West (Osborne 1998; Yntema 2001; Hall 2008; Domínguez 2011; Tsetskhladze and Hargrave 2011; Ampolo 2012). De Angelis's (2009, 57) invitation to consider information deduced from analysis of literary sources independently from that based on archaeological sources seems quite appropriate in this regard: "the union of textual and material sources has to be balanced and aimed at recapturing as many of the complexities as possible of ancient contact zones."

In a careful reexamination of literary sources relating to foundations, Hall concludes that the sources never focus on the moment of foundation, but rather on the first phases of the settlement. He is convinced that these traditions have "more to do with justifying circumstances in the present than with preserving an accurate account of the past."[14] At any rate, the passage in Phlegon – which Hall does not cite – very clearly illustrates, in my opinion, the process of territorial appropriation at the expense of local populations and settlement of the new *polis* by *apoikoi* from Pithekoussai and Euboea. Although the source in question is chronologically quite distant from those events, it recounts a highly significant episode: the foundation of Kyme by the inhabitants of Pithekoussai, at a time (the Hadrianic era) when Pithekoussai had already been abandoned. The passage of Phlegon, like that in Livy, falls into a Pithekoussai-centric historiographic perspective, and underscores the (slight) precedence of the settlement of Pithekoussai. What circumstances at the time of the authors would explain this? We must conclude, instead, that alongside a few later or more recent literary sources mainly interested in backdating current events and episodes, is another type of literary source that recorded, even in later times, significant moments of the foundation of an *apoikia*. In light of this consideration, I cannot detect attempts at updating or alteration to justify a present situation, as Hall would have it. While Strabo (and his source) sets himself up as the "spokesperson" of local antiquity, the accounts of Livy and Phlegon give us an overturned historiographic perspective, in which Pithekoussai is not only founded before Kyme, but actually participates in the *apoikia* of Kyme, combating and driving out local communities, on the same level as Euboean *apoikoi*. This practice is recorded in the cases of the foundation of Rhegion by neighboring Zankle, and of a few Chalcidians led by Theocles after the foundation of Naxos who founded Leontinoi and Katane, after their victory over the Sicels, according to Thucydides (6.3).[15] Thus it seems to me that Livy and Phlegon pass on that alternative version of Kyme's foundation, and consequently the precedence of the *apoikia* on the island. After the island was abandoned due to earthquakes, and the inhabitants had moved to the mainland, we can imagine that the idea of Kyme's precedence over all other Greek *poleis* in southern Italy began to form.

The oldest archaeological material dates to the third quarter of the eighth century BCE (D'Agostino and D'Acunto 2009), and raises a few questions regarding the anteriority or contemporaneousness of Kyme in comparison with Pithekoussai. Pottery fragments from the excavation of the ditch and sector 7 between the Forum and the northern wall are contemporary to the oldest materials from Pithekoussai (D'Agostino, Cuozzo, and Del Verme 2006; D'Agostino and D'Acunto 2009). Aetos 666 *kotylai* and Thapsos cups with panels were found in the settlement and are typical of Pithekoussai's LG I phase, with local imitations. On the south side of the Forum, a dwelling/functional structure was found with material dating to around the last quarter of the eighth/beginning of the seventh century BCE (Greco 2009, 391–408). This chronological framework is confirmed by the sequence of flooring layers in a late Archaic dwelling, in which a post hole with a lining of small stones was uncovered, dating to the last 30 years of the eighth century BCE (D'Agostino and D'Acunto 2009).

So, Pithekoussai and Kyme are two complementary phenomena, not far apart in terms of time, but functionally distant nonetheless (D'Agostino 2009, 172): Pithekoussai, open to integrating peoples from the Levant, Greeks, and indigenous populations, functioned as an external projection of Kyme into Opicia, animated by lively commercial and social dynamics. The city's brief life was brusquely interrupted by conflicts and volcanic phenomena (Strab. 5.4.9; Plin. *HN* 1.203). From a strategic and topographic viewpoint, it is interesting to note that the earliest Euboean *apoikiai* were founded in defensible places aimed at controlling sea routes in the southern and central Tyrrhenian, around the area of the Strait (Zankle and Rhegion, and their respective secondary *apoikiai*, Mylai and Metauros; Naxos), and in the Phlegrean zone (Pithekoussai and Kyme).

According to Thucydides (6.4.5–6), Zankle was inhabited by *lestai* (pirates) and founded by Kyme in Opicia, joined by numerous colonists from Chalcis and the rest of Euboea.[16] This is confirmed by the mention of the *oikistes* Perieres of Kyme and Kratemenes of Chalcis. However, other sources assign the foundation to Naxos, the oldest *apoikia* in Sicily (e.g., Strab. 6.2.3). According to Antiochus, as cited by Strabo (*FGrH* 555 F9), the Zancleans founded Rhegion with the participation of *apoikoi* from Chalcis and the Messenia, led by the *oikistes* Antimnestos.[17] Later, the Zancleans expanded their area of interest, promoting the settlements of Mylai, on the Tyrrhenian coast of Sicily, and Metauros, north of Rhegion. Metauros had a particularly strategic position thanks to its internal connections: in fact, an isthmus linked the Chalcidian settlement with Lokroi,[18] on the Ionian coast, a route still in use in Roman times, when Craxus constructed a palisade and a moat to thwart Spartacus, intending to isolate the *Chersonesos Rheginos* from the rest of the Bruttian peninsula (Plut. *Crass.* 10.4). Archaeological evidence confirms Metauros's close relations with Zankle and the area of the Strait: the settlement controlled a fertile agricultural territory and landing along coastal trade routes toward Campania. Early eighth-century funerary contexts have turned up non-depurative impasto pottery typical of the local culture, sometimes together with imported ones. Based on rituals and the composition of grave goods, it has been deduced that local populations preserved some of their own traditions (such as iron spearheads for warriors), alongside burials characterized by exclusively Greek material. Ties to Zankle, as well as Pithekoussai and Kyme, were very strong during the seventh century BCE, as documented by the presence of the cup shape known as the "Zankle type," found only in these two settlements, as well as cylindrical bottles, "Rhodian-Cretan" *aryballoi* or Pithekoussan imitations thereof. Imported objects from the Aegean and Ionian islands, as well as from Argolis and Laconia, are also attested (Sabbione 2005).

After the Euboean-Chalcidian migrations, there was a phase of apoikistic activity originating from the Greek region of Achaia: geographically, this phenomenon impacted mainly the Ionian coast of Calabria and Basilicata, beginning in the last quarter of the eighth century BCE (Greco 2002). Sybaris was most likely the earliest Achaian city and survived for 210 years, until it was destroyed in 510 BCE by Kroton. Very little is known of its Archaic period, as Thurii (444/443 BCE) and later the Roman colony of Copia (193 BCE) were founded on its ruins. The vast territory of the plain of Sybaris bears the most evident signs of the city's entrenchment and expansion, beginning in the years prior to the settlement of the *apoikia*, over a flat, uninhabited area (Luppino et al. 2012). This phase led to the destruction of the system of local communities, as in the case of the Timpone della Motta site at Francavilla Marittima. Here the remains of a temple from the end of the eighth century BCE constitute the oldest attestation of this type of sacred building in Magna Graecia (Kleibrink, Kindberg Jacobsen, and Handberg 2004; Mertens 2006). The area had been occupied by an Oinotrian community, of which the early Iron Age necropolis at Macchiabate is known, with pits covered by tumuli of stone rubble and containing imported and local grave goods. On the acropolis, some votive objects were unearthed in holes in a small rectangular altar. Given the typological affinities with objects found in the Macchiabate necropolis, these late ninth- to eighth-century offerings allow us to place the Oinotrian phase of the site within this chronological period, along with this area of worship, probably dedicated to a goddess of weaving. During the seventh century BCE, a temple was erected (building 5). Hefty wooden posts were used in its construction, based on a characteristically local technique, and it had a double row of posts on the southern side and a single row in place of its northern wall. The building was made up of an eastern portico (*pronaos*) and an *adyton* on the western side. Around the first half of the sixth century BCE, this building with its wooden poles was replaced by a new structure set on a low pedestal base made of river stones. The acropolis of Timpone exemplifies a very interesting phenomenon, since these mixed-technique buildings were constructed atop earlier Oinotrian structures. Some scholars have suggested that it represents a phase of cooperation and cohabitation between local peoples and Greeks. Moreover, the sanctuary was in use until at least the middle of the fifth century BCE, as documented by importations of Attic pottery (Dehl-von Kaenel 1996).

Sybaris was the mother city of Poseidonia, according to Strabo's account, which had been preceded by a *teichos* (circuit of walls?) along the sea. The *polis* stood in the exceptionally fertile Sele plain, near the prosperous Etruscan city of Pontecagnano, in a strategic position of mediation between Sybaris and local Oinotrian communities (Cipriani and Pontrandolfo 2012). Poseidonia is generally dated toward the end of the seventh century BCE, based on archaeological evidence found in the urban area and in the sanctuary dedicated to Hera at the mouth of the Sele River.[19] The oldest tombs attributable to the *apoikoi* from Sybaris date to this same period, while the city's oldest temple, a small temple on a stone base, dates to 580 BCE (Cipriani and Longo 1996; Mertens 2006).

Myskellos of Rhypai was the *oikistes* of Kroton: according to Antiochus, the oracle of Delphi had assigned the task of founding Kroton to Myskellos, who, exploring the area, noted that Sybaris had been founded on a better spot. He went back to consult the oracle again, and it ordered him to obey the original instructions.[20] Some literary sources credit Kroton with the founding of Kaulonia, considered an Achaian *apoikia* by Strabo and a foundation of Lokroi by Stephanus Byzantinus.[21] Recent investigations in the sacred and urban areas and the *chora* of Kaulonia have clarified the (almost) contemporaneousness of the foundation of Kaulonia and that of Kroton. We have diagnostic material from the sacred area of Punta Stilo from the end of the eighth century BCE (Facella 2011; Parra 2012), which suggests an initial frequentation of this section of coast around the second half of the century. Of particular note among these objects is a bronze appliqué in the shape of a small horse, probably influenced by Corinthian (?) models (Parra 2012, 350–351). The case of Kaulonia clearly illustrates the dialectical relationship between literary sources and archaeological evidence (a thorough analysis in Lombardo 2010). Until a few years ago, Kaulonia was considered a secondary foundation, a subcolony of Kroton, and a strategically and politically "invisible" *polis*, wedged between Lokroi and Kroton. Hence, scholars have endorsed the hypothesis that Kaulonia must have been chronologically successive to the foundation of its mother city, Kroton. In light of what has emerged from investigations, the archaeological material would seem to be contemporary with Kroton, confirming what Strabo recorded. Kaulonia was a primary Achaian *apoikia*, although it must have been subject to Kroton's geopolitical influence in the years following its foundation, and after the city's destruction by Dionysius I, Kaulonia fell within the diplomatic and artistic sphere of influence of Lokroi.[22]

Metapontion is considered a *ktisis* by Sybaris, a bulwark intended to check Taras's expansion toward the plains of Basilicata and to control the Sirites, where a nucleus of Ionians had founded Siris. The moment of the *apoikia*'s settlement was a particularly violent one, considering the destruction of inland sites like Incoronata, as well as coastal ones. The settlement was followed by the organization of the urban space and the occupation of the territory between the end of the seventh and beginning of the sixth centuries BCE. Residential, manufacturing, and public zones were uncovered near the river. In a short time, city walls were erected, urban grids were organized, and construction of monumental public buildings was begun. In the sanctuary area, there is evidence of simple ground altars (*escharai*), which were later replaced with small shrines on stone bases, as in the case of temple C, which was decorated with clay friezes depicting processions. Not until around the mid-sixth century BCE were large public works completed, which gave the city a monumental image. These monuments included the imposing assembly hall (*ekklesiasterion*), the *agora theon*, and two major temples dedicated to Hera and Apollo Lykaios (De Siena 2005; Mertens 2006). Other forms of sacred structure can be distinguished in the territory, evoking the forms of worship practiced in the urban area, as in the Heraion at the Tavole Palatine and at San Biagio della Venella (Lippolis and Parisi 2012).

There are unanswered questions regarding the identification of the site of the *apoikia* of Siris, where the Colophonians arrived around the first decades of the seventh century BCE: Strabo links the Ionians' departure from Asia to the conquest of Colophon by the Lydian king Gyges. The Colophonians took over Siris, drove out the local Chones, and changed the name of the city to Polieion. Tradition attributes the foundation of Siris to the *nostoi*, or return of the Greek heroes from Troy (Lombardo 1998). In fact, according to Strabo, the clue that confirms Trojan origin of the city is the existence of the *xoanon* of Athena from Ilion in the West. On the hill of Policoro, the earliest signs of an East Greek presence date back to the end of the eighth and beginning of the seventh century BCE. Around the mid-seventh century BCE, the hill was occupied and fortified, and between the second half of the seventh and the first half of the sixth centuries BCE, walled structures and kilns were built (Tagliente 1998; Bianco and Giardino 2012).

For Taras, the Delphic oracle is said to have told Phalanthus where to found the city, the only Spartan *apoikia* in the West: "I give you Satyrion and the rich land of Taras to live in, and to become a bane to the Iapygians."[23] According to Antiochus, Phalanthus led a group of Partheniai, the sons of those Lacedaemonians who had been reduced to the status of Helots and no longer enjoyed full rights of citizenship, as punishment for not having participated in the war against Messenia (*FGrH* 555 F13 in Strabo 6.3.2). Thus "the Partheniai, unable to inherit a *kleros* and become full right-holding members of the community, had to be sent elsewhere, both to avoid creating tension and turmoil within their communities of origin, and to give them the opportunity for the full and satisfying existence to which they could have the right, but from which they were excluded in their homeland" (Moggi 2002, 63). This situation has been associated with a passage of Aristotle, in which some *staseis* are transformed into aristocratic-oligarchic regimes:

> when a few aristocrats are too poor and others too rich (this happens in particular in wartime, and is what occurred in Sparta during the Messenian War, as becomes apparent in Tyrtaeus' poem entitled *Eunomia*: a few aristocrats, burdened by problems due to the War, began to demand that lands be redistributed). (Arist. *Polit.* 5.7.3–4 = 1306b; cf. Moggi 2002, 65).

The difficulty in gaining access to land ownership is highlighted by Tyrtaeus, whose writings date to just after Taras's foundation: clear reference is made to a political situation marked by considerable social imbalances among members of the Spartan community, and by the demand for land redistribution.[24] When the Spartans arrived, the Iapygians were living there in scattered huts and their associated cemeteries. Archaeological evidence indicates occupation of the peninsula's extremity (the future acropolis of Taras) and the portion extending east of the channel (Lippolis 2002; Cinquantaquattro 2012). Signs of the new Greek settlement date to the last quarter of the eighth century BCE, and include a small bronze Laconian horse with a perforated base, found in a tomb with a Protocorinthian *aryballos*. The *apoikoi* occupied part of the surrounding territory: the Iapygian village of Satyrion was abruptly abandoned and replaced by a Greek settlement, while at L'Amastuola typical Greek square houses replaced other structures on the site over the course of the seventh century BCE (Burgers and Crielaard 2012). The mention of Satyrion by the Delphic oracle is meaningful, given that archaeological research in the same place east of Taras has brought to light traces of a settlement inhabited since the Bronze Age, in contact with the Mycenaeans. An aetiological myth of precedence may be suggested by the genealogy of the latter city's eponymous hero Taras, the son of Poseidon and the nymph Satyria (Lippolis, Garraffo, and Nafissi 1995; Lippolis 2012).

Lokroi Epizephyrioi was founded by *apoikoi* from Lokris (Ozolia, according to Strabo, Opuntia according to Ephorus), after an initial settlement near Capo Zefirio and the spring of Lokris; three or four years later they settled on Mt. Esopis.[25] Between the end of the seventh and the beginning of the sixth century BCE, the *polis* expanded along the Tyrrhenian coast, founding Hipponion and Medma (Iannelli et al. 2012).

One of the latest Greek *apoikiai* in Magna Graecia, Velia was founded by the inhabitants of Phocaea, who had fled from an attack by the Persians under Cyrus around 545 BCE. They settled for five years at Alalia in Corsica, but were routed by Carthaginians and Etruscans in the Tyrrhenian Sea. With just 20 ships, the survivors took refuge at Rhegion, where a man from Poseidonia showed them where to found the new city, in the territory inhabited by the Oinotrians (Hdt. 1.167; *Velia* 2006; Greco 2012). The citizens of Samos also fled from the tyranny of Polykrates, and found safe haven among the inhabitants of Kyme, in whose territory they founded Dikaiarchia.

From the Archaic Period to the Roman Conquest: Some Highlights

The Archaic and Classical periods laid the groundwork for the Greek cities of southern Italy in all respects.[26] These were their most culturally significant periods.

Metapontion provides the most important example of the development of urban space and the territory (De Siena 2005; Mertens 2006). This internal consolidation was soon followed by a political one, with expansion taking place to the detriment of neighboring populations. In a more expansive instance, Strabo (6.1.13) reports that Sybaris dominated four *ethne* and 25 cities (for discussion, see Ampolo 1994; La Torre 2009). From an archaeological viewpoint, an inscription from Olympia of the second half of the sixth century BCE, mentioning certain *symmachoi* ("allies") of Sybaris (Giangiulio 1992), which were probably independent and not subjugated, and the so-called "coins of the alliance" (Parise 2001), minted by Sybaris and bearing the emblem of the backward-looking bull and with local names of peoples and cities, confirm this complex territorial and politico-diplomatic network.

Substantial financial resources were poured into the construction of imposing architectural projects, particularly from the sixth century BCE on: artistic as well as architectural efforts were greatly encouraged by the rapid development of urban centers and by the phenomenon of converting buildings from wood to stone.[27] From the very earliest manifestations intended to both attract and flout local as well as other neighboring Western Greek *poleis*, these efforts must have been the expression of a very strongly felt sense of self-identification for the community populations (for example, the sanctuary of Hera at the mouth of the Sele River: Torelli and Masseria 1999). The oldest monuments were small in size and built of clay materials for roofs and decorations, as seen at Lokroi (structure Marasà 1) and at Metapontion (structure C1), dating to the first quarter of the sixth century BCE. A very peculiar phenomenon occurred in the Achaian foundations: there was a commingling of proto-Doric and proto-Ionian elements, leading to the development of the style called "Achaian," or "Doric-Achaian," or "Ionian Sea Style," as in the case of the "Basilica" (mid-sixth century BCE) and the later temple of Athena at Poseidonia (Mertens 2006).

Ionian architectural forms spread in the West around the last quarter of the sixth century BCE, in concomitance with the founding of Massalia (today Marseille in France) and Velia. Among the most important examples is Temple D in Metapontion, built around

470 BCE. Its column bases are not typically "Samian"; the *sommoscapus* of the shaft is decorated with sculpted meander motifs and with a wave-motif band, and the capitals with large volutes recall Ephesian exemplars, but differ from them in terms of conception and technique (Mertens 2006). At Lokroi, the Ionic temple of Contrada Marasà marks a break with the previous two architectural phases, with changes in layout and orientation. The stylistic and formal influence of Samian architectural patterns is more clearly identifiable in both the development of the plan and the decoration of the upper parts of the structure, particularly the columns (Costabile 1997).

The importation and creation of sculpture in Cycladic marble began in the middle of the sixth century BCE and can be linked to the increasing use of marble for architectural purposes in the *poleis* (Lazzarini 2007; Adornato 2010a). After initial attempts by local artists to sculpt imported materials, sculptural production in marble spread and came to include quite challenging works (Adornato 2010a). An exemplary case is the Heraion at the Lakinion, near Kroton, where technical and stylistic peculiarities attributable to Cycladic craftsmen have been highlighted. These workers must have created architectural parts and decorations on site, in turn instructing local artists and artisans (Rocco 2010; Belli Pasqua 2010). Set firmly in the Classical period, the marble acrolith of Apollo (440–430 BCE) from the cella of the temple of Apollo Aleus at Cirò (the ancient Krimisa) offers the most exceptional example of acrolithic technique and of the fine expressive quality achieved by local artistic workshops. The head, feet, and left hand have survived, while the bronze wig found alongside the remnants of the acrolith must be attributed to a different cult statue of the second quarter of the fifth century (Adornato 2013, 182 no. 37).

One of the most original and noteworthy of the bronze creations is the statue of Zeus from Ugento, a work created in Taras, as demonstrated by comparisons with other materials from Taras and Magna Graecia, dating to the end of the sixth century BCE, set atop a Doric capital with a rosette-decorated abacus, a characteristically Messapic invention (Adornato 2010b; cf. Lippolis 2012). Bronze production also includes several important larger and smaller exemplars, such as shaped handles of mirrors and *paterai* (shallow dishes), found in all of the *poleis* of Magna Graecia, as well as the original coin *episema* (symbolic badges) (Lippolis 1996).

Magna Graecia has also bequeathed us our oldest surviving example of non-monumental wall painting: in 1969 a tomb was discovered in Poseidonia, with a painted scene of a symposium on all four sides and a covering slab decorated with a depiction of a diving youth, dating to the second quarter of the fifth century BCE (Napoli 1970). Decorative painting and scenes with figures were blended into a single system on the wall of other fourth-century BCE tombs at Poseidonia, and wide evidence has allowed the identification of ateliers with distinctive stylistic-formal characteristics, although the repertoire is not particularly varied. Chariot races, boxing matches, and duels allude to funerary games; the "return of the warrior" celebrates the deceased's skill in battle and his valor. Women are depicted richly dressed in local costumes, engaged in weaving or looking at themselves in the mirror. Beginning in the second half of the fourth century BCE, scenes appeared representing the funerary ritual, from the exposition of the cadaver to mourning, sacrifices, and games (Pontrandolfo and Rouveret 1992).

In terms of Magna Graecia's most significant contributions to the artistic sphere, vase painting from the second half of the fifth and the fourth centuries BCE is indisputably a high point. Although the birth of such production used to be connected to the strategic and military interests of Athens with the foundation of Thurii, we should keep in mind that the *polis* of Metapontion is the source of the earliest materials linked to the activity of a local workshop, around 440 BCE (Denoyelle and Iozzo 2009). Shortly thereafter, Tarantine production began, characterized by the abundant use of images from myths and very large shapes. The highest-quality examples produced in Magna Graecia date to the second half of the century, and were strongly influenced by Attic repertoires and stylistic influences (at least for the first generation), from which they later moved away. Three main groups of pottery have conventionally been identified and distinguished: Apulian, Lucanian, and Campanian (Paestan pottery from the workshops of Asteas and Python is singled out for its peculiarities); the flowering of these types of production was between 440 BCE and the middle of the fourth century BCE (Trendall 1989; Lippolis 1996; Denoyelle and Iozzo 2009).

The second half of the fifth century BCE was marked by the increasingly strong presence of Athens in the political and diplomatic arena of Magna Graecia (Greco and Lombardo 2006), and by the actions of Italic populations – Campanians, Lucanians, and Bruttians (Cerchiai 1995; De Sensi 2008; Intrieri and Zumbo 1995; Cipriani and Longo 1996; Guzzo 1989; Pontrandolfo 2005; Osanna 2009; De Sensi and Mancuso 2011). These peoples, instilled with Hellenic cultural models, came to the fore following the crises that impacted Western Greek cities and institutions during the second half of the century. According to Diodorus Siculus (12.31), the ethnogenesis of the Campanians dates to 438 BCE, with anti-Etruscan and anti-Greek motivations: Capua and Kyme fell, respectively in 423 and 421 BCE, to advancing Campanian populations. The phenomenon of "Lucanization," on the other hand, is seen exclusively in changes in funerary ritual. In the last decades of the fifth century, for example, Poseidonia's tombs were characterized by distinction in groups and hierarchies and the presence of weapons. Later, the semi-roomed tomb type was adopted, with painted slabs and rich grave goods (Pontrandolfo 2005; Pontrandolfo and Rouveret 1992). According to Strabo (6.1.3), the Lucanians had a democratic sort of organization, and elected a king in times of war. The boundaries of *Leukania* extended from the Sele River to Laos, and from Metapontion to Thurii. The Bruttians are sometimes referred to as fugitive slaves of various provenances, and at other times as people subjugated by the Lucanians (Diod. Sic. 16.15; Strab. 6.1.4). The act establishing the ethnos dates to 356 BCE (Diod. Sic. 16.15), and Cosenza was their metropolis (Strab. 6.1.5).

As a result of occupation by Lucanians, Bruttians, and Campanians, the main cities of Magna Graecia underwent a phenomenon of barbarization (Asheri 1999), and then of Romanization: "in reality, these cities are now under Roman control, and these peoples have become Romans" (Strab. 6.1.2). This passage underscores Rome's interest in the geographic and political area (Musti 2005). The first Samnite War (344–341 BCE) supplied Rome with its first opportunity to intervene in the *Ager Campanus* and to gain control of Capua. The Campanian *equites* gained Roman citizenship, while the rest of the population was given *civitas sine suffragio*. After the conquest of Neapolis, Rome set its sights on Apulia and Lucania. As a result of pressure from the Samnites, in 299 BCE the Lucanians asked Rome for aid, which sent 20 000 Latin colonists to Venusia, located on the border between Daunia and Lucania. In 273 BCE, a colony under Roman law was established at Poseidonia, now renamed Paestum (*Poseidonia* 1992; Torelli 1992), and in 272 BCE Taras was also forced to capitulate and become a *socia* of the Romans (Lippolis 1997). After the Apulians and the Lucanians, the Messapians and Salentinians also became *socii populi Romani*, and in 244 BCE the Latin colony of Brundisium was founded. Rome thus came to dominate southern Italy in a single century (Paoletti 1994). Over the course of the second century BCE, Roman control of the entire area became nearly complete: in addition to the *Senatusconsultum de Bachanalibus* of 186 BCE, intended to nip any possibility of revolt in the bud, there is mention of the directive regulating the settlement of the *coloniae civium romanorum*, garrisons made up of 300 armed Roman citizens (194 BCE). Emblematic of the conclusion of Rome's colonizing efforts and the new politico-diplomatic era in southern Italy was the establishment of two colonies under Roman law imposed on Greek cities: Thurii (194 BCE) and Hipponion (192 BCE). Roman names (and concepts) were imposed, creating the cities of *Copiae* and *Valentia*.

ACKNOWLEDGMENTS

I wish to thank Franco De Angelis for inviting me to contribute to the volume; Carmine Ampolo, Donatella Erdas, Antonino Facella, Mariella Gulletta, and Mario Lombardo discussed with me a few problematic questions mentioned here, offering important and fruitful points for consideration.

NOTES

1 *FGrH* 555 F3 in Strabo 6.1.4; Lepore 1988; Ameruoso 1996; *Confini* 1999; Fischer-Hansen, Nielsen, and Ampolo 2004, 249–251; Cordano 2005; Musti 2005, 103–203; on geographical representations of Magna Grecia: Prontera 1986.
2 On *ethne* in literary sources, archaeological evidence, ethnic distinctions and methodological questions: La Torre 2011; see also Cipriani and Longo 1996; Pontrandolfo 2005.
3 On Timaeus (F13): Ameruoso 1996, 13-21; Musti 2005, 103-203. Polybius (2.39.1–6) recalls the burning of the Pythagorean schools and social unrest.
4 Cic. *Tusc.* 4.1.2; Cic. *Lael.* 4.13; see also Val. Max. 8.7.2
5 The use of the comparative *Maior Graecia* is attested from Livy (31.7.11) to Festus.
6 On the distribution of pottery: La Torre 2011, 22-3, fig. 10; on Greek importation to Rome: La Rocca 1982. See Gras 2000; Coldstream 2003; Bartoloni 2005; Kourou 2012.
7 In T1 were a Thapsos-type bowl, a trilobate oenochoe, and a Euboean-type bottle, items that would have been part of a set of drinking ware (symposium?); Facella 2011, 303.
8 Lacco Ameno, Archaeological Museum, sporadic find from the San Montano necropolis, inv. 168813. See Iozzo 2002, 48–49.
9 The grave goods in tomb no. 168 at San Montano comprised four kraters (a form never attested to in contemporary burials) and symposium vases.

10 Gras 1997, 76; Lazzarini 2009, 278; La Torre 2011, 31, speak of direct knowledge of the Homeric epic; here I prefer to use the more general notion of "oral epic tradition." See also Ampolo 2000a.
11 Lacco Ameno, Archaeological Museum, inv. 239083: Dubois, *IGDGG* I 9. Iozzo (2002, 49) reads "Sinos made me"; Lazzarini 2005 with entries; 2009, 280.
12 DeVries 2003, 154. Cf., however, Buchner and Gialanella 1994 and Coldstream 1995, who place the foundation "well before the middle of the eighth century."
13 Liv. 8.22.6. Hall 2008, 398: "even more intractable is the case of Cumae – founded, according to Livy (8. 22. 6), *after* Pithekoussai but, according to Strabo (5. 4. 4), the oldest foundation in the West."
14 Hall 2008, 411, 422 (for citation): "foundation stories ... can reveal a great deal about the early life of a colony but not, perhaps, its ultimate origins."
15 The diagram in Lombardo 2009, 22, table 1, is quite useful, even though the Pithekoussai–Kyme relationship of succession is not taken into consideration. In my opinion, it should be included among cases of precocious subcolonial foundation, within the first generation.
16 The toponym Zankle recalls the Sicilian noun *zanklon*, meaning "sickle" (Thuc. 6.4.5), reproduced in the *parasemon* on coins from the last quarter of the sixth century BCE. On the presence of pirates: Ampolo 2000b.
17 Strab. 6.1.6. Other literary sources attribute the foundation of Rhegion to the Chalcidians (Thuc. 6.86; Diod. Sic. 8.23.2; Strab. 6.1.6). On the role of the Delphic oracle: Hall 2008. On the foundation and the territory: Agostino 2012.
18 In Stephanus Byzantinus Metauros is considered foundation of Lokroi, like Medma and Hipponion.
19 On the function of the sanctuary of Hera at Sele and on Archaic metopes: Torelli and Masseria 1999, see also Cipriani and Longo 1996; on the stylistic influence of Ionic models: Buccino 2010.
20 Strabo 6.1.12 (*FGrH* 555 F10); Diod. Sic. 8.17; Giangiulio 1989; Hall 2008, 400–401; Spadea 2012.
21 [Scymn.], 318; Solin. 2.10; Strab. 6.1.10; Steph. Byz. s.v. Καυλωνία. On Achaian foundations: Greco 2002.
22 Adornato 2004 on the *parasemon* of the incusi from Kroton and Kaulonia in relation to the Delphic sanctuary.
23 Strab. 6.3.2. On all the literary sources for Taras's foundation, see Moggi 2002; Hall 2008, 412–421.
24 Osborne (1998) fails to consider these land distribution phenomena in Greece in connection with *apoikiastic* movements in the Mediterranean.
25 Strabo 6.1.7, citing Ephorus (*FGrH* 70 F138a); Luraghi 1991; Sabbione 2012; Adornato et al. 2018.
26 Ampolo 1987 (on institutions); Diod. Sic. 22.2.2 (on urban space); Osanna 1992; Carter 2006 (on territories); Iozzo 1993, 2002; Lippolis 1996; Denoyelle and Iozzo 2009 (on arts and crafts).
27 Mertens 2006. On approaches to Western Greek art: Settis 1994; Adornato 2010a, 2010b.

REFERENCES

Adornato, Gianfranco. 2004. "CHARAKTHR. Note iconografiche sugli stateri di Kaulonia." In *Kaulonia, Caulonia, Stilida (e oltre). Contributi storici, archeologici e topografici II*, edited by Maria C. Parra, 333–349. Pisa: Edizioni della Normale.

Adornato, Gianfranco, ed. 2010a. *Scolpire il marmo. Importazioni, artisti itineranti, scuole artistiche nel Mediterraneo antico. Atti del convegno di studi (Pisa 2009)*. Milan: LED.

Adornato, Gianfranco. 2010b. "*Bildhauerschulen*: un approccio." In Adornato 2010a, 309–337.

Adornato, Gianfranco. 2013. "Gli acroliti di Morgantina." In *Capolavori dell'archeologia. Recuperi, ritrovamenti, confronti*, 179–183. Rome: Gangemi.

Adornato, Gianfranco, Alessandro Corretti and Antonino Facella, et al. 2018. "*Locri Survey*. La prima campagna (2017)." *AnnPisa*, 2018: 3–39.

Agostino, Rossella. 2012. "*Rhegion* tra *porthmos* e *Sila silva*." In *Origini* 2012, 949–967.

Ameruoso, Michele. 1996. *Megale Hellas: genesi, storia ed estensione del nome*. Rome: Istituto Italiano per la Storia Antica.

Ampolo, Carmine. 1987. "Organizzazione politica, sociale ed economica delle '*poleis*' italiote." In *Magna Grecia. Lo sviluppo politico, sociale ed economico*, edited by Giovanni Pugliese Carratelli, 89–98. Milan: Electa.

Ampolo, Carmine. 1994. "La città dell'eccesso: per la storia di Sibari fino al 510 B.C.E." In *Sibari e la Sibaritide. Atti del XXXII convegno di studi sulla Magna Grecia (Taranto-Sibari 1992)*, edited by Giovanni Pugliese Carratelli, 213–254. Taranto: Istituto per la storia e l'archeologia della Magna Grecia.

Ampolo, Carmine. 2000a. "Il mondo omerico e la cultura orientalizzante mediterranea." In *Principi etruschi tra Mediterraneo ed Europa*, edited by Gilda Bartolini, Filippo Delpino, Cristiana Morigi Govi, and Giuseppe Sassatelli, 27–35. Venice: Marsilio.

Ampolo, Carmine. 2000b. "La funzione dello Stretto nella vicenda politica fino al termine della Guerra del Peloponneso." In *Nel cuore del Mediterraneo antico. Reggio, Messina e le colonie calcidesi dell'area dello Stretto*, edited by Michel Gras, Emanuele Greco, and Pier Giovanni Guzzo, 49–70. Corigliano Calabro: Donzelli.

Ampolo, Carmine. 2012. "Gli storici del XIX e XX secolo di fronte alla colonizzazione greca in Occidente." In *Origini* 2012, 13–34.

Asheri, David. 1999. "Processi di 'decolonizzazione' in Magna Grecia: il caso di Poseidonia lucana." In *La colonisation grecque en Méditerranée occidentale. Actes de la rencontre scientifique en hommage à George Vallet (Rome-Naples 1995)*, 361–370. Rome: École française de Rome.

Bartoloni, Gilda. 2005. "Inizi della colonizzazione nel centro Italia." In Settis and Parra 2005, 345–348.

Belli Pasqua, Roberta. 2010. "Scultura architettonica e officine itineranti. Il caso dell'Heraion a Capo Lacinio." In Adornato 2010a, 171–184.

Bianco, Salvatore, and Liliana Giardino. 2012. "Forme e processi di urbanizzazione e di territorializzazione nella fascia costiera ionica tra i fiumi Sinni e Basento." In *Origini* 2012, 611–641.

Buccino, Laura. 2010. "La scultura in marmo a Poseidonia in età arcaica e classica. Stato della questione e prospettive di ricerca." In Adornato 2010a, 101–126.

Buchner, Giorgio, and Costanza Gialanella. 1994. *Museo archeologico di Pithecusae. Isola d'Ischia*. Rome: Istituto Poligrafico dello Stato.

Buchner, Giorgio, and David Ridgway. 1993. *Pithekoussai I. La necropoli. Tombe 1-723 scavate dal 1952 al 1961*. Rome: Giorgio Bretschneider.

Burgers, Gert-Jan, and Jan Paul Crielaard. 2012. "Mobilità, migrazioni e fondazioni nel Tarantino arcaico: il caso di L'Amastuola." In *Origini* 2012, 525–548.

Carter, Joseph Coleman. 2006. *Discovering the Greek Countryside at Metaponto*. Ann Arbor: University of Michigan.

Cerchiai, Luca. 1995. *I Campani*. Milan: Longanesi.

Cinquantaquattro, Maria Teresa. 2012. "Processi di strutturazione territoriale: il caso di Taranto." In *Origini* 2012, 487–522.

Cipriani, Marina, and Fausto Longo, eds. 1996. *I Greci in Occidente. Poseidonia e i Lucani*. Naples: Electa.

Cipriani, Marina, and Angela Pontrandolfo. 2012. "Mobilità e dinamiche insediative nel Golfo di Salerno." In *Origini* 2012, 987–1013.

Coldstream, J. Nicolas. 1995. "Euboean Geometric Imports from the Acropolis of Pithekoussai." *ABSA*, 90: 251–267.

Coldstream, J. Nicolas. 2003. *Geometric Greece (900–700 BC)*. 2nd ed. London: Routledge.

Confini. 1999. *Confini e Frontiera nella Grecità d'occidente. Atti del XXXVII convegno di studi sulla Magna Grecia (Taranto 1997)*. Taranto: Istituto per la Storia e l'Archeologia della Magna Grecia.

Cordano, Federica. 2005. "*Megale Hellas, Magna Graecia, Italia*: dinamiche di nomi." In Settis and Parra 2005, 33–39.

Costabile, Felice, ed. 1997. *L'architettura samia di Occidente. Dalla cava al tempio. Siracusa, Locri, Caulonia*. Soveria Mannelli: Rubbettino.

Cuma. 2009. *Cuma. Atti del quarantottesimo convegno di studi sulla Magna Grecia (Taranto 2008)*. Taranto: Istituto per la storia e l'archeologia della Magna Grecia.

D'Agostino, Bruno. 2009. "Pitecusa e Cuma all'alba della colonizzazione." In *Cuma* 2009, 171–196.

D'Agostino, Bruno, Mariassunta Cuozzo, and Laura Del Verme. 2006. *Cuma. Le fortificazioni 2. I materiali dai terrapieni arcaici*. Naples: Edizioni Lui.

D'Agostino, Bruno, and Matteo D'Acunto. 2009. "La città e le mura: nuovi dati dall'area nord della città antica." In *Cuma* 2009, 483–522.

D'Andria, Francesco. 1982. "Il Salento nell'VIII e VII sec. a.C.: nuovi dati archeologici." *Annuario della Scuola Archeologica Italiana di Atene*, 44: 101–116.

D'Andria, Francesco. 2012. "Il Salento nella prima età del Ferro (IX–VII sec. a.C.): insediamenti e contesti." In *Origini* 2012, 551–592.

De Angelis, Franco. 2009. "Colonies and Colonization." In *The Oxford Handbook of Hellenic Studies*, edited by George Boys-Stones, Barbara Graziosi, and Phiroze Vasunia, 48–64. Oxford: Oxford University Press.

Dehl-von Kaenel, Christiane. 1996. "Le ceramiche d'importazione." In *I Greci in Occidente. Santuari della Magna Grecia*, edited by Elena Lattanzi, M.T. Iannelli, S. Luppino, et al., 206–212. Naples: Electa.

Denti, Mario 2013. "The Contribution of Research on *Incoronata* to the Problem of the Relations between Greeks and Non-Greeks during Proto-Colonial Times." *Ancient West & East*, 12: 71–116.

Denoyelle, Martine, and Mario Iozzo. 2009. *La céramique grecque d'Italie méridionale et de Sicile. Productions coloniales et apparentées, du VIIIe au IIIe siècle av. J.C.* Paris: Picard.

De Sensi, Giovanna, ed. 2008. *La Calabria Tirrenica nell'antichità. Nuovi documenti e problematiche storiche*. Soveria Mannelli: Rubbettino.

De Sensi Sestito, Giovanna, and Stefania Mancuso, eds. 2011. *Enotri e Bretti in Magna Grecia. Modi e forme di interazione culturale*. Soveria Mannelli: Rubbettino.

De Siena, Antonio. 2005. "Metaponto e la costa ionica della Basilicata." In Settis and Parra 2005, 376–387.

DeVries, Keith. 2003. "Eighth-century Corinthian pottery: Evidence for the Dates of Greek Settlement in the West." In *Corinth, The Centenary: 1896–1996*, edited by Charles K. Williams II and Nancy Bookidis, 141–156. Athens: ASCSA.

Domínguez, Adolfo J. 2007. "Mobilità umana, circolazione di risorse e contatti di culture nel Mediterraneo arcaico." In *La Grecia. 2.3. Grecia e Mediterraneo dall'VIII sec. a.C. all'età delle Guerre Persiane*, edited by Maurizio Giangiulio, 131–175. Rome: Salerno Editrice.

Domínguez, Adolfo J. 2011. "The Origins of Greek Colonization and the Greek *Polis*: Some Observations." *Ancient West & East*, 10: 195–207.

Facella, Antonino. 2011. "Dinamiche generali del popolamento dalla preistoria alla tarda antichità." In *Kaulonía, Caulonia, Stilida (e oltre), III. Indagini topografiche nel territorio*, edited by Maria C. Parra and Antonino Facella, 295–336. Pisa: Edizioni della Normale.

Fischer-Hansen, Tobias, Thomas Heine Nielsen, and Carmine Ampolo, eds. 2004. "Italia and Kampania." In *An Inventory of Archaic and Classical Poleis. An Investigation Conducted by the Copenhagen Polis Centre for the Danish National Research Foundation*, 249–320. Oxford: Oxford University Press.

Gialanella, Costanza. 1996. "Pithecusae: le nuove evidenze da Punta Chiarito." In *I Greci in Occidente. La Magna Grecia nella collezioni del Museo Archeologico di Napoli*, edited by Stefano De Caro, Maria R. Borriello, and Silvia Cassani, 259–274. Naples: Electa.

Giangiulio, Maurizio. 1989. *Ricerche su Crotone arcaica*. Pisa: Scuola Normale Superiore.

Giangiulio, Maurizio. 1992. "La φιλότης tra Sibariti e Serdaioi (Meiggs-Lewis, 10)." *ZPE*, 93: 31–44.

Giangiulio, Maurizio. 2010. *Memorie coloniali*. Rome: L'Erma di Bretschneider.

Giardino, Liliana, and Antonio De Siena. 1999. "La costa ionica dall'età del ferro alla fondazione delle colonie: forme e sviluppi insediativi." In *Magna Grecia e Sicilia. Stato degli studi e prospettive di ricerca*, edited by Marcella Barra Bagnasco, Ernesto de Miro, and Antonino Pinzone, 23–38. Messina: Di.Sc.A.M.

Gras, Michel. 1997. *Il Mediterraneo nell'età arcaica*. Paestum: Fondazione Paestum.

Gras, Michel. 2000. "Il Mediterraneo in età orientalizzante. Merci, approdi, circolazione." In *Principi etruschi tra Mediterraneo ed Europa*, edited by Gilda Bartolini, Filippo Delpino, Cristiana Morigi Govi, and Giuseppe Sassatelli, 15–26. Venice: Marsilio.

Greco, Emanuele, ed. 2002. *Gli Achei e l'identità etnica degli Achei d'Occidente. Atti del convegno internazionale di studi (Paestum 2001)*. Paestum: Pandemos.

Greco, Emanuele, and Mario Lombardo, eds. 2006. *Atene e l'Occidente. I grandi temi. Le premesse, i protagonisti, le forme della comunicazione e dell'interazione, i modi dell'intervento ateniese in Occidente.* Athens: Scuola Archeologica Italiana di Atene.

Greco, Giovanna. 2009. "Dalla città greca alla città sannitica: le evidenze dalla Piazza del Foro." In *Cuma* 2009, 385–444.

Greco, Giovanna. 2012. "Elea: dalla fondazione alla formazione della città." In *Origini* 2012, 1017–1075.

Guzzo, Pier Giovanni. 1989. *I Brettii. Storia e archeologia della Calabria preromana.* Milano: Longanesi.

Hall, Jonathan H. 2008. "Foundation Stories." In *Greek Colonisation: An Account of Greek Colonies and Other Settlements Overseas*, vol. 2, edited by Gocha R. Tsetskhladze, 383–426. Leiden: Brill.

Iannelli, Maria Teresa, Bernarda Minniti, Francesco A. Cuteri, and Giuseppe Hyeraci. 2012. "Hipponion, Medma e Caulonia: nuove evidenze archeologiche a proposito della fondazione." In *Origini* 2012, 857–911.

Intrieri, Maria, and Antonio Zumbo. 1995. *I Brettii. II. Fonti letterarie ed epigrafiche.* Soveria Mannelli: Rubbettino.

Iozzo, Mario. 1993. *Ceramica 'calcidese.' Nuovi documenti e problemi riproposti.* Rome: Società Magna Grecia.

Iozzo, Mario. 2002. "Black-figure Pottery in Magna Graecia and Sicily." In *Magna Graecia: Greek Art from South Italy and Sicily*, edited by Michael Bennett and Aaron J. Paul, in collaboration with Mario Iozzo, 48–67. New York: Hudson Hills Press.

Kleibrink, Marianne, Jan Kindberg Jacobsen, and Søren Handberg. 2004. "Water for Athena: Votive Gifts at Lagaria (Timpone della Motta, Francavilla Marittima, Calabria)." *World Archaeology*, 36: 43–67.

Kourou, Nota. 2012. "L'orizzonte euboico nell'Egeo e i primi rapporti con l'Occidente." In *Origini* 2012, 161–188.

La Rocca, Eugenio. 1982. "Ceramica d'importazione greca dell'VIII secolo a.C. a Sant'Omobono: un aspetto delle origini di Roma." In *La céramique grecque ou de tradition grecque au VIIIe siècle en Italie central et mèridionale*, 45–54. Naples: Centre Jean Bérard.

La Torre, Gioacchino Francesco, ed. 2009. *Dall'Oliva al Savuto. Studi e ricerche sul territorio dell'antica Temesa.* Rome: Fabrizio Serra.

La Torre, Gioacchino Francesco. 2011. *Sicilia e Magna Grecia. Archeologia della colonizzazione greca d'Occidente.* Bari: Editori Laterza.

Lazzarini, Lorenzo. 2007. "Indagini archeometriche sui marmi bianchi della statuaria e architettura della Magna Grecia." *Marmora*, 3: 21–52.

Lazzarini, Maria Letizia. 2005. "L'alfabeto e l'Occidente. Prime testimonianze di scrittura in Magna Grecia." In Settis and Parra 2005, 366–368.

Lazzarini, Maria Letizia. 2009. "L'alfabeto euboico: origine e diffusione." In *Cuma* 2009, 273–283.

Lepore, Ettore. 1988. "La Magna Grecia tra geografia e storia." In *Geografia e storiografia nel mondo classico*, edited by Marta Sordi, 127–144. Milan: Vita e Pensiero.

Lippolis, Enzo, ed. 1996. *I Greci in Occidente. Arte e artigianato in Magna Grecia.* Naples: Electa.

Lippolis, Enzo. 1997. *Tra Taranto e Roma. Società e cultura in Puglia tra Annibale e l'età imperiale*. Taranto: Scorpione.

Lippolis, Enzo. 2002. "Taranto. Forma e sviluppo della topografia urbana." In *Taranto e il Mediterraneo. Atti del convegno di studi sulla Magna Grecia (Taranto 2001)*, edited by Giovanni Pugliese Carratelli, 119–169. Taranto: Istituto per la Storia e l'Archeologia della Magna Grecia.

Lippolis, Enzo. 2012. "Oligarchie al potere: 'gnorimoi' e 'politeia' a Taranto." In *Arte-Potere. Forme artistiche, istituzioni, paradigmi interpretativi*, edited by Marianna Castiglione and Alessandro Poggio (Pisa 2010), 147–172. Milan: LED.

Lippolis, Enzo, Salvatore Garraffo, and Massimo Nafissi. 1995. *Culti greci in Occidente*, 1. *Taranto*. Taranto: Istituto Magna Grecia.

Lippolis, Enzo, and Valeria Parisi. 2012. "La ricerca archeologica e le manifestazioni rituali tra metropolis e *apoikiai*." In *Origini* 2012, 423–470.

Lombardo, Mario. 1998. "Siri e Metaponto: esperienze coloniali e storia sociale." In *Siritide e Metapontino. Storie di due territori coloniali. Atti dell'incontro di studio (Policoro 1991)*, edited by Emanuele Greco, 45–65. Naples: Centre Jean Bérard.

Lombardo, Mario. 2009. "Da *apoikia* a *metropoleis*. Dal progetto al convegno." In *Colonie di colonie: le fondazioni 'subcoloniali' greche tra 'colonizzazione' e 'colonialismo,'* edited by Mario Lombardo and Flavia Frisone, 17–30. Galatina: Congedo Editore.

Lombardo, Mario. 2010. "Caulonia: tradizioni letterarie e problemi storici." In *Caulonia tra Crotone e Locri. Atti del convegno internazionale (Firenze 2007)*, edited by Lucia Lepore and Paola Turi, 7–16. Florence: Florence University Press.

Luppino, Silvana, Francesco Quondam, Maria Tommasa Granese, and Alessandro Vanzetti. 2012. "Sibaritide: riletture di alcuni contesti funerari tra VIII e VII sec. a.C." In *Origini* 2012, 645–682.

Luraghi, Nino. 1991. "In margine alla tradizione sulla metropoli dei Locresi Epizefiri." *Historia*, 40: 143–159.

Mercuri, Laurence. 2012. "Calabria e area euboica." In *Origini* 2012, 971–984.

Mertens, Dieter. 2006. *Città e monumenti dei Greci d'Occidente*. Rome: L'Erma di Bretschneider.

Moggi, Mario. 2002. "Taranto fino al V sec. a.C." In *Taranto e il Mediterraneo. Atti del convegno di studi sulla Magna Grecia (Taranto 2001)*, edited by Giovanni Pugliese Carratelli, 45–78. Taranto: Istituto per la Storia e l'Archeologia della Magna Grecia.

Musti, Domenico. 2005. *Magna Grecia. Il quadro storico*. Rome: Laterza.

Napoli, Mario. 1970. *La Tomba del Tuffatore. La scoperta della grande pittura greca*. Naples: De Donato.

Nenci, Giuseppe, Georges Vallet, Ugo Fantasia, and Carmine Ampolo, eds. 1977–. *Bibliografia Topografica della Colonizzazione Greca in Italia e nelle Isole Tirreniche*. 21 vols. to date. Pisa and Rome: Scuola Normale Superiore and École française de Rome.

Origini. 2012. *Alle origini della Magna Grecia. Mobilità migrazioni fondazioni. Atti del L convegno di studi sulla Magna Grecia (Taranto 2010)*. Taranto: Istituto per la Storia e l'Archeologia della Magna Grecia.

Osanna, Massimo. 1992. *Chorai coloniali da Taranto a Locri. Documentazione archeologica e ricostruzione storica*. Rome: Istituto Poligrafico.

Osanna, Massimo, ed. 2009. *Verso la città. Forme insediative in Lucania e nel mondo italico tra IV e III sec. a.C. (Venosa, 13–14 maggio 2006)*. Venosa: Osanna.

Osborne, Robin. 1998. "Early Greek Colonization? The Nature of Greek Settlement in the West." In *Archaic Greece: New Approaches and New Evidence*, edited by Nick Fisher and Hans van Wees, 251–269. London: Duckworth.

Paoletti, Maurizio. 1994. "Occupazione romana e storia delle città." In *Storia della Calabria antica. Età italica e romana*, edited by Salvatore Settis, 467–556. Rome: Gangemi.

Parise, Nicola. 2001. "Intorno alle serie minori d'incusi di AMI, di PAL-MOL e di SO." In *Il mondo enotrio tra il VI e il V secolo a.C. Atti dei seminari napoletani (1996–1998)*, edited by Maurizio Bugno and Concetta Masseria, 139–143. Naples: Loffredo Editore.

Parra, Maria Cecilia. 2012. "Tra approdo preurbano e stanziamento brettio: due note su Kaulonia." In *Convivenze etniche, scontri e contatti di culture in Sicilia e Magna Grecia*, 347–363. Trento: Tangram Edizioni Scientifiche (Special issue of *Aristonothos. Studi per il Mediterraneo antico* 7).

Peroni, Roberto, and Alessandro Vanzetti. 1998. *Broglio di Trebisacce 1990–1994: elementi e problemi nuovi dalle recenti campagne di scavo*. Soveria Mannelli: Rubbettino.

Pontrandolfo, Angela. 2005. "Le comunità indigene della Magna Grecia." In Settis and Parra 2005, 404–409.

Pontrandolfo, Angela, and Agnes Rouveret. 1992. *Le tombe dipinte di Paestum*. Modena: Panini.

Poseidonia. 1992. Pugliese Carratelli, Giovanni, ed. 1992. *Poseidonia-Paestum. Atti del XXVII Convegno di Studi sulla Magna Grecia (Taranto-Paestum 1987)*. Taranto: Istituto per la Storia e l'Archeologia della Magna Grecia.

Prontera, Francesco. 1986. "*Imagines Italiae*: sulle più antiche visualizzazioni e rappresentazioni geografiche dell'Italia." *Athenaeum*, 64: 295–320.

Rocco, Giorgio. 2010. "Il ruolo delle officine itineranti cicladiche nella trasmissione di modelli architettonici tra tardoarcaismo e protoclassicismo." In Adornato 2010a, 159–169.

Sabbione, Claudio. 1982. "Le aree di colonizzazione di Crotone e Locri Epizefiri nell'VIII e VII sec. a.C." *Annuario della Scuola Archeologica Italiana di Atene* 44: 251–299.

Sabbione, Claudio. 2005. "Le testimonianza di Metauros a Gioia Tauro." In *Lo Stretto di Messina nell'antichità*, edited by Francesca Ghedini, Jacopo Bonetto, Andrea R. Ghiotto, and Federica Rinaldi, 241–252. Rome: Quasar.

Sabbione, Claudio. 2012. "Locri Epizefiri: segni di una città in formazione." In *Origini* 2012, 823–846.

Settis, Salvatore. 1994. "Idea dell'arte greca d'Occidente fra Otto e Novecento: Germania e Italia." In *Storia della Calabria antica II. Età italica e romana*, edited by Salvatore Settis, 857–902. Rome: Gangemi.

Settis, Salvatore, and Maria Cecilia Parra, eds. 2005. *Magna Graecia. Archeologia di un sapere*. Milan: Electa.

Spadea, Roberto. 2012. "Crotone e Crotoniatide: primi documenti archeologici (fine VIII–inizio VII secolo a.C.)." In *Origini* 2012, 721–740.

Tagliente, Marcello. 1998. "Siris-Polieion. Il quadro archeologico." In *Siritide e Metapontino. Storie di due territori coloniali. Atti dell'incontro di studio (Policoro 1991)*, edited by Emanuele Greco, 95–103. Naples: Centre Jean Bérard.

Torelli, Mario. 1992. "Paestum romana." In *Poseidonia* 1992, 33–115.

Torelli, Mario, and Concetta Masseria. 1999. "Il mito all'alba di una colonia greca. Il programma figurativo delle metope dell'Heraion alla foce del Sele." In *Le mythe grec dans l'Italie antique. Fonction et image*, edited by Françoise-Hélène Massa-Pairault, 207–262. Rome: École française de Rome.

Trendall, Arthur D. 1989. *Red-Figure Vases of South Italy and Sicily*. London: Thames & Hudson.

Tsetskhladze, Gocha R., and James Hargrave. 2011. "Colonisation from Antiquity to Modern Times: Comparisons and Contrasts." *Ancient West & East*, 10: 161–182.

Vagnetti, Lucia. 1996. "Espansione e diffusione dei Micenei." In *I Greci. Storia Cultura Arte Società. 2. Una storia greca. I. Formazione*, edited by Salvatore Settis, 133–172. Torino: Einaudi.

Various editors. 1961–. *Atti dei Convegni di Studi sulla Magna Grecia*. 54 vols. to date. Taranto: Istituto per la Storia e l'Archeologia della Magna Grecia.

Velia. 2006. Pugliese Carratelli, Giovanni, ed. 2006. *Velia. Atti del XLV convegno di studi sulla Magna Grecia (Taranto, Ascea Marina 2005)*. Taranto: Istituto per la Storia e l'Archeologia della Magna Grecia.

Yntema, Douwe Geert. 2011. "Archaeology and the *origo* Myths of the Greek *apoikiai*." *Ancient West & East*, 10: 243–266.

FURTHER READING

For the toponyms cited, see the individual entries in Nenci, Vallet, Fantasia, and Ampolo (1977–). On foundations and issues linked to relations with the motherland, local populations, trade, territory, and literary and artistic production, see the indispensable conference series *Atti dei Convegni di Studi sulla Magna Grecia* (Various editors 1961–). On the dynamics of historical memory in the *apoikiai*, see Giangiulio (2010).

CHAPTER FOURTEEN

Sicily

Justin St. P. Walsh

Among the many regions where ancient Greeks lived outside their homeland, Sicily stands out for the intensity of their settlement, the wealth and political influence they collectively acquired, and the historical impact they created throughout the Archaic, Classical, and Hellenistic periods (Map 2). Greek foundations in Sicily appeared as part of the second major wave of Hellenic colonization (after Asia Minor), in the middle of the eighth century BCE, and they continued intensively into the fifth century. Some of the largest Greek city-states in both area and population developed in Sicily, and the island's rich resources became proverbial. Particularly in the Classical and Hellenistic periods, historic events and processes intertwined the island with Greece. At the same time, Sicily's distance from Greece and the continuing presence of tyrants and kings meant that the island maintained an aura of mystery for Greeks in Greece. Sicilian cities, above all Syracuse, also became deeply embedded in struggles with Etruscans, Romans, and other Italic groups for dominance of the Italian peninsula. For modern scholars, all of these issues are of importance, but new questions have also arisen regarding the relationship between Greeks and indigenous Sicilian groups, both at the moment of first contact and as the colonies were founded and developed. A strong indigenous identity was maintained at least down to the fourth century BCE, though influence of one population on the other can be discovered in both directions from the beginning.

Geography

Sicily is often described by Greek historians and archaeologists as being in "the west," a terminology that implicitly marks Greece itself as central. As will be seen below in the discussion of historiographic trends, it is worth noting how this kind of language can be

---

A Companion to Greeks Across the Ancient World, First Edition. Edited by Franco De Angelis.
© 2020 John Wiley & Sons, Inc. Published 2020 by John Wiley & Sons, Inc.

linked to conceptions of colonizing nations as central and dominant, and colonized lands as peripheral and subordinate. Within the geographic area of the Mediterranean, however, it is Sicily that occupies a central location, not Greece.

In order to understand why Sicily became such a significant locus of Greek activity, it is worthwhile to consider the island's geography and climate first. Sicily is the largest island in the Mediterranean (its area is roughly 10% larger than Sardinia, and more than three times the size of Crete). Its central location offered foreigners a stopping point on journeys between Europe and North Africa, or between the eastern and western ends of the sea (Ruiz de Arbulo 1991). At the same time, the island's resources, primarily agricultural, made it naturally attractive in its own right for migrating populations, invading forces, and visiting traders alike. Sicily was famous in antiquity for producing and exporting a wide variety of raw food ingredients, such as wheat, olives, meat, and honey, and finished comestibles such as cheese and wine. The island is not, however, especially rich in metal resources or high-quality stone such as marble.

The landscape of Sicily is highly varied by region. As an island, it has an extensive coastline, but the terrain along the sea ranges from a few broad plains on the island's southern and eastern sides to steep, rocky mountainsides rising immediately from the water (as on the northern coast, between Himera and Messina). There are many fine harbors, and these eventually became the seats of major Greek and Phoenicio-Punic cities: Naxos, Syracuse, Panormos (modern Palermo), Messana (Messina), Soloeis (Solunto), Gela, Akragas (Agrigento), Katane (Catania), Selinous (Selinunte), and others. In some cases, it is clear that these had been indigenous centers prior to contact by Greeks. Some settlements took advantage of the security offered by being founded on smaller islands adjacent to Sicily (Syracuse, Lipari, Motya). Small rivers, probably with greater flows in antiquity than they have today due to extensive modern irrigation, and their valleys provided routes for travel to the interior.

Volcanism has had a significant effect on the island's terrain, most notably in the case of Mt. Etna (at 3300 m above sea level (masl), the tallest volcano in Europe). Etna has an enormous base covering over 1000 km^2, dominating the northeastern part of the island. The Aeolian islands, located off Sicily's northern coast, are also actively volcanic. The black basalt from these volcanoes was often used for building, at least in towns located nearby. This stone was also exported around the island for use in milling grain; the bubbles left in the magma as it cooled provided sharp edges with which to grind. Obsidian was also harvested from Lipari and Pantelleria already in the prehistoric period for use in making tools for cutting (Tykot, Freund, and Vianello 2013).

A major mountain range spans the northern part of the island from Messina to Himera (these are called the Peloritani, Nebrodi, and Madonie mountains as one moves from east to west). These are an extension of the Apennine range that forms the spine of the Italian peninsula. They are mostly around 1000 masl, but can reach up to 2000 masl, and thus they present an effective barrier from southern and central Sicily to the north coast. Few Greek cities were founded in this area, even along the shore (Himera, placed at the mouth of a river whose valley led up into the mountains, was the most notable exception). Other areas are also labeled "*monti*" in Italian, but they are perhaps better thought of as hilly regions (the Hyblaean Hills in the southeast, the Heraean Hills in the center, and the Sican Hills in the northwest). These hills are mostly around 500 masl, in some cases reaching up to 1000 masl. These areas were extensively farmed in antiquity, especially with olives, grapes, and pastoral livestock. Even more significant economically, though also more limited in area, were the coastal plains that must have supplied the bulk of Sicily's grain production (see De Angelis 2000 and 2016 for the most recent assessments of Sicilian farm output). The largest such area is the Plain of Catania, which stretches from Katane to Megara Hyblaia along the eastern coast, and which was bounded by Leontinoi and Morgantina inland. The foundation of these towns was probably at least partly due to a desire to control this fertile territory. Smaller, but still important plains could be found around Gela and at the western end of the island between Selinous and Drepana (modern Trapani).

The island has a typical Mediterranean climate, with hot, dry summers and cool, rainy winters. The terrain is ideally suited for agriculture based on grain (wheat, barley, spelt), olives, grapes, and pastoral animal husbandry (sheep and cattle). At higher elevations (greater than 800 m), fog often enshrouds hillsides during the winter. It even seems that settlements might have been purposely situated away from the highest available land, despite its defensive qualities, to avoid these conditions and to preserve visibility over their territory.

In sum, Sicily was a spacious, fertile island, rich in the kinds of resources Greeks sought. Almost the only area in which it lacked was high-quality stone for monumental buildings and sculptures. In all other respects it was either at least as rich or even richer than Greece itself. What remained was for colonists either to seize the territory they wanted, or to negotiate for it with indigenous populations. Given the stakes involved for both groups, it is probably not surprising that colonization parties usually chose the former rather than the latter.

Historical Sources

Many ancient writers described historical events in Sicily, although not all of these are preserved today (Meister 1990). Most important of all of these for the island's early history is probably the fifth-century historian Antiochus of Syracuse, whose work is lost (Evans 2016). Antiochus was an important source especially for the beginning of Thucydides's Book VI, detailing Sicily's earliest settlement and the order and dates of the foundation of Greek colonies. Thucydides's purpose was to set up his discussion of the disastrous Athenian expedition to Sicily in 415–412 BCE, as well as preceding events (including the Athenian expedition of 427–424) (Harrison 2000; Hornblower 2010). Herodotus also described fifth-century Sicily in some detail, focusing on conflicts between Carthage and the *poleis* of Akragas (modern Agrigento) and Syracuse as a proxy war in the central Mediterranean for the Persian–Greek conflict in the Aegean (Vignolo Munson 2006). Later authors, particularly Diodorus Siculus, born at Agyrion (Agira) on the northern edge of the Plain of Catania, transmitted the history of the island through the early Roman period, while also occasionally clarifying aspects of indigenous beliefs and practices. These relied on another native historian, Timaeus of Tauromenion (Taormina), who lived in the fourth and third centuries. Diodorus was criticized already in the nineteenth century for treating his sources uncritically, but more recently his reputation has been somewhat rehabilitated (e.g., Green 2006).

The pattern of modern historiographic development relating to Sicily is largely in line with those found in other zones of Greek colonization, such as southern Italy and the western Mediterranean. This development can be characterized by terms representing particular models of Greek–indigenous interaction (including the very label of "colonization"). In general terms, historians first focused on Greeks alone (Hellenocentrism), only later investigating the impact of Greek culture on indigenous groups (colonialism, or Hellenization), before finally adopting approaches that considered the agency of all actors (resistance), and the possibility of indigenous influence on colonizers (hybridity/postcolonialism). These kinds of studies, which peer ever more closely and in more nuanced ways at the island's intercultural dynamics, have been balanced by other recent developments spawning from the concept of globalization. Although the modernist approach known as world-systems theory (Wallerstein 1974) did not have much effect on the still-largely "atheoretical" scholarship produced on Sicily, the related concept of visualizing Sicily as the periphery to Greece's hub still held. In the twenty-first century, under the influence of sociology and *longue durée* history (especially Horden and Purcell 2000), and in response to growing pressure from archaeology conducted in non-classical contexts to be more explicitly theoretical, classical scholars began to describe Mediterranean interactions in terms of networks. In this view, islands (or their constituent states) are visualized in the context of the Mediterranean (e.g., Knappett, Evans, and Rivers 2008, Malkin 2011), as nodes in larger networks. The specific impact of such network-theory approaches to Sicilian studies has yet to be seen, but it is clear that, in effect, the island's history is now being investigated at increasingly micro- and macro-levels simultaneously (De Angelis 2016, 21–23).

Around the turn of the twentieth century, western European scholars such as the Briton Edward Freeman (1891) and the Australian Thomas Dunbabin (1948) saw themselves and their nations as heirs to the classical traditions of Greece and Rome (see Urquhart, Chapter 2, this volume). The imperial activities of these countries seemed analogous to Greek colonization efforts because they were a "civilizing" process carried out on lands that were filled with "barbarians" – non-Greeks in the ancient Mediterranean and Black Sea; Africans, Asians, and pre-Columbian Americans in the modern historical context. "Colonization" meant the arrival of order, organization, art, and literature, recognizably similar social and political structures, and economies that were thought to resemble modern empires.

Beginning in the 1980s, archaeologists working in Sicily began to direct closer attention to the process by which indigenous groups adopted Greek cultural practices. In a sense, this was simply a local expression of a long-standing focus of anthropologists called "acculturation," translated as "Hellenization" in the Mediterranean. French and Italian scholars led the way in the earliest of these studies, notably Georges Vallet, Ernesto De Miro, and Giovanni Di Stefano (Ambrosini 1980; Lepore and Nenci 1983) (see Gras, Chapter 3, and De Angelis, Chapter 5, this volume). In the 1990s, English-speaking scholars picked up the thread (De Angelis 1998). Hellenized indigenous sites in the hinterland, such as Sabucina and Morgantina, were widely discussed (Albanese Procelli 1996a; 1996b; 1996c; 1997a; 1997b; Antonaccio 1997, 2001, 2003, 2004, 2005; Lomas 1995, 1997, 2004; Lyons 1991, 1996; Morgan 1997). In several of these cases, the primary point of interest was understanding how contact with Greeks had transformed native societies to the extent that by the late Classical period, it was not possible to distinguish between the two cultures (Albanese Procelli 1997c). Indigenous groups gradually adopted Greek pottery, architectural styles, urban planning, and the alphabet to write short inscriptions in their own language. Soon, native languages, too, would be supplanted by Greek, though given that none of the native languages ever developed a written literature *per se* means that it is difficult to know when or how this transition actually happened. It is notable that earlier scholars of Hellenization not only pinpointed the adoption of material culture, but also often drew the conclusion that these traits signified the adoption of Greek behaviors as well: for example, that the adoption of Greek pottery meant that banqueting in the style of the *symposion* was probably happening in indigenous contexts, too (Shefton 1997). In reality, the record was mixed on such questions (Antonaccio 1999; Walsh 2013; Walsh and Antonaccio 2014; see also Antonaccio and Neils 1995 for Sikel inscriptions on Greek vases using the Greek alphabet, in ways that seem evocative of sympotic behavior, or Lyons 1996 on *klinai* and Greek pottery in elite tombs for women as well as men at Morgantina). The widespread deposition of Greek pottery in Sicilian tombs was something not usually found in the Greek homeland after the Geometric period; instead, it was a common practice in the Italic world. Interestingly, that practice seems to have been picked up by some Greeks, as at Selinous in the Manicalunga necropolis of Selinous (Kustermann Graf 2002) and at Kamarina in its various necropoleis.

Non-Greek Populations

Greek authors are unclear about the number of different indigenous populations or the divisions between them. Thucydides's account (6.2) of three groups – the Sikans, Sikels, and Elymians – is best known. He described all three groups as having come to the island from somewhere else: Liguria in the case of the Sikans, southern Italy for the Sikels, and Troy for the Elymians. These groups reportedly occupied different sectors of the island, with the Sikels in the north and east, the Sikans in the center, and the Elymians at the eastern end of the island (largely confirmed by Diodorus 5.8.1). Strabo (6.2.4), however, mentioned at least two other groups, the Morgetes, the founders of Morgantina, in the island's center, and the Ausoni who settled the Aeolian islands, and then Sicily more generally. Carla Antonaccio (2001, 122–124) has particularly cautioned against accepting Greek descriptions of other ethnic groups at face value; Greek authors may have simplified the true situation or misunderstood it, thus failing to reflect the ways in which indigenes constructed their own group identities. The archaeological evidence, however, does not clearly support the division of pre-Greek Sicilians into three groups or five. The material culture of prehistoric Sicily is comprised of two groups named for type-sites in the east (Pantalica, inland from Syracuse and Megara Hyblaia) and west (Sant'Angelo Muxaro, north of Akragas). The most distinctive products of these two groups seem to be their pottery, with painted decoration more common in the east and incised decoration more common in the west (Trombi 1999). But in the center of the island, as at Morgantina, both types could be found, perhaps indicating that the cultural *facies* merely present regional differences rather than ethnic ones. Linguistic evidence is much more difficult to use in Sicily, since, as already mentioned, local languages were eventually replaced by

Greek and then Latin and the Greek alphabet was sporadically used for generally short inscriptions that reveal their languages to be of Italic origin (Cordano 1992).

Greek Settlement of Sicily

The earliest evidence for Greek goods in Sicily dates back to the Late Bronze Age, with the appearance of Mycenaean imports at Thapsos (Voza 1973, 1986), though it is not clear whether Greeks were the transporters of these vessels. With the collapse of the Mycenaean palace-states in the twelfth century BCE, contact appears to have ceased between Greece and Sicily, only re-emerging in the early eighth century. Three Greek cups were uncovered at Villasmundo, an indigenous site in the hinterland of later Greek Megara Hyblaia. The appearance of such items at indigenous sites has often been described as "trade before the flag," that is, a prelude to eventual colonization (whether or not it was specifically intended at first). The origins of these imports coincide neatly with historical accounts of the earliest colonists. Unfortunately, since we lack firsthand accounts from this period, either by indigenes or by Greeks, it is impossible to say precisely how these groups conceptualized or planned their interactions, how they communicated with each other, how frequent or intense contacts were, over what period of time, by what number of participants, and whether these contacts indicated individual initiatives or community/region-wide efforts.

It is undoubtedly also worth considering the renaissance of intercultural interaction within the larger context of contemporary activities by Greeks across the Mediterranean, as well as within the context of activities by other wide-ranging Mediterranean groups, especially the Phoenicians. As other chapters in this volume make clear, Sicily was but one arena among many where Greeks from different regions wanted to trade and settle. Their reasons for doing so will have been equally complex. Moreover, the earliest settlements in Sicily were founded in the late eighth and early seventh centuries, just as the new form of political community known as the *polis* was coalescing. Since settlements were necessarily created entirely from scratch, scholars assume that their initial plan reflects what contemporary Greeks thought was most necessary for a community at the moment when they were founded (Di Vita 1990; Hoepfner and Schwandner 1994). Settlements such as Syracuse, Megara Hyblaia, Naxos, and Gela have therefore been studied for clues about what features characterized early *poleis*. On its face, this argument has much to recommend it: ideas current at the time of foundation about city- and territory-planning, government, religion, architecture, and many other aspects of life would be reflected in their design and implementation. These ideas would have been brought from the homeland. But the fact also remains that colonial foundations faced different circumstances, pressures, and influences from those prevailing at home. Gabriel Zuchtriegel (2017) has also made arguments that equality was extended only to elites within colonial foundations, not to the general population. It seems increasingly important to examine colonial settlements in a nuanced way that respects both their Hellenic roots and the situations specific to their location far from Greece.

The primary groups of Greeks making colonial expeditions to Sicily in the earliest phase of settlements originated at Corinth and Khalkis. Other Greeks came from Rhodes and

Crete (Gela and Akragas). Their first settlements in Sicily were all founded along the east coast. First was Naxos, followed by Syracuse, Leontini (somewhat inland), Katane, and Megara Hyblaia. It is notable that these early towns all achieved at least one of three goals: control of excellent harbors, access to river valleys leading into the island's interior, and staking out agricultural land. Literary sources describe how some *apoikiai* expelled indigenous people already living there, whereas Megara Hyblaia reportedly received its land (and part of its name) as a gift from a local Sikel king named Hyblon (Thuc. 6.3–4; Diod. Sic. 14.88). If true, then it seems to represent a reality in which Greek relations with indigenes were not simply antagonistic, but were rather more complex and could include negotiation and even friendship.

More colonies followed, especially along the island's south coast. Some of these second-wave and third-wave colonies were actually subcolonies founded by groups from the original colonies. Some were not even full-fledged colonies, but probably more like forts (*phrouria*) designed to maintain control over the hinterland. Akrai and especially Kasmenai could be examples of such a Syracusan fort-town. Syracuse was also active in placing subcolonies to control the southeastern part of the island as far as Kamarina (Di Vita 1954; 1956a; 1956b; 1987; Uggeri 2015). It is likely that these new foundations antagonized the Sikels of the Hyblaian Hills, for when Kamarina revolted against Syracuse in the sixth century, it had indigenous allies (Philistos, *FGrH* 556 F5). Similarly, Megara Hyblaia sent colonists to found the westernmost colony on the southwestern coast, Selinous, Gela founded Akragas, and Messana founded Himera. They allowed their *metropoleis* to extend their influence over other parts of the island. Greek foundations were limited, however, by the presence of indigenes, but also by Phoenicians, who founded their own colonies (Motya, Panormus, and Soloeis) at the western end of the island and allied themselves with the local natives there, the Elymians (Aubet 2009).

The colonies seem to show an interest in equality in land division for settlers from the very beginning. Tréziny (1999) has argued for such equality from the evidence at Megara, where streets in various neighborhoods ran parallel to one another in the original eighth-century plan, and many houses seem to have each had plots measuring approximately 12 m per side. Even though house-lots of different scales were found in different neighborhoods, an overall attempt at standardization appeared. Grid plans found at Naxos, Syracuse, Gela, Akragas, Selinous, Himera, and elsewhere certainly show a high degree of civic organization. Although evidence is largely lacking for the same kind of land division of farmland outside urban centers, it seems likely that the practice did, in fact, extend to agricultural zones. Such apportioning suggests that the literary sources that indicate colonists had an expectation to a share of land even before arrival were in fact true. For example, the poet Archilochus, according to Athenaeus (4.167d), described a Syracusan settler who traded his allotment in return for a honey-cake during the voyage from Corinth.

Sicilian *apoikiai* present some of the best-known examples of agoras and their development over time from anywhere in the Greek world (Ampolo 2012). Megara Hyblaia, forcibly emptied by the Syracusan tyrant Gelon in 483, perhaps most clearly shows an Archaic agora, with small, single-chamber temples in the center and stoas along the edges. The agora of Himera shows similar development in the late sixth century. Grand agoras of the Classical and Hellenistic periods are most clearly evident at Selinous and Morgantina (the latter probably a mixed Greek-Sikel foundation; see below). At these sites, major commercial, religious, and governmental structures define and articulate a space that forms an integral part of the city layout. At Morgantina, for example, the agora is equal in size to six of the city blocks which neighbor it (Bell 1984–1985; 1988). The presence of an *ekklesia* (citizens' assembly), *bouleuterion* (councillors' building), and *prytaneion* (chief councillors' office) indicates how democracy had infiltrated Sicilian political life by the late fifth century at least. At Syracuse, temples to Apollo, Artemis, and Athena took center stage on the island of Ortygia. The Temple of Apollo is one of the earliest, with columns extremely closely placed. Elite competition is evident from the inscription on the stylobate explaining that a certain Kleomenes set up the columns, "beautiful works." At Selinous, increasingly larger temples were also added to the space of the agora during the sixth and fifth centuries. Some included sculptural decoration in their metopes: Temples C and D had an array of mythical stories, some identifiable (Europa and the bull, Perseus slaying Medusa with the assistance of Athena, Heracles and the Cercopes), others generic (male and female deities in chariots, probably apotropaic), and still others unidentifiable. Since high-quality marble was difficult to acquire, especially in the Archaic period, Sicilian Greeks often decorated their temples with painted terracotta. The finest examples are probably the Medusa plaque from the Temple of Athena at Syracuse, and three terracotta altars from Gela. Smaller shrines also appeared in these contexts to the founder, or *oikist*, as a protective hero of the city, and to Zeus Polieus or other civic patron deities (Bell 1999).

Many cities also placed large temples outside their walls, often at liminal points. Syracuse built a temple to Olympian Zeus along the River Anapus, Akragas built a series of temples along its plateau ridge facing south to the sea, Selinous built temples on hills to the west and east of the urban center, and Himera placed one below the city along its shoreline. Non-Greek towns followed suit, with the Elymian city of Segesta building a Greek-style temple (perhaps never fully finished) on a hill overlooking its valley. These were an effective means of broadcasting control, power, and wealth to neighbors, visitors, and the community itself (de Polignac 1995).

Eventually, Sicilian Greeks came to describe themselves as "Sikeliots," a name that unified them while at the same time marking them out as different from the indigenous population and from Greeks in Greece (Antonaccio 2001). A look at Sicilian history raises the question of how deep this unification went. Colonizing groups, for example, were only rarely comprised of Dorian and Ionian Greeks together, and when this happened, or when a new population was integrated (perhaps forcibly) into an existing population, the two groups did not always get along. At Himera, destruction levels have been interpreted as possibly indicating this kind of strife (Allegro 1997). These tensions were particularly evident in the period of tyranny, when the activities of the Deinomenid and Emmenid tyrants seemed focused as much on displacing Ionian populations and concentrating Dorian ones (especially elites, see below) as they did on conquest alone (Braccesi and Millino 2000, 67–101). At the same time, it is worth noting that Hippocrates and Gelon did not only displace Ionian Greeks, but Sikels were also defeated, uprooted, and enslaved or sent away from their towns. Hippocrates attacked Hybla and even tricked his own Sikel mercenaries so he could capture their hometown of Ergetion. In the aftermath of the tyrant Thrasyboulos's removal at the hands of Syracusan democrats in 461, Dorian elites were thrust out of the cities that had been given to them in the previous generation, such as Katane (which had been renamed Aitna). The Aitnaians then took over a Sikel town called Inessa, expelling its inhabitants.

Relatively little is known about events in the Archaic period in Sicily, a fact that is in line with the situation in mainland Greece and Ionia. Until the fifth century, there was no written history, so we are left with fragments of evidence to tell us primarily of various conflicts between *apoikiai*. To the best of our knowledge, Greek colonies in Sicily were governed by oligarchies from the time of their foundation down into the sixth century (De Angelis 2016, 173–179). Unlike in Greece, tyrannies seem not to have emerged in the seventh century. The only early Sicilian tyrant about whom we hear anything substantive was Phalaris of Akragas (Polyaen. 5.1.3–4). He reportedly ruled during the second quarter of the sixth century, and may have succeeded in extending his control over more than one *polis*. Phalaris was notorious for his cruelty, being attributed cannibalism and torture. Not until the end of the sixth century did other tyrants take power in Sicily, but the institution of tyranny was notably long-lived on the island, persisting down to the third century. Tyrants maintained their power through public works and through military activity designed to gain and maintain territory.

We are much better informed about the history of the Classical period. The fifth century was a period in which great personal rivalries, countered by occasional democratic impulses, seem to have dominated political events, and Sicily became a central location in Greek history. The tyrannies that had arisen in the sixth century expanded beyond the *poleis* where they had begun, initiating conflicts to build small empires. In the 490s, Hippocrates led the army from Gela and conquered most of coastal eastern Sicily (apart from Syracuse), including Naxos, Messana, and Leontinoi, and possibly Katane (Luraghi 1994). The Syracusans gave up control of Kamarina to avoid a war with Gela (Sinatra 1998). Archaeological evidence shows that Morgantina may also have been besieged in this period (Sjöqvist 1973). Hippocrates was killed in action in 491. His sons did not succeed him, as their power was usurped by Hippocrates's cavalry commander, Gelon, son of Deinomenes. Gelon continued Hippocrates's campaigns and added the new measure of population resettlement to it (Hdt. 7.156.1–2). Unusually for a tyrant, he also exploited aristocratic sentiment against rising democrats. He allied with Syracusan elites who had been exiled from their city, and, capturing the city, reinstalled them. At the same time, he emptied Kamarina, moving its population to Syracuse, and refounding Kamarina with Geloan colonists. He moved Megara Hyblaia's elite to Syracuse, as well, while selling lower-class Megarians into slavery. The procedure was repeated with another Greek city, Euboea. Lastly, Gelon brought half of Gela's population to Syracuse. In this way, Syracuse became the largest city on the island, and Gelon had the support of an aristocracy that he had created.

Exploiting the traditional *metropolis–apoikia* relationship between Gela and Akragas, Gelon created an alliance with Theron, the Akragantine tyrant. The two supported each other in an effort to extend their joint control over all of Greek Sicily. Theron's capture of Himera in 483, and his expulsion of Terillos, the tyrant of that city, led to a confrontation with Carthage in 480. The Carthaginians, powerful in western Sicily, had been allies of Terillos. Syracuse and Akragas defeated the Carthaginians and cemented their power over Sicily. Mass graves recently discovered in the coastal plain below Himera's plateau offer poignant testimony to the costs of this battle (Bertolino, Alaima, and Vassallo 2017).

Gelon's death in 478 led his brother Hieron (I) to succeed him in Syracuse, while another brother, Polyzalos, ruled in Gela (Bonanno 2010). Hieron continued the "Doricization" of eastern Sicily started by Gelon. He uprooted the inhabitants of the Ionian colonies of Naxos and Katane, sending them to Leontinoi. He refounded Katane as Aitna, serving as oikist, and sending a group from Syracuse to live there. Hieron also extended his interests up Italy's western coast, fighting and defeating an Etruscan fleet at Cyme in 474. Hieron's death in 467, and his replacement by his fourth brother, Thrasyboulos, led to a crisis at Syracuse, however. Thrasyboulos was overthrown by a democratic revolt in 461. This had been preceded at Akragas by a similar revolt against Theron's son and successor, Thrasydaeus. The democrats were supported by their allies from other cities and by the Sikels; as a result, the Deinomenid supporters who had settled at Aitna were driven out.

The Aitnaians fled to the slopes of Mt. Etna, where they displaced Sikels living in the town of Inessa (Strabo 6.2.3, see also Diod. Sic. 11.76.3). This seizure of an indigenous town, very likely seen as only the latest in a series of Greek provocations going back to the Archaic period, triggered a response. A group of Sikel cities joined together as a league, determined to push Greek influence out of the island's interior. It may appear strange, then, that the Sikel army's first endeavor was to attack another indigenous town, Morgantina. The best explanation for this is that Morgantina had been Hellenized, either due to the possible takeover by Hippocrates (mentioned earlier), or through some other infiltration by Greeks. Whatever the case, the result was the destruction of the settlement (Walsh 2011–2012). The leader of the Sikel league, Ducetius (Jackman 2005), moved his hometown, Menai, to a new site, and founded a new town, Palike, at the site of volcanic springs that had long been a locus of Sikel worship (though archaeological remains are scanty: Pope 2006). It is worth noting that Hieron I had already explicitly colonized Sikel myth and religious practice at Palike: in the play Aeschylus had written to celebrate the foundation of Aitna, Zeus was described as the father of the heroes known as the Palikoi, with a local nymph as their mother (Dougherty 1993, 88–91, 94–95). The Sikels recaptured Inessa in 451, in a show of power that agitated both Syracuse and Akragas. After two years of fighting, Syracuse finally defeated Ducetius in 449, but he escaped and sought refuge at an altar in Syracuse's agora, offering his lands in return for preserving his life (Diod. Sic. 11.92). The Syracusans decided to send him into exile at Corinth, and apparently took control over the Sikel league's territory in the center of the island. In an unusual epilogue to the story of the Sikel uprising, Ducetius returned to Sicily, this time as an oikist founding a colony on the north coast called Caleacte that was composed of Greeks and Sikels together, around 440. Such cooperation was exceedingly rare, especially in this period.

Where the Battle of Himera in 480 had made Sicilian Greeks peripheral participants in the Persian Wars, the next phase in the island's history made them a more significant player. When hostilities arose between Leontinoi and Syracuse in 427, the former requested aid from Athens, which sent an expeditionary force that captured Messana (an ally of Syracuse). Kamarina, the other Ionian cities of Sicily, and the Sikels joined Leontinoi as well, facing off against Syracuse and the Dorian cities (except for Kamarina). The result was a stalemate, but when Kamarina and Gela decided to come to terms in 424, the two cities invited all the communities involved to a peace congress at Gela (Thuc. 3.86). Syracuse persuaded the other Sicilian cities to unite in peace and to oppose Athens' imperial interests in the island. The result of the Congress of Gela was for borders to return to their locations in 427, for Kamarina to pay an indemnity to Syracuse, and for Syracuse to give Morgantina to Kamarina. These terms indicate the closeness of Kamarina to its Sikel neighbors, alone among Greek cities, and probably also signals – since there is no other clear explanation for Kamarina's interest in the center of the island – that Morgantina's refoundation in the later fifth century might also have been a joint effort between Greeks from Kamarina and Sikels from the Hyblaian Hills (Bell 2000a; Walsh 2011–2012). One other result of the war of 427–424 was the initiation of relationships between Athens and the Sikels; two Sikel leaders, Archonides and Demon of Herbita, were recognized in a public inscription as *proxenoi* (*IG* 1³ 228).[1]

The Congress of Gela brought peace, but it also set the stage for a much larger conflict between Syracuse and Athens. Again, the conflict seems to have had connections to both Greek and indigenous interests. This time, the call for Athenian intervention in Sicily came from Egesta, an Elymian city in conflict with Selinous. The Egestaeans tricked Athenian ambassadors into thinking they were extraordinarily rich, and Athens saw an opportunity to extend their empire while wounding Sparta's Dorian allies (Thuc. 6.46; though see below regarding their ignorance of the situation). In 415, Athens invaded Sicily, relying on assistance from Sikels and Ionians (who were reluctant to join in). The Athenians besieged Syracuse on land and attacked its harbors with a fleet. Ultimately, however, the Athenian invasion met with bad luck and disaster. Assistance had come to Syracuse from Corinth and Sparta. By 413, the Athenian invasion had failed. Syracuse was now clearly the dominant power on the island. The extent of warfare in this period and later is amply demonstrated by the construction of major fortifications at Syracuse, Gela, and Selinous, all of which survive today.

One of the classic issues debated in the history of the Greeks in Sicily has been the relationship between Sikeliots and the homeland. On the one hand, evidence exists from Panhellenic sanctuaries, particularly Olympia and Delphi, of individual Sikeliots and their cities attempting to build and reinforce relationships with mainland Greece (Scott 2010). These activities came in the form of abundant dedications and treasuries to house them (Selinous and Gela at Olympia; Syracuse at Delphi), as well as participating in the games held at those sanctuaries. Victories by tyrants and their family members in the fifth century were commemorated by odes composed by the superstar artists of their day, Pindar and Bacchylides. Hieron I brought Aeschylus from Athens to compose plays aggrandizing him and his achievements by forging a mythical basis for them. This literature disseminated widely Sicily's (and especially the tyrants') fame and wealth. The victors in games also dedicated tripods and major artworks at Greek sanctuaries in their own honor, such as the bronze charioteer group commissioned by Polyzalos of Gela for Delphi in 478 or 474, and other statues placed in the sanctuary by Hieron I of Syracuse around the same time. This phenomenon is all the more interesting (Scott 2010, 89–91), since it was in contrast to the relative paucity of dedications by mainland *poleis* and individuals. Indeed, it may represent a specifically Sikeliot behavior. It does appear that Sicily was poorly understood by Greeks in Greece. This point was underlined by Thucydides, who attributed the doomed Athenian expedition to just such a misunderstanding (Thuc. 6.1). The Athenians saw wealth and resources for the taking, and the possibility of disrupting their Spartan foes' alliances, but they did not understand the scope of the undertaking.

Sikeliots built monuments to display their victories to one other as well. The most important examples were the series of temples erected at Selinous, Akragas, and Himera following the Greek defeat of the Carthaginians in 480. While Himera built its temple to Nike on the battleground below the city, Selinous and Akragas competed to build many temples and especially the largest Doric temple ever seen (De Miro 1983). Temple G at Selinous (dedicated to Apollo or Zeus) and the Temple of Olympian Zeus at Akragas each measured approximately 50 m wide by 110 m long and were in all likelihood not roofed.

Remarkable artworks were also produced in Sicily throughout the Classical period. The marble sculpture of a *pais* (boy) from Akragas is in keeping with artistic trends at the transition from the late Archaic to the Severe Classical style in Athens and elsewhere (Holloway 1975; Bennett et al. 2002). Slightly later, another marble sculpture depicting a crouching, nude, helmeted warrior was found near the Temple of Olympian Zeus at Akragas. It was not a part of the building's pedimental sculptures, which we know depicted a gigantomachy and the Trojan War, respectively. These themes were aptly chosen for a monument that celebrated a victory of order over "barbarian" chaos and a Greek victory over foes of eastern origin, but also for one so large that it would have needed an extraordinary number of figures to fill its gigantic pediments. Unfortunately, none of these sculptures survive. The temples built at Selinous continued to see decoration in the form of metopes, particularly Temple E (likely dedicated to Hera) on the East Hill (Fuchs 1956). Temple E showed myths of intergender relationships gone awry: Heracles grabbing an Amazon, Zeus seduced by Hera during the Trojan War, Artemis and Actaeon, and Athena and the giant Enceladus. The exposed skin of the female figures was rendered in marble, in contrast to the local limestone that composed the rest of the sculptures. The most spectacular example of a Greek cult statue comes from Sicily in this period, an almost completely intact, over-life-sized acrolithic sculpture of a draped goddess (J. Paul Getty Museum 2007). Again, her body is in limestone, and her head, hands, and feet were in imported marble. The statue was looted, likely from a sanctuary dedicated to Demeter and Kore at Morgantina. It dates to around 425. Demeter and Kore were exceptionally popular at this city shared by Greeks and Sikels, perhaps due to local worship of an indigenous fertility deity who could be syncretized to the cult of Demeter (White 1964; Bell 2008). The famous *contrapposto* sculpture in marble of a charioteer found in a sanctuary at Motya was presumably brought there as a trophy from one of the major Greek cities pillaged by the Carthaginians between 409 and 405; it originally commemorated an athletic victory, likely at a Panhellenic competition in Greece (Bell 1995; Lyons, Bennett, and Marconi 2013).

Sikeliot potters began to produce black- and red-glossed wares copying the sheen of Athenian pottery. Painted images appeared on these vases by the end of the fifth century. The most distinctively Sicilian art made by Greeks, however, came in the form of coinage with relief decoration so fine that the dies included signatures of artists such as Euainetos and Kimon (Lyons et al. 2013). Syracuse and Akragas were the leading cities for these kinds of works, which broke new ground by showing figures with frontal faces. Other metalwork included a remarkable solid gold *phiale*, probably from Himera, which records its weight and dedication by city officials in an inscription along its edge. This object gives vivid life to the story of the Egestaeans tricking the Athenian ambassadors through display of gold and silver plate.

Syracuse's afterglow from defeating Athens was short-lived (Evans 2016). In 409, a Carthaginian campaign began against the Sikeliots responsible for their defeat in 480. The Carthaginian forces first besieged and destroyed Selinous and Himera. In 405, they returned to Syracuse, proceeding down the south coast and doing the same to Akragas, Gela, and Kamarina in turn. An outbreak of plague took its toll on the Carthaginians, however, and they were unable to complete their siege of Syracuse. During the crisis provoked by this war, tyranny again emerged at Syracuse, with Dionysius I taking power over the city (Sanders 1987). In 398, he attacked the Carthaginian island-city of Motya, but the response from Carthage led to another siege of Syracuse, lifted again only because of another outbreak of plague in the Carthaginian camp. Although Dionysius was never able to subdue Carthage, he did extend Syracuse's dominion into the Adriatic Sea, founding cities and intervening in a war in Epirus. He attacked Greek and Etruscan cities along the Ionian and Tyrrhenian coasts as well, especially focusing on Rhegion and its Greek allies. In these ways, Dionysius and Syracuse were performing the same kinds of imperialistic actions carried out by major states across the Mediterranean in the Classical and Hellenistic periods. The cosmopolitan nature of this imperialism was underlined by court life, which, as in the fifth century, included poetry and philosophy. Dionysius I's brother-in-law and chief advisor, Dion, was a philosopher. When Dionysius II succeeded his father, he invited Plato to Syracuse (the visit was ill-fated and eventually cut short, due to court intrigues against Dion, who was Plato's friend and admirer; Plut. *Dion* 5.1–7).

The personality conflicts within the court of Syracuse between Dionysius II and Dion led to an internal crisis in which both men suffered exile at different moments. The instability led some Syracusans to request assistance from Corinth in 344. Corinth sent Timoleon and a small group of ships and soldiers (Talbert 1974; Teodorsson 2005). Timoleon sent Dionysius II into exile at Corinth and took control. Timoleon finally defeated the Carthaginians at the Battle of the Crimissus, in western Sicily, in 339, and the ensuing peace treaty reestablished the status quo, with Greeks controlling the eastern two-thirds of the island, and Carthage agreeing not to make alliances with anti-Syracusan tyrants from other cities. Timoleon's peace held until Syracuse was taken over by a new and ambitious tyrant named Agathocles in 317. He conquered much of Greek Sicily within a few years, and then began hostilities with Carthage. He was unsuccessful in winning that war, but continued to call himself "king of Sicily," and maintained his control over the Greek part of the island.

One important phenomenon that seems to have occurred during the fourth century BCE was the end of a distinct Sikel identity (Antonaccio 2001). Intermarriage had likely occurred since the very beginning of Greek colonization (see, e.g., Thuc. 6.6; Hodos 1999; Shepherd 1999). It is probable that some Sikels lived in Greek cities, and vice versa. By the fourth century, inscriptions in the Sikel language disappear, and other cultural attributes, such as their distinctive painted and incised pottery wares, also ceased to be made. In archaeological terms, it becomes impossible to distinguish Sikels from Greeks. This change can be considered a shift in Sikeliot identity as well, since that moniker gradually included not only people of mixed Sikel and Greek descent, but non-Greeks as well, due not only to intermarriage and cohabitation but also to religious syncretism and economic entanglement.

There was also no clear transition between the Classical and the Hellenistic periods, as happened elsewhere in the Greek world (Wilson 2013, 79). The political history of Hellenistic Sicily continued to be largely a history of Syracuse and its dominance over local affairs. When Pyrrhus of Epirus invaded Italy and attacked the Romans in 280, he was invited by the Greek cities of Sicily to come to their aid against Carthage. The Carthaginians had attacked yet again and were besieging Syracuse; Pyrrhus defeated them in 278 and was proclaimed king of Sicily. He then pursued Carthaginian forces into their own territory, capturing the Elymian citadel at Eryx. The surrender of the other Carthaginian allies in Sicily left Carthage holding only Lilybaeum, but the cost of Pyrrhus's expensive siege of that city became unpopular with the Greeks. They rebelled against him and were ready to join forces with the Carthaginians, until Pyrrhus abandoned Sicily altogether in 275. One of his generals, a Syracusan named Hieron, stepped into this void (Lehmler 2005). Hieron was hailed king in 270 and became known as Hieron II. During his extraordinarily long reign (270–215), he kept Syracuse independent of Carthage and of Rome. He successfully negotiated the perilous rivalry between these two great Mediterranean powers, allying himself with Carthage, and then, following his defeat by the Romans, turning to support them instead.

Under Hieron II, Syracuse again became a cultural center, with the construction of monumental architecture, such as the Great Altar of Zeus and the rebuilding of the Theater of Dionysos (Wilson 2013, 83–90; Bell 1999, 269–276). The kingdom's borders stretched to Naxos along the east coast and as far inland as Morgantina. Messana, northern Sicily, and western Sicily were under Roman control from 241, and by 227 the island, apart from the kingdom of Syracuse, became the first Roman province. The wealth of the period is evident on the frontiers of the kingdom; at Morgantina, several stoas, a fountain-house, and granaries were at least partially constructed (Bell 1988; 2006; Walthall 2013, 2015). This was also the period of Archimedes, the great thinker of Hellenistic Sicily. He was responsible for mathematical discoveries, engineering innovations, and military inventions. The spirit of the period can be seen in the recent discovery of the world's earliest known self-supporting dome and barrel vault, in a bath complex at Morgantina (Lucore 2009). These were constructed of interlocking clay tubes that arched over bathing spaces. This technology seems likely to have been developed at the capital, not on the kingdom's frontiers. Likewise, artistic invention is also evident in this period, as seen from the earliest known tessellated mosaics, again found at Morgantina, but likely invented at Syracuse (Phillips 1960; Tsakirgis 1989). Sicilian metalwork followed trends in Hellenistic art more generally, embracing heightened realism, drama, and the treatment of quotidian subjects. A life-size bronze ram from Syracuse (probably one of a pair), now in Palermo, displays these tendencies. Perhaps the most spectacular examples of Syracusan Hellenistic silverwork are to be found in the service illegally excavated at Morgantina in 1980 or 1981 (Bell 2000b; Guzzo 2003). The gilt silver tondo that was part of this group (formerly in the Metropolitan Museum of Art, now in the archaeological museum at Aidone), depicted Scylla hurling a boulder at the viewer; it is a masterpiece of emotion, fantasy, and drama.

Hieron II's death in 215 brought an end to the independence of Greek states in Sicily. Strife between aristocrats (who favored Rome) and democrats (who favored Carthage) led to Hieron's grandson and heir, Hieronymus, withdrawing from the alliance with Rome.

A Roman army besieged Syracuse for two years, finally capturing the city in 212. Other Greek cities, still calling themselves "Sikeliots" continued to resist until the final holdout, Morgantina, was captured in 211. Coins reading "Sikeliotan" ("the Sikeliot League") found at Morgantina and dating to this final phase of the conflict confirm that the resistance was seen as a Hellenic one, rather than merely Syracusan (Sjöqvist 1960). Rome would rule Sicily for six more centuries.

Conclusion

The history of Greek Sicily owed much to the island's size, agricultural fertility, and location. Colonies became wealthy and populous over the centuries. At the same time, patterns familiar from the homeland also were apparent in Sicily, not least the rivalry between *poleis*, political and economic inequalities that led to tensions between aristocrats and the lower classes, and the emergence of tyranny as a stop-gap solution to social and military problems. The specific context of Sicily, as a space where indigenes and a variety of outsider groups from the eastern and central Mediterranean (Greek, Phoenician/Carthaginian, Roman) were constantly locked in conflict, encouraged different kinds of responses, melding of populations, contesting of territory, and use of resources.

The importance of new, postcolonial assessments of ancient Sicilian history and culture has already been put forward as a more effective way to understand those processes. One relatively recent approach, globalization, deserves reference here as a possible path to developing (or encouraging) future interpretations. Globalization can be described as "processes of increasing connectivities that unfold and manifest as social awareness of those connectivities" (Hodos and Walsh 2017). Shared values and practices are developed, while, at the same time, awareness of differences emerges (Hodos 2017). The adoption of Demeter and Kore worship by indigenous Sicilian communities, for example, was not merely Hellenization or hybridization, but rather it was both of those things simultaneously. The shared worship of agricultural fertility deities allowed Sikels and Sikeliots to find common ground, but also to articulate their own beliefs through divergent practices. Further development will undoubtedly also happen as scholars of Sicily increasingly take note of approaches developed in other fields, such as the social sciences (Canevaro et al. 2018). By recognizing the true complexity of colonial interactions, scholars will continue to gain important new insights into the lives of ancient Sicilians, Greeks and non-Greeks alike (e.g., Berlinzani 2012).

NOTE

1 The names given for these two Sikels in the inscription (and in Thucydides [7.1] for one of them) raise questions about whether they adopted Greek names in their interactions with Greeks, or whether they are simply Greek approximations of translations of the brothers' titles in Sikel. Similarly, Ducetius seems so close to the Latin *dux* that it may also reflect a title as much as a given name (Walsh 2011–2012, nos. 36 and 50).

REFERENCES

Albanese Procelli, Rosa M. 1996a. "Contacts and Exchanges in Protohistoric Sicily." *Acta Hyperborea*, 6: 33–49.

Albanese Procelli, Rosa M. 1996b. "Appunti sulla distribuzione delle anfore comerciale nella Sicilia arcaica." *Kokalos*, 42: 91–137.

Albanese Procelli, Rosa M. 1996c. "Greek and Indigenous People in Eastern Sicily: Forms of Interaction and Acculturation." In *Early Societies in Sicily*, edited by R. Leighton, 167–176. London: Accordia Research Centre.

Albanese Procelli, Rosa M. 1997a. "Importazioni greche nei centri interni della Sicilia in età arcaica: aspetti dell' 'acculturazione'." In *I vasi attici ed altre ceramiche coeve in Sicilia*, vol. 2, edited by Giovanni Rizza and Filippo Giudice, 97–111. Catania: Istituto di Archeologia.

Albanese Procelli, Rosa M. 1997b. "Echanges dans la Sicile archaïque: amphores commerciales, intermédiares, et redistribution en milieu indigène." *Revue Archeologique*, 89: 3–25.

Albanese Procelli, Rosa M. 1997c. "Identità e confini etnico-culturali: La Sicilia centro-orientale." In *Confini e Frontiera nella Grecità d'Occidente. Atti del 36 Convegno di Studi sulla Magna Grecia*, edited by Attilio Stazio, Stefania Ceccoli, Jean-Loup Amselle, et al., 326–359. Taranto: Istituto per la Storia e l'Archeologia della Magna Grecia.

Albanese Procelli, Rosa M. 2003. *Sicani, Siculi, Elimi. Forme di identità, modi di contatto e processi di trasformazione*. Milan: Longanesi.

Allegro, Nunzio. 1997. "Le fasi dell'abitato di Himera." In *Wohnbauforschung in Zentral- und West-Sizilien – Sicilian Occidentale e Centro-meridionale: Ricerche Archaeologiche nell'Abitato*, edited by Hans-Peter Isler, 65–80. Zurich: Archäologisches Insitut.

Ambrosini, Riccardo. 1980. "L'elemento indigeno." In *La Sicilia antica: La Sicilia antica, 2 vols.*, edited by Emilio Gabba and Georges Vallet, 43–51. Napoli: Storia di Napoli e della Sicilia Società Editrice.

Ampolo, Carmine, ed. 2012. *Agora greca e agorai di Sicilia*. Pisa: Edizioni della Normale.

Antonaccio, Carla M. 1997. "Urbanism at Archaic Morgantina." *Acta Hyperborea*, 7: 167–194.

Antonaccio, Carla M. 1999. "Kupara, a Sikel Nymph?" *Zeitschrift für Papyrologie und Epigraphik*, 126: 177–185.

Antonaccio, Carla M. 2001. "Ethnicity and Colonization." In *Ancient Perceptions of Greek Ethnicity*, edited by Irad Malkin, 113–157. Washington, DC: Center for Hellenic Studies.

Antonaccio, Carla M. 2003. "Hybridity and the Cultures within Greek Culture." In *The Cultures within Ancient Greek Culture*, edited by Carol Dougherty and Leslie Kurke, 57–74. Cambridge: Cambridge University Press.

Antonaccio, Carla M. 2004. "Siculo-Geometric and the Sikels: Identity and Material Culture in Eastern Sicily." In *Greek Identity in the Western Mediterranean: Studies in Honor of Brian Shefton*, edited by Kathryn Lomas, 55–81. Leiden: Brill.

Antonaccio, Carla M. 2005. "Excavating Colonization." In *Ancient Colonizations: Analogy, Similarity, and Difference*, edited by Henry Hurst and Sara Owen, 97–113. London: Duckworth.

Antonaccio, Carla. 2009. "(Re) Defining Ethnicity: Culture, Material Culture, and Identity." In *Material Culture and Social Identities in the Ancient World*, edited by Tamar Hodos and Shelley Hales, 32–53. Cambridge: Cambridge University Press.

Antonaccio, Carla M., and Jennifer Neils. 1995. "A New Graffito from Archaic Morgantina." *Zeitschrift für Papryrologie und Epigraphik*, 105: 261–277.

Aubet, Maria E. 2009. *Tiro y las colonias fenicias de Occidente*. 3rd ed. Barcelona: Bellaterra Arqueología.

Bell, Malcolm, III. 1984–1985. "Recenti scavi nell'Agora di Morgantina." *Kokalos*, 30–31: 501–520.

Bell, Malcolm, III. 1988. "Excavations at Morgantina, 1980–1985, Preliminary Report XII." *American Journal of Archaeology*, 92: 318–342.

Bell, Malcolm, III. 1995. "The Motya Charioteer and Pindar's *Isthmian 2*." *Memoirs of the American Academy in Rome*, 40: 1–42.

Bell, Malcolm, III. 1999. "Centro e periferia nel regno siracusano di Ierone II." In *La colonisation grecque en Méditerranée occidentale. Actes de la rencontre scientifique en hommage à George Vallet (Rome-Naples 1995)*, 255–277. Rome: École française de Rome.

Bell, Malcolm, III. 2000a. "Camarina e Morgantina al Congresso di Gela." In *Un ponte fra l'Italia e la Grecia: Atti del simposio in onore di Antonino di Vita*, edited by Giorgio Chessari, 291–297. Padua: Bottega d'Erasmo.

Bell, Malcolm, III. 2000b. "La provenienza ritrovata, cercando il contesto di antichità trafugate." *Antichità senza provenienza, Atti del colloquio international. Supplemento a Bollettino d'Arte*, 101–102: 31–41.

Bell, Malcolm, III. 2006. "Rapporti urbanistici fra Camarina e Morgantina." In *Camarina 2600 anni dopo: nuovi studi sulla città e sul territorio. Atti del convegno internazionale, Ragusa, 7 dicembre 2002/7–9 aprile 2003*, edited by Paola Pelagatti, Giovanni Di Stefano, and Lucilla de Lachenal, 253–258. Rome: Istituto poligrafico e Zecca dello Stato.

Bell, Malcolm, III. 2008. "Hiera Oikopeda." In *Demetra. La divinità, i santuari, il culto, la leggenda, atti del I Congresso internazionale, Enna, 1–4 luglio 2004*, edited by Carmela Angela Di Stefano, 155–160. Pisa: Fabrizio Serra.

Bennett, Michael J., Aaron Paul, Mario Iozzo, and Bruce White. 2002. *Magna Graecia: Greek Art from South Italy and Sicily*. Cleveland: Museum of Art.

Berlinzani, Francesca, ed. 2012. *Convivenze etniche, scontri e contatti di culture in Sicilia e Magna Grecia. Aristonothos*. Scritti per il Mediterraneo antico 7. Trento: Tangram.

Bertolino, Francesco, Flavia Alaima, and Stefano Vassallo. 2017. "Battles of Himera (480 and 409 BC): Analysis of Biological Finds and Historical Interpretation. Experiences of Restoration in the Ruins of Himera 2008-2010." *Conservation Science in Cultural Heritage*, 15(2): 27–40.

Bonanno, Daniela. 2010. *Ierone il Dinomenide: storia e rappresentazione*. Pisa: Fabrizio Serra.

Braccesi, Lorenzo, and Giovanni Millino. 2000. *La Sicilia Greca*. Rome: Carocci.

Canevaro, Mirko, Andrew Erskine, Benjamin Gray, and Josiah Ober, eds. 2018. *Ancient Greek History and Contemporary Social Science*. Edinburgh: Edinburgh University Press.

Cordano, Federica. 1992. "Note sui gruppi civici sicelioti." *Miscellenea Graeca e Romana*, 17: 135–138.

De Angelis, Franco. 1998. "Ancient Past, Imperial Present: The British Empire in T.J. Dunbabin's *The Western Greeks*." *Antiquity*, 72: 539–549.

De Angelis, Franco. 2000. "Estimating the Agricultural Base of Greek Sicily." *Papers of the British School at Rome*, 68: 111–148.

De Angelis, Franco. 2016. *Archaic and Classical Greek Sicily*. Oxford: Oxford University Press.

De Miro, Ernesto. 1983. *Agrigento, the Valley of the Temples*. Novaro: Istituto geografico de Agostini.

De Polignac, François. 1995. *Cults, Territory, and the Origins of the Greek City-State*. Trans. J. Lloyd. Chicago: Chicago University Press.

Di Vita, Antonino. 1954. "Casmene ritrovata?" *Siculorum Gymansiorum*, 7: 264–267.

Di Vita, Antonino. 1956a. "Recenti scoperte archeologiche in provincia Ragusa." *Archivio Storico Siracusano*, 2: 30–44.

Di Vita, Antonino. 1956b. "La penetrazione siracusana nella Sicilia sud-orientale alla luce delle più recenti scoperte archeologiche." *Kokalos*, 2: 177–205.

Di Vita, Antonino. 1987. "Tucidide VI 5 e l'epicrazia siracusana: Acre, Casmene, Camarina." *Kokalos*, 33: 77–87.

Di Vita, Antonino. 1990. "Town Planning in the Greek Colonies of Sicily from the Time of their Foundations to the Punic Wars." In *Greek Colonists and Native Populations. Proceedings of the First Australian Congress of Classical Archaeology Held in Honour of A.D. Trendall, 9–14 July 1985*, edited by Jean-Paul Descoeudres, 343–363. Oxford: Clarendon Press.

Dougherty, Carol. 1993. *The Poetics of Colonization*. Oxford: Oxford University Press.

Dunbabin, Thomas J. 1948. *The Western Greeks: The History of Sicily and South Italy from the Foundation of the Greek Colonies to 480 BC*. Oxford: Clarendon Press.

Evans, Richard. 2016. *Ancient Syracuse: From Foundation to Fourth-Century Collapse*. London: Routledge.

Freeman, Edward A. 1891. *The History of Sicily from Earliest Times*. 2 vols. Oxford: Clarendon Press.

Fuchs, Werner. 1956. "Zu den Metopen des Heraion von Selinus." *Mitteilungen des Deutschen Archäologischen Insituts Romische Abteilung*, 63: 102–121.

Green, Peter. 2006. *Diodorus Siculus, Books 11–12.37.1: Greek History, 480–431 BC, the Alternative Version*. Austin: University of Texas Press.

Guzzo, Pier Giovanni. 2003. "A Group of Hellenistic Silver Objects in the Metropolitan Museum." *Metropolitan Museum Journal*, 38: 45–94.

Harrison, Thomas. 2000. "Sicily in the Athenian Imagination." In *Sicily from Aeneas to Augustus: New Approaches in Archaeology and History*, edited by Christopher J. Smith and John Serrati, 84–96. Edinburgh: Edinburgh University Press.

Hodos, Tamar. 1999. "Intermarriage in Western Greek Colonies." *Oxford Journal of Archaeology*, 18: 61–78.

Hodos, Tamar. 2010. "Globalization and Colonization: A View from Iron Age Sicily." *Journal of Mediterranean Archaeology*, 23: 81–106.

Hodos, Tamar, ed. 2017. *The Routledge Handbook of Archaeology and Globalization*. London: Routledge.

Hodos, Tamar, and Justin St. P. Walsh. 2017. "Religious Activity as an Index for Globalization and Insularity in Archaic and Classical Sicily." Unpublished paper delivered at the Archaeological Institute of America's 118th Annual Meeting, Toronto.

Hoepfner, Wolfram, and Ernst-Ludwig Schwandner. 1994. *Haus und Stadt im klassischen Griechenland*. Munich: Deutscher Kunstverlag.

Holloway, Ross R. 1975. *Influences and Styles in the Late Archaic and Early Classical Sculpture of Sicily and Magna Graecia*. Louvain: Institut supérieur d'archéologie et d'histoire de l'art.

Horden, Peregrine, and Nicholas Purcell. 2000. *The Corrupting Sea: A Study of Mediterranean History*. Oxford: Blackwell.

Hornblower, Simon. 2010. *A Commentary on Thucydides: Volume III: Books 5.25–8.109*. Oxford: Oxford University Press.

J. Paul Getty Museum. 2007. *Cult Statue of a Goddess: Summary of Proceedings of a Workshop Held at the Getty Villa, May 9, 2007*. Los Angeles: Getty Museum.

Jackman, Trinity. 2005. "Ducetius and Fifth-century Sicilian Tyranny." In *Ancient Tyranny*, edited by Sian Lewis, 33–48. Edinburgh: Edinburgh University Press.

Knappett, Carl., Tim Evans, and Ray Rivers. 2008. "Modelling Maritime Interaction in the Aegean Bronze Age." *Antiquity*, 82: 1009–1024.

Kustermann Graf, Anne. 2002. *Selinunte: necropoli di Manicalunga: le tombe della contrada Gaggera*. Catanzaro: Rubbettino.

Lehmler, Caroline. *Syrakus unter Agathokles und Hieron II: Die Verbindung von Kultur und Macht in einer hellenistischen Metropole*. Berlin: Verlag Antike.

Lepore, Ettore, and Giuseppe Nenci, eds. 1983. *Modes de contacts et processus de transformation dans les sociétés anciennes – Forme di contatto e processi trasformazione nelle società antiche*. Pisa and Rome: Scuola normale superior and École française de Rome.

Lomas, Kathryn. 1995. "The Greeks in the West and the Hellenization of Italy." In *The Greek World*, edited by Anton Powell, 347–367. London: Routledge.

Lomas, Kathryn. 1997. "Constructing the 'Greek.'" In *Gender and Ethnicity in Ancient Italy*, edited by Kathryn Lomas and Tim Cornell, 29–42. London: Accordia Research Centre.

Lomas, Kathryn, ed. 2004. *Greek Identity in the Western Mediterranean. Studies in Honor of Brian Shefton*. Leiden: Brill.

Lucore, Sandra K. 2009. "Archimedes, the North Baths at Morgantina and Early Developments in Vaulted Construction." In *The Nature and Function of Water, Baths, Bathing and Hygiene from Antiquity through the Renaissance*, edited by Cynthia Kosso and Anne Scott, 43–59. Leiden: Brill.

Luraghi, Nino. 1994. *Tirannidi arcaiche in Sicilia e Magna Grecia: Da Panezio di Leontini alla caduti dei Deinomenidi*. Florence: Olschki.

Lyons, Claire L. 1991. "Modalità di acculturazione a Morgantina." *Bolletino di Archeologia*, 11–12: 1–10.

Lyons, Claire L. 1996. "Sikel Burials at Morgantina: Defining Social and Ethnic Identities." In *Early Societies in Sicily*, edited by Robert Leighton, 177–188. London: Accordia Research Centre.

Lyons, Claire L., Michael J. Bennett, and Clemente Marconi, eds. 2013. *Sicily: Art and Invention between Greece and Rome*. Los Angeles: Getty Museum.

Malkin, Irad. 2011. *A Small Greek World: Networks in the Ancient Mediterranean*. Oxford: Oxford University Press.

Meister, Klaus. 1990. *Die griechische Geschichtsschreibung von den Anfängen bis zum Ende des Hellenismus*. Stuttgart: Kohlhammer.

Morgan, Catherine. 1997. "The Archaeology of Ethnicity in the Colonial World of the Eighth to Sixth Centuries BC: Approaches and Prospects." In *Confini e Frontiera nella Grecità d'Occidente. Atti del XXXVII convegno di studi sulla Magna Grecia (Taranto 1997)*, edited by Attilio Stazio, Stefania Ceccoli, Jean-Loup Amselle, et al., 85–145. Taranto: Istituto per la Storia e l'Archeologia della Magna Grecia.

Phillips, Kyle M. 1960. "Subject and Technique in Hellenistic-Roman Mosaics: A Ganymede Mosaic from Sicily." *Art Bulletin*, 42: 243–262.

Pope, Spencer. 2006. *The Fourth Century Settlement at Palike, Sicily*. PhD dissertation, Brown University.

Ruiz de Arbulo, Joaquín. 1991. "Rutas marítimas y colonizaciones en la Península Ibérica: Una aproximación náutica a algunos problemas." *Cuadernos de Trabajos de la Escuela Española de Historia y Arqueología en Roma*, 18: 79–115.

Sanders, Lionel J. 1987. *Dionysius I of Syracuse and Greek Tyranny*. London: Croom Helm.

Scott, Michael. 2010. *Delphi and Olympia: The Spatial Politics of Panhellenism in the Archaic and Classical Periods*. Cambridge: Cambridge University Press.

Shefton, Brian B. 1997. "The Castulo Cup: An Attic Shape in Black Glaze of Special Significance in Sicily." In *I vasi attici ed altre ceramiche coeve in Sicilia*, vol. 1, edited by Giovanni Rizza and Filippo Giudice, 85–98. Catania: Istituto di Archeologia.

Shepherd, Gillian. 1999. "Fibulae and Females: Intermarriage in the Western Greek Colonies and the Evidence from the Cemeteries." In *Ancient Greeks West and East*, edited by Gocha Tsetskhladze, 267–300. Leiden: Brill.

Sinatra, D. 1998. "Camarina: Città di frontiera?" *Hesperìa*, 9: 41–52.

Sjöqvist, Erik. 1960. "Numismatic Notes from Morgantina I: The Sikeliotan Coinage." *American Numismatic Society Museum Notes*, 9: 53–63.

Sjöqvist, Erik. 1973. *Sicily and the Greeks: Studies in the Interrelationship between the Indigenous Populations and the Greek Colonists*. Ann Arbor: University of Michigan Press.

Talbert, Richard J.A. 1974. *Timoleon and the Revival of Greek Sicily, 344–317 BC*. Cambridge: Cambridge University Press.

Teodorsson, Sven-Tage. 2005. "Timoleon, the Fortunate General." In *The Statesman in Plutarch's Works, Volume II*, edited by Lukas de Blois, Jeroen Bons, Ton Kessels, and Dirk Schenkenveld, 215–226. Leiden: Brill.

Tréziny, Henri. 1999. "Lots et îlots à Mégara Hyblaea. Questions de métrologie." In *La colonisation grecque en Méditerranée occidentale. Actes de la rencontre scientifique en hommage à George Vallet (Rome-Naples 1995)*, 141–183. Rome: École française de Rome.

Trombi, C. 1999. "La ceramica indigena dipinta della Sicilia dalla seconda metà del IX sec. a.C. al V sec. a.C." In *Origine e incontri*, edited by Marcella Barra Bagnasco, Erenesto de Miro, and Antonino Pinzone, 275–294. Messina: Di.Sc.A.M.

Tsakirgis, Barbara. 1989. "The Decorated Pavements of Morgantina I: The Mosaics." *American Journal of Archaeology*, 93: 395–416.

Tykot, Robert, Kyle Freund, and Andrea Vianello. 2013. "Source Analysis of Prehistoric Obsidian Artifacts in Sicily (Italy) Using pXRF." In *Archaeological Chemistry VIII*, edited by Ruth Ann Armitage and James Burton, 195–210. New York: Oxford University Press.

Uggeri, Giovanni. 2015. *Camarina: Storia e topographia di una colonia greca di Sicilia e del suo territorio. Journal of Ancient Topography*, Suppl. 8. Florence: Congedo.

Vignolo Munson, R. 2006. "Herodotus and Italy: An Alternate World." In *The Cambridge Companion to Herodotus*, edited by Carolyn Dewald and John Marincola, 257–273. Cambridge: Cambridge University Press.

Voza, Giuseppe. 1973. "Thapsos: Resoconto sulle campagne di scavo 1970–71." In *Istituto italiano di preistoria e protoistoria, Atti del XV riunione scientifica*. Florence: Istituto italiano di preistoria e protoistoria.

Voza, Giuseppe. 1986. "I contatti precoloniale col mondo Greco." In *Sikanie: Storia e civiltà della Sicilia greca*, edited by Giovanni Pugliese Carratelli, 543–562. Milan: Garzanti.

Wallerstein, Immanuel. 1974. *The Modern World-System*. New York: Academic Press.

Walsh, Justin. St. P. 2011–2012. "Urbanism and Identity at Classical Morgantina." *Memoirs of the American Academy in Rome*, 56–57: 115–136.

Walsh, J. St. P. 2013. "Consumption and Choice in Ancient Sicily." In *Regionalism and Globalism in Antiquity: Exploring Their Limits*, edited by Franco De Angelis, 229–246. Leuven: Peeters.

Walsh, Justin. St. P., and Carla M. Antonaccio. 2014. "Athenian Black Gloss Pottery: A View from the West." *Oxford Journal of Archaeology*, 33: 47–67.

Walthall, D. Alex. 2013. *A Measured Harvest: Grain, Tithes, and Territories in Hellenistic and Roman Sicily (276–31 BCE)*. PhD dissertation, Princeton University.

Walthall, D. Alex. 2015. "Recenti scavi nei granai monumentali a Morgantina." In *Morgantina ieri e oggi*, edited by Laura Maniscalco, 82–91. Enna: Museo Archeologico di Aidone.

White, Donald. 1964. "Demeter's Sicilian Cult as a Political Instrument." *Greek, Roman, and Byzantine Studies*, 5: 261–279.

Wilson, Roger J.A. 2013. "Hellenistic Sicily, c. 270–100 BC." In *The Hellenistic West*, edited by Jonathan R.W. Prag and Josephine C. Quinn, 79–119. Cambridge: Cambridge University Press.

Zuchtriegel, Gabriel. 2017. *Colonization and Subalternity in Classical Greece: Experience of the Non-Elite Population*. Cambridge: Cambridge University Press.

FURTHER READING

Albanese Procelli (2003) is the first book to synthesize all of the available archaeological evidence to understand intercultural contact in Sicily from an indigenous perspective. Antonaccio (2009) is a reassessment of the categories and epistemologies archaeologists use to define cultural identity in the ancient Mediterranean. De Angelis (2016) is the most up-to-date large-scale history of Greek Sicily. Hodos (2010) is an introduction to the application of globalization theory to the ancient Mediterranean, using Sicily as an example.

CHAPTER FIFTEEN

The Adriatic Sea and Region[1]

Maria Cecilia D'Ercole

Ancient Greeks and the Adriatic Sea: the two terms of this chapter are, at least in part, contradictory, as for centuries this Mediterranean region remained off limits to the lasting settlement of Greek communities (Map 2). The historical process known as "Greek colonization" stopped in the eighth century BC at the gates of the Adriatic Sea, with the Corinthian foundation of Corcyra (modern Corfu) in 733 BC. In the last quarter of the seventh century, the foundations of Epidamnos and Apollonia, on the shore of modern Albania, had a strong impact on the Ionian coast and Balkan peninsula. However, at least until the fifth century BC, the Greeks exerted much less influence on the inner Adriatic space. A wider dynamic of Greek settlement, mostly on the eastern side of the sea (Pharos, Issa, Black Corcyra), started only from the fourth century BC. In spite of this, the relationship of ancient Greeks with the Adriatic does not come down to the mere record of absence. On the contrary, there were many and complex economic and cultural contacts from the Archaic era, with effects on many levels, both material and symbolic, such as economic development, spatial perceptions, and mythical inventions.

Furthermore, the regional approach, which is fruitful for all Mediterranean history (Vlassopoulos 2011), is particularly apt to analyze the historical dynamics of ancient *Adrias*, as is suggested by the geographic morphology of the coastal landscape. At the mouth of the Adriatic Sea the channel of Otranto is only 70 km wide. Its coastline is rather unstable, tending to be submerged by rising waters in the northern Adriatic, but elsewhere advancing as rivers accrue sediments, for example, at the mouths of the Po, on the western side, and of the Drina and Vlora on the eastern one. A narrow coastal strip, formed by sand (Veneto, Emilia, Apulia) or limestone (from Trieste to northern Albania), stretches very near to the plateaux and mountains of the hinterland. Such proximity between plains (Po valley and Tavoliere on the Italian side, the Neretva valley and Myzeqeja in the Balkans) and mountains (Apennines and Eastern Alps) fostered for centuries the

---

A Companion to Greeks Across the Ancient World, First Edition. Edited by Franco De Angelis.
© 2020 John Wiley & Sons, Inc. Published 2020 by John Wiley & Sons, Inc.

practice of transhumance. Finally, the coastal landscape is scattered with promontories (Gargano, Conero), peninsulae (Histria), and islands (the Tremiti on the western side, Kvarner and countless others on the eastern side): they offered not only the landmarks for seafaring, but also the sites for many legends and myths.

Perceptions

> Pythagoras actually recommended that, coming to the end of life, they should not swear but, as when sailing, they should express good wishes with propitious words, as when crossing the Adriatic Sea (Iamblichus, *Life of Pythagoras* 257).

According to Iamblichus (ca. 240–330), this was one the most important precepts left by Pythagoras to his disciples. A recommendation well known to the sailors of Piraeus of the fifth century BC (Lysias XXXII, *Diogeiton*. 25 and fr. XXXVIII) seems to be still popular and forceful in the Roman Syria of Iamblichus; sailing in the Adriatic Sea was an extremely dangerous activity. This negative image may have contributed to the image of the Adriatic as *alimenos*, that is, harborless, recorded in the Augustan period (Strab. 7.5.10; Livy 10.2.4; see D'Ercole 2002, 20–22). There were several elements in this reputation. One was probably only superficial acquaintance with the terrain. Until the Augustan age, the length of Illyria was known, but not its depth (Šašel Kos 2005, 114), and this reveals a maritime perspective in the knowledge of the country's geography. The second element was the real difficulty in coping with winds and sea currents; Ps.-Scymnos (384–387) remarks that the Adriatic could be suddenly shaken by wild storms and dreadful thunderbolts. The last and most important reason arose from various anthropic factors. One was probably piracy, which flourished for centuries in the Adriatic, as we will see below. Another, weightier problem was the political, economic, and cultural organization of the Adriatic peoples which prevented the spread of Greek establishments.

Other ancient perceptions refer to the shape of the sea itself: starting from Hecataeus (*FGrH* I, F90; F93), the Adriatic was considered as a *kolpos*, a gulf which was closed and hard to penetrate. Several Greek authors (Strab. 7.5.9; Ps.-Skyl. 14; 18) assigned to this maritime space a mouth, *stoma*, located at the modern channel of Otranto. Moreover, this closed space also had an internal recess, a *muchos*, in the northern Adriatic (Theopompus of Chios in Strabo 7.5.1; Ps.-Skymnos 387–388; Dion. Per. 92–94). The name itself, *Adrias*, which appears in the Greek language in the last decades of the sixth century BC (Frisone 2008), testifies to the discovery of a coastal region by some groups of Greeks. According to Stephanus Byzantius, this name appeared in the *Periodos gês* of Hecataeus of Miletos referring simultaneously to a river, a settlement, and the sea (*kolpos Adrias*: Hecat., in Steph. Byz. s.v. *Adria*; *FGrH* I, F90).

Already in this ancient level of sources, some trends appear both in historical accounts and in mythological inventions featuring the Adriatic which were to be perpetuated. The first is the contradictory use of the name Adrias. In Hecataeus's fragments, the Liburnians are located in the inner part of the Adriatic gulf (*FGrH* I, F93) and the Histrians are supposed to live on the *Ionios kolpos* (*FGrH* I, F91), whereas they actually dwelt to the north of the Liburnians. Similar confusions existed also between the eastern and western side of the sea: *Iapygia* is the name assigned to two different cities, one in the Italian Peninsula, the other in the Illyrian country (*FGrH* I, F97).

The geographical discovery of the sea and the coastal regions combined contemporary with ethnographic knowledge and allowed the same mistakes and uncertainties to be shared. According to the *Ethnika* of Stephanus Byzantius, Hecataeus was the first to list a sequence of Eastern Adriatic peoples: *Histroi, Liburnoi, Mentores, Taulanti, Chelidoni* (*FGrH* I, F91–94, F99–100). Some of them, like the Histrians and Liburnians, mentioned by several subsequent authors, maintained an importance up until the Roman imperial period. Others, such as the *Suopi, Ithmitai,* and *Habroi*, remained unknown (*FGrH* I, F95–96, F101). On the western shore, Hecataeus speaks of *Iapygia* and the people called *Peuketiantes*, that is, the Peucetians (*FGrH* I, F86, 88–89, 97).

Moreover, some tendencies of Adriatic ethnography can already be noticed in Hecataeus's description of *Europa* and recur often later. A first element is the profusion and high demographic density ascribed by some ancient authors to the Adriatic peoples. Ps.-Skymnos (376–377) estimates that "Adriatic barbarians" amount to around 1 500 000. The same author argues that the Heneti founded more than 50 *poleis* around the Adriatic basin (387–388). Second, some ancient authors are inclined to consider the Adriatic countries as lands of "marvelous things" where exceptional phenomena took place. Stephanus Byzantius, in a passage which seems to go back to Hecataios, underlines the fecundity of the women and animals of the Po valley and attributes the same peculiarity to the *Ombrikoi* (Steph. Byz., s.v. *Adria*; *FGrH* I, F90). Similar statements are repeated two centuries later. Ps-Aristotle describes the fertility of Umbrian women and herds (80) as well as of Illyrian cattle (128). Still in the Hellenistic age, Ps.-Skymnos (378–379) considers all the Adriatic shores as fertile lands where animals procreate several times a year. These testimonies demonstrate an interest in the Adriatic which probably increased during the fourth century BC, as book XXI of Theopompos's *Philippika* suggests. The historian of Chios may have been the source of the demographic appraisal of Pseudo-Scymnos, according to Marcotte (2000, 119, 194–207). Related to the rise of the Macedonian dynasty in the Balkans, this interest in the Adriatic lands probably renewed an image created in the Archaic period (Vattuone 2000, 25–27) and still accepted by some Greek historians in the second century BC. Polybius's account (3.87.3–4; 88.1–3) of the aftermath of the battle of Metaurus, during the second Punic war, highlights the abundance and excellence of every kind of goods in the region of Picenum.

Moreover, in the land of the "Adriatic barbarians," animals can appear singularly civilized. This is the case for the heterogeneous fauna surrounding the shrine of Diomedes at the mouth of the Timavus River. Wolves are supposed to live there among the deer, watching over the precious horses of the Veneto; dogs forbore hunting game when it arrived to shelter in the sanctuary (Strab. 5.1.9). The prodigious dogs of the Daunian temple of Athena, named *Achaia* by Pseudo-Aristotle (*Mir.* 79) and *Ilias* by Aelian (*NA* XI, 5), were known for being friendly with Greeks. It is also the case for the marvelous birds of the islands of Diomedes, able to distinguish honest from knavish men, giving their welcome to foreign people, particularly to Greeks (Strab. 4.3.1). These legendary tales probably imply, at least partially, patterns of contacts between Greeks and native people which developed around places of worship, fostered by some intermediary myths.

Lastly, Greek myths in the Adriatic made it possible to establish links and affinities between various cultural ethnic groups, appealing to the notion of common origin and legendary kinship (*syngeneia*). Among them, the tale of the *nostos* of Diomedes was doubtless the most widespread and forceful (D'Ercole 2000). Starting from the seventh century BC, when the myth was first attached to the Daunian region (Mimnermus, in *Schol. ad Lycophronis Alexandram*, 610), the whole Adriatic shoreline becomes progressively studded by foundations and sanctuaries linked to the Greek hero. Other "returns" of famous Homeric figures are linked to the Adriatic. The connection between Venetus and the Trojan legend could have been already established by a cryptic line in Homer.[2] During the Augustan age, the Trojan links of the Heneti were revived and became very popular. According to several authors (Verg. *Aen*. 1.242–252; Livy 1.1.1–3), the Trojan prince Antenor landed on the Henetian shore and founded Patavium (modern Padua) at the mouth of the homonymous river. Finally, several Greek legends attach a Hellenic origin to the Adriatic people, even if they often deal with a marginal Greekness, at the boundary line with the barbaric people and customs. This is the case for the origins of Daunos and Peucetios, mythical kings of the Daunians and Peucetians, supposed to be the descendants of the Arcadian Lycaon, known in the legendary tradition for his wildness and cruelty (D'Ercole 2005). This is also the case for Illyrius, the eponymous ancestor of the Balkanian people, who, according to Appian's *Illyrica* (1.1), was Polyphemos's son. Various traditions overlapped and coexisted. Another Illyrian group, the Hyllaei, were considered to be the descendants of Hyllaeus, one of Heracles's sons. One of the two harbors of Corcyra is called *limên Hyllaïkon* (Thuc. 3.72). Another flourishing strand of mythical traditions established a link between some Illyrian tribes and the legendary past of Thebes. According to Strabo (7.7.8), the Encheleii, people of Central Illyria, were ruled in the past by the descendants of Cadmos and Harmonia. These mythological kinships provided Hellenic groups with a powerful means to describe and classify other Mediterranean and even continental people. They often provided the background for economic and cultural links, and so it was for Adriatic people.

Regional Contexts

"L'Adriatique est peut-être la plus cohérente des régions de la mer. À elle seule, et par analogie, elle pose tous les problèmes qu'implique l'étude de la Méditerranée entière."[3] This statement by Braudel (1990, 113) provides an excellent introduction to the cultural complexity of the Adriatic civilizations. In fact, one of these "Mediterranean problems" is the interaction between global coherence and local diversity. This contrast is particularly pronounced in the Adriatic case, in which some general trends coexist with a sharp regional variety, as we will attempt to show below.

First, it is worth outlining the main chronological phases of this historical process. A crucial period for the development of the regional groups dates from the end of the Bronze Age and the Early Iron Age, as the archaeological data show. In Slovenia, the process of differentiation starts in the eleventh to tenth centuries and gathers pace during the eighth century, when some microregional groups such as the Dolenjska culture appeared (Turk 2004, 413–414). The regional development of the Illyrian material culture is evident from the Early Iron Age (eleventh to ninth centuries BC) and reached its peak during the sixth to fourth centuries BC, even though the name of the people only began to appear in historical sources in the last decades of the sixth century (Hecataeus, *FGrH* 1, F97, F100). This historical process had several consequences in practices and customs: the occurrence of tumuli, the use of some peculiar kinds of weapons (such as the sword of Glasinac-type, eighth to seventh centuries BC), the local production of matt-painted pottery (like the Devoll-group) and jewels, particularly made of bronze or amber (spectacle- and violin-pins, pendants made with openwork). The material evidence suggests the making of an aristocracy of warriors, which from the seventh century incorporated some Greek defensive weapons in its panoplies (Lippert 2004, 13–16).

Similar processes can also be detected in the Italian peninsula. In the Venetian region, the urban settlements of Padua and Este arose during the eighth century BC, made up of several clusters of cemeteries and places of cult, witnessed by the votive offerings (Capuis 1993, 69–84; 114–116). At the beginning of the Iron Age, great changes occurred in the urban settlement of Bologna, called by Pliny (*HN* 3.112) the major city of Etruria. The three villages extant in the ninth century had by the beginning of the next century consolidated around the area (the modern Villa Cassarini-Villa Bosi) which later became the "acropolis" of the site. This soon became very large, covering over 200 hectares (Sassatelli 2005a, 122–136). Southward, in the Picenian land, developments in the eighth century paved the way for a cultural division between the northern (around Novilara) and southern areas (from Ancona to Ascoli Piceno), apparent later on also in the linguistic tradition (northern- and southern-Picenian inscriptions). Also in Apulia, in the same period, diversities between three areas, the Daunian, the Peucetian, and the Messapian, emerged on the basis of several features such as funerary practice, patterns of settlements, and ceramic productions (D'Andria, 1988; D'Ercole 2005). Starting from the middle of the sixth century, such differences are also detectable in the linguistic field (Marchesini 2013, 20–21).

However, beyond these regional varieties, some cultural features appear to have been so widespread, common to several Adriatic groups, as to justify the impression of the unity evoked above. For instance, similar models of territorial occupation can be observed. Except for some rare cases (Bologna and Marzabotto, which were Etruscan by foundation and culture), at least until the fourth century BC the Adriatic communities kept to the pattern of scattered settlements of different sizes, from the small village to the major poles of territorial control. Strabo (5.4.2) writes that the Picenians used to live in villages (*komedon zôsin*). Up until the fourth century BC, a major settlement of Peucetia, Monte Sannace, was made up of clusters of houses, despite the presence of some stone buildings of large scale (Ciancio, Galeandro, and Palmentola 2009, 313–317). Still in the Apulian region, the great Daunian settlement of Canosa can be still defined, at the end of the fourth century BC, as a "non-*polis*," scattered in different residential areas. This occupation represents a peculiar management of the private and public space which still requires an explanation, as Corrente pointed out (Corrente 2009, 399).

Another common element is the differentiation of burial customs which developed in each regional group following specific and quite coherent dynamics. A first boundary line can be drawn between two wide groups: the societies which emphasize the warrior rule (e.g., the groups of Dolenjska and Glasinac on the eastern side; the Picenians, the Samnite tribes, Daunians, and Peucetians on the western one) and those which exhibit other marks of rank, whether economic or ritual (e.g., the Veneti, the Etruscans of the Po valley, and the Messapians). Second, deep variations existed in the ways of disposing of corpses, often maintained until the Roman conquest: cremation in Venetia, inhumation in the supine position in the western mid-Adriatic groups, and inhumation in a curled-up position in Picenum, in the Liburnian country (around Zadar), and in the three Apulian groups. Within these wide diversifications, each of these practices shows a regional development. In Veneto, a peculiar ritual of cremation in bronze vessels (*situlae*) was possibly inspired by heroic practices. This custom appears in the eighth century BC as a prerogative of the prominent men of the community, as the ritual and the goods of the grave 236 of Este-Ricovero show (Ruta Serafini 2004, 277–278). During the seventh century, this privilege was extended to the women of the local aristocracy. In other cases, burial customs can provide important information on warfare, as the research of Vincenzo D'Ercole (2010, 224–229) on the grave goods of Campovalano (Abruzzo) has well illustrated. In this cemetery, the association between dagger and spear (see below) occurs in most of the grave goods of the eighth to seventh centuries, even for children's burials. From the sixth century BC, the emergence of the sword with crossed grip implies a change in the fighting tactics, now based on individual combat at a distance. The warriors' weapons also appear to have denoted well-defined social hierarchies. In the seventh and sixth centuries BC in the cemetery of Campovalano, most of the warriors owned only a spear, while other weapons (dagger or sword) were apparently the privilege of a restricted elite.

Colonies?

The Greek colonial undertaking in the Adriatic is anything but a linear historical process; on the contrary, this phenomenon was complex and difficult to perceive, as the discrepancy between literary sources and archaeological data illustrates. Therefore, Mario Lombardo (2006) defined most of the Greek foundations in the Adriatic Sea as "phantom-colonies" because of their ephemeral life or indeed because they never got beyond the stage of a project. In spite of that, a long textual tradition among Greek authors testifies to the attraction and interest of this Mediterranean region, although it was long alien and even adverse to Hellenic occupation. According to Plutarch (*Mor.* 293b = *Quaest. Graec.* 11), a group of Eretrians already dwelled in Corcyra before the Corinthian occupation of the island. Strabo (6.2.4) related a different version, maintaining that the Corinthian *apoikoi* led by Chersicrates settled on the island only after the expulsion of its previous inhabitants, the Liburnians (733 BC). This information could be congruous with the practices of the seafaring Euboeans during the Geometric and Archaic period. Moreover, the tradition of the different levels of occupation of Corcyra makes clear the great interest for an island located in a strategic place, holding "the keys of the Adriatic house," as Fernand Braudel (1990, 116) succinctly put it.

In spite of the strong and constant tensions between Corinth and Corcyra, which often led to military conflicts (e.g., Thuc. 1.13.4), periods of reconciliation offered the opportunity for two foundations on the Ionian shore in modern Albania, Epidamnos, in 627, and Apollonia, in 600 BC. Epidamnos was founded in the country of the Taulantians, an Illyrian tribe. Most of the founders were Corcyraeans but, following the ancient customs (*kata dè ton palaion nomon*), the *oikist* was a member of the Corinthian aristocracy, Phalius, son of Eratocleides, claiming a mythic lineage from Heracles (Thuc. 1.24.1). Apollonia, on the other hand, was founded by Corcyrians together with a group of 200 Corinthians, under the guidance of the *oikist* Gylax (Strab. 7.5.8; Steph. Byz. s.v. *Apollonia* and *Gylakeia*). Both settlements were crucial for the economic and cultural contacts with the Illyrian and Epirote people of the hinterland, as a passage in Plutarch (*Mor.* 298 = *Quaest. Graec.* 29) demonstrates. The text explains the function of a public official of Epidamnos called *pôletes* (i.e., "the Seller"), chosen each year among the most reputable fellow-citizens, to organize and control the commercial relationships with the barbarians. In fact, these coastal cities gave access to a long itinerary through the Balkan peninsula, one of the most important routes linking the western to the eastern side of the European continent, which became the Via Egnatia in the Roman period (Braccesi 2003, 47–54; Fasolo 2005; Lolos 2009). This itinerary gave access to the prosperous mining districts of the hinterland, among these, the silver mine of Damastion, a still unidentified settlement in the Balkans, situated by Strabo (7.7.8) between the Illyrian tribes of Encheleii and Lyncestae. The cultural impact of the Corinthian colonies also reached the opposite side of the Adriatic, in the south of the Italian peninsula, as shown by the architectural features of some Messapian public buildings (e.g., at Cavallino), inspired by the Corinthian or Corcyrean style (D'Andria 1988).

In spite of its importance, this Greek presence seems to have been restricted for a long time to the southern maritime regions, between the Adriatic and Ionian shorelines. Only later, during the fourth century BC, was a new colonial undertaking fostered by the political projects of various actors and communities, ranging from Syracusans to Parians. This second phase of Greek colonization penetrated northward into the Adriatic Sea but is, as we mentioned before, less visible in terms of archaeological remains, except for the most important sites like Pharos (modern Hvar) and Issa (probably modern Vis). Pharos was founded by Parian *apoikoi* in 385/384 BC. According to a passage, regrettably fragmentary, in Diodorus of Sicily (15.13.4), in 385 BC the Parians founded an Adriatic colony called Pharos. This enterprise followed the response of an oracle and was achieved with the help of the Syracusan tyrant Dionysius the Elder, who had already founded a colony at Issa some years before. In spite of the Syracusan help, the Parian settlement was still unstable. In effect, a year later, in 384 BC, the native inhabitants expelled from the island joined the Illyrians dwelling on the shore (Diod. Sic. 15.14: *tous peran katoikoûntas Illyriois*) and attacked the Parian colonists using their light and fast-moving vessels. Once again, the Syracusans offered their support to the Greeks of Pharos. The powerful fleet of Dionysios I, based at Issa, overwhelmed the little Illyrian boats, slaughtered more than 5000 barbarians, and captured the others. In a word, the foundation of Pharos was anything but pacific. It was nonetheless lasting, leaving some considerable marks on the land distribution: in this case, archaeological research has found the signs of a deep urban and agrarian reorganization following the colonial foundation. Recent investigations at Stari Grad (on the modern island of Hvar) have brought to light a part of the northern wall of the city as well as a grid of regular division of the land, based on Greek metrology (a modular system of 1 × 5 *stadia*), detectable in the ancient *polis* and in the surrounding *chôra*. A belt of watchtowers was built on the hillforts (Tor, Maslinovik, and Purkin kuk) to control the core of the fertile lands. The area for cultivation (about 1200 ha) could sustain a population of up to 1500; the marginal part of the *chora*, outside the Greek modular division, may have been left for the natives (Slapšak and Kirigin 2001).

The Athenian decision to send a colony to the Adriatic provides a different case in point. This resolution appears in a decree of 325/324 (*IG* II² 1629; *SIG*³ 305; see now Rhodes and Osborne 2003, 512–526) at the end of a typical Athenian naval list. It seems to refer to a previous debate. In fact, the decree states that the deliberation of the Athenian demos concerning the foundation of an Adriatic colony should be achieved "*an tēn tachistēn*," as soon as possible (l. 173–174). Miltiades of Laciadae, a member of the oldest Athenian aristocracy, is called in several passages the *oikistēs* (l. 142, 161, 224), the leader of the expedition; in accordance with the decree, he is said to take over "the triremes and quadriremes and their equipment." This foundation was designed to combat the Tyrrhenian piracy and protect Athenian – and barbarian – trade in the Adriatic, the main object of which was grain, as *sitopompia* is explicitly named (Musti 2010, 108–113). If the context seems fairly clear – the cereal shortage Athens experienced in the last quarter of the fourth century – it seems surprising that this decision was recorded in a text which is on the whole a classical decree regarding territorial defense. Moreover, nothing is otherwise known of this Athenian colonial enterprise, including the putative location of the settlement, identified by some scholars in the south of Italy, for instance on Mt. Gargano, and by others in the Po valley (Braccesi 1979, 298–300; Ferone 2004, 43; Musti 2010). The question has provoked a large debate which still appears hard to resolve, as it is even doubtful whether the colony was ever dispatched.[4] To sum up, at the present time there is no archaeological evidence to show that this event really happened. The Athenian decree seems to give more important information on the economic situation in Athens and on piracy in the Adriatic than on Adriatic colonization.

Economic Exchanges

During the Early Iron Age, trade seems to have been organized on an inter-Adriatic scale involving peoples from the whole extent of the coastline, particularly Daunians, Picenians, and Liburnians. Visible marks of these exchanges are the matt-painted potteries of the Daunian workshops, Baltic amber which probably reached the ports of the northern Adriatic, and the several metal ornaments (fibulae, figured pendants), mostly in bronze, coming from central Europe and the Balkan peninsula (Giumlia-Mair 2011; for the Daunian finds: Mazzei 2010). The circulation of these jewels helped to create a kind of common cultural language between these Adriatic regions. The spread of the characteristic conic crested helmets, which probably had their origin in Picenum, provides another example of the contacts between several Adriatic groups: the Etruscan community on the Adriatic shore (Verucchio), Histria, and the eastern Alps, particularly the cultures of Notranjska and Dolanjska (Teržan 2007, 39). At the edge of the Iapygian peninsula, Messapia represented an exception to this essentially inter-Adriatic network. In this region, direct contacts with Greeks are proved by the impressive quantity of pottery (mostly Euboean and Corinthian), including also some transport vases (Corinthian amphoras "A": Semeraro 1997, 389). Imported vases are particularly concentrated in some places which were crucial for navigation, such as Otranto and Leuca, but they appear also in the hinterland, at Oria (D'Andria 1988, 656–657; Semeraro 1997).

The visible evidence must obviously have been completed by the exchange of commodities which did not leave any archaeological trace, and this is a constant element in the history of Adriatic trade. It is highly probable that already in the Early Iron Age the plentiful grain of the Apulian plains was exported to other Adriatic regions, particularly to the eastern side, while it is almost certain that the Italic region imported raw metals from the Balkans. It is highly probable that some of the natural resources of the Italian peninsula, like the salt formed in several coastal lagoons, would have been exported and generated some particular economic activities such as the production of preserved foodstuffs or tanned leather (D'Ercole 2002, 316–326).

During the seventh century there were some important changes in the features of Adriatic trade. The archaeological evidence from Picenum points to increased contacts with Etruria, allowed by passages through the mountain chain of the Apennines, as well a new appreciation for the precious artifacts of the Ionian and Near Eastern craftsmen, mainly carved ivories and silver vessels. A singular object, an oenochoe from Pitino di San Severino (Macerata), dating from the end of the seventh century BC, provides a case in point. The body of this extraordinary vase is formed by an ostrich egg with golden appliqués while its neck is made of clay with ivory figured appliqués. This object has been compared to Etruscan production, mostly from Vulci, but some scholars have advanced the hypothesis that some of these imported goods derived from direct, although occasional, contacts with Near Eastern and Aegean merchants (Landolfi 1999, 100). In fact, during the seventh century BC direct relationships are also proved at Bologna, by the sudden local development of the so-called proto-Felsinian stelae: about 40 figured slabs of stone dating from the second quarter of the seventh to the first decades of the sixth century BC (Marchesi 2000). These monuments could have inspired the later production of figured stelae in Bologna during the fifth century BC.

Even in the northeastern district, elites were able to obtain heterogeneous luxury goods coming from a far-flung trade. The cemetery of Nesactiom (Istria) provides an excellent case in point. A very lavish grave (Tomb 12) yielded several items coming from Etruria, Magna Graecia, Veneto, and Daunia, probably passed on through several generations from the seventh to the fifth century BC (Mihovilić 1995). On the Italic southern side, Daunia increased a large-scale trade in matt-painted pottery mostly produced by the workshops of the Aufidus lower valley (Foot-Krater Class: Yntema 1990, 234–248).

In this period, Greek merchants probably found in the Adriatic some rare resources required in the production of certain luxury goods. This was the case of the famous iris used in the making of Corinthian perfumes, particularly flourishing under the Cypselid dynasty, which was also central to the colonial undertaking in Illyria. According to Pliny (*HN* 21.40–42), plants of excellent quality grew spontaneously in the upper valleys of the Drinon and Naro (Neretva) Rivers: "*laudatissima in Illyrico, et ibi quoque non in maritimis, sed in silvestribus Drinonis et Naronae.*"

To sum up, Adriatic exchanges during the seventh century seem to have been mainly affected by the needs of local aristocracies, currently defined as princely. These social behaviors left several marks in ritual practices, such as the cremations in bronze situlae, typical of the Venetian region, and figured creations, such as the proto-Felsinian stelae or the images carved on the Daunia *stelai*, which were probably funerary monuments.

A new economic and social phase begins with the sixth century, also marking the start of regular Greek contacts in the *Adrias kolpos*, which took its name, as we have seen, from one of the main centers of the new trade network. These dynamics of circulation could have been at least partly affected by the political changes throughout the Italic peninsula during the last decades of the sixth and the first decades of the fifth century. In 524 BC, an unexpected coalition of Adriatic peoples, comprising of the Etruscans of the Po valley, Umbrians, Daunians, and "other barbarians," launched an attack on Cumae, "the Greek *polis* founded by Chalcis and Eretria in the Tyrrhenian Gulf," undergoing a heavy defeat. Known only from this scanty information in Dionysius of Halicarnassus (7.3.1), this event probably had a strong impact on the social and political structures of Adriatic societies, fostering perhaps the emergence of new elites. A few years later (510 BC), the fall of Sybaris provoked a political earthquake in the area of the Ionian gulf communicating with Adriatic Apulia through the internal valleys of Bradano and Basento. Moreover, the armed conflict between Tarantines and Messapians entered a particularly sharp phase in the last decades of the sixth and the first half of the fifth century BC. These political events must have had an influence on the making of the new Adriatic societies as well as on control of the circulation of goods. It is probably no coincidence if several Iapygian settlements that had flourished until the end of the sixth century disappeared or contracted around 470 BC (Lippolis 2007, 12). On the contrary, in the civilizations of southeastern Alps (Dolenjska), the social and economic conditions improved toward the end of the sixth century, after the stagnation recorded in the first half of the century, probably owing to raids by gangs of Scythian origin on the western edge of the Pannonian plain (Dular and Tecco Hvala 2007, 251–252).

The dynamics of trade in the Po valley have much to say about these wider, new patterns of production and circulation. On the northern side of the Po Delta, Adria, a Venetian settlement with considerable Etruscan elements, received from 580 BC onward several imports of Greek ceramics, mostly Corinthian, but also Laconian. Such imports grew from 540 BC, when Attic pottery increasingly played the main role in these commercial flows. These contacts provoked the reaction of Etruscan people already settled in the region, at Adria as well as in the southern Po valley and in the area surrounding Felsina (modern Bologna). These Etruscan communities probably played the main role in the great reorganization of the Po plain in around 540 BC, when the Etrusco-Venetian emporium of Adria was restructured and the coastal settlement of Spina was founded on the southern side of the delta, at the frontier with the Umbrian country (Sassatelli 1993). The new economic and territorial system probably became attractive for many other groups and individuals, mostly coming from northern inner Etruria (Chiusi and Orvieto) but also from other Italic regions, (Umbrians and Apulians), as the rich onomastic data from Spina suggests. Starting from the second half of the sixth century, this trade network allowed the exchange of several kinds of goods. Among the imports, a major role was played by the fine figured vessels, particularly the Attic ones. Amphoras from Corinth, Attica, Chios, Thasos, and Mende were employed for the transport of wine, except for the so-called Corinthian A, which was used for oil. Some precious materials, such as the marbles of insular and Eastern Greece, also featured in the cargoes of the Aegean ships. In the opposite direction, the valuable tin from continental Europe (coming from Cornwall and possibly also from Bohemia) arrived in these Adriatic emporia, as proved by some grave goods from Spina. In return, Greeks must have acquired various commodities in the Adriatic ports, most of which left no archaeological traces: grain, salt, leathers, probably the valuable horses of Veneto, and maybe slaves. They could also obtain manufactured products from Tyrrhenian Etruria and local craftwork such as worked metals, including bronze vessels and gold ornaments, arm rings, and earrings, which probably flourished in Spina and Adria and certainly in Marzabotto. Yet all this important trade going on in the Po valley seems to have managed entirely without the minting of coinage. To date no trace has been found of a local production of coins or of the circulation of Greek coins in the emporia of the Po valley. Therefore, we can assume that barter was the standard method of exchange. Another important means of exchange was the weight of metals. In the settlements of the Po valley, particularly in Marzabotto, a peculiar production of bars of metal is known; their specific symbol (the "dry branch") was probably a hallmark testifying to their reliability (Pellegrini and Macellari 2002).

Although it is now reasonably clear, the reconstruction of exchanges in the Po valley is nonetheless the outcome of different hypotheses and interpretative patterns that have succeeded one another over time and are still being processed. To limit ourselves to the latest developments, we can emphasize that, starting from 1990, some significant discoveries of amphoras in the settlement of Forcello (on the Mincio River, near Mantua) suggested that most of the goods imported through the Adriatic emporia were directed northward, and reached the rich aristocracies of Celtic Europe along the internal river-borne routes (Sassatelli 1993). In the same years, such connections between Celtic and Adriatic societies were stressed in many other works (e.g., Franchi dell'Orto 1999). Nowadays, this pattern of reconstruction has to be at least partially modified in the light of recent research. Federica Sacchetti (2012) investigated 342 amphoras (from Corinth, Attic, Northern and Eastern Aegean) mostly found in both coastal and internal habitats: Adria and its hinterland (San Cassiano, San Basilio, Le Balone), Spina, Bologna, Marzabotto, and Forcello. The study led to the following conclusions: (i) several settlements of the Po valley seem to have been the main targets for Adriatic trade (more than 30 amphoras were found at Adria-San Basilio, Spina, Bologna, Marzabotto, Forcello; (ii) only a few transport containers (13 out of 342) came from graves and most of them belong to the Corinthian B type; (iii) finally, at least one workshop of Corinthian B amphoras should be located in Corcyra, active between the second half of the fifth and the middle of the third century BC. Other workshops could be located in the Ionian-Adriatic area: Apollonia, Butrint, Pharos, possibly also the country between Taranto and Metaponto (Sacchetti 2012, 36–37). According to these conclusions, the Adriatic area seems to be the place of production and destination of goods, more than a crossroads. On the other hand, the importance of southern Adriatic imported amphoras points to the role of the Corinthian foundation on the Ionian shore. Starting from the sixth and during the fifth century BC, the relationships between the Illyrian people and the coastal Greek *poleis* increased, doubtless because of the exchange of metals (silver, gold, and copper) from the Balkan peninsula and the modern region of Kosovo (Lippert 2004, 17–20; Giumlia-Mair 2011). The settlement of Damastion, mentioned above (Strab. 7.7.8), may have played an important role in this chain of long-distance trade, as is also suggested by the richness of the cemetery found in this region at the modern Trebenischte, near Lake Ohrid. Furthermore, these conclusions tally with some recent studies on the production of wine amphoras at Pharos and Issa.

Their circulation spread essentially through the Adriatic Sea, involving also some significant points of the sea route, like the sanctuaries of Diomedes at Palagruža and Cap Ploca (Kirigin, Katunaric, and Šešelj 2006, 195–203).

This last remark points to one particular feature of ancient Adriatic trade, namely that the places of exchange were often associated with significant landmarks and with cultural traditions. Most of the Adriatic trading centers are in connection with the fluvial network, particularly with the navigable mouths of the rivers. The location of ports in the Po valley (Spina, Adria, San Basilio) provides the most eloquent example, and other cases are known. Pseudo-Skylax (*Periplous*, 24) precisely describes the *emporion* of Nestaioi, at the mouth of the Naron River, modern Neretva (Peretti 1979, 252–261). The trading place was located inside a wide lagoon giving access to the hinterland and the country of the Autariatai. Strabo (4.3.9) knew the *emporion* of *Canousitai* at the mouth of the Aufidus River, where the fluvial waters mingled with the sea creating a wide coastal lagoon that the Greek author calls *stomalimnē*. In these two cases, the coastal hydrography provides an ideal environment for safe anchorage, communication with the hinterland, and the economic activities linked to fishing and the production of salt. In the northern Adriatic, at Timavum, the saltmarsh was controlled by the sanctuary of Diomedes, which also owned a harbor (*limēn*), a thriving wood, and seven springs of water (Strabo, 5.1.8; his sources are Polybius and Poseidonius).

The last example shows another typical feature of several Adriatic landing places, which were often connected with places of worship (Fenet 2005). The *emporion* of Naron was linked to the legend of Cadmos and Harmonia (Ps.-Skylax, 24). Moreover, the strategic position of the cult places sacred to the Greek hero Diomedes suggests the image of a cultic maritime map. Already from the sixth century BC, in the poems of Ibycus of Rhegion, Diomedes appears as the tutelary god of the Adriatic. In the Augustan period, the Greek hero is still described as a kind of Adriatic ruler. According to Strabo (5.1.9) the "Islands of Diomedes," as well as the relationships with King Daunos and the foundation of Argyrippa-Arpi, are evidence of the hero's domination on the sea. Other worship places of the hero are located on promontories. A passage in Pliny (*HN* 3.141) evokes the *promunturium Diomedis*, and recent archaeological research has positively recognized this place, on the Dalmatian coast near Sibenik, at Cap Ploca. A very simple shrine there was dedicated to Diomedes, as proven by some Greek inscriptions on ceramic fragments, inscribed between the fourth and the end of the second century BC. At this place, which is crucial for seacoast visibility and for the direction of streams, various generations of sailors and merchants left their offerings, whether ceramic (more than 65 000 fragments) or coins, confirming the economic importance of this sacred place (Bilić-Dujmušić 2002). Diomedes's cult may also have been connected with the Conero promontory, according to a passage in the *Periplous* of Pseudo-Skylax, 16, placing it in the country of the Umbrian city of Ancôn, and a sanctuary devoted to the hero. Another place linked to the Greek hero's legend lies at the foot of the promontory of Gargano. According to Strabo (6.3.9), Diomedes would have brought his own offerings to *Athena Ilias* in Daunia (known also to Ael. *NA* XI, 5). The holy place could be identified with the worship attested in the Latin colony of Luceria, at least from the last decades of the fourth century BC (D'Ercole 1990).

Finally, the cult of Diomedes seems to be deeply linked with the insular morphology, as the ancient tradition concerning the mythical islands of Diomedes demonstrates, from Pliny

(*HN* 3.151; 10.126) through to Saint Augustine (*City of God*, 18, 16). Traditionally located on the Tremiti archipelago, the shrine has now been conclusively placed on the island of Palagruza, following the excavations of Croatian scholars (1996, and 2002–2007). However, it is not impossible that this island, very near to the western Adriatic coast, was perceived by the ancient sailors as a part of the Tremiti archipelago (Colonna 1998). This possible confusion could explain the traditional location of Diomedes's sanctuary among the Apulian islands. The chronology of sherds and script from Palagruza suggests that Greek sailors used to visit this shrine from the beginning of the fifth century BC through to the Roman period (coins of Dyrrachium, third to first centuries). Moreover, some offerings (*Soleios anetheke*) dating from the beginning of the fifth century in an Aeginetan script show complete similarity with finds from Adria and prove that the island "was a crucial landmark for Greek sailors when sailing the open sea" (Kirigin, Miše, and Barbarić 2010, 65).

Cultural Contacts and Encounters

Objects, especially luxury products and personal ornaments, can hardly circulate without carrying social practices and symbolic meanings. Moreover, the circulation of commodities implies the movement, temporary or lasting, of people of various origins, often middlemen carrying items gathered in several places of trade. Finally, the process of circulation also involves immaterial goods, such as technical knowledge, writing, and figured expression. All these possible cases are well represented in the Adriatic regions. From the eighth to the sixth centuries, the widespread distribution of "spectacle" fibulae from the Balkans, as well as the boat-shaped fibulae with three knobs on the bow, characteristic of Picenum, may signify the assimilation of styles of dress. On both sides of the Adriatic during the Archaic and Classical periods, imported pottery and bronze vessels often show the introduction or imitation of the aristocratic practice of banqueting (Lippolis 2007). Technical knowledge and local figurative patterns became widespread through the trans-Adriatic cultural exchanges, as the art of figured Daunian stelae (seventh century BC) and Venetian situlae (sixth to fourth centuries BC) go to show. Around the middle of the sixth century, the technique of building walls and architectural decoration (capitals, polychrome simae) of an important Messapic settlement, Cavallino (the ancient Carbina?), were probably brought by craftsmen coming from Corcyra (D'Andria 1988, 660–661).

One of the most evident effects of these contacts and exchanges was the creation, whether short-lived or lasting, of mixed societies, a cultural feature that is characteristic of the Adriatic. Already during the Archaic period, some clusters of Greek merchants settled on the Messapian coast. The circumstance can be proved by some graves of the cemetery of Tor Pisana (Brindisi), where the funerary practice (cremation) and the grave goods (Protocorinthian perfume vases, second quarter of the seventh century) are foreign to local customs (D'Andria 1988, 659). Strabo (7.7.8) argues that people of the Ionian coast (Epidamnos, Apollonia) mingled with the Illyrians of the hinterland in Bylliones, Taulantii, Parthini, and Brygi. The epigraphical data can at least partially confirm this information as investigation of the inscriptions of Epidamnos has recognized a little onomastic cluster that could be defined as Illyrian, some Greek names with a native root and some native patronymics of Greek names (Cabanes 1995, 51).

As we stressed before, trade also fostered the formation of mixed clusters on the Po Delta, where various Hellenic groups (Aeginetans, and more generally Dorians, as well as Ionians and Athenians) may have settled and created mixed families. Once again, inscriptions confirm such varying origins through the high percentage of Greek and Etruscan inscriptions, and different Italian scripts from Umbria, Picenum, and Apulia (Colonna 1993). Archaeological evidence provides further confirmation of this multiplicity in the cemeteries of Spina where inhumation and cremation appear to be completely interchangeable. The composition of the grave goods is largely inspired by the Greek practice of banqueting; however, following the Etruscan custom, this practice is extended also to women. That sometimes makes it hard to distinguish the gender of these contexts, such as the lavish goods of grave 128 at Valle Trebba, from the end of the fifth century (Marinari 2004, 269–270). Another mark of this cultural complexity is the particular composition of the grave goods, which often combine Attic pottery and Etruscan bronze vessels, creating a kind of cultural bilingualism.

These contacts would probably have been strengthened by marriages, which sometimes leave a trace in the epigraphic and archaeological data. A funerary monument found near Bologna (Tombarelle), dating from the fifth century BC, belonged to a woman with a Rhaetic name, *Reithvi*, followed by an Etruscan gentilitial in the genitive, *Keisna(s)*, possibly the name of the husband, belonging to the ancient Etruscan tradition (Sassatelli 2005b, 251). The discovery in some children's graves at Spina (end of the fifth to fourth century BC) of *choes*, the ritual vases typical of the Ionian-Attic feast of *Anthesteriae*, could prove that some family clusters which were at least partially Hellenic had settled in this Adriatic community (Maria Cecilia D'Ercole 2010).

Piracy

Rich in islands and inlets, the Adriatic provides an easy channel for long-distance trade, and for centuries this also meant an ideal environment for piracy. Quite endemic in this sea, this activity also represented an economic choice for local societies (Bandelli 2004, 64), explaining perhaps the variety of forms it took during different periods and in different locations. Basically, this predatory process was a spontaneous undertaking by groups of individuals, vis-à-vis the most ancient Liburnian piracy of the eighth and seventh centuries BC. As a matter of fact, about the only historical testimony to the Liburnian "thalassocracy" is the information given by Strabo (6.2.4) on the Liburnian settlement at Corcyra at the moment of the Corinthian occupation. Some centuries later, similar forms of piracy could have been an economic resource for the communities of the Po valley. After the Celtic invasion of 388, Spina was able to maintain its Etruscan character and also its Aegean network of trade, especially with Attica. Unlike other settlements in the Po valley (Marzabotto, Felsina), Spina even experienced demographic growth. This development could be partially explained by the income of piracy, which may have attracted some Etruscan groups from the hinterland (Sassatelli 2004, 21–23). Moreover, passages in Dionysius of Halicarnassus (1.18) and Strabo (5.1.7) state that the Spinitae offered a treasure at Delphi amounting to a tenth of their gains, obtained by their "thalassocracy." This treasure is known also from other reliable sources: Plutarch (*Quaest. conv.* 5.2.675b) and Athenaeus (*Deipn.* XIII.606a), both quoting a great "connoisseur" of the sanctuary, Polemon of Ilion, *proxenus* in Delphi in 177/176. Similar practices are attested for the Cretan pirates, who consecrated a tithe on shipwrecks to Apollo Pythios (*IC* IV, 184, ll. A. 8–19).

The Athenian decree of 325/324, mentioned above, (*IG* II² 1629, ll. 217–232) speaks of *Tyrrhenoi* pirates. According to other interpretations (Braccesi 2003, 112–113), the Etruscan thalassocracy at Spina was actually a kind of "sea policy" designed to counter the attacks of other Adriatic peoples, mostly from the eastern seacoast. Livy's account of the Adriatic expedition of Cleonimos (10.2.4), king of Sparta, at the end of the fourth century BC, describes the Illyrians, Liburnians, and Histrias as fierce peoples known for their maritime raids (*"gentes ferae et magna parte ex latrociniis maritimis infames"*). Another form of Adriatic piracy, which I could define as "parasitic," is also attested by ancient sources in which are implied the control of maritime movements and taking advantage of the weakness or misadventures of merchant ships. That was the case with the piracy of the Frentani, *lēstrikoi anthrōpoi* according to Strabo (5.4.2). On the central Adriatic coast, between Ortônion and Boûka, these wild people dwelt in houses built from the shipwrecks that occurred off their shores. According to Raviola (2004, 116–117), this information can be referred to the fourth century BC. Finally, during the third century BC, another kind of piracy arose, supporting the interests of official powers without giving up its autonomous undertakings. According to Bandelli (2004, 62–63), this could explain the response of the Illyrian queen Teuta to the Roman embassy in 230 BC. In Polybius's version (2.8.8), the queen claimed that she could control the piracy of the country but not the actions of private citizens. Starting from this event and through to the Augustan period, Romans and their allies helped to control piracy in the Adriatic. According to Strabo (7.5.6), the Illyrian people of Ardiaei overran the sea until they were defeated by the Romans. Augustus himself, claiming in *Res Gestae* his victory over maritime piracy (*RGDA* 25, 1), may have been alluding to the Adriatic situation. It is, however, possible that small-scale piracy was never completely eradicated and emerged again during the late Empire (Bandelli 2004, 67–68).

The Turning Point of the Fourth and Third Centuries

Roman policy was undoubtedly a strong factor of change in the Adriatic region, starting from the three last decades of the third century BC, but some new, dramatic shifts had already taken place in the fourth century. The Celtic invasion of the Po valley was a decisive event. Under Brennus's leadership, the northern invaders pushed on as far as Rome in 388/387 BC. According to Pliny (*HN* 3.116), no fewer than 112 Gallic tribes, mostly Boii, settled to the south of the Po River. Polybius (2.17.7) confirms their presence in the area of Felsina. For once, there is archaeological evidence that corresponds to the literary sources; a clear gap can be observed in the rituals and goods associated with Bologna from the second quarter of the fourth century BC. Settlements and funerary rituals point to a demographic collapse as well as a change in patterns of clothing and fighting (Vitali 1992; Minarini 2005, 345–353). However, the Celtic occupation provoked a new arrangement rather than the mere destruction of the ancient society, as there are some signs to suggest that integration of the Boii started at least from the end of the fourth century. The survival of Etruscan customs can be observed in some female burials, while others (e.g., grave Benacci 968) show a possible integration of Etruscan individuals in a cemetery of the Boii. A phase of cohabitation could have followed the first, dramatic clash (Minarini 2005, 355–357).

Another factor of change was the Syracusan interest in the Adriatic, proven, as we have seen, by the account of Diodorus of Sicily of the military garrison in Issa at the time of the founding of Pharos, in 385–384 BC. This presence has been extensively documented by Braccesi (since 1979), also in relation to the likely alliance with the Celts in the Po valley against the Etruscans. However, as this presence does not seem to have had any consequences on cultural expressions in the Adriatic, one is tempted to ask whether Dionysius's projects had a stronger impact on Syracusan policy than on Adriatic development. On the cultural side, the fourth century is perhaps the period of greatest reception of Greek customs in southeastern Italy. Peucetian and Daunian elites show a very deep knowledge of Greek history and myth, as proved by the quality and content of the images on Apulian red-figured vases (Schmidt 2002). A peculiar aspect of the Hellenization of the Apulian elites was the Macedonian mark on some architectural and figurative features in Daunia (Mazzei 1995). These ties with Macedonia open a new, interesting chapter in Adriatic history which has yet to be fully explored.

NOTES

1 Mark Weir (1955-2015) kindly accepted to reread the English version of the text. My chapter is dedicated to his memory.
2 *Il.* 2.851–852: a group of Heneti coming from Paphlagonia were allied to the Trojans. This statement probably contributes to creating the myth of the eastern origin of the Adriatic people (Strab. 13.1.3; 12.3.8).
3 "The Adriatic is perhaps the sea's more coherent region. To it alone, and by analogy, it poses all the problems which the study of the entire Mediterranean implies."
4 Ferone 2004, 34, argues that the Athenian ships (*triacontori*) left because they are missing from the final account of 325/324; a more skeptical position is found in Rhodes and Osborne 2003, 525.

REFERENCES

Bandelli, Gino. 2004. "La pirateria adriatica di età repubblicana come fenomeno endemico." In *Hesperia. Studi sulla grecità d'Occidente 19. La pirateria nell'Adriatico antico*, edited by Lorenzo Braccesi 61–68. Rome: L'Erma di Bretschneider.

Bilić-Dujmušić, Siniša. 2002. "The Archaeological Excavations on Cape Ploca (*Promontorium Diomedis*)." In *Greek Influence along the East Adriatic Coast*, Biblioteca Knjiga Mediterana 26, edited by Nenad Cambi, Slobodan Čače, and Branko Kirigin, 485–497. Split: Knjizevni Krug.

Braccesi, Lorenzo. 1979. *Grecità adriatica: un capitolo della colonizzazione greca in Occidente*. 2nd ed. Bologna: Patron.

Braccesi, Lorenzo. 2003. *I Greci delle periferie: dal Danubio all'Atlantico*. Bari: Laterza.

Braudel, Fernand. 1990. *La Méditerranée et le monde méditerranéen à l'époque de Philippe II*. Paris: 9th ed. Armand Colin Editeur.

Cabanes, Pierre, ed. 1995. *Etudes épigraphiques 2. Corpus des inscriptions grecques d'Illyrie Méridionale et d'Epire I*. Athens: Ecole française d'Athènes.

Capuis, Loredana. 1993. *I Veneti. Società e cultura di un popolo dell'Italia preromana*. Milan: Longanesi.

Ciancio, Angela, Fabio Galeandro, and Palma Palmentola. 2009. "Monte Sannace e l'urbanizzazione della Peucezia." In *Verso la città. Forme insediative in Lucania e nel mondo italico fra IV e III sec.a.C., Atti delle giornate di studio Venosa 2006*, edited by Massimo Osanna, 307–326. Venosa: Osanna Edizioni.

Colonna, Giovanni. 1993. "La società spinetica e gli altri *ethne*." In *Spina. Storia di una città tra Greci ed Etruschi*, edited by Fede Berti and Pier Giovanni Guzzo, 131–143. Ferrare: Maurizio Tosi.

Colonna Giovanni. 1998. "Pelagosa, Diomede e le rotte dell'Adriatico." *Archeologia Classica*, 50: 363–378.

Corrente, Marisa. 2009. "La formazione della città di Canusium." In *Verso la città. Forme insediative in Lucania e nel mondo italico fra IV e III sec. a.C., Atti delle giornate di studio Venosa 2006*, edited by Massimo Osanna, 391–413. Venosa: Osanna Edizioni.

D'Andria, Francesco. 1988. "Messapi e Peuceti." In *Italia. Omnium terrarum alumna*, edited by Giovanni Pugliese Carratelli, 653–715. Milan: Libri Scheiwiller.

D'Ercole, Maria Cecilia. 1990. *La stipe votiva del Belvedere a Lucera*. Collection "*Corpus delle Stipi Votive in Italia*." Rome: Giorgio Bretschneider.

D'Ercole, Maria Cecilia. 2000. "La légende de Diomède dans l'Adriatique préromaine." In *Les cultes polythéistes dans l'Adriatique romaine*, edited by Christiane Delplace and Francis Tassaux, 11–26. Bordeaux: Ausonius.

D'Ercole, Maria Cecilia. 2002. *Importuosa Italiae litora. Paysage et échanges dans l'Adriatique méridionale archaïque*. Naples: Centre Jean Bérard.

D'Ercole, Maria Cecilia. 2005. "Identités, mobilités et frontières dans la Méditerranée antique. L'Italie adriatique, VIIIe–Ve siècles av. J.-C." *Annales. Histoire, Sciences Sociales*, 60(1): 165–181. Paris: Editions de l'Ehess.

D'Ercole, Maria Cecilia. 2010. "Sharing New Worlds: Mixed Identities around the Adriatic (6th–4th Century B.C.)." In *Cultural Identities and the Peoples of the Ancient Mediterranean*, edited by Erich Gruen, 428–451. Los Angeles: Getty Research Institute.

D'Ercole, Vincenzo. 2010. "Approfondimenti sui materiali. G. Le armi e gli armati." In *La necropoli di Campovalano. Tombe orientalizzanti e arcaiche 2*, British Archaeological Reports. International Series, 2174, edited by Cristina Chiaramonte Treré, Vincenzo D'Ercole, and Cecilia Scotti, 223–234. Oxford: Oxford Archaeopress.

Dular, Janez, and Snezana Tecco Hvala. 2007. *South-Eastern Slovenia in the Early Iron Age: Settlement-Economy-Society. Opera Instituti Archaeologici Sloveniae 12*. Ljubljana: ZRC SAZU, Institut za arheologijo.

Fasolo, Michele. 2005. *La via Egnatia I. Da Apollonia a Dyrrachium ad Herakleia Lynkestidos*, Rome: I.G.E.R.

Fenet, Annick. 2005. "Sanctuaires marins du canal d'Otrante." In *Le canal d'Otrante et la Méditerranée antique et médiévale, Actes du Colloque Nanterre 2000*, edited by Elisabeth Déniaux, 39–49. Bari: Edipuglia.

Ferone, Claudio. 2004. "Il IV secolo, Atene e l'Adriatico." In *Hesperia. Studi sulla grecità d'Occidente 19. La pirateria nell'Adriatico antico*, edited by Lorenzo Braccesi, 31–48. Rome: L'Erma di Bretschneider.

Franchi Dell'Orto, L., ed. 1999. *Piceni, Popolo d'Europa*. Rome: Edizioni De Luca.

Frisone, Flavia. 2008. "Ionios poros: storie, rotte e percorsi nella genesi di uno spazio geografico." In *Hesperia. Studi sulla grecità d'Occidente 22*, edited by Lorenzo Braccesi, Flavio Raviola, and Giuseppe Sassatelli, 119–143. Rome: L'Erma di Bretschneider.

Giumlia-Mair, Alessandra. 2011. "Le vie dei metalli dal Medio Oriente al Nord Europa: rame, stagno, oro, argento e ferro." In *Le grandi vie delle civiltà. Relazioni e scambi fra Mediterraneo e il centro Europa dalla preistoria alla romanità*, editied by Franco Marzatico, Rupert Gebhard, and Paul Gleirscher, 103–109. Trento: Castello del Buonconsiglio.

Kirigin, Branko, Tea Katunaric, and Lucijana Šešelj. 2006. "Preliminary Notes on Some Economic and Social Aspects of *Amphorae* and Fineware Pottery from Central Dalmatia, 4th–1st BC." In *Rimini e l'Adriatico nell'età delle guerre puniche. Atti del Convegno internazionale di Studi, Rimini, Musei Comunali, 25–27 marzo 2004*, edited by Fiamma Lenzi, 191–225. Bologna: Ante Quem.

Kirigin, Branko, Maja Miše, and Vedran Barbarić. 2010. "Palagruža – the Island of Diomedes. Summary Excavations Report 2002–2008." In *Dal Mediterraneo all'Europa. Conversazioni adriatiche, Hesperia. Studi sulla grecità di Occidente 25*, edited by Elisabetta Govi, 65–69. Rome: L'Erma di Bretschneider.

Landolfi, Maurizio. 1999. "I beni di prestigio dei principi piceni." In *Piceni, Popolo d'Europa*, edited by Luisa Franchi Dell'Orto, 98–100. Rome: Edizioni De Luca.

Lippert, Andreas. 2004. "Das archäologische Bild des frühen Illyrer." In *Dall'Adriatico al Danubio. L'Illirico nell'età greca e romana. Atti del convegno Cividale del Friuli 25–27 settembre 2003*, edited by Gianpaolo Urso, 11–21. Pisa: Edizioni ETS.

Lippolis, Enzo. 2007. "Beni di prestigio e acculturazione: la diffusione del modello aristocratico greco." In *Dalla Grecia all'Europa. La circolazione di beni di lusso e di modelli culturali nel VI e V secolo a.C.*, edited by Chiara Tarditi, 3–22. Milan: Vita e Pensiero.

Lolos Yannis. 2009. "Via Egnathia after Egnatius: Imperial Policy and Inter-Regional Contacts." In *Greek and Roman Networks in the Mediterranean*, edited by Irad Malkin, Christy Constantakopoulou, and Katerina Panagoupoulou, 264–284. New York: Routledge.

Lombardo, Mario. 2006. "I Greci in Dalmazia. Presenze e fondazioni coloniali." In *Rimini e l'Adriatico nell'età delle guerre puniche. Atti del Convegno internazionale di Studi, Rimini, Musei Comunali, 25–27 marzo 2004*, Archeologia dell'Adriatico 6, edited by Fiamma Lenzi, 19–32. Bologna: Ante Quem.

Marchesi, Marinella. 2000. "La scultura di età orientalizzante in Etruria Padana." In *Principi etruschi tra Mediterraneo e Europa*, edited by Gilda Bartoloni, Filippo Delpino, Cristiana Morigi Govi, and Giuseppe Sassatelli, 336–337. Venice: Marsilio.

Marchesini, Simona. 2013. "Quali lingue, quali popoli nell'Apulia di V e IV secolo a.C." In *La comunicazione verbale tra Greci e indigeni in Apulia nel V–IV secolo a.C.: quali elementi?*, edited by Luigi Todisco, 19–33. Naples: Loffredo.

Marcotte, Didier. 2000. *Géographes grecs. Tome I. Introduction générale. Ps.-Scymnos: Circuit de la Terre*. Paris: Les Belles Lettres.

Marinari, Valeria. 2004. "Il banchetto nei corredi tombali di Spina: un indizio di ellenizzazione?" In *Hesperìa. Studi sulla grecità d'Occidente 18. I Greci in Adriatico 2: suppl. del convegno internazionale Urbino, 1999*, edited by Lorenzo Braccesi and Mario Luni, 267–277. Rome: L'Erma di Bretschneider.

Mazzei, Marina. 1995. *Arpi. L'ipogeo della Medusa e la necropoli*. Bari: Edipuglia.

Mazzei, Marina. 2010. *I Dauni. Archeologia dal IX al V secolo a.C.* Foggia: Claudio Grenzi.

Mihovilić, Kristina. 1995. "Reichtum durch Handel in der Hallstattzeit Istriens." In *Handel, Tausch und Verkehr im Bronze- und Früheisenzeitlichen Südosteuropa*, Prähistorische Archäologie in Südosteuropa 11, Südosteuropa-Schriften 17, edited by Bernhard Hansel, 283–330. Munich and Berlin: Südosteuropa-Gesellschaft, and Seminar für Ur- und Frühgeschichte der Freien Universität.

Minarini, Laura. 2005. "I Celti a Bologna." In *Storia di Bologna. Bologna nell'antichità*, edited by Giuseppe Sassatelli and Angela Donati, 341–361. Bologna: Bononia University Press.

Musti, Domenico. 2010. "Rifornimenti granarii in Grecia." In *Dal Mediterraneo all'Europa. Conversazioni adriatiche, Hesperia. Studi sulla grecità di Occidente 25*, edited by Elisabetta Govi, 107–125. Rome: L'Erma di Bretschneider.

Pellegrini, Enrico, and Roberto Macellari, eds. 2002. *I lingotti con il segno del ramo secco. Considerazioni su alcuni aspetti socio-economici dell'area etrusco-italica durante il periodo tardo-arcaico*. Pisa: Istituti editoriali e poligrafici internazionali.

Peretti, Aurelio. 1979. *Il Periplo di Scilace. Studio sul primo portolano del Mediterraneo*. Pisa: Giardini Editori e Stampatori.

Raviola, Flavio. 2004. "La 'pirateria' dei Frentani." In *Hesperia. Studi sulla grecità d'Occidente 19. La pirateria nell'Adriatico antico*, edited by Lorenzo Braccesi, 109–118. Rome: L'Erma di Bretschneider.

Rhodes, Peter J., and Robin Osborne. 2003. *Greek Historical Inscriptions (404–323 BC)*. Oxford: Oxford University Press.

Ruta Serafini, Angela. 2004. "Il mondo veneto nell'età del Ferro." In *Guerrieri, principi ed eroi fra il Danubio e il Po dalla preistoria all'alto medioevo*, edited by Franco Marzatico and Paul Gleirscher, 277–283. Trento: Castello del Buonconsiglio.

Sacchetti, Federica. 2012. *Les amphores grecques dans le nord de l'Italie. Échanges commerciaux entre les Apennins et les Alpes aux époques archaïque et Classique*. Arles: Edition Errance.

Šašel Kos, Marjeta. 2005. *Appian and the Illyricum*. Ljubljana: Narodni muzej Slovenije.

Sassatelli, Giuseppe. 1993. "La funzione economica e produttiva: merci, scambi, artigianato." In *Spina. Storia di una città tra Greci ed Etruschi*, edited by Fede Berti and Pier Giovanni Guzzo, 153–171. Ferrara: Maurizio Tosi.

Sassatelli, Giuseppe. 2004. "Gli Etruschi di Spina e la pirateria adriatica." In *Hesperia. Studi sulla grecità d'Occidente 19. La pirateria nell'Adriatico antico*, edited by Lorenzo Braccesi, 21–30. Rome: L'Erma di Bretschneider.

Sassatelli, Giuseppe. 2005a. "La fase villanoviana e la fase orientalizzante (IX–VI secolo a.C.)" In *Storia di Bologna. Bologna nell'Antichità*, edited by Giuseppe Sassatelli and Angela Donati, 119–155. Bologna: Bononia University Press.

Sassatelli, Giuseppe. 2005b. "La fase felsinea (VI–IV secolo a.C." In *Storia di Bologna. Bologna nell'Antichità*, edited by Giuseppe Sassatelli and Angela Donati, 235–257. Bologna: Bononia University Press.

Schmidt, Margot. 2002. "La ceramica italiota del IV secolo a.C. in Italia Meridionale: problemi di botteghe e cronologia archeologica." In *La Sicilia dei due Dionisí. Atti Agrigento 1999*, edited by Nicola Bonacasa, Lorenzo Braccesi, and Ernesto De Miro, 253–264. Rome: L'Erma di Bretschneider.

Semeraro, Grazia. 1997. En neusi. *Ceramica greca e società nel Salento arcaico*. Lecce: Martano Editrice-Edipuglia.

Slapšak, Božidar, and Branko Kirigin. 2001. "Pharos and its *chora*." In *Problemi della chora coloniale dall'Occidente al mar Nero, Atti del Quarantesimo convegno di studi sulla Magna Grecia, Taranto 2000*, edited by Attilio Stazio and Stefania Ceccoli, 567–591, Taranto: Istituto per la Storia e l'Archeologia della Magna Grecia.

Teržan, Biba. 2007. "Principi e guerrieri delle due sponde altoadriatiche." In *Piceni ed Europa, Archeologia di frontiera 6*, edited by Mitja Guštin, Peter Ettel, and Marco Buora, 39–65. Udine: Società friulana di Archeologia.

Turk, Peter 2004. "La prima età del Ferro nel territorio a Sud-Est delle Alpi." In *Guerrieri, principi ed eroi fra il Danubio e il Po dalla preistoria all'alto medioevo*, edited by Franco Marzatico and Paul Gleirscher, 411–419. Trento: Castello del Buonconsiglio.

Vattuone, Riccardo. 2000. "Teopompo e l'Adriatico. Ricerche sul libro XXI delle Filippiche (*FGrHist* 115 FF 128–136)." In *Hesperia 10, Studi sulla grecità d'Occidente*, edited by Lorenzo Braccesi, 11–38. Rome: L'Erma di Bretschneider.

Vitali, Daniele 1992. *Tombe e necropoli galliche di Bologna e del territorio*. Bologna: Museo Civico Archeologico di Bologna.

Vlassopoulos, Kostas. 2011. "Regional Perspectives and the Study of Greek History." *Incidenza dell'Antico*, 9: 9–31.

Yntema, Douwe W. 1990. *The Matt-Painted Pottery of Southern Italy*. Galatina: Congedo Editore.

FURTHER READING

Italian and French scholars have conducted much of the research on the Adriatic in last decades. The following works can be recommended for their up-to-date information and illustrations:

Guidi, Federica, ed. 2009. *Adriatico di molte genti. Novità archeologiche tra Veneto, Marche, Abruzzo e Puglia*. Bologna: Ante Quem.

Cabanes, Pierre, ed. 2001. *Histoire de l'Adriatique*. Paris: Seuil.

Čače, Slobodan, Anamaria Kurilić, and Francis Tassaux, eds. 2006. *Les routes de l'Adriatique antique. Géographie et économie. Putovi antičkog Jadrana. Geografija i gospodarstvo*. Bordeaux: Ausonius.

Capuis, Loredana, and Anna Maria Chieco Bianchi. 2006. *Este II. La necropoli di Villa Benvenuti*. Rome: Giorgio Bretschneider.

Dally, Ortwin. 2000. *Canosa, Località San Leucio. Untersuchungen zu Akkulturationsprozessen vom 6. bis zum 2. Jh. V. Chr. am Beispiel eines daunisches Heiligtums*. Heidelberg: Verlag Archäologie und Geschichte.

Gentili, Gino Vicinio. 2003. *Verucchio villanoviana. Il sepolcreto in località Le Pegge e la necropoli al piede della Rocca malatestiana*. Rome: Giorgio Brestschneider.

Govi, Elisabetta, and Giuseppe Sassatelli, eds. 2005. *Culti, forma urbana e artigianato a Marzabotto. Nuove prospettive di ricerca. Atti del convegno di studi, Bologna, San Giovanni in Monte 2003*. Bologna: Ante Quem.

Luni, Mario. 1999. "Rapporti tra le coste dell'Adriatico in età classica e i traffici con Grecia e Magna Grecia." In *La Dalmazia e l'altra sponda. Problemi di Archaiologia adriatica*, edited by Lorenzo Braccesi and Sante Graciotti, 13–40. Florence: Olschki.

Ruta Serafini, Angela, ed. 2002. *Este preromana: una città e i suoi santuari*. Treviso: Canova.

Von Eles, Patrizia, ed. 2002. *Guerriero e sacerdote. Autorità e comunità nell'età del ferro a Verucchio. La tomba del Trono*. Florence: All'Insegna del Giglio.

CHAPTER SIXTEEN

Cyrenaica

Gerald P. Schaus

After limited contacts between Libya and the Aegean in the Bronze Age, Greeks from the island of Thera successfully established agricultural settlements in one section of the North African coast southwest of Crete in the seventh century. These settlements, the most southerly cluster of Greek city-states, were impacted both by special features of regional geography and by local Libyan peoples inhabiting the area.

Geography

The eastern half of the North African coast, stretching from Leptis Magna to Alexandria at the mouth of the Nile, is largely inhospitable desert, almost 2000 km of coastline with few sheltered bays, and little freshwater (Map 2). The exception in this long stretch is right in the middle, Cyrenaica, a 300 km-long massif jutting northward into the Mediterranean Sea, bound on the west by the Gulf of Sirte and on the east by the Gulf of Bomba. Its coastline has several small inlets suitable for harborage, and sufficient sources of freshwater to supply normal human and animal needs.

This prominent land mass rises out of the sea in two abrupt steps of about 300 and 200 m respectively, then rises still further in a broad plateau before it declines slowly southward, changing from rich, well-watered farmland, to drier steppe land, and finally to arid desert (Applebaum 1979, 1–7; Chamoux 1953, 11–17). The narrow coastal plain averages between 1 and 4 km wide except toward the west where it broadens out to ca. 10 km. The middle step is somewhat less narrow (see Figure 16.1). Both of these steep rises are cut by deep gullies (*wadis*), which drain the upper levels in mostly seasonal streams toward the sea. Rainfall, supplemented by heavy summer dews and mists, provides adequate water for both barley and wheat crops, reaching a maximum annual amount of about 500 mm near

---

A Companion to Greeks Across the Ancient World, First Edition. Edited by Franco De Angelis.
© 2020 John Wiley & Sons, Inc. Published 2020 by John Wiley & Sons, Inc.

Figure 16.1 View from Cyrene's theater down across the middle plateau to the sea.

Cyrene. In other areas, rainfall averages closer to 300–400 mm annually, still enough to produce large grain crops in most years (Laronde 1987, 49–51, 259–260; Applebaum 1979, 74–109; land exploitation around Cyrene: Laronde 1996). The total cultivable land in Cyrenaica has been estimated at 16 100 km^2 and Cyrene itself is believed to have controlled about 1750 km^2 directly (35 × 50 km), with a larger zone of settlements further away from this core territory (Laronde 1987, 15–17, 285–313; Austin 2004, 1243–1244). The population of Cyrene, the city and its *chora*, in the fourth century has been estimated at 300 000 (Laronde 1987, 340–342; at only 135 000 by Applebaum 1979, 102).

There are two comfortably habitable zones within Cyrenaica, the plateau including its middle and coastal plains, which received sufficient annual rainfall for agriculture and had a variable depth of fertile red soils derived from insoluable limestone residues, and the steppe to the south of the plateau, which had white soils and only received enough winter rain for seasonal grazing. The former area was the location of the Greek settlements, shared with Libyan agriculturalists and seasonal pastoralists. The best area was around Cyrene, which had the highest rainfall and also water sources from springs due to impermeable marl strata. The area around Barca, the bread basket of modern Libya, was settled later, and although it has the same water-retentive red soils, it depended more on wells. Likewise, the coastal plains around Taucheira, Ptolemais, and Euesperides with smaller amounts of cultivable land depended on wells and cisterns for water during the dry summer months. The steppe land, on the other hand, provided grazing, particularly for sheep, and depended on run-off water in cisterns rather than wells. This was largely occupied by Libyan nomadic herders who returned to the plateau in mid-spring with their flocks (Applebaum 1979, 74–82).

The coast of Cyrenaica must have been visited from time to time by Bronze Age sailors from the Aegean, Cyprus, or the Levantine coast, as excavations at Bate's Island near Marsa Matruh in western Egypt suggest, notably with its Cypriot and Canaanite pottery (Russell 2002; Hulin 2002); however, no secure evidence for Bronze Age Aegean visitors in Cyrenaica itself, even for short stays, has been identified yet (Boardman 1968). Since the desert reaches right to the shore for long stretches both to the east and to the west of Cyrenaica, it is only the proximity of Crete and the prevailing northerly winds that would encourage Bronze Age sailors to use it as a landfall before sailing to Egypt. It was likely first visited by sailors blown off course by storms from the north, as happened twice when Greeks first settled this area in the seventh century (Corobius from Crete [Hdt. 4.151], and Colaeus from Samos [Hdt. 4.152]; also, later two triremes sent by Sparta to Syracuse in the Peloponnesian war [Thuc. 7.50], and mythically, Jason and the Argonauts [Hdt. 4.179, to Lake Tritonis]). While the Nile is 800 km east of Cyrene and Tripolitania (Leptis Magna) is 600 km to the west, the southwest corner of Crete is just 300 km away to the northeast, with prevailing winds coming from a northerly direction (80% of the time in the summer). It must have been common to get caught in a strong gale, and eventually sight the high coast of Cyrenaica while still far out at sea.

Libyans and Egypt

The eastern Libyans are mentioned in Egyptian documents with some frequency. Called loosely *Tjehenu*, tending to refer to Libyans closer to the western Delta, or *Tjemehu*, referring apparently to peoples in more remote regions from Egypt, tribes called *Libu* and *Meshwesh* (*Mashwash*), probably were at home in Cyrenaica, the only region close to Egypt where a denser population could be supported. Herodotus together with Egyptian texts and wall depictions help fill in ethnographic information about native Libyan life in Cyrenaica (Chamoux 1953, 38–68; Barker 1989, 40). From April to October, the tribes would gather within their territorial boundaries in the northern part of Cyrenaica with their herds, taking advantage of permanent sources of water (wells and springs) during the dry part of the year, grazing the stubble left on cultivated fields, and presumably constructing permanent or semi-permanent settlements. When the first rains came between late October and December, the fields were planted with grain and vetches, a portion of the population was left to tend the fields, while the rest led their animals southward to take advantage of grasslands that thrived in the late fall and winter. When the rains ended and grazing along with water sources dried up, herds were led back north, the fields were harvested, and life settled down again in larger communities.

Hunting was practiced as a significant supplement to the crops of the northern plateau and the meat and milk of the herds. Gazelle, antelope, hares, ostriches, wild sheep, and cattle provided both meat and skins for clothing and useful leather products. Migrations of birds, particularly quail, probably offered another source of food, and fish must have been exploited in coastal waters. Plagues of locusts no doubt descended on Cyrenaica periodically devastating crops, but locusts were also eaten as food.

Depictions of Libyan men on Egyptian walls show them wearing long cloaks of colorful animal skins, tied at the neck and open on one side (Bates 1914, plate III). They are light skinned, with sparse beards, and long hair including a braided side knot hanging down in front of their ear, decorated on top with ostrich feathers. A notable feature is the use of tattoos to enliven both arms and legs.

Contact between Libyans and Egyptians was quite regular, especially along the coastal route, and conflicts are well known, particularly in the thirteenth and twelfth centuries (Redford 1992, 247–250). Thousands of Libyan dead are recorded in Egyptian accounts of invasions of the Nile valley from the west. If these numbers are accepted, the population density of eastern Libya, particularly Cyrenaica, must have been quite high, and population pressures relieved through both passive and aggressive migration attempts.

Records give an impressive number of captured cattle, sheep, and goats in these invasions, but there is also mention of substantial quantities of gold, silver, and bronze objects, and reference to Libyan "towns," suggesting that the Libyans had permanent settlements, along with sophisticated exchange mechanisms and craft specialization (White 1994, 37; O'Connor 1983, 272–273). So far, however, these settlements, apart from some graves and shrine sites, have not been securely identified and explored systematically (Hodos 2006, 169–183; White 1994, 38–39; Laronde 1990, 173–174, 177–180; Luni et al. 2010).

Egyptian records tell us that the invasion during Pharoah Merenptah's rule included a very large number of non-Libyan Sea Peoples, presumably from the Aegean region. Their names are mentioned in the texts, but they cannot be located specifically, except perhaps the Lukki, from Lycia, in Asia Minor, and the Eqwesh from the island of Kos (rather than the Ahhiyawa mentioned in Hittite texts) (Redford 1992, 246, table 1, 248–249). They must have been encouraged to join the invading force by the Libyan leader, who recognized their fighting abilities and advanced weapons and armor. The political disintegration in Egypt following the New Kingdom led to the Twenty-second, Twenty-third and Twenty-fourth Dynasties, which were Libyan in origin during the Third Intermediate Period (O'Connor 1983, 274–287).

The Foundation of Cyrene

The first and leading city-state of Cyrenaica was Cyrene. Its foundation and early history are better known than those of any other Greek overseas settlement. It is often used as a model against which other Greek settlements are compared in their development. Yet, at times, its "history" has been obscured by too much available information, including conflicting traditions and questionably authentic documents, which leads occasionally to modern assessments that only accept the bare minimum of facts as trustworthy, leaving aside the rest as possible fabrication based on political or social expediency (e.g., Osborne 2009, 15; see Austin 2008, 189–192). This may have a healthy critical effect on our assessment of ancient written sources, but it also tends to dismiss information that has historical value, misuse other information to serve a modern view of history, or discredit the ability of ancient communities to discern their own history through both oral and written sources lost to us today.

This unusual wealth of source material concerning Cyrene's early history can be summarized briefly. The indigenous Libyans encountered by Greeks in Cyrenaica are mentioned both in Herodotus and by Egyptian art and written sources (discussed above), including details of their appearance and interactions with Egyptians and the newly arrived Greeks. Certain aspects of Cyrene's early development, history, and legends can be gleaned from occasional comments in three victory odes by Pindar (*Pyth*. IV.1–8, 259–262; V.55–67, 79–103; IX.17–70, 103–125) and the *Hymn to Apollo* (65–96) by Callimachus of Cyrene. Much more is learned from Herodotus (4.150–167, 200–205), who provides a detailed account of the primary foundation expedition. He includes two different versions of what motivated Thera to send out the expedition and what its first steps were. He also describes major problems faced by Cyrene in the first century of its existence. On the other hand, a note by a scholiast to Pindar refers to information from a local historian, Menecles of Barca, that suggests an alternate motive for sending out the original expedition (translation Fornara 1983, 17–18, F17). Very rare and unusual is a fourth-century version of the original formal agreement made between those setting out for Libya and those remaining behind on Thera, a document which was acceptable to both Theraen and Cyrenaean citizens of the fourth century (Graham 1960; translation Graham 1983, 225–226). Finally, there is considerable archaeological material which reveals information about life in the settlement's early years, including aspects of the economy, religion, funerary practices, and local society in general. Significantly, archaeology also suggests that other settlements in Cyrenaica were founded quite shortly after Cyrene with Greek settlers possibly from places other than Thera.

It is important to recognize that Herodotus was writing ca. 440 BCE and that his sources were not historical documents but rather local tradition subject to interpretation and change. He (4.147–148) introduces his story of the settling of Libya by going back much earlier to a tradition about the founding of Thera (formerly called Calliste and having inhabitants with a Phoenician origin) led by an elite Lacedaemonian named Theras who had acted as regent for his nephews until they reached maturity and could take their place as kings. At the end of his regency, Theras organized a group of Lacedaemonians and a few Minyans, who were waiting to be executed for some sort of sedition in Laconia, and sailed to Calliste (renamed Thera, after him) in three thirty-oared ships. The island then had three groups of people, Phoenicians, Lacedaemonians, and a small number of Minyans.

Two versions of the foundation story are then clearly delineated by Herodotus, a Theraean version and a Cyrenaean. These have some similar features, but others are difficult to reconcile. Because the events occur two centuries before Herodotus's time and ongoing political factors in the two places no doubt encouraged an emphasis on different aspects of the story, one can only expect that one of the two versions is close to the truth, but both may have truthful elements. To know which of the variant details are fabrications is difficult, but historians have made good attempts (e.g., Sakellariou 1990, 38–65). The gist of the story with features found in both follows here.

An unknown number of generations after Theras's expedition, but presumably not too many (in the middle of the seventh century BCE), a young man descended from the Minyans on Thera, named Aristoteles (according to Pindar), with a second name

"Battus," given to him because of his stammer (Sakellariou 1990, 57–58), went to Delphi either to consult the oracle about his speech impediment or as part of a larger Theraean delegation led by King Grinnos. Battus became the object of an unexpected oracular command. "Battus, you came about your voice, but Lord Phoebus Apollo sends you to sheep-rearing Libya to be founder of a settlement." (Cyrenaean version – Hdt. 4.155). He returned to Thera and, along with other Theraeans, ignored the Delphic command. Over the next few years (seven, in the Theraean version – Hdt. 4.151), a severe drought hit the island, or alternatively, some unspecified but serious problems (Hdt. 4.156), causing the Theraeans to return to Delphi and consult the oracle. The response was again that the Theraeans should send out a group of settlers to Libya. In light of their troubles, a reconnaisance voyage was organized, likely using as a guide a fisherman from Crete who had once been blown by contrary winds to Libya. The mission returned to Thera, and a full fledged expedition was then organized, likely with forced conscription by family (Hdt. 4.153) to bring the numbers up to a point which would secure the success of the settlement. Two penteconters (50-oared ships) left for Libya, presumably with at least 100 men to work the oars fully.

The two versions of the story seem to come together at this point where Herodotus mentions the departure of the penteconters (Graham 1960, 97; but see Ottone 2002, 450 n. 53). The place chosen for settlement was a small island, called Plataea, close to the coast in the Gulf of Bomba (Boardman 1966, 150), with a sheltered anchorage but not ideal for agriculture and without a water source. In any case, the site was poorly chosen, so after two years, leaving a man behind, the Theraeans sailed either home, where they were not allowed to land, or to Delphi to seek further advice. Before long, they returned to Libya and moved to a more promising site at Aziris, described by Herodotus (4.157) as surrounded by the fairest wooded glens with a river running along one side. At this point, we hear for the first time about native peoples. In the seventh year after moving to Aziris, the Libyans entreated the Greeks to leave this place for a better one. The Theraeans were persuaded to move still farther west, although they passed up a site called Irasa, deliberately led past it at night by their Libyan guides, till they reached the site of Cyrene, with its abundant rainfall and full-flowing spring, the Fountain of Apollo (see Figure 16.2).

The site of Cyrene was a major departure from custom for this group of islanders since its location is more than 10 kilometers inland, at an altitude of about 600 m. The advantages must have been persuasive for them to give up close contact with the sea. Fertile soil, an abundant source of water, and protection on three sides by steep hillslopes probably helped confirm their choice, but reaching this decision must have been done much more seriously than Herodotus's story indicates, since being guided blindly by local Libyan escorts is folly. Surely the Greek pioneers at Aziris had explored the coast of Cyreanaica and ventured considerable distances inland during their six years there, and two at Plataea.

Problems with adjusting to life in *terra nova*, a situation faced by so many new Greek settlements at this time, are rarely discussed by ancient sources in any detail. Establishing relations with much larger, and potentially dangerous, indigenous populations with strange customs and language, identifying suitable tracts of land to cultivate and mark ownership, removing rocks, trees, and undergrowth prior to plowing, not knowing local weather and seasonal conditions before risking one's grain seed in a first sowing, suffering through physical and no doubt mental ailments including home-sickness

Figure 16.2 Apollo sanctuary with the acropolis (left), and Fountain of Apollo (in cliff face).

without the normal company of family, must all have been challenging, even with strong faith in divine beneficence. Herodotus (4.156) even records an attempt at giving up on the Libyan expedition and returning home, only to be driven away and forced to try again. The dream of property, prosperity, a peaceful new life, certainly was strong motivation.

What actually compelled the expedition from Thera in the first place is not completely clear. The oracle at Delphi is said to have given a spontaneous command to found a settlement in Libya, but we are equally informed that this was not enough to leave Thera because the oracle was ignored for years. It was what happened subsequently: seven years of drought says Herodotus (4.151) or in the Cyrenaean version, simply misfortunes (συμφοράς), or according to Menecles of Barca, perhaps echoing the Cyrenaean version of events, civil strife (στάσις) on Thera:

> (Menecles) says that the citizens of Thera fell into civil strife, and that Battus was the leader of one of the factions. When the struggle of the factions ended, the result was that Battus' party was driven out of Thera. Renouncing the thought of returning to Thera, they considered founding a colony. Battus went to Delphi and asked whether they should carry on the internal struggle (?) or should establish a colony at some different place. The god responded: 'Your first enquiry is bad, but the second is good.' (Scholiast to Pindar, *Pyth* 4.100, Menecles of Barca, *FGrH* 270 F6 – translation Fornara 1983, 22 F17).

Despite strong arguments in favor of civil strife as the motive for departure, recently restated by Bernstein (2004, 214–222) and reinforced by examining the division of Thera's population between Laconian and Minyan settlers,[1] there is still the clear statement by Herodotus (4.151) that drought was the cause, not *stasis*, and there is the testimony of both Herodotus (4.153) and the Agreement of the Founders that men were forcibly conscripted for the expedition by family, not through political division.

If its contents are indeed authentic, as Graham (1960, 111) and others (e.g., Sakellariou 1990, 62) concluded, the Agreement of the Founders inscription provides a fascinating glimpse into the process of sending out a settlement expedition in times of local stress, but it also indicates that provision was made by the sponsoring state for those citizens who remained at home to take advantage of the benefits of the expedition if it were successful. The purported Agreement is inserted into an inscription whose purpose is to confirm the rights of Theraeans in the fourth century still to move to Cyrene and be given unoccupied land and citizenship including assignment to a tribe, a phratry, and one of the nine Hetaereiae (Companions) based on the original sworn Agreement. There may be both political and economic reasons for confirming the Foundation Agreeement at this time, but we are not told what they are.

Other interesting details in the Agreement are that the Theraeans who sailed with Battus did so as his "companions," although acknowledging him as leader and king, and they

> sailed on equal and fair terms according to family; that one son be conscripted from each family; that those who sail be in the prime of life; and that, of the rest of the Theraeans, any free man who wishes may sail. (translation Graham 1983, 225)

Anyone who tried to avoid this conscription, or who aided someone who tried to avoid it, was liable to punishment by death and loss of all property. This demonstrates the desperate nature of the situation in Thera. The same idea is reinforced by the provision that the expedition could not return to Thera, no matter how badly it fared, for a period of five years. If, however, things continued poorly for five years even with Theraean help, then and only then could members of the expedition return to Thera, and at that point receive back their possessions and their citizenship. Could this Theraean tradition of a foundation agreement, of a time of great stress on the island's populace, of forced conscription by family, of rights of return after five years, and rights to be given land and citizenship in Cyrene if successful, be fabricated in the fourth century, and used to sway the Cyrenaeans successfully so that an inscription was raised in Cyrene? A convincing case has yet to be made to prove such fabrication. Until then, the details of the Agreement, as no doubt examined carefully and accepted by the Cyrenaeans who had little to gain and much to lose in accepting them, offer a unique insight into seventh-century practices.

There is clearly a dire warning in the Agreement about observing the terms laid out in it, and this warning is accompanied by a description of the almost black-magical rites carried out to invoke the consequences of disobedience. Wax images were made, presumably of the oath swearers and their possessions, and then were put into a fire to melt, with a spoken formula, invoking the gods to melt away anyone who did not abide by the sworn agreement, including his descendants and his property. This must have made an impression on the fourth-century Cyrenaeans, especially the most superstitious, when they were reminded of this provision. It also helped the Theraean case when the contract of reciprocity was expressed in the Agreement.

A hundred men or so from a small island 450 km away to the north starting a village in Cyrenaica seems rather insignificant in terms of migration. The local Libyans probably thought of it this way, and may have had earlier contacts with Greeks, or traditions of contact and even alliances going back centuries, with sea travelers from the north. The immigrants may well have been welcomed, if cautiously so, and helped to establish their new community. Trouble only stirred when the Greek settlers increased in number and began taking larger swaths of land for their animals and farms. How long did this take? Herodotus is wonderfully helpful since he tells us some results of his inquiries about the Libyans, their customs, and their relations with the Greeks. This forms part of his narrative about Cyrene, but also a separate anthropological digression on the Libyans, similar to his study of the Scythians earlier in Book Four.

Battus the founder ruled for 40 years, says Herodotus (4.159), presumably from 640/639 BCE (Eusebius's date, using Eratosthenes of Cyrene, Chamoux 1953, 121) when the two ships sailed to Plataea, and so was a young man, no doubt of elite background, when he took on the position. He was succeeded by his son, Arcesilas, who ruled for just 16 years, so presumably until about 584/583. Herodotus (4.159) explicitly states that during this long time, the people at Cyrene remained at the same number as in the original settlement. This is hard to accept, given the archaeological evidence for new Greek settlements during this time at Taucheira, Ptolemais (original name unknown), and Apollonia along the coast. A slow influx, which could easily be absorbed in land that was uncleared and unclaimed by Libyans, perhaps went largely unnoticed. There may be reasons for the slow rate in increasing settlement numbers, but Herodotus could well have exaggerated the situation. In any case, the third ruler, Battus II, the Fortunate (in the list of eight kings who alternated between Battus and Arcesilas), decided to issue an invitation to other Greeks to settle in Cyrene since Thera was too small to supply the desired numbers. Delphi supported him, "Whoever comes to much-loved Libya after the lands are divided, I say he will then regret it" (Hdt. 4. 159).

The result was large numbers of newcomers, and great new tracts of land being claimed away from the territory of the Libyans. Tensions grew. The Libyans were badly treated by the Cyrenaeans, so their king, Adicran, we are told, sought redress not from among other Libyan tribes who might have been sympathetic, but from far-away, powerful Egypt. Perhaps Adicran had a special relationship with Pharoah Apries, who then sent a great army against Cyrene, concerned perhaps himself about the growing strength of Cyrene, only to be defeated at Irasa by the Greeks, with very few of the Egyptian soldiers returning home alive. For this ill-considered debacle, Apries was overthrown by an ambitious young leader, named Amasis, with help from Cyrenaica over a three-year period (570–567 BCE) and two or three battles recorded in Egyptian and Babylonian documents (Boardman 1994, 141 n. 10; "Putu-Yaman" on the Neo-Babylonian tablet (BM 33041 and BM 33053) is conventionally identified as Cyrenaica). From a loss by Egyptians to the Cyrenaeans at Irasa, to a victory by Amasis supported by Greeks including a contingent of Cyrenaeans against Apries and his Babylonian ally, Nebukadrezzar II, we suddenly find that Cyrene is no longer a tiny settlement precariously hanging on to its fragile existence, but an actor on a greater world stage. The role that this Greek settlement played in Egyptian politics may have been exaggerated based on its later size and prosperity, but it was significant enough to be remembered by Herodotus (2.161; 4.159), and confirmed in a Babylonian document.

The relationship between the new pharoah, Amasis, and Cyrene is recorded by Herodotus (2.181) as a close one – both "friends" and "allies." It was even cemented with a marriage between Amasis and a Cyrenaean woman, Ladice (variously Battus's, Arcesilas's, or a certain Critoboulus's daughter: Hdt. 2.181), which resulted in royal gifts being sent to Cyrene (Hdt. 2.181-182). Arcesilas II, nicknamed the Harsh (ca. 566–560 BCE: Stibbe, 1972, 195–201), seems to have benefitted from this close relationship, with support for his tyrranical rule from a contingent of Egyptian soldiers (Stibbe 1972, 199; Plut. *Mor.* 261C) sent by Amasis. This large Egyptian unit was then taken over by Laarchus, the regent of the young Battus, until Laarchus himself was murdered in a plot carried out by Eryxo, Arcesilas's widow (Plut. *Mor.* 260D–261D). The end result though, as told by Plutarch (*Mor.* 261D), was a personal embassy to talk with Amasis by Eryxo, her mother Critola (sister of Battus II, his ally in taking the Egyptian throne), and Polyarchus, Eryxo's oldest brother. Together, they persuaded Amasis of the justice of their murder of Laarchus. This ended Egyptian involvement in Cyrene's affairs until the Persian king, Cambyses, conquered Egypt.

Meantime, two significant events took place during Arcesilas II's poor rule. Very shortly after coming to the throne, he alienated his own brothers to such an extent that they left Cyrene and founded a rival town about 100 km to the west, at a fertile, well-watered place called Barca on the middle plateau. Clearly, a significant number of settlers went with them, and the local Libyans, perhaps happy to find Greek allies against the rule of Arcesilas in Cyrene, were willing to give them land. Second, these brothers succeeded in convincing the Libyans to revolt against Arcesilas, no doubt having been subjugated after the defeat of their Egyptian allies at Irasa ca. 570 BCE. Arcesilas came with a large army to attack the rebellious Libyans, both those around Cyrene and those presumably who assisted his brothers, but they fled out of fear, to the eastern Libyans. Arcesilas, we are told, pursued them, only to be beaten himself, at Leucon, with the loss of 7000 soldiers, a number that strains credibility (Mitchell 1966, 112 n. 73). The upshot was that while Arcesilas continued to rule and Cyrene itself was not attacked by the Libyans, the Libyans must have gained confidence, and respect in their dealings with the Greeks, as well as made close friends at Barca. Interestingly, more native Libyan names have been identified in inscriptions from Barca, Taucheira, and Ptolemais than from Cyrene itself (Masson 1976).

The recent swift growth of Cyrene during the 570s under Battus II, the brutal rule of Arcesilas II alienating the Libyans and many Greeks, along with a major loss to the Libyans at Leucon, brought continuing problems during the reign of Arcesilas's young son, Battus III, the Lame. The Cyrenaeans, perhaps led by a group helping Battus in his early years, decided to consult Delphi, and were told to seek a mediator from Mantineia. Either the oracle had someone in mind, or its words have been reworked after the fact. In any case, the Mantineians offered them their best man, Demonax. Going to Cyrene, studying the situation, Herodotus reports Demonax's solution to the troubles as being twofold: the division of the citizens into three presumably reconstituted tribes, and reducing the lands and priesthoods of the king with the remainder being given to the people. (The elites of Cyrene must have done well by the priesthoods at least.) Demonax did not abolish the kingship, as had happened in so many other city-states in Greece, but its powers and wealth were seriously curtailed.

More interesting is the division of citizens into three "tribes," although Herodotus immediately then describes three "divisions" (*moirai*). This has been regarded as a precurser of Cleisthenes's tribal reforms in Athens ca. 508 BCE, and as indicating that each of Demonax's three divisions was represented in each of three tribes, for nine units altogether (Jeffery 1961, 143–144; Hölkeskamp 1993). Herodotus (4.161) says that the first division consisted of Theraeans and Perioikoi, the second included Cretans and Peloponnesians, and the third contained all the Islanders. This suddenly throws light on developments in Cyrene since its foundation, or more particularly, since the invitation of Battus II to other Greeks to come and settle in Libya. What until now was regarded as a Theraean settlement with a king of Theraean origin, now is only perhaps one-third or one-sixth Theraean. An issue is who were the Perioikoi. Herodotus could have been clearer, and various groups have been proposed. Herodotus a little earlier in his account (4.159) referred to the neighboring Libyans as οἱ περίοικοι Λίβυες, and because Libyans had won new respect at Leucon, some (Applebaum 1979, 18) have thought that these Perioikoi were Libyans. Although unlikely, it would mean that the oldest inhabitants of the area, Theraeans and Libyans, were joined together in this first division.[2] More likely, the Perioikoi were simply later arriving Theraeans (Hölkeskamp 1993, 408) or ones from the six districts outside Thera town (Jeffery 1961, 141).

The second division included Cretans and Peloponnesians, partly reflecting the tradition that a Cretan purple fisher guided the Theraeans to Libya, but also confirming that many other Cretans followed afterwards, probably not waiting for the invitation from Battus II. There is also a tradition that Laconians somehow participated in the settlement, also from an early date. Pausanias (3.14.3) says that Chionis of Sparta, a three-time Olympic victor (ca. 664 BCE), participated in the expedition of Battus, and helped him to found Cyrene and reduce the Libyans (also Isocrates, *Philip*. 5, for a Laconian role). It would seem that the Peloponnesians in the second division then must include a good number of settlers from Laconia, but also a significant number of other Peloponnesians, for example, Arcadians (Austin 2008, 193–194).

The third division, all the Islanders, must certainly include settlers who came at the invitation of Battus II and the Delphic oracle in the 570s or 560s, but there may have been earlier islanders. Thera's neighbors in the southern Cycladic islands, for example, surely heard of the opportunities and responded to them from among the most eager of their young men, especially if the reported drought had affected these islands as much as it had Thera. Pottery at Taucheira and Cyrene supports this (Boardman and Hayes 1966, 73–78; 1973, 34–36; Schaus 1985, 7–9). The Lindian Chronicle records that a group from Lindos on Rhodes joined Battus at Cyrene, but this is often regarded as referring to Battus II and the second wave of settlers. Likewise, Herodotus's reference to good relations between Samos, Cyrene, and Thera, going back to the help given by the Samian merchant Colaeus to the Cretan guide abandoned on Plataea, suggests that some members of the third tribe were from Samos. A mixture of Dorian and Ionian Greeks is probably to be expected. Much pottery produced by Chians and other East Greeks may support their presence as well (Schaus 1985, 49–92, 103–105). In any case, the scope of the migration from the Aegean to Libya over about 90 years from its launch is seen clearly as small in scale at times, but with major influxes, certainly coming from a variety of sources, and possibly including the indigenous Libyans for a significant role in the city's life. This last point is reinforced by Libyan names found on Greek inscriptions throughout Cyrenaica in later centuries (Masson 1976; Laronde 1987, 339).

According to Herodotus (4.162), the reforms held firm during Battus III's long reign (ca. 560–530/525 BCE), but Pheretima, Battus's wife, and mother of his successor, Arcesilas III, was not nearly so content with Demonax's reforms, and loss of authority. When her son became king, both she and Arcesilas demanded a return of their former privileges. A political fight occurred, probably lasting some years, with Arcesilas and his mother defeated and forced to flee to friendlier places. The struggle between monarchy and the form of democracy introduced by Demonax shows the strength of both parties. That Pheretima and Arcesilas split up and headed in different directions to seek military help is noteworthy. She went to Cyprus and was not successful; Arcesilas went to Samos, more likely during the tyranny of Syloson (after 524 BCE). Here he found strong backing for his plan to invade Cyrenaica from individuals who were eager to be offered land in exchange for their fighting skills. This was a migration opportunity of a different kind: conquest of Cyrene, theft of land belonging to earlier Greek settlers, based on the lost rights of the old kingship. One might suppose that a successful army for such a venture numbered in the thousands, and that Samos could not have supplied the full complement. A large mustering occurred on Samos, perhaps more broadly of East Greeks chafing under Persian rule, even though by now, Cyrene, and in particular Arcesilas himself, had medized and offered a payment of annual tribute to the Persian king. Now another Delphic oracle is reported as foretelling that there would eventually be eight generations of Battiad kings, four named Battus and four named Arcesilas. This is suspicious, like something remembered much later when the Battiads were finally overthrown, just before Herodotus's time. In any case, the return of Arcesilas with his army from Samos tipped the balance in his favor. His opponents fled, or were captured and sent away for execution, winding up in Thera, or burned alive when trapped in a fortified tower at Barca (Hdt. 4.162–164).

Since the campaign was successful, and his opponents were dealt with, one presumes that the promised land redistribution took place to reward the men he brought from Samos. Of course, Arcesilas and Pheretima must have taken a fair portion of land and privileges back as their own reward. Arcesilas left his strong-minded mother in Cyrene to administer affairs and even sit in council, while he himself, reportedly fearing an oracle about his early death in Cyrene, retired to Barca where his father-in-law, Alazeir, was king. There, he and Alazeir were indeed murdered by his opponents, victims of the deadly politics of the time (ca. 518 BCE: Mitchell 1966, 101). "Alazeir" is a Libyan name, suggesting that he and his daughter, Arcesilas's wife (who was also related to Arcesilas, Hdt. 4.164), were of Greek-Libyan stock from an earlier mixed marriage, since Alazeir ruled in Barca, the place of refuge offered by the Libyans to Arcesilas II's brothers and rivals, and so presumably a Greek, or Greek-Libyan, settlement.

Cyrenaica and Persia

Cambyses and the Persians took control of Egypt in 525 BCE, with Cyprus and Cyrene offering their support to the Persians rather than the long-ruling Amasis and his son, Psammenitus (Amasis died in 526/525 after 44 years' rule: Hdt. 3.10). Cambyses appreciated this support by sending Ladice back safely to Cyrene, but was unimpressed at the small gift offered by Cyrene after his victory (Hdt. 3.13; 4.165). When Pheretima's son, Arcesilas III, was murdered in Barca by their political opponents, she fled to Egypt, according to Herodotus, and appealed for assistance to the Persian governor, Aryandes, insisting that her son had been murdered for having offered Cyrene in submission to the Persians. To his credit, Aryandes sent a messenger to Barca to inquire who it was that had killed Arcesilas III. The Barcaeans' response was that they murdered Arcesilas for all the many and bad things he had done to them, that is, not because he had medized. Therefore, they all wished to take the blame, or credit, for his death.

Aryandes sent both an army and a fleet of ships to punish the assassins of Arcesilas and King Alazeir, but Herodotus (4.167, 197) uses his judgment to question Aryandes's motive for the expedition. To him, it was more an expedition to conquer the various Libyan tribes unwilling to accept Persian overlordship, and so expand the empire. In the end, Aryandes did not in fact fight the native Libyans at all, only going as far as Euhesperides (Hdt. 4.204), but he besieged Barca for nine months (Hdt. 4.200) until the town was taken by deception (breaking of oaths sworn over a peace treaty). Pheretima took bloody vengence on the most guilty inhabitants, including the mutilation of women, while many other townsmen were enslaved and sent to live in distant Persia (ca. 514 BCE). Herodotus relishes the opportunity to end his narrative about Cyrene by mentioning Pheretima's horrid death from disease soon after.[3]

The long reign of Battus IV (ca. 514–475 BCE) has yielded little ancient historical comment. He must have provided secure, peaceful local government and a regular annual tribute to the Persians, although the Cyrenaean aristocrats may have chafed under his rule. Construction around Cyrene (e.g., agora: the prytaneion, a temple, two porticoes, building F), a good variety of coin issues (Robinson 1927, xviii–xxxv, 1–9 nos. 1–41; for the dating, van Alfen 2016), and a flood of terracotta figurines (Uhlenbrock 2010, 88–89) suggest that the *polis* enjoyed some prosperity. The same is not true of his successor, Arcesilas IV, the last of the Battiad kings of Cyrene, who won the tethrippon (four-horse chariot race) at the Pythian games in 462 and the Olympic race in 460 BCE. In the two odes by Pindar (*Pyth*. IV and V) commissioned to celebrate his Pythian victory, we learn that Arcesilas faced political trouble in Cyrene, one source of which was a certain Damophilus, exiled by Arcesilas and befriended by Pindar himself (*Pyth*. IV, 280–300). Clearly, storm clouds were brewing, especially since Persian weakness after losses to the Greeks at Salamis, Plataea, Mycale, the Eurymedon River, and a troubled succession by Artaxerxes, may have cost Arcesilas key support from that direction. Persian control of Cyrenaica may in fact have ended already by the 460s. Victory in games at Delphi and Olympia followed by raising a mercenary force abroad that was garrisoned at Euhesperides can be seen as steps he took to shore up his rule. Arcesilas IV was murdered, it seems at Euhesperides, by a democratic uprising, or at least a popular one, led most likely by an aristocratic faction in the 450s (Mitchell 1966, 110 n. 62). Cyrene helped the Greeks of the Delian League escaping from the failed expedition to support the Libyan-led uprising against the Persians in Egypt (King Inarus, who initiated the revolt, was Libyan, Thuc. 1.104). Arcesilas IV might still have been alive in 454 BCE when this occurred, though no longer a Persian nominee. On balance, Arcesilas was likely murdered during the Egyptian revolt (between 460 and 454 BCE), bringing an end to the Battiad monarchy (Mitchell 1966, 110, 112).

Two other substantial groups of immigrants to Cyrenaica might be mentioned in passing. One was the large number of mercenaries settled around Euesperides by Arcesilas IV after he hired them to support his regime in its last stages, presumably against aristocratic opponents (Applebaum 1979, 29 n. 149; Theotimus *FHG*, 470 F1, IV, 517, 1 ap. schol.; Pind. *Pyth.V*, 34). The other was the migration during the rule of Ophellas (321–309 BCE) of several thousand (10 000?) Athenians who had suffered under the difficult conditions of Macedonian overlordship (Applebaum 1979, 43). Virtually all of these latter together with their families were lost finally in an attempt to settle in Tripolitania, first during a brutal march across the Syrtic Gulf to assist Agathocles of Syracuse in a war against Carthage (Diod. Sic. 20.40.6), and subsequently in the battles against the Carthaginians and later the Sicilian Greeks. Some, however, may have wound up in Syracuse eventually (Diod. Sic. 20.44.7).

Libyan Tribes and Customs

Herodotus (4.168–199) offers a long tangential discussion on the Libyan tribes of North Africa, proceeding east to west, from Egypt to the farthest reaches known to him or his informers. Some details are worth mentioning since Herodotus himself likely had first-hand experience of some of the tribes. A common theme is an interest in Libyan women, noting such things as dress, sexual promiscuity, and unusual habits.

The Adyrmachidae are noted first, closest to the Egyptians, with customs like the Egyptians but Libyan dress. Women wear bronze anklets on both legs. The Giligamae are next to the west, reaching the eastern boundaries of Cyrenaica where the silphium plant begins to grow. They have Libyan customs. Then tribes having greatest contact with the Greeks are described. First, the Asbystae dwell inland from the Greeks of Cyrene, not reaching the coast because the Cyrenaeans have taken all the coastal land. They are said by Herodotus to imitate closely the customs of the Cyrenaeans, and to be the most interested of all Libyans in racing four-horse chariots, an expensive passion. Two other tribes follow, the Auschisae, south of Barca but with territory reaching the sea at Euhesperides, and a small tribe, the Bacales, whose land touches the coast at Tauchira. Like the Asbystai, the customs of these are close to those of their Greek neighbors. Herodotus then says that the next westward tribe is the Nasamones, which he notes (4.172) is a populous nation, presumably living on the eastern shore of the Gulf of Sirte, south of Euesperides. Like other Libyan nomads, they bring their flocks of sheep to the north for summer pasturage, but then go to the Augila oasis to gather dates growing in great abundance, and he adds that they gather locusts, dry them in the sun, and grind them into powder to add to their milk.

Herodotus (4.187) is impressed with the fitness of the Libyans, regarding them as the healthiest of all men. He says that their nomad diet consisted of meat and milk, but he (4.186) also notes that they do not touch cows' flesh, nor raise pigs. An interesting detail is that the women of Cyrene itself also believe it is wrong to eat cows' flesh, because of the association of Egyptian Isis with the cow. The difference between Cyrenaean women's belief and that of Cyrene's men must be assigned to the intermarriage of Libyan women with Greek settlers in the early years of the city (Marshall 2007).

Libyan religion is summarized briefly by Herodotus (4.188) noting that they only sacrifice to two gods, the sun and the moon, no others. Several sculptural reliefs seem to depict Libyan goddesses amidst scenes with herds (Wanis 1992; Luni 2010). Herodotus also mentions three Greek customs which may have originated among the Libyans: (i) Athena's *aegis* from the hairless tassled goat skins which women wear, (ii) a women's loud ceremonial wail or chant, and (iii) the technique of driving four-horse chariots.

One part of Libya certainly impressed Herodotus (4.198) for its fertility, the Cinyps River region, far to the west in Tripolitania where the soil is black and there is plenty of water, so the harvest yield is 300 fold, three times the amount produced around Euhesperides in western Cyrenaica. A Spartan settlement was attempted there ca. 514 BCE, led by Dorieus and guided by Theraeans (not Cyrenaeans), but it was driven out by Libyans and Carthaginians. Dorieus was assisted by one ship from Cyrene, but paid for by Philip of Croton, an Olympic victor, who had been banished by his home city and found refuge in Cyrene (Hdt. 5.47). The ship he brought was a private one, not supported by Battus IV, who, as a Persian nominee, would have been prevented from helping a Greek settlement in territory claimed by Carthaginians and Phoenicians. What impressed Herodotus (4.199) in Cyrenaica is the different times of harvest of the three elevations of Cyrenaica. The narrow coastal plain is ready first, then the middle plateau (see Figure 16.1), and finally the high plateau of Cyrenaica, so that the whole harvest, he thought, lasted eight months. This is exaggerated (five months perhaps), but it reflects a certain efficiency in the use of manpower to bring in crops from different agricultural zones, of which large landowners took advantage (Applebaum 1979, 94–95).

The Libyans, we are told, had an important role to play in the economy of Cyrene since they alone picked the famous wild silphium plant, a kind of all-purpose medicinal plant. They brought it to Cyrene, whose market was controlled by the Battiads apparently as a personal prerogative, though it is hard to imagine how it was strictly enforced (Applebaum 1979, 122–123). The Libyans must also have found a ready market for other products from their traditional way of life, including wool, perhaps meat, leather goods, and certainly horses, particularly for racing.

Cyrene is located toward the middle of Cyrenaica, yet there are four other city-states to the west and none to the east. The eastern side of Cyrenaica included Irasa, described as the finest of lands (Hdt. 4.158). It was deliberately kept away from the Greeks by Libyan guides when they directed them to Cyrene to settle in the seventh century. This presumably belonged to the Giligamae tribe, which still maintained Libyan customs in Herodotus's day. If it is true that Cyrene controlled 85% of the territory of Cyrenaica by the third century BCE (Applebaum 1979, 104–105), then much of it must have been eastward rather than westward from the city.

Archaeology of the Early Settlements

Material remains support and confirm the broad outlines of the tradition of settlement by Theraeans and other Greeks at Cyrene and places along the coast. They also reveal aspects of this development that written sources do not.

Egyptian paintings provide detailed depictions of various Libyan tribesmen, and these are supplemented by occasional portrait-like heads from Cyrenaica with Libyan features. The so-called Antaios krater by the Athenian vase painter Euphronius (ca. 510 BCE) depicts Heracles wrestling the Libyan giant (traditionally king of Irasa, Pindar, *Pyth.* IX.106 and scholiasts ad loc.), but overall, the evidence for Libyan settlements and culture in Cyrenaica is not particularly good. The cave-like sanctuary at Slonta is well known as a Libyan cult place with some Greek influence in the bead-and-reel molding and Attic pottery going back to the fifth century BCE or so (Luni 2010). Much study has been done of the Libyans by now, and yet the material remains are meager.

Evidence in the form of myths, names, and actual objects has been marshaled to show that Bronze Age Aegean people visited Libyan shores (Ottone 2002, 300–306), but no sites with stratified remains have yet been found in Cyrenaica (Boardman 1968). If sites with Aegean Bronze Age habitation levels are finally identified, they should be located on the coast, near sheltered bays and sources of freshwater, but they likely were semi-permanent or seasonal, without substanial building remains.

Identification of the island of Plataea, the first Theraean landfall, has been suggested for a small island now connected to the mainland by a sandspit, but it has not been explored systematically (Boardman 1966, 149–150). The site of this two-year settlement by a hundred men, struggling to establish a foothold on Libyan shores, may provide a neat snapshot of an exploratory mission if any remains can be found.

Aziris, a six-year settlement (637–631 BCE, based on Eusebius's foundation date for Cyrene of 631 BCE, Chamoux 1953, 120–124), has very likely been located at Wadi el Chalig about 27 km east of Derna. Some brief surface exploration yielded sherds from about the middle of the seventh century, including Protocorinthian, a Cretan spherical flask, an Aeolic gray ware sherd, some likely Cycladic fragments, and East Greek bird bowls and banded cups. The variety of fabrics represented here is surprising, but it may be more reflective of the contacts Theraeans had at home than contacts they had after reaching Libya.

At Cyrene, despite decades of excavation, very little seventh-century pottery has been published yet (Boardman 1966, 152 with refs; Stucchi 1965, 37–44, 60; 1984; D'Angelo 2006; Leone and Mei 2006; Mei 2014). Italian work in the agora area produced much sixth-century pottery; comprehensive study is awaited.[4] An interesting discovery on the east side of the agora is a small sanctuary going back to the late seventh century, apparently dedicated to Ophelles, a healing deity, and nearby a tumulus identified by Stucchi as the tomb of Battus I, the founder, which Pindar (*Pyth.* V, 93–98) says was located on the edge of the agora and where, he maintains, Battus was worshipped as a hero (Stucchi 1965, 32–65). There is little evidence for hero worship in the finds published so far, but the location suits Pindar's comment. Baldassarre (1999, 390–392) proposed that the site of the agora was originally part of agricultural land belonging to the monarchy when Battus was buried here, and that with the wave of new immigration and growth of the city in the 570s leading to Demonax's reforms, land was taken away from the king, including this important location, so that the agora could be laid out on a much grander scale. The tomb of the founder then took its place as a boundary marker of the agora and received heroization. Other kings were buried on the acropolis.

The extramural sanctuary of Demeter at Cyrene has been extremely rich in Archaic votive material, but this only goes back to ca. 600 when the sanctuary was established, not to the earliest years of the settlement (White 1981, 13–19, 25–27). Nevertheless, the picture that emerges is that Cyrene has enough Theraean and Cretan material to confirm the basic foundation story of Herodotus. Clearly, well before the invitation for more settlers was extended by Battus II, Cyrene constructed a sanctuary in Wadi bel Gadir, outside its original city boundaries, where votives were left in considerable quantities and from numerous places: Athens, Corinth, Laconia, the Cyclades, Chios, North and South Ionia (Schaus 1985; Moore 1987; Kocybala 1999). This argues against Herodotus's statement (4.159) that up to this time the population of Cyrene was no larger than at its original foundation. Although perhaps still not large by most standards, it must have been thriving enough to attract Greek ships traveling along the North African coast to or from Egypt, and could well have been a destination itself. Evidence from other Cyrenaican settlements, including Ptolemais (75 km southwest of Cyrene), Taucheira (115 km), and Euesperides (180 km), as well as Apollonia, Cyrene's port, demonstrate that good numbers of Greeks had arrived shortly after the original Theraeans founded Cyrene.

A large deposit of well-preserved votive pottery from another Demeter sanctuary was excavated at Taucheira in the mid-1960s and carefully published shortly thereafter (Boardman and Hayes 1966, 1973). With the exception of a single vase from the mid-seventh century, the sequence of vases begins about 620 BCE (Early Corinthian and East Greek). Comparisons can be made between this deposit and that from the Sanctuary of Demeter at Cyrene (Schaus 1985, 106–107). There was a greater number and variety of Cycladic vases at Tocra ("Melian," "Siphnian," and "Parian"), though no Theran, which Cyrene had. Also, a greater variety of Laconian and Chian vase shapes occurred at Cyrene as well as some other East Greek fabrics, and the quality of the Athenian pottery was better than at Tocra. Several factors have been suggested to explain these differences, including distances and sailing conditions, greater wealth at Cyrene, possible differences in the origins of the settlers, and greater contact with Naukratis for Cyrene. It seems not unlikely, for example, that some inhabitants of Tocra came originally from neighboring islands of Thera.

At Cyrene's port of Apollonia (13 km northeast), the small amount of Archaic pottery found so far goes back to ca. 600 BCE (Boardman 1966, 152–153), but stratified Archaic levels, when found, may put the settlement earlier, since ships were clearly landing on the coast, and this is the best location for Cyrene's needs, sheltered by nearby islands. The same can be said for Euesperides and the settlement later called Ptolemais, although some pottery at both sites goes back even earlier, perhaps like Tocra to ca. 620 BCE (Euesperides: Boardman 1966, 155–156; Gill 2004; for Ptolemais: Boardman 1966, 153, 156).

Before the mid-sixth century, Cyrene had begun to import fine marble sculpture (see Figure 16.3) (White 1971, 2006; Pedley 1971; Kane 1980), and by the late sixth, it was minting its own silver coinage (van Alfen 2016) and constructing impressive temples (Apollo and Zeus: see Figures 16.2 and 16.4) and sanctuaries (Demeter) to accommodate the worship of its gods (Bonacasa and Ensoli 2000, 104–147). Extensive necropoleis include early rock-cut tombs with impressive architectural facades (see Figure 16.5).

Figure 16.3 Sphinx from a votive deposit found outside the city walls, mid-sixth century BC.

Figure 16.4 Temple of Zeus.

Figure 16.5 North necropolis, Archaic portico tombs.

Cyrene also built one of the earlier treasuries at Olympia (ca. 540–520 BCE) to protect gifts which were being left there to Zeus. Subjects on Greek vases occasionally have a Libyan theme (Heracles wrestling Antaios, or the nymph Cyrene wrestling a lion). The most fascinating of these is a Laconian vase found in an Etruscan tomb which depicts a royal figure labeled "Arcesilas" (likely the hated king Arcesilas II) overseeing the weighing and packing of a bulky white material, generally identified as silphium or wool. Given his reputation, his violent death, and the odd reference to Egyptian iconography in the scene, it seems that the vase painter was mocking him (Schaus 2006, 176-78).

Conclusion

The story of Greek settlement along this isolated stretch of the Mediterranean coast is rich in detail. What began as a desperate attempt to escape severe troubles at home on Thera became a complex drama with many acts and unusual characters involving settlers and fighters from other Greek city states, constrained local Libyan tribesmen, and powerful monarchs of Egypt and Persia. In the end, five or six Greek towns were established (the Pentapolis) controlling all the best land of Cyrenaica, dominated by Cyrene until the Hellenistic period. Despite at times conflicting sources, sense can be made of most details in understanding how the original expedition was launched, how monarchy became oligarchy or democracy, how Libyan resistance rose and subsided, and how Egyptian, then Persian, and eventually Macedonian/Ptolemaic political entities dominated these prosperous Greek settlements but had little lasting impact.

NOTES

1 Bernstein (among others, e.g., Dušanić 1978) dismisses the authenticity of the Agreement of the Founders inscription, though he may in part be influenced by his thesis that *miasma* and *katharma* were root causes of other migration expeditions. Graham (1983, 27 n. 3; 1960, 111) argues strongly that the Agreement can be taken as authentic, noting (1983, 41 n. 3) that the scholiast to Pindar, *Pyth.* IV.100, preferred Menecles's reason for the expedition because it was less "mythical." The real choice, he noted, is not myth versus stasis, but rather famine versus stasis as the cause of the expedition.
2 The issue of ethnicity, Hellenic and sub-Hellenic identity, and a conscious distinction of Hellenes from non-Hellenes is interesting in light of the close relations if not possibly shared citizenship between Greeks and Libyans or the establishment of tribes based on sub-Hellenic divisions in Cyrenaica. Hall (2002) makes much of the creation of fictive geneologies in the sixth century as a point of origin of "Hellenicity" rather than earlier contact with non-Hellenes through the diaspora, but others (Mitchell 2006, Domínguez 2006) are skeptical.
3 This version of the story is probably preferable to one ascribed to Menecles of Barca in which Pheretima, after her son's murder, put her grandson, Battus, on the throne, and sent the murderers to Egypt where she then followed, and had them killed. (*FGrH* 270 F5 (iiiA p. 84), translation and discussion in Mitchell 1966, 104–105).
4 A good beginning is Mei 2013. Stucchi (1984, 141) provided percentages of the various fabrics from Italian excavations, but no absolute numbers. This problem has been recognized and is being addressed; e.g., Leone and Mei 2006, 79.

REFERENCES

Applebaum, Shim'on. 1979. *Jews and Greeks in Ancient Cyrene*. Leiden: Brill.

Austin, Michel. 2004. "From Syria to the Pillars of Herakles." In *An Inventory of Archaic and Classical Greek Poleis*, edited by Mogens H. Hansen and Thomas H. Nielsen, 1233–1249. Oxford: Oxford University Press.

Austin, Michel. 2008. "The Greeks in Libya." In *Greek Colonisation: An Account of Greek Colonies and Other Settlements Overseas*, vol. 2, edited by Gocha R. Tsetskhladze, 187–217. Leiden: Brill.

Baldassarre, Ida. 1999. "Cirene." In *La città greca antica. Istituzioni, società e forme urbane*, edited by Emanuele Greco, 385–394. Rome: Donzelli.

Barker, Graeme W.W. 1989. "From Classification to Interpretation: Libyan Prehistory, 1969–1989." *Libyan Studies*, 20: 31–43.

Bates, Oric. 1914. *The Eastern Libyans: An Essay.* London: Macmillan.
Bernstein, Frank. 2004. *Konflikt und Migration. Studien auf griechischen Fluchtbewegungen im Zeitalter der sogenannten Großen Kolonisation.* St. Katharinen: Scripta Mercaturae Verlag.
Boardman, John. 1966. "Evidence for the Dating of Greek Settlements in Cyrenaica." *Annual of the British School at Athens,* 61: 149–156.
Boardman, John. 1968. "Bronze Age Greece and Libya." *Annual of the British School at Athens,* 63: 41–44.
Boardman, John. 1994. "Settlement for Trade and Land in North Africa: Problems of Identity." In *The Archaeology of Greek Colonisation: Essays Dedicated to Sir John Boardman,* edited by Gocha R. Tsetskhladze and Franco De Angelis, 137–149. Oxford University Committee for Archaeology, 40. Oxford: School of Archaeology.
Boardman, John. 1999. *The Greeks Overseas: Their Early Colonies and Trade.* 4th ed. London: Thames & Hudson.
Boardman, John, and John Hayes. 1966. *Excavations at Tocra 1963–1965. The Archaic Deposits 1.* British School at Athens Suppl. 4. London: Thames & Hudson.
Boardman, John, and John Hayes. 1973. *Excavations at Tocra 1963–1965. The Archaic Deposits 2 and Later Deposits.* Annual of the British School at Athens Suppl. 1. London: Thames & Hudson.
Bonacasa, Nicola, and Serena Ensoli, eds. 2000. *Cirene.* Milan: Electa.
Chamoux, François. 1953. *Cyrène sous la monarchie des Battiades.* Paris: Boccard.
D'Angelo, Ivan. 2006. "Imported Greek Pottery in Archaic Cyrene: The Excavations in the Casa del Propileo." In *Naukratis: Greek Diversity in Egypt: Studies on East Greek Pottery and Exchange in the Eastern Mediterranean,* edited by Alexandra Villing and Udo Schlotzhauer, 181–186. London: British Museum Press.
Domínguez, Adolfo J. 2006. "Hellenic Identity and Greek Colonisation." *Ancient West & East,* 4: 446–457.
Dušanić, Slobodan. 1978, "The ὅρκιον τῶν οἰκιστήρων and Fourth-Century Cyrene." *Chiron,* 8: 55–76.
Fornara, Charles W., ed. and trans. 1983. *Archaic Times to the End of the Peloponnesian War.* 2nd ed. Cambridge: Cambridge University Press.
Gill, David W.J. 2004. "Euesperides: Cyrenaica and its Contacts with the Greek World." In *Greek Identity in the Western Mediterranean: Papers in Honour of Brian Shefton,* edited by Kathryn Lomas, 391–409. *Mnemosyne* Suppl. 246. Leiden: Brill.
Graham, A. John. 1960. "Authenticity of the ΟΡΚΙΟΝ ΤΩΝ ΟΙΚΙΣΤΗΡΩΝ of Cyrene." *JHS,* 80: 94–111.
Graham, A. John. 1983. *Colony and Mother City in Ancient Greece.* 2nd ed. rev. Chicago: Ares.
Hall, Jonathan M. 2002. *Hellenicity: Between Ethnicity and Culture.* Chicago: University of Chicago Press.
Hodos, Tamar. 2006. *Local Responses to Colonization in the Iron Age Mediterranean.* London: Routledge.
Hölkeskamp, Karl-Joachim. 1993. "Demonax und die Neuordnung der Bürgershaft von Kyrene." *Hermes,* 121: 404–421.
Hulin, Linda. 2002. "Bronze Age Plain Pottery: Egyptian, Canaanite, and Cypriot." In *Marsa Matruh II: The Objects. The University of Pennsylvania Museum of Archaeology*

and Anthropology's Excavations on Bates's Island, Marsa Matruh, Egypt 1985–1989, edited by Donald White, 17–45. Philadelphia: The Institute for Aegean Prehistory Academic Press.

Jeffery, Lilian H. 1961. "The Pact of the First Settlers at Cyrene." *Historia*, 10: 139–147.

Kane, Susan. 1980. "An Archaic Kore from Cyrene." *American Journal of Archaeology*, 84: 182–183.

Kocybala, Arcadia. 1999. *The Extramural Sanctuary of Demeter and Persephone at Cyrene, Libya: Final Reports. Vol. VII. The Corinthian Pottery*. Donald White, series editor. Philadelphia: University Museum, University of Pennsylvania.

Laronde, André. 1987. *Cyrène et la Libye hellénistique. Libykai Historiai*. Paris: CNRS.

Laronde, André. 1990. "Greeks and Libyans in Cyrenaica." In *Greek Colonists and Native Populations*, edited by Jean-Paul Descoeudres, 169–180. Oxford: Clarendon Press.

Laronde, André. 1996. "L'exploitation de la chôra cyrénéenne à l'époque classique et hellénistique." *Comptes-rendus des séances de l'Académie des Inscriptions et Belles-Lettres*, 140(2): 503–527.

Leone, Roberta, and Oscar Mei. 2006. "Ceramica dal quartiere dell' agorà." In *Cirene "Atene d'Africa"* I, edited by Mario Luni, 79–117. Monografie di archeologia libica 28. Rome: Bretschneider.

Luni, Mario. 2010. "Il santuario *Libyo* della Fecundità a Slonta al confine tra indigeni e greci di Cirene." In *Cirene nell'antichità*, edited by Mario Luni, 62–74. Monografie di archeologia libica 29. Rome: Bretschneider.

Luni, Mario, Oscar Mei, Claudia Cardinali, and Francesca Uttoveggio. 2010. "Tracce della frequentazione libya nel sito di fondazione di Cirene." *Bolletino di Archeologia on line*. http://bollettinodiarcheologiaonline.beniculturali.it/wp-content/uploads/2019/01/1_LUNI_etal.pdf (accessed June 18, 2019).

Malkin, Irad. 1987. *Religion and Colonization in Ancient Greece*. Leiden: Brill.

Marshall, Eireann. 2007. "Marriage Imagery and Gender Dynamics in Cyrene's Foundation Myths: Intermarriage between Cyrenaeans and Libyans." In *Cirene e la Cirenaica nell'antichità. Atti del convegno internazionale de studi. Roma-Frascati, 18–21 Dicembre 1996*, edited by Lidio Gasperini and Silvia M. Marengo, 411–431. Rome: Edizioni Tored.

Masson, Olivier. 1976. "Grecs et Libyens en Cyrénaïque d'après les témoinages de l'épigraphie." *Antiquités Africaines*, 10: 49–62.

Mei, Oscar. 2013. *Cirene e la ceramica laconica: Cirene "Atene d'Africa." VI*. Monografie di archeologia libica, 35. Rome: Bretschneider.

Mei, Oscar. 2014. "Cirene e la ceramic arcaica." In *Cirene "Atene d'Africa" VII*, edited by Mario Luni, 39–55. Monografie di archeologia libica 36. Rome: Bretschneider.

Mitchell, Barbara M. 1966. "Cyrene and Persia." *JHS*, 86: 99–113.

Mitchell, Lynette G. 2006. "Ethnic Identity and the Community of the Hellenes: A Review." *Ancient West & East*, 4: 409–420.

Moore, Mary B. 1987. *The Extramural Sanctuary of Demeter and Persephone at Cyrene, Libya: Final Reports. Vol. III, Part II. Attic Black Figure and Black Glazed Pottery*. Donald White, series editor. Philadelphia: University Museum, University of Pennsylvania.

O'Connor, David. 1983. "New Kingdom and Third Intermediate Period, 1552–664 BC." In *Ancient Egypt, a Social History*, edited by Bruce G. Trigger, Barry J. Kemp, David O'Connor, and Alan B. Lloyd, 183–278. Cambridge: Cambridge University Press.

Osborne, Robin. 2009. *Greece in the Making, 1200–479 BC*. 2nd ed. London: Routledge.

Ottone, Gabriella, ed. 2002. *Libyka. Testimonianze e frammenti*. Rome: Tored.

Pedley, John Griffiths. 1971. "The Archaic Favissa at Cyrene." *American Journal of Archaeology*, 75: 39–46.

Redford, Donald B. 1992. *Egypt, Canaan, and Israel in Ancient Times*. Princeton: Princeton University Press.

Robinson, Edward S.G. 1927. *Catalogue of the Greek Coins of Cyrenaica*. London: British Museum.

Russell, Pamela. 2002. "Aegean Pottery and Selected Cypriot Pottery." In *Marsa Matruh II. The Objects. The University of Pennsylvania Museum of Archaeology and Anthropology's Excavations on Bates's Island, Marsa Matruh, Egypt 1985–1989*, edited by Donald White, 1–16. Philadelphia: The Institute for Aegean Prehistory Academic Press.

Sakellariou, Michael B. 1990. *Between Memory and Oblivion. The Transmission of Early Greek Historical Traditions*. ΜΕΛΕΤΗΜΑΤΑ 12. Athens: Research Center for Greek and Roman Antiquity.

Schaus, Gerald P. 1985. *The Extramural Sanctuary of Demeter and Persephone at Cyrene, Libya: Final Reports. Vol. II. The East Greek, Island, and Laconian Pottery*. Donald White, series ed. Philadelphia: University Museum, University of Pennsylvania.

Schaus, Gerald P. 2006. "Naukratis and Archaic Pottery Finds from Cyrene's Extramural Sanctuary of Demeter." In *Naukratis: Greek Diversity in Egypt: Studies on East Greek Pottery and Exchange in the Eastern Mediterranean*, edited by Alexandra Villing and Udo Schlotzhauer, 175–180. London: British Museum Press.

Stibbe, Conrad M. 1972. *Lakonische Vasenmaler des sechsten Jahrhunderts v. Chr.* Amsterdam: North Holland Publishing.

Stucchi, Sandro. 1965. *L'Agorà di Cirene 1: I lati nord ed est della platea inferiore*. Monografie di archeologia libica 7. Rome: Bretschneider.

Stucchi, Sandro. 1984. "Die archaischen griechischen Vasen und die Kyrenaika: Importe, Imitationen und Einflüsse – ein Überblick." In *Ancient Greek and Related Pottery. Proceedings of the International Vase Symposium in Amsterdam, 12–15 April 1984*, Allard Pierson Series vol. 5, edited by Herman A. G. Brijder, 139–143. Amsterdam: Allard Pierson Museum.

Uhlenbrock, Jaimee P. 2010. "Terracotta Types of Enthroned Females from the Extramural Sanctuary of Demeter and Persephone at Cyrene." In *Cirene e la Cirenaica nell'antichità*, edited by Mario Luni, 85–100. Monografie di archeologia libica 30. Rome: Bretschneider.

Van Alfen, P. 2016. "The Beginnings of Coinage at Cyrene: Weight Standards, Trade, and Politics." In *Le monete di Cirene e dalla Cirenaica nel Mediterraneo. Problemi e prospettive. Atti del V Congresso Internazionale di Numismatica e di Storia Monetaria. Padova, 17–19 marzo 2016*, edited by Michele Asolati, 15–32. Padova: Esedra.

Wanis, Saleh. 1992. "A New Relief from Cyrene with a Libyan Scene." *Libyan Studies*, 23: 41–43.

White, Donald. 1971. "The Cyrene Sphinx, Its Capital and Its Column." *American Journal of Archaeology*, 75: 47–55.

White, Donald. 1981. "Cyrene's Sanctuary of Demeter and Persephone: A Summary of a Decade of Excavation." *American Journal of Archaeology*, 85: 13–30.

White, Donald. 1994. "Before the Greeks Came: A Survey of the Current Archaeological Evidence for the Pre-Greek Libyans." *Libyan Studies*, 25: 31–43.

White, Donald. 2006. "Foreign *Schrecklichkeit* and Homegrown Iconoclasm: Two Faces of Communal Violence at Cyrene." In *Cirenaica: studi, scavi e scoperte. Parte I: Nuovi dati da città e territorio. Atti del X Convegno de Archeologia Cirenaica. Chieti 24–26 Novembre 2003*, edited by Emanuela Fabbricotti and Oliva Menozzi, 191–204. BAR International Series 1488. Oxford: Hedges.

FURTHER READING

Applebaum (1979, 1–52, 74–129) discusses in detail the geography, history, and economy of early Cyrenaica. Austin (2004, 1235–1237, 1240–1249) briefly provides key information about the history, government, and material remains of each individual settlement. Austin (2008, 187–217) also provides an excellent appreciation of the historical sources and detailed account of the foundation and early history according to relevant topics. Bonacasa and Ensoli (2000) contains a beautifully illustrated overview of the major monuments and important finds with a useful bibliography. Boardman (1999, 153–159) has an overview with some illustrations of the Greek settlements and a good summary of the archaeology. Chamoux (1953) is still regarded as an important study on all aspects of the early history of Cyrene. Malkin (1987, 60–69, 204–212, 214–216) examines the role of the Delphic oracle and the tomb and cult of the founder, Battus. Mitchell (1966) examines problems in the sources regarding historical relations between Cyrene and Persia in the late sixth and early fifth century BCE. Osborne (2009, 8–17) uses Cyrene as an example to encourage healthy skepticism of tradition and archaeological evidence when writing history. Sakellariou (1990, 38–67) contains a careful analysis of the oral traditions and written sources for the foundation story of Cyrene.

CHAPTER SEVENTEEN

Egypt

Joseph G. Manning

Geographical and Historical Summary

Greeks, broadly defined, had a long historical relationship with Egypt (Map 3). That is already clear in the Ionian geographers' fascination with Egypt and the Nile River of which Herodotus's *Histories* Book 2 treatise on Egypt was a kind of summa (de Meulenaere 1951; Lloyd 1975–1988; Asheri, Lloyd, and Corcella 2007). Greek speculation that summer monsoonal rains in east Africa caused the annual flood was confirmed by explorers sent to east Africa by the Ptolemies (Malinowski 2014). It remained the best account of Egypt until the decipherment of Egyptian in the nineteenth century opened, for the first time, the understanding of Egypt in Egyptian terms. But the intimate and complex relationship between the Greek world and Egypt extends back a thousand years before that. "Thebes of a hundred gates" is already in Homer (*Il.* 9.383), but we can go deep into the Bronze Age to examine the intimate cultural and economic connections Egypt, especially the Delta, had with other cultures of the Mediterranean (Broodbank 2013). The famous Uluburun shipwreck reveals something of the very wide exchange network in the eastern Mediterranean basin in which Egypt was a part (Pulak 1997, 2008). Archaeological work at the Egyptian Delta site of Avaris has revealed Cretan connections; Greece borrowed from Egypt, never the other way around, according to Herodotus, although it is difficult to imagine, without needing to go as far as Bernal's *Black Athena* hypothesis, to suggest that the Egypt–Greece relationship was not to some extent reciprocal in the Bronze Age. With the emergence of the Iron Age, the relationship is clearer, and the presence of Greeks living in Egypt grew from perhaps a few thousand under the Saite kings of the seventh and sixth century BC to perhaps hundreds of thousands under the Ptolemies, amounting to something between 5 and 10% of an estimated 3.5 million. The Ptolemaic

---

A Companion to Greeks Across the Ancient World, First Edition. Edited by Franco De Angelis.
© 2020 John Wiley & Sons, Inc. Published 2020 by John Wiley & Sons, Inc.

settlement of Greeks throughout Egypt, especially in the Fayyum, had long-term and important historical and socioeconomic consequences for the history of Egypt.

The question of when, if ever, Egypt was a part of the Mediterranean world has often been asked. The answer depends, of course, very much on the kind of evidence one examines. Given Egypt's location in northeast Africa, the answer seems fairly straightforward. It was both *in* and *of* the Mediterranean, to use Horden and Purcell's (2000) distinction. Egyptian civilization indeed cast a very large shadow over the eastern Mediterranean. That shadow is only partially visible to us. The connections, or connectivity, grew stronger through the second and first millennia BC. Even with a quick glance at material coming from the eastern Delta site of Tell el Dab'a (Avaris) from the mid-second millennium BC, one would be astonished at how large and how cosmopolitan it was (Broodbank 2013, 383). Egyptian civilization had a deep and very complex engagement with the eastern Mediterranean, and the issue is an important one not only to sort out the complexities of exchange networks, and the impact of these, but also from the cultural history point of view as to what extent cultural contact and borrowings, formative or constitutive, were part of Egyptian or of classical civilization.[1]

That set of issues is indeed ancient, and is found in the most famous example, throughout the work of Herodotus. The best solution, it seems to me, is Broodbank's (2013, 347), to seek the co-evolutionary processes in the wider Mediterranean world. Already in the Bronze Age, civilizations in the eastern Mediterranean were experiencing profound socioeconomic changes, in part because this was a deeply connected and linked world, with cross-cultural influences that ran in several directions.

It is true that from the perspective of the Aegean, Egypt appears fixed and immobile. But scenes from the noble tombs in Thebes tell a different and far more interesting story. There we see the hurly-burly of ports, of goods being offloaded, scribes weighing and recording, animals moving goods from ships, and by implication we can see here the trade connections between Egypt and the Minoan and Mycenaean worlds. With trade contact came also the exchange of ideas, and imaginative worlds too. The alternative literary tradition of Helen being carried off to Egypt (Hdt. 2.113; derived from Hecataeus?, Lloyd 1988, 46–47) is, perhaps, hinted at in a figural graffito found in Luxor temple at Thebes (Manassa 2009).[2] Herodotus of course is a prime text, but it presents us with the problem of the Greek filtering and the repackaging or "constructing" of Egyptian civilization for Greek audiences (Moyer 2011). The Atlantis myth, preserved *inter alia* in Plato's *Timaeus*, also preserves distant echoes of Egyptian tales. Recently published Demotic Egyptian stories are suggestive of some of the stories told in Herodotus and bring the connection full circle (Ryholt 2006).

The intimate connections between Egypt and the classical world are fraught with controversy, not the least of which is the tendency, still powerful within the discipline of Classics, to deny any role for Egyptian cultural connections in any part of what counts as "classical" history. This has, of course, aroused great reaction (and overreaction) in the form of Martin Bernal's *Black Athena*, among other such revisionary work. This "definitional" problem – what is Egypt, what is Greece, and what influenced how "culture" formed in both places? – runs across two major fields, both Classics and Egyptology, which have tried to isolate and stress the uniqueness of culture in both places. The rich archaeology of the Mediterranean basin, however, tells a rather more complicated story of interaction in the Bronze and Iron Ages.[3]

The Bronze Age/Early Iron Age

Early imports in Minoan Crete, at Knossos for example, and on Samos were Egyptian, from either direct or indirect exchange networks (Boardman 1999, 113; Broodbank 2013, 354). Middle and Late Bronze Age interregional exchange networks between Egypt, the Levant, and the Aegean have produced spectacular material culture. By the seventh century, Egyptian stylists' influence can be seen in Greek architectural styles, sculpture, pottery, bronze work, and musical instruments (Boardman 1999, 143–153; Steel 2010, 461).

More formal networks of exchange between Crete and Middle Kingdom Egypt ca. 1900 BC are fairly well established. The so-called Kamares ware, a prestige good, is found in Egypt in a few late Middle Kingdom burials. Tell el Dab'a (Avaris) is a key Egyptian site in the Delta and shows that it served as an important trade node for Aegean and Near Eastern exchange with Egypt. Even more extensive contact with Minoan Crete occurred in early New Kingdom Egypt, the height of the Egyptian Empire and its most extensive influence in the Near East and the Aegean. Minoan fresco scenes of bull-leaping at Tell el Dab'a dating to Dynasty 18 are the most spectacular examples of at least indirect Aegean contact, although there remains considerable debate about dating and exact context (Bietak, Marinatos, and Palivou 2007). Aegean artistic influence may also be seen at the royal palace of Malkata in western Thebes ca. 1400 BC. Egypt was also connected to an extensive eastern Mediterranean trading network in commodities, including grain. The famous Uluburun shipwreck, dated to ca. 1325 BC (Pulak 1997, 2008; Monroe 2010; a summary in Broodbank 2013, 399–402), is a superb time capsule of Bronze Age trade and preserves many items of Egyptian origin, including a scarab with the name of Nefertiti. Excavations at the imperial center of Amarna, where Akhenaten lived with his bride Nefertiti, have yielded a large amount of Mycenaean pottery (Davies and Schofield 1995; Hassler 2008).

Cyprus, with its important copper sources, grew to become, in the second millennium BC, a major part of a circuit of exchange and diplomacy in the eastern Mediterranean that included Egypt (Rosińska-Balik et al. 2015). These strong links between Egypt and Cyprus would continue down into the Ptolemaic Empire and beyond.

Arguably, then, Egypt had long been a part of the wider Hellenic world by the emergence of the Iron Age at the turn of the first millennium BC. The intense Greek cultural interest in things Egyptian must have been born then, bearing fruit in written form during the first millennium BC (Moyer 2011). By then, Egypt was a different place, run, almost entirely, by outside political forces. Greeks came to Egypt in the seventh century as soldiers and traders and were settled in Naukratis and Daphnae among other places (Vittmann 2003). Greek trading activity was more extensive than has been previously emphasized by those who looked exclusively at Naukratis (Carrez-Maratray and Defernez 2012). While we cannot reconstruct the entire history of Greeks living and doing business in Egypt, we can sort things into two main waves of Greek immigration to Egypt. The first came in the eighth to seventh century BC. The seventh-century BC foundation of Naukratis, whose very name shows that nautical power, that is, Greek (and Phoenician) nautical (and presumably trading) power, was a major force in the first millennium BC.[4] It became an important center of Greek trading networks throughout the Mediterranean and must surely be seen in the context of the long and broader contact with the Greek world. Recent work at the site on the Canopic branch of the Nile suggests that the main port can now be identified.[5] A new sense of the scale of the city, more than 148 acres (60 ha), and the material remains show the extensive trade connections to the East Greek world. The recent underwater archaeological work at the port of Thonis/Herakleion, the very site where Helen had found herself shipwrecked (Hdt. 2.113), also has given us a better sense of trade between Egypt and the Greek world, and its organization and taxation during the first millennium BC (Robinson and Wilson 2011; Robinson and Goddio 2015).

Saite Egypt (656–525 BC)

The Saite period represents an important watershed both in Egyptian history and in the history of Greek–Egyptian relations (Perdu 2014; Agut-Labordère 2013). Here in the mid-seventh century BC, Greeks began to settle in Egypt in significant numbers, primarily as soldiers, at least they are the best documented, and Egypt was not only *of* the eastern Mediterranean world, but a major power in it, checked in the Near East by a rising Babylonian Empire. To some extent, then, blocked in their "traditional" role as a power in the Near East, Saite Egyptian kings turned north and west to the Greek world for alliances. During the seventh and sixth centuries BC, Egypt became part of a political and diplomatic triangle with the Greek world and the Persian Empire. The Saite navy successfully asserted control of Cyprus (Hdt. 2.182; Agut-Labordère 2013, 986; Lloyd 2000). Greeks and Phoenicians were an important element in the Saite navy, and Greek mercenaries played an important role in the Saite Kingdom (Fischer-Bovet 2014, 15–43). Egypt was increasingly opened up to Mediterranean trade.

Under Psammetichus I (Hdt. 2.152; Diod. Sic. 1.68.8), a Greek navy and Greek mercenaries were established, with King Gyges of Lydia providing many of the mercenaries, and they settled in the Delta, around Memphis, and at other key settlements. The reign of Amasis was an important phase in Greek–Egyptian relations and a period, too, of economic expansion and prosperity (Hdt. 2.177); Amasis had extended diplomatic ties to Cyrene, Samos, and Croesus of Lydia (Perdu 2014, 148), and fortified the trading colony at Naukratis.

It was during the Saite period when serious Greek interest in Egypt and Egyptian history and culture began. It is then too that the marginalization of Egypt in Greek history writing began (Burstein 1995, 5). This Greek interpretation of Egypt is, of course, on fullest display in the Egyptian *logos* of Herodotus's Book 2, although as Burstein has correctly pointed out, Herodotus stands apart from other Greek writers on Egypt such as Hecataeus, however much his work shaped Herodotus's framework, in his insistence that Egyptian sources must be used in understanding Egyptian history (Burstein 1995, 12).

Memphis and its cemetery at Sakkara reveal much about Greco-Egyptian cultural interactions. Greek mercenaries played a major role in Saite period Egypt; soldiers left their graffiti on Abu Simbel in 592/591 BC (Hdt 2.161; *ML* 7; Dillon 1997). King Amasis resettled in Memphis the Carian and Ionian soldiers (Hdt. 2.154) who created communities of Caromemphites and Hellenomemphites documented into the Ptolemaic period (Thompson 2012, 14).

The military was a powerful force of cultural integration. The Egyptian called Potasimto, a general commanding Ionian and Carian troops under Psammetichus II in the Nubian campaign, is documented in the famous graffiti at Abu Simbel; the Ionian soldier Pedon, who probably served under Psammetichus I, was rewarded with an Egyptian town for loyal service.[6] Pedon has left us an Egyptian statue with an Ionian inscription that is suggestive of the social integration of Greeks to Egyptian cultural forms in the period (Haider 2001, 200–201). There were other Greeks in the service of Egyptian kings. Under Psammetichus II, the Saite admiral (the first attestation of the office), Hor, also known as Psammetichus, was in command of Aegean troops and served also as advisor to the king on Greek affairs (Agut-Labordère 2013, 990–991).[7]

In the fourth century BC, mercenaries, and fiscal reforms, as elsewhere in the Mediterranean world, became a dominant concern.[8] Greek troops and Greek advisers continued to play an important role in Egypt. The Athenian general Chabrias pushed back Persian attempts of invasion and also provided fiscal advice to King Teos (Arist., [*Oec.*] 25a–b); other Greeks and Greek states like Sparta, under king Agesilaus, were part of an Egyptian–Greek alliance against Persia. Our narrative sources for the period are, in the main, Greek ones, which "reflects the interests of the classical world" (Lloyd 1994, 345). Nectanebo II mobilized some 20 000 Greek mercenaries in his war against the Persian King Artaxerxes III (Diod. Sic. 16.40–48).[9] In the extensive contact with the Greek world, in trading patterns, and in settlements of soldiers and others throughout the country, the Saite period established key socioeconomic patterns of the next great phase of Greek–Egyptian relations, the Ptolemaic period.

Greeks in Ptolemaic Egypt

Alexander's conquest of Egypt in 332 BC, and the subsequent rise of the Ptolemaic dynasty, transformed the relationship of Egypt and the Greek world. Macedonian and Greek soldiers, numbering some 4000 were stationed at Memphis and at Pelusium in the Delta at Alexander's death (Fischer-Bovet 2014, 52). Hiring soldiers was, then, one of Ptolemy's first tasks in order to establish control, although they were hard to keep. Disastrous outcomes in Cyprus after the Battle at Gaza in 312 BC and at Salamis in 306 BC left his army half the size he had recently built. This was a continuing problem (and not just for the Ptolemies, of course) – maintaining and paying for the army in an age of near continuous inter-state war.

Ptolemaic rule also, by way of Alexander's explorer Callisthenes, it seems, ended Greek debates about the causes of the Nile flood (Burstein 1995). Summer rains in the Ethiopian highlands and in the Lake Victoria region were responsible. Ptolemaic rule in Egypt was a culmination of more than a millennium of cultural and socioeconomic exchange (Vasunia 2001; Moyer 2011). Greco-Egyptian civilization of the Hellenistic period should be viewed against the backdrop of the increasingly interconnected Bronze Age world. To be sure, the process of building a new polity in the late fourth century BC by Ptolemy was a watershed moment in the history of the eastern Mediterranean. New energy, new ideas, and now, for the first time, Greek governance in Egypt, changed many things, not the least of which was Egyptian kingship itself.[10] More fundamentally, the immigration and the settling of Greeks changed the demand side of the rural economy through new crops, new kinds of livestock, a new demand for wool, and it altered rural structures. The shift to free-threshing wheat, the wide use of coinage, and the new fiscal system, to name perhaps the three most important, had long-term consequences for the history of Egypt.

The Ptolemaic offshoot of the Achaemenid Empire was the first of the Hellenistic successor states to establish a political equilibrium in its core territory (and therefore also the first to experience difficulties). It reached a peak territorial size ca. 300 BC of 1 million km^2 (60 000 miles^2 or 155 340 km^2 excluding the deserts: Ehrenberg 1969, 144), with a population in Egypt, in my view, between 3 and 4 million, of which between 5 and 10% were ethnically Greek.[11] That would yield an estimate of between 150 000–200 000 on the low end and 300 000–400 000 Greeks on the high end including the urban centers of Alexandria and Ptolemais. A theoretical maximum of arable land in Egypt was 24,800 km^2, a figure that comes from a temple inscription, giving an upper bound of agricultural capacity. The size/time integral of the Ptolemaic state (Taagepera 1978, 181–185 with table 5) was by far the largest of any Hellenistic state, which included Cyrenaica, Cyprus, the most stable parts of the imperial territory, parts of the Aegean, and Caria, which certainly provided an important "source of energy" (Heinen 1984, 415), as did *Koile* Syria in the third century BC (Bagnall 1976; Will 1979). The territory was comparatively large, but also comparatively expensive to control, and subject to fluctuations in agrarian production because of dependence there on the Nile flood with its inter-annual variability.

While this new social environment did not create a "fused" Hellenistic culture as was once thought, beneath elite literary production, certain rituals, and public visual culture, there was a great deal of inter-ethnic interaction, including marriages (the bilingual family archives from southern Egypt are the best evidence), and there was a wide variety of private economic exchange between ethnic groups. That is not an idle observation; exchange across cultural and ethnic boundaries was an important pathway of economic change.[12] The movement of people created new settlements, altered landscapes and exchange patterns, but it also created tensions. At the same time, coinage may have reinforced status dissonances between Greek, and those who adopted Greek culture, and non-Greek populations.[13] Monson's (2015) use of a "structural-demographic" social model that links political instability to population pressure, elite competition for rents, and state fiscal crisis is suggestive. There is very likely even more to it; some of my own recent work suggests a strong link between Nile variability caused by climate forcing events and social instability that strongly suggests agrarian shocks rather than intercultural tensions were a key driver of the social unrest (Ludlow and Manning 2016).

Thanks to the papyri, we can follow, sometimes in great detail, the fortunes and activities of a variety of Greeks who came from across the Greek world seeking a new life under the Ptolemaic kings.[14] Migration of Greeks from all around the Mediterranean in the early third century BC, as merchants, soldiers, and fortune seekers, was a feature of early third-century BC Egypt. The founding of Alexandria had profound effects on Greek culture, becoming effectively the heir of Athens as the cultural center of the Hellenistic Greek world. Here scientists, poets, and scholars gathered – some of the most famous minds in Greek intellectual history. Older views of top-down dominance of Egyptians by Greeks have given way to far richer descriptions of intercultural engagement. The frequent revolts of the period were not, in my view, the result of anti-Greek or "nationalist sentiment" of

Egyptians but, rather, of a concatenation of causes. Among these were the new fiscal system, a major shift in emphasizing free-threshing wheat against the traditional emmer, and a series of Nile flood shocks that can now be identified with climate proxy records.[15]

Early Ptolemaic papyri coming from opposite ends of the country give us a glimpse into Greek social policy in Egypt, however formal it was, as well as a sense of early Ptolemaic Greek settlement across Egypt. First, the well-known and much discussed Peukestas papyrus found at the Sacred Animal Necropolis at Sakkara in the 1972/1973 excavation season appears to suggest that under Alexander's occupation of Egypt there was a sensitive approach to dealing with priestly sensibilities.[16] Memphis, the ancient Egyptian capital city nearby, was a magnet for peoples from all over the basin. Herodotus mentions a Phoenician settlement there ("the Tyrian camp" Hdt. 2.112), and Greek soldiers from around the Aegean were brought into Egypt in the sixth century BC and their descendants were eventually settled by Amasis in Memphis (Thompson 2012, 77). The area of the city was called the Hellenion. Carians, called Caromemphites, had their own section called the Karikon. Second, at the far southern border of Egypt, a Greek marriage contract from Elephantine, a key garrison, demonstrates the variety of Greeks (the man was from Temnos in Asia Minor, and the woman from Kos), and their legal institutions, as well as the scope of Greek settlement.[17]

The ethnic and linguistic diversity among the Greeks in Egypt is well documented in the surviving papyri of the period (Clarysse 1998). Ethnic identities in these documents are representative of the migratory patterns of the age (La'da 2002). Carian language can be found on tombstones from fourth century BC (Thompson 2012, 87). Caria and Carians remained important for the Ptolemies, no better attested than in the best-known archive of the period, the Zenon archive.

This archive, a collection of mainly Greek papyri, presents both a source of great riches for understanding the operations of agricultural estates in the middle of the third century BC in Egypt and also a conundrum for scholars. Fully a third of Ptolemaic-period papyri are represented by this one archive, a little over 1800 usable texts (Clarysse 2009, 2013). The archive itself has still not been fully studied despite a great amount of scholarship on it.[18] It was probably the private archive of Zenon, a Carian, and the estate manager for Apollonios, the *dioiketes* of Ptolemy II and who may also have been from Caria, although the origins of both him and his family remain lost in the mists of time. An association with the new temple of Zeus Labraundaios established in Philadelphia by him might just point in the direction of his hometown pride (Clarysse 2009, 34).

The Zenon papyri document the years 261–229 BC, the height of Ptolemaic state power within Egypt and in the Mediterranean. Zenon was from Kaunos, an assistant of Apollonios from 261 to 258 BC in Alexandria and then in Ptolemaic-controlled Palestine (Clarysse 2013). Eventually Zenon became the manager of the large estate held by Apollonios in the new dynastic-branded town of Philadelphia in the northwest part of the Fayyum, an area reclaimed and settled in the middle of the third century BC. He leaves his service in 248 BC for unknown reasons, but his own work continues. Two brothers lived with him.

The surviving correspondence is in the main written by professional scribes, although some survive in Zenon's own hand, such as letters, memoranda, and the like. They are executed in an "old-fashioned hand," more characteristic of early than contemporary mid-third-century Greek hands, and in an older orthography as well (Clarysse 2009, 42).

The Ptolemaic-period census returns, hardly surviving in anything resembling a complete record of the population, nonetheless give us rich information on the composition and size of households, mainly for Fayyum towns, which were, to be sure, unusual with respect to the rest of Egypt, especially in the higher percentage of Greeks who settled here. The census records also provide firsthand evidence of the taxation of ethnic groups and, to some degree, information about where Greeks settled in Egypt (Clarysse and Thompson 2006). Unsurprisingly, the cavalry settlers, with a 100-*aroura* allotment (ca. 66 acres, 26 ha), were the largest and wealthiest households. Greek soldiers and non-military Hellenes were a privileged tax class, this privilege reflected in the ethnic status titles that appear, for example, in contracts of the period.[19] Non-military Greeks, as well as certain Egyptians, Jews, and Thracians (and some others) in state service (*inter alia* officials, teachers of Greek, athletes, actors), were classed also as "Hellenes" for tax purposes and paid a lower tax rate on the capitation tax (Clarysse and Thompson 2006, 138–147).

The reclamation of the Fayyum under the reigns of Ptolemy II and III was one of the most spectacular achievements of Greek governance in Egypt, with a good Seleukid parallel in the building and settlement of Seleukia along the Tigirs River under Seleukos. The archive of the *architekton* Kleon, a key figure in the Fayyum reclamation, and perhaps an immigrant from somewhere in central Greece (Van Beek 2009, 150), gives us valuable information about the project.[20] We know his family lived in Alexandria from the letters that survive in his archive, but he was spending his days on engineering irrigation works in the Fayyum. He and his family were well connected to the royal court; both of his sons were highly educated and had excellent penmanship, if indeed it was they who wrote their letters and not a professional letter writer (Van Beek 2009, 152)

The role played by the Greeks of Cyrene, the old Greek colony, was vital in the early Ptolemaic state, and in Ptolemaic court culture, of course, not only the work of Callimachus but indeed the entire language of the Ptolemaic inner circle was Doric Greek.[21] Cyrenaean cavalry were the most important force in early Ptolemaic settlement of the country in state-building.

Greeks were concentrated in the urban centers of Alexandria and Ptolemais, but, primarily through military settlement, they were also settled in rural areas, and gradually, through the process of bureaucratization, are found settled throughout the country including ancient centers like Thebes.[22] Gymnasia became a marker of Greek culture throughout Egypt, from the cities and nome *metropoleis* down to villages (Paganini 2011). In certain areas, some Greek communities (from Cilicia, Boeotia, Crete), Jews, Idumaeans, and perhaps others as well (i.e., those classed as "Hellenes" by the state), organized themselves into *politeumata*. These formal social organizations, documented in the second and first centuries BC (but perhaps already in existence by the late third century), were associated with military settlement and appear to have been an instrument of social integration.[23]

Mixed marriages, a Greek husband taking an Egyptian wife, while not widely documented are recorded evenly spread in the surviving documents across the third and second centuries, but the bias toward third-century evidence suggests that they increased over time (Clarysse and Thompson 2006, 328). Ptolemais, situated in the Thebaid not far from Akhmim, was founded as a *polis* ca. 310 BC. Greeks from Cyrenaica, prominent in the army especially as cavalry, may have been among the original settlers of this important town, which, sadly, has been virtually ignored by archaeological investigation.

In ancient Egyptian centers like Thebes, Greeks were a "small minority" of the population (Clarysse 1995, 1), identified by their Greek name, although ethnic identity based on naming practices becomes far more problematic in the second and first centuries BC. Nevertheless, Greeks appear to have played a prominent role as administrative officials, bankers, and in the military.

On the other hand, the state building project of the Ptolemies was, in a sense, incomplete, and created "structural tensions" between Greeks and Egyptians in particular because of a "hierarchy of economic interest in land" that resulted in Greeks having to compete for access to land within the royal sphere (Bingen 2007, 193–194). Ethnic tensions surely existed, but systematic racism is entirely absent, and the very concept, in my opinion, is anachronistic.[24] Examples of ethnic tensions abound in the petitions and records of legal squabbles that survive. Sometimes calling oneself Greek in a petition to the king, it was thought, could enhance one's chances of being heard. On the other hand, in a famous legal dispute, recorded in a long trial record that has one of the most beautiful examples of Greek handwriting from antiquity, the local funerary priests known as *choachytes*, "waterpourers," won their dispute with a high-ranking Greek soldier. The case turned on having the property proof of the title claim to the house under dispute; ethnicity did not matter to the Greek tribunal (Pestman 1992).

Greek tomb owners in western Thebes, the *memnoneia* as it was called in Greek texts, are well represented, an example being a Greek wrestler, which is particularly illustrative of the range of Greeks living in Egypt (Clarysse 1995, 11).

The Ptolemaic period witnessed a major influx of Greeks into Egypt; the exact percentage is debated, but traditionally roughly between 5 and 10% of Ptolemaic Egypt were Greeks. Whatever the exact percentage, though, it is clear that Greek governance of the country had a significant impact on Egyptian institutions. Not the least of these, I have argued elsewhere, was in the realm of Egyptian law (Manning forthcoming). Ptolemaic law, if it is fair to call it that, was bilingual and involved Greek-speaking officials managing or at least monitoring Egyptian legal proceedings. The famous Asyut family trial is the best case in point on how Ptolemaic governance interacted with the ancient Egyptian legal system. Among the most impressive aspects of the adjudication of this small-scale and very local family dispute over ownership of a small amount of land is the fact that we learn that the losing party had made an appeal to officials at the southern capital and administrative center at Ptolemais. Appearing at the head of this appeal panel, at a time of the invasion of Egypt by Antiochus IV and revolt across the country, was none other than Noumenios, the *stratêgos* of the Thebaid, one of the most powerful men in the kingdom.[25] Noumenios also appears in the archive of Horus, the dream interpreter at Saqqara, and, thanks to Polybius, we know that less than two years later he was the lead ambassador who went to Rome, in the aftermath of the Roman expulsion of Antiochus IV from Egypt. Both his son and his grandson would attain very high rank as well.

The Ptolemaic army was of course an important instrument of state power and a powerful tool of state building. Greeks were the dominant force in the military hierarchy, particularly during the third century BC. In rural areas soldiers were stationed in "forts" (*phrouria*) for serving soldiers, and "settlements" (*katoikiai*) for the reservists called kleruchs (Clarysse and

Thompson 2006, 149 citing Polyb. 15.25.17). The newly reclaimed Fayyum region, under Ptolemy II and III, was heavily concentrated with military who had access to new land and were better off economically than others who had moved into the area (Clarysse and Thompson 2006, 151). The Ptolemies devised a two-pronged solution to the universal problem of military mobilization in the Hellenistic word: (i) the use of a combination of professional and mercenary soldiers, and (ii) settled reservists (kleruchs).[26] Garrison communities were established throughout Egypt at strategic locations (Winnicki 1978). Mercenaries were acquired both through local recruiting of those who had come into Egypt (migrations came to an end in the middle of the third century BC) and through outside recruiting efforts by "recruiting officers" (*xenologoi*, Fischer-Bovet 2014, 168–169). Reservists were given plots of land according to rank in exchange for the promise of mobilization in case of need (Fischer-Bovet 2014, table 6.3). By the second century BC the Ptolemies increasingly recruited locally from Egyptians and from Greco-Egyptian families (Fischer-Bovet 2014, 121). Both professionals and kleruchs came overwhelmingly from the Greek-speaking regions of the Mediterranean, including mainland Greece and Macedonia especially (Stefanou 2013). The papyri, Egyptian and Demotic, provide rich details of the changes over time as soldiers settled down, married Egyptian women, became members of local communities, held positions within local Egyptian temples, and played vital roles in building local society. As Fischer-Bovet rightly concludes (2014, 363), the Ptolemaic army was not a tool of colonial power, although it was important in establishing order and security, but it was the core of the Ptolemaic state-building project and the backbone of the Greco-Egyptian local elites who would continue to be prominent in the Roman period.

A fascinating and fairly detailed glimpse into the household of a Ptolemaic soldier and his family living in Upper Egypt comes from the Dryton archive.[27] Dryton, a professional soldier, cavalry officer, and a citizen of Ptolemais, lived a remarkably long life (ca. 195–113 or 111 BC). He was a member of the *politeuma* of Cretans and garrisoned at Pathyris, a military community established in the aftermath of the great Theban revolt ca. 186 BC.[28] His second wife, Apollonia, also called Senmonthis, the daughter of an infantry soldier and identified as "Cyrenaean," was a young Egyptian woman who came from a family who had already to some extent adopted Greek culture. In her own records, she very much appears as a Greek woman, appearing with her *kurios* in Greek-language loan contracts, a requirement of Greek, not Egyptian, law (Vandorpe 2014b, 104). This archive shows us much about the contours of a military family living in Egypt, doing business with both other soldiers and Egyptians and at home in both cultures.

One of the great things about the papyri is that they sometimes hint at compelling stories about the relationships between Greeks and Egyptians at a local level. One interesting story can, I think, be found in two rather ordinary-seeming Upper Egyptian documents from third century BC (Manning 2002). The first is simply a name on the witness list on the verso of an Egyptian contract (*P. Hausw. Manning* 11, a land sale) giving testimony of the act of witnessing an agreement. In a list of 15 Egyptians appears *Hrwtn* son of *Lysmqws*, or Rhodon son of Lysimachus, compete with an Egyptian "h" to accurately indicate the rough breathing of the Greek. The other text is a small Greek text written on a round-topped milestone (*SEG* XLVI 2120) found on the Edfu-Barramiya road at Bir 'Iayyan, a main route to the eastern desert gold-mining region (Bagnall et al. 1996). The text reads as follows:

> From the river to this point, four hundred and sixty-one stades
> In the reign of Ptolemy son of Ptolemy Soter, year 28,
> month of Epeiph; Rhodon son of Lysimachos, from Ptolemais,
> the toparch of the (?) three, set up (this stone).[29]

The small text in fact says a lot. First the Rhodon here was a citizen of Ptolemais, but acting as a kind of governor of a region (the title "toparch of the three" remains mysterious). Second, the name Rhodon son of Lysimachus is reasonably rare, and since we are in the same area as Edfu, out in the eastern desert, we just might have the same person here, separated by some 33 years. If the two persons are one in the same, or even related (perhaps grandfather and grandson), we can then connect Greek administrative officials to the small-scale everyday world of Egyptian legal transactions in places like Edfu and Thebes, which were arguably still quite Egyptian "turf."[30] They present an entirely different picture of social life in Hellenistic Egypt, richer, more complex, and more interesting than the old "fusion" versus "isolation" idea of Greek–Egyptian social interaction. This is something else, neither Droysen's fusion, nor Lewis's "us and them" cultural isolation model. The testimony of Greeks who appear as witnesses in Egyptian contracts suggests not only that Greeks had settled down in urban centers, the usual story, but that, indeed, Greek officials and soldiers could be mobile and conversant with Egyptian life, and were also settled and living throughout Egypt. Many were probably bilingual, and were trusted and respected, if sometimes troublesome, members of local communities.

The latter case, a troublesome Greek living among Egyptians, is perhaps most famously seen in the case of Ptolemy's son of Glaukias, a religious recluse, the son of a Macedonian soldier, who sought refuge in the Serapeum at Sakkara in the second century BC, well known from a series of petitions that have survived (Thompson 2012, 197–246).[31] In them we learn much about religious life in the Serapeum, about economic and religious life in mid-second century BC Egypt, and about inter-ethnic relations and the mutual cultural influences that existed in that sheltered environment. Yet it must also reflect a rather more everyday experience in towns and villages across Egypt where Greeks and Egyptian were neighbors. One of the texts from Ptolemy's papers provides us an extraordinary insight into the machinery of the civil and military bureaucracy and the intricate (and drawn out) process of attempting to enroll (in this case Ptolemy advocating for his younger brother Apollonios) in the Ptolemaic army.[32]

Perhaps even more interesting, and certainly no less dramatic, is the second-century BC Hermias lawsuit that pitted a family of Egyptian mortuary priests, called *choachytes*, against a high-ranking Ptolemaic soldier in a Greek bureaucratic court over the ownership of a house (see above; Pestman 1992). In the long-drawn-out dispute, the Egyptian family emerged the victors on the basis of their possession of the title deeds to the property that proved that they had clear title to the property in dispute, a house in western Thebes. The papyri suggest that legal institutions evolved to some extent under the pressure of the bilingual system. Bilingual family archives such as Dryton show that new legal forms in property transfers and in contracts from the second century BC shape a "Graeco-Egyptian" legal tradition.[33]

However many Greeks there were in Ptolemaic Egypt, the impact of their settlement throughout the country, Ptolemaic governance, and the promotion of Greek language all had long-lasting effects on the culture. The impact of Greek literature and Greek education, for example, with a special interest in Homer, that is well represented in the papyri, can be traced all the way down to the fourth-/fifth-century CE writer Nonnus from Upper Egyptian Panopolis (Akhmim) – a place Herodotus already signaled as having Greek culture (2.91) – and others attest to the long-lasting impact of Greek and Greek literary culture on Egypt. Surely the nearby city of Ptolemais played a role in "Hellenizing" Upper Egyptian culture. It was this Hellenized and urban culture that had become deeply ingrained in the minds of early Christians that the Coptic monk Shenoute powerfully railed against in his sermons. The excellent corpus of women's letters collected by Bagnall and Cribiore (2006) affords us at least a glimpse into the lives of elite women in the period.[34]

The presence of Greeks also changed institutional arrangements. Coinage, for example, was first used extensively in the Ptolemaic taxation system, and the urban centers with highest concentration of Greeks became more monetized than rural areas.[35] The use of coins may have benefitted Greeks more directly; in any case, it certainly changed the institutional structure of the fiscal system well beyond the Ptolemaic period.

In visual culture, hybridized forms began just as soon as immigrants had settled in Egypt. The Carian grave stelae from Sakkara and Abusir (examples shown in Boardman 1999, 136) and the Greek artistic styles of traditional tomb scenes in the Egyptian tomb of Petosiris at Hermopolis in Middle Egypt are just some of the examples from a rich corpus.[36]

Greek language was promoted by the Ptolemaic kings. The adoption, and adaptation, of the Greek language by Egyptian scribes is one of the most fascinating aspects of the study of Greek in Egypt.[37] The Greek language, so well documented in later Egyptian history, is often dismissed as degraded. Clearly the Greek of the period, how it was used, spread, earned, and transformed, shows us that it was a living, breathing, rich, and diverse language, and not a degraded or frozen form of the classical language.

Greeks continued to be an important element of Egyptian society. Indeed, the Greek communities at Alexandria and Cairo were a vibrant part of the fabric of urban life until the Egyptian Revolution of 1952. The poems of Cavafy are perhaps the most evocative example of Greek culture in Egypt in modern times, deeply embedded in a local community while reaching back to the Hellenistic roots.

NOTES

1 The richness of the inter-ethnic contacts in the deep history of Egypt is surveyed by Schneider (2010).
2 On the myth, see Hughes 2005; Edmunds 2016.
3 Boardman (1999, 111–159) provides a good survey.
4 On Naukratis: Möller (2000); Bresson (2005); Villing and Schlotzhauer (2006).
5 British Museum Naukratis Project fieldwork report 2104. https://research.britishmuseum.org/research/research_projects/all_current_projects/naukratis_the_greeks_in_egypt/naukratis_research_project/fieldwork_2014.aspx (accessed December 15, 2019).
6 Agut-Labordère, (2013, 989), with the literature cited in n. 92.
7 The naophorous statue is Manchester Museum 3570, Petrie (1906, 18–19, plates XV and XX): Vandersleyen (2008, 38, 87, 106, no. 217).

8 Overview of fourth-century Egypt in Lloyd (1994).
9 On the narrative of events, see Ruzicka (2012, 151–198).
10 The nature of Ptolemaic kingship has been much pondered. See Samuel (1993).
11 Habicht (1958). The Ptolemaic Kingdom as a state and the royal economy are analyzed in Manning (2010). An excellent and succinct overview of Ptolemaic political history is provided by Vandorpe (2014a). Population estimates vary widely, see Rathbone (1990); Manning (2003); Clarysse and Thompson (2006). I follow Hassan (1994, 170), who estimates 3.23 million at the height of the Ptolemaic period. That figure is low by many other estimates. Fischer-Bovet (2014, 170; 2011) has made a good case for the 5% figure.
12 Cf. Trivellato (2009, 4–15) for the Early Modern Mediterranean.
13 The Ptolemaic legal system with its separate courts for Greeks and Egyptians also certainly reinforced cultural and linguistic boundaries, at least initially. By the end of the second century BC, however, these boundaries had broken down, as the attempts at redrawing social boundaries in a series of royal decrees recorded in *P. Tebt* I 5 (118 BC) obviously show.
14 For a good survey based on some of the papyrological material, see Lewis (1986).
15 Ludlow and Manning (2016). On these revolts, see Veïsse (2004).
16 SB 14.11942. Turner (1974).
17 *P. Eleph.* 1, 311 BC, the earliest dated Greek papyrus from Egypt. See Rowlandson (1998, text 123).
18 Literature on the archive is large. For good orientations, see Pestman (1981); Orrieux (1985); Clarysse and Vandorpe (1995).
19 For a general discussion of "Hellenes" in the Ptolemaic period see Thompson (2001).
20 On the Kleon archive, see Lewis (2001, Chapter 2); Van Beek (2017). On Fayyum reclamation in general, see Thompson (1999).
21 Buck (1946); Clarysse (1998); Dobais-Lalou (2000).
22 On Ptolemaic settlements: Mueller (2006).
23 Honigman (2003); Kruse (2008, 2010); Sänger (2014, 2016).
24 On inter-ethnic relations in the period, see most recently Fischer-Bovet (2015).
25 = *Pros.Ptol.* 196. See the comments by Ray (1976, 128).
26 See Fischer-Bovet (2014, 116–159) for a discussion of the details of military organization and military reforms.
27 Lewis (2001, Chapter 6); Vandorpe (2002); Vandorpe and Waebens (2009).
28 Vandorpe (1995) offers an excellent survey of Thebes and the Theban region under the Ptolemies.
29 Bagnall et al. (1996, 322).
30 Greek-named witnesses are occasionally found in documents coming from Thebes. See Clarysse (1995).
31 The nature of this refuge-seeking, whether motivated by religious beliefs or escape from economic or other social pressures, is disputed. The issues are well summarized by Thompson (2012, 202–204).
32 *UPZ* 14 (158 BC); Thompson (2012, 230–232); Manning (2010, 148–149).
33 Keenan, Manning, and Yiftach-Firanko (2014, 98). On hybrid forms of contract, see Pierce (1972).

34 On the issue of ethnicity here, see Bagnall and Cribiore (2006, 8–9).
35 Von Reden (2007); Manning (2008).
36 Latest analysis of the tomb in Cole (2015), with bibliography.
37 See Vierros (2012). See also Clarysse (2010).

REFERENCES

Agut-Labordère, Damien. 2013. "The Saite Period: The Emergence of a Mediterranean Power." In *Ancient Egyptian Administration*, edited by Juan C.M. García, 965–1027. Leiden: Brill.

Armoni, Charikleia. 2012. *Studien zur Verwaltung des ptolemäischen Ägypten: Das Amt des Basilikos Grammateus*. Cologne: Verlag Ferdinand Schöningh.

Asheri, David, Alan Lloyd, and Aldo Corcella. 2007. *A Commentary on Herodotus Books I–IV*. Edited by Oswyn Murray and Alfonso Moreno. Oxford: Oxford University Press.

Bagnall, Roger S. 1976. *The Administration of the Ptolemaic Possessions Outside Egypt*. Leiden: Brill.

Bagnall, Roger S. 2002. "Alexandria: Library of Dreams." *Proceedings of the American Philosophical Society*, 146: 348–362.

Bagnall, Roger S., ed. 2009. *The Oxford Handbook of Papyrology*. Oxford: Oxford University Press.

Bagnall, Roger S., and Raffaella Cribiore. 2006. *Women's Letters from Ancient Egypt, 300 BC–AD 800*. Ann Arbor: University of Michigan Press.

Bagnall, Roger S., Joseph G. Manning, Steven E. Sidebotham, and Ronald E. Zitterkopf. 1996. "A Ptolemaic Inscription from Bir 'Iayyan." *Chronique d'Égypte*, 71: 317–330.

Bernand, André. 1995. *Alexandrie des Ptolémées*. Paris: CNRS editions.

Bietak, Manfred, Nannó Marinatos, and Clairy Palivou. 2007. "Taureador Scenes in Tell el-Daba (Avaris) and Knossos." *Untersuchungen der Zweigstelle Kairo des Österreichischen Archäologischen Instituts 27*. Vienna: Österreichische Akademie der Wissenschaften.

Bingen, Jean. 2007. "The Structural Tensions of Ptolemaic Society." In *Hellenistic Egypt: Monarchy, Society, Economy, Culture*, edited by Roger S. Bagnall, 189–205. Berkeley: University of California Press. Originally published as "Les tensions structurelles de la société ptolémaïque," in *Atti del XVII Congresso Internazionale di Papyrologia* III. Naples, 1984, 921–937.

Boardman, John. 1999. *The Greeks Overseas. Their Early Colonies and Trade*. 4th ed. London: Thames & Hudson.

Bresson, Alain. 2005. "Naucratis: De l'Emporion à la cité." *Topoi*, 12: 133–155.

Broodbank, Cyprian. 2013. *The Making of the Middle Sea: A History of the Mediterranean from the Beginning to the Emergence of the Classical World*. Oxford: Oxford University Press.

Buck, Carl D. 1946. "The Dialect of Cyrene." *Classical Philology*, 41(3): 129–134.

Burstein, Stanley M. 1995. *Graeco-Africana Studies in the History of Greek Relations with Egypt and Nubia*. New Rochelle, NY: Aristide D. Caratzas.

Carrez-Maratray, Jean-Yves, and Catherine Defernez. 2012. "L'angle oriental du Delta: les Grecs avant Alexandre." In *Grecs et Romains en Égypte: territoires, espaces de la vie et de la mort, objets de prestige et du quotidian*, edited by Pascale Ballet, 31–45. Cairo: Institut Français d'Archéologie Orientale.

Clarysse, Willy. 1995. "Greeks in Ptolemaic Thebes." In *Hundred-Gated Thebes. Acts of a Colloquium on Thebes and the Theban Area in the Graeco-Roman Period*, edited by Sven P. Vleeming, 1–19. Leiden: Brill.

Clarysse, Willy. 1998. "Ethnic Diversity and Dialect among the Greek of Hellenistic Egypt." in *The Two Faces of Graeco-Roman Egypt: Greek and Demotic and Greek-Demotic Texts and Studies Presented to P.W. Pestman*, edited by Arthur M.F.W. Verhoogt and Sven P. Vleeming, 1–13. Leiden: Brill.

Clarysse, Willy. 2009. "The Zenon Papyri Thirty Years On." In *100 anni di instituzioni fiorentine per la papirologia. Atti del convegno internazionale di studi Firenze, 12–13 giugno 2008*, edited by Guido Bastianini and Angelo Casanova, 31–43. Florence: Istituto papirologico 'G. Vitelli.'

Clarysse, Willy. 2010. "Linguistic Diversity in the Archive of the Engineers Kleon and Theodoros." In *The Language of the Papyri*, edited by T.V. Evans and D. Obbink, 35–50. Oxford: Oxford University Press.

Clarysse, Willy. 2013. "Zenon Archive." In *The Encyclopedia of Ancient History*, 1st ed., edited by Roger S. Bagnall, Kai Brodersen, Craige B. Champion, et al. 7170–7171. Chichester: Wiley Blackwell.

Clarysse, Willy, and Dorothy J. Thompson. 2006. *Counting the People in Hellenistic Egypt*. 2 vols. Cambridge: Cambridge University Press.

Clarysse, Willy, and Katelijn Vandorpe. 1995. *Zénon, un homme d'affaires grec à l'ombre des pyramides*. Leuven: Leuven University Press.

Cole, Sara E. 2015. Cultural and Artistic Hybridity: Visual Culture and Elite Identity in Ptolemaic Egypt (ca. 323–30 BC). PhD dissertation, Yale University.

Davies, William V., and Louise Schofield, eds. 1995. *Egypt, the Aegean and the Levant: Interconnections in the Second Millennium BC*. London: British Museum Press.

De Meulenaere, Herman. 1951. *Herodotos over de 26ste Dynastie*. Leuven: Instituut voor Oriëntalisme.

Dillon, Matthew P.J. 1997. "A Homeric Pun from Abu Simbel," *ZPE*, 118: 128–130.

Dobais-Lalou, Catherine. 2000. *Le dialecte des inscriptions grecques de Cyrène*. Karthago 25. Paris: Institut d'art et d'archéologie.

Edmunds, Lowell. 2016. *Stealing Helen: The Myth of the Abducted Wife in Comparative Perspective*. Princeton: Princeton University Press.

Ehrenberg, Victor. 1969. *The Greek State*. 2nd ed. London: Methuen.

Empereur, Jean-Yves. 1998. *Alexandria Rediscovered*. London: George Braziller.

Empereur, Jean-Yves. 2002. *Alexandria: The Jewel of Egypt*. New York: Avrams.

Fischer-Bovet, Christelle. 2011. "Counting the Greeks in Egypt: Immigration in the First Century of Ptolemaic Rule." In *Demography in the Graeco-Roman World: New Insights and Approaches*, edited by Claire Holeran and April Pudsey, 135–154. Cambridge: Cambridge University Press.

Fischer-Bovet, Christelle. 2014. *Army and Society in Ptolemaic Egypt*. Cambridge: Cambridge University Press.

Fischer-Bovet, Christelle. 2015. "Social Unrest and Ethnic Coexistence in Ptolemaic Egypt and the Seleucid Empire." *Past and Present*, 229: 3–45.

Fraser, Peter M. 1972. *Ptolemaic Alexandria*. 3 vols. Oxford: Clarendon Press.
Goddio, Frank, Andre Bernand, Etienne Bernand, et al. 1998. *Alexandria: The Submerged Royal Quarters*. London:Periplus.
Grimm, Gunther. 1998. *Alexandria. Die erste Königsstadt der hellenistischen Welt*. Mainz: von Zabern.
Habicht, Christian. 1958. "Die herrschende Gesellschaft in den hellenistischen Monarchien." *Vierteljahrschrift für Sozial- und Wirtschaftsgeschichte*, 45: 1–16.
Haider, Pieter W. 2001. "Epigraphische Quellen zur Integration von Griechen in die ägyptische Gesellschaft der Saïtenzeit." In *Naukratis. Die Beziehungen zu Ostgriechenland, Ägypten und Zypern in archaischer Zeit. Akten der Table Ronde in Mainz 25.–27. November 1999*, edited by Ursula Höckmann and Detlev Kreikenbom, 175–215. Möhnesee: Bibliopolis.
Hassan, Fekri A. 1994. "Population Ecology and Civilization in Ancient Egypt." In *Historical Ecology: Cultural Knowledge and Changing Landscapes*, edited by Carole L. Crumley, 155–182. Sante Fe: School of American Research.
Hassler, Astrid. 2008. "Mykenisches in Amarna: Funde der Deutschen Orient-Gesellschaft im Ägyptischen Museum Berlin." *Ägypten und Levante*, 18: 129–143.
Heinen, Hans. 1984. "The Syrian-Egyptian Wars and the New Kingdoms of Asia Minor." In *The Cambridge Ancient History, vol. 7.1: The Hellenistic World*, 2nd. ed., edited by Frank W. Walbank, Alan E. Astin, Martin W. Frederiksen, and Robert M. Ogilvie, 412–445. Cambridge: Cambridge University Press.
Hölbl, Günther. 2001. *A History of the Ptolemaic Empire. Abingdon*: Routledge.
Honigman, Sylvie. 2003. "*Politeumata* and Ethnicity in Ptolemaic Egypt." *Ancient Society*, 33: 61–102.
Horden, Peregrine, and Nicholas Purcell. 2000. *The Corrupting Sea: A Study of Mediterranean History*. Oxford: Blackwell.
Hughes, Bettany. 2005. *Helen of Troy*. New York: Knopf.
Johnson, Janet H. 1987. "Ptolemaic Bureaucracy from an Egyptian Point of View." In *The Organization of Power: Aspects of Administration in the Ancient, Medieval and Ottoman Middle East, a Symposium Held at the University of Chicago, Spring, 1983*, edited by McGuire Gibson and Robert Biggs, 141–149. Chicago: Oriental Institute.
Keenan, James G., Joseph G. Manning, and Uri Yiftach-Firanko, eds. 2014. *Law and Legal Practice in Egypt from Alexander to the Arab Conquest: A Selection of Papyrological Sources in Translation, with Introductions and Commentary*. Cambridge: Cambridge University Press.
Kruse, Thomas. 2008. "Das *politeuma* der Juden von Herakleopolis in Ägypten." In *Die Septuaginta – Texte, Kontexte, Lebenswelten. Internationale Fachtagung veranstaltet von Septuaginta Deutsch (LXX.D), Wuppertal 20.–23. Juli 2006*, edited by Martin Karrer and Wolfgang Kraus, 166–175. Tübingen: Mohr Siebeck.
Kruse, Thomas. 2010. "Das jüdische politeuma von Herakleopolis in Ägypten: Zur Methode der Integration ethnischer Gruppen in den Staat der Ptolemäer." In *Volk und Demokratie im Altertum*, edited by Vera V. Dement'eva and Tassilo Schmitt, 93–105. Göttingen: Vandenhoeck & Ruprecht.
La'da, Csaba A. 2002. *Foreign Ethnics in Hellenistic Egypt. Studia Hellenistica 38, Prosopographia Ptolemaica, 10*. Leuven: Peeters.

Lewis, Napthali. 1986. *Greeks in Ptolemaic Egypt*. Oxford: Oxford University Press.
Lewis, Napthali. 2001. *Greeks in Ptolemaic Egypt: Case Studies in the Social History of the Hellenistic World*. 2nd. ed. Oakville, CT: American Society of Papyrologists.
Lloyd, Alan B. 1975–1988. *Herodotus Book II*. 3 vols. Leiden: Brill.
Lloyd, Alan B. 1988. *Herodotus Book II. Commentary 99–182*. Leiden: Brill.
Lloyd, Alan B. 1994. "Egypt, 404–332 B.C." In *The Cambridge Ancient History, vol. 6: The Fourth Century*, 2nd. ed., edited by David M. Lewis, John Boardman, Simon Hornblower, and Murray Oswald, 337–360. Cambridge: Cambridge University Press.
Lloyd, Alan B. 2000. "The Saite Navy." In *The Sea in Antiquity*. British Archaeological Reports International Series 899, edited by Graham J. Oliver, Roger Brock, Tim J. Cornell, and S. Hodkinson, 81–91. Oxford: Archaeopress.
Ludlow, Francis, and Joseph G. Manning. 2016. "Revolts under the Ptolemies: A Paleoclimatological Perspective." In *Revolt and Resistance in the Ancient World: In the Crucible of Empire*, edited by John J. Collins and Joseph G. Manning, 154–171. Leiden: Brill.
Malinowski, Gosciwit. 2014. "Alexander and the Beginning of the Greek Exploration in Nilotic Africa." In *Alexander the Great and Egypt: History, Art, Tradition*, edited by Volker Grieb, Krzystof Nawotka, and Agnieszka Wojciechowska, 273–285. Wiesbaden: Harrassowitz.
Manassa, Colleen. 2009. "A Depiction of Paris in Luxor Temple and the 'eidolon' of Helen." *Zeitschrift für ägyptische Sprache und Altertumskunde*, 136: 141–149.
Manning, Joseph G. 2002. "Rhodon Son of Lysimachos in Edfu (Apollonopolis Magna)." *ZPE*, 138: 146–148.
Manning, Joseph G. 2003. *Land and Power in Ptolemaic Egypt: The Structure of Land Tenure*. Cambridge: Cambridge University Press.
Manning, Joseph G. 2008. "Coinage as 'Code' in Ptolemaic Egypt." In *The Monetary Systems of the Greeks and Romans*, edited by William V. Harris, 84–111. Oxford: Oxford University Press.
Manning, Joseph G. 2010. *The Last Pharaohs: Egypt under the Ptolemies, 305–30 BC*. Princeton: Princeton University Press.
Manning, Joseph G. Forthcoming. "Courts, Justice and Culture in Ptolemaic Law: or the Rise of the Egyptian Jurist." Vienna.
McKenzie, Judith. 2011. *The Architecture of Alexandria and Egypt 300 B.C.–A.D. 700*. New Haven: Yale University Press.
Möller, Astride. 2000. *Naukratis: Trade in Archaic Greece*. Oxford: Oxford University Press.
Monroe, C. 2010. "Sunk Costs at Late Bronze Age Uluburun." *Bulletin of the American Schools of Oriental Research*, 357: 15–29.
Monson, Andrew. 2012. *From the Ptolemies to the Romans: Political and Economic Change in Egypt*. Cambridge: Cambridge University Press.
Monson, Andrew. 2015. "Hellenistic Empires." In *Fiscal Regimes and the Political Economy of Premodern States*, edited by Andrew Monson and Walter Scheidel, 169–207. Oxford: Oxford University Press.
Moyer, Ian. 2002. "Herodotus and an Egyptian Mirage: The Genealogies of the Theban Priests." *JHS*, 122: 70–90.

Moyer, Ian. 2011. *Egypt and the Limits of Hellenism.* Cambridge: Cambridge University Press.
Mueller, Katja. 2006. *Settlements of the Ptolemies: City Foundations and New Settlement in the Hellenistic World.* Studia Hellenistica 43. Leuven: Peeters.
Orrieuxz, Claude. 1985. *Zénon de Caunos, parépidèmos, et le destin grec.* Paris: Les Belles Lettres.
Paganini, Mario C.D. 2011. *Gymnasia and Greek Identity in Ptolemaic and Early Roman Egypt.* DPhil thesis, Oxford University.
Perdu, Olivier. 2014. "Saites and Persians (664–332)." In *A Companion to Ancient Egypt*, edited by Alan B. Lloyd, 140–158. Chichester: Wiley Blackwell.
Pestman, Pieter W. 1981. *A Guide to the Zenon Archive.* P.L. Bat. 21. Leiden: Brill.
Pestman, Pieter W. 1992. *Il Processo di Hermias e altri Documenti dell'Archivio dei Choachiti (P. Tor. Choachiti).* Turin: Ministero per i beni culturali e ambientali.
Petrie, W.M. Flinders. 1906. *Hyksos and Israelites Cities.* London: British School of Archaeology in Egypt.
Pierce, Richard H. 1972. *Three Demotic Papyri in the Brooklyn Museum: A Contribution to the Study of Contracts and their Instruments in Ptolemaic Egypt.* Oslo: Universitetsforlaget.
Pulak, Cemal. 1997. "The Ulu Burun Shipwreck." In *Res Maritimae: Cyprus and the Eastern Mediterranean from Prehistory to Late Antiquity*, edited by Stuart Swiny, Robert L. Hohlfelder, and Helena W. Swiny, 233–262. Atlanta: Scholars Press.
Pulak, Cemal. 2008. "The Uluburun Shipwreck and Late Bronze Age Trade." In *Beyond Babylon: Art, Trade, and Diplomacy in the Second Millennium B.C.*, edited by Joan Aruz, Kim Benzel, and Jean Evans, 289–305. New York: Metropolitan Museum of Art.
Rathbone, Dominic. 1990. "Villages, Land and Population in Graeco-Roman Egypt." *PCPS*, 36: 103–142.
Ray, John D. 1976. *The Archive of Hor.* London: Egypt Exploration Society.
Robinson, Damian, and Andrew Wilson, eds. 2011. *Maritime Archaeology and Ancient Trade in the Mediterranean.* Oxford Centre for Maritime Archaeology: Monograph 6. Oxford: Oxford Centre for Maritime Archaeology.
Robinson, Damian, and Franck Goddio, eds. 2015. *Thonis-Heracleion in Context.* Oxford Centre for Maritime Archaeology: Monograph 8. Oxford: Oxford Centre for Maritime Archaeology.
Rosińska-Balik, Karolina, Agnieszka Ochał-Czarnowicz, Marcin Czarnowicz, and Joanna Dębowska-Ludwin, eds. 2015. *Copper and Trade in the South-Eastern Mediterranean: Trade Routes of the Near East in Antiquity.* BAR International Series 2753. Oxford: Archaeopress.
Rowlandson, Jane. 1998. *Women and Society in Greek and Roman Egypt: A Sourcebook.* Cambridge: Cambridge University Press.
Ryholt, Kim. 2006. *The Petese Stories II (P. Petese II).* The Carlsberg Papyri 6. CNI Publications 29. Copenhagen: Museum Tusculanum Press.
Ruzicka, Stephen. 2012. *Trouble in the West: Egypt and the Persian Empire 525–332 BCE.* Oxford: Oxford University Press.
Samuel, Alan E. 1993. "The Ptolemies and the Ideology of Kingship." In *Hellenistic History and Culture*, edited by Peter Green, 168–210. Berkeley: University of California Press.

Sänger, Patrick. 2014. "The Politeuma in the Hellenistic World (Third to First Centuries BC): A Form of Organisation to Integrate Minorities." In *Migration und Integration. Wissenschaftliche Perspektiven aus Österreich. Jahrbuch 2/2013*, edited by Julia Dahlvik, Christoph Reinprecht, and Wiebke Sievers, 51–68. Vienna: Vienna University Press.

Sänger, Patrick. 2016. "Das politeuma in der hellenistischen Staatenwelt: Eine Organisationsform zur Systemintegration von Minderheiten." In *Minderheiten und Migration in der griechisch-römischen Welt. Politische, rechtliche, religiöse und kulturelle Aspekte (SHM 31)*, edited by Patrick Sänger, 25–45. Paderborn: Ferdinand Schöningh.

Schneider, Thomas. 2010. "Foreigners in Egypt: Archaeological Evidence and Cultural Context." In *Egyptian Archaeology*, edited by Willeke Wendrich, 143–163. Chichester: Wiley Blackwell.

Steel, Louise. 2010. "Egypt and the Mediterranean World." In *The Egyptian World*, edited by Toby Wilkinson, 459–475. New York: Routledge.

Stefanou, Mary. 2013. "Waterborne Recruits: The Military Settlers of Ptolemaic Egypt." In *The Ptolemies, the Sea and the Nile: Studies in Waterborne Power*, edited by Kostas Buraselis, Mary Stefanou, and Dorothy J. Thompson, 108–131. Cambridge: Cambridge University Press.

Taagepera, Rein. 1978. "Size and Duration of Empires: Growth-Decline Curves, 3000 to 600 B.C." *Social Science Research*, 7: 180–196.

Thompson, Dorothy J. 1999. "Irrigation and Drainage in the Early Ptolemaic Fayyum." In *Agriculture in Egypt: From Pharaonic to Modern Times*, edited by Alan K. Bowman and Eugene Rogan, 107–122. Proceedings of the British Academy 96. Oxford: Oxford University Press.

Thompson, Dorothy J. 2001. "Hellenistic Hellenes: The Case of Ptolemaic Egypt." In *Ancient Perceptions of Greek Ethnicity*, edited by Irad Malkin, 301–322. Washington, DC: Center for Hellenic Studies.

Thompson, Dorothy J. 2012. *Memphis under the Ptolemies*. 2nd ed. Princeton: Princeton University Press.

Trivellato, Francesca. 2009. *The Familiarity of Strangers: The Sephardic Diaspora, Livorno, and Cross-cultural Trade in the Early Modern Period*. New Haven: Yale University Press.

Turner, Eric G. 1974. "A Commander-in-Chief's Order from Saqqâra." *Journal of Egyptian Archaeology*, 60: 239–242.

Van Beek, Bart. 2009. "'We Too Are in Good Health.' The Private Correspondence from the Kleon Archive." In *Faces of Hellenis:. Studies in the History of the Eastern Mediterranean (4th Century BC–5th Century AD)*, edited by Peter Van Nuffelen, 147–159. Studia Hellenistica 48. Leuven: Peeters.

Van Beek, Bart. 2017. *The Archive of the architektones Kleon and Theodoros (Collectanea Hellenistica)*. Leuven: Peeters.

Vandersleyen, Claude. 2008. *Le delta et la vallée du Nil, le sens du mot w3d wr*. Brussels: Safran.

Vandorpe, Katelijn. 1995. "City of Many a Gate, Harbour for Many a Rebel: Historical and Topographical Outline of Graeco-Roman Thebes." In *Hundred-Gated Thebes. Acts of a Colloquium on Thebes and the Theban Area in the Graeco-Roman Period*. P.L. Bat. 27, edited by Sven P. Vleeming, 203–239. Leiden: Brill.

Vandorpe, Katelijn. 2002. *The Bilingual Family Archive of Dryton, His Wife Apollonia and Their Daughter Senmouthis (P. Dryton). Collectanea Hellenistica 4*. Brussels: Koninklijke Vlaamse Academie van België voor Wetenschappen en Kunsten.

Vandorpe, Katelijn. 2014a. "The Ptolemaic Period." In *A Companion to Ancient Egypt*, edited by Alan B. Lloyd, 159–179. Chichester: Wiley Blackwell.

Vandorpe, Katelijn. 2014b. "Ethnic Diversity in a Wealthy Household." In *Law and Legal Practice in Egypt from Alexander to the Arab Conquest: A Selection of Papyrological Sources in Translation, with Introductions and Commentary*, edited by James G. Keenan, Joseph G. Manning, and Uri Yiftach-Firanko, 101–110. Cambridge: Cambridge University Press.

Vandorpe, Katelijn, and Sofie Waebens. 2009. *Reconstructing Pathyris' Archives: A Multicultural Community in Hellenistic Egypt. Collectanea Hellenistica 3*. Brussels: Koninklijke Vlaamse Academie van België voor Wetenschappen en Kunsten.

Vandorpe, Katelijn, Willy Clarysse, and Herbert Verreth. 2015. *Graeco-Roman Archives from the Fayum. Collectanea Hellenistica 6*. Leuven: Peeters.

Vasunia, Phiroze. 2001. *The Gift of the Nile: Hellenizing Egypt from Aeschylus to Alexander*. Berkeley: University of California Press.

Veïsse, Anne-Emmanuelle. 2004. *Les "Revoltes égyptiennes." Recherches sur les Troubles intérieurs en Égypte du règne Ptolémée III à la Conquête romaine*. Leuven: Peeters.

Venit, Marjorie Susan. 2002. *Monumental Tombs of Ancient Alexandria: The Theater of the Dead*. New York: Cambridge University Press.

Verhoogt, Arthur M.F.W. 1998. *Menches, Komogrammateus of Kerkeosiris: The Doings and Dealings of a Village Scribe in the Late Ptolemaic Period (120–110 BC)*. Leiden: Brill.

Vierros, Marja. 2012. *Bilingual Notaries in Hellenistic Egypt: A Study of Greek as a Second Language. Collectanea Hellenistica 5*. Brussels: Koninklijke Vlaamse Academie van België voor Wetenschappen en Kunsten.

Villing, Alexandra, and Udo Schlotzhauer, eds. 2006. *Naukratis: Greek Diversity in Egypt*. London: British Museum.

Vittmann, Günther. 2003. *Ägypten und die Fremden in ersten vorchristlichen Jahrhundert. Kulturgeschichte der antiken Welt 97*. Mainz: von Zabern.

Von Reden, Sitta. 2007. *Money in Ptolemaic Egypt*. Cambridge: Cambridge University Press.

Will, Edouard. 1979. *Histoire politique du monde hellénistique*. 2 vols. Nancy: Presses universitaires de Nancy.

Winnicki, Jan. 1978. *Ptolemäerarmee in Thebais*. Wroclaw: Archiwum filologiczne.

FURTHER READING

The early presence of Greek material culture in Egypt is surveyed by Boardman (1999). Broodbank (2013) provides an excellent and up-to-date account of the long history of Greek-Egyptian engagement in the Bronze Age. For the Greek cultural engagement with Egypt, Vasunia (2001) and Moyer (2011) serve as excellent guides.

The study of the Saite period has been revitalized in recent years. A complete survey of Saite institutions, important for understanding later Ptolemaic structure and for early Greek settlement in Egypt, and the role of Greeks in the Saite military, is provided by Agut-Labordère (2013). For Herodotus on Egypt, Lloyd's magisterial work (1975–1988) on Book 2 still stands as an excellent introduction. Moyer (2002) is a critical analysis of Herodotus's (beginning with the passage at 2.143) engagement with the Egyptian past.

Work on Ptolemaic Egypt remains a very active part of Ancient History, with new texts still being published each year, along with major recent assessments of previously published material and analytical work on the structure of the state. A good survey of the Ptolemaic Empire is Hölbl (2001). A good, up-to-date, recent survey can be found in Vandorpe (2014a). Manning (2010) reassesses the structure and the limits of the Ptolemaic state and how the Ptolemaic kings interacted with and used Egyptian society. An important and fresh look at the Ptolemaic army and its evolution in the period can be found in Fischer-Bovet (2014). The shift from Ptolemaic to Roman governance of Egypt, and a new basis of fiscality, is treated well by Monson (2012). For Ptolemaic settlements it is worth consulting Mueller (2006), although it is not the last word on the subject.

The study of the political and social institutions of Ptolemaic Alexandria is still well served by Fraser (1972). Bagnall's study (2002) of the library is incisive. Among the more spectacular aspects of the study of Egyptian this period has been the work of two French teams in the Alexandrian harbors. See for an introduction Bernand (1995); Goddio et al. (1998); Empereur (1998, 2002). On the layout and fabric of the city, see Grimm (1998), Venit (2002), and McKenzie (2011).

The papyri are vital for reconstructing Ptolemaic institutions. For an introduction to Papyrology, see Bagnall (2009). For Ptolemaic period archives, see Vandorpe and Waebens (2009) and Vandorpe, Clarysse, and Verreth (2015).

The Zenon Archive, the largest of the Ptolemaic period, has always been something of an academic puzzle. It provides detailed information for the running of a mid-third-century BC large estate, but exactly how to widen out the interpretation for Egypt as a whole remains problematic. Pestman (1981) still provides an indispensable handbook for the entire archive. The Dryton archive of a Greco-Egyptian family from Pathyris in Upper Egypt has been very well studied by Vandorpe (2002).

The Ptolemaic bureaucracy had been studied from many points of view, and primarily through the lens of the administrative documents in the papyri, and usually from a local point of view. The Menches archive from late second-century Fayyum is the most important collection of texts of the later village bureaucracy, studied by Verhoogt (1998). See also the important study of the office of royal scribe by Armoni (2012), and from the Egyptian point of view, Johnson (1987).

For epigraphy of the Ptolemaic period, the Oxford Corpus of Ptolemaic Inscriptions (CPI) project will be now the standard source: https://www.csad.ox.ac.uk/corpus-of-ptolemaic-inscriptions.

CHAPTER EIGHTEEN

The Phocaeans in the Far Western Mediterranean

Joan Sanmartí

Permanent Greek presence in the far west of the Mediterranean began relatively late, about 600 BCE, when people from the city of Phocaea, in northern Ionia, founded Massalia (today Marseille) on the coast of Provence, not far from the mouth of the Rhone (Map 18.1). Over the next four centuries, until the Roman conquest of this area, the Mediterranean coasts of Gaul and the Iberian Peninsula saw the emergence of numerous Greek sites, and the continued presence of Greek traders (and probably craftsmen) who frequented indigenous settlements, and perhaps even lived in some of them in a more or less permanent way. The Phocaeans were not the first foreigners to trade and settle in these regions, and throughout the above-mentioned period they lived and interacted not only with the indigenous peoples, but also with Etruscans and Phoenicians. They all were the actors of a complex story, where interdependencies between agents and local evolutionary processes overlapped in ways that are still not completely understood. Even if primarily focused on the point of view of one of the parties – the Greeks – a coherent view of this period necessarily needs to consider all these actors and their interactions. I shall begin, then, by showing the ethnic, linguistic, cultural, and political complexity of the western Mediterranean during the first millennium BCE. Then I shall describe the historical dynamics of the Phocaean expansion in that area, and I shall finally deal with the complex relationships the Greeks entertained with the other agents.

The Regional Context Around 600 BCE

By the time when Massalia was founded, the ethnic, linguistic, social, and cultural situation at the western end of the Mediterranean was remarkably complex, as a consequence of both the internal evolutionary dynamics of the autochthonous societies

---

A Companion to Greeks Across the Ancient World, First Edition. Edited by Franco De Angelis.
© 2020 John Wiley & Sons, Inc. Published 2020 by John Wiley & Sons, Inc.

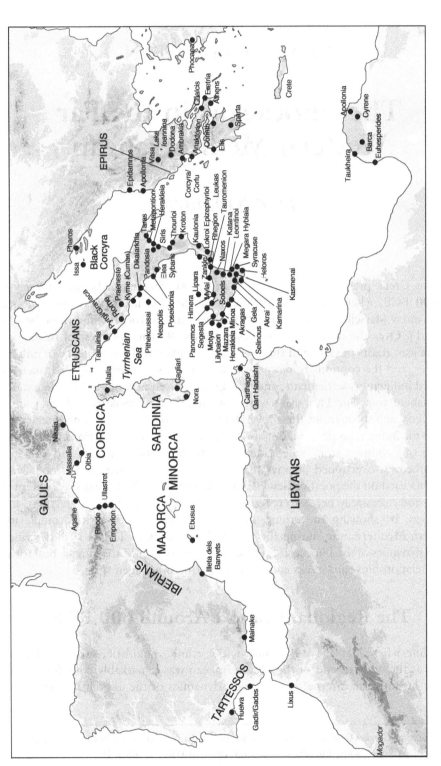

Map 18.1 The far western Mediterranean within the pre-Roman Mediterranean.

and the settlement of foreign people. The presence of Phoenician traders and craftsmen is attested from the ninth century BCE at the indigenous site of Huelva (González de Canales, Serrano, and Llompart 2006), where they arrived attracted by the silver resources of the Río Tinto mines, and also at *Gadir* (Cádiz) (Gener Basallote et al. 2014). Progressively, numerous sites were established on the southern coast of the Iberian Peninsula, as far as La Fonteta, near present-day Alicante, and Sa Caleta, on the island of Ibiza. Others were based in North Africa, so that the whole area around the Straits of Gibraltar became a Phoenician sea (Ramon 2006). Some of them were quickly involved in the production of wine, oil, and perhaps salted fish that were widely exported, particularly to the eastern coast of the Iberian Peninsula (Ramon 2006; Sanmartí 2009).

Toward the end of the seventh century BCE, Etruscan traders also distributed wine amphorae and *bucchero nero* tableware to the Mediterranean coast of Gaul and the extreme northeast of the Iberian Peninsula (Morel 2006a). However, this was a strictly commercial activity, which apparently did not involve the migration of Etruscans, at least in significant numbers. The existence of this trade before the foundation of Massalia has been questioned by some scholars (Bats 1998, 2000), for the imported material dates to not much earlier than 600 BCE – the approximate foundation date of Massalia – and may have been distributed by Phocaean sailors during the period of exploration that would have preceded their permanent establishment.

Regarding indigenous societies of the early first millennium BCE, we have almost no information on the populations of North Africa. In the Iberian Peninsula, the presence of complex settlement patterns has been proposed, despite the poverty of the available data, for the lower Guadalquivir region (Torres 2002, 273–280), known as Tartessos. There, a hierarchical society would have existed, possibly monarchical in nature, if we are to believe the testimony of Herodotus about the legendary king Arganthonios, who established a friendship with the Phocaeans in the late seventh century BCE (Hdt. 1.163). The coast of Mediterranean Andalusia, however, was sparsely populated (Delgado 2008, 34–35). Further east, the populations of the eastern coast of the Iberian Peninsula – that is, the area that the oldest Greek sources designate as Iberia – were organized in simple local communities. The typical settlements were villages of variable size, but these rarely included more than 30 families. These societies experienced a rapid growth in size and political economy from the mid-seventh century BCE, which may be in part related to Phoenician trade. For example, the site of Alt de Benimaquia, near Alicante, witnessed a local production of wine that was certainly controlled by chiefs who used this product as a prestige good (Gómez Bellard and Guérin 1994). Further North, Phoenician wine was widely distributed as a means for increasing prestige and authority by *big men* whose large houses have been found at sites like Aldovesta and Sant Jaume/Mas d'en Serrà (Sanmartí 2009). In Mediterranean Gaul, after a period of some settlement nucleation, the most characteristic feature in the seventh century BCE is the existence of a highly dispersed and unstable population, perhaps due to demographic decrease (Garcia 2004). Consequently, upon the arrival of the Phoceans, there was no powerful political entity in that area, which allowed for their installation at Massalia.

The Societies of the Western Mediterranean from the Sixth Century BCE to the Second Punic War

From the sixth century BCE, coinciding in part with the first stage of the Phocaean expansion, the societies of the far western Mediterranean area underwent major transformations. One obvious shift is the rapid decline of Phoenician trade, which may be related to a reorganization of the Phoenician settlement in southern Spain. This was characterized by the abandonment of some settlements and the concomitant growth of others – *Gadir* (Cadiz), *Malaka* (Málaga), and *Ibosim*-Ebusus (Eivissa/Ibiza) – that eventually became major cities (Ramon 2006).

With regard to indigenous peoples, the so-called Iberian culture developed from the mid-sixth century BCE on the Mediterranean coast of the Iberian Peninsula and as far as the western Languedoc. Although this is hardly definable in terms of material culture, the existence of a non-Indo-European common language throughout the territory gives a reasonable meaning to the notion of "Iberian culture" (Sanmartí Grego 1990). From a sociological and political point of view, its most characteristic aspect is the formation of highly centralized regional polities that were ruled from urban centers of some importance (10–15 ha) by aristocratic groups who developed an administrative system (Sanmartí 2014). This was supported from the late fifth century BCE by extensive use of a specifically Iberian writing system.

On the Mediterranean coast of Gaul, the population expanded in the sixth century BCE, and permanent settlements, usually called *oppida*, gradually formed (Garcia 2004). The apparent absence of large centralized polities and of a writing system until the second century BCE (De Hoz 1999, 231) suggest a lesser sociopolitical development, as compared to the Iberian area.

The Process of the Phocaean Expansion: First Contacts

It is likely that the Phocaean permanent presence in the Mediterranean far West was preceded by other contacts with sailors and merchants from Eastern Greece, including the Phocaeans themselves. We cannot give credence to the tradition, transmitted by Pseudo-Scymnos and Strabo, that attributed to east Greek Rhodians the foundation before the first Olympiad of *Rhode* (Roses), in northeastern Catalonia, close to the Pyrenees. Despite Maluquer de Motes's opinion (1971), it seems likely that this is a legend created in Hellenistic times in Rhodes (Pena 2006), or perhaps in Rhode itself (Domínguez 1990), to ennoble their own origins, since both were new cities, founded respectively in the late fifth and the fourth century BCE. In any case, no archaeological data confirm such an ancient Greek presence.

Herodotus's story (4.152) about a Samian merchant called Kolaios is probably closer to historical reality. After him, shortly before the foundation of Cyrene (631 BCE) Kolaios's ship was diverted by winds from its way to Egypt, and driven beyond the Pillars of Herakles (the Straits of Gibraltar), to Tartessos, where he made an extraordinary profit. Although Herodotus does not mention the products exchanged, we can suspect that

Kolaios returned with a cargo of silver and perhaps Atlantic tin. The finding of several western Phoenician ivory combs dated to 640–630 BCE in the Heraion of Samos – where Kolaios, according to Herodotus, had offered a colossal bronze cauldron – could support the likelihood of this story (Freyer-Schauenburg, 1966).

As mentioned earlier, Herodotus (1.163) attributes to the Phocaeans another extremely profitable contact with Tartessos and King Arganthonios. Although they cannot be regarded as a direct and unequivocal verification of this story, we must mention several findings of Greek pottery dating from the last decades of the seventh century BCE in Phoenician settlements of the Iberian Peninsula, and particularly in Huelva, where wine amphorae from Chios and tableware from Eastern Greece have been found. These luxury products were likely used by the Tartessian aristocracy in banquets aimed at stressing their high social position, and as high-value goods in social transactions (Cabrera 1995). The Greek origin of these goods – only a minority as compared to the Phoenician imports – does not necessarily imply that they were transported by Phocaean merchants. This, however, is a plausible hypothesis, given the Phocaeans' fame as skilled *emporoi* (Ath. 13.576, citing Aristotle), that is, as intermediaries in transactions over long distances. Moreover, it is logical that the Phocaeans' permanent establishment in the far West was preceded by a phase of strictly commercial contacts. The arrival at Huelva of Greek pottery from very diverse origins intensified during the first half of the sixth century BCE, to quickly fade thereafter. By that time, however, the Phocaeans had enlarged their aims and already created one permanent base in the western Mediterranian: Massalia, which eventually became one of the largest and richest cities in that region.

The First Permanent Settlement: *Massalia* and *Emporion*

Leaving aside the above-mentioned tradition about Rhode, the written sources are unanimous in attributing to the Phocaeans an exclusive role in the Greek expansion to the far western Mediterranean region. However, we cannot rule out the possibility that human contingents of diverse origins were involved at the beginning. According to Tréziny (2000), such diversity is suggested by the existence in Massalia of the temples dedicated to Ephesian Artemis and Apollo Delphinios, since the former did not become a panionian cult until the mid-sixth century BCE, and the latter was a distinctly Milesian cult. The more strictly Phocaean identity would have been forged in the late sixth/early fifth century BCE, with the arrival of new Phocaean contingents after the metropolis's seizure by the Persians (Tréziny 2000, 84). However, the weight at Massalia of the cultural traditions from northern Ionia or Aeolis is well attested during the sixth century BCE by a group of votive *naiskoi* (Hermary 2000); they belong to a type particularly common in northwestern Asia Minor, and only attested in Phocaean cities (Elea and Massalia) in the central and western Mediterranean. The importance *ab initio* of the Phocaean component is also noticed in the production of the so-called gray monochrome ware, a characteristically Phocaean pottery type. It is also possible that the first groups established at Massalia included indigenous people. One indication of this is the relatively high percentage of local handmade pottery (15% in the first quarter of the fifth century, which quickly declined thereafter). As Tréziny (2010b) has pointed out, there are different possibilities to explain this: full families, or even small groups, might have coexisted with the Greeks, but it is also possible that this pottery was made by indigenous wives of the Greek migrants, or that it was simply imported, as the Massalians did not produce kitchenware. A similar problem arises from the presence of a significant amount of Etruscan cooking pottery. The hypothesis of an Etruscan community established in the city (probably traders) seems perfectly plausible. To sum up, it is possible that the first settlement at Massalia was a sort of joint venture that gathered people of diverse origins and cultures, which, as argued by Osborne (1998), must have been quite a common situation in the early stages of many *apoikiai*. Nevertheless, the available data indicate that the Phocaean component was very strong, even dominant, from the city's very beginning. Morel (2006b) has gathered consistent data of a varied nature, which prove that Massalia remained faithful throughout its subsequent history to a Phocaean identity that linked her to the metropolis and to Elea.

The site chosen for Massalia was located relatively close (about 50 km as the crow flies) to the mouth of the Rhone, a prime communication route that connects the Mediterranean with central Europe and the Northern Sea (Map 18.1). It also had an excellent port: a deep bay, over 1 km long by 0.5 km wide (Figure 18.1). The new town was located on the

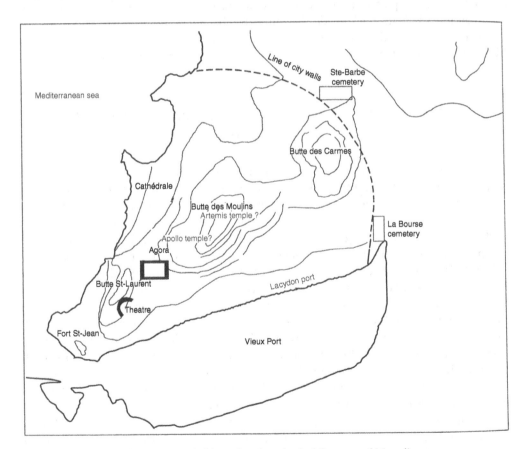

Figure 18.1 Plan of main topographic and archaeological features of Massalia.

promontory that forms its northern side. The material remains of this settlement are scanty, as might be expected in a site that has continuously been occupied to the present, but some debris of modest dwellings date back to the first decades of the sixth century BCE. The importance of maritime activities is demonstrated not only by the numerous Greek and especially Etruscan imports, and the impressive evidence from shipwrecks (Long, Miró, and Volpe 1992), but also by the remains of a pier built in the early sixth century BCE. The few vestiges of the defensive wall are dated to the late sixth century BCE; they prove that the city quickly grew to a substantial extent (about 20 ha).

Within a few decades, Massalia acquired a territory in the Huveaune valley, and toward 540–530 BCE it started the production of amphorae that were used to export its wine production. The existence of the vineyards is confirmed by the finding of planting ditches (Boissinot 2010), while amphora production has been attested in Massalia's eastern suburb. This economic orientation is close to the model of agricultural production intended for trade that was developed two centuries earlier by the Phoenicians in southern Spain, and somewhat later by the Etruscans. The extent of the Massalian *chora* is not known, but it seems that it did not exceed a radius of 8 km around the city (about 60 km^2) until the late third century BCE (Dietler 2010, 115).

Knowledge of the classical city is also limited, but the information available is quite significant. In addition to some typical elements of Greek ways of life (including baths, probably attached to a *palaestra*), the most significant findings are still related to the productive economy and trade (Tréziny 2009–2011). Thus, the amphora production is still attested close to the port, which was shifted to the east, while the Archaic port's area was devoted to the repair of ships. All this confirms the persistence of the economic model established in the Archaic period.

As regards social structure, the most interesting information is provided by the necropoleis of La Bourse and Sainte-Barbe. The burials in the former are all cremations, and both cinerary urns and funerary offerings indicate a significant purchasing power. In Sainte-Barbe, however, the prevalence of inhumation during the fourth and third centuries BCE, as well as the nature of the funerary goods, suggests the cemetery was used by less privileged classes (Bertucchi 1992; Moliner 2013). This seems to confirm the information from the written sources about a strictly oligarchic constitution that persisted throughout the history of Massalia, which is consistent with a highly polarized society.

While Massalia developed rapidly as a large city with a relatively diversified economy, Emporion, which is located in the gulf of Roses, immediately to the south of the Pyrenees, has totally different characteristics. We know from Strabo (3.4.8) that the newcomers settled first on a small island (2 ha) close to the shore and to the mouth of the Fluvià River – which formed a relatively well-protected harbor – and created thereafter a second town on the mainland. As indicated by its name, Emporion was a trading outpost, and remained so to a large extent until Roman times.

The first settlement (or *palaià polis*, as it was known after Strabo) is now a mainland promontory, occupied by the village of Sant Martí d'Empúries. Some excavations have brought to light an indigenous settlement dated to the seventh century BCE. It consisted of rectangular houses grouped in blocks, with walls made of clay and vegetal matter, and it received a significant volume of Phoenician amphorae from Andalusia. From the early sixth century BCE, a small amount of Greek and Etruscan pottery bears witness to the first contacts with Massalia. During the second quarter of the sixth century BCE, a new building phase is attested, also with elongated rectangular houses, but these were made with unbaked bricks on stone bases. There is also a pottery kiln used to produce gray "Phocaean" ware. In addition, the Etruscan and Greek vessels became the majority. These features have been attributed to the creation of the Phocaean *emporion* (Aquilué et al. 2010). Given the continued occupation from the seventh century BCE, and the fact that both the houses and the town planning are reminiscent of contemporary indigenous settlements, the excavators of the site believe that this first *emporion* was a mixed community, in which Greek newcomers lived among local people, a situation not uncommon in the early stages of the contact between Greeks and the native populations of Italy (Osborne 1998, 262–264). An additional argument in favor of the existence of a mixed community is found in the contemporary "northeastern wall necropolis" (so called due to its location in relation to the Roman city). This cemetery is typical of the regional late Urnfield culture, but four out of the 17 excavated tombs are inhumations, which sharply diverts from the common indigenous ritual (Almagro 1955, 359–374). Other scholars, however, believe that the available data are not enough to deny the purely Greek character of settlement at Sant Martí d'Empúries (Moret 2010). Either way, it is logical to assume that the choice of this location was dictated by the existence of the local settlement and its easy access to the interior by river, as Emporion's harbor is mediocre compared to Rhode's (a few kilometers to the north, which was not founded, however, until nearly two centuries later). The apparently intimate coexistence between the native population and the Greeks would suggest that the *emporion* originated as a small-scale private initiative, probably undertaken by freelance Massalian traders, rather than as a state enterprise.

The *emporion* at Sant Martí prospered quickly, since the immediate mainland to the south of the port was occupied already in the third quarter of the sixth century BCE. The first urban structures developed shortly after, and the city grew rapidly to the south, reaching its first southern limit in the second half of the fifth century BCE, when it was given a defensive wall. This enclosed a modest area of only 3 ha, which adds to the 2 ha of the *palaià polis*. The total population has been estimated at about 1500 people (Sanmartí Grego 1992, 29). Two shrines existed, at the port and at the highest point of the settlement, but knowledge of the town plan and the nature of the dwellings remains limited because of the overlap of the Hellenistic and Roman city (Santos, Castanyer, and Tremoleda 2013). We know, however, that in the third quarter of the fifth century BCE an important temple was raised on the southern edge of the city, beyond the wall. At about the same time, Emporion began minting its first, anepigraphic, coins, that were followed in the second quarter of the fourth century BCE by issues with the initials of the city name (*EM/EMP*) (Ripollès 1989). We may conclude that from the second half of the fifth century BCE Emporion developed as an independent *polis*, with a political and economic life of its own, strongly interrelated, as we shall see, with Punic Ebusus and the Iberians. It has been alleged that, in sharp contrast with Massalia, Emporion was a relatively egalitarian society, endowed with a democratic constitution. This is consistent with the fact that the necropoleis indicate no form of economic discrimination (Sanmartí Grego 1992). Indeed, in spite of its urban nature, Emporion probably kept the character and appearance of a commercial outpost throughout its history until the second century BCE, after the Roman conquest, when a relatively large agora was created and new shrines dedicated to Serapis and, probably, to Asclepius were installed in the southern side of the town (see Mierse 1994 and Kaiser 2000 for conflicting views about the reasons for these major transformations).

We cannot dismiss the possibility that the first population of the mainland settlement (often referred to as Neà Polis, although this name is not attested in ancient sources) came directly from Phocaea after the ca. 545 BCE Persian attack, but there are no data to support this. This would account for the two conflicting reports regarding the mother city of Emporion: either Massalia, according to Strabo (3.4.8), or Phocaea if we follow Livy (34.9.1). There are also some fifth-century BCE remains of dwellings outside the wall, immediately to the south, that have been attributed to indigenous people who lived on the outskirts of the city, near the above-mentioned temple, which would have been a meeting place for both communities (Sanmartí Grego 1992; 1993). This would prove the existence of a native community that, following Strabo, ended up fusing with the Greeks to form a single city, which was governed by both Greek and barbarian laws (Strab. 3.4.8). The settlement was enlarged to the South in the fourth century BCE to include the indigenous dwellings, which would reflect this process of integration, although Kaiser (2000) holds that this would have happened only in the second century BCE, under the Roman rule. Another indication of the close relationship between Greeks and indigenous people is the existence at Emporion of a number of inscriptions in the Iberian language and script, including at least six anthroponyms scratched on the bases of Attic cups (Sanmartí Grego 1990; 1993). There are also several Iberian texts on lead sheets, including a letter dated to the late third century BCE (Sanmartí Grego 1990; Velaza 2003). This evidence indicates that a part of the population was ethnically Iberian – but we do not know their status – and that the Iberian language was normally used in the Greek town.

Given its small size, its demographic weakness, and the existence of a firmly organized indigenous power, Emporion was not in the position to control an important territory (Plana-Mallart 2012), which is consistent with the absence of an amphora production. True to its name, it was always engaged in trading activities, of which we have impressive epigraphic and archaeological evidence. The first one is a commercial letter discovered at Emporion itself and dated to the first half of the fifth century BCE (Sanmartí Grego and Santiago 1988). The sender gives instructions to the recipient to undertake certain procedures in relation to the transport of some goods, among which only a reference to wine is preserved. The text explicitly mentions the Emporitai (it is the oldest reference to them), as well as (twice) a third partner, a certain *Basped*[as?] – probably an Iberian name – and an indigenous place name, *Saiganthe*, which has been connected with Saguntum, the famous Iberian city destroyed by Hannibal.

Another extremely interesting document is a text on a lead sheet from Pech Maho, in western Languedoc, which is dated to the second quarter of the fifth century BCE. It describes the acquisition of a boat at Emporion by a dealer called Kyprios. All of the operation's witnesses bear indigenous, mostly Iberian, names (De Hoz 1999, 224–229). The complexity of these contacts among merchants is well illustrated by the fact that the same lead sheet contains an older Etruscan inscription which mentions two merchants who bear an Etruscan (*Venel*) and a Latin (*Utavu*, that is, *Octavius*) name; they were involved in a transaction made in a place called *Matala*, in all probability Massalia.

The nature of the Emporitan business has been further illuminated by the findings of Greek pottery in indigenous settlements of Iberia and by the recent discovery of a Greek, probably Emporitan, shipwreck at Cala Sant Vicenç, in northern Majorca (Nieto and Santos 2009). This was a vessel of about 30 tons, sunk sometime in the late sixth century BCE, loaded with amphorae, mostly Iberian and from Magna Graecia (probably Calabria), plus iron tools (mattocks and pruners) and tin ingots.

Emporion is the southernmost Greek settlement to be archaeologically documented. Several ancient sources, however, mention other Massalian or Phocaean towns, none of which has ever been located. The oldest one is Mainake, as mentioned in Avienus's *Ora maritima*, a fourth-century CE poem that is presumably based on a sixth-century BCE Massalian description of the western Mediterranean shores. It might have been located east of Malaga, in the heart of the Phoenician settlement area. This has led some scholars to suppose that it actually was a Phoenician settlement frequented by Greeks (Niemeyer 1979–1980; Aubet 2005), or a Phocaean outpost in an indigenous milieu (Rouillard 1991, 296–297). Another outpost was Hemeroskopeion, which, according to Strabo, would be *Dianium* (now Dénia, near Alicante), whose Roman name would indicate the existence of a temple dedicated to Artemis of Ephesus, as in other Phocaean settlements (Rouillard 1991, 299–303). Finally, *Alonis* would be located in Santa Pola, also near Alicante, where an indigenous site with evident architectural Greek influence has been excavated (Rouillard 2009, 141–142). Despite the lack of convincing archaeological documents about the real existence of these towns, independent evidence indicates a strong familiarity of the Phocaeans with the southeast of the Iberian Peninsula. On the one hand, the Greek alphabet was employed in this area along with specifically Iberian scripts to record the Iberian language in the late fifth and the fourth centuries BCE. This implies close contact, from which bilingual individuals may arise (De Hoz 1987a, 286–290). On the other hand, the southeast of the Iberian Peninsula and its extension to the interior is the nuclear area of Iberian sculpture, which in some cases shows a considerable influence of Greek models; although this might be due to itinerant Greek artisans, close contact is equally implied (Chapa 1989; Rouillard 1999, 89–90; Croissant and Rouillard, 1996; Rouillard 2009, 143). Finally, a Roman inscription dated to ca. 100 CE refers to this coast as *Litus phocaicus* (Rouillard 1991, 284–285). It would be hard to ignore all this evidence of Greek contact, but it probably indicates the presence of traders and craftsmen based in indigenous settlements, rather than the existence of Phocaean towns (Rouillard 1999; Domínguez 2002).

The Second Phase of the Phocaean Expansion

A second phase of expansion occurred between the late fifth and the third century BCE. It began with the foundation of Agathe (Agde), located at the mouth of the Hérault River, in a place that was already occupied by an indigenous settlement (Dedet and Schwaller 2018). Some 50 years later Rhode (Roses) was founded, just 15 km north of Emporion (Puig and Martin 2006; Puig 2010). Probably it is also a foundation of Massalia (Pena 2006), although attributed to the Emporitans by some sources. In the third quarter of the fourth century BCE, Olbia was created near Hyères, east of Massalia (Bats 1988), and still later, in the first half of the third century BCE, Tauroeis (possibly Le Brusc, at Espeyran) was founded. Further east are Antipolis (Antibes), and Nikaia (Nice), both probably dating from the late third century BCE (Bats 2004). The sources also mention Rhodanoussia and Theline, but their location is uncertain (the latter could be modern Arles). So, in the late third century BCE, the shores of the Gulf of Lion were covered with a string of Greek settlements, to which must be added the presence of merchants and craftsmen based in indigenous sites.

Knowledge of these settlements is still limited, in some cases because of their continued occupation, even down to the present, as with Nikaia and Antipolis. The best known are Agathe, Rhode and, particularly, Olbia. All of them are small and share a common basic structure. Agathe was a rectangle of 257 m by 200 m (about 5 ha); it was protected by a wall and had an internal orthogonal organization. The initial core of Rhode was very small (1.6 ha). It also had a defensive wall, and the few preserved remains of houses suggest an orthogonal layout. Around 300 BCE a new, seemingly unwalled, district was founded further east, following a strictly orthogonal plan. Approximately at the same time, Rhode started minting its own silver coins, so it presumably had become an independent city. As for Olbia, it was a square of 160 m on each side (2.5 ha), bounded by a wall with rectangular towers; the interior was divided into rectangular blocks (11 m × 34.5 m).

Drawing on the testimony of Strabo, who describes these settlements as *epiteichismata* (military outposts), Bats (2004) has suggested that their essential function was to control and protect the coast against indigenous people and piratic actions. In sharp contrast with the *emporion* at Sant Martí d'Empúries, this would have been an essentially state enterprise. This interpretation is supported to some extent by the analogy with some partly contemporary foundations by Athens (Osborne 1998, 252–254), and by the physical similarity between Olbia and Roman *coloniae maritimae* such as Ostia, Minturnae, or Pyrgi. Bats takes this analogy as far as to consider that the Massalian towns were inhabited by citizen soldiers drawn from the lower classes of the metropolis.

The interpretation of these settlements as military outposts seems justified, but this does not exclude other functions. Agathe, for example, controlled a relatively large area, some 20 000 hectares (Garcia 1995), and was well connected with mining areas, so it might have had some economic importance. As for Rhode, it has been suggested that the foundation was the reaction of Massalia keeping her interests in the Iberian Peninsula after the emancipation of Emporion in the fifth century BCE (Puig 2010). Other scholars, however, think that Emporion and Rhode had complementary economies during the third century BCE: Emporion would have preserved a privileged relationship with the immediate Catalan hinterland, while Rhode would have had a particular role in coastal trade (Principal-Ponce 1998), as proved by the wide distribution of its black-glaze tableware production.

Greeks, Phoenicians, and Etruscans

The relationship between Greeks and the Phoenicio-Punic populations has often been considered mainly from the perspective of confrontation, which is justified to some extent by the violent clashes between them that took place in Sicily. In addition, a coalition of Etruscans and Carthaginians ended the Phocaean presence on Corsica, after the battle of Alalia (547 BCE). That being said, one must remember that episodes of confrontation are more easily reflected in written sources than other situations in which peaceful coexistence, and even cooperation, may be common; in any case, local conditions may be extremely diverse and should be analyzed specifically.

We have already mentioned the importance of Phoenician trade in the east of the Iberian Peninsula from the eighth to the early sixth century BCE. However, from the mid-sixth to the late fifth century BCE, the vast majority of imports in that region are of Greek origin, both amphorae (Massalian and others) and tableware. The end of Phoenician trade has been attributed to two unrelated events: the taking of Tyre by the Assyrians, in 574 BCE (which would have changed the demand for products from the far West), and the "arrival" of the Phocaeans, who would somehow have expelled the Phoenicians from the Iberian coast. The role that the local population could have had in these issues and its demand for specific products was simply ignored, drawing on the idea that the indigenous peoples were necessarily fascinated by the novelty and the supposed inherent superiority of *any* Phoenician or especially Greek product. From this point of view, control of markets was a matter for "colonial powers," in which local peoples had little or nothing to say (Dietler 2010, 55–74).

In recent years this view has been modified, considering the fact that the fading of Archaic Phoenician trade in the eastern Iberian Peninsula coincides not only with the presence of the Phocaeans, but also with the formation of the first stratified indigenous societies, which must have favored changes in local demand (Sanmartí 2009). For the late seventh-/early sixth-century BCE *big men* it was necessary to distribute large amounts of goods, including Phoenician wine, in order to maintain or enhance their position. For the new aristocracy that emerged during the sixth century BCE and that was ideologically legitimized, this was no longer necessary, so the demand for Phoenician imports declined. In addition, the elites need to renew regularly the sources of prestige goods, and Phocaean trade provided a remarkable opportunity for this, since it could offer a wide range of new products. Among these, there was high-quality and aesthetically appealing tableware, which must have been appreciated by an aristocracy that certainly practiced elitist banqueting to a much larger extent than the former *big men*. Therefore, changes in the origin, quantity, and nature of the imported material are explained not solely by the Phocaean presence, but also by the internal evolution of Iberian society, which created a demand that the Phocaean traders could fulfill.

For a century and a half, Phocaean trade dominated the eastern coast of the Iberian Peninsula. From the fifth century BCE, however, a new important economic agent appeared: Punic Ebusus, which eventually became a large city (up to 30 ha), comparable to Massalia. During the fifth century BCE Ebusus had developed an intensive agrarian colonization of Ibiza – a comparatively large territory of 570 km^2 – most likely aimed at the production of wine and oil. These products were exported in large quantities to the Iberian coast during the fourth and third centuries BCE; in addition, during the third century BCE, an increasingly substantial number of Carthaginian amphorae were also imported, while their Massalian homologues practically disappeared. It should be noted, however, that Attic tableware continued arriving in large numbers; when it faded, toward the end of the fourth century BCE, the black-glaze vases produced in Rhode took its place. Put another way, while the amphorae in the Iberian settlements are essentially Punic, most tableware is Greek. This pattern indicates the absence of closed commercial areas based on "ethnic" criteria. This impression is further enhanced by the fact that Punic amphorae are also very frequent at both Emporion and Rhode (Sanmartí Grego et al. 1995; Puig and Martin 2006). One final clue in this regard is the fact that Emporitan coinage progressively diverged from Massalia's from the fifth century BCE, to adapt to the Punic weight systems; what is more, during the third century BCE, Emporion minted coins with the symbol of a still horse, a Punic type par excellence (García-Bellido 1994). Moreover, epigraphic evidence from the El Sec shipwreck (Majorca) indicates that Punic-speaking traders participated in the distribution of Attic pottery (De Hoz 1987b). Everything suggests, therefore, that in this period, Ebusus and the Phocaean cities in Iberia worked as partners rather than as commercial rivals, if only because their commodities did not enter into competition, since, as already said, Emporion and Rhode did not base their economies on the export of their own agricultural products.

Regarding the Phocaean–Etruscan relationship, Bats, as already mentioned, has proposed that Massalia had an important role in the distribution of Etruscan vases and tableware in Mediterranean Gaul. This hypothesis is plausible, since the Phocaeans traded very diverse goods that they often did not produce themselves. However, the discovery of shipwrecks with purely Etruscan cargos, such as the Grand Ribaud, indicates that there probably was not a closed Massalian commercial area. This is particularly clear after the discovery at the indigenous port of Lattara, near Montpellier (Eastern Languedoc), of early fifth-century BCE houses attributable to Etruscan merchants (Py et al. 2006). Again, coexistence and even cooperation between traders of different origins seems to be the rule.

The Phocaeans and the Indigenous Populations

As in other Mediterranean areas, the study of Greek expansion in the far West has been strongly influenced by a number of preconceptions about the putative "civilizing role" of the Greeks and their alleged ability to induce deep transformations of the social, economic, and political structures of the societies with which they came into contact (see more fully Chapters 2–6, this volume). This view rests on the idea, firmly rooted in the minds of the European elites, that Greek culture is unique, superior, and the foundation of "Western" civilization. The pride for her Greek origin explains, for example, the magnificent celebration of the 20-century anniversary of the founding of Marseille in 1899. The same holds true for the beginning of the excavations at Emporion, in 1908. These were backed and published by the Institute for Catalan Studies (the National Academy of Catalonia), created one year earlier in order to place Catalan culture at the level of major European cultures. The central role of the notion of "Hellenization" of indigenous peoples is also evident in the famous article by Jacobsthal and Neuffer "Gallia Graeca. Recherches sur l'hellénisation de la Provence" (1933), which inspired shortly thereafter the well-known *Hispania Graeca* by García y Bellido (1948).

Beyond the idiosyncratic aspects, different scholars on both sides of the Pyrenees have also held that Greek influence was a prominent factor of sociocultural change for the indigenous peoples. That is more clearly expressed by Maluquer de Motes. For him the Greeks encouraged production among the indigenous societies, accompanied by an increase in "acquisitive power," social hierarchy, and urbanization. Consequently, the rise of sociocultural complexity was not the outcome of the internal development of indigenous societies, which were conceived as essentially static (Maluquer de Motes 1966). More recently, Domínguez has proposed a form of Greek colonialism close to modern dependency theory, in which the exploitation of the "colonized" population would have been carried out through the indigenous elites, and would have been based on the desire to emulate the (supposedly) hegemonic Greek culture on the part of these; nevertheless, incomplete integration of Greek cultural features would indicate some degree of resistance by the "colonized" (Domínguez 2002, 67–86). The following paragraphs briefly consider these questions from another perspective, starting with a really crucial issue: power relations between Greek and indigenous societies.

It is evident that the Greeks did not subjugate the indigenous peoples of the areas under study. Massalia itself was surrounded by a chain of *oppida* that clearly indicate the limits of its *chora*. Literary sources, especially Justin, confirm this image of a scrutinized and controlled city. Thus, the Massalians controlled the town's access "in peacetime as if they were at war" (Just. 4.3.4). The same author indicates that they fought "great wars with the Gauls and Ligurians," and that by the early fourth century BCE, Massalia was besieged by local peoples. Both archaeological and written evidence indicate that violence was particularly intense during the second century BCE (Dietler 2010, 173–177). It is no surprise, then, that two inscriptions attest the existence of the *ephebeia*, a form of military service, or that Massalia hired Gaulish mercenaries.

It is also clear that neither Emporion nor the Massalian *epiteichismata* could ever have dominated the demographically much more powerful indigenous populations that surrounded them, particularly in Iberia, where strong, centralized polities existed. All this suggests that their relations with the natives must have been peaceful in general, dominated mainly by the common interest of maintaining mutually beneficial transactions; at least in the case of Emporion, they would also be facilitated by the already mentioned ethnic ties.

This brings us to the second issue, namely Greek influence in the emergence of sociocultural complexity among the indigenous societies. The answer is probably different on either side of the Pyrenees. In Iberia, these processes were largely the result of population growth experienced during the early first millennium. This caused the conditions necessary for the emergence of hierarchical *big men*-type societies, whose formation was certainly encouraged by the access to prestige goods offered by the Phoenicians in the seventh century BCE, well before the installation of the Phocaeans at Emporion. The formation of the first urban settlements in Iberia dates back to the mid-second half of the sixth century BCE, shortly after the creation of the *emporion* at Sant Martí d'Empúries, and is obviously unconnected with it (Sanmartí 2014).

In Mediterranean Gaul, on the contrary, demographic growth, sedentary lifestyle, and nucleated settlement developed after the foundation of Massalia, which has led one to suppose the existence of a cause and effect relationship between the processes, and to deny (or to sharply nuance) the role of internal evolution of the indigenous societies: the formation of the "*oppida* civilization" would have been fundamentally the result of changes in the indigenous productive system in order to feed trade with Massalia; in other words, a foreign-induced economic shift would account for population increase and the development of social hierarchy (Py 2012, 133–135; Garcia 2004, 76–80).

Regarding the supposed Hellenization of indigenous peoples, there is no evidence to suggest their assimilation to the Greek (or, for that matter, Punic) culture on either side of the Pyrenees. The acquisition of Greek vases has sometimes been regarded as an indication of acculturation, but, as already stated, these objects were selectively used in indigenous communities according to their own social and cultural patterns, and/or the political purposes of the elites. Suffice it to compare the wide range of Attic pottery shapes used at Emporion (Miró 2006) and Massalia (Gantès 2000) – which is consistent with a Greek lifestyle – with the limited assortment, mostly drinking gear, attested in the indigenous sites (Picazo 1977; different contributions in Sabattini 2000). It is obvious that these objects do not reflect any desire to emulate Greek cultural practices, but were used by the local elites to strengthen social differentiation.

Similar conclusions may be drawn from the analysis of culinary practices. Indigenous cooking instruments are remarkably uniform throughout the area under study; they indicate ways of preparing food presumably different from those of the Greeks. The cooking pot, functionally comparable to Greek *chytrai*, is the most common shape, but there are no indigenous open forms similar to the *càccabos* or the *lopas*, so common from the fifth century BCE in both the Greek and the Punic areas. However, from the fourth century BCE some *càccaboi* are attested in Iberian contexts, generally made locally; besides, during the third century BCE small amounts of cooking vessels made in Carthage are also imported. It is possible, therefore, that from the fourth century BCE some exotic – Greek or Punic – culinary practices were adopted, which is consistent with the increasing importance of dishes among the black-glaze imported pottery (Principal-Ponce 1998). Nevertheless, these vases always constitute a small fraction of the kitchenware, and their presence is documented mainly in sites that for independent reasons may be regarded as centers of aristocratic power. Again, this suggests a selective adoption of certain cultural practices by the dominant social sectors in order to emphasize their high rank, and perhaps to underline their connection to the outside world (Sanmartí 2015).

Similarly, there is no evidence to support linguistic Hellenization. Not only was the Greek language not adopted by the indigenous peoples, but not a single Greek borrowing (nor any Greek personal name) has been attested in the otherwise large number of Iberian texts that have survived, and only a few have been identified in the immediate periphery of Massalia (De Hoz 1999, 230). Of course, there were some (at least) bilingual persons (De Hoz 1999), but they seemingly did not introduce any foreign terms into the local languages.

As for the possible adoption of Greek religious practices, there is some evidence that needs to be discussed, in particular from Ullastret, a large Iberian site, located only 15 km from Emporion. Ullastret was the center of an important regional polity and was inhabited by a socially heterogeneous population that included the local aristocracy. The excavation of the highest part of the site has brought to light three *in antis* Greek-type temples (Casas et al. 2005), with antefixes in the form of *gorgoneia* and negro heads. In addition, two Ebusitan terracotta figurines representing Bes have been found in the site. Nevertheless, the religious life of Ullastret was dominated by indigenous rituals, including such practices so alien to the Greeks as the cult of skulls (Codina et al. 2011). In fact, if we leave aside the temples, Ullastret shows "a stunning coldness towards forms of Greek culture" (De Hoz 1999, 225). It seems plausible, therefore, that the above-mentioned shrines were emporium sanctuaries that placed Greek and Punic traders in a foreign town under the protection and guarantee of the gods. A similar interpretation has been proposed for the Punic-type shrines attested at the Iberian port of Illeta del Campello, near Alicante (García 2003).

Conclusion

The history of the Phocaeans in the far West is still relatively unknown, largely due to the difficulties of reaching the ancient levels of their settlements. However, research carried out in recent decades, especially in Massalia and Emporion, but also at Olbia and Agathe, as well as in a large number of indigenous and Phoenicio-Punic sites that were in constant relation with the Phocaean towns, makes it possible to draw a general picture.

During the first decades of its existence, Massalia was essentially a commercial town, which practiced emporium trade between the two ends of the Mediterranean, reaching as far west as Huelva. However, Massalia soon acquired an agrarian territory, which from ca. 540 BCE onward allowed it to complement its intermediary role with the export of its own production. This consisted mainly of wine that was traded to Italy and particularly to the coast of Gaul and Iberia, where it was distributed through the Phocaean *emporion* at Sant Martí d'Empúries and other indigenous ports like Arles, Pech Maho, the *Saiganthe* mentioned in the letter from Emporion, Ullastret, Illeta dels Banyets, and still others that are labeled with Greek names in the written sources (Mainake or Hemeroscopeion). Closeness between the indigenous population and Greek traders and artisans – including probably sculptors – was one of the main characteristics of these outposts.

From the fifth century BCE this situation progressively changed and two distinct areas emerged. On the one hand, Massalia consolidated its territory and its trade on the Gaulish coast, to the point of creating a kind of maritime empire based on its navy and a string of small military colonies. On the other hand, Emporion and Rhode, the two small independent cities of the Gulf of Roses, still based their economy on emporium trade and the export of the black-glaze pottery made at Rhode. From the fourth century BCE they were progressively integrated in the area of economic influence of Ebusus, another large city that somehow mirrors for the Iberian Peninsula the economic role of Massalia.

This regional status quo remained stable for two centuries and was altered only by events that were external to this area, namely the struggle between Rome and Carthage for supremacy over the western Mediterranean. In these circumstances, the Phocaean towns remained faithful to their traditional friendship with Rome, but the outcome of the conflict represented the start of a new era for the whole region. For Massalia, it involved enlarging her territories, but also an increased dependence on Roman help in her struggle against the indigenous peoples. In addition, its economic base was severely disrupted by the rapid growth of Italic trade in the far West, a fate from which Punic Ebusus did not completely escape either, with the very same consequences.

After this turning point, all the ancient Phocaean towns continued under Roman rule, but they no longer had the specific roles considered in this book. For four centuries they had been major actors, with their Punic homologues, in the history of the far western Mediterranean, not least in that they provided the indigenous societies valuable elements to build and reproduce their unequal social systems, but this did not translate into the adoption of significant traits of Hellenic culture by the local populations. This is probably due to the fact that local elites may have regarded foreign traders as a potential danger for their social status quo, and must have controlled their activities by limiting contact to specific sites under local elite command, that is, in "ports of trade" in the very Polanyian sense of the term; some of these, frequently designated as *emporia*, have been more or less clearly identified (see Rouillard's, Vives-Ferrándiz's, Plana-Mallart's and Gailledrat's contributions in Gailledrat, Dietler and Plana-Mallart 2018). Consequently, it is disputable that the indigenous peoples assumed a subaltern role, or that there was any kind of Greek "cultural hegemony" which enabled the "colonizers" to exert pressure on the "colonized" Iberian elites to guarantee the supply of local commodities (Domínguez 2002, 67, 70). In other words, the natives were not in a position of dependence, exploitation, or marginalization comparable to that imposed by ancient (Carthage or Syracuse, for example) and modern colonialism, or, more recently, by the process of globalization following World War II. I have avoided the terms "colonialism" and "colony" to describe the nature of the Phocaean sites and the relationship they entertained with the indigenous populations of the far western Mediterranean, because they do not adequately describe the actual situation (for a discussion on this conceptual and terminological matter, see, among others, Owen 2005; Hodos 2006, 9–22; Rouillard 2009, 134–135; De Angelis 2010, 19–22; Dietler 2010, 15–24; Costanzi, Chapter 1, this volume). Either way, continued contact caused what Dietler has adequately labeled as "entanglement" between both sides: even Massalia, which clung on to strictly Hellenic (and to some extent specifically Phocaean) traditions, shared some aspects of the indigenous culture (Dietler 2010, 110–111). This must have been particularly true in the cultural interface represented by the small Phocaean towns and the string of indigenous ports of trade along the Iberian and Gaulish coasts. There, reciprocal accommodation and the construction of a mutually comprehensible world (Malkin 2002) took place in ways the adequate understanding of which will be an important point of the research agenda for the coming years.

REFERENCES

Almagro, Martín. 1955. *Las necrópolis de Ampurias. Monografías Ampuritanas*, 3, vol. 2. Barcelona: Seix y Barral.

Aquilué, Xavier, Pere Castanyer, Marta Santos, and Joaquim Tremoleda. 2010. "Grecs et indigenes aux origines de l'enclave phocéenne d'Emporion." In Tréziny 2010a, 65–78.

Arcelin, Patrice, Michel Bats, Dominique Garcia, et al. 1995. *Sur les pas des grecs en Occident… Hommages à André Nickels. Collection Études Massaliètes*, 4. Paris and Lattes: Éditions Errance and A.D.A.M.

Aubet, María E. 2005. "Mainake: The Legend and the New Archaeological Evidence." In *Mediterranean Urbanization 800–600 BC*, Proceedings of the British Accademy, 126, edited by Robin Osborne and Barry Cunliffe, 187–202. Oxford: Oxford University Press.

Bats, Michel. 1988. *Vaisselle et alimentation à Olbia de Provence (v. 350–v. 50 av. J.-C.). Modèles culturels et catégories céramiques*. Paris: Éditions du Centre National de la Recherche Scientifique.

Bats, Michel. 1998. "Marseille archaïque. Étrusques et Phocéens en Méditerranée occidentale." *Mélanges de l'École Française de Rome: Antiquité*, 110: 609–633.

Bats, Michel. 2000. "Les Grecs en Gaule au premier Âge du Fer et le commerce emporique en Méditerranée occidentale." In *Mailhac et le Premier Âge du Fer en Europe occidentale. Hommages à Odette et Jean Taffanel. Actes du colloque international de Carcassonne, Monographies d'Archéologie Méditerranéenne 7*, edited by Thierry Janin, 244–248. Lattes: Publications de l'UMR 154 du CNRS.

Bats, Michel. 2004. "Les colonies massaliètes de Gaule méridionale. Sources et modèles d'un urbanisme militaire aux IV–IIIe s. av. J.-C." In *Des Ibères aux Vénètes*, Collection de l'École française de Rome, 328, edited by Sandrine Agusta-Boularot and Xavier Lafon, 51–64. Rome: École française de Rome.

Bertucchi, Guy. 1992. "Nécropoles et terrasses funéraires à l'époque grecque. Bilan sommaire des recherches." In *Marseille grecque et la Gaule, Collection Études Massaliètes*, 3, edited by Michel Bats, Guy Bertucchi, Gaétan Congès, and Henri Tréziny, 123–137. Lattes and Aix-en-Provence: A.D.A.M. and P.U.P.

Boissinot, Philippe. 2010. "Des vignobles de Saint-Jean du Désert aux cadastres antiques de Marseille." In Tréziny 2010a, 147–154.

Cabrera, Paloma. 1995. "Cerámicas griegas en Tartessos: su significado en la costa meridional de la Península, desde Málaga a Huelva." In *Tartessos 25 años después (1968–1993). Actas del Congreso Conmemorativo del V Symposium de Prehistoria Peninsular (Jerez de la Frontera, 1993)*, Biblioteca de Urbanismo y Cultura, 14, edited by D. Ruiz Mata, 387–399. Jerez: Ayuntamiento de Jerez.

Cabrera, Paloma, and Carmen Sánchez, eds. 2000. *Los Griegos en España: tras las huellas de Heracles*. Madrid: Ministerio de Educación y Cultura.

Casas, Sandra, Ferran Codina Falgàs, Joan Margall, et al. 2005. "Els temples de l'*oppidum* d'Ullastret. Aportacions al seu coneixement." In *Món ibèric als Països Catalans*, XIII Col·loqui Internacional d'Arqueologia de Puigcerdà, vol. 2, edited by Oriol Mercadal Fernández, 989–1001. Puigcerdà: Institut d'Estudis Ceretans.

Chapa, Teresa. 1989. *Influjos griegos en la escultura zoomorfa ibérica*. Colección Iberia Graeca. Serie Arqueológica, 1. Madrid: Consejo Superior de Investigaciones Científicas.

Codina, Ferran, Aurora Martin, Gabriel de Prado, and Bibiana Agustí. 2011. "Ullastret." In *Des rites et des hommes. Les pratiques symboliques des Celtes, des Ibères et des Grecs en Provence, en Languedoc et en Catalogne*, Collection Archéologie de Montpellier Agglomération, 2, edited by Réjane Roure and Lionel Pernet, 158–163. Paris: Éditions Errance.

Croissant, Francis, and Pierre Rouillard. 1996. "Le problème de l'art 'gréco-ibère': état de la question." In *Formes archaïques et arts ibériques*, Collection de la Casa de Velázquez, 59, edited by Ricardo Olmos and Pierre Rouillard, 55–66. Madrid: Casa de Velázquez.

De Angelis, Franco. 2010. "Ancient Greek Colonization in the 21st Century: Some Suggested Directions." In *International Congress of Classical Archaeology: Meetings between Cultures in the Ancient Mediterranean (Roma 2008), Bollettino di Archeologia online*, I, Volume Speciale, 18–30. Ministero per i Beni e la Attività Culturali. http://bollettinodiarcheologiaonline.beniculturali.it/wp-content/uploads/2019/01/5_DEANGELIS.pdf (accessed December 15, 2019).

Dedet, Bernard, and Martine Schwaller. 2018. *Grecs en Gaule du Sud: Tombes de la colonie d'Agathè (Agde. Hérault, Ive–IIe siècles avant J.-C.)*. Collection Études Massaliètes, 15. Aix-en-Provence: Éditions Errance.

De Hoz, Javier. 1987a. "La escritura greco-ibérica." *Studia Paleohispanica: Actas del IV Coloquio sobre lenguas y culturas paleohispánicas, Veleia*, 2–3: 285–298.

De Hoz, Javier. 1987b. "La epigrafía del Sec y los grafitos comerciales en Occidente." In *El barco de El Sec (Costa de Calvià, Mallorca). Estudio de los materiales*, edited by Antonio Arribas, Maria Gloria Trías, Damián Cerdá, and Javier de Hoz, 605–655. Mallorca: Ajuntament de Calvià and Universitat de les Illes Balears.

De Hoz, Javier. 1999. "Identité-différentiation au travers des témoignages linguistiques et alphabétiques: le monde celtique et ibère." In *Confini e frontiera nella grecità d'Occidente. Atti del trentasettesimo convegno di studi sulla Magna Grecia*, edited by Attilio Stazio and Stefania Ceccoli, 213–246. Taranto: Istituto per la Storia e l'Archeologia della Magna Grecia.

Delgado, A. 2008. "'Colonialismos' fenicios en el sur de Iberia: historias precedentes y modos de contacto." In *De Tartessos a Manila. Siete estudios coloniales y poscoloniales*, edited by Glòria Cano and Ana Delgado, 19–49. Valencia: Universitat de València.

Dietler, Michael. 2010. *Archaeologies of Colonialism: Consumption, Entanglement, and Violence in Ancient Mediterranean France*. Berkeley: University of California Press.

Dietler, Michael, and Carolina López-Ruiz, eds. 2009. *Colonial Encounters in Ancient Iberia: Phoenician, Greek, and Indigenous Relations*. Chicago: Chicago University Press.

Domínguez, Adolfo. 1990. "La ciudad griega de Rhode en Iberia y la cuestión de su vinculación con Rodas." *Boletín de la Asociación Española de Amigos de la Arqueología*, 28: 13–25.

Domínguez, Adolfo. 2002. "Greeks in Iberia: Colonialism without Colonization." In *The Archaeology of Colonialism*, edited by Claire L. Lyons and John K. Papadopoulos, 65–95. Los Angeles: Getty Research Institute.

Domínguez, Adolfo. 2009–2011. "Los foceos y sus ciudades, entre Jonia, la Magna Grecia y el Occidente. Diversidad material e identidad étnica." *Empúries*, 51: 9–24.

Freyer-Schauenburg, Brigitte. 1966. "Kolaios und die westphönizischen Elfenbeine." *Madrider Mitteilungen*, 7: 89–108.

Gailledrat, Éric, Michael Dietler, and Rosa Plana-Mallart, eds. 2018. *The Emporion in the Ancient Western Mediterranean*. Montpellier: Presses universitaires de la Méditerranée.

Gantès, Lucien-François. 2000. "La place de la céramique attique dans une cité grecque de l'Extrême-Occident au IVe s.: l'exemple de Marseille." In Sabattini 2000, 131–144.

Garcia, Dominique 1995. "Le territoire d'Agde grecque et l'occupation du sol en Languedoc central durant l'Âge du Fer." In Arcelin et al. 1995, 137–167.

Garcia, Dominique. 2004. *La Celtique méditerranéenne. Habitats et societies en Languedoc et Provence VIIIe–IIe siècles av. J.-C.* Paris: Editions Errance.

García, Josep Miquel. 2003. *La distribución de cerámica griega en la Contestania ibérica: el puerto comercial de La Illeta dels Banyets*. Alicante: Instituto Alicantino de Cultura "Juan Gil-Albert."

García y Bellido, Antonio. 1948. *Hispania Graeca*. 3 vols. Barcelona: Instituto Español de Estudios Mediterráneos.

García-Bellido, María Paz. 1994. "Las relaciones económicas entre Massalia, Emporion y Gades a través de la moneda." In *Iberos y griegos: lecturas desde la diversidad, Huelva*

Arqueológica, vol. 13.2, edited by Paloma Cabrera, Ricardo Olmos, and Enric Sanmartí, 115–149. Huelva: Excma. Diputación provincial de Huelva.

Gener Basallote, María Auxiliadora, María de los Ángeles Navarro García, Juan-Miguel Pajuelo Sáez, et al. 2014. "Arquitectura y urbanismo de la Gadir fenicia: el yacimiento del 'Teatro Cómico' de Cádiz." In *Los fenicios en la bahía de Cádiz. Nuevas investigaciones*, Collezione di Studi Fenici 46, edited by Massimo Botto, 14–50. Pisa: Consiglio Nazionale delle Ricerche.

Gómez Bellard, Carlos, and Pierre Guérin. 1994. "La production du vin dans l'Espagne préromaine." In *Els productes alimentaris d'origen vegetal a l'edat del Ferro de l'Europa Occidental: De la producció al consum*, Sèrie Monogràfica, 18, edited by Ramon Buxó and Enriqueta Pons, 379–387. Girona: Museu d'Arqueologia de Catalunya-Girona.

González de Canales, Fernando, Leonardo Serrano, and Jorge Llompart. 2006. "The Pre-Colonial Phoenician Emporium of Huelva ca. 900–770 BC." *BABesch*, 81: 13–29.

Hermary, Antoine. 2000. "Les naïskoi votifs de Marseille." In Tréziny 2010a, 119–133.

Hermary, Antoine, Antoinette Hesnard, and Henri Tréziny. 1999. *Marseille grecque: la cité phocéenne (600–49 av. J.-C.)*. Paris: Editions Errance.

Hodos, Tamar. 2006. *Local Responses to Colonization in the Iron Age Mediterranean*. London: Routledge.

Jacobstahl, Paul, and Eduard Neuffer. 1933. "*Gallia Graeca*. Recherches sur l'hellénisation de la Provence." *Préhistoire*, 2: 1–64.

Kaiser, Alan. 2000. "Ethnic Identity and Urban Fabric: The Case of the Greeks at Empúries, Spain." *Journal of Mediterranean Archaeology*, 13(2): 189–203.

Long, Luc, Jordi Miró, and Giuliano Volpe. 1992. "Les épaves archaïques de la pointe Lequin (Porquerolles, Hyères, Var). Des données nouvelles sur le commerce de Marseille à la fin du VIe s. et dans la première moitié du Ve s. av. J.-C." In *Marseille grecque et la Gaule, Collection Études Massaliètes*, 3, edited by Michel Bats, Guy Bertucchi, Gaétan Congès, and Henri Tréziny, 199–234. Lattes and Aix-en-Provence: A.D.A.M.

Malkin, Irad. 2002. "A Colonial Middle Ground: Greek, Etruscan, and Local Elites in the Bay of Naples." In *The Archaeology of Colonialism*, edited by Claire L. Lyons and John K. Papadopoulos, 151–181. Los Angeles: Getty Research Institute.

Maluquer de Motes, Juan. 1966. *El impacto colonial griego y el comienzo de la vida urbana en Cataluña*. Barcelona: Consejo Superior de Investigaciones Científicas.

Maluquer de Motes, Juan. 1971. "En torno a las fuentes griegas sobre el origen de Rhode." In *Simposio Internacional de Colonizaciones*, edited by Eduardo Ripoll Perelló and Enric Sanmartí Grego, 125–138. Barcelona: Diputación Provincial de Barcelona.

Marcet, Roger, and Enric Sanmartí Grego. 1989. *Empúries*. Barcelona: Diputació de Barcelona.

Mierse, William E. 1994. "Ampurias: The Urban Development of a Graeco-Roman City in the Iberian Coast." *Latomus*, 53: 790–805.

Miró, M. Teresa. 2006. *La ceràmica àtica de figures roges de la ciutat grega d'Emporion*. Monografies Emporitanes, 14. Barcelona: Museu d'Arqueologia de Catalunya Empúries.

Moliner, Manuel. 2013. "La terre des ancêtres: à propos des nécropoles antiques de Marseille." In *L'Occident grec de Marseille à Mégara Hybaea. Hommages à Henri Tréziny*, Bibliothèque d'Archéologie Méditerranéenne et Africaine 13, edited by Sophie

Bouffier and Antoine Hermary, 35–55. Arles and Aix-en-Provence: Editions Errance and Centre Camille Jullian.

Morel, Jean-Paul. 2006a. "Les étrusques en Méditerranée nord-occidentale: résultats et tendances des recherches récentes." In *Gli Etruschi da Genova ad Ampurias. Atti del XXIV Convegno di Studi Etruschi ed Italici, Marseille-Lattes, 2002*, edited by Stefano Gori and Maria-Chiara Bettini, 23–45. Pisa: Istituti Editoriali e Poligrafici Internazionali.

Morel, Jean-Paul. 2006b. "De Marseille à Velia: problèmes phocéens." *Comptes rendus de l'Académie des Inscriptions*, 150(4): 1723–1783.

Moret, Pierre. 2010. "La diffusion du village clos dans le Nord-Est de la péninsule ibérique et le problème architectural de la *palaia polis* d'*Emporion*." In Tréziny 2010a, 329–332.

Niemeyer, Hans Georg. 1979–1980. "A la búsqueda de Mainake. El conflicto entre los testimonios arqueológicos y escritos." *Habis*, 10–11: 279–302.

Nieto, Xavier, and Marta Santos. 2009. *El vaixell grec arcaic de Cala Sant Vicenç*. Monografies del CASC, 7. Girona: Museu d'Arqueologia de Catalunya. Centre d'Arqueologia Subaquàtica de Catalunya.

Osborne, Robin. 1998. "Early Greek Colonization? The Nature of Greek Settlement in the West." In *Archaic Greece: New Approaches and New Evidence*, edited by Nick Fisher and Hans van Wees, 251–269. London: Duckworth with The Classical Press of Wales.

Owen, Sara. 2005. "Analogy, Archaeology and Archaic Greek Colonization." In *Ancient Colonizations: Analogy, Similarity and Difference*, edited by Henry Hurst and Sara Owen, 5–22. London: Duckworth.

Pena, María José. 2006. "Fuentes literarias sobre la colonia griega de *Rhode* (Iberia)." In Puig and Martin 2006, 41–52.

Picazo, Marina. 1977. *Las cerámicas áticas de Ullastret*. Barcelona: Universidad de Barcelona.

Plana-Mallart, Rosa. 2012. "La présence grecque et ses effets dans le Nord-Est de la péninsule ibérique (VIIe-début du IVe siècle av. n. è.)." *Pallas*, 89: 157–178.

Principal-Ponce, Jordi. 1998. *Las importaciones de vajilla fina de barniz negro en la Cataluña sur y occidental durante el siglo III aC*. BAR International Series, 729. Oxford: Archaeopress.

Puig, Anna M. 2010. "Rhodé (c. 375–195 av. J.-C.)." In Tréziny 2010a, 79–88.

Puig, Anna M., and Aurora Martin. 2006. *La colònia grega de Rhode (Roses, Alt Empordà)*. Sèrie Monogràfica, 23. Girona: Museu d'Arqueologia de Catalunya.

Py, Michel. 2012. *Les Gaulois du Midi. De la fin de l'Âge du Bronze à la conquête romaine*. Paris: Errance.

Py, Michel, Denis Lebeaupin, Pierre Séjalon, and Réjane Roure. 2006. "Les Étrusques et *Lattara*: nouvelles données." In *Gli Etruschi da Genova ad Ampurias. Atti del XXIV Convegno di Studi Etruschi ed Italici, Marseille-Lattes, 2002*, edited by Stefano Gori and Maria-Chiara Bettini, 583–608. Pisa: Istituti Editoriali e Poligrafici Internazionali.

Ramon, Joan 2006. "La proyección comercial mediterránea y atlántica de los centros fenicios malagueños en época arcaica." *Mainake*, 28: 189–212.

Ripollès, Pere-Pau. 1989. "Fraccionarias ampuritanas. Estado de la cuestión." *Archivo de Prehistoria Levantina*, 19: 303–317.

Rouillard, Pierre. 1991. *Les Grecs et la Péninsule Ibérique du VIIIe au IVe siècle avant Jésus-Christ*. Paris: Publications du Centre Pierre Paris.

Rouillard, Pierre. 1999. "Entre Marseille et Huelva." In *La colonisation grecque en Méditerranée occidentale*, Collection de l'École française de Rome, 251, 83–92. Rome: École française de Rome.

Rouillard, Pierre. 2009. "Greeks and the Iberian Peninsula: Forms of Exchange and Settlement." In Dietler and López-Ruiz 2009, 131–151.

Sabattini, Brigitte. 2000. *La céramique attique du IVe siècle en Méditerranée occidentale*. Collection du Centre Jean Bérard, 19. Naples: Centre Jean Bérard.

Sanmartí, Joan. 2009. "Colonial Relations and Social Change in Iberia (Seventh to Third Centuries BC)." In Dietler and López-Ruiz 2009, 49–88.

Sanmartí, Joan. 2014. "Long-term Social Change in Iron Age Northern Iberia (ca. 700–200 BC)." In *The Cambridge Prehistory of the Bronze and Iron Age Mediterranean*, vol. 1, edited by Peter van Dommelen and Bernard Knapp, 107–137. Cambridge: Cambridge University Press.

Sanmartí, Joan. 2015. "Interactions coloniales, cuisine et formes de consommation en Ibérie septentrionale." In *Contacts et acculturations en Méditerranée occidentale. Hommages à Michel Bats*, Bibliothèque d'Archéologie Méditerranéenne et Africaine, 15, edited by Réjane Roure, 171–183. Aix-en-Provence: Éditions Errance.

Sanmartí Grego, Enric. 1990. "Una carta en lengua ibérica, escrita sobre plomo, procedente de Emporion." *Revue Archéologique de Narbonnaise*, 21: 95–113.

Sanmartí Grego, Enric. 1992. "*Massalia* et *Emporion*: une origine commune, deux destins différents." In *Marseille grecque et la Gaule, Collection Études Massaliètes*, 3, edited by Michel Bats, Guy Bertucchi, Gaétan Congès, and Henri Tréziny, 27–41. Lattes and Aix-en-Provence: A.D.A.M.

Sanmartí Grego, Enric. 1993. "Els íbers a *Emporion* (segles VI–III a. C.)." *Laietània*, 8: 87–101.

Sanmartí Grego, Enric, and Rosa A. Santiago. 1988. "La lettre grecque d'Emporion et son contexte archéologique." *Revue Archéologique de Narbonnaise*, 21: 3–17.

Sanmartí Grego, Enric, Pere Castanyer, Joaquim Tremoleda, and Marta Santos. 1995. "Amphores grecques et traffics commerciaux en Méditerranée occidentale au IVe s. av. J.-C." In Arcelin et al. 1995, 31–37.

Santos, Marta, Pere Castanyer, and Joaquim Tremoleda. 2013. "Emporion arcaica: los ritmos y las fisonomías de los dos establecimientos originarios, a partir de los últimos datos arqueológicos." In *L'Occident grec de Marseille à Mégara Hybaea. Hommages à Henri Tréziny*, Bibliothèque d'Archéologie Méditerranéenne et Africaine 13, edited by Sophie Bouffier and Antoine Hermary, 103–113. Arles and Aix-en-Provence: Editions Errance and Centre Camille Jullian.

Torres, Mariano. 2002. *Tartessos*. Bibliotheca Archaeologica Hispana, 14. Madrid: Real Academia de la Historia.

Tréziny, Henri. 2000. "Les lieux de culte dans Marseille grecque." In *Les cultes des cités phocéennes, Études Massaliètes*, 6, edited by Antoine Hermary and Henri Tréziny, 81–99. Aix-en-Provence: Édisud and Centre Camille Jullian.

Tréziny, Henri. 2009–2011. "Marseille antique. Topographie, urbanisme, architecture." *Empúries*, 56: 41–54.

Tréziny, Henri, ed. 2010a. *Grecs et Indigènes de la Catalogne à la Mer Noire. Bibliothèque d'Archéologie Méditerranéenne et Africaine 3.* Paris and Aix-en-Provence: Éditions Errance and Centre Camille Jullian.

Tréziny, Henri. 2010b. "Note sur les céramiques indigènes présentes à Marseille." In Tréziny 2010a, 509.

Velaza, Javier. 2003. "La epigrafía ibérica emporitana: bases para una reconsideración." *Palaeohispanica*, 3: 179–192.

FURTHER READING

There is no authored book dealing with the Greek expansion in the Mediterranean far West on a global scale, but see Domínguez (2009–2011) for an up-to-date summary. Dietler (2010) is an excellent synthesis for Mediterranean Gaul, resting on a solid conceptual basis derived from postcolonial theory. Rouillard (1991) provides the only general authored book, now somewhat dated, about the Greeks in the Iberian Peninsula. Cabrera and Sanchez (2000) is a collection of articles by various specialists who provide a general view on the Greek presence in the Iberian Peninsula. Dietler and Lopez-Ruiz (2009) completes the previous title with an important selection of papers on different aspects of cultural contact in pre-Roman times. Tréziny (2010a) includes a large number of contributions that update the state of knowledge of many aspects of the Greek presence in the far West. Hermary, Hesnard, and Tréziny (1999) is a very good summary, beautifully illustrated, on the history and archaeology of Phocaean Marseille; however, it should be supplemented with Tréziny (2009–2011). Marcet and Sanmartí Grego (1989) is still, although slightly dated, the best overview on Emporion, very well illustrated. Garcia (2004) and Py (2012) provide current overviews on the indigenous cultures of Mediterranean Gaul and their relationship with the Etruscans and Greeks. Sanmartí (2009) summarizes current knowledge of the Iberians and their relations with Greek and Phoenicio-Punic communities. Gailledrat, Dietler, and Plana-Mallart (2018) includes updated papers on the *emporion* and also on the *emporia* of Mediterranean Gaul and the Iberian Peninsula.

CHAPTER NINETEEN

The Northern Aegean

Despoina Tsiafaki

Not all Greeks or the regions to which they migrated have received the same level of modern scholarly attention. Greeks in the western Mediterranean, for example, are much better known than are Greeks in the northern Aegean. Nevertheless, the northern Aegean forms a historically significant chapter in particular for Greeks from the mainland to the south, Ionia, and the islands in between (Map 19.1).

Five main questions are addressed in this chapter. Which Greeks settled the northern Aegean? Was this settlement part of individual and/or common efforts? Why did Greeks settle here and what types of settlement did they establish? How did these settlements change from the Archaic to Hellenistic periods? What kinds of interactions did Greeks have with the non-Greek (or Thracian) inhabitants they encountered, with other Greeks who settled in the northern Aegean, and with the homelands they left behind? In overview, the cultural physiognomy of the northern Aegean Greeks was a matrix of all regional peoples and conditions as they came together and interacted there.

While not easy, answering these pertinent questions requires the ongoing study of, and attention to, our sources. Two main sources to study the Greeks in the northern Aegean exist in the form of scarce ancient authors and archaeological finds. The past 20–30 years have been particularly fruitful, revealing some of the original cultural phenomena we now recognize as northern Aegean. Architectural remains, pottery, coinage, sculpture, and inscriptions, among others, provide clear evidence that Greeks were densely present in the region throughout the periods examined. Our evidence continues to grow for the Thracians and, more recently, for the Phoenicians. Even if the latter are not as well attested, Herodotus (6.47) mentions them searching for metals, singling out the mines of Thasos in particular (Tiverios 2008, 75; Markoe 2000, 173; Lipiński 2004, 160–162). Furthermore, we should not ignore the Persian presence in the northern Aegean (515–479 BC). Persians did not establish towns, but did influence various aspects of life and culture, so far traceable

---

A Companion to Greeks Across the Ancient World, First Edition. Edited by Franco De Angelis.
© 2020 John Wiley & Sons, Inc. Published 2020 by John Wiley & Sons, Inc.

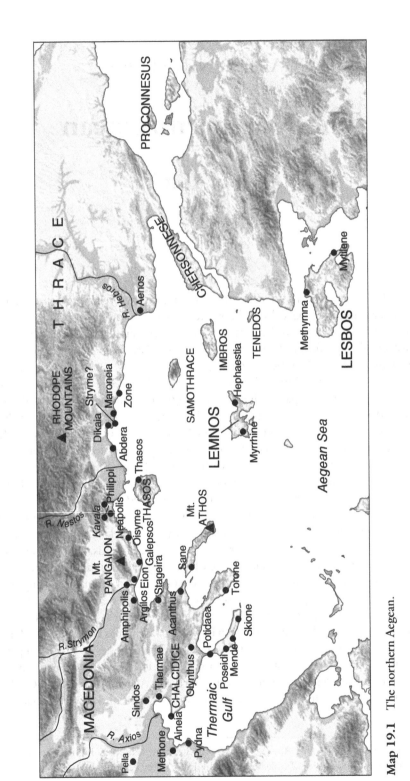

Map 19.1 The northern Aegean.

only indirectly through some limited written and archaeological sources. Nevertheless, the Greco-Persian wars were a significant driver of socioeconomic and political changes, as well as ways of thinking that reconfigured earlier orders and structures in the northern Aegean and, of course, Greece proper. Greek military expeditions and interests shifted to the northern Aegean. Later the Odrysian and Macedonian Kingdoms played important roles, leaving their own indelible mark until incorporated into the Roman Empire.

The Local Inhabitants

The northern Aegean was hardly an unpopulated land before Greeks arrived. Written and archaeological sources prove that settlement was firmly entrenched already from prehistoric times, along with the social systems, ideologies, and cultural customs of their inhabitants. Worth noting is the widespread continuation of many prehistoric settlements down into the historical era (Vlachopoulos and Tsiafaki 2017). The region encompasses Aegean Thrace in the East, the Chalcidice peninsula in the South, and the Thermaic Gulf in the West (corresponding roughly with the seashore part of "Lower Macedonia" in historic times) (Map 19.1). At the time of Greek settlement, the northern Aegean seems to have been populated by different groups, giving it a multicultural character.

Ancient authors refer to this region as inhabited by various pre-Hellenic peoples (Hdt. 7.110–115; Thuc. 2.99.3; Strab. VIIa.1.11.1). Archaeological evidence suggests, on the basis of similar practices and products (such as pottery), the existence of the same or similar peoples. We usually call these prehistoric peoples "locals," to distinguish them from Greek settlers and Macedonians. Even though each community had its own territory, absolute physical boundaries between them are difficult to draw. Primarily organized into groups of tribes (*ethne*), their ethnic identity cannot be identified with certainty. Ancient authors talk about Phrygians and Mygdones who were related to Paiones and Illyrians. The Bottiaioi also lived in the region, and the term was still used even after their expulsion from their homeland by the Macedonians, whereupon they moved to the north of Potidaea in Chalcidice, perhaps already in the seventh century BC. Thucydides (1.65.2) records them in their new land (*Bottike*).

The most mentioned peoples, however, are the Thracians. It is not known whether they were more numerous compared to the others, but they seem to be best known to Greeks. Thracians, until the Macedonian expansion, occupied parts of central and coastal Macedonia, besides Aegean Thrace, as mentioned earlier. Greeks largely encountered and interacted with Thracians, who had the greatest impact on forming their regional cultural identities. Therefore, a brief overview of Thrace and the Thracians is necessary for understanding these cultural dynamics.

According to ancient literary sources, Thracians lived all across the coasts of the northern Aegean and the Black Sea to the Danube River, which formed their northern boundary. The western reaches of this territory, both the land and its rivers (Peneios, Axios, Strymon, and Nestos) were less securely Thracian at times. It is generally accepted that Thracians settled the northern Aegean around the eleventh century BC (Triantafyllos 2017). The Thracians were not a homogeneous group of people, but rather an *ethnos* made up of various tribes. The number and the names of the tribes vary in different sources.

Strabo (7 fr. 48) mentions 22. Herodotus (5.3) calls them the biggest "nation" after the Indians and lists various tribal names, according to their respective territories. The Edoni, Bistones, Kikones, Odomanti, Sapaei, and Satrae are among the best known (Delev 2014). One must never forget, however, that there were many differences in rites, habits, and historic roles among these different Thracian tribes. This is considered to be the primary form of Thracian social organization until it was partially unified under the Thracian Odrysian Kingdom in the fifth century BC.

It should be remembered that the Thracians are chiefly known to us through the literary accounts of others (mainly Greeks). The main focus of these authors was not primarily to describe Thracian history and culture, but rather to provide enough information to set the stage for the issues of direct relevance to them. Consequently, their accounts are haphazard and fragmentary. Archaeology, therefore, takes on extra significance in understanding Thracians. In Aegean Thrace, Thracians mainly occupied the mountainous and lowlands parts of Rhodope and Ismaros close to rivers and water sources. What remains of these communities are fortified citadels, open-air sanctuaries, and cemeteries with their megalithic tombs. Rock carvings with incised linear depictions of human figures, animals, birds, and reptiles, among other symbols, are characteristic and had a magical or apotropaic meaning. Several Thracian settlements are known primarily through ancient authors. One such instance is Pieres between Mt. Symbolon and the Strymon River. Herodotus (7.112) and Thucydides (2.99.3) mention the various towns established here, with Phagres singled out as the most important. Edoni is another instance, with its three known settlements (Ennea Hodoi, Myrkinos, and Drabeskos). In the area around Pangaion, Thracians resided in Prasias Lake in dwellings built on wooden piles, joined to the surrounding land by a narrow wooden bridge (Triantafyllos 2000, 52). The primary activities of those people were livestock raising (sheep, goats, cattle, and horses) and hunting. As agriculturists, Thracians were limited to tiny mountainside fields and the immediate land of their settlements (Triantafyllos 2000, 42–44).

So, unlike elsewhere, Greeks were attracted to the northern Aegean mostly because of its natural resources and geographical position. The region connected the West with the East and the North with the South, especially important in a world of growing connectivity. One of the chief natural assets was the extended forests with their exploitable timber: oak, pine, and, at higher altitudes, fir were widespread in the entire zone. Europe's common pine (*Pinus silvestris*), for example, does not extend any further South than Macedonia, nor silver fir (*Abies alba*), which was the shipbuilder's favorite. Forests and timber also endowed Chalcidice and the Strymon plain. At a time when mobility increasingly characterized Mediterraneans, the high demand for timber suitable for shipbuilding and access to the necessary forests grew in importance. The valleys that were home to these forests also contained diverse environments, including marshland, lakes, meadowlands, and patches of woodlands. In the uplands, conditions did not favor extensive arable farming, but they supported stock-raising. Thracian horses were most popular fauna and were renowned in Greek mythology and history. Cereals, melons, various fruits, and vegetables grew on the coast, as well as the vine for the production of the famous wine of the region (e.g., the Homeric *oinos Ismarikos*). To those should be added other perishable items, such as salt, marine fauna, or animal products, and from the Archaic times onward, olive trees.

The northern Aegean's geology contains some of the most significant mineral resources exploited in the ancient eastern Mediterranean. Metals abounded: iron, copper, silver, and gold are found in various places, with the most characteristic instances being Chalcidice, Mt. Pangaion, the Rhodope area, and Thasos. Chalcidice in particular – because of its fertile plain and wealth in metals and timber – attracted Greeks early on and was a reason for the Peloponnesian War (431–404 BC). Moreover, worth noting is that Athenians named their children after the Echedoros River (present-day Gallikos near Thessaloniki), known for its rich alluvial gold. Mineral resources were among the primary reasons for the Greek presence in the northern Aegean. Nevertheless, we do not have adequate information on how those resources were perceived and exploited in antiquity.

While the region's wealth in metals, timber, and other local products (including slaves) may have been a strong attraction, ease of trade also drew Greeks to the northern Aegean. Promontories, projecting peninsulas, closely situated, advantageous natural ports (such as in the Thermaic Gulf and the Chalcidice), and islands simplified sailing from port to port, even if dangers were never absent. Pydna's harbor was defensible due to its natural features: a long shoreline backed by abrupt bluffs with a gap for easy access to the interior. The way led to a coastal road tending southward and another northward past Methone, Aigai, and onto the Macedonian hinterland. In Aegean Thrace, these natural advantages were more limited, but it is noteworthy how the principal *apoikiai* here (Abdera and Maroneia) were established next to them. Having control of a port was vital for commercial activities. The ease of transport via river and sea routes was always important in the development of civilizations, the northern Aegean being no exception. Coastal zones were connected with their interiors further to the north. The roads along the Strymon River, for example, were one of the possible corridors for northward penetration of Greek arts and crafts (e.g., jewelry). The upper part of Hebros (today Maritsa) was also navigable. Land routes, which connected the western part of the Macedonian Kingdom with the Axios and Echedoros Rivers, as well as with the Thermaic Gulf, would be vital for connecting the coastal settlements with those in the hinterland, providing "access to markets for mountain economies" (Morgan 2009, 28).

Despite the extended scholarly discussion regarding whether the Persian king Xerxes in the early fifth century BC built the road used by him and his troops to march through northern Greece to reach the South (Thessaly and beyond), there is no doubt that there was an inland route (Isaac 1986, 3; Pikoulas 2001, 190–192). Herodotus (7.108–110) is very specific with regard to the existence of regional infrastructure that facilitated Persian travel, which Philip II of Macedonia later took advantage of to create his own road network. Xerxes is known to have built a canal across the Athos peninsula to ensure safe passage of his navy for his invasion of Greece. A bridge crossed the Strymon River (Hdt. 7.22–25), adding further infrastructure to the region, which remained and was exploited long after the expulsion of Persians. The northern Aegean's location along established routes deeply involved it in networks of considerable scale and complexity. The northern Aegean was at the center of communication with particularly Athens (and other points to the south) and the Black Sea, until the late fourth century BC, when these trade routes declined. Thasos, for example, was situated on one of the principal routes between central Greece and the Black Sea, enabling the communication of the southern Greeks and in particular the Athenians. That encouraged the production and export of Thasos's wine, which flourished between about 400 and 250 BC (Tzochev 2016, 250). During this period we witness the emergence of other northern Aegean wine-producing centers, such as Acanthus, Mende, and Samothrace, whose amphoras and their contents were quite popular and widely distributed.

Greeks in the Northern Aegean

This was the context in which Greek settlers arrived in the northern Aegean. Their presence, however, goes back to earlier times, probably long before the establishment of the "official" *apoikiai* starting from the eighth century BC onward. The South already knew of the North in the Bronze Age. Mycenaean finds provide tangible signs of this awareness, while there may be some hints also in the written sources (Tsiafaki 2018). At Torone, for example, the archaeological finds suggest contacts with the rest of the Aegean and represent the earliest Mycenaean pottery fragments found in the northern Aegean (Kambitoglou and Paspalas 2017, 382). The little information, if any at all, for Greek contacts with this region at the beginning of the first millennium BC does not allow much to be said, even though it seems plausible they existed prior to the establishment of the *apoikiai*. The latter, nevertheless, introduced a significant novelty compared to previous centuries, namely permanent occupation and the creation of political and social structures similar to those developed in major cities of the Greek world.

In the Iron Age, Greek presence is documented through literary and archaeological evidence. Before we discuss this in detail, I will summarize its representative characteristics. We may first observe that there was a combination of commercial activities along with the founding of the permanent settlements. Most of them appear to have been coastal cities (see Map 19.1). Even though not all the sites inhabited by Greeks are known yet, they seem to have been in close proximity to one another, mostly oriented toward the Aegean Sea, and close to river mouths, on peninsulas, and/or near good harbors. It is worth noting that even the larger *apoikiai* rarely expanded very far inland to take control of agricultural land or metal resources, implying that maritime orientation remained important and that local people probably had a say in the matter. Abdera might be an exception, since it expanded its territory significantly throughout its history (Kallintzi 2011). After Abdera had securely established itself, it advanced into the Thracian interior and essentially doubled its territory, which originally did not go beyond the Thracian settlement at modern Mandra, marking its presence with the foundation of Bergepolis. The latter lay in a zone that could support intensive cereal crop production and clearly shows the efforts of the Greeks to become established in the region's agricultural heart.

The written sources relate the establishment of various Greek settlements along the seashore extending from the Thermaic Gulf up to the Thracian Chersonese, including the islands of Thasos and Samothrace. Archaeological research, especially that conducted in recent decades, has unearthed parts of the Greek establishments revealing new aspects of their layout. Moreover, it has brought to light a great number of artifacts related to Greek culture, either as original Greek creations or as local imitations and adaptations.

There has been much discussion of Euboeans in the northern Aegean, especially in Chalcidice (Tiverios 2008). Without a doubt, Euboeans are attested in the late eighth century. According to Plutarch (*Aetia Graeca* 293 a–b), Eretrians founded Methone on the coast of Pieria in 733 or 709 BC, after they had been expelled by Corinthians from Corcyra and by their compatriots when they attempted to return home. Thereafter, they made their way to the Thermaic Gulf, to Pieria. Methone is unequivocally described as a Greek city in Ps.-Skylax (*Periplous* 66). Archaeological evidence documents a Neolithic and Bronze Age settlement. It is probable that the Eretrians encountered an already existing community, most likely Thracian Pierians, with whom they coexisted, until the Macedonians expelled them. As a result, the Pierians moved to the east of the Strymon River and named their new settlement Pieris valley (Thuc. 2.99.3). Hence Methone is also known as Thracian Methone, in order to distinguish it from other cities with the same name (Strabo 9.436). After the expulsion of the Pierian Thracians, however, the flourishing Iron Age settlements declined. The latest archaeological evidence suggests that Methone was the most important urban center in the Thermaic Gulf, at least until the Archaic period. Before then, in the Late Geometric period, it was a harbor of great significance not only for the Aegean but also for the eastern Mediterranean. Close to Methone was Pydna, another Greek city, according to Ps.-Skylax (*Periplous* 66), even though we have no other evidence of any Greek settlers here. Pydna reached its peak in the fifth century, when it was a Macedonian city with a harbor playing an important role after the Persian Wars.

Moving to the center of the Thermaic Gulf, several settlements contain Greek presence, even though, again, we have no evidence that they were *apoikiai* (Tiverios 2008, 17–32). For example, ancient Sindos (close to its modern counterpart) could have been an *emporion* with mixed population. Its coastal location explains its floruit in the Geometric and Archaic periods. A Thracian city, Chalastra, was probably located close to it. According to Hecataeus (*FGrH* 1, F163), Therme was a polis *Ellinon Thriikon* (Greeks Thracians), but it is not mentioned as an *apoikia*. On recent thinking, Therme was an established *komedon* (a town in village clusters), with different habitations spread apparently around the head of the Thermaic Gulf. The settlement at Toumba should be its primary nucleus in the Late Bronze and Early Iron Ages, while the coastal town located next to the harbor at Karabournaki became the main part of Therme in the next centuries based on its increased importance in maritime communication and commercial activities. Besides Hecataeus, the Greek presence is also attested through archaeological remains (Tsiafaki 2010). The Persian king Xerxes anchored his fleet and camped at Therme with his army, on his way to southern Greece. Although its location has not yet been verified on the ground, Dikaia, an *apoikia* of Eretria at the head of the Thermaic Gulf close to Therme, is also known. If the suggested location of Dikaia to the east of Therme is correct (Tiverios 2008, 24–26), it would have been located next to Aineia on the Karaburnu promontory, according to the tradition that Aeneas had founded it on his way to Latium after the Trojan War. This combination of myth and history, which includes the Trojan War, is not limited to Aineia.

Thucydides (4.120), for instance, relates that Scione in Chalcidice was founded by Achaeans from the Peloponnese on their return home after Troy's siege. Chalcidice as a whole undoubtedly attracted Greek interest, as literary and archaeological sources demonstrate. It may have been the first place in the entire region where Greeks attempted to found *apoikiai*. Of great importance is Mende, among the earliest *apoikiai* in Chalcidice, established by Eretrians (Thuc. 4.123.1). In particular, the nearby sanctuary at Poseidi, dedicated to Poseidon, shows the appearance of Greek cult practices already in the twelfth century BC. Eretrians appear to be the Euboean settlers for Pallene during the eighth century BC. Among the few *apoikiai* in Pallene, we know their metropolis is Potidaea. It was founded by Corinth, but later than other settlements (*ca.* 600 BC). It is worth emphasizing that it was the only *apoikia* that Corinth established in the entire region. Aphytis is not mentioned as an *apoikia*, but it may also be Greek.

Sithonia was also intensely settled. According to Strabo (7a.1.11), Chalkidians from Euboea founded around 30 colonies already from the eighth century BC. Historical Torone, whether or not it was founded by Chalkis on Euboea, seems, on the basis of its pottery assemblage, to have been receptive to some cultural stimuli from the central Aegean and Euboea. Situated next to a secure natural harbor, it was the most important city in Sithonia, and among the most distinguished in the entire Chalcidice. It seems that most of the cities in Sithonia were located along the coast, but our knowledge of them is very limited, including determining which of them were *apoikiai*. Moreover, archaeological research here has been less extensive than in Pallene. Assa, Galepsus, Pilorus, Sarte, Parthenopolis, and Sermyle are among the cities mentioned by Herodotus and other authors. The minting of silver coins during the sixth and fifth centuries BC places Sermyle as the most important town on Sithonia after Torone.

Discussion of Sithonia cannot omit its best-known city, Olynthus. It was founded by Bottiaioi after they were expelled from their land by Macedonians in the mid-seventh century BC. The Bottiaioi may have coexisted with local populations until the Persians destroyed their city in 479 BC. The new town (Olynthus) built afterward was undoubtedly a Greek city. It prospered and played a significant role in the political, social, and economic life of the region until Philip II destroyed it in 348 BC.

Archaeological evidence diminishes for the third prong of the Chalcidic peninsula, Akte (modern Athos). Its extremely mountainous landscape was, for the most part, not conducive to the establishment of *apoikiai*. According to Strabo (7 fr. 35), Akte's *poleis* were *apoikiai* of Eretria, and Thucydides (4.109.3) states that their populations were mixed. Besides the Greek settlers, we should add people from the northern Aegean island of Lemnos. Ancient authors mention different places (e.g., Dion, Olofyxos, Thyssos, Kleonai, Akrothoon) around the monasteries that later arose in the region.

More Greek *apoikiai* can be found further to the east, in the area of northeastern Chalcidice and Aegean Thrace. However, they differ from those on the Thermaic Gulf and the main peninsula of Chalcidice in terms of their *metropoleis* and time of foundation. The Cyclades and East Greece make their appearance here, but not before the seventh century BC. Andros founded four colonies (Sane, Stageira, Acanthus, Argilos) in this corner of the Chalcidice and at the head of the Strymonic Gulf, all around the mid-seventh century. Argilos is the earliest Greek *apoikia* in the Strymon area, something of great importance, since it is known that the local Thracians (Bisaltians and Edonoi) put up strong resistance to Greeks attempts to settle here, right down to the fifth century. A case in point concerns Amphipolis and the numerous Athenian attempts to settle here.

Another Cycladic island, Paros, showed interest in the region by founding an island *apoikia*, Thasos, at the first half of the seventh century BC. The settlers, led by Telesikles, father of the lyric poet Archilochos, were probably attracted by its mineral resources. From that same time, settlers from various parts of Ionia started to arrive in Aegean

Thrace. The situation here presents some further differentiation than that in Chalcidice and the Thermaic Gulf. With the exception of a few cities, such as Abdera and Maroneia, the rest of the coast was divided into two primary zones, at least during the Archaic period, with each under the control of one of the region's two islands, Thasos and Samothrace. A generation later, the Parians on Thasos founded several settlements on the mainland opposite, creating its *peraia*. Thasos's penetration here between the Strymon and Nestos Rivers lasted from the late seventh until the sixth century BC and was meant either to strengthen Thasos or to exploit and control its mines. Despite Thracian resistance, Thasos succeeded in founding Galepsos, Oisyme, Antisara, and Neapolis. Stryme is mentioned as the easternmost *apoikia*. Its location has been much discussed. Various scholars have suggested that it was the settlement unearthed on the Molyvoti Peninsula. Long afterward, Thasos established Krenides in 360 BC on a site away from the coast that controlled the area and provided access to the gold mines. Soon afterward Philip II conquered it and renamed it Philippi.

Further to the east, Klazomenians and Teians founded Abdera, which dominated the region between the Nestos River and Lake Bistonis. They tried twice to found Abdera in Thracian territory. The first attempt was in the mid-seventh century by Klazomenians under Timisias, whose name is one of the few names of an *oikistes* that survives in the region (others include Telesikles of Thasos and Agnon of Amphipolis). Environmental conditions and ongoing hostilities with the Thracians caused the *apoikia* to decline, but it was strengthened a century later, in the years after the victory of Cyrus the Great over Croesus of Lydia, when the Teians left their homeland and settled in Thrace. Abdera was to become the largest and probably also the richest of all Greek settlements in Aegean Thrace. As mentioned above, to the east of Lake Bistonis is another *apoikia*, Dikaia, whose proposed location must remain tentative, as it has not been excavated to any significant extent. Samians may have founded it not earlier than the second half of the sixth century BC. Maroneia is mentioned as an *apoikia* of Chians (Hdt. 7.109.2; Ps-Skymnos 678) established on the coast of the Thracian Kikones. It was probably located close to a pre-existing Thracian settlement and may have been on good terms with the Thracians living there. The excavations so far have only revealed material dating to Hellenistic and Roman times.

The territory still further to the east was under the influence of Samothrace, founded as a Greek *apoikia* in apparently two phases, initially by Aeolians from the island of Lesbos around 700, and later by Samians in the early sixth century. At almost the same time, the recently installed inhabitants of Samothrace established their own cities on the coast opposite, creating Samothrace's *peraia*, which extended from Maroneia to the Hebros River and included Mesembria, Drys, Zone, Sale, Tempyra, and Charakoma. Apart from Zone, most of these *poleis* are not securely identified or excavated. Zone seems to have been founded on the site of a Thracian settlement, flourishing especially during the fifth and fourth centuries. Geographically speaking, the region under examination reached as far as the Thracian Chersonese. There, sometime during the second half of the seventh century, Ainos received new Aeolian settlers. However, archaeological and literary evidence demonstrates the existence of a significant number of sites in the northern Aegean that are either Greek or preserve Greek presence, but they are not always labeled *apoikiai*. The existence of communities with mixed populations (in both the certain and the tentative instances) has already been referred to, but their identification cannot be established via ancient writings, which are highly fragmented and not intended to provide a full description of all the sites. Moreover, since the northern Aegean was frequently involved in major events in the Greek world (Persian Wars, Peloponnesian War, and so on), these ancient authors write selectively on certain sites and peoples.

Most of the Greek presence in the northern Aegean was established between the eighth and sixth centuries. By the end of the Archaic period, many of the *apoikiai* were thriving and laid the groundwork for the Classical period. This was a hard-won success, but hostilities with the Thracians did not last forever. The existence of strong fortifications, sometimes from a city's earliest phases, proves the need for protection from enemies, who could be, among others, the former inhabitants of the region. Thasos, although probably fortified from the very start, preserves walls that date to the late sixth century. Abdera also had fortifications early on. Moreover, when Miltiades went to the Chersonese, he secured the isthmus with a wall in order to protect Dolonkoi. Even though violence and hostilities often accompanied Greek attempts to found settlements, the long-term development in other cases saw opportunistic groups from both sides align their mutual interests and peacefully coexist (e.g., Methone, Argilos, Thasos, Zone, Samothrace).

Information on the relations between homelands and *apoikiai* is limited. The extent of their contacts and whether the mother city had control over its so-called colony are generally not clear. Corinth, for example, seems to have maintained close ties with its only *apoikia* in the region, Potidaea. Among other things, Corinth sent officials to Potidaea every year, as we know from when Potidaea revolted from Athens before the Peloponnesian War. The Corinthians had considerable presence there. Thasos also had probably long-lasting relations with its mother city, Paros. Abdera similarly maintained close connections with Teos, and may have been under some type of control until the fourth century (Kallintzi 2017, 494). Quite the opposite appears to have been the case with Andros's foundations, which seem to have broken off their relations early on.

That was the regional framework when the Athenian Empire appeared in the fifth century. Athens was largely absent in Archaic settlement. Individual attempts, however, are recorded for the mid-sixth century with Miltiades the Elder in the Thracian Chersonese and Peisistratos in the Thermaic Gulf. The latter, during his exile from Athens, conducted various activities hereabouts, including the foundation of Rhaikelos. Miltiades the Elder was invited by the Dolonkoi, when they were threatened by Apsinthians. He sailed to the Thracian Chersonese with other Athenians, and the Dolonkoi made him tyrant. Miltiades founded or reestablished several cities (Ps.-Skymnos 701–702, 711–712). With the support of the Dolonkoi, the Philaids, his descendants, remained in power until the early fifth century. The most important Athenian settlement in the region, however, was Amphipolis. The Athenians succeeded in establishing it, and in controlling the Strymon valley, after numerous attempts and fighting against the Thracians in 437 BC under the *oikistes* Agnon. Amphipolis was a Greek city, with a mixed population consisting of an Athenian minority and a mixed Greek majority (Thuc. 4.103.5; 106; Diod. Sic. 12.68.3).

The foundation of Amphipolis completed the population profile of the northern Aegean. By this point, the Greeks living there were completely integrated and can also be considered "locals." Thus, in the Athenian Tribute Lists, the inhabitants of Acanthus were known as *Acanthioi*, those of Abdera *Abderites* and not as *apoikoi* of Andros, Teos, and so on. This followed the standard Greek practice of being citizens of the city in which they lived. In the centuries that followed, any changes in the region's settlement and population profile essentially related to military conquests.

The Athenians focused their efforts on coastal Thrace and Thasos, never attempting to expand into Macedonia (Isaac 1986, 23–31). Athenians noted this, and Kimon was accused of such an attempt (Plut., *Cim.* 14). The Delian League (478 BC) was the medium through which Athens gained access and established its control. Beginning with Methone and Aineia in the Thermaic Gulf, continuing with Potidaea, Mende, Torone, and Acanthus in the Chalcidice, and ending with Abdera, Maroneia, and Ainos at Aegean Thrace, it becomes obvious that cities dispersed throughout the region were active members of the League. The Athenian Tribute Lists supply detailed information of the tribute (*phoros*) paid by most of those Greek cities, which demonstrates their dependence on the alliance and their prosperity (Merritt, Wade-Gery, and McGregor 1950). Thasos seems to have been among the biggest contributors, paying 60 talents, in contrast to Aineia, which paid 3 talents. The experience of Thasos (465–463 BC), when it tried to secede from the Delian League, is characteristic not only of the alliance's function and Athens's role in it, but also of the region's importance for Athens. The tribute that Thasos had to pay after its defeat involved losing control of the gold mines in its *peraia* (Hdt. 7.107; Thuc. 1.98.1; 100.2; Plut., *Cim.* 7–8, 14). The northern Aegean Greeks played an important role during the Peloponnesian War (431–404 BC). This war erupted in part because of Potidaea's defection from the Delian League in 432 BC, supported by its mother city, Corinth. During different phases of the War, the northern Aegean was a major theater in which battles between the two opposing sides took place. In 424 BC, the War's center stage moved here when the Spartan general Brasidas besieged Amphipolis, captured Torone, and supported Scione and Mende in their revolt against Athens. The Chalcidean Confederation (*Koinon ton Chalcideon*) was also founded in 432 BC, involving the political unification of 32 *poleis* under the leadership of Olynthus. It dominated the region until Olynthus's destruction at the hand of Philipp II of Macedonia in 348. Acanthus and Stageira were apparently powerful and prosperous enough on their own to oppose Olynthus's pressure to join the Confederation. The Odrysian Kingdom also came into being in the first half of the fifth century (Archibald 1998; Veligianni-Terzi 2004). It had an impact on the northern Aegean by recalibrating the balance of power. The kingdom extended from the Strymon River to the Black Sea and from the Aegean Sea to the Danube River, according to Thucydides (2.97). The Athenians were on good terms with the Thracian kings in various ways. Worth noting is that the kingdom's growth affected the Greek cities and their economies, and resulted in Odryses's controlling trade routes. Thus the economic decline observed for Ainos and Abdera and economic growth observed for Maroneia have been credited to Odryses's actions. Furthermore, the Greek *poleis* in his kingdom also had to pay him tribute (Veligianni-Terzi 2004, 92–97).

The fourth century BC was a period of immense social and demographic change in the northern Aegean (Buckler 2003; Veligianni-Terzi 2004). The Greek cities continued to play a role in the events of the rest Greek of the world, and both main Greek *poleis*, Athens and Sparta, showed interest in the region. During the Corinthian War (395–388 BC), the Spartan king Agesilaos crossed Thrace, making Amphipolis one of his stops. The Athenian general Thrasyboulos attempted to arrange peace with the Odrysian Kingdom. One of the first steps that the Athenians took to rebuild their imperial power in the region involved forming an alliance with Thasos (between 391 and 388) to secure the northwestern Aegean. The end of the war led to the creation of the Second Athenian League in 377, which many cities in the region joined (e.g., Abdera, Dikaia, Maroneia, Ainos, Samothrace). Thebes led by Pelopidas, when it came to the fore (371–362 BC), also showed interest in the region and became involved in the affairs of Macedonia.

This involvement benefited Philip II of Macedonia during his reign (359–336), which marks a decisive turning-point for the Greeks living in the northern Aegean. The Macedonians were self-sufficient in timber, silver, and gold, and had a thriving farming and stock-breeding economy that did not require their participation in Archaic overseas settlement. Instead, as we have already seen, the coastal edges of their state received *apoikiai* from other Greek areas, which were later incorporated into the Macedonian Kingdom. Before Philip II, Macedonia's expansion in the late sixth and fifth centuries impacted the cities mostly located in the Thermaic Gulf. From the mid-fourth century, he expanded into the Chalcidice and Aegean Thrace for reasons different from those that brought previous Archaic Greek settlement. The *apoikiai* established by Philip II, such as Philippi, owed their establishment, rather, to internal affairs related to his imperial expansion in the northern Aegean. One after another all the Greek cities came under his control or were completely destroyed (e.g., Pydna, Methone, Potidaea, and Argilos). Macedonian conquest brought new waves and modes of mobility, as Philip II displaced people across his empire, founded new cities, and interfered with pre-existing economic and political structures.

The picture of the eastern Balkans between 300 and 100 BC indicates, on the one hand, great prosperity, but on the other hand, substantial disruption of overland trade links. Most of those Greek cities in the northern Aegean continued in the Hellenistic period as part of the Macedonian Kingdom, until the Romans incorporated them into their empire.

Regional Cultural Physiognomy

Attempting to outline the cultural physiognomy of any region for a certain time period is an ambitious effort, let alone in the case of the northern Aegean. Here different people and cultures met one other and interacted in various ways depending on the time and place. Cultural interrelations, impacts, and exchanges were a multifaceted phenomenon, which cannot be easily perceived through either archaeological or literary evidence. Similarly, the cultural formation of any region is subject to a wide range of factors closely related to social, political, economic, ideological, religious, and environmental components. A combination of these, along with direct cultural interactions, resulted in a complex network of exchanges that led to this regional cultural physiognomy.

The northern Aegean, owing to its advantageous geographical position and the wealth of its natural resources, became a center for the movement of people, goods, ideas, and cultures, as well as a theater for wars and a target of enemy incursions throughout the Iron Age to the Hellenistic period (Triantafyllos 2000, 35). The key highlights that left their mark include: prehistoric times, Mycenaean influence, Thracian tribes, the Greek *apoikia*, the mixed population communities, the Macedonian Kingdom, the Persian campaigns and presence, the Odrysian state, the spread of Greek language, religion, and art, the widely known Hellenization of Thracians, Macedonian expansion and control led by Philip II and Alexander the Great, and the kingdom of Lysimachos. Phoenician presence, suggested by the written sources (Hdt. 6.47) and the discovery of amphorae at Methone, should also not be ignored (Kasseri 2012; Tiverios 2008, 75–76). Even though the material evidence is scarce and not always documentable, Phoenicians would have been attracted to the region's valued raw materials. The little that is known indicates that they must have had some effect on the region's historical development, especially in regard to the exploitation of its mineral resources (Bourogiannis 2018; Ilieva 2019).

Because of its historical trajectories, the northern Aegean's cultural character appears to have significantly changed between the Iron Age and the Hellenistic period. The process was long and consisted of various parameters, resulting in the symbiosis of peoples and their landscapes. A significant number of the settlements, however, did not attract the interest of the ancient authors; consequently, sparse or practically non-existent evidence exists for their organization or development. Numerous settlements founded here were doubtless multiethnic, since there was permanent contact between migrants and local populations, besides contact between themselves. Radical changes brought forward in the composition of population, in local institutions, and in administration also largely altered culture. From the Iron Age onward, the region was characterized by multiplicity and heterogeneity.

We have only inadequate information for the foundation of the Greek *apoikiai* and *emporia* (ports of trade). The framework remains incomplete, and at present there are more questions than answers. It should be borne in mind that the problem is not limited exclusively to the Greek settlements. Greeks were present in various forms (inhabitants, visitors, merchants, etc.) in different communities, not just those controlled by Greeks. Mixed populations were not uncommon (e.g., Methone, Argilos, Thasos, Zone, Samothrace), and, in certain instances, Greeks resided in local settlements without attempting to found a new city or to organize themselves in any way. For the *apoikiai*, as a rule, we do not know with whom and how the settlers chose to settle, whether according to a pre-organized plan or whether more than one city participated in the new foundation. It is also not known how and why a *metropolis* chose to establish one or more *apoikiai* (e.g., Andros). In any case, some method must always have been in place to ensure that the migrant group had the necessary blend of numbers and skills to survive. Some migrations occurred in conditions of duress: in the late seventh and sixth centuries BC, Milesians and Phocaeans sent out many *apoikiai* to the central Mediterranean and the Black Sea because of the Persian Empire. As in the case of Abdera, foundation occurred twice (see above).

Nevertheless, the *apoikiai* had an overall logic and can be subdivided into three groups, shaped by geography: (i) the Thermaic Gulf, (ii) Chalcidice, and (iii) Aegean Thrace. Based on current evidence, it seems that in the earlier times (Iron Age to Archaic period) there was a clear distinction between the different Greek communities, regardless of the tentative contacts or interrelations among them. It looks as if from the Classical period onward that there were more contacts and interrelations that can be observed, resulting in common attributes, although it cannot be claimed that they ever reached a unified form. The fourth century was a critical turning point for the region in many regards. After the mid-fourth century, the Macedonian conquest reconfigured the regional economy and altered existing Thracian–Greek and Greek–Greek networks. Moreover, Thracians became strongly Hellenized then, if not earlier.

The Greek communities in the region developed "individually" through their diverse relations or contacts with other Greeks, Thracians, or any other people there. Nevertheless, none was independent, all were to a degree dependent on others for consumption and production. Influences, impacts, and interconnectivity played crucial roles. Many *apoikiai* developed into important cities and functioned as commercial hubs not limited to just within the region, but rather as part of the larger networks in the Aegean and Black Seas, and sometimes even beyond. Most Greek cities practiced commerce (e.g., Methone, Potidaea, Mende, Torone, Acanthus, Thasos, Maroneia, Ainos), with agriculture playing a secondary role. That does not exclude the reverse, as with Scione. However, not all of the Greek settlements developed into substantial cities or significant and wealthy centers. Some retained their agricultural character, while at the same time providing access to the interior (Isaac 1986, 12–13).

Even though Hellenization of Thracians and other local cultures has been emphasized in modern scholarship, the reverse has not been as readily addressed. The cultural traffic went both ways and at all levels (economic, social, cultural, etc.), with intermarriage as one example of coexistence, including children born out of those unions. Several instances of intermarriage between male Greeks and female Thracians are known. Hegesipyle, the daughter of the Thracian king Oloros, was the wife of Miltiades and mother of Kimon. Abrotonon, the mother of Themistokles, was from Thrace. Thucydides was the son of Oloros, possibly a Thracian. Thracian male elites also married Greek women, such as the Odrysian king Sitalkes, who took as his wife the sister of Nymphodoros, *proxenos* (consul) of the Athenians in Abdera. Seuthes, the nephew of Sitalkes, married Stratonike, sister of the Macedonian king Perdikkas. Iphikrates and Charidimos, the Athenian generals, married daughters of the Thracian king Kotys I. This must have had an important impact on the demography of the cities as well as in the process of acculturation, especially in the settlements themselves (Isaac 1986, 85). The offspring of these marriages would soon be integrated as citizens of the Greek cities, and they would have developed a sense of belonging because of their citizenship, which put them in a different situation from the non-integrated locals.

The material remains unearthed on the northern Aegean's shores and the surviving literary evidence reveal that the societies living there shared many of the traditions enjoyed by the Greeks living in Greece proper. The way in which we should understand the cultural profile of the northern Aegean Greeks is to assume that material culture reflects behavior and does not prove similarity in lifestyle. Even though "pots do not equal people" and consequently they cannot be used for distinguishing between different "peoples," pottery consumption, albeit not a witness of Greek identity, does indicate a shared common material culture. The import of vases, at least on a systematic level, coincides with the Greek presence in the region, together with the establishment of the Greek residency. Based on the latest findings, the earliest Greek imports in the northern Aegean are Euboean Geometric pottery (Tiverios 2008). Attic Protogeometric and Geometric wares have also been found. Local versions of the same types also appear alongside the imports. Despite the fact that the imports do not necessarily constitute evidence of the Greek character of the community consuming them, in the case of the pre-Classical sites with Greek population, they may have responded to certain needs of the people. Therefore, if the imports were insufficient numerically, these people could have produced their own similar shapes and decorations. We should approach quite differently the imports in these local communities as they could have been status symbols, gifts, exchanged objects, or anything else that current research suggests. For the local versions that imitated the most renowned Greek pottery workshops, their appearance during the early phases of an *apoikia* suggests potters were living there with skills and technologies imported from elsewhere. What that might say about the number and expertise of the founding group cannot be easily determined.

Euboean, East Greek, Corinthian, and Attic pottery represent the main imports from the Iron Age to the Classical period (Tiverios et al. 2012; Manakidou and Avramidou 2019). Although the quantities vary significantly from place to place, the types and chronological range seem to follow similar patterns found in other areas of the Mediterranean settled by Greeks. In addition, their locally produced imitations suggest that demand for the originals exceeded imports. Aside from their consumption by non-Greek populations, who might have had a completely different interpretation of their usage, their use by Greeks could have been similar, although it is more likely that they shared the same practices with other Greeks in the Aegean. Thracians and other non-Greeks in the region also used the same objects (e.g., Attic vases during the Classical period) and shared a similar sense of aesthetics.

The focus of the contemporary research on imports has led to a fixation with trade and a neglect of other modes of interaction between the various peoples of the northern Aegean. Similarities with the rest of Greece in cult, ritual, and burial practices, as well as athletic and military training, can be found in the northern Aegean, while at the same time their own regionalism, such as democracy (e.g., Abdera), its demos (people) and boule (council), was maintained. The architectural remains across many sites speak to public and private life. Urban centers came much later; the prehistoric settlements had already developed their economies, ethnic consciousness, and politico-administrative framework. We possess no written sources for their transition into urban centers. Excavation in these urban centers, however, has often revealed prehistoric remains beneath them, furnishing evidence of their transformation into an organized city with all its characteristic features of town planning, administration, and social structure. Architecture follows types and the styles attested in the rest of Greece, with some individual characteristics and peculiarities that give them a regional flavor. Town planning, especially from the fourth century onward, is similar in most excavated Greek cities of the northern Aegean, which, in turn, share common characteristics with their counterparts in Greece. One must bear in mind, though, that archaeological research is still at an early stage, with most cities not at all well explored.

The material remains provide evidence of their organization and structure dating to early times, if not from the start or at least soon after their foundation. The basement (*Ypogeio*) in Methone forms a representative example in respect of both the variety of its objects and plan (Besios, Tzifopoulos, and Kotsonas 2012). This and other buildings from other sites display not only specialized know-how in construction, but also the existence of specialized craftspeople and project management. Clay products (e.g., pottery, roof tiles, architectural terracottas, loomweights) provide similar evidence. The organization of space, recalling the well-known Greek agora, occurs already in the Archaic times, as, for example, at Methone. The Archaic period witnessed urbanism and the birth of the city, based on the common origin of its citizens and the same laws, traditions, and customs. This included physical features, like fortifications, agoras, public buildings and spaces, religious sanctuaries, private houses, and engineering works, most notably roads, drainage, and water supply. Most cities endured for a long time after developing out of small settlements, sometimes with prehistoric origins. Therefore, the cities were not always highly planned in advance; rather, they could be anarchic or at least follow unspecific rules. However, houses, religious sanctuaries, fortifications, theaters, streets, and cemeteries (namely a city's basic constituent parts) are usually found in cases where organization prevailed. The cities of the northern Aegean during the fourth century and Hellenistic period had a high standard of living and culture (Vlachopoulos and Tsiafaki 2017). In the third century BC, most of the coastal cities of the Aegean Sea and western Black Sea, as well as the chief cities of lower Macedonia and central Thrace, experienced their first significant period of urban expansion, with the emergence of public squares, buildings, and various civic amenities.

The minting of coinage in northern Aegean Greek cities occurred commonly. This began before the end of the sixth century in the form of silver issues at, for example, Dikaia in the Thermaic Gulf, Mende, Scione, Torone, Acanthus, Stageira, Argilos, Thasos, Abdera, and Samothrace. These coins, through their iconographical choices, reflect the values and pursuits of these cities, such as guest friendship (*xenia*), athletics, and games. These were also expressed more widely in other art forms and poetry. The famous painter Zeuxis, for example, adorned the palace of King Archelaos in Pella, for which, Aelian (*VH* 14.7) informs us, Zeuxis was paid 400 mnas. The presence of the Ionian world is also apparent in the sculptures of the late Archaic and early Classical periods found in the region. Euripides also spent time in Pella, staging his tragedy *Bacchae* for the very first time in about 408 BC. Some of the theaters unearthed in the region (e.g., Philippoi, Thasos, Maroneia) not only shared the same architectural features, but probably also hosted the same tragedies and comedies as other theaters did in Greece.

One of the principal parameters forming culture is religion, acting as a link between people. Certainly, the religions of the region's various peoples blended and adapted to one another. Even though our knowledge of mixed and multiethnic settlements is usually limited (for an exception, see De Angelis and Garstad 2006), a brief attempt will be made here. Northern Aegean Greeks shared the same religion, which according to ancient authors (Hdt. 5.7–8) had some culture in common with or similar to those of Thracians (Ares, Dionysos, and Artemis). Sanctuaries to popular Greek gods (e.g., Poseidon, Apollo, and Demeter) are found in the entire region along with deities incorporating characteristics of Greek and pre-existing (e.g., Thracian) cults. This appears to be the case with the cult of Parthenos, popular to the east of the Strymon River, and particularly in the Thasian *peraia* (Isaac 1986). The deity occurs in Oisyme, but it is at Neapolis where she occupies a prominent place. Her sanctuary was the most important one from the Archaic to Hellenistic periods, as evidenced by her impressive Ionian temple of Thasian marble and the dedication of thousands of votive offerings imported from many parts of the Greek world (e.g., East Greece, Corinth, Laconia, and Athens). The adoption of this pre-existing cult as the principal deity of a Greek city might also be seen as an attempt to win the local people over. The cult of Nymphs was also widespread in the region (Tiverios 2008, 39). Apart from Aphytis in Chalcidice and a mention at Abdera, it is found mainly in the Thasian *peraia*, with Neapolis and Oisyme serving as characteristic examples.

The region's extensive forested landscapes favored hunting, a major activity for its inhabitants, and for that reason the cults related to them merit special highlighting. Bendis is the Thracian equivalent to the Greek Artemis. Cross-cultural interactions led to the adaptation and adoption of this goddess into the Greek pantheon, as evidenced by the Athenian state's official adoption of Bendis. A cult of Bendis is also discernible on Samothrace, with Artemis being worshipped in the Athenian colony of Amphipolis (Isaac 1986, 55). We can also suggest that regardless of the hometown or cultic affiliation of worshippers, they could worship in Greek or Thracian sanctuaries. An interesting illustration regards the sanctuary of Apollo in the Greek Zone, where a large number of inscribed Greek pottery fragments are written in Greek letters in a local Thracian dialect. These findings suggest a common cult of Apollo for Greeks and Thracians. On the basis of the research undertaken at the sanctuary of the Great Gods and two sanctuaries of Kybele (Matsas 2005, 93), it can be concluded that something similar probably occurred in Samothrace. The association of the Thracian god of Sun with Apollo is reflected also in the god's regional popularity. Apart from Zone, sanctuaries of the god existed at other places, such as Thasos and Abdera, and Homer (*Od.* 9.197–198) knows of his existence at Ismara (Maroneia).

Demeter was also popular, of course, as protector of cultivated lands and women. Thesmophoria have been revealed in different towns, such as Pella, Abdera, Thasos, and Stageira. For the sea, Poseidon was chief patron, and a sanctuary to him located at Poseidi (Chalcidice) is the earliest Greek sanctuary in the region, active from the Late Mycenaean to Hellenistic periods. Potidaea worshipped this god of their namesake, apparently as the principal deity, and he was depicted on its coins. A sanctuary dedicated to him sat outside the north city wall (Hdt. 8.129.3). There are also myths that connect Poseidon with the foundation of Torone, and Herodotus (7.115.2) records the existence of a sanctuary to him in the Strymonic Gulf.

The employment of religion and/or mythology to interweave relations and common points of different peoples is a longstanding practice of Greeks, with the northern Aegean being no exception, as shown with representative examples in Rhesos and Heracles (Tsiafaki 2018). Heracles's adventures appear to be based around a theme of killing the wild and uncivilized sons of Ares and Poseidon. Rhesos was a famous Thracian king known to Homer (*Iliad* 12.433–511). His cult was apparently widespread in the Rhodope mountains, and known to the Athenians, who conveniently "remembered" him at the time of the colonization of Amphipolis. Following an oracle (Polyaenus, *Strat*. 6.53), they transferred his relics to Amphipolis and erected a memorial to him there. Moreover, various heroes of the Trojan War (e.g., Odysseus, Akamas, Demophon, and Aeneas) wander around northern Greece (Roussos 1986, 58–61; Kakridis 1986, 205–208, 325–335). Thamyris, the famous Thracian musician, is known to have ruled the Akte peninsula in Chalcidice (Strab. 7 fr. 35). Worth noting is how the peak of Athenian interest in the northern Aegean coincides with the popularity Thamyras enjoys in Athenian art, as demonstrated by surviving vases and written sources (Tsiafaki 1998, 94–106).

The Greeks in the northern Aegean also shared language. This cannot be ignored, despite differences existing from place to place. Greek was the *lingua franca* of Greeks and non-Greeks for all communication. Generally understood by all, it formed an important link among people and became a mutual trait. It functioned also as a link with the rest of the Greek world.

Despite the individual characteristics retained or developed within the different communities, common or shared features forming the physiognomy of the region are not unusual, especially during the second half of the first millennium BC. An interesting example is that of the *symposium*, a cultural attribute of the Greeks. Achaemenid Persia also employed banquets in its social life. Under the influence of those two major neighboring and coexisting cultures, Thracians also adopted it, as attested by the discovery of numerous sympotic vessels made of gold and silver. Therefore, already from the first half of the fifth century, communal drinking, the symposium, and undoubtedly wine consumption appear as regional cultural attributes. It is worth noting that in the fourth century bronze and silver kraters, such as the famous one from Derveni, appear typical of Macedonia and Thrace, but not of Greece to the south.

The concept of connectivity (Horden and Purcell 2000) cannot be overlooked in tracking the region's cultural history. Multiple networks apparently coexisted and overlapped in time and space; trade networks with local, regional, and long-distance manifestations overlapped with networks of kinship, cult, and so on. Therefore, it makes sense that the region's cultural physiognomy developed through a long process based on interrelations surrounding imported and exported culture (Gosden 2004, 130). This colorful *potpourri* of locals and transplanted foreigners, including many Greeks, provided the region with its cultural physiognomy.

Conclusion

Rich in natural resources, water, flora, fauna, and natural harbors, the northern Aegean in this period supported a dense population that included Greeks. The latest evidence, however, is not as abundant as ideally needed to give the fullest picture of the activities of Greeks and Thracians. In the Iron Age and Archaic period, Greeks pursued activities in the northern Aegean characteristic of the time: they settled overseas and sought metals. This significantly impacted not only the Aegean basin, but also the wider Mediterranean through trade. It seems that metals, timber, slaves, and other trade products were among the primary attractions for the Greeks. However, each region had its own traits created through the amalgamation of the regional characteristics that existed before and that ensued after the arrival of Greeks, who in turn brought their own individual peculiarities. Their interaction and blending led not only to a *modus vivendi* but also to a regional cultural physiognomy, which hardly remained static but changed over the course of time, thanks to different kinds of dynamics.

Greek presence in the northern Aegean is known well enough through surviving literary sources and archaeological excavations conducted in many settlements. Mixed populations appear not to be exceptional, with Thracian presence strong in the region, resulting in significant, and sometimes vital, impacts on Greek settlement development. Mobility, the spreading and sharing of ideas, technologies, material culture, fashions, as well as the transfer of patterns and ideas on various media, combined. Constant change through connectivity and cross-cultural interaction appear to be major characteristic regional features throughout the time periods considered in this chapter. This led to multiculturalism and the meeting and mixing of peoples and cultures, as well as the ongoing renewal of Greek culture and society (as elsewhere in the Greek world). Ionians, Dorians, Aeolians, alongside their mother cities on Aegean islands, in Asia Minor, and in Greece, took part in multiple networks in especially the Classical and Hellenistic periods. The Athenian Empire was followed by Philip II, and the world created by his son Alexander the Great shaped the Hellenistic world, until in turn it was incorporated into the Roman Empire.

Not always easily documented, the region's communities had a variety of types of administrations. Princely entities such the Odrysian Kingdom existed next to independent territorial polities and Greek civic communities, organized according to the *polis* system. The case of the northern Aegean shows that long-standing connection routes extended deeply into the Balkan peninsula, and the Greek cities emerged and flourished as extensions of these pre-existing networks. Appreciating this allows us to build a more accurate understanding of how technologies, ideas, skills, and materials traveled and crossed boundaries (see more fully Schulz, Chapter 24, this volume).

We may not be able yet to see and fully understand all the micro-aspects regarding the presence and life of the Greeks in the northern Aegean, but we know with certainty that they formed a noteworthy part of the ancient Greek world and that they contributed to its overall culture. Greek migration here and throughout the Mediterranean and Black Seas impacted the history and life of the entire Mediterranean between the Iron Age and Hellenistic period (Osborne 2009, 2–4). Northern Aegean Greeks were a vital part of the ancient Greek world, contributing to the whole, while at the same time forming their own regional cultural physiognomy. As a point of contact of different cultures, it was a place of cultural production (Bhabha 1994), whose impact extended beyond the region and affected the central states of Greek history, especially those of Athens and Sparta.

REFERENCES

Archibald, Zosia Halina. 1998. *The Odrysian Kingdom of Thrace. Orpheus Unmasked.* Oxford: Oxford University Press.

Besios, Matthaios, Giannēs Z. Tziphopoulos, and Antonis Kotsonas. 2012. *Methōnē Pierias: Inscriptions, Graffiti and Trade Symbols on Geometric and Archaic Pottery from the 'Hypogeio' of Methone, Pieria at Macedonia.* Thessaloniki: Kentro Hellēnikēs Glōssas (in Greek). http://ancdialects.greek-language.gr/sites/default/files/studies/methoni_pierias_1.pdf.

Bhabha, Homi K. 1994. *The Location of Culture.* London: Routledge.

Bourogiannis, Giorgos. 2018. "The Phoenician presence in the Aegean during the Early Iron Age: Trade, Settlement and Cultural Interaction." *Rivista di Studi Fenici* 46: 43–88.

Buckler, John. 2003. *Aegean Greece in the Fourth Century BC.* Leiden: Brill.

De Angelis, Franco, and Benjamin Garstad. 2006. "Euhemerus in Context." *Classical Antiquity*, 25: 211–242.

Delev, Peter. 2014. *A History of the Tribes of South-western Thrace in the First Millennium B.C.* Sofia: St. Kliment Ohridski University Publishing House.

Gimatzidis, Stefanos, Magda Pieniazek, and Sila Mangaloglu-Votruba, eds. 2018. *Archaeology across Frontiers and Borderlands. Fragmentation and Connectivity in the North Aegean and the Balkans during the Late Bronze Age and Early Iron Age*. Vienna: Austrian Academy of Sciences Press.

Gosden, Chris. 2004. *Archaeology and Colonialism: Culture Contact from 5000 BC to the Present*. Cambridge: Cambridge University Press.

Horden, Peregrine, and Nicholas Purcell. 2000. *The Corrupting Sea: A Study of Mediterranean History*. Oxford: Blackwell.

Ilieva, Petya. 2019. "Phoenicians, Cypriots and Euboeans in the Northern Aegean." *AURA* 2: 65–102.

Isaac, Benjamin H. 1986. *The Greek Settlements in Thrace until the Macedonian Conquest*. Leiden: Brill.

Kakridis, Ioannis. 1986. "The Return of Odysseus. The Return of Other Heroes." In *Greek Mythology. The Trojan War*, vol. 5, edited by Ioannis Kakridis, 205–208, 325–335. Athens: Ekdotike Athenon (in Greek).

Kallintzi, Constantina. 2011. "The Chora of Abdera: A Contribution to the Archaeology and Historical Topography of the South Region of the Prefecture of Xanthi." Unpublished PhD thesis, University of Thessaly (in Greek). http://thesis.ekt.gr/thesisBookReader/id/31737#page/1/mode/2up.

Kallintzi, Constantina. 2017. "Xanthi. Historical Times. Abdera." In Vlachopoulos and Tsiafaki 2017, 493–501 (in Greek).

Kambitoglou, Alexander, and Stavros Paspalas. 2017. "Torone." In Vlachopoulos and Tsiafaki 2017, 382–383 (in Greek).

Kasseri, Alexandra. 2012. "Phoenician Trade Amphorae from Methoni, Pieria." In Kefalidou and Tsiafaki 2012, 299–308 (in Greek).

Kefalidou, Eurydice, and Despoina Tsiafaki, eds. 2012. *Kerameos Paides: Studies Offered to Professor Michalis Tiverios by his Students*. Thessaloniki: Zitis.

Kiriatzi Evangelia and Stelios Andreou. 2016. "Mycenaean and Mycenaeanising Pottery across the Mediterranean: A Multi-Scalar Approach to Technological Mobility, Transmission and Appropriation." In *Human Mobility and Technological Transfer in the Prehistoric Mediterranean*, edited by Evangelia Kiriatzi and Carl Knappett, 128–153. New York: Cambridge University Press.

Lipiński, Edward. 2004. *Itineraria Phoenicia*. Studia Phoenicia XVIII. Leuven: Peeters.

Manakidou, Eleni, and Amalia Avramidou, eds. 2019. *Classical Pottery at the North Aegean and its Periphery, (480–323/300 B.C.), Archaeological Meeting, 17–20 May 2017*. Thessaloniki: University Studio Press.

Markoe, Glenn E. 2000. *Phoenicians*. London: British Museum Press.

Matsas, Dimitris. 2005. "Samothrace." In *Archaeology. Aegean Islands*, edited by Andreas Vlachopoulos, 92–99. Athens: Melissa Publishing House (in Greek).

Merritt, Benjamin Dean, H.T. Wade-Gery, and Malcolm Francis McGregor. 1950. *Athenian Tribute Lists*, vol. 3. Princeton: The American School of Classical Studies at Athens. https://archive.org/details/bub_gb_1PCnzm6oBhMC_2/page/n4 (accessed December 11, 2019).

Morgan, Catherine. 2009 "Ethnic Expression on the Early Iron Age and Early Archaic Greek Mainland. Where Should We Be Looking?" In *Ethnic Constructs in Antiquity: The Role of Power and Tradition*, edited by Ton Derks and Nico Roymans, 11–36. Amsterdam: Amsterdam University Press.

Osborne, Robin. 2009. *Greece in the Making 1200–479 BC*. 2nd ed. London: Routledge.

Pikoulas, Ioannis. 2001. *The Land of Pieres: Contribution to its Topography*. Athens: Hellenic Research Foundation.

Roussos, Evangelos. 1986. "Akamas and Demophon." In *Greek Mythology. The Heroes*, vol. 3, edited by Ioannis Kakridis, 58–61. Athens: Ekdotike Athenon (in Greek).

Tiverios, Michalis. 2008. "Greek Colonisation of the Northern Aegean." In *Greek Colonisation: An Account of Greek Colonies and Other Settlements Overseas*, edited by Gocha Tsetskhlatdze, 1–154. Leiden: Brill.

Tiverios, Michalis, Vasiliki Misailidou-Despotidou, Eleni Manakidou, and Anna Arvanitaki, eds. 2012. *Archaic Pottery at the North Aegean and its Periphery, (700–480 B.C.), Archaeological Meeting, 19–22 May 2011*. Thessaloniki: Zitis Editions.

Triantafyllos, Diamantis. 2000. "Ancient Thrace." In *Thrace*, 2000: 35–97.

Triantafyllos, Diamantis. 2017. "Thrace. Historic Times." In Vlachopoulos and Tsiafaki 2017, 481–485 (in Greek).

Tsiafaki, Despoina. 1998. *Thrace in Attic Iconography of the 5th century BC. Approaches to the Relations between Athens and Thrace*. Komotene: Morfotikos Omilos (in Greek).

Tsiafaki, Despoina. 2010. "Domestic Architecture in the Northern Aegean: The Evidence from the Ancient Settlement of Karabournaki." In *Grecs et Indigènes de la Catalogne à la Mer Noire. Actes des rencontres du programme européen Ramses2 (2006–2008)*, edited by Henri Tréziny, 379–388. Paris: Bibliothèque d'Archéologie Méditerranéenne et Africaine 3.

Tsiafaki, Despoina. 2018. "Thracians and Greeks in North Aegean." In Gimatzidis, Pieniazek, and Mangaloglu-Votruba 2018, 219–242.

Tzochev, Chavdar. 2016. "Markets, Amphora Trade and Wine Industry: The Case of Thasos." In *The Ancient Greek Economy: Markets, Households and City-States*, edited by Edward M. Harris, David Martin Lewis, and Mark Woolme, 230–253. Cambridge: Cambridge University Press.

Veligianni-Terzi, Chrisoula. 2004. *The Greek Cities and the Kingdom of Odrys from Avdira to the Istros River*. Thessaloniki: Kyriakidi Brothers (in Greek).

Vlachopoulos, Andreas, and Despoina Tsiafaki, eds. 2017. *Archaeology: Macedonia and Thrace*. Athens: Melissa Publishing House (in Greek).

FURTHER READING

Hatzopoulos, Miltiades. 2006. *La Macédoine: Géographie historique, Langue, Cultes et croyances, Institutions. Travaux de la Maison René-Ginouvès no. 2*. Paris: de Boccard.

Lane Fox, Robin J., ed. 2011. *Brill's Companion to Ancient Macedon: Studies in the Archaeology and History of Macedon, 650 BC–300 AD*. Leiden: Brill.

Roisman, Joseph, and Ian Worthington, eds. 2010. *A Companion to Ancient Macedonia* Chichester: Wiley Blackwell.

Sears, Matthew A. 2013. *Athens, Thrace, and the Shaping of Athenian Leadership*. Cambridge: Cambridge University Press.

Tsetskhladze, Gocha R., ed. 2006. *Greek Colonisation: An Account of Greek Colonies and Other Settlements Overseas*. 2 vols. Leiden: Brill.

Tsetskhladze, Gocha R., and Franco De Angelis, eds. 2004. *The Archaeology of Greek Colonisation. Essays dedicated to Sir John Boardman*, revised paperback edition of 1994 original. Oxford: Oxford University School of Archaeology.

Vlachopoulos, Andreas, and Despoina Tsiafaki, eds. 2017. *Archaeology: Macedonia and Thrace*. Athens: Melissa Publishing House (in Greek).

Vlassopoulos, Kostas 2013. *Greeks and Barbarians*. Cambridge: Cambridge University Press.

CHAPTER TWENTY

The Black Sea

Pia Guldager Bilde[†], Søren Handberg, and Jane Hjarl Petersen

Settled between the second half of the seventh and the fifth century BC, the Black Sea region was among the last areas the Greeks moved into (Map 20.1). For them, in many ways, the "new world" of the Pontic area was a challenging environment. The climate was harsher than in the Mediterranean – olives, the Greek crop par excellence, could only grow in a few areas and the flat grass steppe that covers the northern half of the region was an unfamiliar landscape to the Greeks. The indigenous Scythian tribes, who inhabited or frequented the land before the arrival of the Greeks, challenged the Greek way of life: while some were fully sedentary, many were nomads or semi-nomads, a way of living that was traditionally viewed with suspicion (and fear) by the Greek urban dwellers. Many tribes lived peacefully among the Greeks, perhaps mostly in the *chora* of the later Greek towns and cities; however, other tribes were time and again able to put the Greek settlements under substantial pressure, and the steady arrival of new tribes from distant lands posed challenges to the locals, be they Greeks or indigenous.

Throughout the ages, the eastern part of the Black Sea region was and remained more "oriental" than its western part. The Scythian and other nomadic tribes who inhabited the region were of Indo-Iranian decent, and they left a strong cultural legacy. Moreover, the oriental aspect of Pontic culture was further reinforced when, in the late sixth century BC, the Persians conquered the southern half of the region.

Thus, the Black Sea region was not just a Greek environment. There was considerable cultural osmosis between the different ethnic groups of the region: in addition to the Oriental subcurrent, a certain "Hellenization" of the indigenous tribes took place, but equally a certain "barbarization" of the Greeks too. Thus, with three different cultures meeting and sometimes clashing, all three existing on the periphery of the core areas of their respective cultures, the Black Sea was a region where identity was continuously negotiated.

[†] Deceased

A Companion to Greeks Across the Ancient World, First Edition. Edited by Franco De Angelis.
© 2020 John Wiley & Sons, Inc. Published 2020 by John Wiley & Sons, Inc.

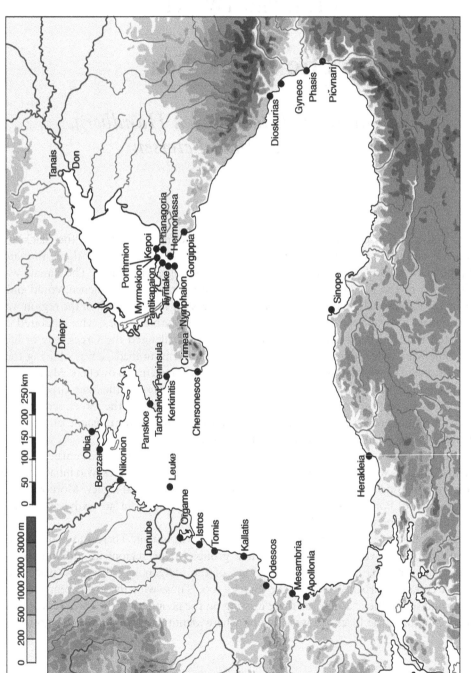

Map 20.1 Map of the Black Sea area with major Greek settlements indicated. Source: © Richard Szydlak.

Early Greek Ventures and Settlements in the Region

Greek interest in the region came late compared with Greek colonization in the Mediterranean, and there is little tangible evidence for Greek presence in the area in the Iron Age, and few literary sources to inform us about the early history.[1] References in Greek literature locate a number of myths in the area, such as the myths of Iphigeneia, Jason and the Argonauts, and Prometheus (Hes., *Theog.* 1.520). The White Island, Leuke, off the mouth of the Danube, is also mentioned in the, now lost, poem Aithiopis by the early Milesian poet Arktinos (Proclus, Chrest. 2). These references have been taken as hints of "precolonial" contacts with the region.

The church historian Eusebius of Caesarea, writing at the beginning of the fourth century AD, provides foundation dates for a number of the earliest Greek *apoikiai* in the region, that is, Istros (657/656 BC), Borysthenes (647/646 BC), and Sinope (631/630 BC). One of the best sources we have for Pontic geography and the dates of the Greek settlements is Pseudo-Skymnos's *Periplus Ad Nicomedem regem*. He provides a later date for the foundation of Istros than Eusebius, namely 627 BC, and gives the date of Apollonia's founding as 610 BC.

The earliest Greek pottery so far identified in the Black Sea area dates to the first half of the seventh century BC and is of North Ionian origin (Kerschner 2006, 239). More common, but slightly later (ca. 650–610 BC), are finds of South Ionian Archaic Ib–c Wild Goat Style pottery. Apart from finds in Orgame, Berezan, and Olbia, most of the early Greek pottery has been found at indigenous sites such as Nemirov and Trachtemirov far up the great rivers in the forest steppe area as well as at fortified sites such as Bel'sk, Nemirov, Bol'tyška, Krivorože, and Čoperskie (Vakhtina 2007; Tsetskhladze 2007). The Greek fineware pottery, which has been found more than 400 km inland, is testimony to "precolonial" and early colonial exchange between the newly arrived Greeks and the indigenous rulers of the land, probably in the form of gift-exchange.

By and large, the overall picture of the earliest settlement patterns in the region in the second half of the seventh century gained from the written sources is corroborated by the archaeological material. Eusebius's date of 647/646 BC for the founding of Borysthens is, for instance, matched by the earliest finds, such as a Middle Protocorinthian kotyle dating to the period 650–630 BC (Solovyov 2010, 90, figure 2).

It is not until the sixth century BC that the Black Sea witnesses a more constant Greek presence. The main body of early Greek pottery at the Greek sites belongs to the South Ionian Archaic Id period, which can be dated to the period between ca. 610 and 580 BC. Thus, the main phase of colonization is as late as the (first half of) the sixth century BC. Numerous cities were founded in this period: Odessos, Tomis, Nikonion, Olbia, Nymphaion, Tyritake, Pantikapaion, Myrmekion, Porthmion, Hermonassa, Phanagoria, and Kepoi, but no precise foundation dates are handed down to us. Also, on the Pontic east coast, Colchis was settled by the Greeks from the mid-sixth century BC, when the presence of Phasis, Gyenos, and Dioskourias is first mentioned or documented (Map 20.1).

Ionian Miletos was already credited in antiquity as the main colonizer with the founding of as many as 90 colonies around the Black Sea (Plin., *HN* 5.122; Ehrhardt 1983); this is evidently an exaggeration, and the material record, especially in the form of pottery, points to the participation of settlers from other areas of the Mediterranean, especially the Aiolian area

(Handberg 2013). In contrast, there are few Doric colonies; among them is Herakleia on the south coast, which according to a number of sources was founded around 550 BC by Megara (Xen. *An.* 6.2.1) or as a joint enterprise of Megara and the Boiotians (Ps.-Skymnos 1016–1017; Burstein 1976), and Mesambria on the west coast, which was founded in the late sixth or early fifth century BC (Hdt. 4.93; Ps.-Skymnos 739–742.; Strab. 7.6.1). Herakleia, in turn, founded Chersonesos in Crimea and Kallatis in the fifth century BC (Hind 1998).

None of the Greek cities were founded inland, and it is characteristic that throughout antiquity the Greek cities were located much further apart than those in the Mediterranean. Furthermore, it is important to notice that the earliest settlements are located the furthest away from the route into the Black Sea through the Hellespont. Surely, the great northern rivers and the interaction with the indigenous hinterland that they enabled must have proved one of the main attractions for settling in the Pontic region.

In the early years, the preferred settlement location was a small peninsula at, or close to, the mouth of a river, from which the settlement's name was typically derived and thus represented a Hellenized version of an indigenous hydronym (Schramm 1973). Thus the oldest colonies were found at the mouth of the great rivers to the north (Borysthenes/Berezan at the confluence of the Dnepr and Bug, Taganrog [Old Tanais?] at the mouth of the Don, and Orgame close to the Donau delta). This location, which was chosen at the expense of sites with natural harbors, was probably preferred because it was easily defendable, and ramparts and ditches are known from some of the settlements, the earliest preserved of which seems to be the recently identified defenses at the settlement of Golubickaja 2 on the Taman peninsula (Kelterbaum et al. 2011). Similar defenses are present at the early settlement of Orgame located on Cape Dolojman west of the modern village of Jurilovka less than 40 km south of the Donau delta.

The earliest dwellings in the Greek settlements consist of semi-subterranean pit houses or dugouts (*zemljanki* in Russian), that is, huts partially dug into the ground. More than 200 such pit houses have been recorded in Berezan. In shape they are round, oval, or rectangular and dug 0.5–1 m into the ground; each hut covers an area of 5–16 m^2. These dugout houses were commonly employed by indigenous tribes as well as by Greek settlers in the north and west Pontic area and they were especially common at settlements in the *chorai*. Even though dugouts are particularly characteristic of the Archaic period, they can still be found in the Classical and Hellenistic periods throughout the region (Tsetskhladze 2004).

In past and current research, a debate has unfolded about the ethnicity of the people living in such huts (Handberg and Jacobsen 2011, 184). Dugout huts were also typical of Greek and indigenous Iron Age settlements in Southern Italy (see Adornato, Chapter 13, this volume), and recent excavations point to Archaic dugouts at Karabournaki in the North Aegean (Tsiafakis 2013). Undoubtedly, all ethnic groups who settled in the region in the Archaic period would have been familiar with this type of dwelling. The construction of dugout dwellings was most likely due to practical reasons, as they represent the easiest way to create shelter.

In the course of the sixth century BC, gradually more and more rectangular houses were built above ground on stone foundations with mud brick walls. In the following centuries above-ground houses dominated, even though the dugouts were never abandoned completely. The practice of digging into the ground was to some extent continued in the houses built above ground, and many of the domestic houses feature one or more basements dug into the ground. In the heyday of the fourth century BC these could be very well constructed out of stone, as for instance examples from the Lower City in Olbia show (Kryžickij and Lejpunskaja 2010).

Worshipping the Healer, the Lady of Apatouron, and the Lord of Scythia

The early Greek settlers brought gods from their homeland with them; this is well documented in the epigraphic record. Of these ancestral gods, one in particular stands out: Apollo. To what extent Greek spiritual life and religious customs were influenced by indigenous religion is much debated; some scholars hold the view that the two religious worlds had little or no impact on each other. Others see a significant fusion of religious epistemologies.

Herodotus tells the story of the Scythian king Skyles (Hdt. 4.78–80), which is a fine example of local code-switching in matters of culture and religion. Skyles's mother was a Greek woman from Istros, who taught him to speak and read Greek. He lived one month a year in Olbia, where he had a house; upon entering the city, he left his army and changed from Scythian to Greek clothes. Later he wanted to be initiated into the local Dionysos Bakchaios cult; this led to his execution at Scythian hands. Even though the episode has a tragic end (and was of course written to portray the *difference* between the two cultures), it shows that code-switching between elements belonging to different cultures could and did take place.

Herodotus's story of Skyles's initiation probably reflects the popularity of a particular Orphic aspect of the cults of Apollo and Dionysos among the inhabitants of Olbia and Berezan, as well as elsewhere in the Black Sea area. This eschatological aspect of the Dionysos cult can be recognized in the archaeological record from as early as the end of the sixth century BC, but it is best exemplified by some inscribed bone-plaques found in the central temenos in Olbia, which have been dated to the middle of the fifth century BC. One plaque is inscribed with the words "life-death-life," which indicates that the cult might have perceived death as a new beginning, a trait that is also a component of indigenous religions, especially the Orphism of the Thracians. The apparent popularity of the cult might also be viewed as a religious response to the traumatic experiences associated with settling in a new world (Guldager Bilde 2008).

Apollo was a prominent deity in the pantheon of Miletos and, on account of his oracles in Delphi and Didyma, of great importance in matters of settling abroad (Malkin 1987). Not surprisingly, Apollo therefore also features prominently in the Greek *apoikiai* in the Black Sea. It is interesting to note that in many places Pontic Apollo was worshipped with an epithet, which we do not find in the Mediterranean,[2] namely as the Healer (Ietros/Iatros). He was thus venerated in Apollonia (*IGBulg*. I² 388bis, 403), Istros (*Inscriptiones Scythiae Minoris graecae et latinae* I.54; *SEG* 37.627), Olbia (Dubois 1996, nos. 55, 59, 65, 90, 99; *SEG* 30.977; 32.801), Berezan (*SEG* 30.880; 32.769; 36.693; 51.969.2), Pantikapaion (*Corpus Inscriptionum Regni Bosporani* [hereafter *CIRB*] 6; 10; 25), Phanagoria (*CIRB* 974), and Myrmekion (*SEG* 48.1006). The first known temple in Olbia was dedicated to Apollo, and no less than two temples were erected in his honor. The earliest temple, which was erected around 500 BC in the western temenos, is referred to as the Ietroon. The temple continued its existence until the third century BC, when the temenos was destroyed, never to be rebuilt. The other temple to Apollo in Olbia, of which

Figure 20.1 Classical lekythos in the shape of Aphrodite appearing from a seashell. From Phanagoria. Height 17 cm. Source: © The State Hermitage Museum, St. Petersburg / photo by Vladimir Terebenin, Leonard Kheifets, Yuri Molodkovets.

very little remains, was constructed in the central temenos slightly later than the first temple and was dedicated to Apollo Delphinios, who is well known from Miletus. An early Classical Attic kylix inscribed with a common dedication to both Apollo Ietros and Apollo Delphinios was found in a Scythian tumulus (no. 400) at Zhurovka, which suggests that the cult of Apollo was appropriated by the local Scythian elite (Rusyayeva 2007, 99–100).

The cult of Apollo Ietros seems to have been particularly important to the Spartocids' rule of the Bosporan Kingdom, and inscriptions relate that members of the royal family were among the priests of Apollo Ietros (Ustinova 2009, 253–254). Although no temple foundations have been found, several architectural elements have been attributed to the so-called temple of Apollo Ietros in Pantikapaion. The reconstruction of the temple, its chronology, and its ascription to Apollo Ietros remain, however, hypothetical.

At least from the fourth century BC onward, the main tutelary deity of the Bosporan Kingdom was Aphrodite (Ustinova 1998, 1999) (Figure 20.1). She was venerated as Ourania in cities on both sides of the Kerč Strait, and inscriptions testify that members of the royal Spartocid family served as priests in her cult (*CIRB* 1041). Her cult apparently arose under local (Scythian and Sindo-Maiotian) influence, which had an oriental imprint, and Herodotus relates her to the local goddess Argimpasse (Hdt. 4.59). Her main sanctuary was in the Apatouron on the Asiatic side of the Bosporos whence she obtained her epithet *Aphrodite Ourania Apatourou medousa*, "Aphrodite Ourania, Lady of Apatouron" (*CIRB* 31; 35; 75; 971; 1111). This sanctuary was situated on the coast of Korokondamitis Bay somewhere in the vicinity of Hermonassa (Strab. 11.2.10), but the precise location has not been identified.

The best-preserved and most ambitious sanctuary, from an architectural point of view, found in the Black Sea region is located at Za Rodinou in the Taman. The temple is a tholos constructed with exterior Doric and interior Ionian columns, and its diameter of 21.2 m falls just 0.5 m short of the ancient world's largest known tholos (the tholos in the Asklepeion at Epidauros). The tholos is located inside a trapezoid courtyard surrounded by stoai with a series of rooms. At least one room (VI) was equipped as a dining hall with room for 18 klinai. The Taman tholos was constructed in the third century BC; some time in the second century BC it fell into ruin and was never reconstructed. Its location far from any town makes it likely that it was a federal sanctuary.

Unfortunately, we do not know to whom the Za Rodinou tholos was dedicated and, because of the excavator's untimely death, it has only been summarily published (Sokol'skij 1976). Nevertheless, this sanctuary could very well have been an Aphrodite sanctuary, since the best parallel to the tholos is the (equally oriental) one at Knidos (Havelock 1995, 59–61).

Achilles might be regarded as a middle-ground figure in the Black Sea area (Hedreen 1991; Hupe 2006). He was much venerated, especially in the northwestern part of the Pontic realm. Already around 600 BC, Alkaios referred to him as "Lord of Scythia" (Page 1968, 89 no. 166 [fr. 48B]). Graffiti found at several sites testify to a widespread cult already in the sixth century BC. In the pre-Roman period he was foremost venerated outside the cities, in the *chora* and especially beyond the *chora*. The most comprehensive collection of finds attesting to his worship in the *chora* comes from the settlement site at Cape Bejkuš located on a small promontory at the confluence of the Bug and Dniepr with the Berezan estuary at what was presumably the southwestern border of Olbia's territory.

The most important sanctuary was on Zmeinyj (Snake) Island located off the Donau delta and probably to be identified as Leuke. The cult of Achilles is attested by a number of graffiti found on the island. A painted sima of the second half of the sixth century BC may document an early cult installation. Situated more than 200 km southwest of Olbia, the island was an important landmark on the sailing route from the Mediterranean to the northwestern Pontic area. Its location in a pan-Mediterranean and pan-Pontic network from at least the fourth century BC onward is well attested by the minting place of the many coins found on the island. Achilles sanctuaries have also been located at other landmarks on the sailing route, such as the Tendra and the Kinburn sand bars; in Antiquity, Tendra was even known as Achilleus's Racecourse (*dromos*) (Hdt. 4.55).

It has been discussed at length whether Achilles was (also) an indigenous divinity, which seems most likely (Burgess 2009). As mentioned, already around 600 BC he was known as "ruler of Scythia." In the Tarchankut Peninsula off the cliffs of Džangul', a cluster of graffiti testifying to the cult of a deity by the name of Targa has been found (unpublished; Hannestad, Stolba, and Ščeglov 2002, plate 4.1.17). Though the graffiti are incised in Greek, the goddess is not of the Greek pantheon. One of the graffiti is a joint dedication to Targa and Achilles. The finds from the site consist of handmade and wheel-made pottery

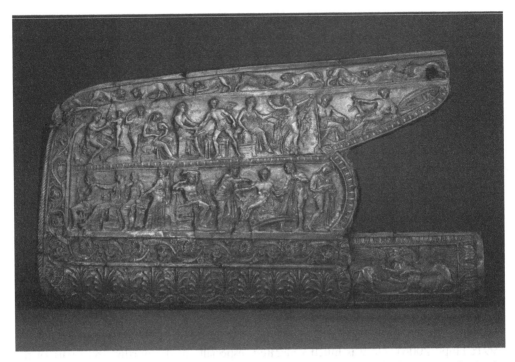

Figure 20.2 Gilded *gorytos* (bow case) of the early Hellenistic period with depictions of episodes in the life of Achileus. From the Chertomlyk Barrow in the Dnieper area. 46.8 by 27.3 cm. Source: © The State Hermitage Museum, St. Petersburg / photo by Vladimir Terebenin, Leonard Kheifets, Yuri Molodkovets.

(amphorae account for almost 50%), glass, and seashells. The find place is located in the distant *chora* of Chersonesos, and, as discussed below, this area was most likely inhabited by a mixed population. Most likely, the sanctuary was common to the local inhabitants notwithstanding their ethnic background.

Achilles was indeed popular among the indigenous elite, as we can gather from the four gold gorytoi, which prominently feature scenes from the myths of Achilles, found in the rich kurgans of Čertomlyk, Il'intsy (lost in World War II), Melitopol, and the Five Brothers kurgan (Daumas 2009) (Figure 20.2). Cultic worship of Achilles continued throughout Antiquity. The passionate idolization of Achilles by the inhabitants of Olbia is rendered by Dio Chrysostom in his Borysthenic speech as a means of portraying the Olbiopolitai as semi-barbarian (Dio, *Or.* 36.9). However, the prominence of the cult of Achilles with the epithet Pontarches in Roman Olbia is well attested from epigraphic material (Burgess 2009, 128–131).

Natural Resources, Trade, and Economy

The Black Sea region is rich in resources. Many species of fish could be caught, of which anchovies were the most important, in addition to mackerel, pike, mullet, tuna, and especially the various species of sturgeon.[3] Grain, especially wheat, but also barley and rye, was cultivated throughout the region. Wine was produced throughout the Black Sea region, whereas the area is by and large too northern for olives to thrive. In the steppe area, pastoral nomadism was carried out by indigenous tribes and Polybios refers to the best quality of cattle coming from the countries around the Black Sea (Polyb. 4.38). Metals may also have been an incentive for settling the region; the Chalybes on the Anatolian north coast were famed for their iron technology (Nieling 2009, 55–57), and copper and iron deposits are available in this area. There were numerous copper mines in Thrace and possibly gold mines in Colchis. However, better metal sources were available in the Mediterranean, so the presence of metal deposits was hardly a decisive factor for settling in the region.

Much of the trade with the Mediterranean is only poorly represented in the archaeological record. Trade in commodities such as fish and fish products (sources collected in Curtis 1991, 118–129), cattle, hides (*FGrH* 328 F162), flax (Xen. *Cyn.* 2.4), and perhaps timber and nuts (Xen. *An.* 6.4.4–5; Strab. 12.3.12; Greaves 2007) can be gleaned from ancient sources, but the archaeological traces are difficult to detect. Polybios, however, paints a vivid picture of the trade going on between the Pontic world and the Mediterranean. He recounts that such necessities of life as cattle and slaves of high quality were imported from the Black Sea (Polyb. 4.38). He furthermore tells us that luxuries such as honey, wax, and salt fish were imported to the Mediterranean in great quantities. In return the Black Sea received olive oil and wine. Very few Pontic transport amphorae have in fact been found south of the Bosporos, so it is obvious that their content (foremost wine) primarily served local consumption. Strabo (11.2.3), who also mentions trade in cattle, slaves, and wine, tells us that the city of Tanais situated at the mouth of the Don River was a favored trading emporium.

The Greek presence in the Black Sea region necessitated the negotiation of a middle ground with an accommodating "language." The earliest coinage, which was produced in the western part of the region from around the middle of the sixth century onward, is a powerful example of such middle ground. This coinage consisted of cast representations of various types. In several cities arrowhead-shaped coins were fabricated, at least in Apollonia (Stingl 2006), Istros (Talmaţchi 2010), Olbia (Zograf 1977), Berezan (Solovyov 2006), and Kerkinitis (Kutajsov 1995). The earliest arrowhead-coins are those of Apollonia, Istros, and Olbia. The ones made in Berezan are trapezoid segments with a relief of an arrowhead and the head of a fish on both sides, whereas the ones from Kerkinitis occasionally combine the arrow shape with the rendering of a sturgeon. In Kerkinitis, more triangular representations of the arrowhead (or a dagger?) were also produced. In the fifth century BC, and thus contemporary with the latter, dolphin-shaped coins were produced in great numbers in Olbia and probably related to the cult of Apollo Delphinios (Zograf 1977, 187–190; Stingl 2005, 121–122), and rarer ones in the shape of a four-spoked wheel (perhaps intended as a solar sign) were made in Istros. The Istrian, Olbian, and Kerkinitian ones were still in circulation as late as the first half of the fourth century BC (Ochotnikov 2006, 82 with references).

Some of these "coins" were marked with the minting city's name and/or symbol, but regardless of the shape of the cast coins, they would have appealed to the indigenous population: most obviously, the arrowhead-shaped ones herald Scythian weapon technology, but even the sturgeon was a powerful symbol in early Scythian imagery (Gavriljuk 2005); the same was true of the solar sign among the Getic tribes (Comşa 1988) and, of course, the wheel signaling the wagon was an equally well-known feature of nomadic life.

It is therefore of interest to note that this early coinage circulated not just in the Greek cities and their *chorai* but also in the indigenous hinterland. The standardization of the coin types therefore probably served as a means of facilitating interregional exchange and trade among both the Greek cities and the local populations.

A number of private letters, the earliest of which can be dated to around 550–525 BC, mention household slaves, slaves engaged in agricultural work, and what appears to be slave trade on a substantial scale (Vinogradov 1998). A lead tablet from Phanogoria contains a request of payment for a slave named Phaulles from Berezan, confirming slave trade between the Black Sea *poleis* in the late Archaic or early Classical period. The extent of the trade in slaves from the region to the Mediterranean is, however, much debated (Avram 2007).

Commercial connections to the Mediterranean can in part also be traced in references to *ateleia* (tax exemption) offered to foreigners. Possibly the earliest mention of tax exemption preserved is a fragmentary graffito on an Archaic bowl found in Berezan. The graffito states that a merchant sold wine, presumably to a local, which he bartered for 20 *medimnoi* of wheat (Vinogradov 1971). Proxeny decrees from the Black Sea bear evidence of mercantile links to much of the Aegean, North Africa, Thessaly, and the Peloponnese (Cojocaru 2009). That Olbia was a center of large-scale trading activities is suggested by the particular formula used in proxeny decrees granting *ateleia* not only to the *proxenos*, but also to his brothers and slaves. This particular, and unique, Olbian formula most likely reflects a conscious political desire to sustain trade (Osborne 2008, 337–339). Sometime around the middle of the fourth century BC, the boule and the citizens of Olbia passed legislation that compelled foreigners, who conducted trade in the city, to exchange their foreign currency to Olbian coins at the *ekklesiasterion* (Dubois 1996, no. 14). The exchange rate of cyzicenes seems to have been favorable, which was probably another way of attracting trade to the city (Bresson 2008, 34–39; 2009).

In Olbia, as in other cities, there is ample evidence for the existence of the *agoranomos* institution (Ivantchik 2012). Three sets of measuring vessels have been found in the so-called East Trading Building in the Olbian agora in the Upper City (Levi 1956, 62–63). The measuring vessels were found in a room filled with imported Attic and local pottery, which might have functioned as storage for goods destined for sites in the *chora*. That Olbia had economic control over its *chora* is suggested by measuring vessels bearing the stamps of Olbian *agoranomoi* at the settlement of Didiva Chata (Ruban 1982, 32–33, figures 1–2), and some graffiti from *chora* sites record commercial transactions.

During the region's period of climatic optimum in the late fifth and especially the fourth century BC, the most important export article to the Mediterranean was probably grain. Particularly well known is the grain trade to Athens from the Bosporan Kingdom in the eastern Crimea and the Taman Peninsula (Dem. 20.32). From its early years, the kingdom cultivated friendly relations with Athens and several rulers received privileges and honors from the Athenians in return for Bosporan grain and military support. Best known is a monumental decree stele found in Piraeus in 1877 and securely dated to 347/346 BC, which records honors to Spartokos II, Pairisades I, and Apollonios (*IG* II² 212; lost in World War II). The relief topping the stele is unusual because it alone renders the honorands, among which there are no Athenians (Figure 20.3). It shows two long-haired and long-bearded males enthroned together, probably the rulers Spartokos and Pairisades, and a male standing to their left, most likely Apollonios.

Figure 20.3 Honorary decree depicting the three Bosporan rulers, Spartokos II, Pairisades I, and Apollonios. Source: © Deutsches Archäologisches Institut.

Cemeteries and Funerary Material

The cities in the coastal zones of the Black Sea region have yielded an abundance of funerary material from numerous identified cemetery areas. Funerary material has continually played a significant role in the scholarly debates on the ethnic composition of the populations of the coastal cities. The various approaches have ranged from traditional cultural-historical studies, equating specific object groups or customs with specific ethnicities, to more recent studies, focusing on aspects related to social status, age, gender, and cultural identity (Petersen 2010, 33–38 with references).

Evidence from the earliest periods comes from Berezan, Olbia, and the cities on the western coast. In Berezan and Olbia the primary grave type was a simple pit burial dug in the ground; some of the more elaborate burials would feature the deceased placed in a wooden sarcophagus, while smaller children could be placed in a ceramic container (amphora or pithos). These so-called *enchytrismoi* burials of children are prominent features in many cemeteries of the Black Sea region and a popular choice in the cases where children received an archaeologically traceable burial. In general, the preserved numbers of child burials vary greatly from locality to locality with a significant number of identified child burials in Archaic Olbia to hardly any in contemporary Nymphaion (Petersen 2010, 212). An interesting feature of many inhumation burials is bedding of eel grass. This custom, perhaps meant to furnish the grave with a comfortable "bed" or "mattress" for the deceased, seems to have been a very common feature of the region from the Archaic period onward, and correspondingly it was used in domestic settings such as dugouts as well (Petersen 2010, 66–67). The long-standing traditional interpretation of this custom – that it was an ethnic Scythian peculiarity – must be confronted with the ancient literary evidence for the use of organic bedding in Greek contexts (Hame 1999, 30–31, 76), as well as finds of eel grass bedding in elaborate wooden sarcophagi in rich Olbian burials thought to belong to the Greek population (Skudnova 1988, 7.) The continuous popularity of the custom in the costal cemeteries and its appeal to various social layers of society seem to point to a custom associated with religious practice rather than a prerogative dictated by ethnicity.

Grave goods of the Archaic period seem again to display great regional variation. In Olbia the Archaic burials range from very modest burials accompanied by a single piece of pottery to elaborate assemblages consisting of imported black-figure or black-glossed Attic pottery, glass and faience vessels, jewelry, mirrors, weapons, tools, terracottas, coins, and even exotica such as alabaster pyxides (Figure 20.4) (Petersen 2010, 94–95).

Figure 20.4 Alabaster pyxis from Archaic grave in Olbia. Naukratis. Second half of the sixth century BC. 11.7 cm. Alabaster. Olbia necropolis, 1912. Burial no. 64. Source: © The State Hermitage Museum, St. Petersburg / photo by Vladimir Terebenin, Leonard Kheifets, Yuri Molodkovets.

Tumuli Burials

Similar assemblages of grave goods came to light during the excavations of the tumuli cemetery of Istros on the western Black Sea coast. Here cremations were placed centrally in the tumuli, which featured remains of sacrificial pits with numerous post-funerary offerings. In three tumuli (XII, XVII, and XIX) the remains of both horse and human sacrifices were identified. Various interpretations have been put forward, mainly concerned with a strong reluctance to connect the practice of human sacrifice to the Greek population. Thus, the tumuli have long been interpreted as burials of the local indigenous elite. However, lately they have been viewed as evidence for "Homeric-style" burials (Damyanov 2005, 82 with references) – an approach which has also been applied in nearby Orgame where the large tumulus TA 95 in particular has been proposed as the heroon of the Milesian founder of Orgame (Lungu 2002, 17).

In general, tumuli or kurgans were prominent features of most cemetery-scapes in the coastal cities of the Black Sea region from at least the fourth century BC onward. Chronologically, they are attested in the region as far back as the Bronze Age. Apart from Istros and Orgame, evidence for substantial use of kurgans in the coastal city cemeteries before the latter part of the fifth and beginning of the fourth century BC is limited. However, it seems that some of the earliest burials in Berezan, which date to the seventh century BC, were placed under modest kurgans, and it has been suggested that a shared funerary culture, a *koine*, existed in the northwestern corner of the Black Sea region among the settlers of Berezan, Istros, and Orgame (Damyanov 2005). The spatial layout of the kurgans differs from location to location, so for example kurgans flank the main roads to and from Nymphaion, tower on the mountain ridges surrounding Pantikapaion, and are separated from the flat ground burials in a designated kurgan cemetery in Kalos Limen (Petersen 2010, 147–149; 215–216; 252); they are completely absent in the city cemeteries of Chersonesos, but frequently met in its rural territories (Nikolaenko 2001). Very elaborate grave goods were often deposited in the kurgans. The Bosporan Kingdom in the Eastern Crimea is particularly outstanding in this respect, and many kurgans from its territories have offered exceptionally rich assemblages of gold jewelry, embroidered textiles adorned with golden dress appliqués, elaborately carved and decorated furniture, and remains of chariots, as well as sacrifices of horses, some in full harness. The burial chambers beneath these kurgans were an impressive masonry achievement, occasionally decorated with wall paintings.

Kurgans have figured prominently in the scholarly debate on the ethnic attribution of various cultural phenomena in the region. They have been regarded as manifestations of the "barbarian" tribes, being a prominent feature of the burial customs of the nomadic elites (Machowski 2011; Meyer 2013). While the elite connotations of the kurgans in the Black Sea region are widely recognized among scholars, several recent studies point to a more complex understanding of their use and multicultural composition; some have interpreted them in terms of culturally complex status markers utilized by local elites to display claims of power rather than ethnicity (Petersen 2009, 2010; Machowski 2011; Rempel 2011; most recently Meyer 2013).

Grave Stelai

The scholarly debate on the ethnic composition of the Black Sea coastal dwellers has also been preoccupied with stelai. Funerary stelai are very common in the Bosporan Kingdom and Chersonesos, while evidence for their production and use is more limited in other coastal settlements. From late Classical and Hellenistic Chersonesos stems a unique body of extraordinarily well-preserved polychrome-painted grave monuments (Posamentir 2010). The shapes of the stelai and the objects depicted on them are gender- and age-specific. Moreover, the material also features a curious type of stele: a combination of anthropomorphic representations, originally painted, set within *naiskoi* which show evidence of wooden shutters or doors at the front (Figure 20.5). The anthropomorphic stelai are traditionally interpreted as yet another feature of the burial customs of the nomadic populations, and some scholars have considered their presence in the coastal cemeteries as a direct sign of indigenous inhabitants in these cities (Posamentir 2010, 377–378 with references). However, it seems that studies such as the one undertaken by Richard Posamentir open up the possibility of viewing the appearance and use patterns of the anthropomorphic stelai in a more complex setting of social and cultural assortment among a population which could play on a variety of culturally diverse strings in their expressions of identity. A similar suggestion has recently been put forward by Patric-Alexander Kreuz in a comprehensive study of Bosporan grave stelai

Figure 20.5 Grave stele from Chersonesos. Anthropomorphic representation in *Naiskos*. Local limestone. Height 26 cm; width 20.5 cm; thickness 14.5 cm. Source: © Richard Posamentir.

(Kreuz 2012). It seems that local and regional strategies of status display often took precedence over ethnic affiliations when it came to the choice and design of grave markers.

Identity in the Afterlife

Another example of the different ways in which statements of identity and social status could be communicated is found in Pičvnari in modern Georgia. Greeks settled here in the mid-fifth century BC in an area that was already inhabited by indigenous tribes. The cemetery was divided into three spatially separated areas: the northern, western, and southern parts (Vickers and Kakhidze 2004). The northern and western parts have caused especial interest, because they show differences in burial practices. In the northern part, the skeleton is placed predominantly in a crouched position with the head toward the north; in the western part, the pit graves frequently contained a wooden sarcophagus and the body in a supine position with the head toward the east. Some tombs in the western cemetery were decisively richer than in the northern one. However, in tombs all over the cemetery the use of "Charon's obols" was widely practiced, primarily in the form of the local Kolkhidki, minted after the Persian weight standard. There is scholarly disagreement as to whether the differences between the more or less contemporary cemeteries are the result of ethnic distinctions or the result of socioeconomic differentiation. The strong Persian influence adds to the cultural complexity of the area, which is manifest not just in the previously mentioned Kolkhidki, but also in the finds of silver phialai and silver and bronze arm rings of Achaemenidizing types. The ability to simultaneously possess and display diverse cultural affiliations is well manifested in another funerary assemblage of the region: Grave no. 24 from Vani, further inland, is an extraordinarily rich burial. The deceased was accompanied by four slaves and a horse. He was wrapped in a shroud decorated with thousands of glass beads, while his clothing was adorned with hundreds of gold appliqués in the form of ducks and eagles. On his chest lay four silver cups, and a silver coin of Pantikapaion, datable to ca. 340–330 BC, lay near his mouth. Among the inventory of the grave were also a Persian-style silver dining set (cup, ladle, sieve, and wine bowl), a Greek bronze jug, a Neo-Babylonian seal stone, two Attic lekythoi, and other Attic pottery, making this an outstanding power display of wealth and status drawing on different cultural components (Kacharava and Kvirkvelia 2008).

A similar case of complex cultural identity is manifested in a particularly puzzling and unique find of the Classical period from the cemetery of Apollonia Pontica: a one-handled cup of local Thracian shape adorned with men in full Thracian dress and attire (Figure 20.6). The cup is undoubtfully of Attic manufacture and has been assigned to the Athenian red-figure painter known as the Eretria Painter (Lezzi-Hafter 1997). The cup, which was most likely a special commission, presents us with a testimony to the ways in which local taste for particular shapes and iconography could be combined with the finest Athenian craftsmanship to accommodate an expression of complex cultural identity.

Figure 20.6 One-handled cup by the Eretria Painter from Apollonia showing Thracian warriors. Preserved height ca. 14 cm. Source: Courtesy of the Archaeological Museum in Sozopol. © Sozopol Archaeological Museum Sozopol.

The City Territories

As mentioned above, the Greek cities and towns were frequently located at a significant distance from each other. This provided the cities with the opportunity to acquire large territories – granted there was peace between the cities and the indigenous tribes of the area. It has become increasingly well documented that the *chorai* were to a significant extent divided into plots (for recent studies on the *chorai*, see e.g., Guldager Bilde and Stolba 2006; Müller 2010, chapters 4–5).

By far the best preserved *chora* – and therefore also the best known in scholarly literature – is the territory of Chersonesos, especially the so-called home *chora* on the Herakleian Peninsula south of the city. This area is a huge triangle of ca. 100 km² framed by the sea on two sides and by the Černaja River and the Sapun Heights on the third and eastern side. There are remains of an early cadastral system dating to the late fifth and first half of the fourth century BC. During the following brief interval between ca. 350 and 325 BC, the Herakleian Peninsula was reorganized with new rectangular plot divisions with stone walls, and at the same time the entire western and northwestern Crimea was incorporated into the Chersonese state as its distant *chora*. There are clear traces of property divisions over large tracts of land in the Tarchankut Peninsula, which testify to the substantial scale of cultivation of the steppe in Chersonesos's distant *chora* (Guldager Bilde, Attema, and Winther-Jacobsen 2012).

In the fourth century BC, the *chora* of Chersonesos was scattered with isolated farmhouses; around 140 are known in the Herakleian Peninsula alone, of which approximately one-fourth have been investigated. Some of the farmhouses were fortified with a tower, and an agglomeration of farmhouses is known from the settlement of Panskoe I (Hannestad, Stolba, and Ščeglov 2002).

Before the Greeks settled the Herakleian Peninsula it was inhabited by members of the indigenous Kizil-Koba culture, the Taurians of ancient literary sources. This agro-pastoralist culture is characterized by a particular type of handmade pottery, significant use of stone tools even in the Hellenistic period, dugout habitations, and low kurgans and cist graves often with multiple burials. Taurian handmade pottery with incised decoration believed to date to the sixth century BC has been found in the Greek city of Chersonesos, which has spurred discussions about a pre-existing Taurian settlement (Handberg and Jacobsen 2011, 187). An inscription, the so-called Diophantes decree, of the late second century BC, refers to "the Taurians who live nearby" (*IPE* I², 352). The finds from inland settlements on the Tarkankhut peninsula consist predominantly of handmade pottery, and the settlements were connected by chains of kurgans located on the watershed between the settlements. Some of the *chora* settlements had large double pens for rearing and milking goats and sheep. Whether the mention of Taurians in the Diophantes inscription, the predominance of handmade pottery, and the kurgans support the view that Taurians were living within the boundary of the Greek *chora*, perhaps as a work force, remains a matter of debate (Carter 2006a, 193; Handberg 2011).

Interaction among the Greek inhabitants of Chersonesos and the Taurians seems also to be reflected in Parthenos, the divine protectress of Chersonesos, who was a fusion of a Greek and an indigenous deity, and whose worship, according to Herodotus, was shared by the local Taurian tribes (Hdt. 4.103; Eur. *IT* 34–41). Although the location of the temple of Parthenos remains uncertain, we know of the erection of public decrees in the pronaos of Parthenos (*IPE* I², 344, 353) and an altar on the acropolis (*IPE* I², 352).

Evidence of the worship of Heracles is a recurrent feature of the Chersonesean *chora*. A number of local limestone reliefs bear witness to his status as the mythological Doric founder of the metropolis, and even terracotta clubs are known from several farmhouses (Guldager Bilde, Attema, and Winther-Jacobsen 2012, 148–149). Most of the relief depictions render a reclining corpulent Heracles, and two of the reliefs (in Čhaika and Kara Tobe) also depict a *gorytos* (Scythian bow case) with his bow suspended above him, a depiction well known from Scythian art. Heracles (or rather, a figure, which the Greeks understood to be Heracles) apparently played a role in the formative history of the Scythian culture, according to Herodotus (Hdt. 4.8–9; Hinge 2008). In the version that Herodotus calls the "Greek" one, Heracles in his pursuit of Geryon's oxen loses his horses while in wooded Hylaia in Olbia's *chora*.[4] There he meets a female with a serpentine lower body (a common image of an epichoric figure related to Aphrodite Apatourion, see above). She orders him to make love to her, and she then promises the return of the horses. The outcome of their meeting is three sons, Agathyrsos, Gelonos, and Skythes, all indigenous

Figure 20.7 Eminakos coin from Olbia with a depiction of Herakles stringing a bow. Source: © The Trustees of the British Museum. All rights reserved.

tribal designations. Heracles left them a legacy, namely bow and belt, which they should master to inherit the land. Only Skythes managed this, and he became the founder of the Scythian tribe (Figure 20.7).

There was also a local legend recorded by the Greek historian Herodoros from Herakleia Pontike (ca. 400 BC) according to which Heracles had obtained his bow and arrow from a Scythian named Teutaros (*FHG*, vol. II. 29, fr. 5). Surely, the bow, with which Heracles is normally depicted, is the Scythian one, the best available technology in the region at the time, and the fact that Heracles would have been viewed favorably by Greeks and indigenous populations at the same time makes him, like Achilles, a likely middle-ground figure (Malkin 2005).

The territory of Olbia has been less discussed than that of Chersonesos, but many reconnaissances have been carried out along the coast of the Dniepr/Bug Rivers and along the Berezan estuary and the numerous ravines that dissect the land. This has led to the discovery of Greek pottery at close intervals already from the Archaic period, and it has been assumed that this signified the presence of *Greek* settlements. A significant number of these sites have been excavated, and the early ones are characterized by dugouts and household pits as well as high quantities of handmade pottery. It is only in the late Classical-Hellenistic period we find large and well-built farms. At Didova Chata, a large Greek farmhouse of the same type better known from Panskoe I has been excavated, and single and double farmhouses, the latter surrounded by a wall, have been identified at Kozyrka 12 and in the Čertovatoe ravine.

Much of Olbia's *chora* was also divided into land plots, but of a quite peculiar type being long and narrow and following the contours of the land. Around 1500 kurgans can be distinguished in the Olbian *chora*, most of them ploughed down. They line the numerous paths through the land, and those found in the plough zone to a great extent respect the plot borders. How far Olbia's *chora* extended is a matter of controversy. Minimalists consider the *chora* to be limited to the area east of the Adžigol ravine, maximalists believe that it stretches as far as Bilozerka on the bank of the Dniepr 25 km east of Cape Stanislav, that is 42 km east of Olbia, and Alexander N. Ščeglov (1992, 242–243) even proposed that Olbia's territory in the late fifth century BC extended as far as the settlement of Panskoe I in the Crimean Tarchankut Peninsula 150 km further south. A middle ground would have the *chora* extend at least 30 km north to the Mykolajiv suburb of Bol'šaja Korenicha, to Glubokaja Pristan' in the east, and to the right bank of the Berezan estuary. It is hardly enough, however, to draw on finds of Greek pottery at a given site as evidence for Greek territorial control over the area, because indigenous tribes made use of Greek pottery to a considerable extent (e.g., Gavriljuk 2008).

As in the case of the Chersonesean *chora*, the interaction between Greeks and indigenous tribes in the territory of Olbia has also been a topic of discussion. In the geographical excursus of Herodotus's Scythian logos (Hdt. 4.17–19) he distinguished between four different categories of Scythians: Plough Scythians, Agricultural Scythians, Nomad Scythians, and Royal Scythians. Closest to Olbia he portrays the Scythian tribes of the Kallippidai, who are "Scythian Greeks," and another tribe called the Alazones. Herodotus relates that the Kallippidai and the Alazones "though in other ways live like the Scythians, plant and eat grain, onions, garlic, lentils, and millet" (Hdt. 4.17). According to the same, north of the Alazones live "Scythian farmers," who plant grain not to eat but to sell (Hdt. 4.17). These tribes must have constituted the vast majority of those cultivating the "Olbian" territory, and the unusual layout of the cultivated terrain may mirror Scythian agricultural practice rather than Greek. In fact, the layout of the plots, unknown from the Greek world, could represent Scythian ploughing technology.

The Crisis in the Third Century BC

Already around 300 BC grain had become a scarce commodity, which is evident from the Chersonesean civic oath of around this date. In this oath, the citizens were obliged to swear that "neither shall I sell grain suitable for exportation which comes from the plain, nor export grain from the plain to another place, except to Chersonesos" (*IPE* I^2 401; Stolba 2005a). Around 270 BC, throughout the north and west Pontic area the *chorai* contracted and the impressive investment in the organization of the arable land that had been made in the fourth century BC was largely abandoned. The crisis was probably a result of a series of interlinked events. The main factor was probably climate changes (Stolba 2005b). The pressure on the resources also led to intensified diplomatic contacts between the Bosporan Kingdom and Egypt during the first half of the third century BC, perhaps in order to secure the import of grain from Egypt (Archibald 2007). Such contact with Ptolemaic Egypt is perhaps reflected in the depictions of a warship in an Aphrodite shrine in Nymphaion (Figure 20.8) that has been interpreted as evidence for an official Ptolemaic visit to the Bosporan Kingdom (Murray 2002).

Figure 20.8 Fragment of a wall from the Aphrodite shrine in Nymphaion covered with a multicolored painting of the Ptolemaic warship "Isis." Plaster and painting with encaustic coating. 160 by 60 cm. First half of the third century BC. Source: © The State Hermitage Museum, St. Petersburg/ photo by Vladimir Terebenin, Leonard Kheifets, Yuri Molodkovets.

At the same time there was also an economic crisis, which resulted in the change of weight standards, the adding of base metals to alloys, over-striking and counter-marking, and the cessation of striking of gold coins (Stolba 2005b). A dramatic increase in lead repairs on pottery seems to reflect the impact of the crisis on ordinary peoples' lives (Guldager Bilde and Handberg 2012).

Even though the worsened climatic conditions may have prevailed for more than a century, the *chorai* of many Greek cities, especially those of the Bosporan Kingdom in Eastern Crimea, were resettled already around 230 BC, and many farms and settlements were now fortified showing that the threat from the outside was real.

In general, the third and second century BC was a time of considerable unrest. New, strong, petty kingdoms turned up among the barbarian tribes, for example the late Scythian Kingdom, which had its capital at Scythian Neapolis in inland Crimea. These Scythians under the rule of King Skilurous conquered land as far away as Olbia, which was under Scythian "protection" for a period of time in the second century BC. There are numerous inscriptions from these centuries that demonstrate how the Greek cities had to maneuver vis-a-vis a partially hostile indigenous population. Epigraphic records, of which the Olbian Protogenes inscription is perhaps the most famous (*IPE* I² 32), allow us to glimpse how wealthy individuals sponsored "protection money" with which to bribe some local tribes to help them against other tribes (Braund 2007, 62–77). In the late second century BC, Mithridates VI Eupator, king of the Kingdom of Pontos (134–63 BC) expanded his sphere of influence to most of the Black Sea area as he "offered his assistance" as "protector" of Greek culture against the frequent "barbarian" assaults on the Pontic cities (Højte 2009). In several Greek cities, honorary decrees were erected celebrating Mithridatic generals (*SEG* 47.1125; 52.735). Best known is the one Diophantos erected in Chersonesos in ca. 106/105 BC (*IPE* I² 352; *Syll.*³ 709; *SEG* 39.692). The inscription mentions that Diophantos was able to deliver a decisive blow against the joint forces of the indigenous tribes, and after this incident, Mithridates became ruler of the Black Sea until his death in 63 BC after prolonged wars with Rome.

Conclusion

The Greeks in the Black Sea were Greeks, but they were also different in a number of ways from the Greeks of the homeland. Local and regional cultural and environmental circumstances influenced their lives and played a significant role in the development and definitions of what it meant to be living in the Black Sea region in this period of Antiquity. While the region was perhaps not primarily settled for trade purposes, there was always a concern toward facilitating trade and exchange of goods, both with the Mediterranean areas and with the indigenous-controlled hinterlands surrounding the coastal areas of the Black Sea. This is not only evident in the archaeological record of the area, but also manifested in the evidence for an early coin *koine* as well as the trade legislations and honorary inscriptions. The efforts to maintain and expand favorable relations seem not to have been restricted only to the trade and exchange of goods, but also defined the ways in which Greeks related to other cultural groupings in the region. Strong influences from very different cultural spheres of central Europe, the steppe regions, eastern kingdoms, and the Mediterranean world inspired, shaped, and drove forward the particular architectural, religious, technological, and material constructs which comprised life in the Greek cities in the Black Sea region. This susceptibility to diverse cultural influences seems to have been a key element in an ongoing negotiation and formation of identity throughout the many centuries of Greek presence in the region.

NOTES

1. Stone anchors of so-called Mycenaean type (if they can be dated at all) and a few oxhide-shaped ingots found on the Bulgarian coast may attest to the actual presence of Mycenaean ships in the Black Sea (Hiller 1991).
2. A recent find of the fourth century BC in Lycian Phaselis proves to be the exception (*SEG* 55.1477).
3. That fish did, in fact, constitute a significant part of the diet of the region's Greek inhabitants has been proven by stable isotope analyses of skeletal material from Apollonia (Keenleyside, Schwarcz, and Panayotova 2006).
4. Hylaia constituted part of Olbia's *chora*. From a Greek letter written on an Archaic potsherd found in Olbia we have the confirmation that Heracles together with Meter and the river god Borysthenes had altars in Hylaia, which "once more" had been destroyed (*SEG* 42.710; Dubois 1996, no. 24, 55–63; see also Braund 2007, 46–48).

REFERENCES

Archibald, Zofia H. 2007. "Contacts between the Ptolemaic Kingdom and the Black Sea in the Early Hellenistic Age." In *The Black Sea in Antiquity: Regional and Interregional Economic Exchanges*, edited by Vincent Gabrielsen and John Lund, 253–272. Aarhus: Aarhus University Press.

Avram, Alexandru. 2007. "Some Thoughts about the Black Sea and the Slave Trade before the Roman Domination (6th–1st Centuries BC)." In *The Black Sea in Antiquity: Regional and Interregional Economic Exchanges*, edited by Vincent Gabrielsen and John Lund, 239–251. Aarhus: Aarhus University Press.

Avram, Alexandru, John Hind, and Gocha R. Tsetskhladze. 2004. "The Black Sea Area." In *An Inventory of Archaic and Classical Poleis*, edited by Mogens Herman Hansen and Thomas Heine Nielsen, 925–973. Oxford: Oxford University Press.

Braund, David. 2007. "Greater Olbia: Ethnic, Religious, Economic, and Political Interactions in the Region of Olbia, c. 600–100 BC." In *Classical Olbia and the Scythian World: From the Sixth Century BC to the Second Century AD*, edited by Sergey D. Kryzhitskii and David Braund, 37–77. Oxford: Oxford University Press.

Bresson, Alain. 2008. *L'économie de la Grèce des cités: (fin VIe–Ier siècle a.C.) II*. 2 vols. Paris: Colin.

Bresson, Alan. 2009. "Electrum Coins, Currency Exchange and Transaction Costs in Archaic and Classical Greece." *Revue Belge de Numismatique et de Sigillographie*, 155: 71–80.

Burgess, Jonathan S. 2009. *The Death and Afterlife of Achilles*. Baltimore: Johns Hopkins University Press.

Burstein, Stanley Mayer. 1976. *Outpost of Hellenism: The Emergence of Heraclea on the Black Sea*. Berkeley: University of California Press.

Carter, Joseph C. 2006a. "Towards a Comparative Study of *Chorai* West and East: Metapontion and Chersonesos." In *Surveying the Greek Chora Black Sea Region in a Comparative Perspective*, edited by Pia Guldager Bilde and Vladimir F. Stolba, 175–206. Aarhus: Aarhus University Press.

Cojocaru, Victor. 2009. "Zur Proxenie in den griechischen Städten des pontischen Raums." *Pontica*, 42: 349–374.

Comşa, Maria. 1988. "Signes solaires sur les bols gétiques imités d'après les coupes déliennes." *Thraco-Dacica*, 9(1–2): 83–100.

Curtis, Robert I. 1991. *Garum and Salsamenta: Production and Commerce in Materia Medica*. Leiden: Brill.

Damyanov, Margarit. 2005. "Necropoleis and Ionian Colonisation in the Black Sea." *Ancient East and West*, 4: 77–97.

Daumas, Michèle. 2009. *L'or et le pouvoir: armement scythe et mythes grecs*. Nanterre: Presses universitaires de Paris ouest.

Dubois, Laurent. 1996. *Inscriptions grecques dialectales d'Olbia du Pont*. Geneva: Librairie Droz.

Ehrhardt, Norbert. 1983. *Milet und seine Kolonien: Vergleichende Untersuchung der kultischen und politischen Einrichtungen*. Frankfurt: P. Lang.

Gavriljuk, Nadežda A. 2005. "Fishery in the Life of the Nomadic Population of the Northern Black Sea Area." In *Ancient Fishing and Fish Processing in the Black Sea Region*, edited by Tønnes Bekker-Nielsen, 105–113. Aarhus: Aarhus University Press.

Gavriljuk, Nadežda A. 2008. "Social and Economic Stratification of the Scythians from the Steppe Region Based on Black-Glazed Pottery from Burials." In *Meetings of Cultures in the Black Sea Region: Between Conflict and Coexistence*, edited by Pia Guldager Bilde and Jane Hjarl Petersen, 237–262. Aarhus: Aarhus University Press.

Grammenos, Dēmētrios V., and Elias K. Petropoulos. 2003. *Ancient Greek Colonies in the Black Sea*. Thessaloniki: Archaeological Institute of Northern Greece.

Grammenos, Dēmētrios V., and Elias K. Petropoulos. 2007. *Ancient Greek Colonies in the Black Sea 2*. Oxford: Archaeopress.

Greaves, Alan M. 2007. "Milesians in the Black Sea: Trade, Settlement and Religion." In *The Black Sea in Antiquity: Regional and Interregional Economic Exchanges*, edited by Vincent Gabrielsen and John Lund, 9–21. Aarhus: Aarhus University Press.

Guldager Bilde, Pia. 2008. "Some Reflections on Eschatological Currents, Diasporic Experience, and Group Identity in the Northwestern Black Sea Region." In *Meetings of Cultures in the Black Sea Region: Between Conflict and Coexistence*, edited by Pia Guldager Bilde and Jane Hjarl Petersen, 29–46. Aarhus: Aarhus University Press.

Guldager Bilde, Pia, and Søren Handberg. 2012. "Ancient Repairs on Pottery from Olbia Pontica." *American Journal of Archaeology*, 116(3): 461–481.

Guldager Bilde, Pia, and Vladimir F. Stolba. 2006. *Surveying the Greek Chora. The Black Sea Region in a Comparative Perspective*. Aarhus: Aarhus University Press.

Guldager Bilde, Pia, Peter A.J. Attema, and Kristina Winther-Jacobsen. 2012. *The Džarylgač Survey Project*. Aarhus: Aarhus University Press.

Hame, Kerri Jeanette. 1999. *Ta Nomizomena: Private Greek Death-Ritual in the Historical Sources and Tragedy*. Unpublished PhD dissertation, Bryn Mawr College.

Handberg, Søren. 2011. "Amphora Fragments Re-used as Potter's Tools in the Rural Landscape of Panskoye." In *Pottery in the Archaeological Record: Greece and Beyond. Acts of the International Colloquium Held at the Danish and Canadian Institutes in Athens, June 20–22, 2008*, edited by Mark L. Lawall and John Lund, 62–66. Aarhus: Aarhus University Press.

Handberg, Søren. 2013. "Milesian Ktiseis and Aeolian Potters in the Black Sea Region." In *Exploring the Hospitable Sea: Proceedings of the International Workshop on the Black Sea Held in Thessaloniki, 21–23 September 2012*, edited by Manolēs Manōledakēs, 1–18. Oxford: Archaeopress.

Handberg, Søren, and Jan K. Jacobsen. 2011. "Greek or Indigenous? From Potsherd to Identity in Early Colonial Encounters." In *Communicating Identity in Italic Iron Age Communities*, edited by Margarita Gleba and Helle W. Horsnaes, 175–194. Oxford: Oxbow.

Hannestad, Lise, Vladimir F. Stolba, and Alexander N. Ščeglov. 2002. *Panskoye I*. Aarhus: Aarhus University Press.

Havelock, Christine Mitchell. 1995. *The Aphrodite of Knidos and Her Successors: A Historical Review of the Female Nude in Greek Art*. Ann Arbor: University of Michigan Press.

Hedreen, Guy. 1991. "The Cult of Achilles in the Euxine." *Hesperia*, 60(3): 313–330.

Hiller, Stefan. 1991. "The Mycenaeans and the Black Sea." *Aegaeum*, 7: 207–216.

Hind, John 1998. "Megarian Colonisation in the Western Half of the Black Sea (Sister- and Daughter-Cities of Herakleia)." In *The Greek Colonisation of the Black Sea Area*, edited by Gocha R. Tsetskhladze, 131–152. Stuttgart: Steiner.

Hinge, George. 2008. "Dionysos and Herakles in Scythia. The Eschatological String of Herodotos' Book 4." In *Meetings of Cultures in the Black Sea Region: Between Conflict and Coexistence*, edited by Pia Guldager Bilde and Jane Hjarl Petersen, 369–397. Aarhus: Aarhus University Press.

Hupe, Joachim. 2006. *Der Achilleus-Kult im nördlichen Schwarzmeerraum vom Beginn der griechischen Kolonisation bis in die römische Kaiserzeit: Beiträge zur Akkulturationsforschung.* Rahden: Leidor.

Højte, Jakob Munk. 2009. *Mithridates VI and the Pontic Kingdom*. Aarhus: Aarhus University Press.

Ivantchik, Askold I. 2012. "Agoranomes dans les cités du Pont nord et occidental." In *Agoranomes et édiles institutions des marchés antiques*, edited by Laurent Capdetrey and Claire Hasenohr, 121–130. Bordeaux: Éditions Ausonius.

Kacharava, Darejan, and Guram Kvirkvelia. 2008. *Wine, Worship, and Sacrifice: The Golden Graves of Ancient Vani*. Princeton: Institute for the Study of the Ancient World, in association with Princeton University Press.

Keenleyside, Anne, Henry P. Schwarcz, and Kristina Panayotova. 2006. "Stable Isotopic Evidence of Diet in a Greek Colonial Population from the Black Sea." *Journal of Archaeological Science*, 33(9): 1205–1215.

Kelterbaum, Daniel, Helmut Brückner, Alexey V. Porotov, et al. 2011. "Geoarchaeology of Taman Peninsula (Kerch Strait, South-West Russia): The Example of the Ancient Greek Settlement of Golubitskaya 2." *Die Erde*, 142(3): 235–258.

Kerschner, Michael. 2006. "Zum Beginn und zu den Phasen der griechischen Kolonisation am Schwarzen Meer: Die Evidenz der ostgriechischen Keramik." *Eurasia Antiqua*, 12: 228–250.

Kreuz, Patric-Alexander. 2012. *Die Grabreliefs aus dem Bosporanischen Reich*. Leuven: Peeters.

Kryžickij, Sergej D., and Nina A. Lejpunskaja. 2010. "Building Remains and Accompanying Finds, 6th–1st Century BC." In *The Lower City of Olbia (Sector NGS) in the 6th Century BC to the 4th Century AD*, vol. 1, edited by Nina A. Lejpunskaja, Pia Guldager Bilde, Jakob Munk Højte, 27–102. Aarhus: Aarhus University Press.

Kutajsov, Vladimir A. 1995. "Cast Money and Coins of Kerkinitis of the Fifth Century BC." *Ancient Civilizations from Scythia to Siberia*, 2(1): 39–59.

Lezzi-Hafter, Adrienne. 1997. "Offerings Made to Measure: Two Special Commissions by the Eretria Painter for Apollonia Pontica." In *Athenian Potters and Painters: The Conference Proceedings, vol. 2, Oxbow Monograph 67*, edited by John Howard Oakley, William D.E. Coulson, and Olga Palagia, 353–369. Oxford: Oxbow.

Levi, Elena I. 1956. "The Olbian Agora." In *Olbia and the Lower Bug in the Ancient Period*, edited by Victor F. Gajdukevič, 35–118. Moscow: Akademia Nauk (in Russian).

Lungu, Vasilica. 2002. "Hero Cult and Greek Colonization in the Black Sea Area." *Revue des Études Sud-Est Européenes*, 40: 3–17.

Machowski, Wojciech. 2011. "Graves beneath Barrows on Ancient Necropoleis in the North-Pontic Area." *Studies in Ancient Art and Civilization*, 15: 127–149.

Malkin, Irad. 1987. *Religion and Colonization in Ancient Greece*. Leiden: Brill.

Malkin, Irad. 2005. "Herakles and Melqart: Greeks and Phoenicians in the Middle Ground." In *Cultural Borrowings and Ethnic Appropriations in Antiquity*, edited by Erich S. Gruen, 238–257. Stuttgart: F. Steiner.

Meyer, Caspar. 2013. *Greco-Scythian Art and the Birth of Eurasia: From Classical Antiquity to Russian Modernity*. Oxford: Oxford University Press.

Müller, Christe. 2010. *D'Olbia à Tanaïs. Territoires et réseaux d'échanges dans la mer Noire septentrionale aux époques classique et hellénistique*. Scripta Antiqua 28. Bordeaux: Ausonius Éditions.

Murray, William M. 2002. "Observations in the 'Isis Scraffito' at Nymphaion." In *7th International Symposium on Ship Construction in Antiquity: Pylos, 26–29 August 1999: Proceedings*, edited by Harry Tzalas, 539–561. Athens: Hellenic Institute for the Preservation of Nautical Tradition.

Nieling, Jens. 2009. *Die Einführung der Eisentechnologie in Südkaukasien und Ostanatolien während der Spätbronze- und Früheisenzeit. Black Sea Studies 10*. Aarhus: Aarhus University Press.

Nikolaenko, Galina M. 2001. *Chora Chersonesa Tavričeskogo. Zemel'nyj kadastr IV–III vv. do n.e. Čast' II*. Sevastopol: Natsional'ni Zapovednik Chersones Tavricheskiï.

Ochotnikov, Sergej B. 2006a. "The *Chorai* of the Ancient Cities in the Lower Dniester Area (6th Century BC–3rd Century AD)." In *Surveying the Greek Chora. The Black Sea Region in a Comparative Perspective*, edited by Pia Guldager Bilde and Vladimir F. Stolba, 81–98. Aarhus: Aarhus University Press.

Osborne, Robin. 2008. "Reciprocal Strategies: Imperialism, Barbarism and Trade in Archaic and Classical Olbia." In *Meetings of Cultures in the Black Sea Region: Between Conflict and Coexistence*, edited by Pia Guldager Bilde and Jane Hjarl Petersen, 333–346. Aarhus: Aarhus University Press.

Page, Denys Lionel. 1968. *Lyrica Graeca selecta. Oxonii*. Oxford: Clarendon Press.

Petersen, Jane Hjarl. 2009. "Kurgan Burials from Nymphaion – A New Approach." In *Meetings of Cultures in the Black Sea Region: Between Conflict and Coexistence*, edited by Pia Guldager Bilde and Jane Hjarl Petersen, 215–235. Aarhus: Aarhus University Press.

Petersen, Jane Hjarl. 2010. *Cultural Interactions and Social Strategies on the Pontic Shores: Burial Customs in the Northern Black Sea Area c. 550–270 B.C.* Aarhus: Aarhus University Press.

Posamentir, Richard. 2010. *The Polychrome Grave Stelai from the Early Hellenistic Necropolis (Chersonesan studies 1)*. Austin: University of Texas Press.

Rempel, Jane. 2011. "Burial in the Bosporan Kingdom: Local Traditions in Regional Context(s)." In *Living Through the Dead: Burial and Commemoration in the Classical World*, edited by Maureen Carroll and Jane Rempel, 21–46. Oxford: Oxbow.

Ruban, Vladimir V. 1982. "The Agoranomos Magistracy in Olbia." *Archeologia*, 39: 30–40 (in Russian).

Rusyayeva, Anna S. 2007. "Religious Interactions between Olbia and Scythia." In *Classical Olbia and the Scythian World: From the Sixth Century BC to the Second Century AD*, edited by David Braund and Sergei D. Kryzhitskiy, 93–102. Oxford: Oxford University Press.

Ščeglov, Aleksander N. 1992. *Polis et chora: cité et territoire dans le Pont-Euxin*. Paris: Les Belles Lettres.

Schramm, Gottfried. 1973. "*Nordpontische Ströme; namenphilologische Zugänge zur Frühzeit des europäischen Ostens.*" Gottingen: Vandenhoeck & Ruprecht.

Skudnova, Varvara M. 1988. *The Archaic Necropolis of Olbia*. Leningrad: Iskusstvo (in Russian).

Sokol'skij, Nikolaj I. 1976. *Taman tholos and the residence of Chrysaliskos*. Moscow: Izdat. Nauka (in Russian).

Solovyov, Sergey L. 2006. "Monetary Circulation and the Political History of Archaic Borysthenes." *Ancient Civilizations from Scythia to Siberia*, 12(1): 63–75.

Solovyov, Sergey L. 2010. "Borysthenes and Olbia. Greeks and Natives Interactions on the Initial Stage of Colonisation." In *Archaic Greek culture: History, Archaeology, Art and Museology*, edited by Sergey Solovyov, 89–102. Oxford: Archaeopress.

Stingl, Timo. 2005. "Fruhe bronzene Geldformen im Nordwestlichen Schwarzmeerraum." In *Bilder und Objekte als Trager kultureller Identitat und interkultureller Kommunikation im Schwarzmeergebiet: Kolloquium im Zschortau/Sachsen vom 13.2.–15.2.2003*, edited by Frederike Fless and Michail Yu Treister, 119–123. Rahden: M. Leidorf.

Stingl, Timo. 2006. "Beobachtungen und Überlegungen zum Pfeilgeld aus Apollonia Pontica." In *Pontos Euxeinos: Beiträge zur Archäologie und Geschichte des antiken Schwarzmeer- und Balkanraume; [Manfred Oppermann zum 65. Geburtstag]*, edited by Sven Conrad and Manfred Oppermann, 97–108. Langenweissbach: Beier and Beran.

Stolba, Vladimir F. 2005a. "The Oath of Chersonesos and the Chersonesean Economy in the Early Hellenistic Period." In *Making, Moving and Managing: The New World of Ancient Economies, 323–31 BC*, edited by Zofia Archibald, John Kenyon Davies, and Vincent Gabrielsen, 298–232. Oxford: Oxbow.

Stolba, Vladimir F. 2005b. "Monetary Crises in the Early Hellenistic Poleis of Olbia, Chersonesos and Pantikapaion: A Re-assessment." In *XIII Congreso Internacional de Numismatica (Madrid, 2003). Actas – Proceedings – Actes*, edited by Carmen Alfaro, Carmen Marcos, and Paloma Otero, 395–403. Madrid: Ministerio de Cultura, Dirección General de Bellas Artes y Bienes Culturales, Subdirección General de Museos Estatales.

Talmaţchi, Gabriel. 2010. "About some Discoveries of Arrowheads: Monetary Signs in South-West Dobruja." *Pontica*, 43: 387–398.

Tsetskhladze, Gocha R., ed. 1998. *The Greek Colonisation of the Black Sea Area: Historical Interpretation of Archaeology*. Historia Einzelschriften 121. Stuttgart: F. Steiner.

Tsetskhladze, Gocha R. 2004. "On the Earliest Greek Colonial Architecture in the Pontus." In *Pontus and the Outside World: Studies in Black Sea History, Historiography, and Archaeology*, edited by Christopher Tuplin, 225–278. Leiden: Brill.

Tsetskhladze, Gocha R. 2007. "Pots and Pandemonium: The Earliest East Greek Pottery from North Pontic Native Settlements." *Pontica*, 40: 37–70.

Tsiafakis, Despoina. 2013. "Architectural Similarities(?) between the Black Sea and North Aegean Settlements." In *The Bosporus: Gateway between the Ancient West and East (1st Millennium BC–5th Century AD). Proceedings of the Fourth International Congress on Black Sea Antiquities. Istabul, 14th–18th September 2009*. BAR International Series 2517, edited by Gocha R. Tsetskhladze, Sümer Atasoy, Alexandru Avram, et al., 61–68. Oxford: Archaeopress.

Ustinova, Yulia. 1998. "Aphrodite Ourania of the Bosporos: The Great Goddess of a Frontier Pantheon." *Kernos*, 11: 209–226.

Ustinova, Yulia. 1999. *The Supreme Gods of the Bosporan Kingdom: Celestial Aphrodite and the Most High God*. Leiden: Brill.

Ustinova, Yulia. 2009. "Apollo Iatros: A Greek God of Pontic Origin." In *Die Griechen und ihre Nachbarn am Nordrand des Schwarzen Meeres: Beiträge des internationalen archäologischen Kolloquiums, Münster 2001*, edited by Klaus P. Stähler and Gabriele Gudrian, 245–298. Munster: Ugarit-Verlag.

Vakhtina, Marina Ju. 2007. "Greek Archaic Orientalising Pottery from the Barbarian Sites of the Forest-Steppe Zone of the Northern Black Sea Coastal Region." In *The Black Sea in Antiquity: Regional and Interregional Economic* Exchanges, edited by Vincent Gabrielsen and John Lund, 23–38. Aarhus: Aarhus University Press.

Vickers, Michael, and Amiran Kakhidze. 2004. *Pichvnari 1. Results of Excavations Conducted by the Joint British-Georgian Expedition 1998–2002*. Oxford: The Ashmolean Museum and Batumi: Archaeological Museum.

Vinogradov, Jurij G. 1971. "The History of Archaic Olbia." *Vestnik Drevnei Istorii*, 1971(2): 232–237 (in Russian).

Vinogradov, Yurij. 1998. "The Greek Colonisation of the Black Sea Region in the Light of Private Lead Letters." In *The Greek Colonisation of the Black Sea Area: Historical Interpretation of Archaeology*, edited by Gocha R. Tsetskhladze, 153–178. Stuttgart: F. Steiner.

Zograf, Aleksandr N. 1977. *Ancient Coinage*. Oxford: British Archaeological Reports.

FURTHER READING

Overviews of the history, topography, and main monuments of most major Greek settlements in the Black Sea region can be found in Avram, Hind, and Tsetskhladze (2004) and Grammenos and Petropoulos (2003, 2007). A valuable introduction to the early phase of Greek presence in the Black Sea is found in Tsetskhladze (1998). Discussions of specific topics such as chronology, landscape, trade, meeting of cultures, and the Persian presence in the Black Sea can be found in several of the volumes in the series *Black Sea Studies*, which were produced at the Centre for Black Sea Studies at Aarhus University. The *Zentrum für Archäologie und Kulturgeschichte des Schwarzmeerraumes* (ZAKS) in Halle/Saale is continuously issuing monographs on a variety of topics related to Black Sea archaeology. Among the many journals that regularly publish articles dealing with the Black Sea in antiquity are *Eurasia Antiqua: Zeitschrift für Archäologie Eurasiens*, published by the German Archaeological Institute, and *Ancient Civilizations from Scythia to Siberia*, issued by Brill. Both provide good starting points for further inquiries.

CHAPTER TWENTY-ONE

The Greeks in the East in the Hellenistic Period

Gerassimos G. Aperghis

Historical Summary

In the wars of the Successors that followed the death of Alexander the Great in 323 (e.g., *CAH* 3.1; Shipley 2000; Erskine 2003), his general Seleukos was first able to gain a foothold in Babylonia in 311 and then gradually take over most of Alexander's Asiatic possessions (Map 3). At his death in 281, Seleukos ruled over an empire that stretched from the Aegean to Central Asia. In the remainder of the third century, the Seleukid state underwent changes in its extent, especially in Asia Minor as a result of conflict with the Ptolemies of Egypt and the emerging Attalids of Pergamon. However, at the beginning of the second century, Antiochos III had mostly reestablished Seleukid control in this region, while taking, in addition, southern Syria, Phoenicia, and Palestine from the Ptolemies.

On the eastern borders, Bactria and Sogdiana, that is, northeastern Afghanistan and the southern regions of Turkmenistan, Uzbekistan, and Tadjikistan, split off. While the manner and timing of the Bactrian secession have been debated, it seems clear that an independent Greek kingdom was in place there by 239 at the latest. This was temporarily subjugated in 206 by Antiochos, but recovered its independence and went on to expand across the Hindu Kush into what are today southern and eastern Afghanistan, Pakistan, and northwestern India. This kingdom eventually fragmented into smaller ones, and these were gradually overrun by invaders between ca. 145 BC and ca. AD 10.

Throughout the third century and even after the defeat of Antiochos by the Romans at Magnesia in 190, which resulted in the loss of western Asia Minor, the Seleukid Empire remained a powerful entity. This is the modern view (Sherwin-White and Kuhrt 1993), in contrast to the older idea of a state in decline from the moment of Seleukos's death.

The Seleukid Empire received its death blow, in fact, only much later, at the hands of the Parthians, an Iranian tribe which had descended east of the Caspian Sea and established

---

A Companion to Greeks Across the Ancient World, First Edition. Edited by Franco De Angelis.
© 2020 John Wiley & Sons, Inc. Published 2020 by John Wiley & Sons, Inc.

itself in the Seleukid satrapy of Parthia, from which it took its name. By ca. 240 the Parthians had acquired their independence in this region and toward the end of the third century began to make incursions further south, though the manner and timing of these moves are debated. Certainly by ca. 140 the Parthians had gradually conquered the greater part of the Seleukid territories in Iran and Mesopotamia, and their conquest was consolidated in 129 after their defeat of Antiochos VII. In this they were helped by the internal dynastic struggles which had considerably weakened the Seleukids. Meanwhile, the Romans had inherited the greater part of western Asia Minor from the Attalids, and the Seleukid state was now restricted to Syria, Kilikia, Phoenicia, and Palestine. By 64 it had been completely dissolved and was in the hands of the Romans (for Seleukid history: Sherwin-White and Kuhrt 1993; Shipley 2000; Austin 2003; summarized in Aperghis 2004, 19–27).

Land, Climate, and the Economy

In the development of Hellenism in Asia an important role was played by the nature of the terrain and the climatic conditions (Map 3). The Mediterranean was familiar to the Greeks, and for this reason they mostly established themselves along its shores. In western Asia Minor, Greek city-states had, of course, existed for centuries, while more sparsely populated areas on the southern coast saw the development of some new foundations in the Hellenistic period. Further inland in Asia Minor, Hellenism progressed more by the establishment of military colonies and the process of osmosis, as local communities adopted Greek culture and were eventually transformed into *poleis* (Brown, Chapter 11, this volume; Cohen 1995). It was in northern Syria under the Seleukids where Greek settlement mainly took place, with the creation of several major cities and many smaller ones from the very beginning of the Hellenistic period. Finally, the coast of southern Syria, Phoenicia, and Palestine was already mostly occupied by native cities, and Greek settlement inland tended again to be in small military colonies (Garnand, Chapter 8, and Manning, Chapter 17, this volume; Cohen 2006). Eventually, Hellenism became quite deeply rooted in this entire region, with a further strengthening in the Roman period.

Far from the Mediterranean, in the Asian interior, the conditions were quite different. The great plain of Mesopotamia received little rainfall, but was irrigated by the Euphrates and Tigris and an extensive network of tributaries and canals, with extremely productive agriculture. Mesopotamia, until its final loss in 129, constituted the population and economic heartland of the Seleukid state, not Syria, as some would argue. Further east stretched the great mountain range of the Zagros and the highlands of Iran and western and southern Afghanistan, extensive, sparsely populated regions. It was only when one crossed the Hindu Kush and attained Bactria and Sogdiana that one encountered again large irrigated valleys, those of the Oxos and Jaxartes (Amur and Syr Daria) and other rivers flowing down from the Hindu Kush and the Pamirs. And since one will also be dealing here with the Indo-Greek kingdoms, one should note the rich, densely populated plains formed by the Indus and its tributaries of the Punjab.

In the Asian interior, apart from the soldiers posted to garrisons, Greek settlers received land in many new city foundations and their main source of income, as with the native populations, was undoubtedly agriculture, whether they farmed their land themselves or had others do so for them. Typically, a settler would receive an allotment in the city, in order to build a house, as well as plots of land for grain production and also vine cultivation, where the conditions were suitable. Trade was mainly local, because transport of bulk goods, such as grain, by land was not normally economical. Thus cities were essentially fed by their hinterlands, though a major river could expand the scope of a city's trade. So could access to the Mediterranean coast, because the sea greatly facilitated transport. Long-distance trade was generally possible only in lightweight goods of high value, such as frankincense and myrrh, spices, ivory, precious woods, stones, and so on, which arrived mainly from southern Arabia, Africa, and India via the Persian Gulf or overland and were then transported to the Mediterranean, at hugely increased prices (Aperghis 2004, 70–78 with references). That some Greeks also settled in existing native cities, such as Babylon, as administrators and traders, and later acquired distinct political rights within the city, a *politeuma*, is evidenced (Spek 1987).

What one notes when comparing the Seleukid Empire with the contemporary city-states of the Greek world is the huge difference in scale. Athens, for example, one of the largest city-states, occupied an area in Attica of some 2500 km^2, supporting probably 200 000 to 300 000 inhabitants, while the Seleukid Empire covered about 3.8 million km^2 at its peak, with a population of some 14 to 18 million (Aperghis 2004, 35–58). Its vastly greater size necessitated a quite different form of civil/military administration compared to the city-state, with power decentralized to the satrapies and their subdivisions: hyparchies, semi-independent native peoples (*ethnē*), and self-governing cities. It also required a different system of financial administration, in which coinage played a key role.

The Establishment of the Greeks in the East

If one excludes the few cases known of individual Greeks in the Persian Empire, such as the doctor Ktesias or the explorer Skylax, or groups that had been exiled to the central and eastern satrapies, such as those Alexander discovered near Persepolis or in Bactria, the first Greeks established in numbers in the Asian hinterland were the garrison troops, mainly consisting of mercenaries, whom Alexander left behind on his march eastward, and the veterans of the army he settled in the Alexandrias he founded on his way. On the basis of the figures given in the Alexander historians, one may estimate the total number at probably not more than 50 000.

It was believed that the Alexandrias in the East were created so that they could serve as centers for the propagation of Greek culture. The truth, however, seems to be that with the exception of Alexandria of Egypt, which from the very beginning was planned to become a large commercial center, of the remaining Alexandrias only five can without doubt be attributed to Alexander (Fraser 1996), and none of these had any significant development. And this was probably because their purpose was different, mainly strategic, since the veterans who were settled there, probably compulsorily, were, along with the garrisons, useful in safeguarding Alexander's lines of communications with India. In addition, however, there was an undoubted economic benefit, since Alexander removed from his army, and its cost, non-productive soldiers, giving them as compensation not money, which was more valuable to him, but land, which he possessed in abundance. This may explain the dissatisfaction of the settlers, supposedly 23 000 in number, who were established in Bactria and revolted immediately after Alexander's death desiring to return to their homelands (Diod. Sic. 18.7).

The real founding of Greek cities in Asia is due to the Seleukids and mainly to the founder of the dynasty, Seleukos, and his son, Antiochos (Cohen 1978; Aperghis 2004, 89–99; 2005 with references). Their purpose may have been entirely different, as will be discussed below.

When Seleukos had conquered the largest part of his empire by 301, with the exception of Asia Minor, which was still in the hands of his main rival, Lysimachos, he faced a serious problem. The wars of the Successors had been conducted since 323 mainly with mercenary armies, which needed to be paid in coin. This was minted principally from the Persian treasures in gold and silver captured by Alexander, valued at 180 000 talents or more, according to Strabo (15.3.9). The greater part of this was eventually coined by Alexander and his generals in order to pay soldiers, but most of the coin moved westward, to mainland Greece and Asia Minor, which were the main theaters of military operations.

The problem for Seleukos was that the greater part of his expenses, for the payment of soldiers, was taking place mainly in coin (Aperghis 2004, 189–205), while his revenue from taxation was being collected mainly in kind, principally from agricultural production and animal husbandry, as had been the case in the Persian state which he had inherited. At some point in time, if the imbalance between revenue and expenses in coin continued, his treasury would be exhausted. To rectify this situation, Seleukos needed to collect most of his tax revenues in coin. But for the farmer or herder to give the Seleukid administration the coin, he first had to acquire it. And this could only be done if he sold his surplus. In practice, however, a farmer or herder does not need to purchase many things that he does not produce or manufacture himself and so has no strong desire to generate a large surplus. However, taxation will force him to do so. Indeed, the more productive the land, with the potential for a greater surplus, the higher the level of taxation that can be imposed by the ruling power; and this is what the Seleukid kings apparently did (Aperghis 2004, 137–180 with references). While the idea that the bulk of Seleukid revenue was received in coin is by no means universally accepted, it is difficult to see how this could not have been so, unless one accepts that the major expense, for the armed forces, was also not incurred in coin (but see below).

The surplus could mostly be sold to those who did not have their own agricultural and animal production, in other words mainly to the inhabitants of cities and towns, and via the markets there to the Seleukid administration, comprising the satrapal offices and garrisons, the royal army and navy, and even the king and his court to the extent that their needs could not be satisfied from the production of royal land, that is, that which was the private property of the king. In order to purchase their foodstuffs, the urban centers earned the necessary coin from the products and services they themselves sold, mainly to the administration, but also to a lesser extent to the countryside. Eventually, both the urban centers and the countryside returned what they earned to the Seleukid administration in the form of rents and taxes. This was the manner in which coin circulated, and in order for the system to work properly, the size of a city had to match the size of the surplus that a region could potentially generate. Too large a city could not be fed, unless the sea was nearby or a river to bring produce from further away. Too small a city would not take full advantage of a region's resources for the benefit of the royal treasury. A catalyst was also required to facilitate the circulation of coin, and this was, to a great extent, the Greek settlers in the new city foundations, with their previous experience of a coin-based economy.

The Seleukid cities seem to have been mostly founded in regions with excess agricultural and herding potential which had not been up to then fully exploited (Cohen 1995, 2006, 2013; Aperghis 2005). Northern Syria, with four large new cities (Antioch, Seleukeia, Apameia, and Laodikeia) and many smaller ones (e.g., Kyrrhos, Chalkis, Beroia, and Seleukeia-Zeugma), did not have any major settlement in the Persian period – Damascus was located further south under Ptolemaic control. The region was quickly filled up with new cities, and access to the Mediterranean helped some of them grow rapidly, Antioch on the Orontes, for instance. By the end of the third century, this city had become the most important Seleukid capital and, after the loss of Mesopotamia, the focus of the empire.

In southern Mesopotamia (Babylonia), ancient cities already existed along or near the Euphrates (Babylon, Sippar, Borsippa, Cutha, Larsa, Kish, Nippur, Uruk, Ur, and others) and there was hardly room for a new one. Instead, the largest Seleukid foundation of all, Seleukeia, was established further east, on the Tigris, near the point where its important tributary, the Diyala, created a fertile plain, a region (Sittakēnē, called Apolloniatis later) where large urban centers did not previously exist and where the irrigation system could be considerably expanded to feed Seleukeia and the other new settlements (e.g., Artemita and Antioch in Sittakēnē). Targeted also were less densely populated regions in northern Mesopotamia between the Euphrates and the Tigris, and also east of the Tigris in old Assyria, which had fallen into decline after the fall of the Neo-Assyrian Empire. In some cases, towns received the status of Greek cities (e.g., Edessa and Nisibis, which were refounded as Antiochs, or Karrhai, which had been a Macedonian military settlement). But other foundations (e.g., an Alexandria in Adiabene and a Demetrias by Arbela) may have been new. In the southeastern part of the Mesopotamian plain, in Susiane, there was also much settlement activity. This region had essentially fed Susa, one of the Persian capitals, but rather as a palatial center, not a large city. Consequently, there was plenty of scope for new Greek foundations. Susa itself was expanded and given the name Seleukeia on the Eulaios, but other cities were also created (e.g., Seleukeia-Hedyphon and Antioch on the Erythraian Sea). Further along the Persian Gulf, there was a new foundation, Antioch in Persis (probably modern Bushire), and at least the three other ones mentioned by Pliny (*HN* 6.159), Arethousa, Chalkis, and Larissa, whose locations are unknown. They may have served simply as staging points for the Seleukid navy, as did Ikaros (Failaka) and probably also Tylos (Bahrain). One final region of the Mesopotamian plain which saw Seleukid city-building on a small scale was the middle Euphrates (e.g., Doura-Europos and the urban site of Jebel Khalid). This, however, was initially a border area for the Seleukids and the settlements there may have been intended primarily as garrison towns, though they served economic needs as well by causing agricultural production to be intensified in the narrow cultivable strip along the Euphrates.

Regarding the Iranian territories, one knows of Greek cities in Media (e.g., Laodikeia-Nehavend in the Zagros, just off the main route crossing the range, and Apameia-Rhagai near Teheran), but of none in the Persian heartland, Persis (Fars), in particular on the

Persepolis plain itself. The *modus vivendi* established by Alexander with the Persians had granted them a privileged status in the empire, and Seleukos remained perhaps the only one of Alexander's generals who did not repudiate his Iranian wife, Apameia. His successors were thus partly Iranian. It may therefore have been considered politic not to establish Greek settlers inside Persis, but rather on the periphery, as Polybios (10.27) reports. In any case, Persis seems soon to have acquired autonomy, but under Seleukid suzerainty, though this last point is disputed (see below). Ekbatana, the Median capital, remained the most important Seleukid administrative center of the region.

Further east, the Seleukids founded several cities. On the road to Bactria, along the chain of oases of Parthia below the southern flanks of the Elburz and Kopet Dag ranges, Hekatompylos became an important admistrative center. An Apameia in Choarene is also noted here. Further north, along the shores of the Caspian, Hyrcania was also settled (e.g., Syrinx and Achaia), while in the oasis of Margiane (modern Merv) in Turkmenistan, the ruins of the fortifications of a very large city, Antioch in Margiane, can still be seen today. For Bactria and Sogdiana further east, there are numerous references to Seleukid foundations, the most interesting of which is the one referred to as Aï Khanoum, whose ancient name is uncertain. One knows very little about the Greek presence in southeastern Iran and western and southern Afghanistan, the Seleukid satrapies of Karmania, Aria, Arachosia, and Drangiane, but a first-century source, the Parthian stations of Isidore of Charax, makes mention of three cities in this region with Greek names (Schoff 1989, 9).

The idea presented here is that the new Seleukid cities served primarily economic needs, rather than political and military ones, as some would argue. But one should not ignore the cities' strategic value, since the concentrations of Greeks settled there were in the last resort the pillars supporting the Seleukid dynasty.

Seleukos had the reputation in antiquity of being a great founder of cities (Amm. Marc. 14.8.6; App. *Syr.* 57). Some, for example Antioch and Apameia in northern Syria and Seleukeia on the Tigris, became important and had a long life. One should not, however, imagine that the new cities were inhabited exclusively by Greeks. The sizes of some can be estimated from the areas enclosed by surviving walls. Antioch and the other three large cities of northern Syria had early on a walled area of some 200–250 ha each. If one takes a figure of about 200 inhabitants per hectare for a city in the Middle East in antiquity, as is often done (Aperghis 2004, 12–15 with references), it would appear that the major Syrian cities were initially designed for about 40 000–50 000 inhabitants each. One does have evidence that the Greek citizens of Antioch and Seleukeia in Syria numbered only about 5000– 6000 (Aperghis 2004, 93) and so with their families some 20 000–25 000, allowing of course for a large number of marriages with local women. Consequently, at least half the inhabitants must have been indigenous populations who had moved there from elsewhere. And this seems clearer in the case of Seleukeia on the Tigris, founded ca. 305, which was designed to cover an area of some 550 ha, roughly twice as much as Antioch, but possibly for just the same number of Greeks. In fact, there is evidence that some of Seleukeia's inhabitants came from three Babylonian cities: Babylon, Borsippa, and Cutha. The earlier idea that Babylon was denuded of its population is now considered incorrect. Only a part of it appears to have made the move and there is no reason to consider that this was forced. A grant of land seems to have been given, and a new capital city would undoubtedly have presented other attractions (Spek 1993, 64–70).

If one were forced to make an estimate, one might conclude that at the time of the first Seleukids there were some 200 000–300 000 Greeks in northern Syria and about the same number in the remaining part of the empire. While the Greeks constituted a relatively large proportion of the population in Syria, they appear to have been a small minority elsewhere.

Aspects of Greek Life

There have been no extensive excavations in most Seleukid cities at levels of the Seleukid period. The remains are, however, sufficient to show clear evidence of Greek life in several sites, and much more so and better known in Asia Minor and Syria. Two examples from further east may be characteristic of what the situation was in the Asian interior.

The first is Babylon, an ancient city which continued to function under the Seleukids in its own fashion, determined mainly by the great temples of its gods. It seems that a number of Greeks were established in the city, probably not as organized settlers but as traders initially, and were then given some kind of separate political status (*politeuma*), probably in the second century. They are distinguished as *politai* from the indigenous inhabitants in Babylonian cuneiform documents. A Greek theater and gymnasium have been excavated in Babylon, as well as houses which seem to show Greek architectural influence (Sherwin-White 1987; Spek 1987).

The other example is a true Greek settlement, Aï Khanoum, in the northeastern corner of Bactria, at the junction of the Oxos and Kokcha Rivers, where a fertile plain is formed that the city could rely on for its provisioning. The city has a triangular plan, with the two rivers along its short sides, and covers a fortified area of some 150 ha. Thus it is likely to have been designed for up to 30 000 inhabitants. The southern corner, where it seems the best houses were located, is at a higher elevation and ends in an acropolis. What survive from the original city are the regular, hippodameian street layout, a palace-administrative center, a theater, a gymnasium and *palaestra*, a *heroon*, temples, and an arsenal. The theater is impressive in size. Semicircular, with a radius of some 42 m, about the same as the theater of Epidauros, it had a capacity of at least five or six thousand spectators. The *palaestra* is also one of the largest known, 100 m along each side. Many architectural details of the city are clearly Greek, but there are also Mesopotamian and Iranian influences. There have also been found inscriptions in excellent Greek, as well as sculpture, small objects, and coins (Bernard 1973 and subsequent volumes concerning the excavations; Bernard 1982; Rapin 1990). It is evident that the population of Aï Khanoum must have had a significant Greek element, which despite being so distant, had close cultural contact with the Greek world to the west and lived in harmony with the local Bactrians. This would perhaps explain why the Greeks were able to retain control in this region for so long, as will be seen below.

One is left with the feeling that Aï Khanoum may not be an isolated example of a Greek city in the East. Bactria and Sogdiana, and indeed many other regions, probably hosted cities quite like it, which are covered today by later habitation and practically lost to us. If this is indeed the case, the Greek presence in Asia at this time would have been nothing short of amazing, small islands of Hellenism within and in harmony with a native sea.

What was the political-military and economic environment in which the Greeks, as well as the indigenous peoples, lived in the Seleukid Empire?

King, Cities, and Friends

For most Greeks in the East, to be subject to a monarchy was a new thing. As Polybios (6.3–10) wrote:

> Kingship is that form of the rule of one person which is voluntarily accepted by his subjects, who are governed by an appeal to reason rather than by fear and force ... Kings are no longer chosen for bodily strength and brute courage, but for the excellence of their judgement and reasoning powers.

The early Seleukids tried to put across to their subjects, particularly the Greeks, the idea that the king was good and just (*dikaios*), militarily successful, and a protector of his people (*sōtēr*). This can be observed in their coinage and the literary and epigraphic evidence. All these constituted the benefits provided to the king's subjects (*euergesia*), who legitimized his rule, in return for loyalty and good-will (*eunoia*).

With the Greek cities in particular, whether pre-existing or newly founded, whether subject, allied, or independent, the Seleukid kings engaged in a diplomatic dialogue, as if between equals, despite the overwhelming imbalance in relative power, so as to maintain the image of benevolent ruler and not tyrant, which the Greek tradition would have found unpalatable (Ma 1999). The subject cities themselves were virtually self-governing, but often, if not always, with a Seleukid supervisor (*epistatēs*).

The senior positions in the civil, military, and financial administration of the empire were in the hands of a relatively small group of officials, the Friends (*philoi*) of the king, as was the case in other Hellenistic kingdoms (e.g., Carsana 1996; Savalli-Lestrade 1998; Habicht 2006). The Friends were mostly Greeks, but not necessarily originally from within the Seleukid realm. There was something like an ongoing search for talented administrators, diplomats, and military commanders, and the Seleukid kings did not hesitate to hire officials from independent Greek cities or rival Hellenistic kingdoms, such as the Ptolemaic. A client ruler might also be admitted into this circle as a matter of policy. The Jewish high priest Jonathan was one such case when rival Seleukid kings were contending for his support in the interdynastic conflicts of the 140s.

The Friends were widely recognized as one of the powers of the Seleukid state, a ruling class, but not a hereditary aristocracy, as had been the case in all the great empires of the Middle East and even in the Macedonian kingdom. In inscriptions of the third century from Greek cities, the king is often referred to with his Friends and his army, whether it is the king making the statement or the *polis*. A city was particularly fortunate if one of its citizens happened to be a Friend and could exercise his influence with the king on its behalf. One belonged temporarily to the circle of Friends, as long as the king so desired, and his successor was expected to confirm the arrangement. A Friend frequently received land for revenue, and the king might take it back when he no longer served. What played an important role was the capability of the official concerned, along with his loyalty to the king, which would partly explain why the Seleukid Empire was so resilient and able to function as an empire for nearly 200 years, at least until the final loss of Mesopotamia to the Parthians in 129.

Initially, there seems to have been just one category of Friends, but in the second century one hears of different grades of increasing importance: Friends, First Friends, Relatives (*syggeneis*). There were certain visible signs of belonging to this circle, for example the right to wear purple and a golden clasp donated by the king.

The Greek Administration

The Seleukids essentially inherited much of the Achaemenid system of administration: the division of the empire into large satrapies and each of these further into smaller administrative units. The satraps, *strategoi* in Greek terminology, seem to have been mainly Greeks, though not necessarily belonging to the circle of Friends. Their powers appear to have been limited to civil/military administration, at least for the western and central satrapies for which there is some evidence. Included within the satrapies were smaller territorial administrative units, the hyparchies, Greek and native cities and "peoples" (*ethnē*). At this lower level, one hears of non-Greek administrators, for example the Babylonians Anu-Uballit Nikarchos and Kephalon or the Jewish high priests Jason, Menelaos, and Alkimos, who were responsible for their respective cities or peoples.

It is often unclear what the ethnicity of an official really is, unless the patronym or city affiliation is also given. Thus, though most of the names of known Seleukid officials are Greek (Grainger 1997), it is quite possible that one may be overestimating the proportion of actual Greeks in administrative positions. Indeed, the relatively rare occurrence of native revolts suggests that the empire must have co-opted many members of the local elite into government. This is clearly seen in the case of Judaea, for which the evidence is more extensive. It is worth noting that the Maccabean revolt faced by the Seleukids there had mainly religious causes and pitted the Hellenized upper stratum of Jewish society against the more conservative religious elements of the population (Bickerman 1979; Aperghis 2011a and 2011b with references for different views).

The need for the Seleukids to carefully manage their finances was previously noted. Thus the financial administration in many satrapies, certainly those in the west and center, was, it seems, independent of the satrap and subject to a satrapal *dioiketes* and his subordinate *oikonomoi*, who also managed the king's private land in each satrapy. The *dioiketes* corresponded with the king directly, and certain decisions had to be taken jointly with the satrap, while there was also cooperation at the lower administrative level, the hyparchy or *oikonomia* – probably the same administrative unit with a different name according to the function of interest. This was a clever system when the ultimate power, the king, was located so far away and did not wish for too much power to be vested in the satraps. The role of native administrators at the top levels of financial administration is not evidenced, since all the names of actual or possible *dioiketai* and *oikonomoi* known are Greek. Since the Seleukid kings kept this crucial aspect of their administration under their personal control, it is not unlikely that they did so using a central cadre of solely Greek senior administrators (Aperghis 2004, 263–295 with references).

The multitude of taxes in the Seleukid state is impressive. All those categories of taxes which are described in pseudo-Aristotle's *Oikonomika* are to be found there: on the natural products of the land, for example metals, water, and salt, on agriculture and animal husbandry, on transportation, on trade and other economic transactions, on people and their work. The total revenue from taxation is estimated at between 15 000 and 20 000 Attic talents annually at the empire's peak under Antiochos III, the greater part of which in coin. And this for the simple reason that the mainly military expenses of the state had to be covered, which were also in coin. For comparison, the public revenue of Athens, rich by Greek standards, was normally only a few hundred talents annually (Aperghis 2004, 117–179, 248–251 with references).

The Greek inhabitants of the Seleukid Empire do not seem to have had any special privileges compared to the indigenous peoples with regard to taxation. Because, however, most of then lived in cities, they were subject to the lower direct taxation of the cities, as were the Babylonians, Phoenicians, and others, probably because the cities were useful to the Seleukids as the driving force of a monetary economy.

Coinage

An innovation that the Seleukids introduced into Asia was the extensive use of coin, which could more easily be dealt with initially by the Greeks, with their experience of coin-based economies. Alexander had made the first move in this direction when coin was minted at Babylon and Susa, principally for the payment of his troops (Waggoner 1979). This is not to say, however, that some of the indigenous peoples did not use precious metals in their transactions, the Babylonians, for instance, and quite extensively. But to accept a gold or silver coin at its nominal value, rather than treat it as precious metal and weigh it, was a significant step forward and required time to be implemented widely. A consistently high precious metal content and correct weight, allowing for some loss due to wear, were absolutely necessary to maintain confidence, and this the Seleukids managed to achieve in their precious metal coinage for all of the third and the first part of the second century, after which a gradual debasement of the currency set in. Where the innovation was more marked, however, was in the introduction of small-denomination bronze coins for everyday use. This was a completely fiduciary coinage, where the nominal value of the coin was usually much greater than the value based on metal content. Indeed, the Seleukid kings after Seleukos I hardly minted silver coins smaller than a drachm, but used bronze coins instead (Houghton and Lorber 2002; Houghton, Lorber, and Hoover 2008).

The Seleukid coins were not intended to be the sole currency within the empire. Indeed, Seleukid gold and silver circulated in a minority until at least the middle of the second century, though their share of the total coin in circulation was gradually increasing all the time. This was because the Seleukids mainly minted new coin to replace what was withdrawn from circulation by loss and wear and also to finance important military campaigns. There was never any attempt to replace foreign currency *en masse* (Aperghis 2004, 213–246 with references). Unlike the Ptolemies, the Seleukids opted for an economy "open" to the Greek world further west and allowed all coins minted on the Attic standard, as were the numerous "Alexanders" and their own, to circulate freely. One reason, of course, was necessity, since their long, porous borders with their neighbors would have made mandatory exchange very costly to implement – the Ptolemies could impose this efficiently at their main port of entry to Egypt, Alexandria. But another reason may well have been the desire of the Seleukids to attract Greek settlers and traders with a policy of open physical and economic borders. Considering the relatively few Seleukid coins found in hoards outside the empire and the many foreign coins found within, it seems that the Seleukid balance of payments must have been positive most of the time in the third and early second centuries.

The iconographic material of Seleukid coins is essentially Greek. To begin with, the coin types and name of Alexander were used on the gold and silver minted by Seleukos. This was essentially an attempt to seek legitimacy for his rule as the successor of Alexander in the eyes of the Greeks and of his army, for whom the coins were mainly destined. The king's head on the obverses of most precious metal issues began to be displayed with the next ruler, Antiochos I, and is typical of other Hellenistic coinages, but the reverses, as well as both obverses and reverses of the bronze, are quite varied. The Seleukids usually displayed there their patron gods and demi-gods, mainly Zeus and Apollo, but also Athena, Artemis, Herakles, Nike, the Dioskouroi, Dionysos, Hermes, Helios, Poseidon and others; or the attributes associated with these. This was a statement in the eyes of their subjects of the kings' piety and the support they received from the gods. But the Seleukids also projected themselves as warrior-kings primarily, charged with the security and welfare of their subjects, and their coins served this purpose at a time when a coinage circulating widely across the empire was the nearest thing to today's mass media. The depiction of the goddess Nike on coin issues of a particular mint, for example, is nearly always an indication of some victory in the region. Here the Seleukids were obviously catering primarily for their Greek subjects and army, who would have understood the significance of the iconography, and it is interesting that they did not consider it necessary to address themselves directly to the native populations. This was probably in line with a policy to rely only on native elites to govern, who could be expected to acquire some knowledge of the Greek language and culture if they wished to participate in the administration or deal closely with it.

One other characteristic of Seleukid coins of the third and early second centuries is that they normally display two monograms on their reverses, often associated with a particular symbol. It has been suggested (Aperghis 2010), though this goes against the views of most numismatists, that the monograms on Seleukid coins reflect the dual system of civil/military and financial administration discussed earlier, that is, that the monograms depict both the name of the issuer of coin, typically representing the financial administration, and that of the recipient, who belonged to the civil or military administrations, while the symbol usually identifies the intended end-user of the particular coin issue, who is typically a branch of the royal army (infantry, cavalry, elephant corps, support services), a specialized military unit (e.g., archers), or a satrapal garrison.

The Armed Forces

The king ultimately imposed his authority by means of his armed forces and so was able to collect the tribute and taxes owed him. These were then expended mainly in pay and support for his soldiers and sailors. Here the Seleukid Empire was no different from other empires, the Roman, for instance, and the military expenses of the state constituted a huge proportion of total expenses (Aperghis 2004, 189–205 with references).

While the army played a role in the selection of the king in the Macedonian kingdom, this soon disappeared in the Seleukid, because the army there did not, in my view, come mainly from the ranks of Greeks. The idea that the Greek settlers, who were given land, or at least their sons, had the obligation to serve in the royal army is quite widespread (e.g., Bar-Kochva 1977). Though this was certainly a system used by the Ptolemies to attract foreign soldiers, there is no convincing evidence for the Seleukids. It is more likely that the Seleukid army was a paid force composed in large part of non-Greeks. Even from the time of Seleukos I, it is argued that the bulk of the cavalry was Iranian and that the heavy infantry also included Babylonians and Iranians, while the greater part of the coinage issued was intended for military pay (Aperghis 2020, and see below).

The view expressed here is that the Greeks who were established in the Seleukid cities certainly obtained a land grant, but apparently without the obligation to serve in the army, except in critical circumstances. They were much more useful to the king as administrators and basic catalysts in the economic life of the cities, so that coin could flow smoothly to and from the royal treasuries. A decisive defeat – and the Seleukids suffered several, and not only at the hands of the Romans at Magnesia – would have seriously affected the Greek element, if it had been serving in large numbers in the armed forces, and shattered the foundations of the empire, but this never happened until the Seleukids' last-ditch effort against the Parthians in 129, where they did have recourse to Greek citizens from Antioch and probably elsewhere. Only in certain frontier areas, and especially in western Asia Minor, where the conditions were not favorable for the founding of large new cities, because of the existence of so many already, and where it was necessary to defend the frontiers, were military colonists installed in smaller *katoikiai*, some of which developed much later into *poleis*.

The regular army, consisting of both Greeks and others, was apparently paid, even in peace time. Antiochos III's army mutinied in 222 because of arrears of pay (Polyb. 5.50.1–5); Demetrios I offered to enroll Jewish soldiers at the same rate of pay as his other troops (1 Macc. 10.36); Demetrios II provoked dissatisfaction when he disbanded soldiers who had been paid even in peacetime so as to be ready for a call-up (Joseph. *AJ* 13.130). The regular army was reinforced by mercenary soldiers of different origins, not only in the satrapal garrisons but also for important campaigns.

The Spread of Greek Culture

There was at one time a widespread belief that one of the objectives of Alexander the Great – and of the Seleukid kings who followed him – was to systematically propagate Greek culture, thus bringing the benefits of a superior Greek civilization to the masses of Asia. It was recognized later that this view was simply a product of its times, the age of imperialism and colonialism, when the great European powers justified their expansion into other continents in these same terms and pointed to Alexander as their example. The view today is considerably more down-to-earth. Advanced civilizations, such as those of the Babylonians, Persians, and Phoenicians, already existed in Asia when Alexander crossed over, and required very little from the Greeks, while Alexander's own interest was primarily in conquest. However, when the region became politically and militarily subject to Alexander and the Seleukids, it became quite natural for the indigenous elite and those who had dealings with the administration to wish to learn the Greek language used in government and on official documents and to acquire a certain degree of Greek culture so as to be able to participate in the benefits of cooperation with the ruling power. As noted earlier, locals were active in government and some even took Greek names. The process of Hellenization was obviously stronger where there were many Greeks, especially so in the cities and in certain regions like northern Syria and western and southern Asia Minor. But it was certainly not a forced process, only what one might call "Hellenization by osmosis" (Sherwin-White and Kuhrt 1993, 141–187).

In the sphere of religion also, no attempt appears to have been made to impose the worship of Greek gods, the case of the Jews during the Maccabean revolt being open to other interpretations (Aperghis 2011a and 2011b with references). Indeed, one can observe widespread syncretism, that is, the linking together of different gods as essentially one, for example Zeus of the Greeks with Ba'al of the Phoenicians or Marduk of the Babylonians. One can also see this in the forms of worship – for example, dedications by Seleukid kings in Babylonian sanctuaries or their participation in the great New Year festival in Babylon or sacrifices made for their wellbeing as in a Greek temple (Kuhrt and Sherwin-White 1991). It is debatable whether the Seleukid kings wished to be worshipped as gods. The honours offered to them were initially voluntary, by Greek cities of the Aegean, and only much later, ca. 200, did Antiochos III inaugurate his own official cult and those of his ancestors, with high priests and revenues to serve them. But these cults were not apparently for true gods, only for men whose achievements had raised them above the level of others and given them the right to be so recognized (Chaniotis 2003; Potter 2003). On their coins, the Seleukid kings usually depicted themselves in a very simple way, with only the royal diadem, a ribbon tied round their forehead, to distinguish them. Up until the first quarter of the second century, epithets were added to their names only rarely, but these become more common later, and two in particular, *theos* ("god") and *epiphanēs* ("illustrious" or "made manifest"), may be considered to relate to cult worship (Houghton and Lorber 2002).

Continuity under the Persians and Parthians

It is sometimes considered that the Persian heartland, Persis, modern-day Fars, broke away from the Seleukid Empire at the time of the death of Seleukos I in 281 or soon after and that there was a violent reaction against Greek settlers in this region. The opposite view, first presented by Strabo (15.3.24), is that the Seleukids maintained overlordship over Persis until the Parthian conquest ca. 140 and that this is reflected in the coins issued by the Persian rulers (*fratarada*), which seem to show satrapal rather than royal symbols, and by the presence of Persian troops in Seleukid armies (Wiesehöfer 1994; Müsseler 2005–2006).

Hellenism survived in Mesopotamia and Iran under the Parthians after their conquests of these regions in the second century. A nomadic people to begin with, the Parthians took over a number of practices from the Greeks among whom they settled. One can see this mainly in the attempt of the upper class to acquire Greek culture. The kings used the Greek script and language on their coins, and several even took epithets of Greek kings, and also that of *philhellene*, that is, friend of the Greeks (Shore 1993). Indeed, it is said that the annihilation of the Roman army under Crassus in Mesopotamia in 53 was announced in the theater while the king and his court were attending a performance of the *Bakkhai* of Euripides, when the head of Crassus was thrown onto the stage as part of the performance (Plut., *Crass.* 33.2).

From inscriptions of the Parthian period one can see a certain degree of continuity with the Seleukid in the administration of Mesopotamia, attesting to the continuing Greek presence there (see Further Reading). It is interesting that from much later, the first years of the Sassanian dynasty, which succeeded the Parthians in the 220s AD, there is a bilingual Greek-Persian inscription at Naqsh-e Rajab near Persepolis, which must have been intended also for a significant Greek element of the population. Next to it is a rock carving in which the supreme god of the Persians, Ahuramazda, hands over power to the Sassanian king, Ardashir. There are two small figures below, in what appears to be an amicable relationship. One idea is that they represent a Persian and a Greek, as the dress may show.

The Greco-Bactrian and Indo-Greek Kingdoms

In Bactria and Sogdiana, the most distant satrapy of the Seleukid state, under the continuous threat of nomads from the north, the Greek satrap, Diodotos, seems to have gained his independence at the latest by 239 and declared himself king (Sherwin-White and Kuhrt 1993, 107–113; Holt 1999). The continuation of this kingdom is of great interest, but very little is known, because there are so few written sources. Thus one relies more on the coinage for a historical reconstruction.

It is generally accepted, however, that commencing around 200, the Greeks crossed the Hindu Kush into southeastern Afghanistan, Pakistan as far as the mouth of the Indus, and part of northwestern India. One knows the names of a few kings from written sources, but over 40 from their coins. The original kingdom soon split into smaller ones, which gradually fell to nomad invaders from the north and west: Bactria around 130, the Kabul valley and Gandhara, the region west of the Indus, by about 55, and finally the Punjab perhaps as late as 10 AD (Bopearachchi 1991), though the dating has been the subject of much discussion.

One knows very little about the Greeks in these regions, but one can make interesting speculations about their history and cultural impact (Karttunen 1997, 253–320; Coloru 2009). Archaeological work in Bactria and Sogdiana has shown that these were quite densely inhabited areas, with extensive irrigation networks. Bactria is even referred to in ancient sources as "of the thousand cities" (Just. 41.4.5; Strab. 15.1.3). When ca. 128 Chiang Qien, the envoy of the Chinese emperor, arrived in Sogdiana, an event which one associates with the opening of the so-called Silk Road, he found the region under the control of the nomad Yueh-Chi, but was impressed by the number of fortified towns and the extensive road network, possibly a result of the urbanization program which, as in so many other places, may be associated with the Seleukids (Tarn 1984, 474–477).

One is surprised by the quantity and quality of the coins of the Greek kings of Bactria and India. They are among the finest from an artistic point of view, and if one also takes into account the quality of the architectural and other remains from Aï Khanoum and the advanced level of Greek used in the inscriptions there (see Further Reading), one can accept that the Greek kingdoms in this part of the world must have been flourishing at certain times. Indeed, the largest coins in the Greek world come from Bactria – a gold 20-stater piece of Eukratides and a double dekadrachm of Amyntas (Bopearachchi 1991).

An interesting question is how far the Greeks did actually advance to the north and east. One knows that in the time of the first Seleukos, as Strabo (11.7.1–3; 11.11.5) writes, his general, Patrokles, explored the Caspian Sea, while Pliny (*HN* 6.18.49) notes that another, Demodamas, had been sent on an expedition across the Jaxartes (Syr Darya). Strabo (11.11.1) adds that the Greek kings who came later went further than Alexander and that Menandros had reached the Himaos River (if this report was true) and Demtrios Patalene and the Kingdoms of Saraostos and Sigerdis. And that furthermore the Greeks had also advanced as far as the Sēres and Phrynoi.

Alexander ceased his eastward march at the Hypanis (Beas) in the Punjab, while the Himaos is the Jumna, which flows through Agra. Patalēnē is the region of the mouth of the Indus, and the kingdom of Saraostos may be equated with Saurastra in India. Between the two lies the Cutch peninsula, where the kingdom of Sigerdis is probably to be located.

The Ferghana valley, mainly in what is today Kyrgyztan, is a natural extension of Sogdiana and was very likely included in it. From there a wide pass at an altitude of nearly 4000 meters leads across the Pamirs to China and can be traversed easily in the summer. It was never a great obstacle to the movements of nomadic peoples westward. There are indications that the Greeks knew of this route mainly from the reference to the Sēres, the silk people, the name given in antiquity to the Chinese. One should probably think here only of commercial contacts via middlemen in the region of Kashgar, a later important hub on the Silk Road. If the Sēres are considered to be somewhere to the northeast, the same may apply to the Phrynoi, who are linked to them by Strabo. An appropriate region would be that around lake Izyk-Kul in northeastern Kyrgyztan, on a more northern branch of the Silk Road.

At the other extremity of the Greek advance, in northern India, one has much more concrete evidence. First, there are the locations of coin finds, which extend to the Indus delta, the Punjab, and further east (Bopearachchi 1991). The best-known Indo-Greek king was Menander, who ruled ca. 155–130 in Pakistan and the Punjab, perhaps even as far as the region of Delhi. From Indian sources, one knows of the capture of Pataliputra (modern Patna) by the Yavanas or Yonakas (Ionians), as the Greeks were called. A siege of Madhyamika in southern Rajasthan by these same Greeks is also noted (Tarn 1984, 225–269).

What remained of the presence of the Greeks in Pakistan and northern India? Their coins circulated until at least the first century AD. Characteristically, the obverse displays the head of the king and his name in Greek, while the reverse shows this in the Indian language and script, often with Indian iconography. It was obviously necessary to make concessions to the Indian population so that it could be successfully ruled by a small Greek minority.

The nomads who took over from the Greeks – Sakas, Kushanas, and others – used the Greek language on their own coins initially and, later, their own language in Greek characters, in some cases even as late as the fifth century AD. But one does not know whether the names of Yavanas recorded in Indian inscriptions of the first century AD are those of Greeks who were residents or visitors at trading stations, such as Barygaza and Barbarikon, serving the sea trade with Roman Egypt that had begun to flourish at this time, or whether they refer to Greeks who had been established in these places earlier, at the time of the conquests of the Hellenistic period.

Where Greek influence appears stronger, however, is, surprisingly, in Buddhism. This had developed in northern India from the fifth century and seems to have been supported by Indo-Greek kings. A Buddhist text, the *Milindhapana*, the Debate of King Menander, presents a dialogue between the king and the sage Nagasena in Menander's capital, Saghala (probably modern Sialkot). Until that moment, Menander had apparently been dissatisfied with his debates with Indian sages, but he now apparently recognized the superiority of the arguments of Nagasena when expounding Buddhist doctrine (Pesala 1991). Plutarch (*Mor.* 821 D, E) also notes that when Menander died, the cities of his kingdom quarreled as to which one should receive his remains. The dead king was cremated, his ashes divided among the cities, and monuments built over them. This may point to Buddhist stupas, which cover some relic of an important man, but does not necessarily mean that Menander converted to Buddhism at the end of his life, as the *Milindhapana* maintains. It does show, however, how a Greek king needed to appear to his subjects if he wished to gain their acceptance. The policy of the Seleukids was similar in Babylonia, for example, where they participated in the great New Year festival of the local gods and bore the title of King of Babylon.

The Buddha was not initially depicted as a person, but only symbolically, as a lotus, or the wheel of *dharma*, or his footprint. For perhaps the first time he appears, along with his disciples and Boddhisatvas, in human form as another Apollo in the Greco-Buddhist art of Gandhara of the first to fourth centuries AD. The realism of the figures, the fall of their clothes, and the expressiveness of their features all point to Greek influence. The sculptors who carved the images were almost certainly local, but they had originally been taught by Greeks. The Greek kingdoms had by then disappeared, but vestiges of their culture remained for a long time.

Conclusion

In northern Syria and western and southern Asia Minor, the Greeks had a strong numerical presence from the beginning of the Hellenistic period, and their influence spread rapidly in these regions and was further reinforced during the Roman period. East of the Euphrates, a Greek presence existed right to the end, in many cases even taking the form of authority. Because they were so few, however, the Greeks were eventually submerged in the native populations. That their rule lasted as long as it did in many places – Iran to the middle of the second century, Mesopotamia until ca. 140, Bactria until ca. 130, southeastern Afghanistan (Arachosia) and the Kabul valley (Paropamisadai) until ca. 70, Gandhara until ca. 55, and the eastern Punjab until perhaps AD 10 – is evidence of their ability to administer their territories effectively and cooperate well with their native subjects. The Greek influence, however, was more long-lasting in the use of the Greek language and script, in coinage and sculpture, and probably also in the areas of civil/military and financial administration, for which the evidence lies in the practices one sees used by the nomadic peoples who followed them, and also in the traditions. In the Hindu Kush and elsewhere, there are beliefs that certain tribes are descendants of the Greeks, for example the Kalash of northwestern Pakistan. There may be some truth in this, but certainly not from soldiers of Alexander the Great, as is the usual idea. Possibly, however, from the Greeks of Bactria, who found refuge in the mountains in the face of nomad invasions. Whatever the truth, the story of the Greeks of Asia is an interesting episode in the history of Hellenism.

REFERENCES

Aperghis, Gerassimos G. 2004. *The Seleukid Royal Economy: The Finances and Financial Administration of the Seleukid Empire*. Cambridge: Cambridge University Press.

Aperghis, Gerassimos G. 2005. "City Building and the Seleukid Royal Economy." In *Making, Moving and Managing. The New World of Ancient Economies, 323–31 BC*, edited by Zosia H. Archibald, John K. Davies, and Vincent Gabrielsen, 27–43. Oxford: Oxbow.

Aperghis, Gerassimos G. 2010. "Recipients and End-users on Seleukid Coins." *BICS*, 53: 55–84.

Aperghis, Gerassimos G. 2011a. "Jewish Subjects and Seleukid Kings: A Case Study of Economic Interaction." In *The Economies of Hellenistic Societies, Third to First Centuries BC*, edited by Zosia H. Archibald, John K. Davies, and Vincent Gabrielsen, 19–41. Oxford: Oxbow.

Aperghis Gerassimos G. 2011b. "Antiochos IV and his Jewish Subjects: Political, Cultural and Religious Interaction." In *Seleucid Dissolution. The Sinking of the Anchor*, Philippika. Marburger Altertumskundliche Abhandlungen 50, edited by Kyle Erickson and Gillian Ramsey, 67–83. Wiesbaden: Harrassowitz.

Aperghis, Gerassimos G. 2020. "The Armed Forces of Seleukos I, with Help from Coins." In *New Perspectives in Seleucid History, Archaeology and Numismatics in Honor of Getzel M. Cohen*, edited by Roland Oetjen. Berlin: de Gruyter.

Austin, Michel M. 2003. "The Seleukids and Asia." In Erskine 2003, 121–133.

Austin, Michel M. 2006. *The Hellenistic World from Alexander to the Roman Conquests*, 2nd ed. Cambridge: Cambridge University Press.

Bar-Kochva, Bezalel. 1977. *The Seleucid Army*. Cambridge: Cambridge University Press.

Bernard, Paul. 1973. *Fouilles d'Aï Khanoum*, vol. 1: (*Campagnes 1965, 1966, 1967, 1968*). Mémoires de la délégation archéologique française en Afghanistan (DAFA), no. 28. Paris: Klincksieck.

Bernard, Paul. 1982. "An ancient Greek City in Central Asia." *Scientific American*, 246: 126–135.

Bickerman, Elias. 1938. *Institutions des Séleucides*. Paris: Geuthner.

Bickerman, Elias. 1979. *The God of the Maccabees. Studies on the Meaning and Origin of the Maccabean Revolt*. Leiden: Brill.

Bopearachchi, Osmund. 1991. *Monnaies gréco-bactriennes et indo-grecques. Catalogue raisonné.* Paris: Bibliothèque Nationale.

Burstein, Stanley. M. 1985. *The Hellenistic Age from the Battle of Ipsos to the Death of Kleopatra VII* (Translated Documents of Greece and Rome, vol. 3). Cambridge: Cambridge University Press.

Capdetrey, Laurent. 2007. *Le pouvoir séleucide. Territoire, administration, finances d'un royaume héllenistique (312–129 avant J.-C.).* Rennes: Presses universitaires de Rennes.

Carsana, Chiara. 1996. *Le dirigenze cittadine nello stato seleucidico.* Como: New Press.

Chaniotis, Angelos. 2003. "The Divinity of Hellenistic Rulers." In Erskine 2003, 431–445.

Cohen, Getzel M. 1978. *The Seleucid Colonies.* Historia Einzelschriften 30. Wiesbaden: Steiner.

Cohen, Getzel M. 1995. *The Hellenistic Settlements in Europe, the Islands, and Asia Minor.* Berkeley: University of California Press.

Cohen, Getzel M. 2006. *The Hellenistic Settlements in Syria, the Red Sea Basin, and North Africa.* Berkeley: University of California Press.

Cohen, Getzel M. 2013. *The Hellenistic Settlements from Armenia and Mesopotamia to Bactria and India.* Berkeley: University of California Press.

Coloru, Omar. 2009. *Da Alessandro a Menandro: il regno greco di Battriana.* Studi ellenistici 21. Pisa: Fabrizio Serra.

Erskine, Andrew, ed. 2003. *A Companion to the Hellenistic World.* Oxford: Blackwell.

Fraser, Peter M. 1996. *Cities of Alexander the Great.* Oxford: Oxford University Press.

Grainger, John D.A. 1997. *A Seleukid Prosopography and Gazetteer.* Leiden: Brill.

Grainger, John D.A. 2014. *The Rise of the Seleukid Empire (323–223 BC).* Barnsley: Pen and Sword Books.

Grainger, John D.A. 2015a. *The Seleukid Empire of Antiochus III (223–187 BC).* Barnsley: Pen and Sword Books.

Grainger, John D.A. 2015b. *The Fall of the Seleukid Empire (187–75 BC).* Barnsley: Pen and Sword Books.

Habicht, Christian. 2006. "The Ruling Class in the Hellenistic Monarchies." In *The Hellenistic Monarchies. Selected Papers*, edited by Christian Habicht, 26–40. Ann Arbor: University of Michigan Press.

Holt, Frank. 1999. *Thundering Zeus: The Making of Hellenistic Bactria.* Berkeley: University of California Press.

Houghton, Arthur, and Catharine Lorber. 2002. *Seleucid Coins: A Comprehensive Catalogue. Pt. I*, 2 vols. New York: American Numismatic Society and Classical Numismatic Group.

Houghton, Arthur, Catharine Lorber, and Oliver Hoover. 2008 *Seleucid Coins: A Comprehensive Catalogue*. Pt. II, 2 vols. Lancaster: American Numismatic Society and Classical Numismatic Group.

Karttunen, Klaus. 1997. *India and the Hellenistic World.* Studia Orientalia 83. Helsinki: Finnish Oriental Society.

Kosmin, Paul J. 2014. *The Land of the Elephant Kings.* Cambridge: Harvard University Press.

Kuhrt, Amelie, and Susan Sherwin-White. 1987. *Hellenism in the East.* London: Duckworth.

Kuhrt, Amelie, and Susan Sherwin-White. 1991. "Aspects of Seleucid Royal Ideology. The Cylinder of Antiochus I from Borsippa." *JHS*, 111: 71–86.
Ma, John. 1999. *Antiochos III and the Cities of Western Asia Minor*. Oxford: Oxford University Press.
Mairs, Rachel. 2011. *The Archaeology of the Hellenistic Far East: A Survey*. BAR International Series 2196. Oxford: Oxbow.
Mairs, Rachel. 2013. The Archaeology of the Hellenistic Far East: A Survey. *Supplement 1*. https://www.academia.edu/2645099/R._Mairs_2013_The_Archaeology_of_the_Hellenistic_Far_East_A_Survey._Supplement_1_Hellenistic_Far_East_Bibliography_ www.bactria.org (accessed December 6, 2019).
Musti, Domenico. 1984. "Syria and the East." In *The Cambridge Ancient History, vol. 7.1: The Hellenistic World*, 2nd ed., edited by Frank W. Walbank, Alan E. Astin, Martin W. Frederiksen, and Robert M. Ogilvie, 175–220. Cambridge: Cambridge University Press.
Müsseler, Wilhelm. 2005–2006. "Die sogennanten dunklen Jahrhunderte der Persis – Anmerkungen zu einem lange vernachlässigten Thema." *JNG*, 55–56: 75–103.
Narain, Awadh K. 1957. *The Indo-Greeks*. Oxford: Oxford University Press.
Pesala, Bhikkhu. 1991. *The Debate of King Milinda. Buddhist Traditions, vol. 14*. Delhi: Motilal Bararsidass.
Potter, David. 2003. "Hellenistic Religion." In Erskine 2003, 407–430.
Préaux, Claire. 1978. *Le monde héllenistique: la Grèce et l'Orient de la mort d'Alexandre à la conquête romaine de la Grèce, 323–146 avant J.-C.* 2 vols. Paris: Presses universitaires de France.
Rapin, Claude. 1990. "Greeks in Afghanistan: Aï Khanoum." In *Greek Colonists and Native Populations: Proceedings of the First Australian Congress of Classical Archaeology held in Honour of A.D. Trendall, Sydney 9–14 July 1985*, edited by Jean-Paul Descoeudres, 329–342. Oxford: Clarendon Press.
Rostovtzeff, Michael. 1941. *Social and Economic History of the Hellenistic World*. 3 vols. Oxford: Oxford University Press.
Savalli-Lestrade, Ivana. 1998. *Les philoi royaux dans l'Asie hellénistique*. Geneva: Droz.
Schoff, Wilfred H. 1989. *Parthian Stations by Isidore of Charax*. Chicago: Ares. Orginally published in 1914.
Sherwin-White, Susan. 1987. "Seleucid Babylonia." In Kuhrt and Sherwin-White 1987, 1–31.
Sherwin-White, Susan, and Amelie Kuhrt. 1993. *From Samarkhand to Sardis*. London: Duckworth.
Shipley, Graham. 2000. *The Greek World after Alexander 323–30*. London: Routledge.
Shore, Fred B. 1993. *Parthian Coins and History. Ten Dragons against Rome*. Quarryville, PA: Classical Numismatic Group.
Spek, Robert J. van der. 1987. "The Babylonian City." In Kuhrt and Sherwin-White 1987, 57–74.
Spek, Robert J. van der. 1993. "New Evidence on Seleucid Land Policy." In *De Agricultura*, edited by Heleen Sancisi-Weerdenburg and Pieter W. de Neeve, 61–77. Amsterdam: Gieben.
Tarn, William W. 1984. *The Greeks in Bactria and India*, 3rd ed. Cambridge: Cambridge University Press.

Waggoner, Nancy M. 1979. "Tetradrachms from Babylon." In *Greek Numismatics and Archaeology. Essays in Honor of Margaret Thompson*, edited by Otto Mørkholm and Nancy M. Waggoner, 269–280. Wetteren: Cultura Press.

Welles, Charles B. 1934. *Royal Correspondence in the Hellenistic Period: A Study in Greek Epigraphy*. New Haven: Yale.

Widemann, François. 2009. *Les successeurs d'Alexandre en Asie central et en Inde du nord-ouest et leur heritage culturel*, 2nd ed. Paris: Riveneuve.

Wiesehöfer, Josef. 1994. *Die 'dunklen Jahrhunderte' der Persis*. Zetemata 90. Munich: Beck.

Wiesehöfer, Josef. 2001. *Ancient Persia, from 550 BC to 650 AD*. London: Tauris.

Will, Edouard. 1979–1982. *Histoire politique du monde héllenistique*. 2 vols. Nancy: Presses universitaires de Nancy.

FURTHER READING

The general background for the Greek presence in Asia during the Hellenistic period is given in *The Cambridge Ancient History*, vol. 7.1: *The Hellenistic World*, and in Shipley (2000) and Erskine (2003). On the Persian background, see in particular Wiesehöfer (2001).

The starting point for the study of the Seleukid Empire could well be Sherwin-White and Kuhrt (1993), a revisionist view of a "strong" empire with its base in Mesopotamia rather than on the Mediterranean coast, something recognized in later studies (Shipley 2000, 271–312, 320–325; Austin 2003; Kosmin 2014; Grainger 2014, 2015a, 2015b). Of interest also are Musti (1984); Kuhrt and Sherwin-White (1987); and the relevant sections in Will (1979–1982); and Préaux (1978). For the administration of the empire, Bickerman (1938) is still valuable, while Capdetrey (2007) provides the most recent discussion. Rostovtzeff (1941) is sometimes useful as a reference, but the economy of the empire and its financial administration are handled much more extensively in Aperghis (2004), which also deals with some related matters, for example, city-building and land grants, military aspects, and coinage. Cohen (1995, 2006, 2013) include all the Hellenistic foundations in Asia. Ma 1999 brings to life the interaction of a Seleukid king with Greek cities; and the collection of papers on the Seleukids in *Topoi*, Suppl. 6, 2004 is also useful. For Seleukid coinage, the catalogs of Houghton and Lorber (2002) and Houghton, Lorber, and Hoover (2008) also provide the necessary references. For Seleukid and Parthian Mesopotamia see, in general, the work of van der Spek; and for Iran in the Seleukid and later periods that of Wiesehöfer.

The older and contrasting views on the Greco-Bactrian and Indo-Greek kingdoms are given in Tarn (1984; and older editions) and Narain (1957). Holt (1999) is good for the transition period to an independent Bactria, and Bopearachchi (1991) for the coinage, though more recent numismatic research has somewhat modified the historical picture. The latest syntheses are those of Coloru (2009) and Widemann (2009). The findings of the French-led excavations at Aï Khanoum headed by Bernard (1973) are published in a series of *Memoires* of the Délégation Archéologique Française en Afghanistan. Archaeological work and Greek-period finds to date in this entire area, with references to the relevant publications, are summarized in Mairs (2011) and its first supplement, Mairs (2013).

The main ancient literary sources for the Greeks in the East in the Hellenistic period are Diodoros Siculus, Polybios, Livy, Appian, and Justin, with 1 and 2 Maccabees and Josephus useful for the later Seleukids. Epigraphic evidence is collected in Welles (1934) concerning royal correspondence with the Greek cities. Interesting literary and epigraphic texts are translated in Austin (2006) and Burstein (1985), and also in Ma (1999) and Aperghis (2004). For the Babylonian view of Seleukid history and the Greeks, as expressed in cuneiform documents, one can refer to the ongoing publications by Spek and Finkel on the www.livius.org website.

PART III
THEMES

CHAPTER TWENTY-TWO

Greeks and Cultural Development in the Pre-Roman Mediterranean

Tamar Hodos

The promotion of the classical tradition in eighteenth- and nineteenth-century Europe inculcated in European thought a sense of Greek cultural superiority. During the twentieth century, this continued to impact, influencing our interpretations of the nature and extent of Greek influence upon those populations with whom they came into contact. A superficial look around the Mediterranean will show widespread commonality in a number of material features during the first millennium BCE, features that derive from the Greeks, including artistic and architectural forms, motifs, and plans, ceramics, and numismatic and alphabetic concepts. This has suggested the presumed adoption of the practices, values, and beliefs that accompanied the use of such artifacts and styles in Greek contexts. This phenomenon, seen especially among those who had close contact with the Greeks resulting from Greek colonization, has traditionally been regarded as evidence of Hellenization: the adoption of Greek culture.

Hellenization is often interpreted as a binary, unidirectional process. The Greeks maintain cultural, social, political, and economic superiority, and immunity from any such influence by those who were Hellenized, adopting Hellenic culture wholesale and unquestioningly. There is little consideration of agency or reciprocity. This perspective, which dominated interpretation for decades, is characterized by conclusions such as, "in the West, the Greeks had nothing to learn, much to teach" (Boardman 1999, 190).

During the 1990s, such interpretations began to be replaced by views informed by postmodernist perspectives, which sought to break down generalized narratives put forward by dominant powers. As a result, more recent scholarship on the Greek colonial phenomenon has focused on two aspects. One is the differences in cultural practices among those we collectively identify as Greeks. This deconstructs the notion that Greek culture was homogeneous and timeless (a similar approach appears in Phoenician studies: Hodos 2009; Garnand, Chapter 8, this volume for further discussion). The other has explored the colonial phenomenon from the perspective of the colonized to better understand the impact and mechanisms of interaction and influence between the Greeks (and Phoenicians) and those already existing in areas of colonization (e.g., Dietler 2010; Hodos 2006; van Dommelen 1998). Many of these postmodern interpretive frameworks examine the means by which identities are created, perpetuated, projected, and perceived. The role of the middle ground, the development of hybridized cultures, and the significance of agency have been the focus; they intersect in the development of social identities (Hodos 2010b with references).

Individual and group identities exist by definition through their distinction from others. Our understandings of these in the past therefore entail appreciation of the roles the use and reuse of goods and ideas play in identity projections and reflections. To assess these, we must examine not only the things that were consumed but also the ways in which they were consumed. This differs from assuming that, for example, the presence of Greek pottery means that those users were using the pottery in a Greek manner and considered themselves Greek, interpretations that underlie the Hellenization model. Equally important are rejected or ignored goods or ideas. Consumption and demand cannot be regarded as simple or automatic responses to the availability of goods. Rather, they are culturally, temporally, and politically specific. Taking this approach distinguishes contemporary interpretations from past ones, which regarded consumption as a direct consequence of production and distribution.

This drilling down into differences between Mediterranean communities, whether Greek colonies or indigenous settlements, has encouraged study of the very localized (for discussion of whether it is appropriate to use the term "colony" to characterize such enclaves of Greeks abroad, see Hodos 2006, 19–22 with bibliography, as well as the Introduction and Chapter 1, this volume). As a result, it has been suggested that we have lost sight of the fact that there are shared characteristics that contributed to the structural, overarching understandings of previous generations in the first place (Hodos 2009, 2012; Domínguez 2012). The fact remains that Greek material culture forms played a major role in shaping the Mediterranean during the first millennium BCE. The aim of this chapter is to recontextualize these aspects into contemporary discourse; Sicily and France provide comparative case studies.

The Greeks and Mediterraneanization

A number of features that derive from the Greeks were widely adapted by a variety of populations around the Mediterranean. Almost everywhere Greeks settled, their wine and associated drinking wares quickly became integrated with local tastes and customs, and their ceramic assemblages influenced regional indigenous outputs. Many settlements share Greek-derived architectural forms. The Greek alphabet was adapted to express local languages, and many native communities borrowed the Greek system of coinage. Even religious syncretism developed over time.

These adoptions and adaptations of Greek cultural characteristics were not wholesale replication, however. Instead, features were utilized selectively, and always in a way that accorded with local practices, tastes, and traditions. Furthermore, they were not adopted immediately, or uniformly. Rather, over time, these modified ways became normalized such that we can argue for a Mediterraneanization (Morris 2003): a global Mediterranean both bonded by shared (but not identical) features and distinguished by localized differences (as derived from globalization theory [Hodos 2010b], and to which Morris explicitly references Mediterraneanization. Others have suggested *oikumenization* to characterise this known, "inhabited world" [e.g., Seland 2008] instead of globalization. Given that not all regions of the ancient *oikumene* participated in the shared features we associate with globalization, *oikumenization* is inappropriate to characterize such a conceptualization; see Hodos 2014a for further discussion). This works in several arenas. One is among the various Greek communities themselves. During the Greek colonial era, "Greek" identity coalesced into something broadly identifiable, despite differences between individual Greek settlements (and similarly for the Phoenicians). Greek culture, as much as we can discuss it as a single concept, was constantly evolving. Furthermore, each Greek settlement was hybrid in its various articulations, born in response to its own localized geographic, social, cultural, and political interactions with its neighbors. Another arena is among those populations living around the Mediterranean coastline who engaged with the Greeks (and Phoenicians) through various social, commercial, and political networks. These, too, are regarded as constantly evolving, hybridizing cultures. The developments we see in their material, economic, political, and religious practices over the first millennium BCE are similarly born from their particular circumstances. The networks that connect these arenas, and others (e.g., the Phoenician world), contribute to the gradual evolution of a globally integrated Mediterranean over the first millennium BCE.

Urban Development

Discussions of urban development today focus on urbanization, an active, developmental process. Integral to it are the ways increasingly densely populated settlements developed socially, politically, and economically. This perspective is crucial to interpreting the changes and developments in Mediterranean settlements during the first millennium BCE.

The most famous Greek urban concept is the *polis*, with its dual meaning of both nucleated settlement and political community. Built features we have come to associate with the *polis* – such as a centralized market place, civic, religious, and residential zones, a grid system, rectilinear houses articulated along blocks, and a city wall – developed gradually, and not universally. For instance, grid planning was used by Greeks in Sicily and southern Italy during the late eighth and seventh centuries, but adopted in the Aegean only in the sixth century and more widely during the fifth century (Shipley 2005). There was also variation. In Sicily, for example, some cities had houses aligned on parallel, equidistant roads with groups of oblique cross-streets (Megara Hyblaea), others had true orthogonal plans (Naxos; Syracuse), or parallel streets without cross-streets (Kasmenai). City walls are often regarded as a sixth-century development, but a number of Greek settlements had them well before then (Frederiksen 2011). The placement of elements such as public buildings in specifically selected locations within a townscape also took diverse forms (see *passim* in this volume). In terms of the relationship between such physical features and political forms, it has been argued that no fixed relationship can be determined between the evolution of Greek town planning and Greek political and social concepts (including democracy; Shipley 2005). Thus, the widespread adaptation by others of Greek town planning forms, from the sixth century, does not necessarily reflect the adoption of Greek ideologies. Indeed, the concept of a walled city with carefully planned and located community administrative, economic, and cultic buildings, and freestanding, uniformly oriented domestic structures, has origins in the Early Iron Age Levant. Tyre, for instance, was a densely populated, constantly evolving settlement between the eleventh and eighth centuries, with multistory buildings, centralized civic buildings (royal residences, archives, and treasuries), religious structures, and substantial urban works, including a city wall. Late ninth-century Sarepta had an orthogonal layout. The Phoenicians brought their sophisticated urbanism to the central and western Mediterranean during the late ninth and eighth centuries (e.g., Carthage: Niemeyer et al. 2007), prior to the Greeks.

The reaction to these urban features differed from place to place. Precolonial Sicilian settlements usually consisted of clustered circular structures articulated without a planned or organized layout. It is only during the later seventh century and throughout the sixth century that such communities began to adopt urban elements, notably rectilinear architectural forms, orthogonal street patterns, and substantial city walls. Monte Saraceno di Ravanusa, in the hinterland of Gela, is one such example. Originally, the settlement consisted of circular houses, some of which were quite sizeable and perhaps served a community or religious function. The settlement was redesigned in the sixth century to accommodate multi-roomed rectilinear structures; they were articulated along regularized blocks in an orthogonal layout of major avenues and minor cross-streets. A city wall was built at this time to encompass both the upper and the lower settlement terraces. During the sixth century, other Sicilian sites also adopted urban plans involving blocks articulated along large and narrow streets, rectilinear architecture, and encircling city walls, such as Monte Bubbonia, Monte Iato, Vassallaggi, Sabucina, and Morgantina (Hodos 2006, 105–112 with references).

Not all settlements adopted the full range of features, however. Rather, selective elements were interpreted in accordance with local social and political practices. For instance, Sicilian communities did not necessarily reserve a central area equivalent to the Greek agora, which characterizes Greek cities of this period. City walls were generally not constructed before the sixth and fifth centuries, despite evidence of conflict between the Greeks and their indigenous neighbors from the late eighth century. Many Sicilian settlements were hilltop sites with naturally restricted access, which obviates significant need for a city wall. Therefore, the construction of a city wall during the sixth and fifth centuries, while suggesting contemporary threat, may also reflect what had become a common expression of urban development by this time. The same may be said for orthogonal layouts and rectilinear structures. Phoenician Motya also consolidated its urban center during the sixth century through constructing city walls, the Cappidazzu temenos, and an enclosed harbor, and linking the island to mainland. Indeed, several Sicilian Greek cities underwent redevelopment during the fifth century, themselves, like Syracuse, Megara Hyblaea, and Selinus, adopting new orientations, street plans, and in some cases house plots. These changes may be associated with inter-site competition and display, perhaps mediated by political ideologies, like tyranny. In sum, urban expressions were constantly evolving, and as the different cultures of Sicily continued to interact, their frames of reference for collaboration and competition coalesced into shared forms such that by the fifth century, Greek, Phoenician, and Sicilian settlements utilized common features (albeit of largely Greek and Phoenician origins).

A similar pattern of a gradual, diverse urban evolution took place in France. During the eighth and seventh centuries, one-room, oval-shaped, or rectangular post-framed wattle-and-daub structures characterized the domestic architecture of many indigenous coastal and hilltop settlements. During the late seventh and the first half of the sixth centuries, after Massalia's foundation, stone foundations slowly started to replace posts, and gradually mud brick was used for walls, especially among coastal communities. Buildings became articulated in a strictly rectangular formation and were tightly aligned in contiguous rows organized along rectilinear street plans. Ramparts began to be constructed. These developments should not be interpreted as direct imitations of Massalian practices, however. Rampart construction in France predates the foundation of Massalia (e.g., Saint Blaise, last quarter of the seventh century). There is also diversity in rampart form and construction techniques among French settlements in the Massalian region between the sixth and third centuries: those closest to Massalia preferred only a few rounded towers instead of the regularly spaced rectangular form used at Massalia itself. It has been argued that the development of rectilinear organization among French settlements was not the result of a preconceived plan but the result of generations of experimentation. Indeed, Massalia's own zoned orientation emerged only by the fifth century. The gradual adoption of these features demonstrates that they had become just as much a part of normative indigenous practices as Massalian, and were not a feature of Hellenization (Dietler 2010).

Exchange and Consumption

The widespread circulation of Greek pottery, especially wine wares, around the Mediterranean contributed significantly to the Hellenization interpretation of cultural impact. The consumption of Greek wine, and its specialized shapes for mixing, pouring, and drinking, is a much more complex affair than simple emulation, however. Nor is it exclusive desire to demonstrate social status. Such cross-cultural appropriation has more to do with the distinctions and expressions of concurrent social identities within individuals and groups. Thus, the spread of Greek wine and wine wares deserves careful reconsideration. It is particularly these vessels, rather than other ceramic forms, such as serving vessels, plates, and other ritual shapes, that attracted the interest of many Iron Age Mediterranean communities. Wine became a standardized commodity. One of the reasons may have been its ability to travel, enabling it to serve as a gift or good. Its higher alcohol content than many indigenous drinks, which contributed to its storage longevity, imbued it with a more potent psychoactive impact. This may have rendered it appealing for use in rituals where inebriation played a role in observance and celebration. Wine was never a complete replacement for other alcoholic forms, but among many Mediterranean communities, it quickly became an important feature in social practices (ritual, burial, domestic).

Wine wares were transported across the Mediterranean by ship, and usually were the main cargo; less often are other foodstuffs found. Vessels operated according to a cabotage system, in which goods were acquired at successive ports through a series of short, coast-hugging journeys, or at major redistribution centers, where goods were gathered together for secondary export. Ships carried single-origin or multiple-origin cargos. For example, the sixth-century Écueil de Miet wreck (France) carried Etruscan amphoras and black bucchero kantharoi, while the late sixth-/early fifth-century Grand Ribaud F wreck (France) contained nearly 1000 Py 4 Etruscan amphoras, some 40 bronze basins and a few Greek and other Etruscan finewares. On the other hand, the Giglio wreck (Italy) carried Etruscan, Greek, and Phoenician amphoras and finewares, while the Gela wreck (Sicily) transported a mix of Greek (Chian, Lesbian, Corinthian, Attic transport) and Phoenician amphoras, alongside other ceramics, and the Pointe Lequin 1A wreck (France) contained a substantial cargo of nearly 100 Aegean amphoras (most of which were East Greek), over 700 Attic black-figure cups, and around 500 Ionian B2 cups (manufactured in Italy: Krotscheck 2008). The early sixth-century Rochelongue wreck (France), which carried 800 kg of copper ingots, some tin ingots, and 1700 bronze objects of Iberian, Atlantic, Central European, and Italic types, reminds us that wine was not the only valued cargo at this time.

From the eighth century, Etruria was a major exporter of wine. Etruscan trade with Carthage, for instance, was dominated by wine, evidenced by over 800 wine amphoras and 60 bucchero vessels (although Etruria was just one importer to Carthage at this time; Phoenicians regularly imported a mix of Greek, Phoenician, and Etruscan wines and tablewares: Hodos 2006 with examples). After the middle of the seventh century, however, Carthage no longer extensively imported wine from central Italy (but Etruscan perfumed oils became popular). Instead, wine was imported from East Greece. Evidence for the shift being consumer-driven, rather than producer-promoted, can be seen in the fact that the Etruscan wine trade flourished in France from the end of the seventh century: the first foreign imports to France date to this time and are exclusively Etruscan wine amphoras and kantharos drinking cups. Even Greek Massalia imported over 80% of its wine from Etruria from its foundation ca. 600 BCE until the late sixth century. After 540 BCE, Massalia began its own wine production, with exports becoming a major commodity from the last quarter of the sixth century. Massalia also remained a global consumer, importing wine from around the Greek world, Phoenician Spain, and Etruria.

In France, interest in wine had thus taken hold long before Massalia's foundation. At Lattes, Etruscan and then Massalian amphoras make up nearly 50% of the ceramic assemblage for most periods and are distributed throughout the site itself, indicating that consumption was not restricted by class or other social status. By the end of the fifth century, Massalian wine amphoras make up 60% of the ceramic assemblage at Espeyran and nearly 75% at Cailar. These sites functioned not only as redistribution nodes into the interior, but also as consumers themselves, since consistently substantially more is found in these settlements than went upriver. Little else suggests Massalian or Etruscan foundations, although Massalian and Etruscan enclaves are known, such as at Lattes.

With widespread wine consumption came other influences, especially in ceramic manufacture. Greek and Phoenician settlements around the Mediterranean began to produce their own pottery styles, albeit derived from their imported cultural repertoire. Thus, in Sicily, we see the advent of Sikeliot (Sicilian Greek) pottery, which borrowed from Corinthian, Attic, and East Greek traditions (Hodos 2006, 2010a). In France (Massalia), we see the development of Colonial Cream Ware and Gray Monochrome, the former of which became the settlement's standard tableware (Dietler 2010). The Phoenicians of Sardinia, Sicily, Malta, and Carthage shared a regional production *koine* that was mostly derivative of eastern Mediterranean forms (e.g., bichrome geometric amphoras, "mushroom" jugs, trefoil-lipped jug, urns, plate forms: Hodos 2014b).

In both Sicily and France, features of colonial Greek wares were incorporated into indigenous productions. In Sicily, for example, Sicilian communities rapidly adopted the use of the trefoil oenochoe and drinking cups. They had little interest in mixing bowls until the sixth century (and even then they were never hugely popular). Furthermore, their stylistic development often took different trajectories from colonial outputs of the same shape. For example, Sicilian trefoil oenochoai of the sixth and fifth centuries continued to use motifs derived from seventh-century imports, rather than contemporary motifs that the Greek colonies themselves produced and imported. Interest in *ungeuentaria* is even more particular: the Sikels of eastern Sicily had virtually no interest in these small perfume jars, even though they were important products in the Greek world, and our knowledge of their typological development comes from the vast quantities interred in the *necropoleis* of Syracuse and Megara Hyblaea. The Sikans of central Sicily, however, did have an interest in these vessels and their contents, and frequently used them from at least the seventh century, in domestic and funerary contexts (Hodos 2010a).

In France, Colonial Cream Ware and Gray Monochrome were first produced by Massalian potters in the early sixth century. By the end of the first quarter of the sixth century, they were also being produced in indigenous workshops using the potter's wheel and controlled draft kilns, technologies adopted from the Greeks. But these were not direct copies of colonial prototypes. Rather, the indigenous output was hybrid in nature, integrating traditional forms and motifs, and variations of, and developments from, Massalian shapes and decorations. In contrast to Sicily, these two outputs remained discrete productions among indigenous communities, ceasing by the mid-fourth century, having had no impact upon the rest of the local repertoire or techniques. Thus, their rise and fall may relate to the social value of wine in general, rather than to an emulation of Greek ways of life; they did not occur in isolation from other commodity exchange networks, like grain production and natural resources, but were completely integrated with them (Dietler 2010).

Thus, what we see is not an immediate demand for specifically Greek wine around the Mediterranean during eighth and seventh centuries, when Greece was rapidly establishing colonies around the Mediterranean. Over the course of the sixth century, however, Greek wine comes to dominate the Mediterranean. In the Rhône valley, Massalian wine, specifically, becomes exclusively consumed, a taste that lasts until the second century (Dietler 2010). Carthage, too, imported wine from the Levant, Etruria, and Greece between the eighth and sixth centuries, but before the end of the sixth century imported wine almost exclusively from the Greek world (Bechtold and Docter 2010). Even Sicily, in addition to being a major producer and exporter of wine, was also a consumer of other, mostly Greek, varieties: Corinthian and East Greek wine amphoras are regularly found throughout the island; Massalian types are found to a substantially lesser extent, and Etruscan to an even more diminishing one (Hodos 2006, 130 with references). Political turbulence in the Tyrrhenian during the sixth century, which may have affected Etruria's ability to produce and export its own products, may have enabled the sale of Greek wines to flourish. There is no doubt that Greece played a major role in fostering an interest in wine consumption, especially in places like Sicily, but it was not the driver in all places, such as in France, among Phoenicians in the central Mediterranean, and even in North Africa, where the indigenous communities of Cyrenaica demonstrated no interest in Greek goods for three centuries (Hodos 2006). Thus, the consumption of Greek wine and use of Greek wine-drinking vessels are not connected to any kind of Hellenization, *per se*, but reflect a far more complex system of economic, social, political, and cultural networks in an increasingly connected, and expanding, milieu.

The Alphabet

One of the most striking features of the first millennium BCE is the dissemination of the Greek alphabet across the Mediterranean. Derived from the Phoenician alphabet at the end of the ninth century BCE, early extant examples of the Greek alphabet are often to do with a sense of ownership, through single letters, dedicatory inscriptions, and possessive graffiti. It is not appropriate to think of this as literacy, since literacy requires both reading and writing skills. In the ancient world, these skills may not necessarily have been mastered by the same person. Social emphasis was on the importance of oral agreements and witnesses rather than the production of written documents (although they did exist). The skills of literacy, therefore, were in the hands of the few. The material contexts of inscriptions themselves further suggest that writing served more diverse social purposes beyond linguistic communication. With this in mind, the spread of writing to non-Greeks and non-Phoenicians must be regarded within a social realm.

In Sicily, Greek script is first adopted during the sixth century by local populations to express spoken dialects, and usually follows the form of the nearest Greek settlement. Phoenician, used by Phoenician settlements in Sicily from the sixth century, was not adopted. Thus, communities around Etna used the script common at Catania, while those in the Hyblaean hills and around the Catania plain chose the variant of Syracuse and Megara Hyblaea. Gela provided the alphabetic model for those settlements in its central Sicily hinterland, while Selinus did much the same for surrounding communities in western Sicily. Minor variations in letter forms among a particular group of communities says more about local identities in an evolving world than a sense of wanting to become Greek. For example, in eastern Sicily, there is a clear alphabetic *koine* based upon the use of the Sikel alpha, with more localized alphabetic distinctions. These are nevertheless distinct from the linguistic corpus of western Sicily, which derives from the Selinus alphabet (Hodos 2006, 147–152). The inscriptions are often little more than brief expressions of ownership or greeting, etched onto drinking cups, suggesting a relationship between wine consumption and writing, the inscription perhaps enhancing the status of the vessel owner.

But how influential was the written word? In France, writing in and around Massalia served a variety of purposes, including commercial contracts (see below). At Lattes, for example, Etruscan was used from the sixth century and Greek from the middle of the fifth century, but neither was adapted more widely to express local dialects until several centuries later, and then it was Greek. The Ionian form of the Greek alphabet, used in Massalia, was eventually adopted by lower Rhône basin communities to express their Celtic dialect in marking funerary and votive personal property, but only from the end of the third century BCE. Among communities around Greek Emporion, in Roussillon and western Languedoc, the alphabetic model that was adopted to serve the local languages, in the mid-fourth century, was Iberian, which had developed directly from the Phoenician alphabet in seventh-century southern Spain (Dietler 2010, 70–72).

In Sicily, Greek becomes the language of official communication by the fourth century. This is not to say that the use of Greek to communicate political systems indicates that those systems were of a Greek nature, however. The bronze decrees from Entella exemplify the complexity of the situation. Entella had originally been an Elymian city, which allied with the Carthaginians during the late fifth century; the city was reduced by Dionysius in 368 BCE but still subjected to Carthaginian control before being liberated by Timoleon. One may presume, therefore, that its liberation came with new political requirements. These decree tablets, dated by some to the late fourth and by others to the middle of the third century BCE, are written in Greek and refer to an assembly, a council, leaders, military alliance, citizenship rights and juridical procedures, institutions, and processes familiar to a Greek and which presumably followed common practice in other Greek cities of the time. There are, however, points of procedure outlined in these decrees that are distinctly un-Greek, such as the nomination of three wise men to resolve property conflict by a system of lots. This suggests a developed political system that incorporates traditional (perhaps even Elymian?) political traditions alongside Greek ones.

This exemplifies the constantly evolving, hybridizing nature of the era. Rather than outright adoption of the Greek alphabet and its functions, the use of these letters was modified to fit with local values and procedures. The long evolution of their adaptation also suggests emulation is not the aim. In sum, the nature and extent of the use of Greek and/or the Greek alphabet beyond Greek colonial settlements depends more on local historical circumstances determined by the particulars of the settlement and its regional connections and interactions, rather than any general pattern or rate of linguistic development, or sense of Hellenization.

Coinage

Coinage was a Lydian invention of the seventh century BCE. Using electrum that occurred naturally in the river silts of Sardis, lumps of consistent weight were struck with designs, usually an animal. By the last third of the seventh century, Ionian cities such as Ephesus, Phocaea, and Klazomenai were also producing coins, and sometimes stashing hordes of them. The concept soon spread to other Greek communities (but not others in western Asia Minor, despite its multicultural nature during this period). Aegina, Athens, and Corinth began minting mostly silver coins by the middle of the sixth century; well before the start of the fifth century, many other Greek mainland cities, and Greek settlements in Italy, Sicily, North Africa, and France, were doing the same. It has been argued that the Greeks produced coins for a number of political purposes, such as facilitating state payments, collecting taxes and tribute, and demonstrating a polity's ability to define standards of value. More recent discoveries of smaller denominations of silver coins suggest that they also played a role in retail trade from its inception in the Greek world (Kurke 1999).

Coinage was not quickly nor uniformly adopted beyond Greek communities. It has long been noted that the Phoenicians did not mint coins until the middle of the fifth century. It is also at this time that other communities began minting coins, although only occasionally, gradually, and with regional differences. For example, during the first half of the fifth century, indigenous communities in Sicily created a system of metallic exchange based upon the bronze pound, or *litra*, rather than on minted, or silver, coins (although they did produce silver coins, as well). This bronze *litra* corresponded to a Greek silver *litra* of 13.5 g. Zancle, which, along with Naxos, Himera, and Selinus, was one of the first Sicilian Greek cities to mint coins (ca. 540 BCE), struck silver coins of this weight, which was also one-fifth of the Attic drachm. As a result of a convenient conversion, and no doubt to facilitate exchanges with the Sikels, Sikans, Elymians, and other local populations, the *litra* became an additional denomination among Sicilian Greek cities, especially those minting to the Attic standard (and Euboic). To distinguish the slightly heavier *litra* from an *obol*, cities gave them different types. At Syracuse, for instance, the *litra* displayed a cuttlefish, while the *obol* depicted a wheel. The *litra* eventually supplanted the *obol* in Greek Sicilian issues. This may relate to Syracuses's political domination, one result of which was the near island-wide use of the Attic weight standard.

The emphasis on the low-value, bronze *litra* among non-colonial Sicilian communities led to the wide production of small denominations in bronze among the Greek cities of the island, a feature not seen to such an extent elsewhere in the Greek world (although Greek communities in the Black Sea began to mint bronze denominations at the same time). Their value was not based on their material worth but on a fixed exchange rate with silver coins, such that an individual could exchange bronze coins for silver in the market. Akragas was the first to produce such a "denomination," around 450 BCE, initially casting the metal into a small shield-like or triangular form, rather than a coin shape, but it quickly cast a coin shape before finally striking bronze coin forms. By this time, Segesta and Himera also began to strike bronze coins, but these, too, were fiduciary only and not worth their weight in metal. By 430/420 BCE, Syracuse began to mint fiduciary bronze coins, and the concept soon spread to Greek communities in Italy, and back to mainland Greece itself (Fischer-Bossert 2012).

In France, Massalia began minting coins during the last quarter of the sixth century. Communities immediately around Massalia very sporadically produced imitations of Massalian silver *oboles* during the fifth century, but there is little evidence of other indigenous communities in France minting coins until the second century BCE (Dietler 2010). Yet it is clear that settlements beyond the Massalian hinterland were cognizant of coinage. A fifth-century legal document on a lead tablet from Pech Maho, in western Languedoc, discusses in Ionian Greek payment by coin as partial means of purchasing a ship (see further Sanmartí, Chapter 18, this volume). The other side of the tablet is inscribed in Etruscan, in which Massalia can be deciphered. The multilinguistic nature of the tablet in a settlement with a substantial indigenous population, as well as Greeks and Etruscans, and the lack of any comparable use of coinage among Gallic communities should make us question the roles that coinage itself played. Clearly, coinage served no substantially better means of exchange than existing mechanisms within non-Greek contexts. This suggests that the use of coinage among non-Greeks, when adopted, served purposes beyond the practical ones of making payment. The fact that coins minted by indigenous Sicilian communities during the fifth century, such as Eryx and Segesta, used non-Hellenic coin legends reinforces this perspective (and additionally suggests that the traditional language of western Sicily continued to play an official role at this time: Hodos 2006). The logical conclusion is that coinage functioned as much as political expressions of achievement and power as practical means of making payment on behalf of a polity or individual.

Clearly, the commercial benefits provided by coinage in Greek systems of exchange were not applicable to the means of commerce in non-Greek communities. Coinage did not provide any advantage over extant value exchanges to foster its adoption. Yet clearly these groups were widely involved in local, regional, and international trade and exchange networks, given the widespread commodity exchange noted above; their lack of need for coinage to facilitate such systems successfully suggests that coinage did not develop for economic reasons but from internal needs in response to local social demands.

Religious Syncretism

One development from these increasingly enmeshed political and social interactions is religious syncretism. The fusion of Greek Zeus with Egyptian Amun is perhaps the most famous. Greek knowledge of the Egyptian deity is probable from at least the seventh century, when Greek merchants came to Naucratis to facilitate trade with the mighty Egyptians. By the end of the sixth century, Cyrene began to strike coins with the image of Zeus-Ammon, as a bearded head crowned by a pair of ram horns, and had constructed an enormous Doric temple dedicated to him (see further Schaus, Chapter 16, this volume). It has been argued that the Greeks recognized Ammon as comparably supreme to Zeus, which led to their acceptance of Ammon as another title of Olympian Zeus. Political strategy may have shaped this syncretism, as well. The syncretism between Greek Zeus and Egyptian Amun no doubt protected the Greek annexation of Cyrenaica, as much as and perhaps in conjunction with the royal marriage between the Egyptian Pharaoh Amasis II and the Cyrenian princess Ladice in 548 BCE. Justification for territorial annexation is a common feature of foundation tales, often "recorded" centuries later, and religious sanctions feature frequently. In this instance, Pindar, composing in the middle of the fifth century, explicitly equates the land of Libya with the precinct of Zeus-Ammon.

Frequently, we see the outward use of Greek traits in local religious practices to an extent that initially it seems that the community converted to Greek religion outright. In sixth- and fifth-century Sicily, for example, sites such as Monte Saraceno, Monte San Mauro, Monte Bubbonia, and Vassallaggi used variations of the Greek-derived *oikos* form in their religious structures; similar variations are also found among contemporary Sicilian Greek religious architecture, at Gela, Himera, Megara Hyblaea, and Selinus (Hodos 2010a, 90). This does not necessarily mean that the cults celebrated in indigenous contexts were Greek, however. The appropriation of Demeter attributes in local cult practices is a case in point. The synergy between Demeter's chthonic characteristics and the agro-pastoral features of indigenous Sicilian religion have been used to identify and explain a widespread adoption of Demeter cults. Yet sometimes this must be questioned. For instance, in a small shrine in a domestic quarter of Sabucina, a number of Demeter statuettes were found in association with a model of a pitched-roof temple with animal *protomes*, an incense burner, offering cups, bronze jewellery, and a ram figurine. Is it really Demeter being worshipped? Demeter figurines have not been found elsewhere at the site, and both the ram figurine and the pitched temple model are characteristic of contemporary indigenous cultic rituals and spaces. It is more likely a local deity being worshipped, for whom Demeter's form and attributes were acceptable means of veneration, rather than Demeter herself.

A similar example can be seen in Sardinia. A series of fourth-century BCE shrines in former *nuraghi*, each with a number of Greek lamps, was initially interpreted as dedications to Demeter, since lamps are strongly correlated with Demeter worship in the Greek world. A close examination of one such shrine suggests otherwise. Sardinian lamps and Punic incense burners in the assemblage, associated with Punic cults, imply that Punic rituals were being observed (which may include Demeter, who joined the Punic pantheon of deities in the early fourth century). The high proportion of oil lamps also reflects continuity of Sardinian cult practices, which used lamp light (although a minority are of Sardinian types). The context of the nuraghe itself also suggests specifically Sardinian traditions. Considering these together, it has been argued instead that the original provenance and connotations of the objects were incorporated into new practices and meanings constructed in, and specific to, the culturally mixed environment of colonial Sardinia (Hodos 2010a with references).

Indeed, the Greeks themselves were not immune to adopting and adapting foreign divinities. The best example of this is the cult of Kybele, the Phyrgian mother of the gods (*Matar*), and divinity of fertility, motherhood, and mountains (*Matar kubileya*, of the mountain, in Phrygian). From the late seventh century, knowledge of her began to spread from Asia Minor across the Greek world, and by the fourth century, the cult of the Mother Goddess, as *Meter* or *Meter Kybele*, with acknowledged Anatolian origins, was found in nearly every Greek city. Although widely worshipped, she remained recognized as a foreign divinity, and a number of rituals associated with her worship were attributed to Anatolian traditions, such as ecstatic rites and mystery practices. Her characteristics share features with other Greek divinities, which may explain her popularity: as with the Potnia Theron, she is mistress of animals; like Rhea, she is mother of the gods; her fertility role links her to Demeter. Her earliest Greek depictions, which come from Asia Minor, are on votives that show her as a standing divinity in Greek dress framed within a *naiskos*. By the middle of the sixth century, she is depicted as a seated goddess within the *naiskos*, and with a lion attribute. The lion is the only animal she appears with in Greek contexts, although the bird of prey was her most ubiquitous symbol in Phrygian contexts. It is the leonine form that was carried to the Aegean and mainland Greece, Italy, Sicily, and the far West (Massalia). The late sixth-century inclusion in her Greek iconography of the *tympanum*, an Oriental instrument (although not specifically a Phrygian one), is a distinctly Greek addition (Roller 1999).

Conclusions

The adaptation of Greek forms and practices is but one facet of the multiple exchanges of ideas and practices that took place during the first millennium BCE. As evident in the examples above, the coalescence of shared and differing practices was a gradual evolution, uneven and far from uniform. Rather than serving as evidence of widespread replication of Greek practices, the examples above reveal the selective choices individual communities made as they engaged with the wider Mediterranean world. As a result, these developments are better characterized by a globalization framework of interpretation, which simultaneously fosters the shared practices that give rise to the sense of one-placeness we associate with globalization while articulating the differences between those same connected communities. The widespread adaptation of Greek goods and ideas is part of that sense of one-placeness associated with globalizing processes: these are shared practices, rather than identically replicated (by Greeks themselves, and others). Their slow adaptation suggests that it is not emulation at play, but normalization that emerges from long-term commonalities. These commonalities established foundations for an interconnected Mediterranean that gave rise to Carthage and Athens as the classical world power players. In turn, they set the stage of established networks that enabled Alexander the Great to develop political oversight over a vast swathe of the eastern Mediterranean, and which Rome ultimately used to its advantage (see further Aperghis, Chapter 21, this volume).

REFERENCES

Bechtold, Babette, and Roald Docter. 2010. "Transport Amphorae from Punic Carthage: An Overview." In *Motya and the Phoenician Ceramic Repertoire between the Levant and the West 9th–6th Century BC*, edited by Lorenzo Nigro, 87–116. Rome: Missione Archeologica a Mozia.

Boardman, John. 1999. *The Greeks Overseas*. 4th ed. London: Thames & Hudson.

Dietler, Michael. 2010. *Archaeologies of Colonialism*. Berkeley: University of California Press.

Domínguez, Adolfo. 2012. "Local Responses to Colonisation: Some Additional Perspectives." *Ancient West & East*, 11: 205–218.

Fischer-Bossert, Wolfgang. 2012. "The Coinage of Sicily." In *The Oxford Handbook of Greek and Roman Coinages*, edited by William Metcalf, 142–156. Oxford: Oxford University Press.

Frederiksen, Rune. 2011. *Greek City Walls of the Archaic Period, 900–480 BC*. Oxford: Oxford University Press.

Hodos, Tamar. 2006. *Local Responses to Colonization in the Iron Age Mediterranean*. Abingdon: Routledge.

Hodos, Tamar. 2009. "Colonial Engagements in the Global Mediterranean Iron Age." *Cambridge Archaeological Journal*, 19(2): 221–241.

Hodos, Tamar. 2010a. "Globalization and Colonization: A View from Iron Age Sicily." *Journal of Mediterranean Archaeology*, 23(1): 81–106.

Hodos, Tamar. 2010b. "Local and Global Perspectives in the Study of Social and Cultural Identities." In *Material Culture and Social Identities in the Ancient World*, edited by Shelley Hales and Tamar Hodos, 3–31. Cambridge: Cambridge University Press.

Hodos, Tamar. 2012. "Paradigm Shifts in Mediterranean Archaeology: A Response to the Discussion on Hodos, *Local Responses to Colonization in the Iron Age Mediterranean*." *Ancient West & East*, 11: 247–259.

Hodos, Tamar. 2014a. "Stage Settings for a Connected Scene: Globalisation and Material Culture Studies in the Early First Millennium BCE Mediterranean." *Archaeological Dialogues*, 21(1): 24–30.

Hodos, Tamar. 2014b. "Colonisation and Cultural Developments in the Central Mediterranean." In *The Cambridge Prehistory of the Bronze and Iron Age Mediterranean*,

edited by A. Bernard Knapp and Peter van Dommelen, 215–229. Cambridge: Cambridge University Press.
Krotscheck, Ulrike. 2008. *Scale, Structure and Organization of Archaic Maritime Trade in the Western Mediterranean: The Pointe Lequin 1A*. Unpublished PhD dissertation, Stanford University.
Kurke, Leslie. 1999. *Coins, Bodies, Games and Gold: The Politics of Meaning in Archaic Greece*. Princeton: Princeton University Press.
Morris, Ian. 2003. "Mediterraneanization." *Mediterranean Historical Review*, 18(2): 30–55.
Niemeyer, Hans Georg, Hans R. Baldus, Roald F. Docter, and Karin Schmidt, eds. 2007. *Karthago; die Ergebnisse der Hamburger Garbung unter dem Decumanus Maximus*. Mainz: P. von Zabern.
Roller, Lynn. 1999. *In Search of God the Mother: The Cult of Anatolian Cybele*. Berkeley: Univerisity of California Press.
Seland, Eivind H. 2008. "The Indian Ocean and the Globalisation of the Ancient World." *Ancient West & East*, 7: 67–79.
Shipley, Graham. 2005. "Little Boxes on the Hillside: Greek Town Planning, Hippodamos, and Polis Ideology." In *The Imaginary Polis: Symposium, January 7–10, 2004*, edited by Mogens H. Hansen, 335–403. Copenhagen: The Royal Danish Academy of Sciences and Letters.
van Dommelen, Peter. 1998. *On Colonial Ground: A Comparative Study of Colonialism and Rural Settlement in First Millennium BC West Central Sardinia*. Leiden: University of Leiden.

FURTHER READING

Theoretical approaches: Hodos 2010b. Outlines the development of the theoretical interpretation frameworks in the study of cultural interactions in the ancient world.
Urbanization: Hansen, Mogens H., and Thomas H. Nielsen, eds. 2004. *An Inventory of Archaic and Greek Poleis*. Oxford: Oxford University Press. Introduces all aspects of the development of the Greek *polis*.
Osborne, Robin, and Barry Cunliffe, eds. 2006. *Mediterranean Urbanization 800–600 BC*. Oxford: Oxford University Press and the British Academy. A valuable collection of regional case studies for Greek and non-Greek urbanization in the Mediterranean.
Trade and exchange: Morley, Neville. 2007. *Trade in Clasical Antiquity*. Cambridge: Cambridge University Press. Offers a succinct overview to our understanding of trade, consumption, demand, and exchange in the ancient world.
Writing: Powell, Barry. 1991. *Homer and the Origin of the Greek Alphabet*. Cambridge: Cambridge University Press. This remains the primary source on the development of the Greek alphabet.
Jeffery, Lilian H. 1990. *The Local Scripts of Archaic Greece*. Oxford: Clarendon Press. This remains the most modern, detailed survey of Greek inscriptions.
Coinage: Metcalf, William, ed. 2012. *The Oxford Handbook of Greek and Roman Coinages*. Oxford: Oxford University Press. Provides the most up-to-date synthesis of evidence for coinage and how it was used in the ancient Greek world.

Religious syncretism: Johnston, Sarah I. ed. 2004. *Religions of the Ancient World*. Cambridge, MA: Harvard University Press. A valuable comparative volume that outlines the various religions of the ancient world.

Demetriou, Denise. 2013. *Negotiating Identity in the Ancient Mediterranean*. Cambridge: Cambridge University Press. Examines the role cultic practices at five Greek-founded, multicultural trading settlements played in creating common understanding while maintaining sociocultural distinctions.

CHAPTER TWENTY-THREE

Relations with Homelands: *Apoikia* and *Metropol(e)is*

Frank Bernstein

A movement, which intensified during the eighth century BC and which we still call, against better knowledge, "Archaic Colonization," led to a rapid extension of the world of the Greeks. Certain regions of the Mediterranean and the Black Sea began to be marked by aggregations of Greek places. The world of the Greeks, which had long since been polycentric, stretching from the so-called mother country over the Aegean to Asia Minor, was further expanded (Bernstein 2019). This process was, however, not grounded in the "expansion" of individual communities. For this term does not describe a random movement in space but rather a movement that is aimed explicitly at extending space, one which naturally seeks to link the new foundations to their home country following territorial acquisition. This objection is important in the context of the process considered here. For the movement that is described as "colonization" was driven by various causes, reasons, and motivations, and occurred in no less a manifold number of ways. The process of the dispersal of the Greeks instead takes the shape of a diffusion characterized to an equal extent by migration and mobility.

Many of the coasts of the Mediterranean and the Black Sea became a place for habitation and of movement. The typology of the Greeks, who frequented these regions as warriors or pirates and mercenaries, farmers or traders and craftsmen – to differentiate migrants from mobile groups – is no less imprecise than the concept of "colonization." Such differentiation fails to pay sufficient attention to the fact that Greeks could be all of this in sequence, and also simultaneously. This polymorphy of living conditions explains not only the vagueness of the ancient terms *apoikía* and *empórion* but also the ongoing discussions of categorizing Greek places as areas of habitation and/or trading places.

It is clear that in a world that is characterized by migration and mobility, the relationships between individuals and communities took various forms. It is not surprising that recent research on this topic has been inspired by network theory, and that it created

A Companion to Greeks Across the Ancient World, First Edition. Edited by Franco De Angelis.
© 2020 John Wiley & Sons, Inc. Published 2020 by John Wiley & Sons, Inc.

corresponding models to pay tribute to this polymorphism (Malkin 2011; Ulf, Chapter 7, this volume). In such a networked world, however, it is still highly relevant to ask about the relations with homeland. Identity is and remains linked to one's regional and, in particular, local origin. It is a result of the lack of better sources that it is nearly impossible to say much with any certainty on the level of the individual. In poetry we find instances of an at best constructed discourse on the sensitivities and longings of the individual abroad. Possible relationships with homelands can, if at all, be documented for communities with actual, or at least pretended, shared local or even regional origin. *Apoikíai* also emanated from *éthnē*, yet relationships are hard to trace – which, however, does not prove their inexistence. Quite to the contrary, the search for collective relationships leads rather to the world of the *póleis* and thus to the important questions of the rapports and relationships between "colony and mother city," *apoikía* and *mētrópolis*.

This problem will be reexamined critically in what follows. It is linked (i) to considerable heuristic and methodical problems, and (ii), above all, to conceptual problems. Such difficulties do not negate the existence of relationships, yet they present a challenge to every model employed to explain the phenomenon. At the same time, it is important to seek alternatives, which can allow the typological representation of the relationships between *apoikíai* and *mētrópoleis* taking into consideration also (iii) the respective prerequisites and conditions.

Heuristic and Methodical Problems

Dispersed literary testimonies compare the relationship between "colony and mother city" with that of a child to its parents (Pl. *Leg.* 6.754 a–b; Polyb. 12 fr. 9.3; Diod. Sic. 10 fr. 34.3). It is hence surprising that the term "daughter city," *thygatrópolis*, has not (yet) been found. These rare ancient voices have led to the characterization of this relationship as one of reverence in modern research. Yet it is impossible to evaluate the nature of such links. It is difficult to establish whether military aid was naturally granted, how far legal agreements were signed, and how far the *mētrópolis*'s social organization and political and religious institutions were replicated in the *apoikía* upon its foundation. It is above all a problem of sources, as testimonies of the Classical and even Hellenistic age prejudice past as well as more recent research, prompting at times generalizations that are too bold.

For a long time, Thucydides's narrative had a considerable impact on reconstructions of the rapport between *apoikía* and *mētrópolis*: the dispute between Corcyra and Corinth regarding Epidamnos, a foundation of the Corcyraeans and hence a "grandchild" city of the Corinthians (1.24.1–1.55.2). The conflict, which broke out in 435 BC and which took on a fatal dynamic, was considered by the historian as the first *aitía*, "cause," of the Peloponnesian War. The "grandmother" insisted on the duty of the "daughter" to pay reverence to her. However, this model is not a useful one for thinking about the relationships between *apoikía* and *mētrópolis*. The Ionian island, like other foundations of the Corinthian Cypselids in western Greece or even in Thrace, is rather a phenomenon *sui generis* which points to the expansive, if not hegemonic, ambitions of individual *póleis*. It is not a coincidence that this example has often been linked to a further prominent point of reference: Athens, whose claim to political influence was articulated in the single bold statement that it was the *mētrópolis* of all of Ionia.

A prominent epigraphically attested Attic decree on the establishment of the *apoikía* Brea in Thrace from ca. 440 BC (*ML*² 49 = *IG* I³ 46 = Osborne and Rhodes 2017, no. 142) contains detailed directions of the *mētrópolis* for the city to the founded. It obliges her, *inter alia*, to send her donations to the gods for the most important city festivals of Athens. In addition, violation of these directions would have been penalized. This decree hence constituted an external settlement that was closely linked to its mother city. However, this example of the foundation of a "colony" carried out by public institutions, regulated by fixed procedures, and sanctioned by law, should not be considered as a *pars pro toto*. For the *apoikía* Brea is too similar to the cleruchies, the garrisons of the so-called Athenian Empire. That said, a later decree from the late fifth century BC differentiates clearly between *apoikía* and *klēruchía* (*IG* I³ 237 l. 9). Yet, despite this distinction, which cannot be used for this earlier period, both documents are testimonies of the "imperial colonization" of Athens in the age of its naval supremacy. Such foundations, like other foundations of the fourth century BC, a period when the former hegemon sought to reestablish its leadership, are comparable in their shape and aims to Roman *coloniae* rather than to the multiple Greek foundations, which, starting from the eighth century BC, increasingly bordered the Mediterranean and the Black Sea regions. Already here it is important to stress that these *apoikíai* were founded as autonomous and politically independent communities. It is hence not helpful to consider the daughter cities of Athens in this context. But other documentary testimonies of relationships between autonomous and sovereign *apoikíai* and their *mētrópoleis*, which are important for the present inquiry, cannot easily claim to be representative of the phenomenon, but perhaps even rather narrow the perspective.

The Brea decree is part of the group of so-called foundation decrees. Only a few have been preserved, a fact which calls for caution. A testimony such as the probably early Hellenistic inscription, which contains a decree on the foundation of Corcyra Melaina in the Adriatic Sea by the Greek community Issa with the collaboration of Illyrian dynasts (*Syll.*³ 141 = *StV* III 451), is too compelling in its level of detail. There are penal regulations regarding the distribution of land, which carefully distinguish the area for construction within the city to be walled from the land in the *chōra* of the *pólis* that is to be established, with precautionary additional regulations on this matter for future settlers. In particular, however, this inscription closes with lists of the first settlers from Issa, which are arranged in three columns under their names as Dymanes, Hylleis, and Pamphyloi according to their respective *phylḗ*, "tribe." This document hence powerfully demonstrates the transferral of the civic subdivisions of the mother city, in this case the transferral of the Dorian *phylaí* structure. Even so, is it possible to take this example as the general rule? Is it a different story with foundations which assembled settlers emanating from Ionian *phylaí*? Here, a prominent example, which sheds light on the nature of legal agreements between mother city and its daughter, is instructive on the methodological problem of so-called representativeness.

An often-cited foundation inscription from the first half of the fourth century BC that appears in most of the standard treatments of Greek history could point to a so-called *isopoliteía* between Thera and its *apoikía* Cyrene in Libya which would put their citizens on an equal footing. It appears to corroborate an ancient right from the time of foundation and thus contains also an "oath of the settlers." I will return to this in more detail below; here we may briefly mention it to illustrate the methodical problems involved. For it is necessary to inquire whether such close relationships were the rule or the exception, whether these inscriptions, which are compelling in their informational value, influence *a priori* our assessment of the rapport and even its institutionalized relationships between *apoikía* and *mētrópolis*. But, above all, it is important to be aware of the fact that, in view of the shortage of sources, these epigraphic testimonies easily induce drawing over-hasty parallels. And these reservations highlight further difficulties.

Conceptual Problems – and Possible Solutions

In tune with the formerly privileged legalistic approach, many treatments painted a far too cohesive picture (e.g., Busolt and Swoboda 1926, 1264–1280). Thereafter scholarship sought a more subtle approach. The comprehensive surveys of Seibert (1963), Graham (1964), and Werner (1971) have, more than any others, given new impetus to research. Their case studies looked at the relationships between *apoikía* and *mētrópolis* in a broader context, also provoking fruitful criticisms (see in particular Ehrhardt 1987). Detailed comparative studies of the social, political, legal, and religious institutions in *mētrópoleis* and *apoikíai* (Ehrhardt 1988; Robu 2014) have encouraged more differentiation. But as much as such studies have advanced our understanding, they *nolens volens* contributed to viewing relationships too quickly as the norm.

Against this background, an explanation had to be sought as to why no links between a certain mother city and "her" "colony" could be established in the sources, provoking perhaps the hint of an *argumentum e silentio*. And how easily can a static picture indeed be gained – particularly under the impression of a legalistic perspective of the conditions? Miletus, however, to cite an easily comprehensible example, will simply not have been in a position to maintain close and enduring links with its "colonies." The Ionian *mētrópolis* was razed by the Persians in 494 BC and remained for a long time under their rule before it regained its independence and former status in the fourth century BC.

Hence, the possible relationships between *mētrópolis* and *apoikía* were probably not static but rather dynamic. We should bid farewell to wanting to present consistent interpretations of the disparate source situation. Change is to be expected. For that there were possibly no relationships at the beginning, perhaps because they could not exist; for that they developed in some places only due to some particularly fruitful conditions over time, but not everywhere, in particular not in instances where the daughter city had gained more importance than the mother city; for that special links could also break, be refounded, or be simply invented, all this is not only possible but is also reflected in the evidence. But there is more: the possibility that the arrangement of a place was the result of a collaboration of several mother cities goes beyond the scope of the traditional model. *Strictu sensu* there can be only one "mother." And that the self-awareness of the *apoikía* could profoundly change in the wake of *époikoi* ("additional settlers"), that so-called secondary foundations perhaps modified existing links, that special closeness or distance between mother city and "colony" had perhaps considerable influence on the nature of the relationships, such issues, to name only the most self-evident ones, have to be considered to equal extent if one wants to grasp not only the dynamic but also the variation of possible relationships.

Such an accentuated overview of the phenomenon cannot be achieved if the different relationships are analyzed in an accumulated manner. For then it would again seem as if the rapports were characterized not by variation but by a congruence of types. In order to address the above-posed questions appropriately, it is necessary to look at possible relationships in their historical context, in order to reveal the respective preconditions and, thereby, the importance of change. Of course, the world of the fifth and fourth century BC is not that of the early Archaic period when Greeks settled in the western Mediterranean basin. The available sources, however, do not allow a strictly diachronic approach, yet some examples allow the types of relationships and their prerequisites as well as conditions to be outlined.

Types of Relationships, Their Prerequisites and Conditions

Established relationships between communities necessitate the existence of a certain concept of state. In the eighth century BC, the *pólis*, which is both city and state, was however only just emerging, so that her characteristic institutions and procedures were not yet fully developed; this step in its development is by now rightly called "proto-state." It is hence not possible to speak of a state-led initiative to found colonies or even a stately organized "colonization movement" in this period, and probably not even for most of the seventh century. A regulated procedure, such as the Brea decree of the *ekklēsía* of Athens discussed above reveals, is in any case unthinkable.

The question is rather whether the development of the *pólis* was far more than is commonly thought the result of the early "colonization," with the arrangement of an *apoikía* as an opportunity to experience and to experiment. For now the affairs of the new community had to be regulated from the ground up, and there was probably more need to equilibrate interests than in the homeland. The need to order the community offered the possibility of questioning established forms and of venturing new solutions. This particular path to the "political," which the Greeks, oddly enough, chose at this stage in their history, and which led to the development and realization of political institutions such as magistracies, the council, and the people's assembly and which increasingly transformed the *pólis* to a polity of citizens, was a difficult and, above all, a slow process. In turn, this means that the concept of a mother city which sent out not only people as settlers but also institutions of the settlement to be established is more than doubtful. For how can the *apoikía* have been a "likeness," as is often said, of her *mētrópolis* in these circumstances?

This conjecture is even more doubtful considering the fact that *apoikíai* were, as far as we know, independent communities from their foundation, not linked in a relationship of dependence to their mother cities. On this there is, however, agreement in scholarship. The uncontroversial autonomy and sovereignty of the *apoikíai*, however, is directly linked with the much-discussed question of the causes, reasons, and motives of their foundation (Costanzi, Chapter 1, this volume). This question shapes, as it were, right from the beginning the assessment and evaluation of possible relationships with the *mētrópolis*, and is hence worthy of close consideration.

Trade interests, population pressures, droughts, and sociopolitical disintegration drove the "colonization movement." The picture is multifaceted. And hence it was above all necessity or coercion (leaving aside trade interests) that prompted this new movement in the eighth century BC. Emigration and the foundation of an *apoikía* literally offered a way out of the problems of the homeland. Overall, it is hence misguided to talk about *mētrópoleis* actively sending out settlers; rather, they only ceded people. They were thus not able to appoint a *ktístēs* or rather an *oikistḗs*, for the "founder" was in many cases probably only the leader of those who were willing or forced to emigrate. He must have been an energetic figure, probably in most cases an aristocrat. But what we call his *mētrópolis* was in the first instance only his place of origin, no more, no less.

"According to old rites," so Thucydides writes (1.24.2), did the Corcyraeans appoint the *oikistḗs* from their mother city Corinth at the foundation of Epidamnos. But the reference to a *nómos palaiós* raises the wrong expectations, for his comment is to be understood against the background of the above-mentioned hegemonic interests of Corinth. In his "Sicilian Archaeology" the historian himself reports that the founder of Catane stemmed from Naxos (6.3.3) and not – as to be expected – from Chalcis. But then the foundation of Selinus, which originated from Megara Hyblaia, can, if one follows this logic, indeed be called a grandchild city, for the *oikistḗs* was once fetched from Megara – so says Thucydides in a later passage (6.4.2). Automatism is hence not to be expected. And here can only be hinted at the fact that not every founder will have left his homeland under peaceful conditions, quite a number might indeed have been fugitives.

When Archias founded Syracuse around 734/733 BC, this happened as the result of a sociopolitical disintegration of the noble lineage of the Temenids in Corinth, which was dominated by the Bacchiads (Bernstein 2004, 45–77). Against this background it is very unlikely that at first there were any relationships between the far distant *apoikía* on Sicily and their *mētrópolis* on the Isthmus at all. Nonetheless, 400 years later it was Timoleon, who was of all things an *oikistḗs* from Corinth, who was responsible for the refoundation of Syracuse after it was struck by multiple disasters. The long period between initial foundation and refoundation was governed by dynamics; however, due to the available sources, those can only be glimpsed in instances, yet they adumbrate that the relationships between *apoikíai* and *mētrópoleis* were constantly subject to change.

"Foundation" was a process concluded upon the death of its founder. The veneration of the deceased *oikistḗs* employed the formalized language of the hero cults, a framework in which the memory of the origins of the *apoikía* gained in density, until finally merging into a *ktísis*, a "foundation story." It was of invaluable importance as a means of identification for, at the latest, the second generation born and raised in the new community. This explains all the more why it could be constantly retold, and this retelling was necessary. However often it was updated, both the deeds and the origin of the *oikistḗs* remained central to the *ktísis*. The people whom he had gathered around him probably were his *hetaíroi*, his "followers," and those will have included people from other cities – or so it was told. The arrangement and extension of a settlement abroad, if this enterprise was successful, was a great deed which commanded respect, a fact which leads us in our present inquiry to a further important aspect. For what is probably at stake in the narration of a *mētrópolis* of the *oikistḗs* is in fact probably often only a port of emigration.

It is impossible to know the extent to which people willing to emigrate gathered in places like Chalcis, Corinth, Megara, or Miletus from their hinterland or even neighboring communities to set sail. Such movement appeared as a colonization enterprise only in retrospect. Is it the chance nature of the available sources that almost no relationships can be documented in the case of the so-called Megarian colonies, which were so numerous? Or does the coming together of settler groups from different origins, and the fact that an *epoikía*, an "influx of settlers," fostered the development of an *apoikía*, reveal that many foundations were undertaken not just by one or even several cities, or even by regions, which considered themselves to be the *mētrópoleis* or which were considered as such by the *ápoikoi*? How strong was the impact of chain migrations? In any case, it is in fact the social and political background of the emergence and development of *apoikíai* that explains why, first, they were from the beginning autonomous and politically independent unities, and why, second, in some cases there could not be the one *mētrópolis*, and why she was in most cases not an "emissive" city. And yet, *apoikíai* were linked to their *mētrópoleis* in a strong feeling of belonging, as is often said.

Against this background, it is perhaps best to speak in general about a feeling for and of the homeland, which was stored in collective memory. The flexible *ktísis* will have furthered this sentiment, thereby forging groups of very different origin into one community of descent. It is, however, impossible to say how far the continuation of established forms of community organization like *phylaí* and *phratríai* (Jones 1987) reinforced such sentiments. Yet it is clear that they document the regional origins of the *apoikíai* in a similar way as do linguistic patterns, that is to say the rapid propagation of the Greek dialects especially since the eighth century BC and the use of certain scripts (Schmitt 1977; Jeffery 1990). It cannot be overestimated how far these at first diffuse similarities could eventually develop into an overarching concept of identity. Herodotus will later emphasize *en passant* that *tò Hellēnikón*, "the Hellenic," was characterized by a common origin, a common language, common buildings, and sacrifices to the gods as well as common rites (8.144.2). Emotional links to their homeland in the sense just established, however, will have articulated themselves in particular in the religious sphere. In the institutional organization of the *apoikíai* it is the calendar and cult which provide points of reference.

Calendars did not merely structure time in the course of the year, they also recorded the sacred times of regular simple sacrifices as well as festivals which cemented the community of gods and men. Identical names of the months and their sequences as well as the proliferation of certain festivals of the gods point to noticeable similarities of numerous communities of the Greek world (Trümpy 1997, and, still, Nilsson 1906). The use of a common calendar expresses a certain link of the *apoikíai* to their *mētrópolis*. At first sight, then, not only were the first settlers connected to their former places of living through religious practice but in a similar way their descendants were also linked to their origins. Yet, on closer inspection, there are problems. Sacred rituals, which were fixed in the calendars through the recording of sacred times, as well as the conception of the gods that lay at their core, could in fact be very different.

Traditionally, these are imagined in a very schematic way. It is thought that cults were imported at the foundation of an *apoikía* and, in a similar vein, that strong links to the *mētrópolis* were established through their identical organization. It is true that comparative studies such as that of Ehrhardt (1988) have revealed through the sensible analysis of often scattered findings the likelihood of such exports, even if this is difficult to prove on the level of the individual. The erection of an altar of Apollo Archēgétēs at the foundation of the Sicilian Naxos through the Chalcidians (Thuc. 6.3.1; cf. App. *B Civ.* 5.109.454–455), perhaps only an innovation, does already seem to be an exception from the rule. Overall, it seems that the cult that was established upon the death of its *oikistēs* was the first cult "that, by definition, was explicitly the colony's own and not imported from the *metropolis*" (Malkin 2011, 113).

This statement is influenced by the idea of a cult identity which sees similarities in external characteristics such as divine addressees of festivals in order to postulate congruencies. Of course, the paths of men dictate the paths of the gods as well as the forms of their reverence. It is to be expected that the first settlers adopted the established and hence proven cultural institutions of their homelands, which they introduced, perhaps unintentionally, in their new place of living. That said, reference to cult identity is often rather unspecific, allowing, for instance, to speak of congruence of practices if it is possible to document a cult of Apollo in *apoikía* x and *mētrópolis* y, even if the respective rituals as well as the concepts of the divine on which they are based are unknown.

Greek polytheism was a very flexible religious system. Conceptions and practices could continuously be modified, and there were no models of orthodoxy or orthopraxy of later periods. Apollo's sacred festival, the *Kárneia*, of Cyrene, a city founded around 630 BC, would, for instance, at first sight suggest that it had transferred a Doric cultural institution of their mother city Thera to Libya. However, in the *apoikía*, god and festival were reconceived as festival of the divine founder, and cult practices were profoundly changed as regards ritual. The reason for such accentuations is probably to be located in the forced migration (Bernstein 1998, with 2004, 171–222). The cult allowed the reenactment again and again of the traumatic foundation history. This example can, of course, not be generalized; it is mentioned here to indicate the varied prerequisites and conditions of possible relationships, which are to be taken into consideration whenever typology is to be established. Cult identity in its literal sense cannot be excluded, yet here it is important to issue a warning against assuming that certainty can be established in these (cult) matters. That said, cult is not to be reduced to rituals fixed in calendars; dedications and even participation or sharing in cult practices are also signs of religious relationships.

It is not always possible to distinguish between official and private dedications, that is, those set up by individuals on their own account. An inscription from Samos, probably dating to the early sixth century BC, documents the dedication of two Perinthians to Hera, the prominent divinity of the Aegean island (*IG* XII 6.2.577). Perinthos, possibly founded a generation earlier on the Thracian coast of the Propontis, was an *apoikía* which depended on Samos. As a result, its dedicatees could call themselves "Perinthian kinsmen" (ll. 3–5; Graham 1964, 162–163). However, it cannot be excluded that they acted while on an official mission, and the inscription does not give away whether it was set up in order to meet a duty of the *apoikía* to its *mētrópolis*. But it is not possible to establish such as duty with reference to parallel examples. For this conclusion rests on the assumption that relationships between *apoikía* and *mētrópolis* had existed as a general rule, an assumption which the discussions above have revealed as in need of revision, or at least indeed to be put into perspective. At this point, I would like to return to the conflict between Corinth and Corcyra, the prominent example which served also as a point of reference in religious relationships. For the Corinthians blamed the Corcyraeans for not sending the conventional offerings to the common festivities and for not ceding the best piece of a sacrifice to the Corinthians as the other *apoikíai* did (Thuc. 1.25.4). But this accusation cannot be taken as evidence for such obligations, again being rather an expression of the hegemonic demands of Corinth.

Of course, the fact that a citizen of the mother city was able to participate in the cults of the "colony" is recorded in a Milesian inscription from the late fourth century BC. The stone contains several agreements between the Ionian *mētrópolis* and the *apoikía* Olbia in the northern Pontic area, some of which reinforce earlier regulations (*Milet* I 3, 136 [cf. VI 1 p. 170–171] = *Syll.*³ 286 = *StV* III 408 = Rhodes and Osborne 2003, no. 93). Already in the first few lines we can read (ll. 1–6):

> The following are traditional for the Olbiopolitans and Milesians. The Milesian in Olbiopolis shall sacrifice like an Olbiopolitan at the same altars and frequent the same public religious rites in the same way as the Olbiopolitans.

We do not know whether these agreements rested on reciprocity, as here it is only renewed. Nor is it clear whether obligations of the *apoikía* can be deduced from this text. Perhaps the privilege for citizens from Miletus emerged in a particular situation, which was granted by Olbia. Again, generalization is impossible. At the same time, this is yet another example of the fact that our understanding of the rapport between *apoikía* and *mētrópolis* rests on the individual case. A sense of belonging, which could but did not have to be expressed emotionally in religion, could find other expressions, too. The Milesian inscription offers an important hint. The above-cited agreement is immediately followed by this regulation (ll. 6–7): "There shall be exemptions from taxes (*ateleíai*) for the Milesians as there were before." These exemptions, which here remain rather vague, touched upon the problem of the legal relationships between *apoikía* and *mētrópolis*.

Agreements of a legal nature between autonomous and at the same time sovereign cities could only exist where there was a particular interest to establish them. Banal as this statement might appear, it underlines that the respective prerequisites and conditions will also have influenced this type of relationship. Both sides need not have been equally interested in such links, a one-sided dictate can only be conceived under the auspices of "imperial colonization" and will hence not be examined here. One has to remember that some *apoikíai* were not or could not have been interested in establishing legally sanctioned relationships because of the reasons of their emergence, of particular regional interests or constraints, perhaps even because of their growing political success at a time when their *mētrópolis* incurred political defeats. This could explain the fact that only few such legal agreements have come down to us in the sources. This also means that the few epigraphic testimonies from the Classical and Hellenistic period cannot be taken as proofs for a possible system of regular legal relationships, which emerged in the Archaic period.

It is certainly no coincidence that the just-cited document from Miletus starts off with a call upon *tà pátria*, "the traditional principles" (l. 1), probably something like legal principles based on usage, which were perhaps fixed for the first time in this decree and which open up inquiring into the possible (but not necessarily so) informal nature of even regular legal relationships between *apoikía* and *mētrópolis*. Historians should always be particularly wary whenever sources refer to traditions. An even more important problem is to situate these rare finds in the broader research context, and hence to address them appropriately.

Thasos in the northern Aegean was founded probably in the seventh century BC by the Cycladic island of Paros. In a dedicatory inscription to Heracles from the late sixth century BC the dedicatee, a certain Akeratos, is keen to stress that he was the only one (*mónos*) to serve as *árchōn* in both Thasos and Paros (*IG* XII *Suppl.* 412 = *CEG* 416 = vER I 80 ll. 1–2). This occasional find raises several questions. For instance, did Akeratos hold the archonship(s) jointly or (even necessarily) in sequence? The problem lies in differentiating whether he possessed double citizenship or whether there was generally *isopoliteía* or even *sympoliteía* between Thasos and Paros. More on this in due course. First, however, a second example.

Abdera in Thrace was probably reestablished around 545 BC by settlers from the city of Teos in Asia Minor, who had fled from Persian pressures. An epigraphic find, a new fragment of the so-called *Teiorum dirae*, probably to be dated to the second quarter of the fifth century BC (*SEG* XXXI 985 = K 79 = vER I 105), contains regulations for both mother and daughter city. This testimony hence documents a particularly close sense of belonging together and thus has led scholars to propose that there existed, at least in the earlier period, if not a formal link, one that was similar to a *sympoliteía* between the Abderites and the Teians, as if "the two cities formed a single political entity" (Graham 1992, 56). It is tempting to pose the question of whether a basic common state structure could exist between *apoikía* and *mētrópolis* outside of hegemonic legal relationships when both sides were autonomous and independent from each other. Abdera and Teos, however, remain puzzling. Perhaps the best explanation is to be found in the very special circumstances of the foundation of the *apoikía*, that is to say the flight of the Teians from the expanding Persian Empire. But it is just as unrepresentative as the *árchōn* Akeratos in Thasos and Paros.

Those two examples show again how inappropriate it would be to integrate all these divergent finds into one single system to explain the relationships between *apoikía* and *mētrópolis* and thereby to negate their differences (in this context, see Giangiulio 2008). Relations of a legal nature, wherever they were forged, were similarly dynamic, being dependent on particular political demands and developments. And as the discussion so far has already suggested, by this time citizenship had also emerged as a factor of major importance in the Greek world. It guarantees the rights to participation in the institutions of the *pólis*, be it in cult or political office. Outsiders are *ápolis*, "without homeland." It is hence not surprising that this formal affiliation was of importance also in legal agreements between states. Legal relationships between *apoikía* and *mētrópolis* concerned are often, and above all, problems of citizenship.

The group of so-called foundation decrees includes also a much-discussed settler law of the Eastern Locrians for Naupactus in the Western Locris dating to the first quarter of the fifth century BC (*IG* IX 1².3.718 = *Syll.*³ 47 = ML² 20 = K 49 = vER I 43). However, this text does not document the foundation of an *apoikía* but rather concerns regulations for immigrants, who were to settle in the already existing city in the Ozolian Locris. It would hence be more appropriate to speak of an *époikoi* document. It is important to note that the Hypocnamidian Locrians, that is the Eastern Locrians, were probably represented by the "Opuntians" (l. 11) or assembly of the "thousand Opuntians" signing the "statute" (l. 46). The *pólis* Opus probably acted as the *mētrópolis* of the Eastern Locrians (Beck 1999). Remarkably, however, the decree ordered on the one hand that every immigrant was to be removed from his old citizen group to become a citizen of Naupactus; on the other hand, the decree ruled that he and his descendants should permanently (!) benefit from the right to take part in the cults of their home city and its civic subdivisions, even if only as a *xénos*, as a "foreigner" or rather a "guest-friend" (ll. 1–4). Leaving and at the same time attachment to the old city are linked in this regulation, which questions the traditional equation of civic rights and cult participation (Walter 1993, 130). In addition, the new Naupactian is granted both the right of return under certain conditions and the permission to rejoin the old citizenship group free of charge as if he was returning as a volunteer or as persecuted (ll. 6–10). These individual regulations might appear contradictory at first yet can be explained with reference to the particular political situation of Locris. The Western Locrian Naupactus was in need of military reinforcement to assert themselves against the neighboring Aitolians. Eastern Locrians hence had to be lured to move to Naupactus, a risky move which had to be made as easy as possible. Their right of return brings to mind a clause of the *hórkion tōn oikistērōn*, the "oath of the settlers" from Cyrene mentioned above, who allegedly were sent out from their *mētrópolis* Thera in 630 BC to found an *apoikía* in Libya.

To underline its importance, this oath agreement is attached to a decree of the Cyrenaeans from the first half of the fourth century BC (*SEG* IX 3 = *ML*[2] 5 = *Verbum* 17, 1994, 244–46 [cf. *SEG* XLIII 1185]). The *psēphisma* grants citizenship only to the Theraeans according to the agreements (ll. 4–5), hence pretendedly just confirming an ancient right. For as it is said in the *hórkion*, among others, the assembly of the Theraeans once regulated that those sent away were for a certain time entitled to return with the protection of their property and their citizenship, if they were unable to assert themselves in their settlement abroad (ll. 33–37). These detailed and written agreements are difficult to imagine in the period around 630 BC and hence raise doubts about the authenticity of the oath. In addition, its authenticity is also called into question by Cyrene's own foundation history (see above), which was the result not of a sending out of the *mētrópolis* but rather of expulsion from Thera, underlining again that the entire document, that is the *psēphisma* and the *hórkion*, has to be analyzed against the background of the political conditions and demands of the fourth century BC (Bernstein 2004, 180–185). A huge degree of dynamism, not of conformity, characterized the relationship between mother and daughter city. To deduce an established right of return for settlers from this example would again – as in the case of the Naupactians – generalize highly contextualized regulations. That said, it is clear that with this example we touch upon the legal concept of the *isopoliteía*, the reciprocity of civic rights in different *póleis*.

Unlike the *sympoliteía* (see above), the *isopoliteía* neither touches upon the autonomy of the partners nor does it restrict their independence regarding foreign policy. It is difficult to establish how far such diverse citizenship agreements between *apoikía* and *mētrópolis* go back in time, because other documents emphasize, similar to the decree of the Cyrenaeans, that they do not establish new rights but confirm older privileges (Gawantka 1975, 97–101, 111–113). However, as already emphasized, this invocation of tradition is deceptive, and even if it is not fictive, it may be a recent development. Is it hence only due to the source situation that no cogent testimony of *isopoliteía* for the period prior to the fourth century BC has been preserved? Even the above-cited inscription from Miletus, which pretends to affirm established agreements with her daughter city Olbia and which is rightly a commonly cited example for this phenomenon, does at closer scrutiny in fact not document a general grant of *isopoliteía*. A formal *isopoliteía* document between the Ionian *mētrópolis* and her *apoikía* Cyzikos on the southern coast of the Marmara Sea is, however, preserved in a contemporary fragment of a marble stele (*Milet* I 3, 137 [cf. VI 1 p. 171] = *StV* III 409). It contains the Milesian decree, yet given its fragmentary state it does not allow us to establish whether the formal agreement was renewed.

In any case, legal relationships between *apoikía* and *mētrópolis* were hence subject to often very dynamic political developments especially when they pertained to the reciprocity of civic rights. As regards Miletus, such obligations will have been a rather recent development, given the chaotic history of this important Ionian city. It also has to be emphasized that an involvement in the citizenry in fact limited the autonomy of the *póleis* and will hence not be a common phenomenon. Scholarship has thus underlined that regulations on *isopoliteía* did not necessarily mean to achieve an assimilation of the citizens but aimed rather at strengthening the friendly relations between the two parties involved (Schmitt 1988, 541). This also explains the emergence of kinship discourses in diplomacy, the fact that *syngéneia* was celebrated between *apoikía* and *mētrópolis*, too – even in the case where it was, at first glance, lacking.

An inscription from 242 BC found in the Asclepieion of Cos (*IG* XII 4.1.222) explains the *asylía* for the city Camarina with the fact that the Coans were *synoikistaí*, "co-founders" (l. 9) of the Sicilian *apoikía*. As a result, so the Camarinaeans confirmed in the *asylía* document, the Coans would enjoy in Camarina the greatest and most important privileges, namely kinship (*syggéneia*), close relationship (*oikeiótēs*), and *isopoliteía* (cf. ll. 10–12). The obviously one-sided grant of *isopoliteía* is not of interest here; what is far more irritating is that Camarina was founded in the early sixth century BC from Syracuse. Coans were probably not involved. Their status as *synoikistaí* is rather to be explained with reference to the refoundation of Camarina by the above-mentioned Timoleon in 339 BC (Diod. Sic. 16.82.7). This finally underlines that not only the involvement of more than one city in the foundation of an *apoikía* (not to mention the *époikoi*), but the multiple "refoundations" of a "colony" also further complicate the issue of the relationships between *apoikía* and *mētrópolis*. To take Camarina as an example, this was, as far as is known to us, founded four times. A "close relationship," such as is emphasized by the *asylía* document, could, so far as it existed, of course dissolve easily, yet it could also be retied quickly. How would we interpret this testimony were it not for the report of Diodorus Siculus?

Conclusion

The rapports and relationships between *apoikía* and *mētrópol(e)is* were shaped by a high degree of dynamism and variation. This typological survey has brought to the fore seemingly accelerated developments as well as the simultaneousness of the dis-simultaneousness. In all cases, it was vital to pay attention to respective prerequisites and conditions. Of course, not every aspect of this phenomenon could be examined. A systematic analysis of the relationships of secondary foundations that compares the regional aggregations and networks of Greek presence would have deserved our attention, like many other related issues. However, this contribution has aimed at highlighting one particular problem: to put into perspective the model of "colony and mother city." This necessitated close engagement with the heuristic and methodical problems as well as possible resulting conceptual problems. Only then could questions of possible relationships between *apoikía* and *mētrópolis* be addressed with the help of some examples.

If we finally consider the high number of *apoikíai* which can be documented and the comparatively low number of cases where relationships with their *mētrópoleis* can be proven, then this underlines how little we actually *know*. Scholarship often attempts to meet such an empirical gap with the provision of models, yet the logical coherence of these must remain self-referential and hence hermetically closed and can, if at all (as in the case of ancient history and archaeology), be validated only from the outside by new findings. The desperate use of a model, however, determines our *thinking* – and hence our *understanding*. Only if we understand the discussed examples as "ideal types" in the Weberian sense are they able, if used alongside all finds and findings, to provide a glimpse of the singularity of past realities. Differentiation, not the leveling of the empirical through the use of models, is necessary, for the relationships between *apoikía* and *mētrópolis* were all but self-evident. The individual case is and remains crucial.

REFERENCES

Beck, Hans. 1999. "Ostlokris und die 'Tausend Opuntier'. Neue Überlegungen zum Siedlergesetz für Naupaktos." *ZPE*, 124: 53–62.

Bernstein, Frank. 1998. "Transfer und Distanz: Thera, Kyrene und die Gründung der Apoikie im Kult." In *Religion – Wirtschaft – Technik. Althistorische Beiträge zur Entstehung neuer kultureller Strukturmuster im historischen Raum Nordafrika / Kleinasien / Syrien*, edited by Leonhard Schumacher, 1–19. St. Katharinen: Scripta Mercaturae.

Bernstein, Frank. 2004. *Konflikt und Migration. Studien zu griechischen Fluchtbewegungen im Zeitalter der sogenannten Großen Kolonisation*. St. Katharinen: Scripta Mercaturae.

Bernstein, Frank. 2019. "'Ionische Migration' vs. 'Große Kolonisation der Griechen': Kategorien und Konsequenzen." *Historia*, 68: 258–284.

Busolt, Georg, and Heinrich Swoboda. 1926. *Griechische Staatskunde II: Darstellung einzelner Staaten und der zwischenstaatlichen Beziehungen*, 3rd ed. Munich: Beck.

Ehrhardt, Norbert. 1987. "Die politischen Beziehungen zwischen den griechischen Schwarzmeergründungen und ihren Mutterstädten. Ein Beitrag zur Bedeutung von Kolonialverhältnissen in Griechenland." In *Actes du IXe congrès international d'épigraphie grecque et latine I*, edited by Alexander Fol, 78–117. Sofia: Trinovi.

Ehrhardt, Norbert. 1988. *Milet und seine Kolonien. Vergleichende Untersuchung der kultischen und politischen Einrichtungen I–II*, 2nd ed. Frankfurt: Lang.

Gawantka, Wilfried. 1975. *Isopolitie. Ein Beitrag zur Geschichte der zwischenstaatlichen Beziehungen in der griechischen Antike*. Munich: Beck.

Giangiulio, Maurizio. 2008. "I rapporti tra *metropolis* e *apoikia* e i limiti della *polis*. Teo e Abdera, Paro e Taso." In *Forme sovrapoleiche e interpoleiche di organizzazione nel mondo greco antico. Atti del convegno internazionale, Lecce, 17–20 settembre 2008*, edited by Mario Lombardo, 251–257. Galatina: Congedo.

Graham, Alexander John. 1964. *Colony and Mother City in Ancient Greece*. Manchester: Manchester University Press.

Graham, Alexander John. 1992. "Abdera and Teos." *JHS*, 112: 44–73.

Jones, Nicholas F. 1987. *Public Organization in Ancient Greece: A Documentary Study*. Philadelphia: American Philosophical Society.

Jeffery, Lilian H. 1990. *The Local Scripts of Archaic Greece: A Study of the Origin of the Greek Alphabet and Its Development from the Eighth to the Fifth Centuries B.C.*, rev. ed. with a Supplement by Alan W. Johnston. Oxford: Clarendon Press.

Malkin, Irad. 2011. *A Small Greek World: Networks in the Ancient Mediterranean*. Oxford: Oxford University Press.

Nilsson, Martin P. 1906. *Griechische Feste von religiöser Bedeutung mit Ausschluss der attischen*. Leipzig: Teubner. Reprint (with Introduction by Fritz Graf) Stuttgart: Teubner, 1995.

Osborne, Robin, and Peter J. Rhodes, eds. 2017. *Greek Historical Inscriptions, 478–404 BC*. with Introduction, Translations, and Commentaries. Oxford: Oxford University Press.

Rhodes, Peter J., and Robin Osborne, eds. 2003. *Greek Historical Inscriptions, 404–323 BC*. with Introduction, Translations, and Commentaries. Oxford: Oxford University Press.

Robu, Adrian. 2014. *Mégare et les établissements mégariens de Sicile, de la Propontide et du Pont-Euxin. Histoire et institutions*. Bern: Lang.

Schmitt, Hatto H. 1988. "Forme della vita interstatale nell'antichità." *Critica Storica*, 25: 529–546.

Schmitt, Rüdiger. 1977. *Einführung in die griechischen Dialekte*. Darmstadt: Wissenschaftliche Buchgesellschaft.

Seibert, Jakob. 1963. *Metropolis und Apoikie. Historische Beiträge zur Geschichte ihrer gegenseitigen Beziehungen*. Dissertation, University of Würzburg.

Trümpy, Catherine. 1997. *Untersuchungen zu den altgriechischen Monatsnamen und Monatsfolgen*. Heidelberg: Winter.

Walter, Uwe. 1993. *An der Polis teilhaben. Bürgerstaat und Zugehörigkeit im Archaischen Griechenland*. Stuttgart: Steiner.

Werner, Robert. 1971. "Probleme der Rechtsbeziehungen zwischen Metropolis und Apoikie." *Chiron*, 1: 19–73.

FURTHER READING

There is, to my knowledge, no monograph which deals with the relationship between *apoikía* and *mētrópolis* with attention to the above-noted general prerequisites and conditions. The seminal works of Seibert (1963) and Graham (1964) have lost none of their importance, and their case studies still offer the best way into the subject. Werner's thoughtful article (1971), which also covers a wide range of material, deals with far more than the legal relationships cited in its title, as does Ehrhardt's paper (1987).

CHAPTER TWENTY-FOUR

The Making of Greece: Contributions from the Edges[1]

Raimund J. Schulz

Greek history is generally portrayed as a developmental process determined by the center of Aegean settlement. Within this framework, "colonization" too is a one-way street. Accordingly, the development of these marginal regions proceeded largely independently of the *poleis* of the Aegean region. Thus, more recent publications have mostly treated these two areas separately. I consider this separation inappropriate for gaining a full understanding of Greek antiquity. My chapter therefore attempts a switch in perspective: It sets out from intensive interactions and interdependencies between all the Greek settlement areas and their border zones and explores the consequences. To what extent did the local situations of the peripheral areas lead to developments in power politics, the military, and the economy, as well as in religion and philosophy? What repercussions did they have on the "homeland"? Did they leave a substantial imprint on Greek history? In tackling these questions, let us first take a look at the challenges that Greeks had to face overseas.

The Situation in the Peripheral Regions

When Greek adventurers set out to seek their fortunes on faraway coasts from the ninth century BC, they set their sights on resource-rich regions with urban or proto-urban societies (De Angelis 2003, 10; Petropoulos 2005, 10, 26; Descoeudres 2008, 362). If they did not want simply to be feared (and despised) as pirates, they had to establish themselves as specialists in areas that impressed the native peoples and surpassed their competitors. Mercenaries and privateers offered their combat experience. Engineers built fortifications for Celtic sovereigns and warships for the Mesopotamian kings. Traders and artisans supplied Sicilian and Thracian elites with oil, wine, and pottery for the maintenance of a status-securing lifestyle (Stein-Hölkeskamp 2006, 318; Isaac 1986, 37).

A Companion to Greeks Across the Ancient World, First Edition. Edited by Franco De Angelis.
© 2020 John Wiley & Sons, Inc. Published 2020 by John Wiley & Sons, Inc.

Emigrants founding their own settlements (*apoikiai*) in the eighth century could also exploit the contacts of those men. Cases of aggressive occupation surely did exist. Overall, though, life for the first generations was defined by cooperation rather than confrontation, at an unmitigated intensity foreign to the Aegean world; in many new foundations, native inhabitants settled together with the colonists (Lomas 2000, 173–175; Greco 2006, 178). Mixed marriages with indigenous women resulted in bilingual children (Coldstream 1993; Petropoulos 2005, 27; Antonaccio 2007, 217; Lomas 2000, 176; Isaac 1986, 85; Tiverios 2008, 33, 112). Bilingualism was a precondition for the Greeks in the marginal areas to adopt the Phoenician alphabet (Morris 2007, 240). Research has noted distinct "mobility across ethnic boundaries" even for Cyrene, where the arrivals encountered semi-nomadic natives (Lomas 2000, 175; cf. Morgan 1999; Austin 2008, 207–208).

This mixing principle also applied to the Greeks themselves; however, the bands of mercenaries, traders, or colonists originated almost without exception from different communities and linguistic groups (Malkin 2009, 378; Morris 2007, 217, 238). Whereas mercenary soldiers and traders could change their places of residence, colonists had to be quick to integrate within a stable settlement community; and this was often done incorporating native segments of the population as well (Greco 2006; Link 1994, 174–175). Whether one conceives the development into a *polis* as a lengthier process (Osborne 1998, 264–266; Stein-Hölkeskamp 2006) or concentrates its development on the founding act of an *oikistes* (Malkin 1987; 2009, 377), in either case, no ready models, conventions, or recipes were available for the task of forming an *apoikia*.

As a result, in many places there were phases of experimentation and conformance to indigenous settlement structures. Circumstances demanded more liberal planning from the outset (Greco 2006, 182–185; Malkin 2009, 377–379). The partitioning of the municipal region in some Sicilian *apoikiai* into a sacred district, a public area with a large *agora*, and a private area with regularly divided blocks of houses differed markedly from old *poleis*, such as Sparta, Corinth, or Athens, which had developed by accretion and fusions of village settlements over a longer period of time (Greco 2006, 189; Antonaccio 2007, 212; Fischer-Hansen 1996; Descoeudres 2008, 356). If the thesis of recent research is valid that colonization certainly did not everywhere presuppose the existence of the *polis* in the homeland (Malkin 1987, 12; Hansen 1994, 15), then this finding supports that particular peripheral regions gave a substantial boost to the development of city institutions, because under the creative pressure of circumstances much had to develop and merge more rapidly.

We unfortunately have no information on how the transition from a settlement founding to its political constitution proceeded. However, on one point all *apoikiai* were alike in that a "frontier situation" evidently impairs the emergence of a dominant group within a settlement community (De Angelis 2003, 51). With very few regionally conditioned exceptions (Cyrene), leaders of the colonist expeditions did not manage to remold their leadership role into a permanent monarchical post (Malkin 1987, 89; Greco 2006, 170). The settlement founders (and their advisers) must have realized from the start that the only way to meld together heterogeneous groups of settlers into a conflict-resistant unit was to grant all the colonists equal political rights: As a rule, the entire party of settlers formed the city council and claimed council seats for their descendants. Each colony foundation thus led to the creation of a settler aristocracy *ex nihilo* (Vinigradov and Kryzickij 1995, 1).

Some researchers believe that this equality of mixed segments of the population propelled a general trend "toward egalitarianism" and caused a "collapse of aristocratic forms of government in the motherland" (Robinson 1997, 71–72). Others take it as a model function for a reshaping of the entire citizenry (Athens) (Léveque and Vidal-Naquet 1996). However, there is a total lack of evidence for such connections; and they are not very plausible, either. Colonization surely did secure political stability for the "mother cities" insofar as it steered internal tensions abroad; and it undoubtedly accelerated the formation of institutions needed to organize emigration. Furthermore, trans-Mediterranean exchanges may well have taken place due to problems experienced in the boundary regions. That concrete instructions for action by *poleis* in the homeland grew out of them is unlikely, however, not only because ties to the *apoikiai* were quite loose, but because their conditions for survival differed in many respects from those of the "mother cities."

Thus the peripheral regions always remained a preferred field of action for aristocratic ambitions, where they could develop with much less inhibition. Political equality among the new settlers was also an aristocratic principle that did not exclude differentiations in status and property. All colonists may have held claim to equally large shares of land drawn by lot prior to arrival, yet these were tradable against other goods or services at all times, as the well-known episode about the exchange of a share of land for one honey cake while still on the passage illustrates (Archilochos fr. 293 W; Athen. 4, 167d). For that reason, after a transitional period, landownership concentrations also arose in the colonies in the hands of some families (such as the Syracusan *gamoroi*), who moreover would have sought to set themselves apart from later settlers. All of this rather speaks for a strengthening rather than for a weakening of the aristocratic principle.

Since landownership was easy to sell and the lure of more lucrative activities to get rich (as a mercenary or pirate) was strong, a high fluctuation among the colonists has to be taken into account. Whereas the mother cities enforced a process of exclusion by sending out segments of their populations, the early *apoikiai*, conversely, had to expend much energy on keeping their population figures stable and augmenting them by facilitating immigration. Kathryn Lomas has shown that the native inhabitants of the southern Italian colonies could obtain citizenship rights with comparatively little difficulty (Lomas 2000, 168). Many colonies could also hope that their agrarian bounty and their locations at the crossroads of important travel routes would attract traders and artisans interested in resettling. Perhaps the great liberties within the municipal areas of the western colonies served as a reserve pool for follower settlers (Hansen 2006, 45). In any event, the repartitioning of large areas of land according to a regular grid plan occurred here only in the sixth century (Osborne 2007, 287).

All these measures did not eliminate a structural deficiency; if anything, they only mitigated it. In Sicily, Italy, and Thrace, the settler aristocracy established itself as a very rich cavalry elite and prevented the development of a strong hoplite class (Dunbabin 1948, 404; Mitchell 2000, 96; Isaac 1986, 85). This became a military problem when, at the beginning of the sixth century, conflicts were mounting between the *apoikiai* and the Carthaginians and Etruscans. Many western colonies started to build fortifications at this time to shore up their defences (Fischer-Hansen 1996, 334–335). Some restricted the sale of landed property to halt fluctuation within their populations and to strengthen the hoplite militias

(Arist. *Pol.* 1266b [19]; Link 1994, 172). Others rather counted on an influx of hoplites from the Aegean area. The challenges that thereby arose, namely, making life attractive for new settlers without short-changing those already there, were complex, although in western Locris one could still reserve land lots for new hoplites from undistributed real estate. In Cyrene, a redivisioning of the entire population into tribes (*phylae*) had to be carried out.

One alternative was to deploy mercenaries. Because, as a rule, they were only called up for concrete battle commissions, the problem of land procurement was eliminated. But mercenary soldiers always pose a power potential difficult to control. When the large landowners of Syracuse solicited help against rebellious immigrants and native field workers, the cavalry general Gelon used the chance to erect a tyranny with the help of hired professional warriors. In 485 he relocated half of Gela's population and Camarina's aristocrats to Syracuse and created a new city society with the subsequently settled 10 000 mercenaries (Berve 1967, 1:142; De Angelis 2016, 104–105). Such population shifts were only possible in the border areas with their tradition of new social and political structures combined with the mixing principle and a general social fluidity. Gelon considered his measures a new foundation and let himself be honored as a heroic *oikistes*.

The Pulsating Sixth Century: Formations of Power and Intensifying Overseas Trade

Population shifts were, furthermore, a first step toward empire building based on "dynastic" ties with other tyrants. Other colonies like Sybaris, Croton, or Thasos used their hinge function between Mediterranean trade and the fluvial or territorial exchange systems of the barbaric countries to build up politically integrated trade regions and minor empires supported by subcolonization (Eich 2006, 136–149; Greco 2006, 194–196). They thus followed a trend observable in the Mediterranean region since the beginning of the sixth century. In the west the Carthaginians and Etruscans expanded into the Greek settlement areas, in the east the Lydian kings pushed their kingdom up to the Aegean coast, and in Egypt the regents of Sais solidified their dominion over the Libyans. All powers developed an enormous demand for mercenaries and maritime shipping technology. It is not surprising that military innovations like the trireme first appeared not in the Aegean area but in the Phoenician/Carthaginian sphere of power or in Egypt and were later adopted by Sicilian and southern Italian tyrants to build larger fleets (Dunbabin 1948, 419; Berve 1967, 1:143). Also in this respect, the wealth and open-mindedness of the colonial regions acted favorably toward promoting innovation by specialists.

The explosive growth in demand by the marginal powers for armament technology and mercenaries stimulated Mediterranean trade enormously. Each mercenary was accompanied by at least one slave and only additional slaves could fill the warships' rower benches. Because since the beginning of the sixth century the period of widespread enslavement had passed within the Greek homeland, and bonded labor was forbidden (Van Wees 2003), this demand could only be covered by the "barbaric" regions, such as Thrace. Traditionally the target of raids, their sovereigns also profited from the enslavement of their own populations (Rihll 1996, 97, 103). The sale of slaves probably also contributed toward the distribution of coinage into Greece and the western colonies by Greek mercenaries from Lydia (Rihll 1996, 104–106). Greeks employed in the service of garrisons in Egypt, Palestine, and Syria expected, in addition, a constant supply of *hetaerae*, oil, wine, and tableware, which were surely also desired by their contractors (Haider 1996, 75, 93, 103). Within about the same period of time, specialized markets for ceramics and marble sculptures from the Aegean region formed in Etruria, Spain, Italy, and by the Black Sea.

Initially, the *poleis* located along central trade routes profited by this development, making customs gains and operating as producers, intermediary deliverers, or carriers of the desired goods and services. The success stories of Chios, Aegina, and Samos indicate the opportunities that opened up. Because they possessed only modest agrarian resources, they concentrated on long-distance trade of specialized wares and products. Chios was the center of the Aegean slave trade and shipped out slaves from Thrace and Phrygia to Lydia, Egypt, and into the Levant, hence regions that engaged many Greek mercenaries (Sarikakis 1986; Möller 2000, 50, 78, 199, 210; Rihll 1996, 90–91; Greaves 2015, 71–86; Isaac 1986, 145). At the same time, traders from Chios supplied the Nile territory with Thracian silver and the eastern Mediterranean coastal regions with tableware (Möller 2000, 80). Samos exported wine and sculpted marble, and under the rule of Polycrates assumed the transport of mercenaries on ships specially designed for the purpose (Wallinga 1993, 93–96). Aegina also traded slaves and, like Chios and Samos, supplied the western Mediterranean and Egypt (via Naucratis) with Ionian, Corinthian, and Athenian ceramics (Möller 2000, 123, 460; Osborne 1996, 32–33). Herodotus counts the merchants Sostratos of Aegina and Colaeus of Samos among the wealthiest men of their guild; Chios belonged, next to Corinth, among Greece's richest *poleis* (Möller 2000, 80; Thuc. 8.45.4). Chios, Samos, and Aegina possessed the strongest war fleets of the Aegean area. When the nobility of the Aegean coastal cities, stimulated by eastern (Lydia) and western (Sybaris/Croton) models, developed an increasingly luxurious lifestyle, the profitability spread to merchants from other *poleis*, such as Athens, which exported pottery, oil, and wine.

But how could cities with few agricultural resources and an economy specialized in export products, such as wine, mastic oil, and pottery, feed their growing populations and still afford the luxury of entire fleets of warships? The obvious answer is by importing grain from the regions they supplied with their own products. The grain bounty of Sicily, southern Italy, Cyrene, and Egypt exceeded that of the Aegean region many times over (De Angelis 2009, 239; for Sicily: De Angelis 2016, 226–234, whereas Ober 2015 still sees the Aegean *poleis* in an economically strong position). Silos in Megara Hyblaea suggest surpluses as early as 700 BC that were exported not just within the regional trading system but also into the Greek peninsular area (De Angelis 2003, 51; 2009, 241; Morris 2007, 239; Osborne 2007, 283). A shift toward intensive agriculture in the sixth century has also been shown for Metapontion, permitting large surplus production (Carter 2000, 88). It is probable that Corinth imported grain from the west (Salmon 1984, 129; Van Wees 2009, 459). Samos utilized its mercenary-transporter vessels (see above) to import Egyptian grain on the return passages. Besides that, Chios and Aegina probably established themselves as importers of grain from Egypt and (since the middle of the sixth century) from the Black Sea region (Isaac 1986, 143; Möller 2000, 80). According to Herodotus, the Persian king Xerxes allowed grain ships to pass through the Hellespont on their way to Aegina and the Peloponnese (Hdt. 7.147; Möller 2000, 210). These were certainly modest quantities – otherwise the king of Persia would have consumed them (Noonan 1973). The decisive point is that channels of communication were laid, along which bulk amounts could be delivered regularly and also for military purposes. The fact that, according to Herodotus, Gelon offered to provide the entire army of Greeks with grain for the duration of the Persian war, shows that corresponding export capacities were, or at least were assessed to be, available (Hdt. 7.159).

Organization of Hegemonial Rule after the Persian Wars

A significant increase in demand for supply goods from the marginal regions resulted out of the developing power politics in Athens over the course of the Persian wars. The build-up of the Delian League into a hegemony encompassing the entire Aegean area, the strategic displacements (although not documentable until 431) of entire city populations (Aegina), and the maintenance of a large trireme fleet recall the minor empires of the tyrants (Eich 2006, 155; Aegina: Ellis 1969, 10–11). They were not, however, based on contracts exclusively defining maritime obligations. Persian instruments of domination were more important: the organization of tributes, the sending out of official emissaries to the confederated cities, the deployment of supply ships and horse transporters, and the ability to carry out sieges by land and sea are such a distinct break with the limited forms of organized rule and war-making in the Greek area up to then, that they are hardly conceivable without any Persian-Phoenician models (Raaflaub 2009, 88–89).

Different from the Persian Empire, there was in the case of Athens a stark incongruity between expanding dominion and its material foundation. Until then the Aegean area had largely been independent of metal imports (apart from tin and gold) (Treister 1996; Descoeudres 2008, 360). Later, maintenance of the fleet alone required regular importation of an abundance of supplies and raw materials, ranging from copper, tar, pitch, and timber from Macedonia, to sail cloth and flax from Egypt, tin from Spain and the British Isles, and hides from the Cimmerian Bosporus. The processing of *matériel*, the rise of Piraeus as the most important overseas harbor, the manning of warships, and not least the tying down of Athenians in time-consuming democratic institutions, additionally generated a powerful stream of slaves particularly from Thrace (Hunt 1998). As a result, the inhabitants of Athens and its vicinity climbed to 350 000 individuals. Based on conservative estimates, even in the best years of rainfall, two-thirds to three-quarters of the grain demand had to be imported (Garnsey 1988, 87–133; Moreno 2007, 3–76). Foreign policy correspondingly had to draw into consideration the rich agrarian zones of the Aegean even more than before, hence Euboea, Thrace, and Macedonia, as well as Sicily and Egypt.

Similar to how the forming of minor colonial empires and expansionist Carthaginians and Etruscans mutually stimulated each other, the Athenian model animated other *poleis* to set afloat fleets and reactivate colonial networks for their upkeep. The fact that the Peloponnesian War was ignited at the most important junctions of the grain and timber trades, such as Kerkyra and Potidaea, and that the Athenians tried to close off the harbor city Megara from its colonial markets, shows the degree to which the *poleis*, under the pressure of maritime resource accumulation, tried to broaden their influence on the peripheral regions and to cut off competitors from such ties (cf. Thuc. 1.36 and 6.90.4).

Twenty Athenian warships set out in 427 to "stop the grain importation from Sicily to the Peloponnese and to make a preliminary attempt at whether they could not take hold of the matter in Sicily" (Thuc. 3.86.4.; Salmon 1984, 129). Ten years later the attempt would become reality with the largest fleet ever to sail for the West. Prior to that, Sparta had tried by land to gain control over the Thracian and Macedonian timber reserves so important for the Athenian fleet. Expeditions into the northern Aegean may additionally have served to relieve the militias, overtaxed by the war's temporal and spatial expansion, by integrating slaves and mercenaries.

Ultimately, all attempts at gaining longer-term access to the border regions failed for lack of military means and essential governance tools. Although the Peloponnesian War led to trans-Mediterranean ties between hitherto autonomous warring regions, the belligerent powers' dependence on the resource-rich border regions was strengthened further. Significantly, the war was decided not by the major expeditions by Athens or Sparta but by Persian subsidies.

The Periphery Strikes Back: The Rise of Marginal Powers in the Fourth Century

In the West, besides Carthage, Syracuse in particular profited by the ongoing war. Syracusan ships first appeared in the Aegean after the Athenian invasion had been fended off (Thuc. 8.77; Hunt 1998, 86–87). Ten years later, Dionysius drew the most skilled engineers away from Carthage and the Greek world into his court to design four-tiered military vessels and new catapults as well as to transform Syracuse into the strongest fortress of the western Mediterranean. At the same time, he maintained his own army of mercenaries, which was sent out in its entirety as settlers of new colonies at strategically important positions. These are clear traits of territorial rule reaching beyond treaties and personal relationships that for a while extended up to the Adriatic (Parke 1933, 69–70).

The *poleis* in the homeland lacked the material means and political preconditions for such power structures. Consistent adaptation of new kinds of weaponry and techniques, such as a light infantry or catapults, prevented the hoplite ethos. Athens still proved to be the most flexible; but the elimination of the naval league constrained its financial maneuvering room and strengthened its dependence on grain- and slave-exporting regions (Moreno 2007). Just as the *poleis* of the Aegean had formerly profited as intermediary caterers to the demand by the warmongering border regions for slaves, mercenaries, and silver, now some of the peninsular regions, formerly less affected by the wars, made use of this constellation. In Thessaly, Jason of Pherae became the most powerful man of Central Greece because there the dominance of the noble cavalry elites was much more firmly built upon the basis of serfs (*penestai*); his ascent was not obstructed by the institutions of the *polis*. Yet precisely this supposed independence bore the germ of decline. If luck failed on the battlefield, the war lords' power collapsed again a short while later under the rivalries among the nobility.

Conditions in Macedonia were more favorable. There the *polis* as a restrictive institution against territorial dominance was largely lacking. Yet Macedonia had a monarchy which had long understood that defense of the country required military mobilization. In addition, the country availed itself of enormous ship-timber and grain resources and had access to valuable precious metals. Philip II put this constellation to use and drew the following consequence out of the strengths and weaknesses of prior military potentates: in order to stifle resistance by the nobility, he summoned their sons to his palace. Like Dionysius of Syracuse, he engaged the best engineers and, unhampered by internal checks by the *polis*, adopted from Syracuse and Thessaly the military innovations on developing an army. Owing to its specialization in weapons technology and quality training, it was superior to the *polis*'s militia. To strengthen the country's defense capabilities and to secure its conquests, he undertook major population displacements, built up newly founded cities into fortresses, and employed mercenaries as garrison troops (Ellis 1986, 58–71; Parke 1933, 159–163). Philip thus used Dionysius's imperial methods to construct a territorial government that, step by step, cut off Greece's *poleis* – particularly Athens – from their resource sources, from Chalkidike up to the Bosporus. The victory by the Macedonians near Chaeronea was the keystone to a development ending in the marginal regions' resources and openness toward innovation carrying the day.

Religion, Philosophy, and Science

The rise of Macedonia and Syracuse reveals once again that the history of the Aegean settlement area and the marginal regions did not, by any means, proceed independently. It was, rather, defined by boosts of influence that set in motion irreversible developments and feedback effects in the economy, military, and power politics. Without the cooperation of native inhabitants and the acquisition of settlers and mercenaries from the homeland, the *apoikiai* of the seventh century would not have been viable and would not have subsequently experienced the boom that, in its turn, was a precondition for the wealth of the Aegean harbor and trader cities in the sixth century. Without regular imports of grain and raw materials, neither the construction of imperial systems of rule after the Persian wars, such as the Attic naval league, nor long hegemonial wars, that in dimension exceeded all precedents, would have been possible. Yet most Aegean *poleis* lacked the political and material preconditions, in the form of import-independent resources of their own, for imperial territorial domains to form. Monarchically governed marginal regions, like Syracuse and Macedonia, profited by this weakness. They tended to invest their material and agricultural wealth more consistently and flexibly in adapting innovative war technology and conducting expansionary wars.

Changes of such bearing evidently not only opened up new opportunities but also carried along enormous burdens. The sense of being torn between optimistic awakening and power-political weakness may not have been less widespread among large segments of the Aegean *polis* world of the fourth century than inside the early *apoikiai*. In between lay an endless series of military conflicts and political convulsions: the siege and destruction of entire cities, ever longer campaigns, a growing dependence on imported goods, the rising danger of fatal epidemics attending population growth and large standing armies of mercenaries, and the experience of an ever-expanding world permeating the various settlement areas. All of these heightened the need for a sense of security, orientation, and assurances for the future. So, an army of charismatic healers, seers, oracle sayers, and purgatorial priests flooded the Greek world from the end of the seventh century, all of them specialized in banishing insecurity and crises of the here and now through absolution and prophecies.

The colonial regions were particularly receptive to such arts because their heterogeneous communities in the midst of an alien world demanded identity-forming and confidence-building acts. Colonial legends stylize the *oikistai* as leaders who – legitimated by the oracle of Delphi – cleanse the *apoikia* of a domestic *miasma* by the cathartic act of foundation and safeguard it against all unclean things (Bernstein 2004, 224). Their proximity to alien cultures made the colonies much more open-minded also toward "barbaric" practices, if they promised some orientation and security for the future. Men like Aristeas of Proconnesus familiarized the Greeks of the northern Pontus region and southern Italy with shamanistic purging and ecstatic practices. Mercenary leaders like Phanes of Halicarnassus, who according Herodotus "was initiated into every detail of all the circumstances in Egypt" (Hdt. 3.4), brought along to Greece and Sicily amulets of a "purging" effect (*pharmaka*) and magical spells from Carthage (De Salvia 1991). Settlers in Samothrace, an important stop-over for seafarers, traders, and colonists, adopted elements of Thracian mysticism for their own Dionysus cult (Tiverios 2008, 112, 129).

The special achievement of the Greek peripheral areas was their selective elaboration of their own traditions from among the numerous options into coherent thought structures. Over the course of the sixth century, the mysteries of profound purging rituals joined with borrowings of Egyptian, Indian, and Iranian origin to form a new conception of an immortal spiritual soul that must reincarnate itself in different bodies (metempsychosis) before it can come home in heaven (Parker 1995, 502). Orpheus from Thrace was the mythical ancestor of these movements. In the second half of the sixth century, Orphic itinerant priests developed an intricate cosmogony and anthropogeny that spread principally in the colonial regions of Sicily and southern Italy, on Crete, and in Thrace and the northern Pontos region. In the fifth century, Orphic cult communities in southern Italy, Sicily, and the northern Aegean (Olbia) conducted initiations and buried their dead with gold leaves bearing instructions on how to act in the world of the dead (Parker 1995, 484–495).

Why, of all places, Orphic eschatology and spiritual doctrine were so well received in colonial regions and were only later "domesticated" (in the form of the Eleusinian mysteries) in some homeland *poleis* remains an open question. The "mixing principle" of Greek and indigenous cults made the elites more receptive to alternative religious currents. Eschatological promises of salvation, initiatory secret knowledge, and purification rituals evidently cater to a sense of insecurity that cannot be overcome by traditional religious and social authorities anymore. And finally, the need – not atypical of colonial societies – to provide a special religiously underpinned identity for oneself in a foreign land probably also played an important part.

The success around 530 of the charismatic Pythagoras of Samos in Croton was especially attributable to these framing conditions. Disease had ravaged the city a few years before. After a devastating defeat against Locris and Rhegion, the aristocrats had to tolerate being accused of leading an effeminate life of luxury. By taking up the Orphic doctrines, turning the postmortem existence of the divine soul, dependent upon moral merit in this world and upon purity, into an ethical postulate within the framework of a strictly regulated way of life, Pythagoras began a process of "moral rearmament." The Pythagorean life corresponded in this regard to efforts, also evidenced in the contemporary poetry, by a nobility on the defensive, to set itself apart from its social inferiors through moral qualities of "internal goodness, moderation, and intellectual superiority" (Donlan 1980, 77–99). Vegetarianism (perhaps only feasible in grain-rich South Italy?) came out of this spiritual wandering, and the notion that the body was just an appendage to the divine soul fundamentally contradicted the norms of the *polis* world. But precisely for that reason it made space for some dignity not just promising to alleviate aristocrats from the charge of degenerate luxury and military incompetence, but also opening up the possibility to set themselves apart from the rebellious *demos*, perhaps also from aristocrats of the homeland *poleis* (Parker 1995, 501).

This is what made the doctrine of soul migration and related cults so attractive to the colonial tyrants. It diverted attention away from the bare fact of despotism and offered a chance to stabilize theologically their politically precarious position. The path from a divine soul to a godlike human is short. It is no coincidence that the origins of a ruler cult should be sought in the period under Dionysius I in Syracuse (Sanders 1991). The new spiritual teaching is no longer in reaction to crisis but an expression of optimistic self-confidence growing out of the described military successes and power politics of the monarchically ruled marginal regions.

Alongside princes, bards, and seers, physicians represented the highest rank attainable by the soul in its cycle of reincarnations. Sicknesses were traditionally interpreted as consequences of impurity. It is certainly no coincidence that the arrival of Pythagoras in southern Italy concurred temporally with one of the greatest epidemics to befall Croton. The Pythagorean ban on eating beans was in response to a sometimes fatal hypersensitivity to broad beans (Zhmud 1997, 127–128). The remedy of the Pythagoreans was to recommend moderation and abstinence; for, "overindulgence" – says the master – "ruins not only people's fortunes but also their bodies, because most sicknesses come from undigested meals and this is the consequence of excess" (Diod. Sic. 10.7).

The warning against luxury as a problem of political ethics is combined with a diet that together with gymnastics and music became the basis of the southern Italian "school of doctors" at Croton (perhaps also at Cyrene). Its representatives, all of them Pythagoreans or receptive to Pythagoras's doctrines, thought that ailments should be cured or prevented without seeking a religious explanation, by observing manners of living and circumstances with a view to their natural causes. Croton's doctors, such as Democedes, spread their art eastward, in the opposite direction to Pythagoras's westward path. Trading cities, such as Aegina and the at times tyrant-ruled *poleis* Athens and Samos, were stops along his way to the Persian court where he would flourish (Nutton 2004, 62–63). This once again reveals a basic phenomenon that the wealth of the western colonies and export-orientated *poleis*, along with their receptiveness toward innovations, acted as magnets to charismatic specialists. Particularly tyrants (later, the Hellenistic kings) availed themselves of the material means to pay these specialists and let them work unhampered by social constraints. In this regard, there is a remarkable convergence between "progress" in scientific philosophy and militaristic power politics. The mathematical and mechanical theories of the Pythagorean Zopyrus of Tarentum made possible the development of the catapult at the courts of Dionysius in Syracuse and Philip in Pella (Zhmud 1997, 200; Kingsley 1995, 146–147).

As well, we encounter another phenomenon typical of the edge areas. Colonists and seafarers had to keep an acute eye out on the world and nature along with its changes, in order to survive. The successes of charismatic specialists, too, were based on the observation and explanation of nature (Parker 1995, 488, 492–493). Empedocles from Acragas, one of the most famous Pythagorean seers, physicians, and prophets, composed a treatise, not only on "purifications" but also "on nature." Peter Kingsley has pointed out the degree to which his cosmology is influenced by the natural Sicilian surroundings and traditions. The same can be said of Euhemerus of Messene and his construction of the utopian society of Panchaea (De Angelis and Garstad 2006; Kingsley 1995). More recent research has equivalently emphasized Pythagoras's own interest in the order of the world. Antiquity owes to it, among other things, the hypothesis of a spherically shaped Earth.

The wise men of the West received essential inspiration from the coastal *poleis* of Asia Minor. Even Pythagoras's place of origin, Samos, the foundations of the Phocaeans in southern Italy (Elea), and Democedes's travels imply a constant exchange of knowledge and experience. The *poleis* of Asia Minor differed from the agrarian colonies of the West on two essential points, however. Their perception of the world was much more strongly marked by the practical challenges of far-ranging voyages by ship and the prospects of success through overseas trade. It was not without reason that the wise men, whom we call natural philosophers, occupied themselves intensely with geography, nautical astrology, and the navigational arts. They, furthermore, had much closer ties with the cultivated kingdoms of the East. Both these points may explain why they attempted to answer questions about the origin and laws of change governing the material world by taking recourse to Eastern books of wisdom and cosmologies, while refraining from making eschatological prophecies of salvation and defining ethical rules of living.

On one point, however, they converged with the charismatics of the West, and this common ground formed a culmination point for all philosophical efforts of the sixth century, namely the quest for a sensible order of the expanding and ever-more-rapidly changing world. Pythagorean number theory and theses of natural philosophy about the forces of change in the cosmos were not the only outcomes of this quest. These were also the propelling factors for an attempt to fit the expanded knowledge about the world and its inhabitants into geographical and ethnographical ordering patterns. Without an extended horizon of experience beyond known limits and without a constant readiness to make contact with foreign cultures and ethnicities, these developments would not have been possible.

This surely also explains why the wise men's results did not reach the world of the *polis* of the homeland, or if they did so, only much later on, and why Athens became a focal point for "teachers of wisdom" (sophists) only in the fifth century when maritime trade and the naval league brought the offing into view. The politicians of democracy needed the help of specialists, and disappointed aristocrats needed alternatives.

They found them, among other things, in the Orphic itinerant priests, who according to Plato (*Resp.* 364b–c) peddled their books on the doorsteps of the rich, after the shocks of the Peloponnesian War. The fact that Plato himself gained inspiration in Sicily and southern Italy from the Pythagoreans in developing his theory of ideas, that he founded the Academy after the model of Pythagorean living communities, and tried in Syracuse to turn into reality the model ideal ruler, shows that the awakening in the border regions was understood as an escape, a chance and inspiration, even 400 years later.

NOTE

1   Translated by Ann M. Hentschel, Stuttgart.

REFERENCES

Antonaccio, Carla M. 2007. "Colonization: Greece on the Move, 900–480." In *The Cambridge Companion to Archaic Greece*, edited by H. Alan Shapiro, 201–224. Cambridge: Cambridge University Press.

Austin, Michel. 2008. "The Greeks in Libya." In *Greek Colonisation: An Account of Greek Colonies and Other Settlements Overseas*, vol. 2, edited by Gocha R. Tsetskhladze, 187–217. Leiden: Brill.

Bernstein, Frank. 2004. *Konflikt und Migration: Studien zu griechischen Fluchtbewegungen im Zeitalter der sogenannten Großen Kolonisation* (Mainzer Althistorische Studien 5). St. Katharinen: Scripta Mercaturae Verlag.

Berve, Helmut. 1967. *Die Tyrannis bei den Griechen*. 2 vols. Darmstadt: Wissenschaftliche Buchgesellschaft.

Carter, Joseph C. 2000. "The *Chora* and the *Polis* of Metaponto." In *Die Ägäis und das westliche Mittelmeer. Beziehungen und Wechselwirkungen 8. bis 5. Jh. v. Chr.* (Akten des Symposions, Vien, 24 bis 27 März 1999, Österreichische Akademie der Wissenschaften, Archäologische Forschungen 4), edited by Friedrich Krinzinger, 81–94. Vienna: Verlag der österreichischen Akademie der Wissenschaften.

Coldstream, J. Nicolas. 1993. "Mixed Marriages at the Frontiers of the Early Greek World." *Oxford Journal of Archaeology*, 12(1): 89–107.

De Angelis, Franco. 2003. *Megara Hyblaia and Selinous: The Development of Two Greek City-States in Archaic Sicily*. Oxford: Oxford University School of Archaeology.

De Angelis, Franco. 2009. "Ancient Sicily: The Development of a Microregional Tessera in the Mediterranean Mosaic." In *Société et climats dans l'Empire romain: Pour une perspective historique et systematique de la gestion des resources en eau dans l'Empire romain*, edited by Ella Hermon, 235–250. Naples: Editoriale scientifica.

De Angelis, Franco. 2016. *Archaic and Classical Greek Sicily: A Social and Economic History*. Oxford: Oxford University Press.

De Angelis, Franco, and Benjamin Garstad. 2006. "Euhemerus in Context." *Classical Antiquity*, 25(2): 211–242.

De Salvia, Fulvio. 1991. "Stages and Aspects of Egyptian Religious and Magic Influences on Archaic Greece." In *Akten des 4. Internationalen Ägyptologischen Kongresses München 1985*, vol. 4, edited by Sylvia Schoske, 335–343. Hamburg: H. Buske Verlag.

Descoeudres, Jean-Paul. 2008. "Central Greece on the Eve of the Colonisation Movement." In *Greek Colonisation: An Account of Greek Colonies and Other Settlements Overseas*, vol. 2, edited by Gocha R. Tsetskhladze, 289–382. Leiden: Brill.

Donlan, Walter. 1980. *The Aristocratic Ideal in Ancient Greece: Attitudes of Superiority from Homer to the End of the Fifth Century*. Lawrence: Coronado Press.

Dunbabin, Thomas J. 1948. *The Western Greeks*. Oxford: The Clarendon Press.

Eich, Armin. 2006. *Die politische Ökonomie des antiken Griechenland*. Vienna: Böhlau.

Ellis, John R. 1986. *Philipp II and Macedonian Imperialism*. London: Thames & Hudson.

Fischer-Hansen, Tobias. 1996. "The Earliest Town-Planning of the Western Greek Colonies, with Special Regard to Sicily." In *Introduction to an Inventory of Poleis: Acts of the Copenhagen Polis Centre*, vol. 3, edited by Mogens H. Hansen, 317–373. Copenhagen: Munksgaard.

Garnsey, Peter. 1988. *Famine and Food Supply in the Graeco-Roman World: Responses to Risk and Crisis*. Cambridge: Cambridge University Press.

Greaves, Alan M. 2015. *The Land of Ionia: Society and Economy in the Archaic Period*. Chichester: Wiley Blackwell.

Greco, Emanuele. 2006. "Greek Colonisation in Southern Italy: A Methodological Essay." In *Greek Colonisation: An Account of Greek Colonies and other Settlements Overseas*, vol. 1, edited by Gocha R. Tsetskhladze, 169–200. Leiden: Brill.

Haider, Peter W. 1996. "Griechen im Vorderen Orient und Ägypten bis ca. 590 v.Chr." In *Wege zur Genese griechischer Identität. Die Bedeutung der früharchaischen Zeit*, edited by Christoph Ulf, 59–115. Berlin: Akademie Verlag.

Hansen, Mogens Herman. 1994. "*Poleis* and City-States, 600–323 B.C.: A Comprehensive Research Programme." In *From Political Architecture to Stephanus Byzantius: Sources for the Greek Polis*, edited by David Whitehead, 9–17. Stuttgart: Franz Steiner Verlag.

Hansen, Mogens Herman. 2006. *The Shotgun Method: The Demography of the Ancient Greek City-State Culture*. Columbia: University of Missouri Press.

Hunt, Peter. 1998. *Slaves, Warfare and Ideology in the Greek Historians*. Cambridge: Cambridge University Press.

Isaac, Benjamin. 1986. *The Greek Settlements in Thrace Until the Macedonian Conquest* (Studies of the Dutch Archaeological and Historical Society 10). Leiden: Brill.

Kingsley, Peter. 1995. *Ancient Philosophy, Mystery, and Magic: Empedocles and Pythagorean Tradition*. Oxford: Clarendon Press.

Lévêque, Pierre, and Pierre Vidal-Naquet. 1996. *Cleisthenes the Athenian: An Essay on the Representation of Space and Time in Greek Political Thought from the End of the Sixth Century to the Death of Plato*. Trans. and edited by David A. Curtis. Atlantic Highlands: Humanities Press.

Link, Stefan. 1994. "Zur archaischen Gesetzgebung in Katane und im epizephyrischen Lokroi." In *Rechtskodifizierung und soziale Normen im intellektuellen Vergleich*, edited by Hans-Joachim Gehrke, 165–177. Tübingen: Gunter Narr Verlag.

Lomas, Kathryn. 2000. "The *Polis* in Italy: Ethnicity, Colonization, and Citizenship in the Western Mediterranean." In *Alternatives to Athens: Varieties of Political Organization and Community in Ancient Greece*, edited by Roger Brock and Stephen Hodkinson, 167–185. Oxford: Oxford University Press.

Lomas, Kathryn, ed. 2004. *Greek Identity in the Western Mediterranean: Papers in Honour of Brian Shefton*. Leiden: Brill.

Malkin, Irad. 1987. *Religion and Colonization in Ancient Greece*. Leiden: Brill.

Malkin, Irad. 2009. "Foundations." In *A Companion to Archaic Greece*, edited by Kurt A. Raaflaub and Hans Van Wees, 373–394. Chichester: Wiley Blackwell.

Mitchell, Barbara. 2000. "Cyrene: Typical or Atypical." In *Alternatives to Athens: Varieties of Political Organization and Community in Ancient Greece*, edited by Roger Brock and Stephen Hodkinson, 82–102. Oxford: Oxford University Press.

Möller, Astrid. 2000. *Naukratis: Trade in Archaic Greece*. Oxford: Oxford University Press.

Moreno, Alfonso. 2007. *Feeding Democracy: The Athenian Grain Supply in the Fifth and Fourth Centuries BC*. Oxford: Oxford University Press.

Morgan, Catherine. 1999. "The Archaeology of Ethnicity in the Colonial World of the Eighth to Sixth Centuries B.C.: Approaches and Prospects." In *Confini e frontiera nella Grecità d'Occidente. Atti del trentasettesimo convegno di studi sulla Magna Grecia, Taranto 3–6 ottobre 1997*, 85–145. Naples: Istituto per la storia e l'archeologia della Magna Grecia.

Morris, Ian. 2007. "Early Iron Age Greece." In *The Cambridge Economic History of the Greco-Roman World*, edited by Walter Scheidel, Ian Morris, and Richard Saller, 211–241. Cambridge: Cambridge University Press.

Noonan, Thomas S. 1973. "The Grain Trade of the Northern Black Sea in Antiquity." *AJPh*, 94: 231–242.

Nutton, Vivian. 2004. *Ancient Medicine*. London: Routledge.

Ober, Joshia. 2015. *The Rise and Fall of Classical Greece*. Princeton: Princeton University Press.

Osborne, Robin. 1996. "Pots, Trade and the Archaic Greek Economy." *Antiquity*, 70: 31–44.

Osborne, Robin. 1998. "Early Greek Colonization? The Nature of Greek Settlement in the West." In *Archaic Greece: New Approaches and New Evidence*, edited by Nick Fisher and Hans Van Wees, 251–269. London: Duckworth.

Osborne, Robin. 2007. "Archaic Greece." In *The Cambridge Economic History of the Greco-Roman World*, edited by Walter Scheidel, Ian Morris, and Richard Saller, 277–301. Cambridge: Cambridge University Press.

Parke, Herbert W. 1933. *Greek Mercenary Soldiers: From the Earliest Times to the Battle of Ipsus*. Oxford: Clarendon Press.

Parker, Robert. 1995. "Early Orphism." In *The Greek World*, edited by Anton Powell, 483–510. London: Routledge.

Petropoulos, Elias K. 2005. *Hellenic Colonization in Euxeinos Pontos: Penetration, Early Establishment, and the Problem of the "Emporion" revisited* (BAR International Series No. 1394). Oxford: Hadrian Books.

Raaflaub, Kurt A. 2009. "Learning from the Enemy: Athenian and Persian 'Instruments of Empire'." In *Interpreting the Athenian Empire*, edited by John Ma, Nikolaos Papazarkadas, and Robert Parker, 89–124. London: Duckworth.

Rihll, Tracey. 1996. "The Origin and Establishment of Ancient Greek Slavery." In *Serfdom and Slavery: Studies in Legal Bondage*, edited by Michael L. Bush, 89–111. London: Longman.

Robinson, Eric W. 1997. *The First Democracies: Early Popular Government Outside Athens* (Historia Einzelschriften 107). Stuttgart: Franz Steiner Verlag.

Salmon, John B. 1984. *Wealthy Corinth: A History of the City to 338 B.C.* Oxford: Oxford University Press.

Sanders, Lionel J. 1991. "Dionysios I of Syracuse and the Origins of the Ruler Cult in the Greek World." *Historia*, 40: 275–287.

Sarikakis, Théodore C. 1986. "Commercial Relations between Chios and other Greek Cities in Antiquity." In *Chios: A Conference at the Homereion in Chios 1984*, edited by John Boardman and C.E. Vaphopoulou-Richardson, 121–131. Oxford: Clarendon Press.

Shapiro, H. Alan, ed. 2007. *The Cambridge Companion to Archaic Greece*. Cambridge: Cambridge University Press.

Stein-Hölkeskamp, Elke. 2006. "Im Land der Kirke und Kyklopen: Immigranten und Indigene in den süditalischen Siedlungen des 8. und 7. Jahrhunderts v.Chr." *Klio*, 88: 311–327.

Tiverios, Michalis. 2008. "Greek Colonisation of the Northern Aegean." In *Greek Colonisation: An Account of Greek Colonies and Other Settlements Overseas*, vol. 2, edited by Gocha R. Tsetskhladze, 1–154. Leiden: Brill.

Treister, Michail Y. 1996. *The Role of Metals in Ancient Greek History*. Leiden: Brill.

Van Wees, Hans. 2003. "Conquerors and Serfs: Wars of Conquest and Forced Labour in Archaic Greece." In *Helots and Their Masters in Laconia and Messenia*, edited by Nino Luraghi, 33–80. Washington DC: Harvard University Press.

Van Wees, Hans. 2009. "The Economy." In *A Companion to Archaic Greece*, edited by Kurt A. Raaflaub and Hans van Wees, 444–467. Oxford: Wiley Blackwell.

Vinigradov, Jurij G., and Sergej D. Kryzickij. 1995. *Olbia: Eine altgriechische Stadt im nordwestlichen Schwarzmeerraum* (Mnemosyne Suppl. 149). Leiden: Brill.

Wallinga, Herman T. 1993. *Ships and Sea-Power before the Great Persian War: The Ancestry of the Ancient Trireme*. Leiden: Brill.

Zhmud, Leonid. 1997. *Wissenschaft, Philosophie und Religion im frühen Pythagoreismus*. Berlin: Akademie Verlag.

FURTHER READING

Descoeudres (2008) discusses the relations between colonial regions and the Greek peninsula. The collection in which his chapter appears provides a reliable survey of all the colonial regions. De Angelis (2016) provides a fundamental study on the development of Greek cities in Sicily in their geographical and historical settings, building on his earlier studies on the topic. Eich (2006) contains the only comprehensive modern account of the relationship between economics, politics, and power in the Greek world from antiquity into the fourth century BC. Hunt (1998) convincingly documents the important role that slaves played in the armies of the Greek *poleis*. In general, pertinent articles by renowned scholars on essential themes of Greek antiquity also relevant to the present chapter (such as, the economy or founding myths) are contained in Shapiro (2007). Various research approaches to the issue of the "specialness" of the western Greeks indispensable for any further study in this area can be found in the collection Lomas (2004). Kingsley (1995) is a fascinating study on the development of the Pythagorean Empedocles at the same time as being a modern intellectual history of the western colonies during the classical period. Ellis (1986) gives a comprehensible and readable overview of the ruling mechanisms of the Kingdom of Macedonia under Philip and points out parallels and models. Moreno (2007) critically assesses research on Athens's dependence on grain exports, especially during the fourth century.

Index

Abdera, 164n52, 413–414, 417–425, 508
Abrotonon, 422
Académie des inscriptions et belles-lettres, 53, 54
Academy, 524
Acanthus, 414, 416, 418–419, 422–424
Acco ('KK), 151, 162n14, 162n17
acculturation, 47, 298
Achaeans, 415
Achaemenid, 173–175, 177, 181, 187–190
  see also Persia
Achaia, 319
Achilles, 437–438, 448
Acholla, 163n27
Acra (R°Š ŠYG°N), 156
acropolis, 321
actor-network theory, 126
Adicran, 347
Adžigol Ravine, 449
administration, 93, 102, 109, 142–144, 148, 183, 186, 188–189, 239, 257–258, 263–264, 350, 371, 373, 383, 388, 421, 423, 427, 461–462, 466–469, 471–472, 475, 486
Adn/Adonis (Phoenician), 256
Adrias, 317–319, 326–329
Adriatic, 317–337
Adyrmachidae, 352
Aegean (Basin and Sea), 139, 140, 142, 144, 150, 175, 179–182, 184–185, 190, 409–429, 434, 440, 459, 471, 513–514, 516–521

Aegina, Aeginetan, 149, 329–330, 491, 517–518, 522
Aelian, 319, 424
Aeneas, 146
Aeolia, Aeolian, 224–228, 231, 233, 236–239, 241, 417, 427, 433
Aeolian League, 228, 241
Aeolian Migration, 226
Aeolic order, 233
Afghanistan, 108–109, 459–460, 464, 472, 474
Africa, 142–143, 147, 150, 156, 159, 161n3, 440, 461
Agathe (Agde), 394–395, 400
Agathyrsos, 447
agency, 47, 124, 126, 129
Agenor, 162n21
Agesilaos, 419
Agnon, 417–418
agora, 142 see also market
agoranomos, 440
agreement, legal, 500–501, 503, 507–510
Agreement of the Founders (Cyrene), 346–347, 358n1
agriculture, 14, 17, 43–44, 77, 91, 105–107, 109–110, 140, 141, 147, 148, 151, 156, 159–161, 180, 199–200, 206, 250, 276–277, 279, 296–297, 301, 309, 323, 339–340, 344, 353–354, 368–369, 391, 396, 397, 400, 414, 422, 440, 449, 460, 462–463, 468, 517, 520

A Companion to Greeks Across the Ancient World, First Edition. Edited by Franco De Angelis.
© 2020 John Wiley & Sons, Inc. Published 2020 by John Wiley & Sons, Inc.

agro-pastoral(ism), 447
Aḫḫiyawa, 223
Aḫtâ, 182
Aigina *see* Aegina
Aï Khanoum, 464–465, 473
Aineia, 415, 419
Ainos, 417, 419–420, 422
Aiolia *see* Aeolia
Aithiopis, 433
Akeratos, 508
Akkadian, 142–144
Akragas, 296–297, 299, 301–304, 306, 492
Akrothoon, 416
Akte (Athos), 416, 425
Alalia, 160, 395
Alashiya, 251, 257
Alcaeus *see* Alkaios
Alazeir, 350–351
Alazones, 449
Albania, 6n2, 317, 322
Alberti, Leandro, 86
Alcibiades, 17, 28n13
Alexander the Great, 108–109, 149, 174, 177, 190, 421, 427, 459, 461–462, 464, 468–471, 473, 475
Alexandria, 368–370, 374, 383, 461, 463, 469
Alkaios, 185, 437
Al Mina, 44, 150, 183–184
Alonis, 394
alphabet, 139–140, 142, 149, 483, 484, 490–491, 514
Alps, 317, 324, 326
Altertumswissenschaften, 69, 74, 77–79, 84
Amari, Michele, 69
Amarna, 144, 162n18, 164n49
Amasis, 347–348, 350
Amathous, 162n6, 253, 257–261
Amathus *see* Amathous
amber, 321, 324
America, American, 38–39, 42, 47
Amphipolis, 416–419, 425
amphora, amphorae/amphoras (pl.), 202, 206, 208, 211, 324, 326–327
Amun, 493
Amyclaeum, 150, 163n41
analogy, 39, 40
Anatolia, 176–177, 179, 181, 184–185, 188, 221–245
ancestor, putative, 141, 161n4, 162n21
Ancona, 321
Andros, 416, 418, 421

Anglophone, 37, 41–43, 45–47
Anna, 146
Antaradus, 153
Antenor, 320
Anthesteriae, 330
anthropology (theory), 122
anthropomorphism, 444
anti-classicism, 92–93
Antimenidas, 185
Antioch, 463–464, 470
Antiochos, 459–460, 462, 468–471
Antipater, 18
Antipolis (Antibes), 394–395
Antisara, 417
Apatouron, 435, 437
Apennines, 317, 325
Aphrodite, 252, 260–261, 264, 277, 436–437, 447, 449–450
Aphrodite Apatourion, 447
Aphrodite Ourania, 436–437
Aphrodite-Turan, 150
Aphytis, 416, 425
Aplāja, 186
apoikia, apoikiai (pl.), 1–2, 37, 42–45, 102, 104–106, 141–142, 150, 413–418, 420–423, 433, 435, 499–512, 514–515, 520–521
apoikismos, 16, 26
apoikization, 16, 26, 124
apoikoi, 322–323
Apollo, 54, 181, 212, 260, 281, 284, 302, 306, 331, 343–344, 355, 389–390, 424–425, 435–436, 469, 474, 506
Apollo Archēgétēs, 506
Apollo Delphinios, 436, 439
Apollo Ietros, 436
Apollonia (Albania), 56, 63, 317, 322, 323, 327, 329
Apollonia (Black Sea), 433, 439, 446, 451n3
Apollonia (Libya), 347, 355
Apollonia Pontica, 103, 435, 445 *see also* Apollonia (Black Sea)
Apollonios, 369, 373, 440–441
approach, legalistic, 502–503
Apries, 347
Apsinthians, 418
Apulia, 317, 321–322, 325–326, 329–330, 332
Arabia, 461
Arachosia, 189
Aradus (ʿRWD), 144, 146, 151, 153–154, 160, 161n4, 164n50

Aramaean, 144, 146, 150, 159, 162n22
Aramaic, 239
Arcado-Cypriot, 250
Arcesilas I, II, III, IV, 347–348, 350–352, 357
Archelaos, 424
Archias, 149, 504
Archilochos, 416
architecture, 54, 60–61, 118, 156, 203–204, 226–227, 232–234, 240–241, 251, 260, 283–284, 299–300, 308, 323, 329, 332, 355, 365, 394, 409, 423, 424, 436–437, 465, 473, 483–487
árchōn, 508
Arganthonios, 387, 389
Argilos, 416, 418, 420–421, 424
Argimpasse, 437
Argonauts, 433 *see also* Jason
Argyrippa-Arpi, 328
Aristeas of Proconnesus, 521
aristocracy (ᵓDR"chief"and RB"elder"), 149, 514–516, 521–523 *see also* elite
Aristophanes, 175
Aristotle, 15, 16, 19, 24, 159
Arktinos, 433
Arles, 395, 400
army, 461–462, 466, 469–470, 472 *see also* cavalry; hoplite; mercenaries; navy; soldier
Arqa, 146
Arrian, 22, 24, 29n27
Arsinoe, 264
Artemidorus, 19
Artemis, 226, 231–233, 237–239, 261, 302, 306, 389–390, 394, 424–425, 469
artist, 14, 23, 25, 26
Arwad, 186
Aryandes, 351
Arzawa, 223–224
Ascalon, 164n42
Ascoli Piceno, 321
Ashurnasirpal, 162n24
Asia
  Central, 101, 108–110, 459–462, 465, 468, 470–471, 474
  Minor, 72, 174–175, 179–181, 185, 459–462, 465, 468, 470–471, 474, 523
Askalon, 186
Asklepeion (Epidauros), 437
Assa, 416
assembly (ᶜM/ᶜam), 149
Assos, 230, 233–234, 236
Assyria, Assyrian, 142–144, 146–147, 151, 257

ᶜAštart, 150, 164n45
Astarte, 252, 260
astrology, 523
asylía, 510
ateleia, 440
Athena, 212, 233–234, 238–239, 281, 283, 302, 306, 319, 328, 353, 363–364, 469
Athenaeus (of Naucratis), 24, 176
Athenaios *see* Athenaeus
Athens, Athenian, 148, 150, 248, 259–260, 297, 304–307, 324, 331, 332n4, 413, 416, 418–420, 422, 424, 425, 427, 440, 445, 491, 495, 500–501, 503, 514–515, 517–520, 522–523
athlete, 14, 24, 26
Atlantis, 364
Aufidus, 325, 328
Auschisae, 352
Ausonia, Ausonian, 274
Australia, Australian, 42
Autariatai, 328
autochthonous, 253, 261, 265 *see also* indigene; local populations; native populations
autoevolution, 93
Auza, 144, 146, 162n18
Avaris (Tell el-Dab'a), 363–365
Axios, 411, 413
Aziris, 344, 354

Baalmilk, 256, 259
Babylon, Babylonian, 176–182, 184–189, 459, 461, 463–465, 467–468, 470–471, 474 *see also* Neo-Babylonian
Baᶜal, 156
Baᶜalazor (BᶜLᶜZR), 163n25
Bacales, 352
Bacchiads, 504
Bactria, 108–109, 459–462, 464–465, 472–474
Baetis, 153
Bakabaduš, 189
Bakambama, 189
Balawat Gates, 146, 162n23, 163n25
Balkans, 317, 319, 323, 325, 329
banausic, 159
banqueting, 329–330 *see also* symposium
Barbarian, 73, 438, 443, 450
Barbarization, 103, 107, 431
Barca, 340, 343, 345, 348, 350–352, 358n3
Bargylus, 151

Baria, 164n52
Barron, William, 39
barrow, 101–103
barter, 327 *see also* exchange; trade
basileus, 254, 257–261
Battiads, 350–351, 353
Battus I, II, III, IV, 25, 344–351, 353–355, 358n3
Bayer, Theophilus, 108
Bazbaka, 188–189
Beazley, John, 37, 44
Bengtson, Hermann, 78–79
Bérard, Jean, 54–57, 66
Bérard, Victor, 55–57
Berezan, 433–435, 437, 439–441, 443, 448–449
Bergepolis, 414
Berve, Helmut, 77–78
Betyllium, 164n47
Bible, Hebrew, 177
big-man, 122
bilateral, 104
Bilozerka, 449
bioarchaeology, biogeoarchaeology, 120
Birgi, 153
Bistones, 412
Bistonis (Lake), 417
Black Corcyra, 317 *see also* Corcyra Melaina
black-magic rites, 346
Black Sea, 101–107, 118, 179, 431–457, 517
Blakeway, Alan, 44
boat, 323, 329 *see also* ship
Bohemia, 202–203
Boii, 331–332
Boiotians, 434
Bologna, 321, 325–327, 330–331
Bol'šaja Korenicha, 449
Bol'tyška, 433
Bonaparte, Napoleon, 86–88
Borysthens, 433–434, 451n4
Bosa, 147, 163n31
Bosporan Kingdom, 436, 440–441, 443–444, 449–450
Bosporos *see* Bosporus
Bosporus, 101–103, 106, 437, 439, 518, 520
Bostan eš-Šeiḫ, 190
Bostrenus, 156
Botrus, 144, 162n18
Bottiaioi, 411, 416
Bottike, 411
Brasidas, 419
Brea, 501, 503

Breisach, 202
Brennus, 331
British Isles, 518
Britain, British, 37–51 *see also* Anglophone; colonial; colony; imperialism; politics, modern
bronze, 140, 142, 143, 146, 147, 159, 200–203, 205–213, 221, 223–227, 233, 235, 238, 239, 320–322, 324–325, 327, 329–330
Bronze Age, 143, 159, 339, 341, 354, 443
Brunšmid, Josef, 76
Brygi, 329
Buddhism, 474
Bug, 101–103, 105, 434, 437, 448
Bugfeld, 204
Bulgaria, 104–105
Bull of Corcyra, 156
Burckhardt, Jacob, 69, 70, 72–75
burial, 201–212, 223–226, 229–231, 233–235, 239, 321–322, 332, 436, 441–447 *see also* barrow; cemetery; cremation; funeral; inhumation; tumulus
Buthrotum, 156, 158
Byblos *see* Byblus (GBL)
Byblus (GBL), 143–144, 146, 162n14, 186
Bylliones, 329
Byrsa, 146
Byzacena, 142
Byzantium, 104–105, 164n42

Cadmos *see* Cadmus
Cadmus, 142, 164n21, 320, 328
Caere, 150, 164n44
Cailar, 488
Cala Sant Vicenç, 394
calendar, 505–506 *see also* month(s)
Callatis, 104–106
Callimachus of Cyrene, 343
Callisthenes, 367
Calpe, 164n52
Camarina, 510, 516
Cambyses, 149, 348, 350
Camirus, 163n41
Campania, Campanian, 273, 275, 279, 285
Campovalano, 322
Canaanite *see* Phoenician
Canada, Canadian, 42
Canosa, 321
Canousitai, 328
Cape Bejkuš, 437
Cape Dolojman, 434

Cape Stanislav, 449
Cappadocia, 180
Cap Ploca, 328
captive, 122–123, 125
Capua, 285
Carchemish, 144
Caria, Carian, 103, 164n46, 179, 185–186, 225–226, 228, 231, 233, 236–239, 241, 369
Carmel, 151
carnelian, 146
Carthage (QRTḤDŠT), Carthaginian, 40, 47, 141–142, 144, 146–149, 151, 156, 158–160, 163n27, 163n29, 163n36, 395–396, 399–401, 486, 488–489, 491, 495, 515–516, 518–519, 521
Carthago Nova (QRTḤDŠT), 142, 153, 164n52
Cartia, 164n52
Caspian Sea, 179, 459, 464, 473
Castillo Doña Blanca, 153
Catane, Catania, 490, 504
Cavallino, 323, 329
cavalry, 515–516, 519
cedar, 151
Celts, 212–214, 327, 330–332
cemetery, 441–447
center and periphery, 120, 125 *see also* periphery
Centre Jean-Bérard, 61
Ceos, 148
ceramics *see* pottery
Čertomlyk, 438
Čertovatoe Ravine, 448
Chabrias, 367
Chaeronea, 520
chain migration, 121, 505
Chalcidice, 179, 411–417, 419–421, 425, 520
Chalcis, Chalcidian, 76, 159, 164n59, 416, 504–505
Chalkidian *see* Chalcis, Chalcidian
Chalkidike *see* Chalcidice
Chalybes, 439
Charakoma, 417
Charchedon, 144, 146 *see also* Carthage
Charidimos, 422
charisma (authority), 521–523
Châtillon-sur-Glâne, 202
Chelidoni, 319
Chersicrates, 322
Chersonesos, 106, 118, 434, 438, 443–444, 446–449, 451

Chersonesus *see* Chersonesos
Chersonesus Taurica, 102, 104, 118
chiefdom, 122
Chinese, 472–473
Chionis of Sparta, 349
Chios, Chian, 417, 517
Chiusi, 326
Choes, 330
Chones, 273, 281
chora, 102–103, 107, 118, 141, 156, 161n5, 431, 437–438, 440, 446–447, 449, 451n4, 501 *See also* hinterland; territory
Chytroi, 257
Ciaceri, Emanuele, 90–92
Cicero, 156
Cilicia (Que), Cilician, 144, 151, 162n16, 179, 184, 186, 460
Cilix, 162n21
Cimmerian Bosporus, 518
Cimmerians, 101–104
Cinyps (river region), 353
circular migration, 121
Cirta (KRT), 150, 164n43
citadel, 142, 146, 149 *see also* stronghold
Citium (KTY/QRTḤDŠT), 142, 144, 162n6, 162n17, 164n42, 251–253, 256–260, 264
citizen(ship), 17, 18, 22, 24–26, 38, 64, 77, 80, 90, 105–106, 141, 142, 149–150, 159, 228, 260, 263, 282–283, 285–286, 302, 323, 331, 343, 345–346, 348–349, 358n2, 372–373, 395, 418, 422, 424, 440, 449, 464, 466, 470, 491, 501, 503, 507–510, 515
city, 460–467, 500–511
city foundations, 24
city gate (*šaʿar*), 142
city-state, 122, 141, 143–144, 148, 460–461 *see also* macro-state; micro-state; *polis*
civic subdivision, 501, 509
civilization, 140, 160
civilizing mission, 40, 45, 72, 141
classical economic theory, 120, 121, 124, 127
Classical Tradition, 4–5
clay brick wall (Heuneburg), 203–205
Clearchus, 21
Cleonimos, 331
cleruchy, 14, 501
climate, 460
clothing, 331
Cnidus, 149, 437
coalition (of Adriatic peoples), 326

code-switching, 435
coercion, 122, 127
cohabitation, 332
coinage, 212–214, 230–231, 237, 239–241, 260, 264, 461, 466, 468–470, 472, 475, 491–493, 517 see also economy; exchange
Colaeus (of Samos), 149, 341, 349, 388–389, 517
Colchis, 103–105, 433, 439
collective memory, 505
colonia, 501
colonial, colonialism (ancient and modern), 3, 37–40, 44–45, 47, 48, 85, 89, 124, 250, 263, 265
colony, American, 38–39, 42
colony, ancient Greek, 37–39, 41–46
colony, colonization (ancient and modern), 1–3, 102–106, 109, 118, 124, 199, 204, 317, 322–324, 433–434, 460, 470, 499–507, 510–511, 513–517, 519, 521–523
commerce, 14, 20, 28nn18–19 see also exchange; trade
commodity, 125
Communism, 1
community, autonomous and sovereign, 501, 503–505
comptoir (Kontor), 143 see also port of trade
Conero promontory, 318, 328
conflict theory, 123, 131
conscription (of citizens), 344, 346
constitution, 148
consumer city, 129, 151
consumption (theory), 128–129, 131, 484, 487–490
contact zones, zones of contact, 126–127, 130–131
context of migration, social and cultural, 121–128, 130
Copenhagen Polis Centre, 142, 148
Čoperskie, 433
Copiae, 286
copper, 151–152, 248–252, 257–259, 262–263, 327
Corcyra, Corcyraean, 156, 158–160, 317, 320, 322, 327, 329–330, 500, 504, 506–507, 518
Corcyra Melaina, 501
Corinth, Corinthian, 76, 81, 140, 148, 149, 156, 159–161, 176, 177, 180, 181, 300–301, 304, 305, 307, 317, 322–327, 329–330, 416, 418–419, 424, 488, 489, 491, 500, 504–507, 514, 517
Corsica, 60, 160

Cos, 150, 163n41, 510
Cosenza, 285
cosmology, 523
cosmopolitan, 144, 150
cost-benefit calculations, 120–121, 127
counter-culture, 130–131
craftsmen, 325, 327, 329
cremation, 322, 329–330
Crete, Cretan, 150, 179, 339, 341, 344, 349, 354–355
Crimea, 434, 440, 443, 446, 449, 450
Croesus, 366
Croton, 273, 276, 280–281, 284, 287n22, 516–517, 521–522
cult (identity and practice), 504–509
cultural actor, 129
cultural affiliation, 445
cultural change, 119–135
cultural complexity, 445
cultural contact, 119–135
cultural division, 321
cultural drift, 124
cultural grouping, 451
cultural identity see identity
cultural osmosis, 431
cultural self-image, 128
cultural space, 124, 126–127, 129
cultural sphere, 451
culture, 13, 15, 25, 26, 119–135, 431, 435, 443, 447, 450, 470–471
Cumae, 87, 159, 287n13, 326
cuneiform, 144 see also writing
Cuoco, Vincenzo, 88–89
Curtius, Ernst, 69, 71–75
customs, 320–322, 329–330, 332
Cyclades, 179, 416
Cypro-Minoan, 250, 252–253
Cypro-Syllabic/Cypriot syllabary, 253–256, 259, 261–262, 264
Cyprus, Cypriot, 142, 144, 146, 151, 178, 341, 350, 365–368
Cypselids, 325, 500
Cyrene, Cyrenaica, 53, 56, 64, 93, 181, 339–362, 366, 370, 493, 501, 506, 509, 514, 516, 517, 522
Cyrnus, 149 see also Corsica
Cyrus, 21, 29n28, 232, 234, 239
Cythera, 150
Cyzikos, 510

Daedalus, 22
dagger, 322 see also weapon

Damascus, 144, 146
Damastion, 323, 327
Danube, 433
Daphnae, 365
Darius I, II, 173, 177, 187–188
daughter city, 500–502, 508–510
Daunia, Daunian, 319–321, 324–330
Daunos, 320, 328
de Bougainville, Jean-Pierre, 53
decision theory, 120–121, 125, 127
decree, 501, 503, 507–510
dedication, 506 *see also* votive offering
Deinomenids, 17
Delian League, 518
Delos, 23, 25, 150, 163n41, 180
Delphi, 23–26, 29n35, 74, 124, 156, 280, 282, 287n17, 287n22, 330–331, 344–345, 347–351, 435–436, 439, 521
Demeter, 306, 309, 355, 425, 493–494
Democedes (of Croton), 23, 522–523
democracy, 18, 43, 263, 285, 302–304, 350–351, 358, 392, 423, 485, 523
Democritus (of Ephesus), 176–177, 181
demography, 319, 330–331 *see also* population
Demonax (of Mantineia), 348–350, 354
demos, 522 *see also* democracy
dependency, dependent (persons), 125, 127 *see also* captive; slave
de Polignac, François, 43
Dercylidas, 19
dialect, 141, 505 *see also* language
diaspora, 3–6, 15, 16, 26, 27, 124, 127
Dicaearchus (of Messina), 19
Dido, 146, 149
Didova Chata, 448
Didyma, 435
diffusionism, 124
Dikaia (Aegean Thrace), 417, 420
Dikaia (Thermaic Gulf), 415, 424
Dikaiarchia, 283
Dio Chrysostom, 438
Diodorus Siculus, 18, 19, 22, 323, 332
Diogenes Laertius, 16
Diomedes, 319–320, 328–329
Dion, 416
Dionysius I, 16, 150, 307, 323, 332, 519–520, 522–523
Dionysius of Halicarnassus, 16, 326, 330
Dionysos *see* Dionysus
Dionysus, 150, 424, 435, 469, 521
Diophantes (decree), 447
Diophantos, 451

Dioskourias, 103, 433
Dioskurias *see* Dioskourias
discourse(s), 130–131
disease, 521
ditch, 434
Dnieper, Dniepr, 101–103, 105, 437, 448, 449
Dniester, Lower, 101, 105
Dobrudja, 105, 107
Dodecanese, 89, 179
dog, 319
Dolenjska culture, 320–321, 326
Dolonkoi, 418
Don, 434, 439
Donau Delta, 434, 437
Dora, 147
Dorian, Doric, 105, 330
Dorieus (of Sparta), 149, 156, 159, 353
°DR (*'adīr*), 149 *see also* aristocracy; elite
Drabeskos, 412
Drina River, 317
drought, 344–346, 349
Drys, 417
Dryton (archive), 372–373, 383
dugout, semi-dugout, 104, 434, 442, 447–448
Dunbabin, Thomas J., 37, 41, 46

East Greece, East Greek, 227, 230–231, 235–236, 241, 349–350, 354–355, 416, 424
Ebusus (Eivissa-Ibiza), 163n27, 388, 392, 396–397, 400
Ebysus *see* Ebusus
Echedoros, 413
Ecole française d'Athènes, 55, 57, 59, 60, 63
Ecole française de Rome, 55, 56, 58, 59, 61, 64
ecology, 120, 363–364
economy, 16, 41, 44, 56, 58, 75–76, 94, 102–107, 109, 180, 185, 199–201, 210–211, 231, 240, 248, 251–253, 257, 261, 263, 297, 298, 307, 309, 318, 320, 322–330, 343, 346, 353, 363, 366, 368, 371, 373, 375n31, 387, 391–392, 395–398, 400, 413, 416, 419–423, 438–441, 460–461, 463–464, 466, 468–470, 483, 485, 486, 490, 493, 517
see also agriculture; agro-pastoral(ism); amber; bronze; coinage; copper; exchange; *garum*; gold; goods; grain; iron; lapis lazuli; lead; metal; objects; ostrich egg; pastoralism; perfume; purple dye; salt; silphium; silver; timber; tin; trade; tuna; wine

Ecueil de Miet (shipwreck), 487
Edoni, 412
egalitarianism, 122
Egibi, 188
Egypt, Egyptian, 143–144, 146, 150, 151, 162n14, 164n46, 164n49, 176, 181, 183–186, 189–190, 341–343, 347–352, 354–355, 357–358, 358n3, 449, 516–518, 521
Elea (Velia), 160, 283, 389–390, 523
Eleusinian Mysteries, 521
Eleutherus, 151
Elîšā, 176
Elissa, 146, 149 *see also* Dido
elite, 104, 106–107, 122, 125, 127, 322, 325–326, 332, 436, 438, 443 *see also* aristocracy
Ellišu, 182
Elymian, 159, 491–492
Emesa, 151
emic, 128, 140
emigration, 504, 514–515
Empedocles (of Acragas), 523
empire, 37–39, 44, 231–232 *see also* Assyria; Athens; Macedonia; Neo-Babylonia; Persia; Lydia; Ptolemy I; Ptolemy II; Seleucid
empirical gap, 511
Emporiae *see* Emporion
Emporion (Empúries-Ampurias), 143, 155, 156, 389–395, 397–400, 439, 490
emporion, emporia (pl.), 38, 42–45, 61–62, 104–105, 127, 141–144, 150, 328, 415, 499 *see also* economy; exchange; market; port of trade; trade
Emporium *see* Emporion
Encheleii, 320, 323
England, English *see* Britain
Ennea Hodoi, 412
enoikismos, 125, 141–143, 150
Enosis (°Y NSM), 153, 155
Entella, 491
Ephesos, 176–177, 181, 223, 225–228, 231–234, 238, 240–241, 491
Ephesus *see* Ephesos
epic, 159
Epidamnos, 317, 322–323, 329, 500, 504
epikouros see mercenaries
Epirus, 323
epoikía, 505
epoikos, 502, 508, 510

Eratosthenes, 151, 163n34
Eretria, Eretrian, 142, 159, 415–416
Eretria Painter, 445–446
Eryx, 156, 492
Eryxo, 348
Esarhaddon, 143, 181
Espeyran, 488
essentialism, 140, 148, 164n48
Este, 321–322
Eteocretan, 253
Eteocypriot, 250, 252–253, 260–261, 264
ethnicity, 122, 431, 434, 438, 441–445 *see also* identity
ethnos, 122
etic, 128–129, 140
Etruria, Etruscan, 59, 60, 62, 78, 88–89, 140, 159–160, 275, 304, 307, 321, 324–327, 330–332, 487–490, 492, 515–518
Euboea, Euboean, 159, 179, 180, 303, 324, 416, 422–423, 518
Euhemerus (of Messene), 523
Euhesperides, 351–353
Eumaios, 180
Euphrates, 143–144, 146, 151
Euripides, 424
Europe, Central, 199–220, 323, 324, 326–327, 451
Eusebius, 433
Evagoras, 254, 260–261
Evelthon, 255, 259
evidence, the heuristic problem of, 502, 507 *see also* methodology
excess population, 119, 124
exchange, 122–125, 127, 433, 440, 451, 487–489, 491–494 *see also* trade
exile, 15, 18–19, 27, 122, 125
expense, 462, 468, 470
exports (grain, etc.), 107, 161, 183, 190, 250, 252, 296, 325, 387, 391, 396, 397, 400, 413, 426, 440, 449, 487–489, 505–506, 517–519, 522, 528 *see also* economy; exchange; trade
expulsion, 509

facies sicula, 275
factory (*feitoria*), *fondaco* (*funduq*), 143 *see also* port of trade
family, 120, 330, 440, 448
farmhouse, 106, 447–450
Fascism (Italian), 85, 89, 91–92, 94 *see also* Nazism

Fazello, Tommaso, 86, 92
feasting, 201, 203–204, 207–209, 212 see also banqueting; symposium; wine
Felsina, 326, 330–331
Ferri, Silvio, 93
festival, 501, 505–506
fibulae, 324, 329
figuration, 128–130
Finley, Moses, 42–43
Five Brothers kurgan, 438
flax, 518
fleet, 323 see also boat; navy
Forcello, 327
foreigner, foreignness, 93–94, 125–126, 130–131, 440 see also outsider
forum (Rome), 142
Fossakultur, 275
foundation, 143, 146–147, 149, 153, 160–161, 162n15, 162n18, 163n27
story, 343, 355, 500–504, 506, 508–510
founder, 143, 146, 149, 163n27, 504, 506, 510 see also oikistes
France, French, 53–67, 484, 487–492
Freeman, Edward, 46–47
Frentani, 331
friend, 466–467
fugitive, 504 see also exile
funeral, 123, 209–210
fusion, 40, 46

Ǧabalal-Aqra', 183
Gades (°GDR), 153–154, 159, 387–388
Gadir (Cadis) see Gades
Galen (of Pergamon), 23–24
Galepsus, 416, 417
Gargano promontory, 318, 324, 328
Garibaldi, Giuseppe, 90
garrison, 332, 460–463, 469–470 see also army
garum, 153
Gaudalete, 153
Gaza, 161n4, 183
Gela (shipwreck), 486, 488, 490, 493, 516
Gelon, 18, 21, 156, 301–304, 516, 518
Gelonos, 447
gender, 330, 441, 444 see also woman
geography, 119, 121, 125, 127–128, 523
Georgia, 103–104, 445
Gephyraean, 142
Gergis, 164n54
Germany, German, 4, 61, 69–84, 85, 199, 202, 204–205, 208, 457

Getae, Getic, 105, 107, 439
gift exchange, 122, 124, 127, 210, 213, 433
Giglio (shipwreck), 488
Gigthis, 164n54
Giligamae, 352–353
Gillies, John, 39–40, 45
Glauberg, 204
globalization, 120, 298, 309, 485, 494–495
see also network
Glubokaja Pristan, 449
god, 465, 469, 471–472, 474, 505–506
gold, 146, 151–152, 163n28, 325, 327
Golubickaja 2, 434
goods, 120, 122, 125, 127–129 see also objects
Gordion, 229–230, 235, 239
government see big-man; citizen(ship); city-state; democracy; egalitarianism; hierarchy; kingship; law; macro-state; micro-state; monarchy; oligarchy; *polis*; politics; tribe; tyrant
Grächwil, 202
Grafenbühl, 203–204, 206–211
grain, 148, 151, 161, 324, 325, 327, 517–520, 522 see also agriculture; land
Gramsci, Antonio, 94
grandchild city, 500, 504
Grand Ribaud F (shipwreck), 488
Grand Tour, 88, 90
Graviscae, 150
Greco-Bactrian, 108–109, 472–474
Greco-Macedonian, 108–109
Greece, Greek, 101–109, 118, 123–127, 150–151, 156, 159–161, 161n2, 161n4, 162n17, 163n34, 164n43, 164nn45–46, 317–337, 483–497, 519
culture, 470–471
language, 469–475
script, 465–466, 470–475
Grimaldi, Francesantonio, 87–88
Grote, George, 40–41, 46, 90
Gūzānu, 188
Gyenos, 433
Gyges, 228, 230, 232, 366
Gylax, 323

Habroi, 319
Hadrumetum, 159
Halpa, 144
Halycus, 160
Hamath, 146, 151
Hanî, 174

harbor, 156, 160, 223, 228, 258, 274, 296, 301, 305, 318, 328, 339, 383, 391, 392, 413–416, 426, 434, 486, 518, 520
Harmonia, 320, 328
Hasebroek, Johannes, 76–77
Hathor, 258, 260
Hazor, 151, 162n14, 164n49
Hebros, 413, 417
Hecataeus, 318–319, 415
Heeren, Arnold Herrmann Ludwig, 75–76
Hegesipyle, 422
Hegewisch, Dietrich Hermann, 70, 72
Hellas, Hellenes, 140 *see also* Greece, Greek
Hellenism, 45, 103, 106–107, 460, 465, 471
Hellenium, 164n45
Hellenization, 40, 45–46, 103, 107–109, 118, 160, 332, 431, 434, 471, 483–484, 487, 490–491
Hellenocentrism, 298
Hellespont, 434, 517
helmet, 324 *see also* warfare; warrior; weapon
Hemeroscopium, 160, 400
Hemeroskopeion *see* Hemeroscopium
Heneti, 319–320, 332n2
Hera, 54, 150, 233, 261–262, 273, 280, 281, 283, 287n19, 306, 389, 424, 425, 506
Heraclea (Italy), 88, 274
Heraclea Pontica, 25, 104–105, 118, 160, 434, 446–448
Heracles, 233, 302, 306, 320, 323, 354, 357, 425, 447–448, 451n4, 469, 508
Heraklea *see* Heraclea (Italy)
Herakleia *see* Heraclea Pontica
Herakles *see* Heracles
Hermann, Karl Friedrich, 74
Hermione, 177
Hermitage Museum, The State, 102, 108
Hermonassa, 433, 437
Herodotus, 18–25, 341, 343–353, 355, 363–364, 366, 369, 374, 409, 412–413, 416, 425, 435, 437, 447, 449, 505, 517–518, 521
hero, heroon, 443, 504
Heroönpolis, 150, 164n46
Hesiod, 20, 240
Hetaireiae, 346
Heuneburg, 202–206, 208, 211
Heyne, Christian Gottlob, 75
Hiarbas, 146
hierarchy, 130
Hieron I, 18, 21, 304–305
Hieron II, 308

Himera, 160, 492–493
hinterland, 141–142, 151, 156, 161n5, 163n33, 434, 440 *see also chora*; territory
Hippocrates (doctor), 23
Hipponion, 160, 273, 282, 286, 287n18
Hipponium *see* Hipponion
Hiram (ʿḤRM/Aḥīram), 144, 149
Hirschlanden, 204
historiography, 2–5, 37, 40–43, 46, 47, 295, 298
Histria, Histrian, 318–319, 324, 331
Histroi, 319
Hittite, 143–144, 223–224, 229
Hochdorf, 202, 204, 206–211
Hohenasperg, 202–206, 208, 211
Holm, Adolf, 69, 71
Homer, 56, 88, 180–181, 190, 225, 229, 238, 240, 363, 374, 425
hoplite, 515–516, 519 *see also* army; soldier
Horn of Africa, 89
horse, 276, 281, 282, 319, 327
house, 143, 149, 153, 180, 188, 200, 226–228, 232, 233, 259, 275, 282, 301, 305, 321, 331, 371–373, 387, 391–392, 395, 397, 424, 461, 465, 485–486 *see also* dugout; farmhouse; pit house
Huelva, 387, 389, 400
human capital, 120
Ḥume, 186
hunting, 341
Hyblon, 160
hybridity, 164n48, 298, 309
Hyenos, 103
Hylaia, 447, 451n4
Hyllaei, 320
Hyllaeus, 320

Ialysus, 163n41
Iamblichus, 318
Iaones, 180–181
Iapygia, Iapygian, 273–274, 282, 319, 324, 326
Iatnana, 257
Iberia, Iberian, 488, 490
Idalion, 254–260, 264
[Iddin]-Nabû, 189
ideas, 123, 125–128
identity, 139–141, 161n2, 247–248, 250, 253, 264–265, 431, 441, 444–445, 451
Ietros, 435–436
Il'intsy, 438
Illeta dels Banyets, 400

Illyria, 318–320, 322–323, 325, 327, 329, 331
Illyrius, 320
Imgur-Enlil, 146 *see also* Balawat
immigration *see* migration
imperialism, 3, 70, 75–76, 85, 89–90, 93, 124
Incoronata, 275, 281
India, 109, 459, 461, 472–474, 521
indigene, indigenous, 46–47, 139, 148, 150, 159–160, 431, 433–435, 437–440, 443–451 *see also* Barbarian; elite; local populations; native populations
Indo-Greek, 472–474
inhumation, 322, 330
innovation (military), 515–516, 518–520, 522
inscription, 321, 328–330
Institute of Ligurian Studies, 59
Insulae Purpurariae (MGDL), 153
integration, 331–332
internal strife, 123 *see also* stasis
internationalism, 85, 88, 93–95
Ionia, Ionian, 43, 102–103, 105, 173–176, 180–181, 221–245, 259, 325–330, 409, 416, 424
Ionian League, 228, 241
Ionian Migration, 226–227
Ionian Revolt, 225, 228, 239–240
Ionian Sea, 317, 322–323, 326–327, 329
Ionian Sea Style, 283
Ionic order, 233
Ipf, 202, 204
Iphigeneia, 433
Iphikrates, 422
Iranianism, 107
Iran, Iranian, 459–460, 463–465, 470–471, 474, 521
Irasa, 344, 347–348, 353–354
Irdaparna, 189
iris, 325
iron, 140, 147, 151–152
Iron Age, 199–201, 204–207, 209–210, 213–214, 221, 223–227, 241, 433–434
Islanders, 344, 349
Ismaros, 412
Isocrates, 15, 25
isopoliteia, 501, 508–510
Israel, 144, 163n35
Issa, 317, 323, 327, 332, 501
Istria, 103, 106
Istros, 433, 435, 439, 443
Italia, 273–275
Italy, Italian, 85–100, 150, 160, 434, 515, 517, 521–524

Ithmitai, 319
Ithobaʿal (ʾTBʿL), 144, 163n25
itinerant craftsmen, 122–125, 127
itinerant diviner, 122–123, 125
ivory, 238, 325

Jason (Argonaut), 443 *see also* Argonauts
Jason (of Pherae), 519
Jeconiah, 186
Jerusalem, 144
jewelry, 321, 324
Jew, Jewish, 15–16, 466–467, 470–471
Jordan, 151, 161n4
Judah, 144
Jurilovka, 434

Kalhu, 162n24
Kallatis, 434
Kallippidai, 449
Kalos Limen, 443
Kamares (ware), 365
Kanesh, 142–143
Karabournaki, 415, 434
Karatepe, 161n5
KAR-Esarhaddon (Sidon), 143
Kárneia, 506
KAR-Shalmaneser (Til-Barsip), 143
Kasmenai, 485
Kaulonia, 273, 275–276, 281, 287n22
Kepoi, 433
Kerč, 101–102, 436
Kerkinitis, 439
Kerkyra *see* Corcyra
Kikones, 412, 417
Kilikia *see* Cilicia
Kinburn (sand bars), 437
Kingdom of Italy, 88
Kingdom of Pontos, 450
Kingdoms of Sicily and Naples, 86–87
kingship, 102, 104, 106–109, 118, 256–259, 263, 459–460, 462, 466–474, 513, 516, 522 *see also* monarchy
kinship, 140–141, 149, 320, 510
Kinyps, 156
Kition *see* Citium
Kittîm, 176
Klazomenai, Klazomenian, 227, 231, 232, 234–235, 417, 491
Kleinaspergle, 202, 206, 208–211
Kleon (*architekton*), 370, 375n20
Kleonai, 416
klēruchía, 501 *see also* cleruchy

Knidos *see* Cnidus
Knossos, 365
Koinon Kyprion, 265
Kolaios *see* Colaeus
komedon, 415
komedon zósin, 321
Kopet-Dag, 108
Korokondamitis Bay, 437
Kotys I, 422
Kourion, 253–254, 257
Kozyrka 12, 448
Krenides, 417
Krivorože, 433
Kroton *see* Croton
kārum, kāru, karāni, 142–143, 162n10 *see also* port of trade
ktísis, 504–505
ktístēs, 504
Kuban, 102–103
Kushite, 146
Kvarnar Island, 318
Kybele, 232, 238, 494
Kypris, 264

Laarchus, 348
Lacedaemonian, 343
Laconia, Laconian, 343, 346, 349, 355, 357
Ladice, 348, 351
La Fonteta, 387
land (plots, etc.), 14, 24, 66, 71, 77, 79, 88, 89, 103, 105–106, 118, 188, 189, 199, 206, 248, 258, 263, 282, 287n24, 297, 301, 323, 339–341, 344, 346–348, 350, 352–354, 357, 368, 371–372, 411–414, 416, 421, 425, 449, 460–462, 464, 466–468, 470, 515–516 *see also* territory
Langlotz, Ernst, 78, 79
language, 139–141, 144, 225, 230, 238–239, 469–475, 505 *see also* alphabet; inscription; script; syllabary writing
Languedoc, 58, 59, 64
Laos, 273, 285
lapis lazuli, 146
Lapithos, 257–258
La Tène style, 212–214
Lattara (Lattes), 397, 488, 490
law, 19, 24, 38–39, 54, 64, 70, 74, 86, 95, 120, 143, 285–286, 322–323, 371–373, 393, 424, 440, 451, 491, 492, 500–502, 507–510, 512, 523 *see also* customs
lead, 151–152

leather, 325, 327
Lebanon, 151, 176, 178, 183
Ledra, 257
Lemnos, 416
Leontes, 151
Lepore, Ettore, 94
Leptis Magna (QRTḤDŠT), 142
Lesbos, 417
Leuca (Adriatic), 324
Leucon (Cyrenaica), 348–349
Leuke (Black Sea), 433, 437
Levant, Levantine, 142–144, 146–151, 159, 180–185, 486, 489, 517
Libanus, 151
Liburnians, 318–319, 322, 324, 330–331
Liburnoi, 319
Libya, Libyan, 89, 92–93, 146, 156, 159, 181, 341–345, 347–358, 358n2
Libyphoenician, 159
life-long stay, 125
lifestyle, 124, 129, 131
Limassol, 162n6
limên Hyllaïkon, 320
Lindian Chronicle, 349
links, social, religious, political, legal, institutional, and emotional, 500, 502, 505, 507, 508
literary tradition, 225–226, 229, 237
Livy, 318, 320, 331
Lixus (LKŠ), 156, 159, 164n56
local(ism), 431, 435–441, 443–445, 447, 448, 450, 451
local population, 123–128, 130
Locris *see* Lokris
Lokris, Lokrian, 282, 287n18, 516, 521
Lombroso, Cesare, 89
Lucania, Lucanian, 285–286
Luceria, 328
Lycaon, 320
Lycia, Lycian, 179, 221, 223, 228, 235, 237, 239, 241
Lydia, Lydian, 186, 221, 225, 228–229, 231–239, 241, 516–517
Lyncestae, 323
Lysimachos, 421

Macedonia, Macedonian, 106, 108–109, 174, 319, 332, 411–413, 419–421, 424, 426, 518–520
macro-economic approaches, 120
macro-state, 144

macro theories/models, 120
Maenace, 142, 150, 160, 163n29, 164n52, 394, 400
Maeotian, 102, 104, 107
magistrate (ŠPṬ/*sufes*), 148–149
Magna Graecia, 86, 91, 94, 273–274, 276–277, 280, 283–285 *see also* Megale Hellas
Mago, 151
Mainake *see* Maenace
Makkadūnu, 174
Malaca, 164n52
Malkata, 365
Malkin, Irad, 42–43
Malta, 488
ᶜM (ʿam) 149 *see also* assembly
Manni, Eugenio, 94
Mannzmann, Anneliese, 78, 80
Mansur-depe, 108
Marathus, 153–154
Marduk-nāṣir-apli, 188
Margiana (Merv Oasis), 108–109
marginalization, 86, 90
Marienberg, 202
Marion, 257–258
maritime *see emporion*, exchange, harbor, port of trade, sailing route, trade
market, 120, 142–143, 159, 162n9, 162n11 *see also* agora
Maroneia, 413, 417, 419–420, 422, 424–425
marriage, 330 *see also* family; woman
Martin, Roland, 60–61
Marxism, 94
Marzabotto, 321, 327, 330
Mäšäk, 180
Maslinovik, 323
Massalia (Marseille), 57, 62, 160, 385, 387, 389–401, 487–490, 492, 494
Mattan (MTN), 146
Mazzarino, Santo, 1, 4
Mazzocchi, Alessio Simmaco, 87
Meẓad Ḥashavjāhû, 185
Mediterranean, 122–125, 139–141, 143, 148, 150–152, 156, 159–161, 431, 433–435, 437, 439, 440, 451, 460–461, 463
Mediterraneanization, 484–485
Medma, 273, 282, 287n18
Megale Hellas, 273–274 *see also* Magna Graecia
Megara Hyblaea, 55, 57, 58, 60–62, 64, 149, 159–160, 485–486, 489–490, 493, 504, 517
Megara Hyblaia *see* Megara Hyblaea

Megara, Megarian, 140, 159–160, 434, 504–505, 518
Megiddo, 151, 162n14, 164n49
Melita, 163n27
Melitopol, 438
Melkiathon, 260
Melqart, 146, 148, 153, 260
Memphis, 150, 366–367, 369
Menander, 162nn17–18, 163n35, 164n53, 473–474
Mende, 414–415, 419, 422, 424
Menecles of Barca, 343, 345, 358n1, 358n3
Meninx, 153, 159
Mentores, 319
mercenaries, 21–22, 26, 27n4, 29nn22–23, 29nn25–26, 122–123, 125, 127, 141, 150, 164n46, 212–214, 500, 513–514, 516–517, 519–520
merchant, 122, 123, 125, 127, 325, 328–329 *see also* exchange; trade
Merv Oasis (Margiana), 108–109
Mesambria, 104, 417, 434
Mesopotamia, 460, 463, 465, 467, 471–472, 474
metal, metallurgy, 147, 151, 159 *see also* bronze; copper; gold; iron; lead; mining; silver; tin
Metapontion, 149, 273–275, 281, 283, 285, 517
Metaponto *see* Metapontion
Metapontum *see* Metapontion
Metauros, 279, 287n18, 319
Metaurus *see* Metauros
methodology, 2, 5–6, 94, 501–503, 511
Methone, 413, 415, 418–424
metropolis, 38, 41, 42, 71–73, 78, 80, 139–140, 143–144, 148, 149, 151, 153, 156, 163n27, 447, 500–512
Micali, Giuseppe, 88–89
microregional(ism), 3, 253, 298, 320, 409, 411, 413, 418, 420–426, 442, 445, 451, 484, 488, 491, 493, 500, 505, 511, 514, 517
micro-states, 144, 146–147
micro theories/models, 120–121, 126–129
middle ground, 126–127, 131, 221, 227–228, 241–242, 437, 439, 448
Midi (France), 59
migration, 3–6, 107, 119–135, 224–227, 238, 241, 250, 254, 342, 347, 349–350, 352, 358n1

migration (cont'd)
   forced, 15–19, 27, 29n26, 122–123, 504, 506
   motivations, 121–123
   theories, 119–129
Miletos, Milesian, 103, 221, 223–228, 230–232, 235, 237–238, 240–241, 433, 435, 502, 505, 507, 510
Miletus *see* Miletos
military, 322, 332, 515–516, 518–520, 522
   see also army; cavalry; hoplite; navy
Miltiades, 324, 418, 422
Mimnermus, 320
mining, 323 *see also* metal
Minyan, 343
Mitford, William, 39, 40, 46
Mithridates VI Eupator, 101, 107, 450–451
mixed settlements, 125
mixed societies, 329–330
MLK, 148 *see also* monarchy
mlk (Phoenician), 256
mobility, 3–4, 6, 13–36, 119–135, 499
model, the conceptual problem of, 500, 502, 506, 511
Molyvoti Peninsula, 417
Momigliano, Arnaldo, 2, 4, 94–95
monarchy, 109, 122–123, 148, 163n35 *see also* kingship
Monte Bubbonia, 486, 493
Monte Iato, 486
Monte San Mauro, 493
Monte Sannace, 321
Monte Saraceno di Ravanusa, 486, 493
month(s), names and sequences of, 505 *see also* calendar
Morgantina, 297–299, 301–306, 308, 486
mother city, 500–504, 506–507, 511 *see also* metropolis
motherland, 143 *see also* metropolis
Motya (MṬW), 153–154, 159, 486
movers, 122
MQMḤDŠ, 162n8 *see also* Neapolis
multicultural(ism), 443
murex, 151, 153
music, 123, 522
Mussolini, Benito, 89–91
Mušēzib-Nabû, 186–187, 189
mutual misunderstanding, 127
Mycenae, Mycenaean, 140, 144, 223–225, 414, 420, 425
Mygdones, 411
Mykolajiv, 449
Myriand(r)us, 144, 150

Myrkinos, 412
Myrmekion, 433, 435
Mysteries *see* Eleusian Mysteries
MḤZ, 142–143 *see also* port of trade

Nabonidus, 185
Nabû-ereš, 186
Nabû-uṣalli, 186
Naron, 325, 328
narrative, historical, 3
Nasamones, 352
nationalism, 2–3, 69, 85, 89–93
National-Liberation Movement, 108
native populations, 40–41, 44–47 *see also* indigene; local populations
natural philosophy *see* philosophy
Naucratis, 142, 150, 164n45, 231, 237, 365–366, 517
Naukratis *see* Naucratis
Naupactus, 508–509
navy, 462–463 *see also* boat; fleet; sailor; ship
Naxos, 296, 300–301, 303, 304, 308, 485, 492, 504, 506
Nazism, 77–78, 94
Neapolis (as concept), 142, 148
Neapolis (Italy), 154, 273, 285
Neapolis (Sardinia), 158
Neapolis (Scythia), 450
Neapolis (Sicily), 155, 160
Neapolis (Spain), 155, 160
Neapolis (Thrace), 417, 424–425
Nebuchadnezzar II, 175–176, 181, 186
Nemirov, 433
Neo-Babylonian, 445 *see also* Babylon
neo-classical theory, 120
Neretva Valley, 317, 325, 328
Nesactiom, 325
Nestaioi, 328
Nestos, 411, 417
network (social, economic, etc.), 25, 109, 121–122, 129–131, 140, 161, 174, 180, 201, 213, 283, 298, 324, 326, 328, 330, 363–365, 413, 420, 422, 426–427, 437, 460, 472, 485, 489–490, 493, 495, 499–500, 511, 518
New Zealand, New Zealander, 42
Nicaea (Nice), 160, 394–395
Nikaia *see* Nicaea
Nikonion, 433
Nile (Delta and River), 150, 517
Němčice, 212
nomad(ism), 431, 439, 443, 444, 449

non-*polis*, 321
Nora, 147, 163n31
norm, social and cultural, 121, 129–130
Notranjska culture, 324
Noumenios (*stratêgos*), 371
Novilara, 321
Nymphaion, 433, 442–443, 449–450
Nymphodoros, 422
Nysa, 108

oath, 501, 509
obelos, 250, 252
objects, 13, 63, 119, 122, 125–127, 207–213, 230–231, 240, 252, 254, 280, 281, 306, 325, 342, 354, 399, 423, 441, 444, 465, 488, 494
Odomanti, 412
Odrysian kingdom, 411, 412, 419–420, 422, 427
Oehler, Johann, 69, 76
oenochoe, 325
oikistes, oikistai (pl.), 14, 323–324, 417–418, 504, 506, 514, 516 *see also* founder
Oinotria, Oinotrian, 273, 275, 280, 283
Oisyme, 417, 424–425
Olbia (Black Sea), 102–103, 106, 142, 433, 435, 437–442, 447–450, 451n4, 507, 510
Olbia (Hyères), 394–395, 400
Olbia (northern Aegean), 521
Olbia (Sardinia), 162n7
oligarchy, 228, 282, 303, 358, 391
olive, 151, 160
Olofyxos, 416
Oloros, 422
Olympia, 146, 156
Olynthus, 416, 419
Ombrian, 330
Ombrikoi, 319
Onesilos, 259
Onuba, 147, 156, 163n29, 163n31
open contact zones, 126–127
'Ophir, 162n10
Opicia, 279
Opus, 509
oracle (Pythian, etc.), 14, 24–26, 28n9, 435 *see also* Delphi
Orgame, 433–434, 443
Orientalism, 90
Orientalizing, Orientalization, 160, 231, 233, 236
Orontes, 150–151
Orpheus, Orphism, 435, 521, 524

Orsi, Paolo, 90–91
Orvieto, 326
ostracism, 15
ostrich (egg), 325
otherness, 125
Othoca (ʿTQ), 156, 158
Otranto (channel), 317–318, 324
Ourania, 436–437
outsider, 122–123, 125 *see also* foreign
overpopulation, 71, 75–78
Oxus, 118, 190

Pace, Biagio, 90–93, 95
Padua, 320–321
Paestum, 87 *see also* Poseidonia
Paiones, 411
Pairisades I, 440–441
Pais, Ettore, 90–92
Pakistan, 459, 472–473, 475
Palaepaphos, 250–251, 263–264
Palaetyrus, 153, 155, 164n53
Palagruza Island, 328–329
paleography, 147
Palermo, 91, 94 *see also* Panormus
Palestine, 459–460, 517
Pallene, 416
Pamphylia, 230, 238
Panchaea, 523
Pangaion, 412–413
Panhellenism, Panhellenic, 24–25, 102, 259, 305–306
Panionion, 174
Pannonian plain, 326
Panormus (ṢYṢ), 156–157
Panskoe I, 447–449
Panticapaeum, 101–103, 433, 435–436, 443, 445
Pantikapaion *see* Panticapaeum
Paphos, 252–254, 256–259, 261–262, 264
Paros, 416, 418, 508
Parsu, 186
Partheniai, 282
Parthenopolis, 416
Parthenos, 447
Parthia, 108–109, 460, 464, 467, 470–472
Parthiena, 108
Parthini, 329
participation/sharing (in cult practices), 506, 508–509
Pasargadai, 190
pastoralism, 340 *see also* agriculture; agro-pastoralism

Patavium (modern Padua,) 320
patrilineage, 141
Pech Maho, 393, 400, 492
peer polity, 122
Peisistratos, 418
Pelasgian, 88
Pella, 424, 523
Pelodes, 156
Pelopidas, 420
Peloponnese, Peloponnesian, 224, 349, 415, 440, 517–519, 524
Peloponnesian War, 341, 413, 418-419, 500, 518–519, 524
Pelusium, 150, 164n46
Peneios, 411
Pentathlus, 149
penteconters, 344
peraia, 417, 419, 424–425
Perdikkas, 422
perfume, 325
Perinthos, 506
periodos, 24
Perioikoi, 349
periphery, 2, 431 *see also* center and periphery
Periplous (Pseudo-Skylax), 328
Persepolis, 177–179, 187–190
Persian Gulf, 461, 463
Persia, Perisan, 106, 149, 164n46, 229, 232–235, 239–241, 348, 350–351, 353, 358, 409, 411, 413, 415, 418, 420–421, 426, 431, 445, 461–464, 470–472, 502, 517–520, 522
Peucetia, Peucetian, 319–321, 332
Peucetios, 320
Peuketiantes, 319
Phagres, 412
Phalius, 323
Phanes of Halicarnassus, 521
Phanogoria, 433, 435–436
phantom-colonies, 322
Pharos, 323, 327, 332
Phasis, 103, 139, 433
Phaulles, 440
Pheritima, 350–351, 358n3
Philip II, 413, 416–417, 420–421, 427, 520, 523
Philippi, 417, 420
Philistia, Philistine, 144, 183, 186
Philistus, 144, 146
Philo (of Alexandria), 24

philosophy, 513, 520–523
Phocaea, Phocaean, 140, 149, 159–160, 224, 226, 228–231, 233–235, 237–238, 385–407, 491, 523
Phocaia *see* Phocaea
Phocion, 18
Phoenicia, Phoenician, 42, 44–47, 56, 71–72, 87, 139–171, 181–186, 343, 353, 421, 459–460, 462, 470–471, 483–486, 488–491, 514, 516, 518
phratría, 505
Phrygia, Phrygian, 180, 221, 229–230, 232–233, 236, 239, 241, 517
phylé, 501
physician, 522–523
Picenum, Picenian, 319, 321–322, 324–325, 329–330
Pichvnari, 105
Pieres, 412
Pieris valley, 415
Pilistu, 183
Pillars of Heracles, 139–140, 151
Pilorus, 416
Pindar, 17, 343, 345, 351, 354, 358n1
piracy, pirate, 180, 184, 279, 318, 324, 330–331, 395, 499, 513, 515
Piraeus, 142, 150, 440, 518
Pirindu, 186
Pithecussae, 150, 154, 159, 182, 273, 277–279, 287n13, 287n15
Pithekoussai *see* Pithecussae
pit house, 434 *see also* dugout
Pitino di San Severino, 325
Pičvnari, 445
place of destination, 121, 123–125
place of residence, 121, 123
place of utility, 121, 124–125
Plataea island, 344, 347, 349, 354
Plato, 70, 75, 524
Plutarch, 16, 177, 322–323, 330, 415
Po (River and Valley), 317, 319, 322, 324, 326–328, 330–332
Pöhlmann, Robert, 70, 74, 76
Pointe Lequin 1A (shipwreck), 488
Polemon of Ilion, 331
pôletes, 323
Polieion, 281
polis, poleis (pl.), 2–3, 37, 38, 40, 42–43, 72–74, 78–79, 102–107, 109–110, 122, 141–142, 144, 147, 148, 150, 161n5, 224, 233, 237, 239–240, 250, 254, 259,

260, 263, 460, 470, 485, 501, 503, 508–509, 514, 519–520, 522–523
politeuma, 372
politics, ancient, 14–16, 18, 26, 27, 121–122, 124, 128, 130–131, 148–149, 177, 201, 204, 210, 223–229, 232–233, 235, 237–241, 259–265, 274, 282–283, 285, 295, 298, 300, 302–303, 308–309, 318, 323, 326, 342–343, 346–347, 350–351, 358, 365–366, 368, 375n11, 385, 387–388, 391–392, 397, 399, 411, 414, 416, 419–420, 440, 461, 464–466, 483–486, 489–492, 495, 500–505, 507–510, 514–516, 519–520, 522
politics, modern, 1–5, 37–118
Polyaenus, 425
Polybios *see* Polybius
Polybius, 156, 328, 331, 439
Polycrates, 517
Polyphemos, 320
Pompeius Trogus, 146, 163n26
Pontecagnano, 280
Pontus (Black Sea), 521 *see also* Black Sea
population, 120, 340–342, 346, 355, 460–461, 464–465, 467, 472–474 *see also* demography
Porthmion, 433
port of trade, 127, 141–143, 162n12
Portus Sigensis, 156
Poseidi, 415, 425
Poseidium, 164n47
Poseidon, 174, 282, 416, 424–425, 469
Poseidonia, 61–62, 273, 280, 283, 284, 286 *see also* Paestum
postcolonial(ism), 3, 45, 47, 79–80, 92, 128
postmodernism, 483–484
Potidaea, 411, 416, 418–420, 422, 425, 518
pottery, 200–206, 208–209, 211, 214, 223, 225–227, 229–232, 235–236, 240, 275–277, 279, 280, 285, 286n6, 321, 324–326, 329–330, 484, 487–488
power, 120–121, 126–128, 131
precolonial, 103–104, 433
pre-Roman history, 87–88, 91
prestige goods, 122
priest, 521, 524
Prometheus, 433
Protectorate, Scythian, 106–107
Protogenes, 450
Provence, 58–59

proxenos, proxeny, 440
Pseudartabas, 175
Pseudo-Aristotle, 319
Pseudo-Skylax, 328, 415
Pseudo-Skymnos, 319, 433
psychology, social, 120, 125, 127, 128
Ptolemais, 340, 347–348, 355, 368, 370–374
Ptolemy I, 253, 257, 262–263
Ptolemy II, 263–264
Pumayaton, 257
Pumayyaton (PMYTN), 146
Punic *see* Phoenician
Punicum, 164n44
Punicus/Porphyrusa, 163n41
Punjab, 460, 472–474
Purkin kuk, 323
purple dye, 151, 163n41 *see also murex*
push and pull factors, 120–121
Pūṭu-Yaman, 181, 347
Pydna, 413, 415, 420
Pygmaliōn *see* Pumayyaton
Pyrgi, 150
Pythagoras, 87–88, 91, 318, 521–524

Qarqar, 146
QRT *see* city-state
QRTḤDŠT *see* Carthage, Neapolis
Que *see* Cilicia
Qurdi-Aššur-lāmur, 180, 182–184

race, racism, 3, 39, 40, 46, 89–91, 95
radiocarbon, 147–148
raid, 326, 331
rampart, 434 *see also* stronghold
Raoul-Rochette, Désiré, 69
Ra's Ibn Hāni', 183
rational choice actor, 120
Ravenstein, Ernest George, 119
RB (*rab*), 149, 163n37 *see also* aristocracy
Rōdānîm, 176
reception (of Classicism), 4–5
refoundation, 504, 510
refugee *see* exile
regionalism, 320–322 *see also* microregional(ism)
reification, 131
relationships and rapports (between communities and states), 38–41, 500, 502–503, 507, 510

religion, 16, 43, 45, 46, 79, 91, 93, 102, 105, 123, 124, 140, 149, 156, 174, 220, 233, 238, 260, 263–265, 300, 302, 304, 307, 343, 353, 373, 375n31, 399, 420, 424–425, 435, 442, 451, 471, 493–494, 505–506, 513, 520–524
representativeness, the methodological problem of, 501 *see also* methodology
resident alien, 143, 150
revenue, 183, 264, 462, 466, 468, 471
Rhaetic, 330
Rhaikelos, 418
Rhegion, 273–274, 278–279, 283, 287n17, 521
Rhodanoussia, 395
Rhode (Roses), 388–389, 392, 394–397, 400
Rhodes, 150, 163n41, 179–180
Rhodope, 412–413, 425
right of return, 509
ritual, sacred, 505–506 *see also* religion
Rochelongue (shipwreck), 488
Romania, 105
Romanticism, 85, 87, 94
Rome, Roman, 85–87, 89–93, 146, 153, 285–286, 286n6, 298, 308, 451, 460, 470, 472, 474
Roscher, Wilhelm, 70
Rostovtzeff, Michail I., 102–103, 106, 108, 118
Rēši-ṣūri, 182
ruler cult, 264 *see also* kingship; monarchy
Russia, Tsarist, 101, 103, 105–107

Sabucina, 486, 493
Sa Caleta, 387
sailing route, 437
sailor, 318, 328–329
Saint Blaise, 487
Sais (Saïs), 150, 516
Sakkara, 366, 369, 373–374
Salamis, 248, 251, 254–255, 257–262, 264
Sale, 417
Salinas, Antonino, 92
salt, 153, 325, 327–328
Samaria, 144
Samnites, 273, 285
Samos, Samian, 149, 190, 365–366, 417, 506, 517, 521–523
Samothrace, 414, 417–418, 420–421, 424–425, 521

sanctuary, 14, 20, 22–26, 127, 319, 328–329
Sane, 416
Sant Martí d'Empúries, 391–392, 395, 398, 400
Sapaei, 412
sarcophagus, 441, 442, 445 *see also* burial
Sardinia, Sardinian, 142, 146–147, 153, 156, 160, 162n16, 163n36, 488, 494
Sardis, 189, 226–229, 232–233, 237–240, 491
Sarepta, 486
Sargon II, 257, 261
Sarmatian, 102, 107
Sarmatization, 103, 107
Sarte, 416
Satrae, 412
satrapy, 460–462, 464, 467, 469–472
Satyrion, 282
Scione, 415, 419, 422, 424
Scopas of Paros, 23
Scramuzza, Vincent, 94–95
script, 329, 465–466, 470–475, 505 *see also* alphabet; inscription; syllabary; writing
sculpture, 22–23, 63, 93, 108, 201, 204, 233, 237, 240, 241, 258–259, 284, 297, 302, 306, 353, 355, 365, 394, 409, 424, 465, 474–475, 517
Scythia, Scythian, 102, 104–107, 118, 326, 431, 435–437, 442, 447–450
Scytho-Sarmatian, 109
sea peoples, 144, 342
sea policy, 331
secondary foundation, 502, 511
seer, 521–523
Segesta, 492
Seleucid, 108–109, 459–474
Seleukeia, 463–464
Seleukid *see* Seleucid
Seleukos, 459, 462, 464, 468–471, 473
self-identity, 128, 131 *see also* identity
Selinus, 156–157, 159, 486, 490, 492–493, 504
Seneca, 75
Sennacherib, 184
Septuagint, 15–16
Sermyle, 416
settlement, 144, 146–161, 162n22, 164n47, 164n51, 164n54, 200–206, 208, 213, 214, 317–318, 321, 323–324, 326–327, 329–330, 460, 463, 465, 501, 503, 504, 509

settler, 122, 124–125, 460–465, 469–471
  additional, 502, 505, 508 *see also epoikia, epoikos*
Seuthes, 422
Sexi, 164n52
Shalmaneser, 143, 146, 162n23
Shem, 141
shipwreck, 331, 363, 365, 487–488
short journey migration, 119, 124, 125
short-term stay, 125
Shuksi, 164n47
Siannu, 182
Sianu, 146
Sican *see* Sikan
Sicily, Sicilian, 17, 18, 21, 25, 28n9, 38, 39, 42, 46, 47, 86–87, 90–92, 94, 150, 153, 156, 159–160, 163n32, 163n36, 295–315, 484–486, 488–494, 515, 517–519, 521, 524
Sidon (ṢDN), Sidonian, 142–146, 151, 156–157, 161n4, 162n24, 162nn14–15, 163n27, 163n39, 164n42, 183, 190 *see also* KAR-Esarhaddon
Siga, 156
Sikan, 71, 489, 492
Sikel, 71, 160, 299, 301–307, 309, 489, 490, 492
Silk Road, 472–473
silphium, 352–353, 357
silver, 146, 151–152, 323, 325, 327
Ṣimirra, 182
Sindian, 102, 104
Sindos, 415
Sinope, 103, 433
Sippar, 186
Siris, 275, 281
Sitalkes, 422
site selection, 140, 151, 153, 160 *see also* city; foundation; settlement
Sithonia, 416
situla, situlae (pl.), 322, 325, 329
Skilurous (King), 450
SKN, 148 *see also* viceroy
Skyles, 435
Skythes, 447–448
slave, slavery, 122–123, 125, 141, 327, 448, 516–519
Slonta, 354
Slovenia, 320
small world effect, 130

Smith, Adam, 75
Smyrna, 224, 226–228, 231–234, 237–239, 241
Snodgrass, Anthony, 42
social space, 121, 127–129, 131
society, 122–123, 129–131
sociopolitical (context), 122, 124, 126, 130
Sogd, 108–109
Sogdiana, 459–460, 464–465, 472–473
soldier, 461–462, 469–470, 475 *see also* army; hoplite; mercenaries; military; warrior; weapon
Solomon, 144, 149
Solon, 16, 19
Sophist, 523
Sostratos *see* Sostratus
Sostratus (of Aegina), 149, 517
soul migration (metempsychosis), 521–522
Southern Question, 90–91
Soviet Union, 1, 7n2, 101, 103–109
ŠPṬ (*sufes*), 148, 163n35 *see also* magistrate
spaces of contact, 127–128
Spain, 4–5, 58, 142, 147, 160, 162n16, 163n36, 181, 231, 385–407, 488, 490, 517–518 *see also* Iberia
Sparta, Spartan, 148, 149, 156, 159, 419, 427, 514, 519
Spartocid, 436
Spartokos II, 440–441
spear, 322 *see also* weapon
Spina, 326–328, 330–331
Spinitae, 330
Stageira, 416, 419, 424–425
Stamp Act (of 1765), 38
Stanyan, Temple, 38
Stari Grad, 323
stasis, 346, 358n1 *see also* internal strife
state, 120, 122–123, 503, 508 *see also* city-state; macro-state; micro-state; *polis*
status, 120–123, 130, 441, 443, 445, 447
stela, stelae (pl.), 325, 329
Stephanus of Byzantium, 318–319
stomalimne, 328
Strabo, 142, 151, 153, 164n51, 320–323, 328–331, 412, 416, 439
strategos, 263–264
Stratonike, 422
stronghold, 142, 149, 161n5
Stryme, 417
Strymon (River), 411–413, 415–419, 424

Strymonic Gulf, 416, 425
style, 58, 63, 66, 148, 212, 214, 226–227, 234, 236–237, 241, 250, 252, 259–260, 283, 299, 302, 306, 323, 329, 365, 374, 423, 433, 443, 445, 483, 488, 489
subcolonization, 516
Sulcis (SLKY), 153, 155, 159, 164n55
Suopi, 319
supply and demand, principle of, 120, 124, 127
supporter, 123
Susa, 177, 188–190
sustenance organization, 120
sword, 321, 322 *see also* weapon
Sybaris, 91, 274, 280, 281, 283, 326, 516–517
syllabary, 253, 254, 261, 264
symmachia, 106
sympoliteía, 508–509
symposion *see* symposium
symposium, 204–205, 207–208, 277, 284, 286n7, 286n9, 299, 426
syncretism, 107–109, 233, 238, 493–494
syngeneia (syngéneia), 320, 510
synoikistai, 510
Syracuse, 144, 150, 155–156, 159–160, 295–297, 299–309, 323, 332, 485–486, 489–490, 492, 504, 510, 516, 519–520, 522–524
Syria, Syrian, 151, 179, 184, 186, 187, 460, 463–465, 471, 474, 517
Syrtis, 156

Tadjikistan, 108
Taganrog, 434
Takhti-Sangin, 108
Taman, 434, 437, 440
Tamassos, 257, 262
Tanais, 434, 439
Tanakh, 141, 151, 161n4
Taphians, 180
Taras, 274, 282, 284, 286, 287n23
Tarchankut Peninsula, 437, 447, 449
Tarentine Gulf, 76
Targa, 437
Tarquinia, 150
Taršíš, 176, 181
Tarsus, 162n16
Tartessos *see* Tartessus
Tartessus, 156, 159, 162n16, 387–389
Taucheira (Tocra), 340, 347–349, 355
Taulanti, 319

Taulantians, 322
Tauris, Taurian, 447
Tauroeis, 394
Tauromenium, 146
taxation, 462, 468–469 *see also* economy
Taymā', 185–186
Tūbal, 180
techne, 22, 23, 26
technology, 329, 516, 520 *see also* innovation
Telesikles, 416–417
Tell Kabri, 185
Tell Sukas, 184
Tell Tayinat, 184
Temenid, 504
temenos, 435–436
temple, 16, 54, 87, 108, 118, 148, 153, 162n9, 164n45, 190, 226, 228, 232–234, 238, 239, 250–252, 260, 264, 280, 281, 283–284, 301–302, 306, 319, 351, 355–356, 364, 368, 369, 372, 389–390, 392–394, 399, 424, 435–437, 447, 465, 471, 493 *see also* architecture; festival; priest; religion; sanctuary; style
Tempyra, 417
Tendra, 437
Teos, Teian, 417–418, 508
territory, 59, 63, 66, 105–106, 443, 446–449 *see also* chora; hinterland
Teuta, 331
Teutaros, 448
thalassocracy, 330–331
Tharrus, 156, 158
Thasos, Thasian, 55, 56, 60–61, 150, 162n21, 163n41, 409, 413, 414, 416–422, 424–425, 508, 516
Thasus *see* Thasos
Thebes (Boeotia), 142, 320
Thebes (Egypt), 370–373
Theline, 395
Themistokles, 422
Theopompos, 318
theoroi, 14, 25, 26, 29n35
Theras, 343
Thera, Theraean, 339, 343–347, 349–350, 354–355, 357, 501, 506, 509
Thermaic Gulf, 411–421, 424
Therme, 415
Thessaloniki, 413
Thessaly, 174, 440, 519–520
"Third Greece," 2
Thirlwall, Connop, 41, 43, 46

Thonis/Herakleion, 366
thoroughfares (ḥuṣôt), 142
Thrace, Thracian, 409, 411–422, 424–426, 435, 439, 445–446, 515–518, 521
Thrasyboulos, 419
Thucydides, 14, 17, 18, 20, 21, 143, 156, 163n32, 305, 309n1, 411–412, 415–416, 419, 422, 500, 504
Thurii, 273–274, 280, 285–286
thygatrópolis, 500
Thyssos, 416
Tiberii Julii, 107
Tiglatpilesar III, 180
Til-Barsip, 143 *see also* KAR-Shalmaneser
Tilla-tepe, 108–109
Timaeus, 146, 163n26
Timavum, 328
Timavus River, 319
timber, 151, 153
time-limited encounters, 122–123, 127
time, sacred, 505
Timisias, 417
Timoleon, 504, 510
Timpone della Motta (Francavilla Marittima), 280
tin, 146, 152, 518
Tinnit, 156
tithe, 331
Tombarelle, 330
Tomis, 433
tophet, 156
Tor, 323
Torone, 414, 416, 419, 422, 424–425
Toumba, 415
Trachtemirov, 433
trade, 122–124, 127, 201–202, 211, 213, 324–330, 438–440, 451, 461, 465, 468–469, 474 *see also* barter; exchange
trader, 513–518, 520–521, 523
trading post, 72, 75–78, 140, 142, 160–161, 164n50 *see also emporion*; port of trade
transfer, institutional, 501, 506
translation, 2, 4
transnationalism, 4, 69
travel, 14, 19–27n6, 29n33, 29nn30–31
traveling concept, 126
Tremiti (Archipelago and Island), 318, 329
Trendall, Arthur Dale, 42
tribe, 320–323, 331, 411–412, 420
triggers for migration, 13–36, 120, 123, 124, 128, 130

Tripolitania, 142, 156, 341, 352–353
trireme, 516, 518
Troad, 179, 224, 226, 230–231, 233–236 *see also* Troy
Trojan War, 143, 146, 320
Troodos, 248, 258
Troy, 223–224, 226–227, 238, 241 *see also* Troad
Tsarist *see* Russia, Tsarist
tumulus, tumuli (pl.), 234, 321 *see* burials
tuna, bluefin (*Thunnus thynnus*), 151, 153, 156
Turkestan, 108
Turner, Frank, 47
typology, ceramic, 143, 147–148
tyrant, 516, 518, 522
Tyre (ṢR), 141–142, 144–146, 148–151, 153, 155, 160–161, 162n24, 162nn14–15, 163n27, 163n35, 163n39, 164n50, 176, 180, 183, 186, 486 *see also* Zorus
Tyritake, 433

Üetliberg, 202
Ugarit, 162n15
Ukraine, 103
Ullastret, 399–400
Uluburun (shipwreck), 363, 365
Uni-ᶜAštart, 150
Uni-Hera, 150
Unqi, 144, 151, 164n47
urbanism, urbanization, 60–61, 102–103, 109, 118, 139–143, 147–150, 485–487
Uruk, 178, 186
Ushnatu, 146
Uštāna, 187–188
Utica, (ᶜTQ), 144, 146, 156, 158–159, 164n56
Uzbekistan, 108

Valle Trebba, 330
Vassallaggi, 486, 493
Velia *see* Elea
Venetus, 320
Verucchio, 324
Via Egnatia, 323
viceroy, 148, 162n6
Vico, Giambattista, 87
Villa Cassarini-Villa Bosi, 321
village, 321
vine, 151 *see also* wine
violence, 127

Vix, 203, 205, 209–210
Vlora River, 317
Volga, Lower, 103
votive offering, 321 *see also* dedication
Vouni, 258–259
Vulci, 325

Wachsmuth, Wilhelm, 74
wanassa, 252, 254, 261–262
wanax, 254, 256
Wandering Poets, 122–123, 125
warfare, 14, 17 *see also* army; hoplite; solider; sword; warrior; weapon
warrior, 321–322
weapon, 321–322
Weber, Max, 76
Wenamun, 143, 162n15
Werekter, 143
Wilcken, Ulrich, 76
Wilusa, 223
wine, wine wares, 484, 487–490 *see also* pottery; symposium; vine
woman, 28n10, 73, 180, 201, 207, 284, 299, 319, 322, 330, 351–353, 369, 372, 374, 422, 424, 425, 435, 464, 514
world system, 120
World War I, 92
World War II, 92–95, 103, 108
writing, 213–214, 239, 490 *see also* alphabet; inscription; script; syllabary

xenia, 424
xenoi, 22
Xenophon, 15, 19, 21–22, 26–27, 29n22
Xerxes, 413, 415, 517

Yaman, 173–174, 176, 178–181, 183–186, 189
Yamanāya/Yamnāya, 173–175, 177, 180–182, 184, 186–189
Yariris, 144
Yauna, 187

Zadar, 322
Zakarbaᶜal (ZKRBᶜL), 146
Zancle, 159, 492
Za Rodinou, 437
Zenon (archive), 369, 383
Zeus, 233, 260, 264, 284, 302, 304, 306, 308, 355–357, 369, 469, 471, 493
Zeus-Ammon, 493
Zeuxis, 424
Zhiga-tepe, 109
Zmeinyj, 437
Zone, 425
zones of intense contact, 126–127, 131
Zopyrus (Taras), 523
Zorus, 144, 146 *see also* Tyre